Praise for *Before Official Multiculturalism*:

"Combining painstaking archival research with sharp analysis, Franca Iacovetta's *Before Official Multiculturalism* offers us an important account of English Canada's particular version of multiculturalism. Studying the work of women associated with Toronto's International Institute in the 1950s and 60s, Iacovetta's book offers us new ways of thinking about the possibilities and, perhaps more importantly, the enduring limitations of liberal, plural multiculturalism, both then and now."

Adele Perry, Professor of History and Women's and Gender Studies, and Director of the Centre for Human Rights Research, University of Manitoba

"Meticulously researched and accessibly written, this study of Toronto's International Institute offers a much needed and explicitly gendered intervention into our understandings of mid-century migrant settlement efforts. Emphasizing women's engagement at and with the Institute, Iacovetta deftly untangles the potential and paradoxes of white settler-based liberal cultural pluralism and efforts at multiculturalism before it was made 'official' in Canada."

Rhonda L. Hinther, Professor of History, Brandon University

"This magnificent work makes it clear why Franca Iacovetta is one of the leading scholars of gender, labour, and migration history in Canada. In a finely tuned analysis, Iacovetta explores the double-edged nature of pluralism at the International Institute of Metropolitan Toronto from 1956–1974. *Before Official Multiculturalism* offers critical insights that help us better understand the significance of ongoing contestations over culture, community, and belonging in the present."

Laura Madokoro, Associate Professor of History, Carleton University

STUDIES IN GENDER AND HISTORY

General Editors: Franca Iacovetta and Karen Dubinsky

Before Official Multiculturalism

Women's Pluralism in Toronto, 1950s–1970s

FRANCA IACOVETTA

UNIVERSITY OF TORONTO PRESS
Toronto Buffalo London

© University of Toronto Press 2022
Toronto Buffalo London
utorontopress.com
Printed and bound by CPI Group (UK) Ltd, Croydon, CR0 4YY

ISBN 978-1-4875-4563-5 (cloth)   ISBN 978-1-4875-4565-9 (EPUB)
ISBN 978-1-4875-4564-2 (paper)   ISBN 978-1-4875-4566-6 (PDF)

Studies in Gender and History

Library and Archives Canada Cataloguing in Publication

Title: Before official multiculturalism : women's pluralism in Toronto, 1950s–1970s / Franca Iacovetta.
Names: Iacovetta, Franca, 1957– author.
Series: Studies in gender and history ; 53.
Description: Series statement: Studies in gender and history ; 53 | Includes bibliographical references and index.
Identifiers: Canadiana (print) 20220281815 | Canadiana (ebook) 20220282013 |
  ISBN 9781487545642 (paper) | ISBN 9781487545635 (cloth) | ISBN 9781487545659 (EPUB) |
  ISBN 9781487545666 (PDF)
Subjects: LCSH: International Institute of Metropolitan Toronto – History – 20th century. |
  LCSH: Women social workers – Ontario – Toronto – History – 20th century. |
  LCSH: Immigrants – Services for – Ontario – Toronto – History – 20th century. |
  LCSH: Cultural pluralism – Ontario – Toronto – History – 20th century. |
  LCSH: Community activists – Ontario – Toronto – History – 20th century. |
  LCSH: Social integration – Ontario – Toronto – History – 20th century. |
  LCSH: Toronto (Ont.) – Ethnic relations – History – 20th century.
Classification: LCC FC3097.9.A1 I23 2022 | DDC 305.8009713/541 – dc23

We wish to acknowledge the land on which the University of Toronto Press operates. This land is the traditional territory of the Wendat, the Anishnaabeg, the Haudenosaunee, the Métis, and the Mississaugas of the Credit First Nation.

This book has been published with the help of a grant from the Federation for the Humanities and Social Sciences, through the Awards to Scholarly Publications Program, using funds provided by the Social Sciences and Humanities Research Council of Canada.

University of Toronto Press acknowledges the financial support of the Government of Canada, the Canada Council for the Arts, and the Ontario Arts Council, an agency of the Government of Ontario, for its publishing activities.

To my father, Giovanni Lombardi Iacovetta (1920–1983), for believing in the power of education and in the potential of his rebellious daughter

Contents

List of Illustrations   ix

Acknowledgments   xi

Part One: Introduction

1 The Case Study   3
2 The Scholarship   23

Part Two: Narrative, Subjectivities, and Affect in the Multicultural Social Welfare Encounter

3 Toronto Counsellors and International Institute Social Work Theory and Practice   31
4 Professionals, Narrative, and Gendered Middle-Class Subjectivities   50
5 Marital Conflict, Emotions, and "De-culturalizing" Violence   76
6 Generational Conflict: Intimacy, Money, and "Miniskirt" Feminism   101

Part Three: Community-Building Experiments, Integration Projects, and Collective Belonging

7 Making Multicultural Community at the Institute   131
8 Community Projects for Rural Villagers: Health and Occupational Training   165
9 Food as Charity, Community-Building, and Cosmopolitanism on a Budget   194

Part Four: Ethnic Folk Cultures and Modern Multicultural Mandates

10 Immigrant Gifts, Pluralist Spectacles, and Staging the Modern City and Nation   223
11 Handicrafts, High Art, and Human Rights: Cultural Guardianship and Internationalism   257

Conclusion   291

Appendix   307

Notes   315

Index   407

Illustrations

Nell West and colleagues at Institute open house 13
IODE volunteer and new citizen at a citizenship reception 13
Two female bank tellers 114
Young men with motorcycles and a convertible 116
Institute staff and volunteers with coffee and posters of house events 136
Playing cards at the International Institute 142
Outdoor group members at Rice Lake 143
A crowded dance floor in the Cabaret Theatre on College Street 149
Institute "personalities" at a house party 150
A woman carrying a burlap bag of produce on her head in Kensington Market 170
Children eating fruit during Greek Orthodox Easter celebrations on "the Danforth" 171
Santa's arrival at an Institute Christmas party 205
Nell West hosts a sit-down Christmas dinner 206
Performers sing carols during an Institute Christmas show 207
A Croatian dinner at the Institute 212
A Community Folk Art Council bake sale 213
Stephen Vojtech, master chef of Metro Caravan 214
Carnival night at the International Institute 232
Folk singer George Brown performs at the Institute 235
Women in Lithuanian national dress with hand-crafted dolls and a decorative spinning wheel 236
A Latvian folk-dance troupe 237

Young women perform traditional Chinese dances at the Institute 237

Chinese dragon dance in the Toronto Ward 238

Nell West hosting John Yaremko and a priest at the Institute 240

Outdoor Bavarian beer garden at Berlin pavilion 246

Women sell candelabras and decorative cards at an Institute craft show 268

A man sells paper flowers and other handmade items at an Institute craft show 268

Refugee artist Edward Volkman holds up his painting 269

Greek performers dance at an outdoor concert at Nathan Phillips Square 274

Mayor William Dennison and Miss Caravan contestants in Nathan Phillips Square 283

Commissioner Daniel Hill and others at an Ontario Human Rights Commission dinner at the Institute 287

Invited "ethnic leaders" and members at an Ontario Human Rights Commission dinner 288

Acknowledgments

When, thirty-five years ago, I ordered my first files from the International Institute of Metropolitan Toronto records at the Ontario Archives, I did not fully realize that it offered an entry into the neglected history of women's multiculturalism. Over the years, I returned to the collection for various projects. Then, I decided to take the plunge and conduct a project of historical recovery, one that led me to write both a Toronto- and Canadian-based and a cross-border North American study of women's pluralism that also addresses the longer roots of pluralism in Canada and the United States. I did not have the foresight to plan to write this book in time for the fiftieth anniversary of the official adoption of multiculturalism in Canada, but the desire to offer a left feminist historian's intervention into the heavily male and elite-dominated historical scholarship helped me to finish it.

I am pleased to acknowledge the debts that I have incurred along the way. The archivists at the Archives of Ontario were both helpful and patient with a scholar who, in an era before cameras became such a critical tool of the historian's trade, ordered far too many photocopies of their materials. I thank as well the archivists at the City of Toronto Archives. A fellowship with the Immigration History Research Center Archives at the University of Minnesota facilitated my research into the US International Institute records. There, I benefited enormously from the professional assistance and expertise of archivist Daniel Necas and from the unflagging support of then director Donna Gabaccia. I offer a special thanks to Michael Moir (University Archivist) and especially Julia Holland, both of the York University Clara Thomas Archives and Special Collections, and to the staff of the Archives of Ontario, for helping me to access photographs while navigating holiday and COVID-19 lockdowns. Jesse Munroe generously shared with me items from his impressive personal archive of Canadian National Exhibition materials.

A generous Principal's Research Award from the University of Toronto Scarborough provided critical funding for this project. I also received student assistantships and other support through the Department of Historical and Cultural Studies at UTSC and the Graduate History Department at St George. A heartfelt thank you to the generous scholars who wrote in support of this project: Lynn Abrams, Dirk Hoerder, Alice Kessler-Harris, and Veronica Strong-Boag.

I greatly appreciated the opportunity to deliver papers based on this research at several venues. These included the *Gender & History* symposium on Migrations, Institutions, and Intimate Lives at the University of Bristol; German Canadian Studies Conference in Grainau; Colloqium Series of Western University's Centre for Research on Migration and Ethnic Relations; Canadian Studies in Italy Conference in Milan; Department of History, Vaxjo University, Sweden; Social Science History Association meeting in Montreal; Berkshire Conference on the History of Women, Genders, and Sexualities held at Hofstra University; Department of History at the University of South Florida, Tampa; Canadian Historical Association meeting in Ottawa; L.R. Wilson Institute, McMaster University; Health, Medicine and Mobility Conference at University of Prince Edward Island; St Mary's University (with hosts Women's Studies, CERIS Maritimes, and Pier 21); and the Toronto Public Library.

As countless colleagues and students spent the first year of the pandemic pivoting every which way possible, I enjoyed the privilege of being able to write this book during a final paid leave from my university. As people continued to adapt and innovate, I completed revisions in the first few months of my retirement from the University of Toronto. But during the lengthy process of thinking and drafting the book, I benefited from the curiosity, support, and feedback from various colleagues. My thanks to Heidi Bohaker, Laurie Bertram, Donna Gabaccia, Sean Mills, Jeffrey Pilcher, Steve Penfold, James Retallack, Lynn Viola, and Natalie Zemon Davis. A special thank you to Russell Kazal, who generously shared with me his own research on the history of pluralism in the United States and offered invaluable feedback on earlier drafts of my work.

For their advice, feedback, and camaraderie at home and away, I thank Bettina Bradbury, Marlene Epp, Dirk Hoerder, Claudia Rapp, Susana Miranda, Wendy Mitchinson (who is sadly missed), Silke Neunsinger, Roberto Perin, Gabriele Scardellato (also sadly missed), Katrina Srigley, Marc Stein, Jorge Olivares, Molly Ladd Taylor, Cynthia Wright, and Stacey Zembrzycki. I am grateful to Robert Cupido, Tina Chen, Gilberto Fernandes, Michael Akladios, Kassandra Luciuk, Yukari Takai, and Funké Aladejebi for generously answering my questions about individuals, ethnic spectacles, and Cold War politics.

My thanks to the York University and University of Toronto members of the Toronto Immigration History Group for their feedback on earlier versions of certain chapters. Working with graduate students has been central to my professional life at the University of Toronto and I continue to derive much intellectual pleasure from it. More specifically, co-writing an article on the US

Institutes with Erica Toffoli helped me to move forward with my book. So, too, did my conversations with Sheyfali Saujani, Lauren Catterson, Amanda Whitaker, Jennifer Evans, Edward Dunsworth, Sanchia de Sousa, and Simon Vickers. Jason Romisher of Western University helped me over a pandemic hurdle by conducting some London-based research.

For this project, I was able to expand considerably an existing database of Institute case files (from just over 1,000 to 7,000 files). I thank Amanda Wedge for her work on the final database, for responding efficiently to my endless requests for a run of cases of this or that type, for assisting with the chapters in part 1, and for generating the tables in the appendix. Before taking up their own professional posts, Nadia Jones-Gailani, Dennis Kim, and Jared Toney provided critical research assistance. Kate Grisdale provided some valuable editorial assistance.

My reading of the case files has benefited from various workshops with undergraduate students who have taken my course on historical methods. For going over "my numbers" and catching my mistakes, I thank Tracy Stewart. I owe an intellectual debt to my anonymous readers (and one of them in particular) for their rigorous, engaging, and generous reading of my manuscript. At University of Toronto Press, Len Husband provided support and good cheer as he shepherded the manuscript through the review process. Thanks as well to the Press's Christine Robertson, for keeping me on schedule, to copy editor Anne Laughlin, for improving my prose and posing thoughtful questions, and to Judith Clark for the index.

I was lucky enough to be on leave and not teaching online during this pandemic. But the isolating process of writing under various stages of lockdown was helped enormously by the many walks with friends (including Kathy Scardellato, Marcel Martel, Roberto Perin, Danyelle Boily); the virtual visits with friends (including Cynthia Wright, Paul Eprile, Debbie Honickman, Russell Kazal, Debbie Gesensway, Maggi Redmonds, Mariana Valverde, Molly Ladd Taylor, Tracy Stewart, and Bob Allan), the biweekly virtual dinners with friends (Donna Gabaccia and Jeffrey Pilcher), and virtual cocktails and dinners with family (Lorna Wright and the "Iacovettas" – Mario, Brenda, Tony, Sandy, Bruno, Fran, Sandra, Duane, the nieces and nephews, and the grandnieces and grandnephews.) My siblings and their partners will know that my effort to handle with respect and sensitivity the material contained in the case files is informed by our own experiences with the type of encounters, struggles, heartbreak, and loss they document.

I owe a very special thanks to three scholars and good friends who kindly read a rambling draft of this big book and offered cogent advice on how to make it better: Mariana Valverde, Craig Heron, and Ian Radforth. As my life partner, academic colleague, and ally, Ian has never failed to offer me his professional and personal support, and his love and intellectual talents have sustained me through yet another challenging project.

PART ONE

Introduction

Chapter One

The Case Study

Visiting Toronto's International Institute

For almost two decades before Canada adopted multiculturalism as an official policy in 1971, the International Institute of Metropolitan Toronto was actively promoting pluralism as a city- and nation-building project. Both a social welfare agency and a socio-cultural organization, the Institute applied what were later called multicultural approaches in its immigrant counselling and casework. Women played key roles in the Institute as leaders, community organizers, and front-line social workers. They comprised a significant proportion of its diverse immigrant clientele and its ethnically mixed membership. During the multi-ethnic festivals that the Institute mounted with its allies and collaborators, women performed on the stage and behind it as organizers. The wealthier women also participated in the making of an urban bourgeois aesthetic that traded in ethnic folk performance and arts and crafts.

The Toronto Institute was officially founded on 1 October 1956. At that time, two existing agencies merged and joined the international institute movement, a US-wide network of pluralist agencies with origins in early-twentieth-century women's reformism. During its heyday in the 1960s, the Toronto Institute was located for several years at 709 College Street in the immigrant west end. The two buildings – an auditorium that had once been a Protestant church and then a synagogue, and a three-storey school building – were connected by a rear passageway. The two-level auditorium was renovated and a basement-level cabaret space was created. The renovated school-turned-main-building housed a lounge, a library, two exhibition spaces, several meeting rooms, and staff offices. Entering the premises meant stepping into a multicultural but heavily European space.

Let's imagine what visitors to the Toronto Institute in, say, 1964 would have observed. The tour's host was Canadian social worker Nell (Nellie) West, the agency's first director and its longest-serving administrator. Greeting the visitors in the front hall of the main building, she likened the agency to "a bridge whose traffic is the interpretation of the newcomer to the Canadian, and of the Canadian society to the newcomer." Speaking in a deliberately slow and calm manner, West described her heavily immigrant staff as uniquely placed to fulfil the dual goal of integrating immigrants into Canadian society while preserving their distinctive cultures and promoting ethnic diversity. The Institute, she declared, represented a bold experiment in the making of an international community, or local United Nations, that could act as a model for a more robust multicultural nation. She noted, too, that "native-Canadians," not only newcomers, had to undergo a process of "re-education" that would instil in them a respect for cultural diversity. While admitting to the need for more Canadian-born members, West then invited her visitors to see for themselves how newcomers and Canadians together were pursuing "common purposes on a basis of mutual respect, equality, and non-discrimination in regard to race, nationality, and religion."[1]

As the visitors toured the main building, which was open all week from 8:30 am until 11 pm, they took in various scenes. The tense faces of the men and women waiting for an intake interview in the reception centre or for their appointment with one of the multilingual counsellors conveyed considerable anxiety. One visitor swore that she could hear muffled shouting from behind a door. The chatter and music that could also be heard signalled more upbeat scenarios. In the main floor rooms that were set up with card tables, a dozen men and women of Dutch, German, and other origins were playing bridge or chess, their friendly banter obviously annoying the serious-minded club leaders who wanted quiet concentration. Across the hall, a visitor walked into a group discussion on democratic citizenship. Another joined a group watching a National Film Board documentary on the Calgary Stampede. In an upstairs room near the kitchen, the supper club members were enjoying their monthly dinner, the featured Portuguese meal the work of a cook and some of its fifteen members. Next door, the heavily Eastern European outdoor group was planning weekend camping trips. In the other rooms, some of the Institute's three dozen affiliated groups, the few non-European among them being the Chinese Canadian Association and the West Indian Student Association, were holding their own meetings.

The English classes and conversational tutorials brought a few hundred people into the Institute each weekday afternoon and evening. Finding a tutorial being held in a stairwell, one visitor watched as a blind teacher used a small china dog and some wooden dolls to help her Italian, Greek, and Colombian students learn English. Nearby, some social workers and a public health nurse were learning Italian. Bypassing the lounge, where two women were leafing through magazines, another visitor took in the refugee art show in one of the exhibition rooms.

As for the music heard in the main building, it came from three rooms. In one of them, an affiliated Latvian choral group was rehearsing for a civic holiday performance at City Hall. In another, a Macedonian folk-dance troupe was getting ready for a popular television show. In the third, some young Hungarian men were listening to jazz records. A visitor who went into the cabaret theatre in the auditorium building found the International Institute Folk Dancers rehearsing for an upcoming festival. On Saturday nights, people took over the space to dance to the contemporary music of orchestras like Jim O'Neil and His Boys or Salvatore's Orchestra, though men always outnumbered women. Had our visitors returned for the opening concert of an Institute United Nations or Ethnic Week program, which was usually held in the main auditorium, they would have witnessed a colourful and eclectic show. By decade's end, someone tracking the Institute's efforts to promote multiculturalism on a wider scale would have attended the first Metro International Caravan in summer 1969. A mega-festival with many organizers and sponsors, dozens of pavilions showcasing ethnic folk culture and food, and hundreds of thousands of tourists and local participants, Metro Caravan's longevity would help to solidify Toronto's image as the most culturally diverse city in Canada.

Women's Pluralism

This book is a study of a model of liberal pluralist multiculturalism in which women were the primary agents. Drawing on the rich archive of Toronto's International Institute and research on the US Institutes,[2] and other sources, it examines multiculturalism as social work and community organizing as well as cultural and nation-building practices. I argue that the Toronto Institute women promoted a progressive but flawed mandate to integrate immigrants and refugees into an increasingly diverse city. And by extension it offered a model of multiculturalism to the rest of the nation.

The study investigates the contradictions between, on the one hand, the women activists' desire to celebrate ethnic diversity and build a pluralist community, and, on the other, their implication in a nation-building project that sought to manage that diversity and ensure loyalty to the state. To paraphrase and modify Benedict Anderson's notion of imagined communities, their practices of nation-building included the use of popular spectacles and dissemination of a multicultural vocabulary through different types of media to shape a public narrative of Toronto and Canada as a robust multicultural society during an era of mass migration.[3] Drawing on the feminist, class, and anti-racist critiques of nation-building and the scholarship on spectacle and commemoration, I show that these practices involved the manipulation of the Canadian past, the staging of eclectic but packaged displays of ethnic folk cultures, and the inventing of a pluralist tradition meant to allay anxieties and ensure social order at a time of rapid change.[4]

The book probes the fundamental tensions within liberalism – including the liberal social work variant – between democratic ideals and hierarchies of influence and power by scrutinizing the on-the-ground interactions, negotiations, and conflicts that marked the individual counselling sessions as well as the group and community relations at the Toronto Institute. Among these hierarchies, the imprints of gender, race, and class relations – and often gender, ethnic/race, and class systems based on national or ethnic origins – shaped both quotidian life at the Institute and its community projects and cultural programs.[5]

In offering a warts-and-all analysis of women's pluralism in Canada through a broadly cast case study of the Toronto Institute, this book also reflects an engagement with North American, cross-border, and international as well as national debates and developments. My main goal was not to write an institutional history, but to use the institutional record to explore themes related to women and multiculturalism. But I certainly address the Institute's origins and its demise.[6]

This is also a Toronto story. Pluralism, like all ideologies, can have regional or local variants and inflections. Pittsburgh has its Cathedral of Learning and Winnipeg its International Centre. In both cases, ethnic groups were invited to decorate a room that reflected their heritage culture.[7] Toronto's multiculturalism is a bold, even brash, brand. That Toronto is the most diverse city on the globe comes trippingly on the tongue of its boosters. A statue entitled *Monument to Multiculturalism* stands prominently in the centre of town, a gift from the Italian community. The claim that UNESCO recognizes Toronto as the world's most diverse city is an urban myth by which many Torontonians live. The city's self-styled image is wrapped up in a super pluralism and hyper-diversity brimming with over-the-top food-and-festival spectacles driven by populist ideology and business tourism.[8] The Raptors-mania during the 2019 National Basketball Association championship turned a Toronto basketball team composed primarily of African Americans (but also with a president and two key players of African origins) in a US league into a symbol of Toronto and Canadian multiculturalism. The victory parade put the city's diversity on a national, North American, and global stage.[9] The pluralist boosterism of the Toronto Institute and its allies was aided by the city's growing population, its rise as the country's financial centre, and its increasing influence as a media centre as well as a tourist destination that could project its vision to national and even some international audiences.

Precursors

Toronto's International Institute was part of a US-based umbrella organization with roots in the Progressive era (1890s–1920s), but its origins were local. The initial impetus came from a group of professionals and volunteers who responded to the arrival of refugees in postwar Toronto by organizing practical support and cultural activities involving interactions with Canadians. As immigration continued, the Toronto Welfare Council (TWC), later the Social Planning Council of Metropolitan Toronto (SPC), secured a commitment from people with links to social and volunteer agencies to expand the existing services for newcomers and to create a community centre where old and new Canadians could meet each other. By 1952, two agencies were formed. The New Canadians Service Association of Ontario (NCSA) focused on securing social services for the newcomers while Old St Andrew's Church Memorial House offered cultural and recreational programs.[10]

With funds provided by several charitable groups, St Andrew's ran its friendly house out of an old downtown Presbyterian church building at 415 Jarvis Street, a location removed from the immigrant areas. Initially, the programs were largely a continuation of the intellectual and cultural activities organized by a group of University of Toronto professors for the early arriving Eastern European refugee intellectuals and professionals. (It was called the Hart House Group after the Gothic-style building on the university campus where the meetings were held.) After St Andrew's assumed operations, the membership and range of activities grew. By 1954, the latter included a lecture series, a series of English tutorials, and "a library of Canadiana" to be used as resource materials. The much-valued intercultural groups – defined as groups where "the Canadian and the newcomer participate equally" – organized some of the social and recreational activities.[11]

The TWC reports undertaken in connection with St Andrew's application for funds from the Community Chest of Greater Toronto (later the United Community Fund and United Appeal Campaign) issued some concerns. One was that programs geared mainly towards a "well-educated clientele" might undercut the goal of building a democratic community by scaring off "uneducated" newcomers. Another was the (not surprising) anti-German sentiment expressed by immigrant and Canadian members towards a large cluster of German newcomers.[12] The arrival of Southern Europeans of humble rural origins diversified the class and ethnic profile, but Eastern Europeans from middle-class backgrounds would remain a strong presence in Institute programs.

In response to criticism from the members, the St Andrew's board rescinded an English-only policy meant to discourage Old World animosities and attract more English Canadian members. Significantly, the decision followed a discussion of the International Institutes' philosophy of encouraging immigrants to retain their cultural heritage while also accepting the dominant US culture. English Canadian nationalism continued to inform Toronto Institute pluralism, but so, too, would the insistence that Canadians not simply create programs for newcomers but also participate in cross-cultural activities that would make them better citizens too. A visit by a St Andrew's delegation to Detroit's Institute influenced later developments.[13]

The NCSA's orientation and referral services focused initially on the Eastern Europeans who used St Andrew's House. It, too, enjoyed the support of sponsors. The funds provided by the Imperial Order Daughters of the Empire (IODE) allowed the agency to rent downtown office space. In 1954, the wealthy Anglo women of the Junior League of Toronto adopted the NCSA as a charitable project. The NCSA moved into St Andrew's and hired West as director. A pluralist by virtue of her social work training and experience in interwar Chicago, West (and colleagues) spoke of modelling the NCSA after the International Institutes. Two years later, the NCSA and St Andrew's merged and joined the American Federation of International Institutes.[14]

The IODE's involvement with the NCSA and then the Institute requires some additional comment given its history as an imperialist organization that had long promoted the assimilation of immigrants into a British-defined Canada. After the Second World War, the IODE, like many other English Canadian groups, shifted its focus away from Britain, whose status and prestige in the world had declined, and towards North America and to Canada in particular. In the process, notes Katie Pickles, a belief in the racial hierarchies that had undergirded imperialism gave way to a preoccupation with what made Canada unique. Active Cold Warriors as well, the IODE women proclaimed Canada's uniqueness by emphasizing the values and institutions the Communists sought to destroy. In highlighting such virtues as liberalism and parliamentary democracy, they also confirmed the continuing value of a British heritage. As for newcomers, the IODE's assimilationist stance gave way to an integrationist one that accepted the immigrants' cultural distinctiveness provided they adopted the dominant norms of Canadian society.[15]

An upper-middle-class women's organization associated with charitable activities both elite (as in support for the Toronto Symphony Orchestra) and popular (clothing drives), the Toronto Junior League's decision to "adopt" the NCSA and then support the Institute arose out of the overlapping networks among influential volunteers within the respective organizations. But its spokeswomen also spoke of the desire to foster "a community project" in immigrant integration that would involve many more Canadians. The continuing support that both the IODE and the Junior League offered an agency serving non-English-speaking immigrants also reflected other postwar developments, including the decline in animosity towards ethnic minorities occasioned by the revelations of Nazi and Communist atrocities, the rise of global movements in human rights and ethnic consciousness, and the resurgence of liberal internationalism.[16]

Toronto Institute Profile

The Toronto Institute, like its US counterparts, was a volunteer agency heavily reliant on the community chest funds collected to support municipally based, semi-private charity agencies. Admitted to the United Community Fund in 1956, it received most of its funding from the UCF/United Appeal organization.

(In 1964, a good year, the agency's income stood at $34,547.) Occasional grants came from private charity organizations, from various departments within the federal and provincial governments, and from Metropolitan Toronto Council.

The Institute functioned with a volunteer board of directors, a director (or executive director) and other paid staff, and volunteers. In 1960, the budget allowed for sixteen full-time staff positions, which consisted of professional and semi-professional social workers with training in group work or counselling as well as half a dozen clerical and secretarial staff, and two maintenance workers. The multilingual secretaries also did duty as home visitors. The annual membership numbers ranged from a low of about 600 to just over 2,000, with more people attending the major cultural events. Male members outnumbered female ones.

The International Institutes, including Toronto's, combined the settlement movement concept of a neighbourhood house with that of a community hub, or social centre, that drew people from beyond the neighbourhood. After spending its first years of operation in the cramped quarters of St Andrew's, the Toronto Institute acquired the lease on the College Street address in 1959 and moved in after completing the renovations. In winter 1966, it moved again, to 321 Davenport Road. By 1973, a newly decentralized Institute consisted of four offices spread across Metropolitan Toronto.

Personnel

All together, the Institute was more ethnically diverse than the city's mainstream agencies and government departments. Overall, women outnumbered men in paid and volunteer posts, though at various points in time, a majority of the board members and senior administrators were men.

The greatest degree of ethnic diversity existed among the combined staff of the Department of Group Services, which oversaw the clubs and house programs, and the counselling staff of the Department of Individual Services. In addition to the professional social workers and semi-professional practitioners, staff included social work students who were placed as group workers (but not counsellors) and educated newcomers who received on-the-job training. In keeping with a now familiar multicultural principle, the Institute deliberately recruited from the immigrant communities it served, though most of the staff it employed were from a middle-class background. The previous occupations of those who were retooled as counsellors included teacher, engineer, trade official, lawyer, doctor, and university student. By 1970, a more racially diverse staff included social workers from Korea, India, and Guyana, but the financial and other troubles that led to the agency's demise by the end of 1974 meant their terms were short-lived. Even so, the refugee or immigrant profile of many Institute staffers precludes a simple categorization of them as so many

Canadian bourgeois agents of Canadianization acting upon poor and marginalized foreigners.

The multi-ethnic Institute board included politicians, businessfolk, professionals (lawyers, accountants, dentists), and social welfare personnel who supported immigration and saw in pluralism a means by which to preserve social order in a time of rapid change.[17] Prominent male members included the Russian-born David Croll, a leading Liberal and Canada's first Jewish senator. Progressive Conservatives included lawyer and city councillor William Archer and, later, Allan Grossman, a Jewish Canadian cabinet minister in the Ontario government. C.D. Milani, an Italian Canadian developer who subsidized the Institute's summer outdoor fundraiser, and Leon Kossar, a Ukrainian-Canadian journalist and festival promoter, were among the ethno-Canadian (as in neither British nor French in origin) men who served on the board.

The educators who served board terms included, early on, J. Roby Kidd, director of the left-leaning Canadian Association for Adult Education, and later, Freda Hawkins, a political scientist specializing in immigration policy at the University of Toronto. The Institute was a non-denominational though heavily Protestant agency, but the presence of Catholic leaders such as Father C.J. Mulvihill, an administrator of Catholic immigrant services and charities, was a nod to the many Catholic immigrants entering Toronto. A civil servant with expertise on English and citizenship programs, Stephen Davidovich belonged to the "nationalist" or mainstream Ukrainian Canadian community.[18]

Many of the board's female members came through the Institute's networks. Social worker Charity Grant worked with the SPC and the federal Canadian Citizenship Branch while Helen Ignatieff (who married into the celebrated Russian Canadian family) was a curator of "Canadiana" at the Royal Ontario Museum. Well-connected Canadian volunteers included Mrs Douglas (Margaret or Peggy) Jennings, considered "foster mother" to the Institute for having secured the Junior League's support for the NCSA.[19] Ethno-Canadian members included Mrs S. Di Giacomo of the Catholic Women's League (CWL) and Jean Lumb, the Chinese Canadian businesswoman and human rights activist. A wartime arrival who had worked with the Red Cross and the Allied intelligence services in Europe, and later became an immigrant counsellor with Canada's department of labour, the multilingual Irene Ungar represented the Canadian Polish Congress (Toronto District) and Canadian Polish Women's Federation.[20] In the early 1970s, Dr Nalla (Nallamma) Subramaniam Senathirajah, a sixties-era professional immigrant of Sri Lankan origins who held faculty, government, and private positions as an urban planner and policy analyst, became one of the few racialized members on the board. One of the few women to serve as board president was Mrs S. Gordon (Elizabeth or Betty) Isserstedt (née McBain), a long-time volunteer who in 1962 married a German Canadian.[21]

The half-dozen people who served as Institute director were predominantly white middle-class Anglo-Canadians, though they were not a monolithic group. The first director, Nell West (1897–1973), began her career in the mid-1920s as a prairie schoolteacher. The eldest of six daughters of Protestant Irish-Canadian farmers in Manitoba, West (née Wark) later claimed that teaching Hungarian and Finnish immigrant children in Saskatchewan and Alberta gave her insight into the challenges facing newcomers. Inspired by reform and suffrage leader Nellie McClung, whom she knew as an adolescent in Winnipeg, West later turned to social work. After graduating from Winnipeg's Wesley College (later United College), she went to the University of Chicago, where she earned a social work degree under the supervision of settlement movement leader Edith Abbott, and then worked in the settlement movement. She also spent time at the London School of Economics and at the American College of Education in Vienna. On returning to Canada, she spent more than a decade in public welfare administration in Windsor, Hamilton, and St Catharines, Ontario. In 1934, Croll, then minister of public welfare in the Ontario government, hired West as an assistant deputy minister.

In 1940, West married a man twenty-two years her senior, and at whose request she retired. Two years later, however, she accepted a wartime invitation from the federal government to head the Division of Voluntary Services in the Department of National War Services. At war's end, a recently widowed West accepted a position overseas with the United Nations Relief and Rehabilitation Administration (UNRRA), becoming chief welfare officer for the displaced persons operations in Austria. West's subsequent involvement with the NCSA and Toronto Institute combined her experience in refugee and public welfare work. Her Chicago training in social work mirrored that of many of her US Institute counterparts. As did her love of international travel: she made several trips to Europe and visited India and the Soviet Union. After stepping down as Institute director in 1962 amid a budget crisis attributed to an inept assistant director,[22] West became director of services, overseeing the group services and counselling departments. Upon retiring in 1965, she joined the board until her death in 1973, a year before the Institute ceased to exist on 31 December 1974.

There is a touch of sexism in the nickname that colleagues gave West, a childless widow, in acknowledgment of her "zealous" devotion to the agency: Mrs International Institute. But she also received formal tributes. Upon her retirement, Senator Croll called her "a pioneer in a pioneer field" (immigrant services) and reaffirmed her position that for pluralism to take root both the newcomer and the Canadian had to undergo a transformation or re-education. A few years later, Archer said of West that "without ... the foundation she built," the Institute would not exist. West later received an Order of Canada for a distinguished career of service.[23]

Apart from Black Trinidadian Milton Philip (1966-7), none of West's successors matched her professional credentials. Philip was part of a small but important wave of university-bound Caribbean immigrants who entered Canada well before its adoption in 1967 of a nominally race-neutral immigration policy (the points system).[24] The Institute's only director of colour, Philip held a bachelor's degree in social work and a master's degree in sociology from the University of British Columbia.[25] West's longevity, combined with the high turnover in directors, also helps to explain her continuing influence within the Institute.

If we include John Gellner, a Czech-Canadian writer with Liberal Party connections who served as interim director in 1962, three of the directors were retired officers with the Royal Canadian Air Force. After settling the Institute's 1962 budget crisis, Gellner returned to the board. West's official successor as director was H.C. Forbell (1962-4), who claimed expertise in immigrant cultures largely on the basis of having commanded a multinational NATO (North Atlantic Treaty Organization) squadron in Europe.[26] John T. Seaman (1964-6), who had served with a reconnaissance aircraft squadron in England and Europe during the war, became director after retiring from the Air Force College in Toronto.[27] He then left to join the staff of the Royal Commission on Bilingualism and Biculturalism (B&B, 1963-9), created by the Liberal government in response to growing unrest among nationalists and separatists in Quebec. Prime Minister Pierre Elliott Trudeau's "unexpected" response to the B&B, which highlighted French-English relations and led to sweeping changes in French-language education across the country, was to officially endorse multiculturalism within a bilingual framework.[28]

The only other female director, Mrs M.D. (Tine) Stewart, held the post during the agency's last five years. A Dutch war bride, she had been a long-time Institute volunteer. Two other women deserve brief mention. Kay Brown served as assistant director during the early 1970s, following earlier stints as group work supervisor and editor of the Institute's newsletter, the *Intercom*. Veteran social worker Edith Ferguson directed two major community projects out of a branch office of the Institute.

The mainly female and middle-class volunteers were more ethnically mixed than the directors. Whether volunteer group workers, reception staff, or teachers, most of them worked part-time. The IODE supplied many of the Anglo-Protestant volunteers but also some Canadians of European origins. Other volunteers came through the Young Women's Christian Association (YWCA), the SPC, and the CWL. Some Anglo volunteers spoke languages other than English, but many of the bilingual and multilingual volunteers came from women's groups or branches connected with ethno-Canadian organizations. Some working-class women, including immigrants, volunteered their labour to Institute events. The male volunteers came from the Institute membership and service groups such as Rotary Clubs.

The Case Study 13

Nell West and colleagues host an Institute open house. Archives of Ontario, F884-2-9, B427166.

An IODE volunteer assisting the Institute offers a congratulatory handshake and a picture book on Canada to a new citizen during a citizenship reception at Toronto City Hall in May 1959. Archives of Ontario, F884-2-9, B427166.

Members and Clients

The people who used the Toronto Institute, and helped to shape its character, differed in terms of their class and cultural capital. The fee-paying members who joined the intercultural clubs and groups played an active role in running the house programs. In the mid-1960s, the membership represented about sixty different "nationality" groups.[29] The members and their guests made the Institute a lively place, though newcomers always outnumbered the Canadian-born. Middle-class members outnumbered their working-class counterparts, and men dominated overall.

The immigrant clientele that tapped the Institute's counselling services was much larger and more culturally diverse than the membership. There were many more women clients than female members, but men dominated the clientele as well. Newly arrived and usually speaking little if any English, clients sought assistance for a range of problems. Altogether, the clients in my database of 7,000 case files for the period 1952-72 represent 120 different nationality or ethnic groups. At any given time, however, that number was much smaller. The single largest number of case files were referrals to the Institute for English classes, which were quickly processed. The most common request was help with employment, but many of the clients who booked a counselling session were facing a range of problems, from inadequate housing and mounting debts to marital conflict and mental illness (see Appendix). By 1960, the initial staff of three counsellors had more than doubled, and could provide services in more than two dozen, mostly European, languages. The social work sessions involving Institute staff and clients thus constituted multicultural encounters.

The Institute's mandate to serve non-English-speaking newcomers explains why only a small number of white immigrants from the United Kingdom became clients. (A handful of British immigrants did become members.) The presence of the Jewish Immigrant Aid Society and other Jewish agencies in Toronto surely explains the Institute's small number of Jewish clients. The clients of the late 1960s and the early 1970s included English speakers from the Caribbean, South Asia, and Africa, though the scarcity of information in many of the post-1967 case files hinders an in-depth analysis of their encounters with Institute staff.

My large database of confidential case files represents a significant sample of all the files preserved in the collection of the Toronto Institute at the Archives of Ontario. The Appendix explains the process of selection and provides a profile of the clients and types of cases. The anonymized case files featured throughout the book include both brief and lengthy files, but the thick files involving more complicated cases receive more attention. My scrutiny of the featured files is informed by a familiarity with all the cases in my database, but, setting aside the referrals for English classes, the examined files cover two-thirds of the total files in the database.

The American International Institutes

While Canadian precedents also mattered, West et al. chose to embark on their ambitious project by joining a forty-six-year-old American movement. Historians such as Raymond Mohl and Kristin Hoganson have examined the women's reform movement that propelled the creation of the Institutes and their evolution into pluralist organizations. The initial impetus came from the US-based YWCA movement, which had responded to the growing presence in US cities of new immigrants by providing immigrant women and their daughters with social services and recreational activities. In 1909, the national YWCA hired Edith Terry Bremer, a University of Chicago–trained settlement worker who had worked with the Chicago Juvenile Court, the Women's Trade Union League, and the United States Immigration Commission, to help them address immigration matters. Under the auspices of the YWCA, Bremer – who would go on to become the long-term head and national spokesperson of the international institute movement – created the first Institute in New York City in 1910. Within five years, local YWCA branches had established affiliates in Pittsburgh, Los Angeles, and elsewhere. The rapid spread of Institutes after the First World War then led the YWCA to create a separate department devoted to a whole range of immigration concerns. By the 1920s, fifty-five Institutes existed, mainly in industrial cities with large immigrant populations. Most served primarily Eastern and Southern European newcomers, but West Coast Institutes served Asian immigrants too.[30]

Almost from the start, the Institutes expanded beyond the initial aim of aiding foreign-born women and began working with immigrant families and immigrant communities as a whole. In the 1920s, Bremer's conversion to cultural pluralism would have a major impact on the Institutes, making them vocal advocates of pluralism. Certainly, the liberal assimilationist currents that had circulated within the Chicago-based academic and settlement networks in which Bremer initially trained rejected the calls for immediate Americanization. They also advocated for services to facilitate immigrant adjustment and showed a sensitivity towards ethnic cultures. But they expected the children of immigrants to become assimilated through their participation in the schools and other institutions of modern American society.

Bremer's transition to pluralism, which endorsed ethnic diversity as a permanent feature of American life, stemmed from her experience in immigrant work and her opposition to the wartime Americanization campaigns. The pluralist turn taken some years earlier by Chicago settlement leaders such as Jane Addams and Edith and Grace Abbott also played a role. As did the writings of interwar ethnic pluralists such as Isaac B. Berkson, a Jewish-American educator who endorsed pluralism as a form of cultural democracy. By the 1930s, Bremer was entertaining the radical ideas of Louis Adamic, a left-wing

Slovenian-immigrant-cum-popular-US-author whose pluralism celebrated the contributions of the immigrant working classes and denounced racism and fascism. Berkson and Adamic themselves belonged to a broadly leftist tradition of intellectual pluralism whose origins lay in the writings during the 1910s by intellectuals such as Randolph Bourne, who praised the virtues of cosmopolitanism, and Horace Kallen, the German American philosopher credited with coining the term cultural pluralism. Kallen envisioned America as a federation of autonomous and enduring ethnic communities.[31]

During the interwar decades, the Institutes ran active pluralist programs that owed much to the energetic leadership of Bremer, who also helped to found new affiliates and lobbied for immigration reform. In opposition to the era's reigning assimilationist forces, the Institutes promoted an ideology of immigrant cultural gifts, which preached that immigrant customs did not threaten but rather enriched US society. Integration, they added, required not only the immigrants' acceptance by the wider society, but their ability to participate fully in American life while also remaining ethnically distinct members of a culturally pluralist society.

The Institutes rejected the biological determinism that informed racialist theories of superior and inferior races and instead applied a modestly relativist understanding of culture to ethnic and race relations. Institute directors, many of them female professional social workers, sought out representatives from the ethnic communities to help shape programs. They spoke of building multi-ethnic community centres. The policy of hiring immigrant and ethnic staff distinguished the Institutes from other agencies. Young foreign-born and first-generation women with social work training became nationality workers providing services in different languages and liaising with the immigrant communities.

The YWCA's founding of the institute movement had reflected its shift from a more evangelical concern with moral uplift to a greater engagement with social reform issues such as public health, labour reform, and women's suffrage.[32] During the 1930s, however, many Institutes abandoned the YWCA largely because of its more melting-pot approach to immigrants. YWCA staff might speak of peoples of diverse origins fusing to make a new people, but conformity to Anglo-American ideals was paramount. The Institute folks spoke instead of a mosaic where ethnic groups maintain their distinctiveness while functioning as a part of the whole society. The Institute affiliates then incorporated as a new national organization, the name of which became the American Federation of International Institutes (AFII) in 1944.

The Institutes were independent entities but they were expected to pay fees to the central body in New York City and abide by its training and program guidelines. The ethnic make-up of many affiliates was heavily European, but it also varied depending upon a city's demographic profile. Besides the educational and cultural programs, the Institutes offered clients concrete help in navigating the web of immigration laws and bureaucracy, though, as Andrew Urban notes, they never advocated subverting them. The interwar staff of the San Francisco Institute procured legal aid services for the Chinese, Japanese, and Korean clients negotiating the era's anti-Asian exclusionary regime. In Boston, they assisted Armenian Americans desperate to sponsor relatives fleeing the genocide.[33] To carry out their goal of promoting a more pluralistic society but with one common loyalty to the nation, the Institutes, argues Hoganson, pursued a contradictory agenda that combined celebrations of ethnic folk cultures with instructional programs aimed at Americanization[34] – a point to which I return below.

The post-1945 US Institutes navigated a contested terrain. Reformist impulses that championed a tolerant and democratic nation bumped up against Cold War discourses that, as Donna Gabaccia notes, celebrated America's ability to enforce straight-line (one-directional) assimilation and "the acquisition of a distinctive American 'national character.'"[35] Growing demands for ethnic inclusion and liberalization of the immigration laws stood alongside calls for conformity to conservative gender and family models.[36] A strict immigration regime remained in place until 1965, but the door was opened to refugees from the Soviet Union and Europe. A product of US imperialism, waves of migrants from Puerto Rico and the Philippines also arrived. Caribbean and Latin American migration increased markedly largely in response to postwar labour demands.[37] In response, the AFII reaffirmed its goals, though leaders varied in their estimation of its accomplishments. In 1949, Bremer optimistically claimed that pluralism, helped by the war, the United Nations, and decades of Institute work, had replaced "the old Americanization concept." William Bernard, who replaced the retiring Bremer in 1954, admitted that pluralism still had many opponents and that much work needed to be done.[38]

A Canadian International Institute in Toronto

One of several new Institutes created after the Second World War, Toronto became the AFII's lone Canadian affiliate. There was talk of founding a Vancouver or Montreal Institute, but neither materialized. Still, the Toronto Institute's networks included plenty of liberal and progressive Canadians as well as US Institute colleagues. Other social agencies and groups in Toronto and in other Canadian cities, including London, Ontario, developed similar mandates.[39]

The post-1945 US Institutes initially focused on time-consuming refugee resettlement and naturalization cases, though many later renewed active social and cultural programs. Toronto immediately adopted a wide-ranging social and cultural mandate that more closely resembled that of the interwar US Institutes. Far from being merely derivative of US patterns, that mandate, as we shall see, drew as well on a history of Canadian pluralist experiments that, through a mix of celebration and appropriation, portrayed Canada as a mosaic of integrated cultures.

As Canada's most popular immigrant destination, Toronto made sense as the site of a Canadian Institute. As did the timing. In Canada, too, officials initially adopted a cautious approach to liberalizing the admission laws, but they would open the doors more widely than did their US counterparts. Between 1946 and 1971, a period of virtually continuous immigration, more than 3.5 million immigrants entered Canada. In proportional terms, that volume rivalled the intake of the ten times more populous United States. The newcomers who arrived in Toronto, which drew one-quarter of the nation's immigrants, added to its British population, at least initially, and significantly boosted its European profile. Already by 1954, when the City of Toronto and its surrounding suburbs became Metropolitan Toronto, the increased density of the downtown immigrant areas led middle-class Canadians to move out. Some immigrants, among them Eastern Europeans and Germans, followed them to the suburbs. The rates of suburbanization among groups such as the Italians grew markedly in the 1960s while the post-1967 immigrants settled more broadly across the northern suburbs and the Greater Toronto Area.[40]

Post-1945 migration challenged really for the first time Toronto's Anglo-Protestant profile. Despite the importance of Irish Catholics in the city's history, the sheer number of Protestants, and their dominance within the city's and the province's elites, ensured that Toronto was still very much a WASP city into the 1970s. The hegemony of Protestant culture also owed something to the blue book laws that upheld "Toronto the Good" moralism, though different groups of immigrants would contest the restrictions on outdoor gatherings and other activities.[41]

With 37 per cent of its population composed of foreign-born persons in 1971, Metropolitan Toronto had become an ethnically diverse but still primarily white city.[42] Canada's points-based immigration system contributed to the substantial increase in immigration from Asia and the Caribbean, the proportion increasing from 10 per cent in 1965–6 to 23 per cent in 1969.[43] In 1971, though, still only 20 per cent of Canada's newcomers were born outside Britain or Europe.[44] In Toronto, the members of the "other" ethno-racial groups represented only 5 per cent of the 2.6 million people across the Toronto metropolitan census area. Of these "others," East Asians topped the list (61,785), followed by those from the Caribbean (15,325), Africa (12,135), and South Asia (5,650). Apart from the East Asians, all these immigrant groups, as well as Toronto's Indigenous and Canadian-born Black population, represented less than 1 per cent of the metropolitan census population. The figure for East Asians was just over 2 per cent.[45] Continuing immigration from "new" source countries would certainly impact Toronto, which in 1981 recorded a major spike in the number of newcomers from South Asia, the Caribbean, and South and Central America. By then, however, the Institute had long shut its doors.[46]

The Toronto Institute's immigrant membership and especially its clientele reflected the broader patterns of migration to Canada and Toronto. During the 1950s, Eastern European refugees, the most numerous of them Hungarian refugees of the 1956 revolution, dominated programming and counselling work. But there were also clusters of German, Dutch, and other immigrants from Western Europe. Southern European immigrants of rural origins dominated the agency's 1960s-era counselling, community, and charitable work. In the late 1960s, Institute counsellors were serving Czechoslovakian refugees of the 1968 invasion as well as newcomers from Asia (including from South Korea and India); the Caribbean (including Jamaica and Trinidad); and Latin and South America (including Ecuador, Uruguay, Colombia, and later Chile). A handful of Arab immigrants from the Middle East and North Africa were involved in Institute programs.[47]

The Institute women were promoting pluralism in an increasingly heterogeneous though mostly white city, but they also witnessed the racism that white Torontonians unleashed on the South Asian and other racialized immigrants who began arriving in significant numbers in the 1970s.[48] The presence of racialized newcomers, some of whom arrived before 1970 and became Institute members or clients, created an opportunity to recast, or at least to begin to rethink, pluralism in a less Eurocentric fashion. The materials dealing with the post-1967 newcomers are disappointingly sparse, but they do allow me to talk about opportunities both taken and missed.

Possibilities, Limits, and Paradoxes

Like the debates over multiculturalism, the US-based scholarship on the International Institutes is heavily polarized. Those who emphasize the US Institutes' progressive features argue that they represented the humanitarian as opposed to social control side of immigrant social welfare. The multi-ethnic events, they add, offered a critical means by which to preserve im/migrant cultures and present them to wider US audiences.[49] The critics argue that the Americanizing forces that inflected Institute festivals and other activities betray a delayed melting-pot stance that accepted diversity "only for the present,"[50] and that turned ethnic folk cultures into tourist commodities.[51]

The Canadian and American scholarship on pluralism more broadly is similarly polarized between those who praise and those who damn multiculturalism (see chapter 2). The observation applies as well to the wider international arena. It is not only that polarized debates also rage within individual nations such as the United Kingdom. The spectacle of state leaders declaring the failure of multiculturalism in Europe also reflects very different understandings of this liberal ideology from that within self-defined nations of immigrants. Instead of the positive connotations historically attached to pluralism in North America and Australia (however contested or unevenly implemented), multiculturalism in post-1945 European countries such as France, Germany, and the Netherlands was more about managing the diversity of foreign guest workers who were supposed to, but did not, return "home" when their labour was no longer needed. Europe's "immigrant crisis" predated the more recent arrival of refugees fleeing violence and war in the Middle East and Africa, but their presence both in the United Kingdom and on the Continent further fuels the multiculturalism backlash.[52]

Moving beyond a dichotomy of liberal pluralism as either a progressive or retrograde ideology, my analysis of the Toronto Institute, and of multiculturalism more broadly, offers a more complex framing that probes the possibilities and limits as well as the paradoxes of an influential (if now besieged) approach to incorporating immigrants into the nation-state.[53] The study sheds light on several themes. Here, I note two of them.

One is that the Institute espoused a double-edged pluralism marked by positive and negative features. A desire to encourage integration so as to preserve distinctive traditions and promote cultural diversity existed alongside the insistence that immigrants absorb core Canadian values. As its theoreticians posit, ethnicity is socially constructed, or invented. Also, pluralism and assimilation are not simple opposites, and a given cultural event might well contain elements of both. But frequent blurring of the lines between integration, assimilation, and Canadianization produced ambiguity and confusion.[54] In their group, community, and counselling work, Institute staff sometimes served as empathetic and progressive pluralists; other times they operated as intrusive experts. The popular festivals they mounted harnessed traditional folk cultures to a modernist nation-building project that also traded in nostalgia, market tourism, and an elite culture. Mobilized in support of a model of "good" citizenship and to celebrate a liberal internationalism in a Cold War context, the pageants and folk arts sidelined Indigenous peoples and racialized immigrants while also turning them into colourful folk figures.

A second theme concerns the Toronto Institute's mixed record of success and failure and its uneven legacy. The cultural activism of the women and their male colleagues and various partners, I argue, helped to lay the groundwork for a later acceptance of multiculturalism among many ordinary Canadians. But it never resolved the tensions owing to the paradox of simultaneously celebrating and appropriating immigrant customs for city- and nation-building ends. Staff efforts to apply pluralist, or social-cultural, approaches in their counselling practices have not been entirely forgotten, but their categorical characterization as assimilationist by some social work scholars underscores the slipperiness of the concepts used.[55]

A Book in Four Parts

The book is organized thematically. The Introduction, or part 1, is divided into two chapters: the case study just presented and a discussion of the extensive scholarship on multiculturalism. The three sections that follow part 1 roughly correspond to the Institute's major types of activities: counselling and casework, group and community programs, and promoting cultural diversity among wider publics. Just as the focus of the different but overlapping activities shifted, so too does the scale of investigation. The initial focus is on the individual clients (or couples) and their counsellors; it then shifts to the clubs and community projects meant to foster a collective sense of belonging and to ensure the integration particularly of low-income immigrants. Finally, the lens is on the cultural events and festival spectacles intended to delight, inform, and inspire the audiences in attendance to embrace cultural diversity.

In part 2, Narrative, Subjectivities, and Affect in the Multicultural Social Welfare Encounter, the chapters draw on my database of case files in order to examine the interactions particularly between the immigrant counsellors and immigrant clients. Like other social welfare scholars, I highlight the "theatre of encounter" captured, albeit unevenly, in the social worker's case file. Moving beyond the dichotomized debates over whether these texts reflect reality or the file-maker's fiction, I approach the case records as professional constructions that create clients, authorities, problems, and solutions, but that also often include the narrative traces of the client's subjectivities. I interpret them through a narrative and an emotions framework and highlight the affective dimension of these interactions.[56] Paying attention to both the material and the discursive, my analysis considers how front-line workers sought to apply the contradictory demands of the Institute's agenda while experimenting with different narrative forms of case-record writing, and how the clients' subjectivities, their grim circumstances, and their compliance or resistance entered the story. I also draw comparisons between Institute and contemporary multicultural approaches to immigrant counselling.

The chapters in part 3, Community-Building Experiments, Integration Projects, and Collective Belonging, explore the theme of building a democratic pluralist society from different vantage points and spatial scales. They address the multifaceted, even contradictory, character of the Institute – as a multicultural, intercultural, and intermediate social space[57] as well as a contact zone marked by hierarchical relations[58] – and how it affected individual and group identity formation and social dynamics. The analysis of the Institute's charity, health and welfare, and vocational training projects examines the Institute's community-based efforts to improve access to health and welfare resources and trade-training programs. Together, the chapters explore social work as both a progressive and a regulatory practice.

Turning to cultural spectacles, folk revivals, gendered performances, and nation-building, the chapters in part 4 – Ethnic Folk Cultures and Modern Multicultural Mandates – explore the cultural scripts, contestations, and negotiations that shaped the Institute's popular pluralism. The analysis probes the Institute's immigrant-gifts pluralism and the cross-border links that shaped its eclectic multicultural extravaganzas. It highlights the cultural assertion of the ethnic elites who engaged in a dialectical dance of accommodation and resistance with the Institute.[59] Another focus is the roles that women played in shaping and enacting Institute pluralism during an era that saw a resurgence in liberal internationalism and a folk revival movement. Attention is given to how middle-class and wealthy women embraced their role as guardians of ethnic folk culture and cultivated a bourgeois aesthetic built around the collection of immigrant arts and crafts. The section also looks at the ways in which women's and men's costumed bodies performed an attractive, even therapeutic, pluralism, and one that aligned with conventional gender norms. Finally, I explore how the young women who performed the traditional folk culture scripts navigated Canadian modernity.

Chapter Two

The Scholarship

Many Canadians mistakenly believe that a mosaic ideology has long reigned in Canada while the melting pot still enjoys hegemony in the United States. This is not so. Over the course of the twentieth century, multicultural ideologies displaced dominant assimilationist ones often called Anglo-conformity in Canada and the melting pot in the United States. Multiculturalism became a formal state policy in the former but not in the latter, though in neither case was the trajectory from a minority to a leading if contested creed a linear or straightforward one.

The Canadian federal policy adopted in 1971 initially emphasized an ethnicity-based multiculturalism and provided funding for ethnocultural organizations interested in the preservation of cultural heritage and for research on ethnic groups. By the 1980s, most provincial governments, some of which had earlier passed similar policies, had their own multiculturalism policy. In 1982, multiculturalism was recognized by the Canadian Charter of Rights and Freedoms, which superseded the 1960 Canadian Bill of Human Rights. In 1988, the Canadian Multiculturalism Act was passed. In response to the growing calls to combat racial discrimination against newer immigrants, the 1980s also saw the creation of some equity- or rights-based policies and programs. Official multiculturalism has always attracted critics, but the experts report that it remains popular with Canadians, though to a far less extent in Quebec.[1]

American Multiculturalism

American ideologies of multiculturalism were less codified but no less far-reaching and, in some cases, more insurgent in questioning existing hierarchies of race and gender. In the United States, the term "multiculturalism," while it surfaced in the 1970s, rose to prominence in the late 1980s and early 1990s to describe movements in universities and the public schools demanding greater curricular attention to non-European groups in American life. The term quickly spread beyond the academy to take in popular affirmations of the value of diversity. As an ideology or a set of ideologies, American multiculturalism holds, in David Hollinger's 1995 formulation, that "the United States ought to sustain rather than diminish a great variety of distinctive cultures carried by ethno-racial groups." Ideologies of multiculturalism thus share a baseline commitment to American diversity as a positive good – with "diversity" functioning as a keyword and defined ethno-racially or even more broadly to include gender and sexuality – and reject assimilatory stances promoting greater cultural homogeneity.[2]

Such ideologies were expressed in movements, especially in education, and in academic and popular discourse, and became institutionalized in state policies such as affirmative action, where the keyword "diversity" figures as a "compelling state interest" that can justify using race as a criterion in university admissions.[3] As Russell Kazal notes, historians have tended to delineate different versions of post-1970 American multiculturalism, often cast as dichotomous pairs, as in "hard" versus "soft" and "radical" versus "liberal." While these dichotomies run along varying axes, the first terms tend to denote a greater emphasis on group boundaries and autonomy and an insurgent questioning of racialized inequality and structures of power, often aspiring to "Third World" coalitions of peoples of colour. The second terms express concerns that tended to value, respectively, the American nation understood as diverse – a feature of state-sponsored celebrations – interaction and harmony among groups, and the freedom to choose identities.[4] However varied, multiculturalist ideologies were never hegemonic in the United States, contending from their inception with racially exclusionary and nativist views and movements that became particularly evident in and after the 1990s.[5]

A number of historians have argued that American multiculturalism, in its different strains, grew out of the crises of the 1960s, with Black nationalism serving as a key source. As Bruce Schulman argued, Black Power's rejection of integrationism in the late 1960s and stress on group autonomy and identity hastened the demise of liberal universalism and assimilationism and became a model for other groups, helping to fuel the Chicano, AsianAmerican, and American Indian movements and what came to be called the "white ethnic revival." For Schulman, the ideal of "diversity" emerged in the 1970s as an answer to the question whether the United States could effectively merge several different types of cultural nationalism. Affirmative action policies in hiring, government, and universities shifted their rationale from integration to diversity on the grounds that "welcoming" racial and cultural differences into institutions would reflect US society's multicultural character. Such changes signified an ideological shift that reconceived the nation as less a melting pot than as "discrete peoples and cultures sharing the same places." The "center of gravity," in other words, "had drifted toward multiculturalism." Gary Gerstle similarly traced the rise of "soft" and "hard" versions of multiculturalism as part of a larger crisis of American nationalism triggered by the civil rights movement and the Vietnam War. In his study of the post-1945 white ethnic revival, Matthew Frye Jacobson located roots of both a contemporary "Ellis Island whiteness" and a left "brand of multiculturalism," the latter initially fostered in part by white ethnic New Leftists and feminists pushed by revivalist strains towards radically pluralist positions.[6]

Such readings tended to cast post-1970 multiculturalism as fundamentally new, in marked contrast to the cultural pluralism of the early and mid twentieth century. The latter was Eurocentric at its inception and, some scholars argued, limited in popular reach and substance, betraying an assimilationist undertow.[7] Yet, as Kazal argues, more recent work has depicted American pluralist ideologies before the 1960s as far more robust, with wider popularity and stronger roots in particular communities and institutions. Such histories have tracked ethnic pluralist expressions that not only predated Horace Kallen and his early-twentieth-century intellectual contemporaries (see chapter 1), such as Kazal's work on late-nineteenth-century Pennsylvania, but also mid-twentieth-century variants of bottom-up, egalitarian, and at times interracial pluralisms. One example is the radical 1930s unionism of the International Ladies Garment Workers Union. Another is the interwar cultural gifts movement in education. Yet another is the left and left-liberal political and civil rights mobilizations that crossed multiple colour lines in interwar, wartime, and postwar Southern California.[8] Nor should we forget the revolutionary multiculturalism of the Industrial Workers of the World. The Wobblies' organizing strategies among African American, foreign, and women workers included the use of interpreters, multilingual materials, ethnic intermediaries, "folk" music, and storytelling.[9] Some of this work, in fact, points to continuities between mid-century pluralisms and the multiculturalisms, both liberal and radical, that emerged during and after the 1960s.[10]

Canadian Multiculturalism

A Eurocentric cultural pluralism was more clearly a precursor to official multiculturalism in Canada. But here, too, more light is being shed on the earlier roots of intellectual and popular as well as social work pluralism. As the studies of the US Institutes suggests, though, US historians have done more than their Canadian counterparts to trace the longer community roots of women's pluralism (see chapter 1). By contrast, the Canadian scholarship, whether sympathetic or critical, highlights the ideas and actions of male elites. These include colonial and Dominion officials, prime ministers, politicians at every level of government, intellectuals, state-recruited academic experts, policy-makers, ethnic leaders, senators, civil servants, royal commissioners, political philosophers, and promoters of mega folk festivals.

Whether revered or reviled, Canada has its "fathers" of multiculturalism. They include Trudeau, of course.[11] And Ukrainian Canadian Paul Yuzyk. The third-force argument in favour of multiculturalism so closely associated with the high-profile Conservative senator, nationalist Ukrainian Canadian leader, and Cold Warrior tapped into a settler ideology of nation-builders.[12] In Toronto, the Institute women cultivated a relationship with a range of ethnic elites, including other conservative Ukrainian Canadians who would lay claim to the title.[13] At least one scholar has awarded the title to the federal civil servants of the Canadian Citizenship Branch.[14]

To be sure, one-half century after Canada's official multicultural turn, the writing on the subject is both vast and varied. There are the many volumes that consider the challenges and national debates of the post-1945 and sixties eras and the continuing machinations surrounding the making of citizenship, human rights, and linguistic as well as multicultural policy and its implementation.[15] Next to them stand the now numerous critiques of the (evolving) multicultural state and society. Drawing on feminist, critical-race, post-colonial, Marxist, Foucauldian, and postmodernist insights, these studies highlight the state's regulatory power over the lives of racialized immigrants and Canadians, particularly women but also over-policed youth and men, and the hyper-surveillance since 9/11 of Arab, Muslim, and other dark-skinned people.[16]

The paradoxical nature of Institute-style multiculturalism certainly owes something to the slipperiness of the term and of liberal ideologies more generally. In Canada, as elsewhere, multiculturalism has been invoked to refer to a wide range of phenomena. In addition to referencing a social reality and a government policy, Canadians scholars have discussed it as a progressive ideology in support of ethnic diversity, an ethno-political or multicultural movement that challenged the dominant two-nations narrative of Canada, a promoter of civic virtue and a more open society, and as an anti-racist or equity rights strategy.[17] Leading liberal theorists such as Will Kymlicka have approached multiculturalism as a liberal theory of minority rights and as a cultural resource assisting immigrant adaptation into the mainstream. Charles Taylor's definition of multiculturalism as a politics of identity recognition builds from the assumption that people's feelings of self-worth and self-esteem are possible only when they are positively recognized for who they are.[18] Scholars have also examined multiculturalism as a state strategy for managing diversity, whether viewed in terms of managing majority-minority relations or politically polarized ethnic groups, in war, peace, and Cold War contexts.[19]

In arguing for the detrimental or superficial impact of multiculturalism, popular and scholarly critics have invoked such terms as "cultural apartheid" (as in the emphasis on how cultural difference retards integration into the mainstream and reduces cross-cultural interactions) and a "food and festivals" brand of "aestheticized difference."[20] Or featured small-town white Canadian-born Ontarians who use the white-settler term "*Canadian* Canadian" to distinguish themselves from everyone else.[21] Almost sixty years after John Porter coined the term, the "vertical mosaic" includes many more culturally varied racial groups and shows greater extremes of privilege and disadvantage than the European ethnic groups Porter studied.[22] One scholar has invoked the term economic apartheid to underscore what the COVID-19 pandemic has laid so bare: the overrepresentation of racialized workers, many of them women, in low-paying and precarious jobs, and living in racially segregated, poor, and unhealthy housing and neighbourhoods.[23] In another iteration of multiculturalism-as-hypocrisy, feminist anti-racist scholars remind us that the era of liberal multicultural policy-making also introduced the illiberal domestic worker and other temporary worker schemes that continue to create unfree pools of racialized labour in Canada.[24]

The strongest rebuke to Canada's oft-cited liberal philosophers comes from feminist anti-racist and left scholars such as Himani Bannerji and Richard Day, who locate Canada's "troubled" experiments in state pluralism in a history of conquest and colonialism. The policy agenda that its makers and supporters claim will finally solve the nation's supposedly ongoing crisis of diversity and national unity, they argue, derives instead from a long history of treating others, be they Indigenous peoples, conquered colonials, or mixed-ethnic populations, as problematic entities to be managed, dispersed, interned, or exterminated. In her own oft-cited critique of official multiculturalism, Bannerji notes that the ethnocultural identities assigned to "visible minorities" are official categories of belonging that reify culture and serve the interests of English Canada in its ongoing rivalry with Quebec.[25] Meanwhile, the liberal analyses as well as the insistence on pluralism's benefits continue apace.[26] So, too, do the acrimonious debates in Quebec over reasonable accommodation of religious diversity that led to the establishment of the Bouchard-Taylor Commission.[27]

Where Are Canada's Women Multiculturalists?

Some women do appear in the literature on Canadian multiculturalism, whether as early-twentieth-century US or Canadian popular writers[28] or late-twentieth-century academic experts.[29] There were women on the staff of the Royal Commission on Bilingualism and Biculturalism (B&B) and among those who presented briefs. The Toronto Institute brief stressed the value of a cosmopolitan citizenship.[30] Accustomed to negotiating with Toronto's ethnic elites, Institute women were familiar with the "we are nation builders too" politics waged by the Ukrainian-led ethnic lobby during the lengthy commission.[31]

The women-centred and gendered immigrant histories penned by feminist historians such as Frances Swyripa, Marlene Epp, and Laurie Bertram offer critical insight into the cultural hybridity of women's everyday pluralism. Or into the deployment of female images, roles, and myths by the male advocates of an ethnic group's cultural politics. But most of them focus on the cultural adaptations within an individual group.[32] An exception is Swyripa's recent book on the everyday socio-religious multiculturalism being practised by European groups on the prairies already in the late-nineteenth century through place-naming, the erection of places of worship and cemeteries, public commemoration, and more private observances.[33] Canadian studies of the roots of pluralism date the rise of an intellectual pluralism in late-nineteenth- and early-twentieth-century debates among English Canadian academics and reformers, and that of organized ethnic pluralist movements in the interwar era.[34] The Toronto Institute's cultural mandate echoed that of John Murray Gibbon, impresario of the well-studied interwar folk festivals and author of the 1938 book that popularized the idea of the "Canadian Mosaic."[35]

Women receive significant attention in two twentieth-century histories of bottom-up pluralism that highlight the lived experiences, negotiations, and mutual accommodations of individuals, groups, and communities. Robert Vipond's study of a west end Toronto school that reflected Toronto's transformation from an Anglo-Protestant to more European and then global city offers a lively analysis of how teachers, parents, and students grappled with the challenges posed by differing waves of immigrants and the intervention or indifference of officialdom. In their important synthetic treatment of immigrants in western Canada, Royden Loewen and Gerald Friesen propose a regional model of urban prairie pluralism. It posits that the adaptations of sequential waves of immigrants, who both created their own rich ethnic webs (such as family, church, and ethnic associations) and interacted with others in imagined boundary zones (sites of interaction with the hosts that could be negative or positive), encouraged a distinctive form of ethnic diversity and hybridity in prairie cities.

While instances of racism, failure, and compromise are noted, the main portrait in both cases is of well-intentioned men and women who, in Vipond's case, arrived at solutions, such as ESL (English as a second language) classes, that were later called multiculturalism. According to Lowen and Friesen, after 1945, the process of mutual accommodation and cultural reimagining was aided by open-minded civic and community leaders who sometimes relinquished control of the social agencies and civic institutions to the immigrants and their children. The lack of a sustained gendered analysis in Vipond's case, however, obscures women's particular experiences and contributions to the making of a school- and community-based pluralism. A similar problem with Loewen and Friesen's book, which certainly incorporates histories of immigrant women, reflects the privileging of theories of ethnic boundary-making and the like that privilege men's activities.[36]

Nevertheless, I share with the scholars just cited, and with the feminist and anti-racist scholars cited here, a desire to do more than simply excoriate Canadian multiculturalism. In assessing a women-led, and deeply flawed, variant of multiculturalism against today's horrific realities, I ask whether it offers any lessons for our current times. The question animates the whole study, but I return to it explicitly in my conclusion.

PART TWO

Narrative, Subjectivities, and Affect in the Multicultural Social Welfare Encounter

Chapter Three

Toronto Counsellors and International Institute Social Work Theory and Practice

Two of the women hired by the International Institute of Metropolitan Toronto to staff its Department of Individual Services were Margarete Streeruwitz, a political refugee from Communist Czechoslovakia who arrived in Toronto in the early 1950s, and Effie Tsatsos, a Greek schoolteacher who immigrated to Canada towards the end of the decade.

Hired to carry out the Institute's pluralist-integration mandate by providing counselling and casework services meant to ensure individual and family adjustment, neither Streeruwitz nor Tsatsos was a professional social worker. (The job description called for a bachelor of social work degree or equivalent.) A one-time client of the Institute precursor, the New Canadians Service Association (NCSA), Streeruwitz evidently had some practical experience, however. Like other Europeans hired at the Institute in the 1950s, she may have worked for one of the many social welfare organizations serving refugees in Europe after the war. Before moving to Toronto, Tsatsos spent her first year in Canada employed as a dishwasher in a Vancouver restaurant owned by the relatives who had sponsored her. In Toronto, before joining the Institute, she taught Greek-language classes to (presumably tourism-bound) Canadians and, having learned English in Canada, English classes to Greek women looking for work. In keeping with the Institute's strategy to recruit educated and bilingual or multilingual staff from the communities being served, director Nell West and colleagues considered Tsatsos' teaching background sufficient qualification for the job.

As Institute recruits who trained on the job while carrying heavy caseloads, Streeruwitz and Tsatsos were expected to apply the casework method central to social work practice with the sensitivity and insight required by the social-cultural perspectives adopted by the affiliates of the American international institute movement. Besides West, there were a few, mostly male, professional social workers who initially carried out the training. As front-line workers who were themselves refugees and immigrants adjusting to life in

Canada, Streeruwtiz, Tsatsos, and their co-workers sought to negotiate the contradictory imperatives imbedded in both the casework method and the social-cultural approach. While both women embraced their role as cultural intermediaries between the newly arrived and the host community, their relationship to the Institute differed. Five years after being hired in 1965, Tsatsos left the Institute to focus full-time on a daycare centre she had established for immigrant working mothers. As the daycare's initial Greek clientele expanded to include the children of South Asian, Caribbean, and other European immigrants, Tsatsos hired a Pakistani immigrant with nursery school experience as her second-in-command.[1] By contrast, Streeruwitz had a much longer career with the Institute. Hired in spring 1957, she moved quickly through the ranks from trainee to counsellor and later head of the Institute casework committee. She also did a stint as reception centre supervisor, which involved training and supervising the volunteers. Streeruwitz retired in 1971, her fifteen-year career making her the Institute's longest-serving paid counsellor.[2]

This chapter offers a profile of the Toronto Institute's counselling staff and examines the nature of International Institute social work theory and practise. Forgoing the polarized depictions of the Institutes as either integrationist or assimilationist institutions,[3] it argues that the theories and approaches that comprised the institute movement's liberal pluralist, or multicultural, approach towards the incorporation of immigrants contained contradictory elements. In addition to addressing the contradictory imperatives of the casework method, it highlights a central paradox that characterized the social-cultural approach. Like their US counterparts, Toronto's counsellors and caseworkers rejected the biological determinism that undergirded racialist ideologies and promoted instead a degree of cultural and moral relativism. Yet they viewed the integration process as completed only once the economically and otherwise adjusting immigrant had absorbed a common core of the hostland's values about work and personal ethics, democracy, and marital and family life. Veering onto the slippery terrain of assimilation, that stance created ambiguity and confusion over the meaning of such key terms as integration, assimilation, and Canadianization (or Americanization). Equally important, though, is that while administrators and departmental supervisors included professional Canadian social workers, the staff's heavily newcomer and "semi-professional" profile preclude reductionist portraits of the Institute as an Anglo-Canadian agent of Canadianization. Nor did the tensions within Institute social work practice necessarily render the workers incapable of providing clients with concrete support.[4]

Counsellors and Caseworkers

Histories of social work practice (as opposed to theory or policy) usually feature middle-class women of the dominant majority and their working-class, poor, and immigrant or racialized clients. By contrast, Toronto Institute counsellors were also immigrants and refugees and their clientele included both middle-class and working-class newcomers.[5] Having earlier recruited immigrant and first-generation women trained in social work, many of the post-1945 US Institute workers were second- and third-generation Americans of varied origins who had trained in the immigrant social service field, though some immigrants were also hired.[6] The social work encounters in Toronto instead involved counsellors and clients who were both "foreigners" adjusting to life in Canada, though their status and power differed. In subsequent chapters, both counsellors and clients are anonymized out of respect for their privacy and that of their families. But here I offer a brief profile of the heavily female but mixed-gender counselling staff.

Across two decades, the Toronto Institute, including its precursor, the NCSA, hired approximately two dozen counsellors, though the length of term and full- or part-time status varied. Apart from Nell West, the paid counsellors were immigrants or refugees. The reception centre volunteers who offered orientation services and conducted the occasional home visit or counselling session were mostly Anglo- and ethno-Canadian women of European origins. Altogether, women outnumbered men in the counselling department. A man usually (but not always) held the position of departmental supervisor while several female counsellors oversaw new staff and volunteers. Initially mainly Eastern European in composition, the counselling staff became more ethnically, and then racially, diverse in response to the changing composition of the clientele, but remained heavily European to the end.

By the early 1960s, there might be eight or nine counsellors filling the staff's six full-time positions at a given time. Together, they provided services in more than two dozen, mostly European, languages. The Caribbean and South Asian counsellors hired in 1970 worked mainly in English. In many instances, so, too, did the bilingual and multilingual European workers, though they differed with respect to training and experience. The departmental supervisor and the members of the casework committee usually held professional social work credentials or had the "equivalent" in social work experience. In addition to training and supervising the counsellors and volunteers, casework committee members handled their own caseloads.[7]

The counselling staff shared a middle-class urban background as well as differing personal circumstances, including those based on gender. In occupational terms, the staff included, besides the few trained social workers, a former teacher and teaching program graduate, an engineer, a trade official, a lawyer, two self-identified business people, and some university graduates. Professional credentials or practical experience was important, but a linguistic and cultural fit also mattered. Institute efforts to hire front-line workers from within the immigrant communities represented in their clientele was not simply a pragmatic response to the lack of "foreign-speaking" personnel in the mainstream agencies and government departments. It also reflected an inclusive, or multicultural, strategy meant to facilitate meaningful social work interactions. The impracticality of hiring counsellors from every ethnic group meant, however, that linguistic abilities, along with the "transferable skills" of well-educated or accomplished applicants, were often the deciding factors in hiring.

Institute administrators preferred educated applicants with a capacity for "sound" judgment and an ideological affinity with the values of liberal capitalist democracies and the North American "modern" way of life. Like their middle-class clients, most newcomer counsellors had experienced downward mobility before joining the Institute. Some file entries capture a counsellor's own efforts to understand Canadian models, the grammatically imperfect writing a reminder that English was not their first or second or even, in some cases, their third or fourth language. Overall, however, the dynamics exhibited by the counsellor-client interactions reflected a variety of configurations with respect to class, gender, and ethnicity/race or culture.

Politics also mattered. Very few pro-Communists of any ethnic origin visited the anti-Communist Institute and no leftist of Eastern European origin joined the staff. In hiring Greek and Portuguese staff, senior staff chose candidates that they hoped would be viewed as neutral by the left and right factions within these groups. Political divisions among Greeks predated the Civil War (1946–7), the Cold War's first hot spot, but the post-1945 immigrants were divided between the small but vocal pro-Communist Greeks, who were largely the children of the 1946 revolution, and the majority of non-Communists. The Portuguese included those sympathetic to the long-standing Salazar dictatorship and the smaller number of leftists who opposed it.[8]

The initial multilingual counselling staff of two women and one man comprised two workers, Streeruwitz and Serbian refugee N.S. Bojovic, and secretary Ida Mertz, a German immigrant who also conducted home visits. Together, they spoke a dozen European languages, including German, the largest group of independent immigrants to first use the department's services being Germans, and the languages of the displaced persons, such as Polish and Ukrainian.

A professional social worker with a master's degree in social work (MSW), Bojovic was hired in fall 1956 as departmental supervisor and head of the casework committee. A speaker of half a dozen Eastern European languages as well as Italian and English, he prepared reports, publicized the department's work, held training and debriefing sessions, and handled some of the more complicated cases requiring more in-depth casework. Bojovic earned praise as a "very mature" caseworker who understood the social-cultural approach and as a fine trainer of staff.[9] Also multilingual, Streeruwitz spoke several Slavic languages as well as German. Her ability to speak Hungarian helped the Institute to face its first major challenge with the arrival of the Hungarian refugees of 1956. One of four Eastern European female counsellors, Streeruwitz's reputation among colleagues as "a warm and understanding personality" and "a capable ... person" reportedly extended to many Institute clients.[10]

The Institute initially planned to focus on offering orientation services, such as translating documents, making referrals, and providing information about jobs and housing, along with periodic consultation for agencies needing help with non-English-speaking clients. In response to the mounting outside requests, however, it expanded its counselling and casework services.[11]

Subsequent counsellors included Hungarian Dr George Nagy, an early-fifties arrival active in the Hungarian Canadian community who was hired to assist with the many Hungarian "56ers" using the Institute, and Clara Tirkantis, a woman engineer.[12] Dutch-born John Henselmans, who supplemented his interrupted university training in sociology and psychology in The Netherlands with social work courses at the University of Toronto, was hired as a social worker in 1960. He, too, spoke several languages, including German, French, and Spanish. A few years later, when Bojovic left for a better-paid position with the Toronto Board of Education's Child Adjustment Service (a counselling department),[13] Henselmans became departmental supervisor. Ironically, given his role as a facilitator of immigrant integration, the "devoted" Henselmans, as a board member described him, later returned to Holland.[14] Irene Szebeny, a multilingual Hungarian refugee who came to Toronto via Brazil, juggled duties as bookkeeper, home visitor, and occasional counsellor. The long-serving staffer was considered a "dedicated" worker who "cheerfully worked overtime" without pay.[15]

The Southern Europeans hired in the 1960s handled many of the growing number of cases involving their compatriots, but, like other counsellors, they also dealt with many clients of other ethnic origins. The Italian-speaking staff increased with the hiring of additional multilingual counsellors. They included Yugoslavian-born Anton Justi, who spoke French, German, and Italian as well as five Eastern European languages. A former government official and businessman in the import-export trade, Justi had worked in Europe before coming to Toronto. He made a distinct impression with his accumulated "knowledge" of different European "culture[s] and customs."[16] An avid bridge player who later became president of the Canadian Yugoslavian Professional Association, Justi counts among the few counsellors who harboured ambitions as part of an ethnic elite. Maria Cosso was first hired as a fieldworker with the Institute's extension office, but the university-educated Genoese woman joined the main counselling staff in the late sixties. So did Vincent Castellano, a lawyer from Palermo who had worked in construction before landing the Institute job. Like a few other immigrant staffers, he eventually earned a bachelor of social work degree (University of Toronto). He later moved to the Catholic Welfare Bureau.[17]

The mainly female Greek counsellors included Tsatsos and some part-time workers. A former lawyer, the male Greek counsellor Thanos Panagiotis resigned a few years after joining the staff in the early 1970s because he was caught sharing his clients' confidential information with the Greek Consulate. If the plan had been to "out" Communists to the Greek government, he would surely have disappointed his superiors.[18]

The mostly female Portuguese counsellors also spoke Spanish, so they carried a caseload of Latin American clients (both Spanish-speakers and Portuguese-speaking Brazilians) in addition to those from Portugal and elsewhere. First recruited as a volunteer, Maria Mota reportedly became "a much sought-after" interpreter for the Family and Juvenile Court. University-educated and married to a businessman, she was praised for her "knowledge" of the North American way of life. She, too, was described as a "very conscientious" and "dependable" counsellor with "a pleasant and cheerful personality" who also worked long hours and sometimes received clients at home. Her correspondence with her female co-workers during her periodic trips to Portugal in order to give birth or accompany her husband on a business trip suggests warm relations: at one point, she thanks them for a Christmas cake and describes being "deeply moved" by the baby and holiday greetings.[19] But like Henselmans, Mota and family later returned to Portugal. We know little about Zia Taveres, who began as a maternity replacement for Mota and later joined her mother in the United States. A parish priest who retrained as a community worker, Ezequiel Pereira da Silva joined the staff in the early 1970s. The credentials of Javier San Martin, a Spanish-speaking counsellor assigned to new clients from Central and South America, remains a mystery.

Through a special arrangement with the federal Department of Manpower (formerly Labour), in 1970 the Institute hired Royston C. Jones as West Indian (Caribbean) counsellor and Murali Nair as South Asian (Indian) counsellor. Both professional social workers, each man combined social work duties within Toronto's Black and South Asian communities, respectively, with part-time counselling at the Institute. Originally from Guyana, Jones was educated in Britain and, before coming to Toronto, had worked with Black community groups in London, Ontario. During his three years with the Institute, he earned a reputation as an insightful counsellor, cooperative colleague, and fine administrator.[20] A social worker from India, Nair left the Institute not long before its demise in 1974. Hired mainly as a group worker, Catherine Lee, a Korean social worker who had trained in the United States, handled some Korean and Japanese clients.[21] The by now financially crippled Institute hired no new counsellors in response to the later clients arriving from Africa, Indonesia, and other new source locales.

The reception centre staff who also conducted home visits included recruits from such organizations as the Catholic Women's League (CWL), ethnic organizations (such as the Greek Ladies Philanthropic Association and Italian Immigrant Aid Society Women's Auxiliary), the Imperial Order Daughters of the Empire (IODE), and the Toronto Junior League. The multilingual volunteers included Vera Peruklijevic (who spoke Greek, Arabic, and Macedonian) and Olga Spaajkovic (who spoke several Slavic languages), both likely CWL recruits. Anna Garcia spoke Portuguese and English. Some of the Anglo-Canadian volunteers also spoke a few different languages. The volunteer supervisor of the reception centre (who usually also had some counselling experience) familiarized her staff with the available services through tours of government and agency offices and explained the rules governing skills-training and professional accreditation programs.[22]

The criteria used in recruiting volunteers included evidence of "an interest in helping immigrants" and the absence of "prejudice to race or religion." As a precaution against "burn-out," they, too, attended debriefing sessions.[23] Supervisors generally thought the volunteers handled a difficult job with "patience and understanding."[24] Retention was a challenge, whether due to marriage, pregnancy, a husband's relocation, or burnout, but the repeated references to a second or third year of service suggest that some women found the work satisfying.

Casework, Social-Cultural Perspectives, and Cross-Border Conversations

By the time the Toronto Institute, through its precursor, the NCSA, established an immigrant counselling service in 1952, the casework method so central to the professionalization of social work in the United States and Canada was established practice. This individualized approach to social problems and solutions, notes Karen Tice, ushered in "a textual revolution in social work," but plenty of debate occurred over how best to create a case file. Some casework leaders advocated a dispassionate, hence more objective or scientific, account of what front-line workers observed, while others urged them to preserve some of the "local colour" (by, for instance, quoting a client) so as to underscore the uniqueness of each situation. Still others called on workers to elevate the probative value of their work by organizing the details into typologies or client types. While social work's elder disciplines, such as psychology and sociology, called for the removal of undesirable "subjective" and "feminine" content, a minority of casework leaders encouraged front-line workers to include the clients' own stories through verbatim quotation.[25]

The casework method dominated by the fifties and sixties, but discussion over the most effective way to create a case file continued. As subsequent chapters show, case records differed among co-workers within the same agency. In practice, the Institute's newcomer counsellors – most of whom resembled the professionalizing female social workers of an earlier era than the products of the latest professional social work schools – struggled to negotiate the contradictory imperatives between, on the one hand, offering (feminine) sympathy and nurturance, and, on the other, (masculine) objectivity and dispassion. We find a mix of specialized and colloquial language as well as objective and subjective evaluations.

As members of the international institute movement, Toronto Institute counsellors were expected as well to apply the social-cultural perspective with which the US affiliates had been experimenting for two decades. The approach drew on anthropological and psychological theories that emphasized the defining role played by group-defined culture – from attitudes and feelings to laws and institutions – in shaping behaviour. Pluralist social work assumed a progressive respect for diverse cultures yet also applied theories inflected with a degree of cultural determinism. US Institute instructional materials that informed the training in Toronto reveal, too, that the application of social work methods derived from a (modest) cultural relativist position often generated hypotheses of immigrant pathology. The theoretical and training materials that comprised the integrationists' repertoire also reveal a certain slippage between integrationist and more assimilationist goals.

Within the wider social work profession, the social-cultural approach represented a specialized but growing field of training. Professional social work in early-twentieth-century Canada, like academic sociology and anthropology, was underdeveloped compared with its counterpart in the United States, making it difficult to track emerging pluralist social work approaches. Leading Canadian social reformers such as J.S. Woodsworth, the liberal-intellectual-turned-socialist, came to endorse pluralism, but one in favour of eventual assimilation, or what social service personnel called "Canadianization." In other words, a liberal assimilationist position. As Susan Bellay shows, between the publication of *Strangers within Our Gates* (1909) – an early sociological tract that peddled a hardline assimilationist stance and indulged in racial typographies of European immigrants – and the First World War, Woodsworth's thinking evolved to include a more cosmopolitan view of ethnic relations and nation-building. Influenced by postwar liberal internationalism and the pluralist turn in the US settlement movement, he replaced a pro–British Canadian stance wherein "ethnic-mingling" with "others" led to social deterioration with a more pluralistic (and culturally relativist) one in which heterogeneity had a role to play in the "moral regeneration" of the Canadian community and nation. His more inclusive approach was decidedly Eurocentric, however, with respect to who was to be educated into Canada's lofty national ideals. The mix of progressive and regressive elements in Woodsworth's interwar pluralism resembles the tensions that existed between the integrationist and assimilationist elements in the US Institutes' Americanization efforts.[26]

By the early 1960s, Canadian advocates of social-cultural perspectives in social work with immigrants, most notably Benjamin Schlesinger, then an "up-and-coming and highly prolific sociologist of the family" with the University of Toronto's School of Social Work,[27] argued that Canada lagged behind the United States. Already in the 1940s, he noted, even mainstream US social agencies facing a growing volume of "ethnic cases" were incorporating social-cultural factors in casework. Like West, Schlesinger urged greater adoption of these methods in Canada in light of renewed large-scale migration and the upsurge in immigrants and ethno-Canadians using the social services of the country's expanded welfare state.[28]

Schlesinger was not officially linked to the Toronto Institute, but some of his students were surely placed with the agency. He attributed the increase in teaching social-cultural perspectives in social work programs in North America to renewed immigration and the lobbying efforts of the Council on Social Work Education of the United States and Canada.[29] The liberal-minded Schlesinger, notes John Graham, "optimistically claimed" that the rising rates in divorce and remarriage in North America as well as the growing number of working women and single-parent households were becoming a part of the fabric of modern society and ought not be stigmatized. His arguments in favour of paying closer attention to the social-cultural aspects of a case drew on those of US colleagues such as Hertha Kraus, a German American social worker who had worked for the Roosevelt New Deal administration before joining the faculty at Bryn Mawr College, and Katherine Newkirk Handley, who taught social welfare administration at the University of Illinois. Schlesinger's publications on social-cultural casework with immigrants and minoritized Americans made use of (anonymized) US Institute cases.[30]

Prominent Canadian social work theorist Charles Fine argued instead for a distinctively Canadian pluralist approach even as he cited US advocates of social-cultural approaches. Fine acknowledged the contributions of US colleagues like Kraus, whose principles of orientation counselling were widely discussed. Kraus stressed the psychological importance of steering immigrants immediately towards the "community resources" that met basic needs like housing and employment because it gave them "a sense of achievement" early on that could help sustain them through the long spell before "material achievements may become possible." Also citing Canadian authors, Fine attributed the similarities in social-cultural models in both countries to the shared values associated with liberal democracies, such as the worth of the individual and a society's responsibility for its citizens' welfare. He conceded that the integration model promoted by US figures such as Kraus and William Gioseffi, a caseworker in the Veterans' Administration of the US government, had enjoyed some success in mediating the call for total conformity with American ways. But he claimed that Canadian efforts in this regard surpassed those in the

United States in the development of a model by which national unity would be achieved through a cross-pollination of heterogeneous cultures. A national strategy that prioritized the "harmonizing" of host and immigrant cultures, and that recognized the "unique contributions" of ethnic groups to the host society, he asserted, was gaining proportionally more adherents in Canada than south of the border, thereby laying a stronger basis for the spread and legitimacy of multicultural practices in social work.[31]

Canada's adoption of official multiculturalism in 1971 no doubt bolstered Fine's exaggerated nationalist claims, and many Canadians still know little about US pluralism or the cross-border conversations about pluralism that Fine himself acknowledged.[32] Such exchanges were of course quite direct in the case of the Toronto Institute, whose training sessions and consultations drew on US Institute materials developed by the central body in New York City. Toronto in turn supplied Institute headquarters with examples of cases and with summary reports for use in training materials that were produced and distributed to member affiliates.[33]

In the United States, liberal social work academics served as consultants and instructors for the Institutes. They included two New York City–based colleagues, Mary E. Hurlbutt of New York University's School of Social Work and Morton Teicher, a former University of Toronto professor who became the founding chair of the Social Work School at Yeshiva University. Their social-cultural approach borrowed insights from influential anthropological texts such as E.B. Taylor's *Primitive Culture* (1895). In it, Taylor defined culture as "that complex whole which includes knowledge, belief, art, law, morals, customs, and any other capabilities and habits acquired by man as a member of society" and into which individuals are socialized. Also influential was Ruth Benedict's *Patterns of Culture* (1946), which issued the oft-quoted phrase in support of cultural relativism: "No man can thoroughly participate in any culture unless he has been brought up and has lived according to its forms, but he can grant to other cultures the same significance to their participants which he recognizes in his own."[34]

In lectures and publications, social workers with links to the US Institutes outlined how individuals were socialized into the value systems, behavioural norms, traditions, institutions, and even "emotional structures" of their respective group in support of the progressive principle that all cultures were deserving of respect. Rejecting, at least theoretically, the notion that one culture was superior to another, they warned against issuing moral judgments about "other" cultures. They insisted that to be effective facilitators of integration, social workers with clients from different ethnic groups, and thus different "dominant behavior" patterns, had to solicit detailed life histories and other information that offered insight into a client's socio-cultural heritage in order to determine the cultural adaptations required for a healthy adjustment to (North) American culture. An understanding that humans are shaped by their culture, they added, allowed them to scrutinize dispassionately the values of their own culture without falling into a blind relativism that sanctioned any kind of behaviour, the result of which would be chaos.[35]

Some allowance was made for individual variation, as suggested by the insight, usually attributed to sociologist Lawrence Frank, that psychological factors or membership in a political or social "subculture" might account for differences in the behaviour of the members of a given cultural group. Even so, in the training-based demonstrations of how social-cultural approaches were to be applied to immigrant cases, the analysis could slip into a cultural determinism whereby ethnicity, often understood as a "nationality group" such as Poles and Italians, but with further distinctions drawn for subgroups such as Polish Jews and Southern Italians, dictated immigrant behaviour (see below). Another source of tension derived from the related idea that, as Kraus put it, the immigrant must undergo "drastic" change in order "to enter successfully into a cultural community substantially different from the one or several cultures in which the individual has lived before entering the new world."[36] It begs the question whether cultural transformation as a requisite for positive adaptation trumped respect for "other" cultures.

Post-1945 social workers associated with the Institutes asserted as well that social science knowledge garnered from the study of the impact of class, religion, ethnicity, and other social phenomena on human behaviour would enrich the medical and psychological knowledge informing social work methods. Hurlbutt predicted that, having embraced psychiatric concepts in the early twentieth century, and then having experimented with public welfare concepts during the Great Depression, social work was now poised to more fully absorb cultural concepts. Teicher similarly argued that the profession's understanding of "man in society" rooted so firmly in psychological and psychiatric knowledge was being "augmented, buttressed and fortified" by insights gained from "understanding man in cultural terms." A common example used in support of such claims was that cultural awareness would prevent caseworkers from miscasting as socially deviant or psychologically ill a client whose seemingly volatile or emotional behaviour was normal within their cultural milieu. These knowledge-based claims did not imply dismissal of psychological approaches – Teicher himself warned against replacing "father psychiatrist" with "mother social scientist" – but stressed the value of combining approaches.[37] The advice meted out by the casework supervisor with the Milwaukee Institute, Frieda Heilberg – to focus first and foremost on people's universal need for "understanding, acceptance, a feeling of belonging" – reflected the continuing importance of psychological approaches in social-cultural casework.[38] Indeed, many used the terms psychosocial and social-cultural interchangeably.

Beginning with institute movement founder Edith Terry Bremer, advocates of a social-cultural approach stressed that application of its insights allowed workers to identify the cultural stresses that produce an individual's social pathology, which might present in any number of ways, from stomach troubles or self-harm to anti-social and violent behaviour. Such discussions involved frequent adoption of a psychological language of pathology. Senior Institute personnel such as Milwaukee's Heilberg and Cleveland's Boris Clarke offered common variants of this pathologizing discourse, warning that, without appropriate counselling, those who were plagued by "inner conflicts" or "bewildered" by strange new living patterns, and ignorant or suspicious of existing social services, would cling to old beliefs and customs and remain ill-adjusted.[39]

The observations could apply to everyone, from middle-class refugees exhibiting emotional problems caused by war and Communist repression to humble rural folk unfamiliar with the "cultural climate and code of ethics and behavior" of the big city, though the former were expected to adapt more quickly than the latter to modern urban life.[40] Southern European immigrants and racialized migrants from within the US empire, such as Puerto Ricans and Filipinos, fell into the designation of more backward rural groups requiring greater degrees of adjustment to American ways. The persistence of low socio-economic status in one's sending and one's adopted country was expected to contribute to mental distress.[41] A similar logic was evident in Toronto Institute reports written by veteran Canadian social worker Edith Ferguson regarding the challenges facing the city's rural Europeans.[42]

A related claim was that an awareness of the heavily symbolic nature of people's behaviour enabled the social worker, under certain circumstances, to predict behaviour, though the examples given mainly involved an immigrant's expected reactions to a situation. A typical example drawn from actual cases was that peasant parents invited to live in the upscale home of their Americanized (or Canadianized) adult children would experience discomfort. If told about the situation after the fact, the caseworker's strategy was to resolve such tensions by negotiating a compromise whereby the parents moved into modest accommodation without losing their children's support, and both couples worked to restore family relations.[43]

The training materials in the Toronto Institute archive are limited, but the available reports align with institute movement positions about, for instance, approaches to addressing the cultural stresses faced by clients in adjusting to the new conditions. Following Kraus' line of argument, Toronto counsellors noted that even the many employment cases required sensitivity to the social-cultural factors that might impede adjustment or cause conflict because an immigrant's experience of being misunderstood on account of language or cultural barriers could generate profound disappointment and threaten their sense of security. Senior social workers told public audiences that many clients suffered from "emotional problems" that resulted in "nervous breakdowns," and also that, with the "proper" help, many newcomers adjusted either quickly or eventually. They taught as well that a social-cultural perspective offered the social worker "some detachment from the value of one's own culture," enabling the worker to avoid making judgmental assessments.[44]

The records of the central body of the International Institutes and a dozen city affiliates offer further insight into how front-line workers were being trained in social-cultural methods. Particularly helpful are the detailed handouts and notes related to a ten-day training session that Hurlbutt held at the San Francisco Institute in 1945 with staff and students invited from Institutes in Oakland, Fresno, Los Angeles, and Hawaii. In anticipation of the postwar work that lay ahead of them, Hurlbutt extolled the virtues of a social-cultural approach in helping to shape behaviour to facilitate "Americanization." Citing the aforementioned anthropological texts attesting to the importance of group-generated "attitudes, folkways, mores, ways of behaving and feeling" in shaping society's institutions, individual behaviour, and a sense of belonging, she also reaffirmed the Institutes' belief in the "equal validity of difference in customs." Viewed within the context of the era's anti-immigrant and assimilationist discourses, the Institutes' liberal position comes through clearly in Hurlbutt's assertion that in the United States "there is a great deal of prejudice." She attributed the discrimination experienced by even US-born groups such as Armenians in Fresno, California, and Italians in New Haven, Connecticut, at the hands of dominant-majority "Anglo-Americans" to both "the fear of loss of economic and political control" and a "lack of knowledge" about such groups.[45]

Turning to the social casework method, Hurlbutt stressed that it was necessary to first collect detailed information, including through life histories, that captured the cultural factors shaping a client's life, and then to "break down" the client's "nationality background into many differentiations: regional, class, religious, vocational, etc." Even "a family unit," she added, imparts certain cultural patterns of behaviour to its members. Rejecting assimilationist notions of immigrants "becoming" Americans "in a definite and static sense" on the grounds that immigration had made America a "multi-group society" and a "highly dynamic" culture, she explained the caseworker's role in encouraging gradual integration. The process involved first determining the cause(s) of a client's ill-adjustment, paying special though not exclusive attention to the social-cultural elements involved, whether related to language or religious beliefs, attitudes towards authority or family, or a deep-seated resentment over their circumstances. Next, offering the appropriate treatment, be it specific advice, in-depth counselling, or referral to a more specialized agency, to affect the desired change. In making the changes necessary to resolving the problem, which invariably included some modification in cultural attitudes or behaviour, the client advanced further along the path towards integration.[46]

The training materials demonstrate the challenges of implementing social-cultural methods and some of their ironic consequences. As a pluralist,

Hurlbutt stressed the importance of a gradual and voluntary process of integration but also insisted that newcomers adopt "a common core" of American values. She explained that "deciding" whether the Institutes advocated "integration or assimilation" was "partly a problem of terminology." Insofar as integration "deals with putting together parts to make a whole" and assimilation "with absorbing and making a whole which is uniform," the Institutes certainly advocated "integration." She had no qualms, however, about using the term assimilation to apply to the newcomer's "necessary absorption of American ideals."[47] A desire to encourage integration so as to preserve "ethnic" cultures and promote a pluralist nation thus existed in tension with the perceived necessity to ensure newcomers' compliance with the dominant codes of the host society.

The paradoxical character of Institute pluralism is most evident in such unresolved efforts to "balance" calls for integration and assimilation. On the one hand, Institute personnel conceived of integration as a "two-way street" where, to quote Heilberg, the aim was not "relinquishing" one's national and cultural background, but instead "a gradual growing into the new surrounding" and "developing the ability of combining or amalgamating the old and the new to fit into the new environment." Patient and understanding hosts offering early and effective assistance could help immigrants make a "positive, constructive" transition from being recipients of social services to "givers" who also contributed to American "civic, social, cultural, economic life."[48] On the other hand, the immigrants, as Hurlbutt asserted, were required to adapt to a core of American values that, though "constantly changing and developing," nevertheless encompassed a set of widely shared ideas "about child life, about civil liberties, about education, about freedom of the press, etc." That core, she added, helped to define appropriate behaviour and thought regarding social and political values as well as marital and family relations and childrearing. Going further, she argued that the existence of this "tangible entity" meant that "mere integration is not sufficient" as it "would deny the acceptance of a "common core of ideas" and "just make for a pluralism which is incompatible with the existence of an American culture." While acknowledging that the degree of transformation expected of immigrants would depend "on the meaning we want to give to the common core," she made clear that experts like herself and the staff she trained would define the ideals and urge their adoption.[49]

Cases that offered post-1945 Institute staff textbook scenarios of migrant maladjustment included Milwaukee's Puerto Ricans. According to Willette Pierce, head group worker at the Milwaukee Institute, her staff had encountered "quite a number of difficult marital situations" owing to "extremely and unreasonably" suspicious and jealous husbands who accused their wives of "having affairs with other men." Consequently, the women, some of them wage-earning wives, were under tremendous stress. The explanation given for the tensions, namely that old cultural patterns based on the assumption that "the man" is "ruler over the family" were being "threatened by the new environment which recognized and gave more freedom and rights to the women," also supplied the treatment: individualized counselling aimed at modifying male behaviour through exposure to American ways. A well-intentioned aim thus, paradoxically, served to reinforce both the idea of immigrant pathology rooted in culturally deterministic models of behaviour and that of the superiority of American values.[50]

The US Institutes had a much longer history than the Toronto Institute of interacting with racialized clients, and their records provide far more evidence than do Toronto's of how the application of progressive social work models could both reflect and reinforce processes of racialization. How Hurlbutt's 1945 training session treated the insight that clients' behaviour was also conditioned by their group's unique emotional structure illustrates the paradoxical processes at play. The teaching cases used to demonstrate how such knowledge helped a caseworker determine which adaptations to advise offer striking examples of how, in its application, an insight ostensibly free of moral judgment highlighted pathology.

A teaching case file on a "White Russian émigré" who fled the Bolshevik Revolution with her family for Manchuria before later migrating to the United States concluded that she clearly exhibited the "cultural attitudes" associated with her group, none of them positive. They included "apathy" and "self-humiliation and self-pity" (this "being a teaching of the Greek Orthodox religion") as well as a "deep concern over changes in social status" common in the "upper middle class in Russia." Workshop discussion of an Italian American woman who, reverting to an Old World Sicilian custom, staged "a prearranged kidnapping" in order to obtain a church blessing for a second marriage concurred with the caseworker's conclusion that the Sicilian emotional make-up "differs from that of a Northern Italian." Both caseworker and trainees thus located the client's cultural script (or ostensibly ingrained cultural predispositions) in a historically pathologized region. These examples, like the psychiatric reports regarding the mental deficiencies of Eastern and Southern Europeans, serve in turn as a caution against the tendency within current whiteness studies to subsume all "white ethnics" into a normative and monolithic category of "white." Doing so can obscure the complicated identities and stigmatizing stereotypes that still applied to various groups of Europeans.[51]

Training cases involving racialized American clients suggest a resort to a more deeply pathologizing discourse. One of the Red Cross cases involving African American soldiers posted in wartime Europe featured a private who suspected his wife of cheating on him. The female caseworker interpreted his "ingratiating, almost servile" behaviour as typical of how Black Southerners interacted with whites, and his indirect way of issuing complaints as "a form of passive resistance" stemming from the "feeling" that being drafted into the army was "as arbitrary and meaningless" as any other experience caused by white rules. She characterized his request for help in solving his marital problem as symptomatic of being "culturally conditioned to leave all major responsibilities to the whites." Finally, she noted that, in evading responsibility for his family problems, he exhibited yet another African American cultural pattern, this one "directly connected with the essentially matriarchal structure of many negro families." In short, the analysis drew on a theory about women's dominant role in African American families sapping men's capacity to compete in white society that Black feminists have long rejected as misogynist as well as racist.[52]

Reading with and against the Grain

The heavily female and European counselling staff carrying out the Toronto Institute's pluralist-integration agenda mirrored more the professionalizing social workers of earlier decades than the graduates of fifties- or sixties-era professional schools of social work.[53] (Even the few professionally trained refugee and immigrant social workers had to make some adjustments to Canadian paradigms.) As social work practitioners handling heavy caseloads and, in the women's case, family responsibilities as well, they sought to identify the social-cultural (and other) elements of a case and convey to clients such lofty but vague Canadian ideals as democracy and the egalitarian family. They also used their own common sense and occasionally drew on their own experiences of loss, migration, and resettlement. Expanding caseloads and limited resources meant a greater focus on shorter-term counselling rather than in-depth casework requiring several visits and appointments with medical and other authorities, but plenty of case files indicate return visits to a counsellor over a lengthy period of time.

Case files were a primary site where heavily polarized debates over "representation" (the discursive) and "reality" (the material) occurred, but subsequent efforts to integrate key insights from materialist and post-structuralist approaches have produced a rich body of scholarship.[54] My database of 7,000 confidential files created by Toronto Institute counsellors – for which there is no equivalent in the US context – allows for a more in-depth analysis of front-line social work practice among newcomers than is possible for the US Institutes as well as other social agencies. My access in certain instances to the original case file as well as the circulated human interest story that staff constructed from it allows me to trace the various layers of mediation involved.[55]

Once again, investigation into what Mark Peel calls the "everyday world of welfare in case files" shows plenty of mismatch between prescription and practice. As social workers of an immigrant social agency, Institute counsellors were expected to be sympathetically disposed towards immigrants and, as previously noted, certain female workers developed a reputation as a caring worker, though they, too, occasionally expressed annoyance with a non-compliant client. In their sessions with a client, however, counsellors were supposed to practise empathy (an ability to perceive and understand a client's feelings while possessing the self-awareness and emotional self-regulation needed to avoid experiencing the client's feelings of grief or loss) rather than sympathy (in the sense of sharing a client's feelings to the point of experiencing their grief or loss) or pity (feeling sorry for them). Instead, we find a mix of sympathy and pity as well as efforts at empathy, and a contradictory mix of objective and subjective assessments.[56] The encounters sometimes blurred the boundaries of public and private, as when workers gave a client money out of their own pocket for food or bus tickets or accepted an invitation to a family event. Female staff were more likely than their male counterparts to bring a woman client home for lunch but, occasionally, a male caseworker did the same with a male client.

All this has implications for how we interpret the case files. Certainly, front-line counsellors were the authors of these texts. They largely controlled the description of a client's appearance or the emotion(s) a client expressed – doing so with such signifiers as "pleasant," "arrogant," "confused," or "upset" – as well as the social conditions they observed. Even when interacting with middle-class clients, they enjoyed the power that issued from their position as knowledge-based professionals. In relation to working-class or low-skilled clients, they enjoyed tremendous class privilege. Certain male caseworkers could be exceedingly heavy-handed in their negative assessment of a woman client. Reading the case files with the grain, then, offers us insight into how front-line workers used a professional narrative form like the case file to order evidence on a person and determine a diagnosis and solution.[57]

At the same time, as a wide range of social welfare scholars assert, possibilities arise for reading against the grain of these dominant accounts. One can look for the narrative traces of a client's subjectivities in the "openings provided by the conflictual interplay of professionals and clients."[58] The case file constitutes a professional intervention, but the narrative practices of caseworkers also create opportunities for dialogue with the attentive historian.[59] The files penned by the Institute's immigrant counsellors generally lacked the conceptual tidiness, and turgid or specialized language, of the tightly organized case records produced by the male-dominated professionals, such as psychiatrists, with whom they sometimes interacted, and whose reports sometimes made it into their client's file. The counsellors' more colloquial or descriptive wording and frequently rambling style sometimes allow traces of clients' subjectivities to surface. The observation also applies to other contents in the file, including the personal statements or cover letters that clients had dictated to or had translated by a volunteer or counsellor. These narratives, too, were mediated by agency staff who may have coached a client on what to say or who in translating the document altered some wording, but they contain traces of a client's mode of self-representation.

Similarly, the counsellors' training, however piecemeal, guided their selection of the relevant "facts" (and some were too quick to apply a medical label to a client), but entangled in the incongruous mix of differing or contradictory impressions, events, and judgments, a client's opinions and feelings occasionally surface in the story. As Tice notes, a client's subjectivity was "professionally transmuted," but it was "never completely erased." It is captured or hinted at in the recorded instances of a client's defiance or resistance to a worker's analysis or advice. In a worker's expression of approval or disapproval, we catch glimpses of an acquiescent or unruly client. That the files created by the female counsellors offer more possibilities than those produced by their male colleagues for reading against the grain confirms what feminist and gender scholars of social work practice have identified as a distinctive type of knowledge produced by the practitioners of a long female-dominated enterprise.[60]

The women counsellors' files are qualitatively different from the men's partially because they spent more time than male workers listening to female clients and thus felt a greater professional proximity to them. As workers who escorted women to a clinic or government office, or helped them place a child in temporary care, or dispatched a public health nurse to visit them, they knew better than their male colleagues the domestic side of poverty, prejudice, and marginalization.[61] But this did not preclude the possibility that, as Linda Gordon bluntly put it, some female workers were "worse" than their social agency.[62] Or that men occasionally really listened to a female, or male, client.

Conclusion

The Toronto Institute's counselling offices, like its recreational and social spaces, constituted both an intercultural site where cross-cultural encounters occurred, and a contact zone where the interactions took place within a context of asymmetrical power relations. These offices, and the other places where counsellors met with clients, whether a local coffee shop, a street corner, or a counsellor's or client's home, constituted as well an intermediate space located somewhere along the spectrum between the public and private. Drawing on my database of case files, the subsequent chapters in part 2 probe the multicultural social welfare encounters that occurred within the ragged, even liminal or transitional, spaces between immigrant private life and the wider Canadian hostland.[63]

The files in my database are both rich and frustrating sources that contain an uneven and overlapping mix of difficult conversations as well as competing, confirming, and, if only rarely, entangled narratives as well as multiple negotiations. Many include a notable amount of detail but many others do not. Most cases end abruptly, making it difficult to assess outcomes, though such files are revealing in other ways. The counselling staff wielded considerable power over clients in these local sites, though, in many cases, Foucault's putative "gaze" amounted to a "glance," or judgments hastily made on the basis of initial impressions, but never exercised full control.[64] A judicious use of the database enables in-depth analysis of the "theatre of encounter" captured, albeit unevenly, in the social worker's case file.[65]

The files scrutinized in subsequent chapters are the product of outside interventions into people's intimate lives, though a blurring of public and private also occurred.[66] Whether the result of invited or imposed intrusions, the highly mediated glimpses into the intimate realm offered by these texts reveal a social welfare encounter that was a far more uneven, messy, and emotional process than that suggested in social work teaching materials. We find plenty of negotiation and frustration on both sides, but there is evidence here, too, of the bonds of trust that occasionally developed, particularly when both counsellor and client were women. The files shed further light on social-cultural insights about emotional structures and also invite informed speculation about the emotional reactions of counsellors and clients. In the three chapters that follow, I explore the role of narrative and gendered subjectivities as well as emotions and affect in the social welfare encounter through an examination of case files (and other sources) that deal, respectively, with downwardly mobile professionals, marital conflict, and generational conflict within families.

Chapter Four

Professionals, Narrative, and Gendered Middle-Class Subjectivities

In a 1959 letter sent to the Department of Individual Services of the International Institute of Metropolitan Toronto, a female scientist from Bulgaria thanked the counselling staff for its "kindness, patience and moral support" in helping her to land a job in her field. For months after arriving in Canada, she wrote, she had wandered from government office to social agency and even church group asking about meaningful work only to hear about low-level jobs. At the Institute, however, she found someone who took "an interest in me" and who understood the difficulties of adapting to a new life. As a result, she added, revealing an attachment to a professional status and identity, disappointment and desperation gave way to "a ray of hope in my soul." Promising to become an Institute member and volunteer, she pledged to help others forced to escape persecution in their Communist "Fatherland" to "become honest and useful people."[1] The Institute counselling staff, who knew the value of a compelling narrative, helped the author with the final version of her letter, which appeared in subsequent reports. In addition, her involvement in Institute activities would have reinforced the multi-ethnic but heavily Eastern European character of an agency whose democratic stance both reflected the main tenets of a postwar liberal capitalist welfare state and bore the mark of a transplanted anti-Communism.

As a woman, this refugee scientist belonged to a minority. But Institute staff used her letter of appreciation and that of other grateful or successful clients to justify the receipt of community chest funds and to generate other funds. They appeared in the publicity materials and in updates sent to Institute headquarters in New York City as proof of the efficacy of their professional interventions. The counsellors publicly circulated the human interest stories they gleaned from selected case records for the same purposes, the character profiles, twisting plotlines, and hopeful endings being key features of the publicity stories used in support of their liberal pluralist project.[2] Containing elements of drama, suspense, and humour, the human interest narratives that animated the

Institute reports and presentations delivered to both professional and popular audiences reveal the counsellors' heavy editorial hand. While also mediated sources, the case files speak to the need or desire of many clients to tell their story, however selective, truthful, or fanciful. So, too, do the letters contained in a file, whether its contents had been dictated to or translated by a counsellor or volunteer. The client narratives contained in a caseworker's notes capture, albeit partially, elements of the "theatre of encounter" that played out between social worker and client.[3]

This chapter examines the interactions between the Institute's professional clients and their mostly female but also male counsellors, highlighting the role of narrative and class-based gendered subjectivities in shaping the multicultural social welfare encounter. The Institute's employment files are not a reliable predictor of eventual success or failure, though they do challenge the popular misconception that immigrants with a professional background, then and now, experience an easier transition than do other immigrants. A careful reading of the more detailed professional files sheds light on the gendered subjectivities of middle-class newcomers in much-reduced circumstances navigating a restrictive professional landscape. Close scrutiny of the fragmented narratives in these files sheds light on social welfare interactions where counsellors and clients were both middle-class newcomers (and often both of European origins) seeking to rebuild professional careers and lives in Canada. My assessment of the files shows, too, that the Institute's counselling methods both prefigured key aspects of contemporary multicultural career-counselling principles (such as recruiting counsellors from within the immigrant communities being served) and exhibited the familiar shortcomings of career-counselling for "foreign" professionals, such as urging clients to markedly reduce expectations rather than try to resume or realize their professional aspirations.

Scholars in the fields of refugee studies and social work have documented, albeit in different ways, the importance of a convincing narrative. The traumatized refugee must narrate a "credible" and compelling story that will convince a judge or tribunal to grant asylum, and the community agency compiles its success stories in order to secure private or public funds.[4] We know, too, that storytelling, particularly in safe spaces, can help those with traumatic pasts to heal,[5] and also that those with ugly histories to hide, including war criminals, manufacture alternative narratives.[6] Reading the case files alongside the publicity stories and thank-you letters provides insight into the role of the material and the discursive in shaping Institute social work practices.[7] As for gendered identities, the preponderance of files on male clients means paying particular attention to masculinity. Neither Canadian ethnic historians nor Canadian historians of masculinity have scrutinized the masculinities of twentieth-century professional or bourgeois refugee and immigrant men. My assessments draw on the now extensive and feminist-informed literature in historical masculinities highlighting the relational, hierarchical, fluid, and unstable character of masculinity.[8] Feminist scholarship on the subject informs the briefer but no less considered analysis of the professional female clients.[9]

Professional Selves

Contemporary scholars of immigration have documented the fervent desire of immigrants with professional backgrounds to re-establish careers in new contexts as well as the structural and cultural barriers that stand in their way. Rejecting dichotomized debates over whether individual attributes (such as speaking fluent English and host-society work experience) or institutional barriers (certification rules and employer prejudice) explain the difficulties in obtaining accreditation, they have critically examined the licensing controls limiting the entry of "foreigners" into the professional associations. They have also documented the ways that the social and career-counselling agencies that have emerged to help newcomers resume careers (or realize careers for which they have trained) emphasize compliance with these heavily self-interested institutional rules.[10]

These observations apply to Canada. Historians of Canada's post-1945 refugees have critiqued the institutional regulations and devaluation of "foreign" education and experience.[11] Until recently, however, in their focus on the success achieved by white European "good material" or "cream of the crop" refugees, they have been out of step with contemporary social scientists, especially in regard to lesser-skilled immigrants and working-class Canadians. Milda Danys attributes the success of Lithuanian displaced persons in postwar Canada to their being an "exceptional people" with a "psychology predisposed to be successful." Jan Raska is more attentive to the supports extended to the different waves of refugees from Czechoslovakia and acknowledges failure, but, again, the dominant portrait is of model middle-class citizens.[12] By contrast, more contemporary studies of racialized newcomers from the Global South seeking to re-establish (or attain) professional careers in Global North nations like Canada show how hostland racism and claims to "universal" measurements that denigrate "foreign" training and justify deskilling and "decredentializing" often lead to a drop in the newcomers' professional identity and status and, in some cases, a permanent descent into lower-skilled work.[13] One of the exceptions to the dichotomy just drawn is Shezan Muhammedi's recent history of the Ugandan Asians who between 1972 and 1974 became Canada's first major group of non-European, non-white, and predominantly Muslim refugees. While he, too, concludes that Ugandan Asians became successful, integrated Canadians, his textual and oral history sources document the considerable employment and everyday racism experienced by many of these "high quality" but racialized refugees.[14]

Contemporary insights can enhance understandings of the mainly white-on-white encounters that occurred at the Toronto Institute, provided we do not simply equate anti-immigrant sentiment against Europeans with anti-Black or anti-Brown racism. The findings of present-day multicultural adult education experts, anthropologists, and clinical psychologists regarding the gendered subjectivities of professional immigrants also have a wider applicability. One important socio-cultural insight concerns the tensions produced by the paradox of professionals who self-identify as such being forced by the host society's rules to "regain" a professional identity through post-migration "education," whether via formal examination or retraining.

Another is that the institutional rules construct the immigrant as "a deficient self" and play a role in a process whereby one may internalize the negative descriptor in order to survive, psychologically and emotionally, in the new society. Some immigrant professionals resist the process by challenging the dominant norms, by ceasing to pursue a career, or by returning home. Certain groups, such as journalists and artists, may try to resolve the problem by seeking self-employment within their ethnic community. But many others acquiesce to the constraints imposed. When that happens, these experts argue, the professional client views the social agencies as existing mainly to help them overcome a personal deficiency while they accept lower-paid jobs in the belief that they must acquire the qualifications for professional posts even when they possess them. To deal with the disappointment, they lower their pride by internalizing a notion of a "deficient self" constructed largely through the host society's institutional rules. Cross-cultural difficulties with interpersonal and presentational skills also produce anxiety among migrants unfamiliar with the host's cultural code, and those who are unemployed are likely to experience high levels of stress. Consequently, many end up accepting entry- or end-level jobs for which they are overqualified in order to support their families. They suffer a deterioration in their mental health, the manifestation of which is also gendered. Professional wives, for example, attribute their husband's increasingly "unstable" or "aggressive" behaviour to persistent unemployment and the anxiety it generates. Pressure from similarly burdened kin may compound the problem to the point that the individual loses a sense of hope and motivation.[15]

Publicity Narratives

Most people who used the Institute's counselling services, including professionals, wanted help with securing work. The Institute staff emphasized that early success or failure on the job market had a lasting impact on a newcomer's attitude towards the new society and their integration. As one report put it, a person "employed in his own trade or profession – will become a happy and adjusted settler – and in years – a Canadian citizen."[16] The value attached to integrating professionals also reflected a dual logic: Canada's economy could benefit hugely from their specialized knowledge while the failure to adapt could produce pronounced maladjustment.

Drawing on North American studies that linked severe "ill-adjustment" to the wide gap between aspirational and achieved levels of employment among professionals, the Institute lobbied, unsuccessfully, to secure a dedicated government employment counsellor (from the National Employment Service, NES) to help clients with the certification process. A press release articulated the liberal principles involved, declaring that in a competitive capitalist society, immigrants should have "equal" access to the "community resources" that will enhance their participation through a proper "clarification" of their skills. It also included the Bulgarian female scientist's letter and the following caution: "the human being may learn the hard way by trial and error, but one wonders how many mental illness[es] and crimes could be prevented, if a human being was helped in his effort to make a happy and productive life."[17]

The counsellors circulated the narratives they gleaned from selected professional files for similar reasons. As casework supervisor, Margarete Streeruwitz explained that a failure to expose the obstacles could mislead the public into thinking "the main difficulty lies with the individual himself" when "his" primary goal is employment.[18] Another reason was to cast a favourable light on the counsellor's actions, an author's "flourishes and dramatic momentum" turning narratives drawn from cases into what Mark Peel calls "speaking stories" that often exaggerated the positive interventions involved.[19] The initial worker might write a draft and senior staff might polish it, with the use of the authorial "we" ensuring anonymity and indicating a common purpose.[20]

Neither tales of total triumph nor of abject failure, the publicity or human interest stories produced by Institute counsellors noted early disappointments and ended on a hopeful note. Most featured male clients, but referenced their families. The Institute counsellor and/or other understanding Canadians usually played a pivotal role in the optimistic ending. An early example featuring a young German architect "resentful" about a first Canadian winter spent unemployed stressed the importance of a timely intervention. On his landlady's suggestion, he visited the Institute, enrolled in English classes, and "became less bitter." Opening up about his feelings, he recounted his arrival in Halifax; he and some friends had been so overtaken by "fear and anxiety" at hearing the Immigration official say they were now "on their own" that "they sunk down on a bench ... immobile for half an hour" before deciding to continue with "the adventure to make good in Canada." (The one dissenting "boy" booked a return passage home.) The story ends with an endorsement of the Institute's timely and positive intervention.[21]

Another story featuring Germans had several twisting plots. Mr S. was an engineer with an outstanding resume; however, because of his poor English, he was unable to find employment, adding "a psychic pressure" to the anxiety of sponsoring family and adapting to life in Canada. Owing to the "intellectual differences" between him and the working-class German family with whom he resided, he "had no one to whom he could talk" and felt lonely. The Institute's entry into his life improves matters, as he begins English classes, gets documents translated, and is referred to jobs. But just as he finds work and his wife and son arrive, an unexpected setback comes in the form of a "puzzling and disturbing" spot on his lung detected during a company medical exam. Sent to a sanitarium, he harbours fears of deportation. Meanwhile Mrs S. loses her job and suffers "a nervous breakdown," and once discharged is embarrassed to accept welfare support. Then, finally, the ray of hope. The "mysterious spot" remained fixed and Mr S. is issued a clean bill of health. The couple decide to stay in Canada, their ability to speak English underscoring the importance of the Institute's services.[22]

A story that highlighted the gratitude but also resilience of newcomers who benefited from the Institute's timely assistance involved an older unemployed Estonian businessman, age 58, and his wife. After hearing the man's "sad tale" (he was desperate to help the son who had sponsored them), the counsellor phoned an employer looking for "a young man with fair English" to work as "a candy packer" and urged him to instead hire "our applicant." While awaiting an answer, the writer continues, "we found out that the client had his own chocolate factory and shop in his country," adding that "he even produced small snapshots – and with tears in his eyes said this was all he had left." To everyone's "great delight," the man was hired. He later visited the Institute, giving "every girl" in the office "a chocolate bar ... a hand-shake and a big grin."[23]

Two narratives intended to highlight the Institute's role in helping talented men overcome their discomfort over job interviews also contain elements that speak to the masculine subjectivities of professional newcomer men frustrated by their inability to regain a professional life. The first man, an engineer, age 29, said his "heavy" Eastern European accent was putting off prospective employers. The counsellor's decision to contact employers directly to make the man's case elicited the expected gratitude. The client's comments about the "pleasure" derived from being able to converse with other professional men struck a hopeful chord while also illustrating his attachment to a professional identity.[24] The source of anxiety for the second man, a Dutch academic, was that his "dark skin" caused "difficulties" in interviews. In the only staff-shaped narrative to touch on race and colonialism – the dark skin is attributed to an Indonesian grandmother – the focus is on the counsellor's ability to help his client distinguish between perceived racism and "insufficient" qualifications. In other words, the European counsellor's approach to this mixed-race client assumed a "deficient self" and discounted racism. Convinced the main problem was the man's "insufficient" credentials, "lack of confidence," and "expectations of rejections," the caseworker arranged follow-up sessions that reportedly helped the client to improve his interview style and his "attitudes" towards others.[25]

Curiously, given the presence of usable material, the narratives featuring women were few and brief. An amusing one involved the manager of an upscale "apartment house" who said she liked the "nice" chambermaid she had been sent by the agency, but "to please send her someone else" as the former ballerina was a lousy housekeeper. "By now," the writer notes, the residents "knew all about her stage career, her husband, her divorce, etc. but the apartments were not cleaned properly."[26] None of the uncovered staff-crafted publicity stories featured post-1967 racialized clients or counsellors.

Cases and Scenarios

The noteworthy presence of middle-class newcomers among the Toronto Institute's clientele is reflected in my database, one-third of which involve clients from professional backgrounds.[27] The subset of 335 case files to which I now turn were selected because they contain enough qualitative content to permit some meaningful observations. The subset, though small and skewed heavily in favour of European and pre-1967 clients, captures a wider range of scenarios as well as many more negative or abrupt endings than do the publicity stories. Men (59 per cent) outnumber women. Eastern European refugees (74 per cent) dominate both the total group and the male and female groups (74 and 75 per cent respectively). Immigrants from Western Europe are a distant second (22 per cent), and the non-Europeans a very distant third (4 per cent).[28]

The Institute's involvement in every government-subsidized refugee resettlement scheme enacted during its history is reflected in the subset. The Eastern Europeans who dominate the refugee clientele include the early arriving Polish veterans who had served with the British forces in the Second World War and the displaced persons who followed them to Canada shortly afterwards. Both groups arrived on labour contracts for specific industries, with wives and children joining them later. The Hungarian refugees of 1956 were part of the 40,000 refugees resettled in Canada through a government-led scheme following the Soviet Union's defeat of the uprising. The Czechs and Slovaks were among the 12,000 refugees who arrived in a similar fashion following the Soviet-led invasion of Prague in 1968. Czechs outnumber Slovaks in the subset (66 and 34 per cent respectively).[29]

The remaining professional refugees, about whom the small number of case files say very little, include a handful of Chileans and Ugandan Asians. The Chilean refugees were not the leftists who fled Chile following the 1973 military coup that ousted Salvador Allende's democratically elected socialist government and installed General Augusto Pinochet's authoritarian regime; the leftist refugees' admission was delayed by Canada's security forces. Rather, they were late-1960s and early-1970s refugees of Hungarian, Czechoslovakian, and Yugoslavian origin who had escaped after the Second World War to South America, and some of their Chilean-born adult children. The observation also applies to the post-coup Chileans who were clients of the Institute in 1973 and 1974. Unlike most of the 7,000 Chileans who comprised the first major group of leftist refugees to be settled in Canada, the Institute's Chilean clients resented both Allende and Pinochet and claimed to have been "persecuted" as "foreigners."[30] The few Ugandan Asian clients were among the almost 8,000 refugees admitted into Canada following General Idi Amin's 1972 order to expel South Asians from Uganda.[31]

The immigrants were mostly Germans who arrived in the fifties and early sixties following the lifting of exclusions in 1950, a few early arriving Dutch, and a handful of post-1967 Chinese and Asian Indian immigrants who arrived under the points system, which based admission on probable economic contribution to Canada. The Institute's Chinese clients arrived mainly in the late 1960s and the early 1970s. The case files do not state birthplace or citizenship, but few would have come directly from mainland China. The 1967 points system allowed Chinese families from South America, the Caribbean, Southern Africa, and Southeast Asia to immigrate to Canada. With Canada's recognition of the People's Republic of China in 1970, immigration gradually grew, becoming significant after 1972. Like those who followed them during the peak period of 1972–8, most of the Chinese who became Institute clients in 1972 (my cut-off year) would have come from Hong Kong, with much smaller numbers arriving from Taiwan and Malaysia. The few point-system Asian Indian professionals were men who became Institute clients in the early 1970s, at the start of a decade that would see a dramatic increase in immigration from South Asian countries.[32]

There were commonalities among the numerically dominant Eastern Europeans in the subset of cases, including their anti-Communism, but there were also differences. For example, whereas the early refugees had refused to return to Communist-run homelands at the end of the Second World War, the Hungarian "1956ers" and Czechoslovakian "1968ers" had lived under a Communist regime for a lengthy period of time, the "68ers" having done so the longest. They shared a middle-class hostility towards Communism, but their status and trajectories varied. Some men had enjoyed privileged and influential positions and elite status in pre–Second World War homelands and then languished in camps for years before securing refuge in Canada, while others had faced occupational stagnation due to the anti-bourgeois policies of their Communist homeland state. The experience with state arrest and imprisonment also varied.

In addition to the men who dominate the most prestigious professions, such as law and medicine (89 per cent), the subset includes a large cluster of engineers (21 per cent) and smaller groups of journalists, accountants, teachers, and university graduates.[33] A minority of the women are in the elite ranks (11 per cent), but the noteworthy proportion of female professionals (39 per cent) reflects in part state mandates that encouraged women's participation in Communist economies.[34] Teachers and nurses account for just over half of the professional women, with the former outnumbering the latter.[35] A majority of the men and women are in their thirties and forties (65 and 54 per cent respectively). Two-thirds of the men are married, the majority of them fathers. Just over half of the women are married, and just over half of them have children. Almost two-thirds of the clients were counselled in their own language, while a minority of those from non-English-speaking nations spoke "fair" or "good" English. They learned about the Institute from family, neighbours, landladies, and friends, or through referrals from other agencies or government departments.[36]

As for counsellors, women (6) outnumbered men (4) in the subset. Three European female counsellors (two refugees and one immigrant) handled a majority of the cases (61 per cent) overall and close to two-thirds of the female ones. An Eastern European refugee and Northern European immigrant were the most active male counsellors. The counsellors describe male doctors, lawyers, and academics as "brilliant" and "distinguished," and others as "bright" and "excellent." They praise men for possessing "active" and "alert" personalities or the "aggressive" look of determination. On occasion, as with the Eastern European female worker who described a Chinese teacher keen to improve his English as "a very nice, cheerful person," they complimented men for possessing less obviously "masculine" traits.[37] The female counsellors applied descriptors such as "intelligent" and "bright" to a number of women professionals.

That praise reflected a client's homeland status, though the sympathy-laden (as opposed to empathetic) observations speak as well to the counsellors' own profile as middle-class newcomers rebuilding lives and careers in Canada. In some cases, a counsellor shared the same national or ethnic group affiliation, and gender, as his or her client. Sometimes counsellors with anti-Communist inclinations recounted clients' stories of state persecution and escape in their letters to prospective employers, vouched for their willingness to start at the bottom, and recommended them as people "of trust and of great integrity."[38] While attuned to the shifting targets of anti-immigrant prejudice, and the need to counter it, the heavily European counselling staff saw itself as part of a white population even if this understanding was not solidified until the early 1970s with the increase in the number of racialized clients.[39]

The professional group also stood out because it required "longer and more intensive counselling" than did less-skilled immigrants, largely due to the certification rules created at the provincial level by the professional associations. The College of Physicians and Surgeons of Ontario (CPSO), for example, required an applicant to provide proof of medical training, pass an English-language exam, submit letters of reference, formally declare one's intention to become a Canadian citizen, and complete a one-year internship in an approved Canadian hospital. The dentists, which included women since dentistry was a heavily female occupation in some Eastern European countries, had to repeat a three-year university program, though some were given a year's credit. A portfolio for a doctor or engineer could include twenty or thirty letters; many delays occurred for various reasons, including papers lost in wartime, insufficient English, and a shortage of hospitals willing to provide internships.[40] Staff also identified the complex "human factors" involved, from a client's personality or "state of mind" to the time and sensitivity involved in raising a client's morale and helping them to "regain" their self-respect.[41]

Male Professionals

The initial "occupational" plan for these clients involved a short-term strategy to meet immediate needs through "sub-marginal placement" and a longer-term one to reach the "desired goal" of accreditation and desirable employment. But it was quickly compromised by the many referrals received from government departments and social agencies that lacked personnel with the linguistic skills or cultural "knowledge" to handle "foreign" professionals. As they increasingly involved male professionals who, one, two, and three years after arriving in Canada were still stuck in manual jobs and showing signs of psychological stress,[42] the staff focused on a pragmatic strategy of securing low-level white-collar jobs.

The recorded comments (or narrative traces) in the men's files offer revealing if mediated glimpses into a middle-class newcomer masculinity marked by status anxiety. The oft-expressed preference for "cerebral" rather than "heavy" labour is a case in point. Fifties-era examples include a Latvian lawyer who said that while his wife was working as a warehouse "packer" he wanted "to use his brain" in an office with a decent salary, and a Ukrainian journalist-turned-factory-worker who said he wanted a job "which would require rather my intellectual capacities than those of my muscles" and provide a salary sufficient to support his family.[43] Other men expressed their professional subjectivity by protesting the unfairness or absurdity of Canadian disregard for homeland credentials and, in the case of the Eastern European refugees, insufficient appreciation of the courage shown in defying or escaping Communism. The 1952 letter of a Bulgarian veterinarian and former government meat inspector annoyed over the Ontario Veterinarian Association's rejection of his diploma from Sofia University noted his role in combatting an outbreak of foot-and-mouth disease in Bulgaria and in arranging his family's escape from "Communist tyranny."[44]

In response to their clients' complaints about delays or difficulties in accessing courses or exams, Institute counsellors admonished them to appreciate that one could not just "jump into a career" in Canada and to be patient.[45] Conversely, the stoicism of a former physics professor from Lithuania employed for a year as a janitor to help support his family earned him praise. Calling him "well-adjusted [because he is] able to face the situation and understands it," his immigrant male counsellor found him a nominally better-paying job in a department store.[46]

On occasion, however, a counsellor expressed embarrassment over the failure to offer a highly accomplished man meaningful work. An Eastern European female counsellor conveyed such sentiments in her fifties-era files on two refugee lawyers from Yugoslavia – a Serb, age 43, who also edited a Toronto-based newspaper, and a Yugoslavian, age 59, who had also been an academic. When the "trustworthy" and English-speaking Serbian lawyer-turned-logger-then-hospital-janitor about whom she was confident of placing in a "clerical position" ended up in a bakeshop, she wrote "we should try something better." (The paper trail then ends.)[47] She was equally disappointed over her failure to secure the older Yugoslavian law professor employed as a night watchman a college teaching contract. Some postwar Eastern Europeans did land university jobs, but no academic in this subset of cases did so, including a younger Chilean (age 32) engineer, on whose behalf a female counsellor wrote the meteorology department of a Montreal-based university.[48] It was also difficult to place older journalists with Canadian newspapers, whose editors said they lacked an understanding of the local context and colloquial language. Hence, immigrant journalists, then as today, would often pursue work within their ethnic community. A Ukrainian refugee journalist who had been actively involved in anti-Communist activities in Europe did just that, becoming a prominent leader among nationalist (conservative) Ukrainians.[49]

In one of just three cases that addressed racism, a 31-year-old Chinese teacher from Malaysia who spoke fluent English expressed frustration with "the apparent excuses" given "for not hiring him." He told his European worker about a principal in Hamilton, Ontario, who "told him they were only looking for a teacher who was familiar with the particular school environment he had to teach in." Although "disappointed" to encounter this racism-by-evasion not only in the United States, where he had spent some time, but also in Canada (even if "more of an undercurrent"), he preferred to "succeed" in Canada. During a follow-up call to report that the private school referrals had not panned out, he offered the kind of praise that made for a good publicity story: Institute staff in Toronto, as in Buffalo, were "trying to help a person right away instead of only talking about it as many others do."[50]

The one file that features both a racialized counsellor and client contains the recorded complaints of K.M., a young Ugandan Asian accountant, age 26, who notes that, two years after arriving in Canada, yet another employment counsellor (from Canada Manpower Centres, CMP, formerly the NES) had told him "to forget the certification for now" and take a factory job as a shipping clerk. The job, he says, involved "cutting textiles" as well as clerical work, but it was the low wages ($2 per hour) that led him to abandon it for a temporary but better-paying job at a gasoline station. The counsellor refers K.M. to an agency that would help him to prepare his resume (the Institute no longer provided the service) so that he could fill out an application to the Certified General Accountants of Ontario. This surely pleased K.M., though the notes do not explicitly say it. Nor do they say whether counsellor or client thought racism explained the repeated advice to defer certification. CMP offices were involved in the Ugandan Asian resettlement scheme and the advice itself was familiar enough. Still, the other three Ugandan Asian men in the subset, each with a different Institute worker, were given the same referral. It suggests that Institute counsellors were more sympathetic than their mainstream counterparts to the men's desire to re-establish their professional lives. As an active member of the Uganda Committee of Toronto, which was coordinating re-settlement efforts, the Institute also shared a widely held assumption that an early success rate would temper anti-Asian racism.[51]

"Emotional and Psychological Fallout"

Clinical psychologists studying barriers faced by today's professional migrants recommend the adoption of a "multicultural" career-counselling model that resembles the Institute's pluralist approach. Using Institute-like language, they claim that counsellors knowledgeable about their client's cultural background can be more effective intermediaries, interpreting the hostland's institutional rules and cultural norms to the immigrant, and the immigrant's homeland credentials and experience to hostland employers, agency staff, and the wider public. A related suggestion that counsellors familiarize themselves with the prejudices of the wider society and address their own biases was encouraged in Institute training and debriefing sessions (see chapter 3).

There is also overlap with respect to storytelling techniques. Multicultural career-counselling experts advise that the counsellor, having formed an opinion of a client's cultural norms and beliefs from initial meetings, help the client to gain greater self-knowledge by completing exercises, such as writing a "future biography" or an obituary, that reveal how the client envisions their life unfolding. By addressing the client's stereotypes and experiences of discrimination as well as past successes, the counsellor, they add, can further assist the client in developing appropriate career goals that are also compatible with their integration into the host culture.[52] Institute counsellors did not use these specific narrative tools, but they certainly understood the value of storytelling in dealing with what we now call migrant trauma, and in facilitating adjustment as well as in promoting their work. Such efforts are evident in the files on clients described as "dejected and frustrated" men who, "having wandered from place to place" without receiving appropriate guidance or support, exhibited a "pattern of disappointment and psychological or emotional fall-out."[53]

That determination reflected in part a professional imperative to organize individual details into higher-level or more "scientific" categories such as client types (see chapter 3), but the constructions themselves can also be read in terms of masculinities. Two main types were identified. First, there were the once-prominent judges, surgeons, and academics who had undergone a stressful transition from the privileges of an elite or hegemonic masculinity, and the sense of entitlement it engendered, to a subordinated and marginalized one, initially as displaced persons or escapees in refugee camps and then as struggling refugees in Canada. Second, the counsellors identified a middling stream of professional such as engineers and teachers who, having experienced the limits placed on their career, status, and freedom by the anti-bourgeois policies of their Communist homeland, are re-embittered by the realization that resuming a career in Canada will be far more difficult than promised or assumed.[54]

The counsellors' recorded complaints of male clients in many files constitute narrative traces that convey not only a resentment against Communist officials and Canadian professional associations alike, but also a sense of diminishment at finding themselves still a long way from resuming or rebuilding a professional career and a middle-class way of life. These sentiments are captured in the many references to being "compelled" or "forced" to toil at degrading work despite professional credentials. Even allowing for the worker's input, the professional subjectivity of a Hungarian lawyer-turned-physical-education-teacher who insisted on being referred to as "Doctor" can be gleaned from a letter in the file that is addressed to the minister of education. In it, he complained that, despite Canadian assurances to the contrary, his application had been rejected by fifteen schools. In spite of two diplomas, the letter reads, "I am compelled to work as [a] night cleaner." Calling his situation absurd given the reported need of teachers "in many parts of Canada," and his willingness to go anywhere for "a position in my profession," he asks the minister to assist a newcomer who is "unable to go further" on his own. The letter notes other achievements, including coaching the "world-famous Hungarian Vasas" soccer team, and his political courage ("I was imprisoned 4 years because of my anti-communist activities in Hungary"). Like others, he also conveys a sense of shame over his inability to support his wife and children. The last point suggests that, despite the greater presence of women in the professions in Communist states as compared to Canada, many Eastern European men who arrived in Canada espoused a breadwinner ideology familiar to Canadians, though some may have done so in support of their claims.[55]

Angry Young(er) Men

Although Institute counsellors were trained to consider the social-cultural and psychological elements of a case, the files under review focus more explicitly on the psychological maladjustment of elite and middle-class men experiencing downward mobility and status anxiety than on matters related to specific group-defined cultures (see chapter 3). They do, however, view many of these clients as members of a particular subgroup, namely Eastern Europeans victimized by Communism who needed help in readjusting to life in a Western capitalist society.

The first "problem" type was the angry younger man in his thirties or forties who blamed his Communist homeland for denying him the life he rightfully deserved, and Canada for denying a high-quality newcomer the opportunity to resume a career. A Ukrainian engineer resentful about his demotion to draftsman also dismissed his co-workers as "all communist." His counsellor felt equally compelled to "explain" that the workers' "anti-European attitude" was due to fears over "job security" and not left-wing ideology.[56] Complaints that Canadian immigration officials in Europe or Halifax misled them about Canadian conditions were also common, but these were often framed in the context of Institute publicity stories that stressed the importance of its services.[57]

The many files noting registration for courses or preparation for exams suggest that a majority of these men acquiesced to the regulations, at least initially. So, too, do the files on the cluster of engineers of European, Asian Indian, and Chinese origins who, having failed to gain admission into the Association of Professional Engineers of Ontario, reduced their aspirations and enrolled in a drafting course or applied for jobs as an entry-level draftsman.[58] Although facing fewer obstacles than their Asian counterparts, the European engineers who resumed their careers nevertheless experienced less prestige in Canada than they had in Europe. But they did participate in the postwar "modernization" of Canadian industry that saw the rise of new factories and massive public works projects. Although neglected by Canadian historians of masculinity, the "technical experts" who filled the post-1945 ranks of Canada's "modern men" included those of "foreign" extraction.[59]

The few explicit cases indicating a rejection of the certification rules included men who demanded help in finding work in the United States. One example involved a 37-year-old married German doctor employed as an attendant at a Toronto mental health facility, a physically demanding job that included restraining patients. No doubt aware of the "anti-Nazi" sentiment aimed at Germans, he explained his Russian origins and recounted his war story. It included conscription into the Russian army as a medic, serving as a POW in a surgical clinic in Berlin, and, at war's end, fleeing to the US zone, where he worked in a refugee hospital until receiving an exit visa, which allowed him to enter Canada. He then complained about a recent twist in his story, noting that just as he secured a hospital internship, the medical rules were changed; they now required English-language exams in more subjects than was previously the case. Claiming that his counterparts in Los Angeles were already gainfully employed doctors, he demanded help in joining them. The caseworker, who surely knew of similar difficulties south of the border, agreed to make enquiries, but no update appears in the file. A few cases involving engineers wanting to find work in the United States, or return to Europe, also end abruptly.[60]

64   Narrative, Subjectivities, and Affect

Institute staff were not surprised to encounter frustrated men, even recommending some of them for media interviews or conferences. They were critical, though, of "arrogant" clients who resisted their advice or were otherwise less-than-compliant clients. A Canadian female volunteer counsellor accused a former Polish judge who complained about being "compelled to work as an unskilled industrial labourer without any hope for the future" of possessing a "bitter" and "defeatist attitude," but also begrudgingly admitted that "I suppose one cannot blame him for it." He reportedly declared that four and a half years after arriving in Canada, "I can't call myself a hapy [sic] well adjusted Canadian." After failing to place him as a law clerk, she suggested that a bookkeeping or (basic) accounting course would make him more employable. The advice, then, was to reduce his lofty expectations and aim for a more realistic goal, a white-collar job preferably in his field. Once retrained, she added, he should advertise in a legal newsletter as "a Polish judge, speaking good English and desiring legal clerical work."[61] We do not have his response, but the curt dismissal of a Latvian statistician given similar advice suggests, too, that clients' refusal to condescend to clerical posts frustrated Institute counsellors and their colleagues.[62]

One of the best storytellers was T.B., a 35-year-old teacher imprisoned in Hungary for his anti-Communist activities and then barred from his profession. The differing responses he elicited from his female and male counsellors offers as well an example of how gender influenced the theatre of encounter. The harried woman counsellor who first handled his request for a job while he awaited the results of his application to teacher's college offered a negative judgment: "I do not know whether the prison affected him that way, but he seems very hard to handle – conceited, does not care about anybody else." An effort to secure the multilingual T.B. a teaching contract with the University of Toronto failed. Then, a male immigrant counsellor with social work training became T.B.'s counsellor, perhaps because he objected to the female worker. This counsellor's different portrayal of T.B. as "nervous and timid" suggests that T.B. was willing to share his anxieties with another man. The counsellor attributed T.B.'s "nervous" demeanour, and obviously poor health, to "his difficult past." In an observation that suggests he considered the file a potential publicity story, he adds that T.B. will "improve" when "he gets his place in Society," though "everything" depended on his health.[63]

Institute staff, many of them avid newspaper clippers, learned more about T.B. through a Toronto newspaper article on Hungarians that interviewed him under a pseudonym. Clearly impressed by T.B.'s story, the reporter recounted the man's five-year imprisonment in Hungary and his escape in 1956, his experience with certification "red tape," and his plans to publish a memoir. The journalist ended on an optimistic note, writing that, besides selling real estate (using a "late-model" car supplied by his firm) and "doing private tutoring," T.B. and his wife now lived in a "spacious" but "simply" furnished flat in the (more middle-class) Casa Loma district and that their (middle-class) social life revolved around the Hungarian Helicon Society (est. 1951), an arts and letters club.[64]

By contrast, the case file goes on to record T.B.'s deteriorating health, his "quit[ing]" real estate, and his failure to secure admission into teacher's college. As the situation worsened, the counsellor contacted a charitable organization with a plea to help out a former political prisoner who suffered "great moral degradation from 'brain washing' and other evil practices," and who was now "in the middle of a crisis" that, unless circumvented, may cause "a breakdown," forcing the whole family to go "on relief." He adds, the course was the man's "last chance to obtain a license and practice his profession" at age 36. Referencing T.B.'s breadwinner status, the counsellor also notes that "he is haunted by the spectre of his family being unsheltered and hungry," and asks that funds to cover living expenses for the duration of the course be provided, preferably as a gift, but, alternatively, as an interest-free loan.[65]

T.B.'s mental anguish presented as a crisis in masculinity and his male counsellor's attentiveness to the anguish of a client who fit both a Cold War and "good material" script underscored its value as a publicity story. So, too, did the ending. T.B. may not have taken that teacher's course, but his luck did change over the next few years. First, he received approval as a substitute high school teacher from a suburban board of education and entered teacher's college. Then a high school in Fort Erie, Ontario, responded to an ad he placed in an educational newsletter, though he declined the job. Finally, he moved to Buffalo and landed a job with the city welfare department. Perhaps the fact that the happy ending occurred in the United States explains why the case was never turned into a "speaking story."[66]

An articulate 1956er whose anti-Communist views were also featured in the Toronto media explained middle-class resentment towards Eastern Bloc states in terms of the contradictions of a well-resourced technical education system that combined demanding standards with state-directed favouritism towards students whose parents were workers or party members. This practice, he argued, discriminated against the "class-alien" elements: the bourgeoisie, wealthy peasants, and non-Communist intelligentsia. In a differently gendered scenario, he used his rhetorical skills to convince a sympathetic female counsellor to find a (female) donor willing to help him start a cleaning business, and then disappeared with the money.[67]

One of the few cases where staff attributed a young man's excessive anger to serious psychological dysfunction also sheds light on the limitations of the Institute's career-counselling approach. Noting the "great deal of hostility" expressed by J.R., a Yugoslavian refugee, towards the manager of his research laboratory for reneging on a promise to promote him, the Eastern European caseworker aimed to help him gain insight into his situation. According to his notes, he first convinced J.R. that abandoning the job was a mistake because it meant he could not collect unemployment insurance or enrol in a hospital training course that interested him. Then, the caseworker explained that J.R.'s rationale for considering a move to Montreal – that Quebeckers would be more "welcoming" than Anglo-Torontonians towards someone who had lived in France and spoke French – was a misplaced effort to "escape from stress." And, finally, he helped J.R. "to realize that his present difficulties were related to his personality problem," which J.R. then attributed to his negative refugee camp experiences having made him a "nervous person." But there is no further follow-up.[68] In another scenario, a female counsellor, pleased that her success in securing a "very bitter" Ukrainian accountant a bookkeeping job had turned him into a happy and appreciative client, expressed her professional pride in a way that aligned with the Institute's liberal capitalist ethos. She wrote that in helping immigrants to achieve a better life, the host society benefited from the human capital they represented: "we were able to do a job which saved a man from loosing [sic] his self-confidence, but also the community from loosing [sic] a man with a good professional skill." She was also celebrating what was in effect a demotion from professional accountant to low-level bookkeeper.[69]

Depressed Older Men

The efforts to place professional clients in low-level white-collar work was particularly pronounced in the case of men who fit the second main type of ill-adjusted professional, the "older" man in his fifties and sixties who was "depressed" or "very depressed." In a typical example, the female counsellor of a 60-year-old Yugoslavian banker repeatedly rejected for managerial posts told the one bank manager who expressed an interest in him that his depression was strictly situational (that is, linked to his difficult circumstances). Given the chance, she added, the "intelligent, capable" man would "prove a very reliable, conscientious worker" who could "offer some input." The job in question was a clerical one.[70]

In pursuing a strategy that involved deskilling and decertification, counsellors hoped that office work would produce an income and halt a further decline in the men's mental health. As an enticement, they presented low-level clerical posts as providing the accoutrements of a respectable middle-class, if not an intellectual, scientific, or legal, pursuit, and a better-than-minimum-wage income. Implementing the white-collar strategy was not easy, however; the relevant files feature mostly women counsellors trying to assist men for whom they felt sympathy, even pity, rather than empathy. A European female worker who thought the "very well educated and honest looking" academic who had gone through several dead-end jobs during his first year in Canada would find even "an easy clerical job" too "difficult" nonetheless suggested a library technician or bookkeeping course. When he mentioned a chauffer's licence, she wrote "an excellent plan," her enthusiasm indicating relief over his having seriously reduced his expectations.[71] Her female co-worker, also European, conveyed sympathy towards a Yugoslavian engineer and his wife in her plea to an indifferent personnel manager in the city's landscaping division to show compassion towards a "distraught" couple "desperate" to sponsor their daughter by giving the man a job. A refusal even to help with the application form made the manager the anti-immigrant villain in this story. An Institute volunteer assumed the role of friendly Canadian by hiring the wife as a maid, but the file ends without news of the daughter.[72]

In the main exception to this pattern, a few cases show female counsellors asking about locales where the accreditation process might be less strictly enforced than in Ontario. An ethno-Canadian volunteer counsellor went this route with a 54-year-old Bulgarian dentist upset over the Ontario Dentistry Association's refusal to recognize his diploma from the University of Lille, France, or the dentistry practice he had in Bulgaria and France. Concerned the "enterprising" man was getting "progressively more depressed" over his inability to break a two-year cycle of odd jobs, she contacted a Japanese Canadian doctor based in the Yukon who had written an article in a Japanese Canadian newspaper to which the Institute subscribed about the need for medical personnel in the territory. Making a case for her client's suitability, she wrote that he had greatly enjoyed his one short-lived contract with the Quebec Health Service in Harve St Pierre – which she revealingly describes as an "isolated place on the edges of Labrador" – because he could "practice his profession."[73] The dentist's file, like those of an older journalist and lawyer also willing to move away to practise their respective professions, does not include a record of the eventual outcome.[74]

The only proven successful case of this type involved Dr N.J., a Polish doctor, age 53, who had been working as a hospital cleaner while preparing for his medical exams. He complained about the CPSO rules now requiring the follow-up internship to be a rotating one, saying the arbitrary change threatened to sabotage his plans. Noting the fifty or so rejection letters in his file, his European female counsellor sympathized, writing that she could understand why he "did not believe that anyone could help him," and why "he resented very much being a cleaner in a hospital where he saw other young doctors doing the work he had done for 20 years." She also observed his pronounced mood swings, reporting that he alternated between "behav[ing] very dignified" and "laps[ing] into a very excited state of mind," and that he had mentioned killing himself and his children. She did not recommend hospitalization, however. Convinced that his depression was situational – the details of which indicate a "crisis in masculinity" triggered by persistent status and male-breadwinner-anxiety – she instead advised him to persevere in the hope that securing an internship might allow him "to become his own self." After he passed the exams, her resourcefulness and some good luck produced a hopeful outcome. She contacted a former client who had held an internship with an out-of-town hospital to ask about possible openings. Now a resident, he offered to visit Toronto with a colleague and interview the client. Three weeks later, Dr N.J. began an out-of-town internship while his wife and children stayed in Toronto. There is no update in the file, but the actions of the former-client-turned-resident underscores the importance that the reacquisition of a career in a (still male-dominated) prestigious profession played in the adjustment of "elite" male newcomers to Canada.[75]

Professional Women

The vast majority of the female professionals in my subset of cases are Eastern European refugees. The exceptions include a Chinese teacher who, arriving amid the Christmas rush of 1970, was told to apply for sales work in a department store. Of the two young Chilean-born professionals, both daughters of Eastern Europeans, one was a social worker keen to work with the Institute. The female counsellor helped the woman, who spoke fluent English, with the application and said that the Institute director Tine Stewart would interview her, but in the end she was not hired. The counsellor's advice that the client also apply for an advertised job with Planned Parenthood not only made good sense, but also indicated her own support, one she shared with other female staff, for women's reproductive rights.[76] The other young Chilean professional, an architect, was visiting her parents, both of whom were also Institute clients, but she, too, was looking for a job in her field. The file ends without an outcome, but she may have been a visitor ("tourist") hoping to apply for immigrant status while in Canada (as a matter of policy eligibility for all such applications would be revoked in November 1972).[77]

The women's files contain less narrative content than the men's, but there is enough information to draw some comparisons. As to similarities, they, too, document initial downward mobility, marked examples of which include an architect-turned-waitress and an agronomist-turned-babysitter. Like their male counterparts, a handful of female university graduates gained acceptance into engineering or other professional schools, mainly at the University of Toronto.[78]

We also find recorded expressions of disappointment over downward mobility in cases of middle-class professional women. Only a few, however, were like Dr P., a Polish doctor in her thirties whose attachment to her professional status and identity was demonstrated through a grim determination to resume an elite career. She also had a compelling story to tell. According to her cover letter, she trained as a general practitioner in Crimea and then worked in a transit camp hospital in Germany during the war, earning a medical diploma. After the war, she worked as a doctor with the International Refugee Organization in Europe before migrating to Brazil, where she practised as a physician until

Professionals, Narrative, and Gendered Middle-Class Subjectivities   69

moving to Canada in the mid-1950s. Dr P. came to the Institute after failing to secure a rotating internship. A few years later, she returned to report that she had secured and completed an internship and taken the medical exams, but that difficulties with English led to her failing one of them. In a hopeful ending reminiscent of a publicity narrative, the counsellor referred Dr P., who was married without children, to a private tutor with a nursing background and recommended a university course in English conversation.[79]

Even allowing for the translator's input, the few employment letters in the women's files shed light on the women's mode of self-representation as well as desire to impress prospective employers. Most echo that of a 32-year-old Polish engineer, a married woman without children, who articulated her professional identity within an anti-Communist discourse. Her plot-twisting narrative began at the end of the Second World War, when she earned a degree in agricultural studies. Having held positions with a number of university laboratories and cattle-breeding stations, the letter notes, she pursued further studies in animal breeding and served as editor of a series of engineering textbooks published by Krakow University. But her fortunes changed with the "tighten[ing] of "the communistic attitude" following the Communist victory in 1948. She noted, "I was not allowed to continue with my professional work being a descendent of an intellectual "bourgois" [sic] family," but "continued to keep my professional knowledge by reading books and periodicals."[80]

The letter of a female engineer hoping to find work with a research agency not only expressed an attachment to a professional profile; it also issued one of the two explicit references in the subset to sexism in the professions. An ethnic Ukrainian from Poland, she began by narrating her war story. Having moved with her family to Poland after graduating from a university in Soviet Ukraine, the letter notes, she was working in a metallurgical laboratory "when the Germans overran Poland" and sent her to Auschwitz for the remainder of the war. Arriving in Canada on a domestic labour contract, she later found marginally better paid work as a nurse's aide in a Toronto hospital. Then came her big break: a contract to work in a metallurgical lab with a research institute and a generous supervisor who, knowing her diploma was lost in the war, provided a reference letter attesting to her skills. She acknowledges "the gap" in her work experience, but insists that she is "still only 36, and prepared to start as a technician at any level whatsoever." She reaffirms her professional attributes, saying she is a "specialist in metallography, microphotography, and microstructures." She then adds that, besides having to contend with the "handicap" of being a foreigner, "there is the circumstance that women are not commonly employed in this field by industry." The file had speaking-story potential and, in hiring her, the Ontario Research Foundation fit the role of generous Canadian employer.[81] A more specific case of male bias involved a young (25-year-old) Hungarian geologist described by her female caseworker as a "very intelligent, very pleasant intellectual lady." The geology company refused to hire a woman for their advertised "junior geologist" position because it entailed "supervising small prospecting groups" of men in "isolated areas."[82]

More striking, however, are the differences in the situation of male and female professionals. These included the lower wages of the female placements and a reluctance to accept night-shift work. Women also differed from their male counterparts in their response to the accreditation regulations. Close to two-thirds of them chose, largely for pragmatic reasons borne of structured patriarchy, not to pursue a lengthy certification process but instead to opt for lower-status jobs within their field or even outside it. This was particularly true of older women who, like the fifty-something Latvian refugee dentist and pharmacist, said they were "too old" and financially insecure to "redo" a university program and asked for work as a lab technician or, failing that, office work. Although there is no record of her saying so, the same reasoning likely applied to the 52-year-old Chinese doctor who arrived in 1970 with a husband and children and speaking "poor" English.[83] An earlier-arriving Russian gynecologist and pediatrician, age 43, was more blunt, saying she could not "look for" an internship because she had to look after her children.[84] Younger women in their thirties, among them an Eastern European refugee doctor and engineer, similarly said they could not repeat their training because they now had a family.[85] Evidently less daunted by the rules regulating their respective professions in Ontario, many of the teachers and nurses, both single and married women without children, tried to secure their Canadian "standing," though few had done so as indicated in their Institute file (see below).

The prevailing gender norms regarding women's reproductive roles and caring labour both informed women's middle-class femininity and limited their ability to resume a career. While cognizant of the impact that pregnancy or a supportive male partner had on women professionals, Canadian ethnic historians have not closely scrutinized the gender dynamics involved.[86] By contrast, current studies of dual-career couples emphasize the detrimental impact of "traditional" gender-based expectations within the migrating family unit on the integration of female spouses, especially when mothers or other female kin are not available to help provide domestic support. Women, they show, are usually the trailing spouse, and the unpaid caring labour expected of them disadvantages them in the professional labour market. Also, migration often alters the gender dynamics within dual-career families so that women who were full-time professionals back home feel pressured to sacrifice "personal" gains in order to ensure the family's well-being in the hostland.[87]

Arriving amid the rapid social changes of the late sixties, the Czech and Slovak female professional refugees of the Prague Spring, many of whom had lived for two decades in a Communist state that sanctioned women's wage earning and state-run childcare, were struck by the lack of such facilities in Toronto.

Like other working mothers, they tapped the available facilities, such as church-run nurseries and orphanages as well as subsidized and private daycare centres. The relevant files capture their frustration over insufficient spots. Raska explains Czech women's underemployment in Canada vis-à-vis the Czech Soviet Republic in terms of the fewer jobs available for skilled women in Canada and the sexism of Canadian Immigration officials who sometimes refused to place them in English- or French-language programs. We could add the absence of a "nationalized" (provincialized) daycare system – something for which feminists were then lobbying – as well as interruptions or delayed entry into the labour force due to childbirth. That no alliance was forged between Canadian feminists and women "68ers" despite agreement on the need for more childcare services is not surprising, though, given their opposing views on state intervention and the left or the left-liberal politics of many feminist activists.[88]

Predictably, Institute counsellors supported women's pragmatic decision to lower their professional aspirations in order to immediately earn an income and meet family expectations. A partial exception to the pattern hints at the difficulty of abandoning a career: a Czech engineering instructor, who first declared that "she did not want a factory or cleaning job" but "to work in her own profession and hopefully return to teaching," reappeared some months later to say she was "desperate for work" and would take anything. Applying the white-collar-job strategy, her Eastern European woman counsellor advised her to take her translated certificates and university diploma to the local banks and libraries and ask for an interview. She also supplied some clothing and furniture donations and placed the child in a nursery. More generally, the absence in these files – for gaps or omissions in the files can be as revealing as verbatim quotations or narrative traces – of recorded laments over careers suspended or cancelled by children underscores both the impact of transplanted "traditional" gender roles on women, including those from Communist homelands, and the pragmatism with which most women handled the demands of motherhood. Some of them, though, may have sought re-entry into their field once their children were older.[89]

A file on a 68-year-old widowed Russian psychologist determined to secure a clerical job with "a psychologist or psychiatrist" shows a woman trying to hold on to a vestige of her homeland status and identity by seeking a position where she believed she could make use of her expertise as well as multilingual skills. The notes of her European male worker, a trained social worker, capture her disappointment and his counselling approach. He writes that, because she was so "certain" about attaining her goal that she was "unable to consider" any other clerical job, he supported her plan to contact several doctors as a corrective strategy. Two weeks later, she returned upset over being repeatedly told that she was "too old" to practise in Canada, and asked him why he had not stressed just how futile her quest would be in their first interview. The counsellor, who claimed to have spent a "considerable" amount of time with the woman, replied that as she was not then "ready" to hear the bad news, he "thought it advisable for her to find out for herself." With some professional self-satisfaction, he adds, she agreed with him, thereby offering proof that he helped her to attain a greater degree of self-awareness. There is no follow-up, but the final entry implies that she was now willing to accept any type of office work.[90]

Only two women, an older Latvian pharmacist, age 56, and a young Polish academic, age 25, expressed satisfaction with a downward career move. Having failed the qualifying pharmacy exams, the pharmacist worked as a nurse's aide before retooling as a cook. Several months after her European female worker placed her in a tourist lodge, she sent a thank-you letter to the counselling staff. "Although I have not great experience in the culinary art," it reads, "I am not without knowledge and I say, cooks are not born – they are made – by their own efforts," adding, "So I shall do my best in this new art." Whether or not she received help in writing it, the letter indicates that she was able to derive validation from a less-skilled job by redefining it as a new career.[91] One of the Institute's few Jewish clients, the Polish academic wanted a clerical job in order to sponsor her parents and a sister from Brazil. Once hired, she wanted to buy her counsellor a gift. He demurred, saying her good news was enough reward and that professional codes prohibited the practice. Since this worker, like others, accepted invitations to family dinners and celebrations from appreciative clients, his insistence on maintaining professional/private boundaries in this instance is noteworthy. As for the woman, who, like the Bulgarian scientist of our opening story, volunteered at the Institute, she simply found his home address and had her husband (an Austrian journalist) drop off a gift.[92]

Trailing Professional Spouses

Among the women in the professional subset who belonged to a dual-career marriage were nurses and teachers. Under the auspices of the Canadian Nurses Association, many immigrant nurses were initially placed as nurse orderlies in hospitals. Ostensibly meant to help them acquire the Canadian knowledge required for the exams, the exhausting labour involved could interfere with their studies.[93] It explains why a Chinese nurse who was seriously injured at work planned to prepare for the nursing exams while convalescing: she was told the certificate would help secure a less physically demanding job in a clinic. The female counsellor found her a volunteer tutor to help with her English.[94]

In addition to attaining sufficient English, immigrant teachers had to secure a letter of standing from the Ontario Department of Education or earn a teacher's certificate in order to practise their profession. Meanwhile, some of them worked in factories and as waitresses and domestics. While nurses and teachers enjoyed less prestige than doctors or lawyers, they, too, maintained a professional ethos. In a written thank you to the Institute for arranging an interview with the Metropolitan Toronto Board of Education, a Ukrainian teacher referred to the "pleasure" of conversing with another professional woman. She also did some volunteer (translation) work for the Institute.[95] The case files involving translated résumés and diplomas, notes as to preparation for nursing exams, and applications to teacher's college indicate a determination to resume a career as well as interruptions due to family duties, whether related to pregnancy or the arrival of children from overseas. They show, too, how some women's options were limited by a husband's aspirations, such as pursuing a post-graduate degree in order to advance in his field. Or, alternatively, how his success or good luck (such as landing a job with a firm that covered the cost of his Canadian training) allowed them to leave low-level jobs and pursue their own certification.[96]

Institute counsellors routinely invoked the white-collar-job option with their teacher clients, urging those with sufficient English to apply for work as bank tellers and office clerks on the premise that these respectable jobs (which did not require typing skills) were more attainable. A case from the late 1960s illustrates the great lengths to which a young Yugoslavian teacher in her mid-twenties went in an effort to resume a career she valued, and her eventual acceptance of an alternative one. A CMP job counsellor referred the married woman, who spoke fluent English, to a particular European female counsellor at the Institute. Afterwards, she dutifully made the rounds, visiting the local Immigration Department, the Toronto Board of Education, and a high school principal's office. Discouraged from teaching, she asked about nursery and daycare positions only to be told about the training course requirement. When, a year later, she was still unemployed and her physician husband was still struggling with the CPSO licensing requirements, the counsellor recommended a bank teller position, saying it was a "good" job and that dealing with the public would acclimatize her to "the Canadian way of life." After putting up some initial resistance, she relented. A dozen calls later, she was sent to interview with a bank, but failed the English test. Another slew of phone calls to employers interested in "bright young women for office [work]" led to a job with an Ontario public health agency; this time, she passed the English test and became a clerk in the accounting department. The final entry describes her as "happy" and "grateful" – the perfect client. Having reduced her aspirations in order to secure a much-needed income, she also fits the profile of the professional wife rationalizing the value of accepting less fulfilling work.[97]

The records under review contain no direct evidence of frustrated husbands becoming more belligerent towards their wives. In one case that suggests the possibility of male aggression, the European male worker thought the Hungarian lawyer/husband and teacher/wife "both appear a bit depressed as a result of their unsuccessful search for a position." But the husband dominated the meetings, at one point dismissing his poor-paying "salesman" job, then refusing to retrain as a welder, and then denouncing Canadians for not hiring him. One might well imagine that the silent wife bore the brunt of his growing anger, even if he did not turn violent (a theme discussed in chapter 5).[98]

Finally, a few disgruntled couples decided to return to Europe, in one case doing so separately. The latter case involved a Czech female teacher married to a graphologist who first attributed their unhappiness to her husband's frustration over learning English. She appeared to be doing well, completing an English course and securing a letter of standing. When she could not find a teaching job, her female counsellor suggested that, as a fluent Russian speaker, she contact the University of Toronto about the possibility of teaching Russian. A month later, the woman reported that the university required a PhD, that her husband had returned to Czechoslovakia, and that the Immigration department wanted the repayment on her passage loan. She pursued teaching possibilities over the next few months, suggesting the couple had separated, but the final entry says that she also returned home.[99]

Conclusion

Toronto Institute counsellors, particularly the women, clearly sympathized with their professional clients, particularly the compliant ones, and, at least initially, assumed they could make significant contributions to Canada. These clients' struggles also resonated personally with the counsellors, most of whom themselves were educated middle-class newcomers working to rebuild new careers in Canada in the aftermath of war, loss, and displacement. The evidence suggests, too, that they treated the post-1967 racialized professionals without racial animosity, though the scant information in the relevant files, along with the charges of racism occasionally laid against Institute personnel (see chapter 7), renders this observation highly speculative. At the same time, however, the counsellors, whether formally trained or Institute-schooled, viewed their clients through a professional filter, as evidenced by the typology of angry younger men and depressed older men. Shaped partly in response to the Eastern European refugees' deep resentment towards Communist regimes that stole their freedom and careers, the typologies were also informed by Cold War narratives. The absence of similar female typologies may be explained by the pragmaticism that made many of them compliant subjects.

An analysis of both the case files and publicity stories reveals the strengths and weaknesses as well as paradoxes of liberal pluralist social work practices. On the one hand, they prefigured key aspects of contemporary multicultural career-counselling methods. This included hiring counsellors and caseworkers who came from the immigrant communities represented by the clientele and who, whether before or after their on-site training, possessed a knowledge of and sensitivity to the cultural attributes of the ethnic groups (and subgroups) which the clients belonged – though there was little explicit evidence of their applying this social-cultural perspective. On the other hand, the advice meted out exhibited what these same experts consider the shortcomings of career counselling for "foreign" professionals. While impressed by their accomplished clients, Institute staff ultimately wanted them to significantly reduce expectations rather than try to resume or realize their professional aspirations, or to lobby for changes in the accreditation rules. As for the clients, both women and men experienced significant downward mobility, at least initially, but also showed a grim determination to recoup a professional and middle-class way of life. However, facing greater restrictions, women were more likely than men to trade in career goals for more attainable white-collar jobs that also allowed them to meet familial obligations. Finally, while these employment files offer some glimpses into the emotional life of clients and even counsellors, it is the case files dealing with marital conflict and with generational tensions, the subjects of chapters 5 and 6 respectively, that lend themselves to a more sustained analysis in this regard.

Chapter Five

Marital Conflict, Emotions, and "De-culturalizing" Violence

A case of marital conflict that came before the counsellors of the Department of Individualized Services at the International Institute of Metropolitan Toronto involved a Greek couple referred by the Ontario Family Court in winter 1968. In keeping with the court's "socialized justice" mandate to investigate and mediate conflict and effect a reconciliation, the court social worker wanted the couple to receive counselling from someone who knew their language and culture. The European female counsellor assigned to them had been the court interpreter during their recent hearing, so she already knew that, one year after arriving in Canada through the family sponsorship system, the wife had laid a claim of non-support against her husband/sponsor. She accused him of squandering his wages, disappearing for long periods at a time, and neglecting the children. The file entries convey her resentment towards the in-laws, with whom she lived, for encouraging him to "treat her badly." The worker's notes on the "long talk" she had with her client about her in-laws "not respect[ing]" her refer to the client by her first name, suggesting that a degree of intimacy had also been quickly established.[1]

In keeping with the pro-family stance of the Institute and the Family Court, and the social welfare state more broadly, the counsellor advised the wife "to be patient" with her husband, who had skipped the session, and work towards reconciliation. Since the woman asked the worker to reform her husband's ways as she did not want to "break her family," the advice also aligned with her wishes, though the counsellor suspected it had more to do with her concern for the children's welfare than her husband's. As for the meddling in-laws, the counsellor urged the woman to try to convince her husband to find separate housing, her imperfect English indicating her own status as an immigrant, albeit that of an educated middle-class urbanite. I "advised" her, she writes, "to try her best to make husband to find an apartment to live out of the parents and brothers and sisters in law." While it reflected a private nuclear family ideal, the advice was, under the circumstances, a reasonable if inadequate strategy; limited finances and the husband's family ties probably rendered it moot. The counsellor suspected the marital problems were due in part to the class difference between the wife, a former city clerk with a higher-than-average education (among Greek immigrants), and her husband and in-laws, who came from a rural village. So she also advised her client, then employed as a hospital cleaner, to apply for a government-subsidized English and commercial studies course that might lead to a better-paid clerical job. The woman followed the advice and, in a follow-up call several months later, said she was "very happy" with the course and her husband. Shortly afterwards, however, she reported on his backsliding, saying he had quit his job, was again coming home late at night, had disappeared already for a week, and was again being "careless for [the] children." In response, she renewed her claim of non-support.[2]

A major theme illuminated by this case is the emotional suffering the wife endured at the hands of a husband (and in-laws) who lacked any emotional investment in or affection for her or her children. Like the majority of the women featured here, she was not a victim of wife battery, but, like them, she endured much soul-destroying emotional abuse. Ironically, given the era's Canadian stereotypes of the rigidly patriarchal European family, the husband justified his actions on the grounds that Canada had freed him from the community constraints of his homeland. The wife said that, whenever she confronted him about his hurtful behaviour, he countered that in Canada he could do as he wished, cynically invoking "Canadian" ideals of freedom and democracy in defence of a system of gender oppression that crossed class, cultural, religious, and political boundaries. Many of the other husbands featured here similarly sought to reassert their authority over a wife who challenged them. A notable minority of them did so not through verbal and emotional abuse alone, but also by resort to physical violence, one of the means by which, as leading feminist scholar Shahrzad Mojab notes, male power is reproduced in economic and class systems, cultures, and societies around the globe.[3] A handful of men appeared to suffer emotional abuse due to marital conflict.

This chapter explores how Toronto Institute counsellors dealt with cases of marital conflict, highlighting the role of emotions and the impact of female counsellors in the multicultural social welfare encounter.[4] In addition to probing the recorded interactions between counsellors and clients for what they reveal about intimacy and affect, I engage the debates surrounding case file–based research and those regarding a supposed correlation between "foreign" ethnic cultures and male violence against women. With respect to the counsellors, the files under review allow me to explore a central paradox, or tension, identified by feminist and other social welfare scholars, namely that, however progressive, social workers are involved in an inherently intrusive profession and are subject to class-based biases. At times, however, individual workers, particularly women, might "really listen" to a female client.[5] Like the case records involving professional clients (see chapter 4), these files contain little explicit discussion of social-cultural factors, but much of the advice meted out reflected the staff's training in social work models that depicted Canadian (North American) models of marriage and family life as more modern and superior compared with European ones. Cases of marital conflict brought counsellors into contact with women from working-class and poor as well as middle-class backgrounds. There were also strong commonalities among the female clients, whose struggle to rebuild lives for themselves and their children in unfamiliar and reduced circumstances was further jeopardized by their conflicts with intimate partners. That the women counsellors handled close to two-thirds of the wife assault cases under review allows me to probe the affective dimension of interactions where both worker and client were newcomer women. I also ask whether the emotional labour that workers performed took a toll on their own emotional well-being.

My analysis engages as well the theory and method debates among historians researching emotions in the past through critical scrutiny of highly mediated textual sources.[6] An emotions frame that is sensitive to both discursive and materialist contexts in which newcomer couples in conflict conveyed their emotions, or had them interpreted by newcomer counsellors, particularly women, managing their own emotions, enriches our understanding of this theatre of encounter.[7] Drawing on historical and contemporary feminist studies of spousal conflict and intimate partner abuse, I argue, too, that the numerical dominance of the physically non-violent cases permits a more nuanced portrait of immigrant marital conflict in post-1945 Canada than studies, including my own, that focused almost entirely on domestic violence cases.[8] Finally, I draw some comparisons between the plight of the mainly European women featured here and that of more recent women from non-Western cultures enduring abuse in Canada and elsewhere. As regards the current debates over the need to "de-culturalize" so-called honour killings and situate them within the broad spectrum of violence against women,[9] the historical evidence presented here and elsewhere supports feminist arguments that systemic racism accentuates, rather than replaces, the material and ideological inequalities that give rise to violence against women.[10]

Emotions and Feminist Scholarship

Historians of emotions utilize divergent theoretical and methodological approaches, but generally subscribe to a social constructionist position. While recognizing a biological and cognitive element to feelings, they view the experiences, expressions, and interpretation of emotions as largely shaped by the societies and cultures in which they are imbedded. Depicting emotions as signifiers of social interaction, impactful cultural forces, and historical change agents, historians have examined the norms governing emotions and individual and collective responses to them; further they have tracked dominant, alternative, and oppositional emotional communities or regimes.[11] Histories of affect have fruitfully explored the ways in which intimacy within local, cross-cultural, and transnational sites has been marked by both tender and tense ties.[12]

Here, I have incorporated certain insights from this literature into a feminist framework attuned to both the material and discursive. While rejecting the rigid post-structuralist stance that descriptors of emotion (or "linguistic labelling") can never convey real feelings (somatic expressions), I have, for example, applied Nicole Eustace's advice that, in searching for patterns of emotional expression and regulation in texts, we try to distinguish between who is articulating – or trying to articulate – or performing a given emotional state.[13] Or, put another way, one can recognize that the social worker's gaze (to invoke Foucault) is informed by training as well as subjectivity without relegating to fiction every observation of a client.[14] Similarly, while I do not accept the primacy that historians such as William Reddy and Frank Beiss have assigned to emotions, I have incorporated their valuable insights into emotional suffering and how its communication affects others in both intended and unintended ways.[15]

Historian Barbara Rosenwein's guidelines for interpreting sources produced by members of what she calls "emotional communities"[16] also have wider applicability. She advises us to consider the frequency and weight of emotional terms and phrases in our sources, and to look for whether body gestures are noted. We ought not rely solely on descriptors, but look, too, for what "individuals define and assess as valuable or harmful to them" because people express emotions about such matters. They also express emotions by how they label others. Rosenwein also urges us to read the metaphors (as in "I blew my stack"), because they can signify an emotion, and the silences, because unemotional texts can be as revealing as overtly emotional ones.[17] Once again, these files constituted professional narratives, but careful scrutiny of the recorded emotional (and unemotional) vocabulary, expressions, bodily gestures, and performances of the clients sheds light both on the newcomers' intimate lives and on the affective dimension of social work interactions that occurred within a multicultural but heavily white European context.

Feminists across the globe locate the roots of wife abuse and domestic violence in patriarchy, a hierarchically organized system of gender-based power that is universal but manifests in particular ways through historically specific economic and socio-cultural forms. Histories of sexuality, divorce, and spousal violence in Canada and beyond highlight the ideological and structural factors involved, including the patriarchal family and unequal contests over limited resources, and the recurring patterns, such as men's efforts to isolate, control, and humiliate intimate partners. Feminists note the role that factors such as economic dependency, isolation, shame, and fear of losing the children play in silencing women. They also acknowledge the particular disadvantages faced by immigrant women.[18]

Marital Conflict Cases

A subset of 100 cases from my database of 7,000 Institute case files involves marital conflict, and it is roughly divided between clients from "better-off" backgrounds (professionals, skilled technicians) and those of more plebeian status (former peasants, factory workers, labourers). But all of the cases involve financial struggle, and conflict over money, and men's control of it, is a source of tension. Almost twenty national or ethnic groups are represented, though six Eastern and Southern European groups account for two-thirds of the cases.[19] The ages range from mid-twenties to early-fifties, but many clients are in their thirties. The five European women counsellors who together handled just over half of all cases involving marital conflict and two-thirds of the wife assault cases include two Eastern European refugees and three Southern European immigrants. Of the four male workers, two Europeans (a refugee and an immigrant) handled all but five of the cases assigned to men; a different European immigrant and a racialized immigrant counsellor handled four and one of the five cases, respectively. In handling these cases, workers invariably invoked the egalitarian Canadian family ideal and other models and insights their training taught them, but the women in particular expressed a mistrust of certain husbands.

Three-quarters of the cases (75) in the subset of 100 cases include no evidence of physical violence, but a minority of them (25) clearly do. The ethnic profile of the first cluster[20] and the second[21] resembles that of the total subset, though each includes a higher percentage of "better-off" clients than the overall subset. Given the links between emotional and physical abuse, I stress that, while my categorization is carefully considered, the boundaries between the two were hardly rigid. Most of the women in the non-violent disputes were not Family Court referrals, and many already knew about the Institute, whereas the wife assault victims were mainly Family Court referrals. That women in both groups frequently requested help in placing children temporarily with an agency or orphanage so they could work reflected their grim material realities and the availability of (low-wage) female jobs in Toronto as well as a strategic use of "foster care" facilities. A few professional women asked about government-subsidized training courses, but most requested or held lower-skilled jobs. Most Family Court referrals laid a claim of non-support against husbands, though some filed for a legal separation or divorce. For most wives, after other strategies failed, the court was a last-resort legal strategy to pressure husbands into stopping their "bad" behaviour. A few husbands filed for separation.

In important respects, these women's situation and the overall patterns of abuse parallel those documented for women, both citizens and immigrants, in earlier and later eras in Canada[22] as well as in Europe, Britain, Australia, the United States, and elsewhere.[23] Such experiences were rooted in a patriarchal family form that crossed lines of class and culture, and that involved contests over power and resources in which women were seriously disadvantaged, given their economic, social, and psychological subordination to male privilege. The traces of male narratives in the files reflect the presumed right of husbands to autonomy, to control both family resources and wives, and to exert authority over children. The recorded words and actions of women reveal the agency and courage of financially precarious and often isolated women who sought to use the limited options available to deal with a miserable or abusive marriage. They speak as well to the particular vulnerability of immigrant women who arrived as a sponsoring husband's dependent: fear of deportation on the grounds of "indigency" or "unsuitability" undoubtedly kept some of them from leaving husbands or seeking a divorce.[24]

The significant presence of women who fought with male partners without being physically beaten is noteworthy given the era's cultural stereotypes of "foreign" men as quintessential wife beaters and their women as the paradigmatic assault victim.[25] Women who taunted or deserted husbands or took lovers exposed themselves to accusations of immorality, however. Emotionally damaged husbands also require attention, but without losing sight of the fact that men who are emotionally or physically abusive, or both, towards their intimate partners cut across class, race, cultural, and other social categories of difference.

Women in Non-violent Disputes

Many of these 75 cases involve wives who complained about neglectful and irresponsible husbands who "foolishly" squandered wages – usually on drink, but also girlfriends, guitars, and cars – while ignoring "important things" like the bills and feeding children. Some made it clear, too, that their husband also demeaned them. They often did so not by describing feelings of anger or personal diminishment, but through recorded utterances of emotional phrases that appear repeatedly in the file entries: "he doesn't give me money for food" or "he drinks and locks me out of the house." Women also conveyed their hurt feelings, or emotional suffering, through recorded body gestures, including hand-wringing and tears. In 1958, an Austrian woman who collapsed into tears in her female worker's office said her husband "refuses to give her any money" and "tells her to get out of their place." But like others, she secured help in getting a job (cleaning) to support herself in case he left. A decade later, a Greek woman fought through tears to tell her female counsellor that "she is left out of the house" and that her "husband doesn't like her anymore." Convinced that a meddling brother-in-law was partially to blame, this counsellor, like the one in the chapter's opening story, recommended a separate residence. Again, the advice was reasonable, given the many immigrant women who were, then as now, compelled or forced to live with hostile in-laws, but the outcome is not recorded in the file.[26]

By contrast, a few women explained their decision to leave irresponsible husbands in ways that indicate their having undergone a shift in their emotional state from anger or despair to a firm resolve to leave the marriage. Instead of emotion words ("angry") or metaphors ("I blew up") there is an unemotional or matter-of-fact tone to the recorded entries. A former nutritionist from Germany, age 42, explained that the last straw was her husband opening an account with a department store in her name (she had a job), putting them further into debt. There is no venting of emotions, even though emoting may have increased her male counsellor's sympathy towards her. Instead, she revealed her plan to place an ad in a newspaper announcing that she would no longer cover his debts, apply for a legal separation, and hold on to the house. A 26-year-old nurse from Belgium who had secured legal aid in Toronto to apply for a legal separation from her husband in northern Ontario reported that, after recovering from two hospitalizations for "nervous depression" because of his irresponsible actions, she had moved on. Given the many women compelled to remain in loveless marriages, her decision to move miles away is noteworthy. That she left, initially, without her daughter suggests, too, that she was not afraid of his hurting the girl. Still, her file, which records her landing and losing a live-in babysitting job because her (jealous?) employer thought she paid insufficient attention to her children, underscores the precariousness of life as a single mother even in a city with plentiful low-wage jobs for women. One might argue that the apparent absence of a display of emotion meant these women suppressed their "real" feelings or feigned indifference. Seen through the now widely shared view that emotions contain rational, cognitive elements based on evaluations of what will increase or decrease one's emotional suffering or well-being, we might consider instead that these women managed to shed emotional investment in their husbands.[27]

A few women were despondent over failed love affairs, though none of the men, even the two-timing fiancés, were batterers. A young Portuguese live-in domestic whose fiancé was being deported to Portugal for having entered Canada illegally (as a ship stowaway) rejected her female worker's advice to stay put as she might later be able to sponsor him. She then returned "very upset" over the news he had "another girlfriend" in Canada, but also wanting a new job. A German clerk fed up with a waffling "fiancé," also the father of her child, asked her European male worker to pressure him into either marrying her or leaving them alone. She was reportedly "pleased" with the news that he agreed to a financial settlement in lieu of marriage. His name suggests a Middle Eastern heritage, but nothing is said about this being a mixed-ethnic union.[28]

Most inconsolable of all was a Filipina nurse, age 30, whose brother took her to the Institute in 1970, following a suicide attempt triggered by the actions of her fiancé, a doctor from India, who was backtracking on the marriage plans. It is the only case in the total subset of 100 cases where client and counsellor were both racialized immigrants from non-Western nations. The woman told her male counsellor, a trained social worker, that after she and her fiancé had met as co-workers in a US hospital, they fell in love and moved in together, and discussed plans to get married. After she moved to Toronto in 1969 for a job, they had maintained a long-distance relationship, with him doing most of the visiting. However, as the fiancé began to argue that "the vast difference in Cultural and Religious background" would make life as his wife in India far too difficult – which she dismissed as "excuses" – happiness turned to despair. According to the file entries, the woman used a mix of medical diagnoses (depression, persistent suicidal thoughts) and descriptions of her behaviour (extremely irritable, short-tempered) to convey her despair. She added that the flare-ups had escalated during recent visits, though the fiancé "never" lost his temper (an observation that her brother confirmed), and that she had kicked him out. The file makes clear that she was also a dutiful daughter of a large transnational family. She had sponsored her brother (an engineer working as a security guard) and sister-in-law, a nurse, to Toronto, and financed her mother's recent visit. When the counsellor – who described her as "short stocky" but "neatly dressed" and a "cohesive" if "slow" thinker – raised the race issue, she insisted that race had not derailed the relationship. When he asked about other pressures, she said there were none.

The counsellor agreed with his client's diagnosis of depression, though the discussed follow-up sessions, including with the fiancé, never transpired. His advice that she own up to her suicide attempt as a step towards "greater self-awareness," and to apologize to her "boyfriend" because her "nasty temper" likely "hurt his feelings," seems heavy-handed. In an era marked by acute prejudice against mixed-race unions – so much so that Institute staff usually advised against them – his willingness to consider "the possibility of a smooth relationship" was liberal-minded. But the pluralist stance was undercut by the sexist assumption that his client would need "to convince her boyfriend of her willingness to sacrifice everything for him, and the sake of married life."[29] While this, too, was common enough in the period, the women counsellors, as we shall see, did think women could make some demands in a relationship.

The few women who expressed discomfort with their husband's sexual demands without reference to violence or fear of violence highlight sex as an unequal site of marital conflict and suggest that sexual conflict between "foreign" couples did not necessarily end in physical violence. Upon entering the office of her female counsellor, a young Hungarian bookkeeper interested in applying for a training course reportedly blurted out that she had been so "shocked" by her husband's "behavior" on their honeymoon night in Toronto that she left him and moved in with some "Hungarian friends." She explained that she had agreed to an arranged marriage after her Austria-based father responded to a marriage ad in a Hungarian newspaper from a man in Toronto. Having just lost the grandmother who raised her, she agreed to marry the man in order "to get out of Hungary." Still, some intimacy must have developed in the relationship because a few months later she noted that, while she still could not talk about that night, she was "considering a reconciliation" as he "is nice to her and willing to compromise" in the bedroom.[30]

By contrast, a Ukrainian mother of two who in fall 1959 left her husband of seven years because of sexual dissatisfaction seemed the female villain in a sad tale of marital "breakdown" that left the husband deeply depressed. A referral letter to the Institute from a sympathetic senior social worker with the husband's psychiatric hospital said he suffered from "agonizing loneliness" and "nightmarish" dreams of "his wife torturing him with abusive words, as she used to in real life." She advised that, since the marriage "appears hopelessly broken," the focus be on finding the "amiable" man some friends through the Institute. The European male worker handling the case may well have had little trouble accepting the social worker's speculation about the man's depression being linked in part to his Catholicism given that social-cultural theories drew such connections.[31] After meeting the man, he concurred with the diagnosis.

Yet, other contents in the file reference the wife's emotional struggles. The excerpts from a letter she had sent to her husband's doctors claimed that, for years her "religious morals" had led her "to hide their unhappy intimate relationship," keeping up the façade of an "ideal" marriage for the "neighbours" even though she had "not derived any satisfaction from their intercourse." Then, after suffering a "nervous breakdown," her psychiatrist (whose own staff may have helped her with the letter) recommended against reconciliation. The caseworker wondered, instead, whether the wife's problems were due to menopause, thus also implying that she was depressed. The woman's refusal to let her daughters visit their father does beg the question whether her own pain had prevented her from feeling any sympathy for the emotional suffering her decision had caused him. Perhaps the answer lies partly in the hospital worker's observation that he was "still very much emotionally involved" with his wife, though he also expressed the hope that he might find some female as well as male companionship at the Institute. For a man accused of not being able to satisfy his wife, he may have viewed a new relationship as confirmation of his manhood. The Institute caseworker later proclaimed that the two counselling sessions had been of therapeutic value for the man, who expressed appreciation for the support, and registered him into the Institute's house program.[32]

Emotional Struggles

We find, too, some women ensnared in ugly debates triggered by their or their husband's suspicion and jealousy, again without evidence of battery or the threat of it, though the files indicate men's efforts to reassert their authority. A woman who complained about her husband sending money to, and even visiting, a former lover and their "illegitimate" son in Portugal while she supported a family of five on a teenage daughter's meagre wages, said the constant shouting matches had caused her to develop a heart condition, forcing her to quit work. The husband countered that he had "nothing to do with that woman," but sent only small gifts of money to the boy. After two sessions with him, the immigrant female counsellor optimistically reported that he had agreed "to treat his family well," which included giving his wife more money and even opening a joint savings account. The wife initially confirmed they were "very happy" and "living well together," but a few months later renewed her claim of non-support.[33]

An "infuriated" Greek man filed for legal separation after his pregnant wife visited Greece while he was in a Toronto sanitarium receiving treatment for tuberculosis (TB). In a reversal of the usual gender pattern, the wife, a skilled dressmaker, had sponsored him to come to Canada following a long-distance courtship and marriage by proxy. After meeting with them separately, the European male counsellor recorded their competing stories. He accused her of having an affair in Greece (or in Montreal or Vancouver), and of depleting their savings even though she was the breadwinner. Having earlier refused to do his laundry, he added, she waited a week after returning to Toronto before visiting him in hospital. Accusing her of wanting to reconcile only because she was pregnant, he also wanted proof that "the child belongs to him." She said she had visited family in Greece because she was pregnant, sick, and temporarily homeless after her husband's aunt had forced her to leave her house so she could rent it. Noting they had spent little time together because his TB symptoms manifested a few months after he arrived in Toronto, she spoke, too, of needing "a change" after putting up with his obnoxious behaviour during her hospital visits. She also said that she wanted to reunite as she was generally "pleased" with him (and his aunt), and wanted to keep the child, adding that she could earn enough to support it.

Of the husband, the European male worker noted that any mention of his wife sent him into "confused outbursts" during which he could not be reasoned with, and attributed his troubles to emotional immaturity. The man's refusal to negotiate appeared to offer him a sense of reasserting his authority (or saving face) over an employable and strong-willed wife. The counsellor recommended delaying further counselling until the husband's health improved, and then to refer the couple to a better-resourced family agency that might help him see his way towards reconciliation.[34]

There are also a few women who, sapped of the psychic and emotional reserves needed to live with a mentally ill husband, and guilt-stricken over their adversely affected children, walked out. The professionally transmuted expressions of emotion contained in these files (see chapter 3) convey a sense of the very real havoc that such prolonged emotional suffering wreaked on the women. A European male counsellor said of a Dutch woman determined to leave her schizophrenic husband despite her church elders' disapproval because of her son's worsening "emotional problems," that she, too, appeared to "suffer mentally" from the situation. Although sympathetic, his advice – to "try to improve her appearance a bit for herself and the children's sake," and try some "forms of relaxation" – was not terribly helpful.[35]

The lengthiest (one-year) file in this group features a 35-year-old Slovakian woman, Mrs H., who left a decade-long marriage to a man institutionalized in both Czechoslovakia and Canada while he was undergoing electroshock therapy in Toronto. The entries track her efforts to use every option available to secure a decent home for herself and their two children. They capture both her fears of deportation and her remarkable resilience. When she first visited the Institute, she admitted to the European woman worker assigned to her case that her welfare officer's talk of deportation had scared her into finding any type of work – but also that she was "very worried about the children," especially a son exhibiting his father's pronounced mood swings. Clearly, the government worker had used the threat of deportation to force Mrs H. back to work rather than try to extend her welfare supports so she could deal with her children. A refugee who had fled Communism, she was clearly terrified by the prospect of being sent back to Czechoslovakia. Significantly, the Institute counsellor addressed both issues. First, she referred Mrs H. to a Hungarian-speaking psychiatrist for her son, explaining that, given her situation, the Department of Public Welfare (DPW) would cover the cost. Then, she found her a job with one of the many middle-class Toronto women who hired Institute clients as "cleaning ladies."

A few months later, Mrs H. announced that she was "living common law" with a Czech man she knew from home and was pregnant by him. She added, with obvious delight, that he would "put the whole family" on his insurance coverage, only to report soon afterwards that he had returned home. At her wit's end, she applied for a visitor's visa to the United States to see her parents, whom she now hoped to join permanently. But her plans were undermined, first by an operation to remove a painful gallstone, and then by the refusal of a visitor's visa because she was a welfare recipient. She then faced pressure from the social workers at her husband's hospital to care for him at home. Her caseworker helped her to pen a reply that says she is "in no position" to do so as she now "has 3 children to care for." The case ends with her applying for Ontario Housing (subsidized housing) and filing for a legal separation from her husband.[36]

Angry and Damaged Husbands

The handful of cases involving husbands who were angry, even vengeful, but also damaged emotionally by a wife's actions, catch some of the male losers of these disputes.[37] One Hungarian man was "so upset" to learn his wife in Hungary had disappeared with a lover and abandoned their teenage daughter that he began drinking heavily, lost his job, got further depressed and, on Christmas Day 1958, attempted suicide. His female counsellor then expressed concern about his befriending a "very neurotic" female client, but later admitted the "friendship" was helping him. A decade later, a Portuguese man whose wife reportedly left him and their two children because of his bitter "dissatisfaction" with Canada, became an Institute client. His complaint about the police refusing to "bring her back to him" suggests he was further embittered by her rejection of his authority. The recorded observations of his European male caseworker also speak to the emotional suffering of a father who needed to work but who could not bring himself to place his children in a temporary foster home. So, too, does the frustrated caseworker's complaint about the man's crying upsetting the children. (His parents had remained in Portugal to care for a "retarded" child so he had no family to help him with his children.) "Whenever a suitable foster home is found," an entry reads, "he comes up with objections." These comments also suggest that, notwithstanding the social-cultural principle of respecting "other" cultural norms regarding emotional expression, this Northern European worker thought his Southern European client overly emotional. His last entry notes that the client's "emotional outburst" in front of the latest potential foster parents will likely again end badly.[38]

Some estranged husbands who felt humiliated or diminished as a man or outraged by a hostile wife's taunts, sexual infidelities, or treatment of children tried to enlist the Institute's help in punishing her for her "immorality." As the following two cases illustrate, a wife's evident culpability could differ enormously. The first file tracks the efforts of an increasingly desperate Hungarian man whose wife called him too lazy to work despite debts, then threatened to move in with her mother in Montreal, and finally "kicked him out" and took in a lover, to recruit various counsellors into stopping her welfare supports. He first claimed that she gave the lover money out of her welfare cheque, but neglected the children, who he claimed wanted to live with him. Then he reported (disingenuously) that, since spending just one night in jail because of a late night "quarrel" with his rival, she tormented him with shouts of "criminal." (Like other estranged couples, they lived near each other.) He returned wanting help in tracking down a joint account he thought they had opened, only to be told he needed a lawyer for that. And, finally, that she had admitted to having just "tried to provoke an abortion herself," saying she hoped it "would work again" as it had a year previously. While the counsellors already thought the wife a less-than-ideal mother, his efforts stopped neither her affair nor her welfare payments. She got her divorce. Meantime, the seemingly hapless man got injured on a job he had recently begun and asked for help in filing a claim with the Ontario Workmen's Compensation Board.[39]

The second wife, whose estranged husband, a Hungarian tradesman employed as a dishwasher, accused her not only of having sex with men in front of their daughter but also of sexually abusing the toddler is the only such case in my entire database. Written in a tone of disgust and outrage, the husband's letter to police justifying his abduction of the girl is the main source of information about the wife's sexual trysts, her late-night fights in restaurants with ex-lovers, and occasional prostitution (oral sex for $5). The male lovers, who, along with a female neighbour, were listed as potential witnesses for the divorce and child custody case, had clearly provided many of the lurid details. The man's letter, which may have had a co-author, was blunt. It noted that his daughter sometimes climbed on top of him and, using sexual language, "demonstrated the usual movements of sexual intercourse." Turning to the sexual abuse he said he witnessed, he wrote that his wife dismissed his objections, first to encouraging the girl to masturbate alongside her while they watched television, and then to "play[ing] with her "in this way," by saying "it was her daughter" and she could do as she wished. (If true, her excuse echoed that of abusive men towards their wives.) Meanwhile, the husband added with dripping sarcasm, she had the welfare agencies convinced she was "moral." The European female counsellor expressed her own hostile feelings towards the wife (who denied everything in court) in two ways. First, she called the wife's words in a letter she sent to her husband as "terrible" and "disgusting." (The letter is not in the file and we do not know whether she is its sole author.) Second, the worker dubs the woman a sexual outcast ("nymphomaniac"), though the labelling also reflected her suspicion that she was mentally ill.[40]

Wife Assault Cases

Institute counsellors were witnesses to the pain and trauma of wife battery. It was particularly true of the women who handled two-thirds of the twenty-five wife assault cases. The files record cases of husbands of Ukrainian, Italian, Hungarian, and other ethnicities who repeatedly hit, slapped, punched, and kicked their wives, or poisoned or drugged them. The files also record the degrading insults and threats, the controlling behaviour, and the heavy drinking that often accompanied the beatings. Portuguese, Slovakian, and Greek wives who criticized husbands who came home late from drinking his or, in some cases, her, wages, were beaten, sometimes until they were "black and blue." So, too, were Austrian, Yugoslavian, and other wives who challenged their husbands' authority over the children. Husbands taunted wives with talk of "girlfriends" and then beat them for demanding or begging them to give them up. They accused them of infidelity, claiming they slept with a male neighbour or a relative, a boarder in their rooming house, or the man in the "upstairs" flat. There were violent outbursts from estranged husbands who showed up to torment a wife, or rape her, or to abduct a child. A few men did jail time for the attempted murder of wives they accused of infidelity.[41]

Most husbands rejected Institute counselling, even when the court ordered it, their absence a reminder of those who, as Annalee Golz observed for an earlier era, used "stony silence" as a defence strategy.[42] A European male counsellor handled one of the few cases where an abusive husband, a Greek immigrant, joined his wife for counselling at the Institute. The wife, who had recently undergone a fifth hospital surgery, explained how her husband, a diagnosed alcoholic and referral from the Research Addiction Foundation, excused his drinking, obnoxious behaviour (he ruins every wedding and party, she said, and made her feel ashamed), infidelity (girlfriends), and beatings – which he called "spankings" – of their "mentally retarded child." In words recorded in the file, she also conveyed the emotional effect of life in a loveless marriage: "when he comes home he does not even ask his wife what she wants, give her a kiss and love the children" but "just goes out to drink." Aware that the staff of the institution where she hoped to place her child thought the woman in danger of a "break down," the counsellor also recorded her descriptions of her husband's controlling behaviour. He would not let her book a hair appointment, "dress properly," or "go out alone." He used the pretext of a shaving kit that had shifted slightly from the spot where he had left it to accuse her of infidelity. In a twist to the usual pattern, he hit her or the child not when drinking, but when told not to drink.

The counsellor noted that the husband's "red" face betrayed a serious drinking problem. Then that he spent much of the session blaming his financial woes and "nervous" condition on his parents, whom he said beat him as a child, his medication (too strong), and on the child, whom he disowned. He also expressed much envy towards his better-off brothers. We know that victims sometimes "talk back" to their abusers or "act out," whether by smashing dishes or taking lovers. But in suggesting that she shared some blame for the abuse because she accused her husband of being weak, the counsellor engaged in victim blaming. In the end, though, he attributed the problem mainly to the husband's emotional immaturity, and the case ends with the plans for the child's institutionalization moving forward. Meanwhile, the husband was scheduled for treatment at a mental health clinic, making this case also one of several where wives tried to stop the violence by getting a husband whom they thought was suffering from mental illness committed.[43]

Emotions Work

In handling the wife assault cases, female counsellors conveyed feelings of sympathy towards their clients. Did they develop bonds of trust with them? And did the emotions work they performed cause them emotional suffering? Recent studies on the emotional and physical toll of providing caring labour in the human services field and on "compassion fatigue" among "helping" professionals and volunteers offer constructive ways of addressing these questions.

The Institute female counsellors differ markedly from the flight attendants who provided the basis for sociologist Arlie Russell Hochschild's affect-based theory of the harm done to human service workers forced to feign, and encouraged to internalize, emotions intended to keep customers and profit-making corporate owners happy. But it is helpful to think of them in terms of a "managed heart."[44] The requirement to constantly perform as the knowledgeable, empathetic, confident, and persuasive social worker no matter one's own feelings could be stressful, especially given the emotionally demanding caseloads involving angry, anxious, sad, despondent, and desperate clients.[45] As for the early clinical evidence indicating compassion fatigue, or secondary trauma syndrome (STS), among social workers, human rights workers, and others who work extensively and for lengthy periods with trauma victims, I have neither private diaries nor clinical records that document counsellors referring to STS symptoms. Only recently, in the aftermath of the 11 September 2001 terrorist attacks, have experts acknowledged compassion fatigue, or STS, among those who work extensively with trauma victims as a phenomenon. The syndrome is not limited to women, but, given women's predominance in social work practice, many are vulnerable to it. Mirroring those of their clients, the symptoms range from irritability, sadness, numbness of feelings, and depression to avoidance of work, and flashbacks in which one has a sense of "reliving" (the client's) experience.[46]

My sources do, however, contain evidence of the stress and anxiety of counselling work, and the emotional wear and tear of handling many traumatic stories and difficult conversations. Most husbands might have rejected Institute counselling, even when ordered by the Family Court, but they showed up to try to charm, intimidate, or harangue female counsellors about their wives. A few of them charged into the offices, demanding to see the "lady" who helped his wife. One husband punched a male counsellor, drawing blood and sending him to hospital.[47] As frequent court interpreters, female staff heard men spout all-too-familiar accusations (she's low-class, a prostitute, a whore) and excuses (it's because of drink or poverty or some other perceived unfairness). That a few of them took a leave in order to deal with their own family crises, sometimes abroad in Europe, is also suggestive. As is the significant turnover (with a few exceptions) in the counselling staff. The admittedly fragmentary personal correspondence among staffers suggests, too, that women's friendships helped them to deal with the emotional demands of the job.[48] The following assessment of a number of the wife assault cases handled by two of the Institute's female workers takes account of this larger context.[49]

The woman counsellor who handled most of these cases was one of the Institute's multilingual refugees from Eastern Europe. She carried a diverse caseload that included clients from Asia and Central and South America as well as Europe. The second counsellor was one of the Portuguese immigrant counsellors who hailed from a city in mainland Portugal, spoke Spanish and Portuguese, and dealt with Central and South American as well as Southern European clients. As middle-class European women who landed jobs in Canada as social workers (even if not fully accredited ones), these staffers were differently situated than the wife assault victims, including those of middle-class origins. But their handling of these cases reveals a strong capacity for sympathy, albeit one that sometimes bordered on pity, if not the empathy expected of the fully professional social worker. And clearly their concern was not limited to clients who shared their own class or ethnic background.[50]

The Eastern European counsellor's response to Mrs A., a former Dutch nurse who confessed that years of physical and emotional abuse had made her an alcoholic, fits this pattern. Despite a large caseload, she took the time to have "a long talk" with Mrs A., whose husband had recently deserted her, in order "to keep her spirits up" because "she was very, very upset." She recorded having applauded the woman for recently joining Alcoholics Anonymous, which she claimed was helping. In response to the client's nearly destitute state – which made her vulnerable to deportation – the worker promised to provide more help. Her efforts paid off when a Dutch embassy official agreed to provide Mrs A. with additional financial help and a lawyer for the divorce. An ability to listen to a client also characterizes this worker's response to a "very upset" working-class Hungarian client. When she first raised the possibility of reconciliation, the woman retorted that "she had a terrible life with that man," who, she found out, had been through three wives, and was "a very questionable character ... not able to look after a family." Having "heard" her client, the worker, in implicit defiance of Catholic Family Services, which was pressuring the woman to return to her husband, helped her get a separate flat, a job, and some second-hand clothing and furniture.[51]

The Portuguese counsellor's file entries on her Portuguese clients also suggest strong feelings of sympathy towards women enduring wife assault. A tone of sadness bordering on pity informs her notations about a young woman whose husband had poisoned her when she was pregnant in hopes of killing the baby. First there is the explanation that the woman had to send her "very ill" child to her parents in Portugal because they were dependent upon her Toronto wages. Then an acknowledgment that this dutiful daughter's critical role in a transnational family economy was suffering from an emotional transnationalism ("she cries a lot because she is far away from her baby") rooted in women workers' painful separation from their own children.[52]

The same worker's advice to a pregnant hairdresser whose husband kept threatening "to beat her in the tummy so she will lose the child" to "stay with him until the baby arrives [as] maybe he will change" illustrates the prevailing pro-family approach. A genuine concern for the woman is nonetheless evident from her accompanying advice that, should he not change, "to leave him because she is too young to start suffering this way." Her wait-and-see advice might have still rankled.[53] A mix of sympathy and pity similarly marked the Portuguese counsellor's response to a former telephone operator who was supporting a teenager and mother on the low wages of a hotel chambermaid. After hearing about the beatings and a hernia operation gone terribly wrong, she took the Portuguese woman home for lunch, and then escorted her to the local welfare office to apply for support. She also found her cleaning work.[54]

On occasion, these counsellors did lose their patience with a wife assault victim whom they believed was lying or making poor choices. To draw from the refugee counsellor's larger caseload, she bluntly told one abused wife separated from her husband that she would lose her mother's allowance support if she did not stop allowing the husband back into the house.[55] She was equally blunt with another mother's allowance recipient who had left her abusive husband and moved into a midtown apartment with new furniture that she could not have possibly afforded, saying that if she did not drop her story about an American cousin helping her out, and seriously downgrade, she would lose her support. She issued the ultimatum after home visits conducted by DPW staff revealed evidence of a man (not the cousin) living in the flat (men's clothing scattered about). Her young children unwittingly undermined her claim to be doing a friend's laundry when they attested to a Mr G. living with them a few days a week. The woman agreed to move to DPW-approved housing, though she had to make a fuss in order to avoid being located near her husband. She also got her divorce, though securing child support became more complicated after he returned to Hungary. The worker also helped the woman renegotiate the payment schedule for the furniture debt with which her ex-lover had saddled her.[56]

Like her colleagues, this counsellor could also be ineffectual, as evidenced by the file on the one racialized victim of wife assault. Although a teacher, Mrs G., age 33, and her young son arrived in Toronto from India in 1969 as the sponsored dependants of her husband, a skilled technician who undoubtedly entered Canada under the points system.[57] The woman's harrowing tale of arrival dominates the file. The ordered structure of the story and some probable editorializing on the counsellor's part reminds us that we are reading a professionally rendered narrative. But the verbatim quoting of the client and the piling up of details contain critical traces of the woman's voice and her courageous effort to seek help. The one lengthy entry explains that Mrs G. spent hours at the airport waiting for her husband before calling a male friend of his, who helped her to rent a bachelor apartment in the building where his family lived. The husband then showed up at the apartment, but, instead of "look[ing] after his family," he "took away her passport, and Jewels" and said he was sending her "back to India." Tapping the few networks at hand, she contacted and moved in with another family from her home village who lived in Brampton, a neighbouring city and a magnet for South Asian immigrants. But after the man "molested" her, she returned to Toronto. Telling the counsellor that she wanted to remain in Canada, Mrs G. asked her not to divulge her current address to anyone as her husband was trying to track her down and had even contacted the police. The counsellor ensured her complete confidentiality and asked her permission to contact a family agency that might help, but her notes on the phone call with the agency worker reveals the irony of the Institute's family approach. Despite Mrs G's desperate desire to stay away from her husband, the two social workers prioritized reunification. To that end, the Institute counsellor agreed to first "interview" the (completely elusive) husband in order to "explain his responsibilities" as a sponsor to support his wife, and to inform him of Canadian laws against wife battery. She added that, should he not cooperate, Mrs G. would be referred to a legal aid officer for help in getting established on her own. The case ends, though, with the counsellor telling a frustrated Mrs G., also in need of a job, that she cannot register with the government employment service (Canada Manpower) without a passport.[58]

The lengthiest files involving wife assault reflect interactions, albeit interrupted ones, across a lengthy time period and offer insight into the circumstances in which female counsellors developed bonds of trust with a wife assault victim.[59] The cases follow a general pattern by which the counsellor, faced with compelling evidence that the marriage is beyond repair, abandons efforts at reconciliation and becomes the client's ally. That evidence often came from female neighbours who corroborated a woman's stories of the husband's verbal and physical abuse, including in legal affidavits. Some workers also witnessed the men's erratic or threatening behaviour during home visits, in court, or at the Institute. A positive evaluation of the woman's reputable behaviour also played a role, but so, too, did her distraught state.[60] The cases in question also hint at the emotional wear and tear experienced by female counsellors from their professional, and personal, investment in the women. Here, I highlight three examples.

As court interpreter for the case, the Portuguese counsellor already knew a depressing amount about Mrs S., a Portuguese Family Court referral who had left her husband two years previously because of regular beatings. Shortly before giving birth to her third child, he had beaten her "so badly" that "the baby was born with black marks all over his body." The worker also knew that for this immigrant woman, the challenges of living with hostile in-laws had reached grotesque proportions. Mrs S. had managed to run away during an incident in which the mother-in-law pulled her by her hair along the house corridor while a brother-in-law covered her mouth to keep her quiet. She eventually broke free and the neighbours, hearing her screams, called the police. When Mrs S. returned for her children, the husband released only one of them. The worker's notes on a counselling session with the couple record an exchange in which the husband, who came to further torment, not reconcile with, his wife, rudely dismissed the (familiar) suggestion that they find an apartment "without his family." He said "he would rather have a prostitute as a wife." Expressing her

94   Narrative, Subjectivities, and Affect

contempt for him, the counsellor wrote, "if they would reconcile, it would only be to get [her] pregnant again, and she would be left with three children to support." Abandoning talk of reconciliation, she now advised Mrs S. to apply for the government-subsidized commercial-skills course in order to improve her ability to support her children "in case her husband runs away and does not give any financial support." The suggestion of a training course (with subsidy) that promised better returns than the usual dead-end jobs lined up for clients reflected the worker's sympathy for, but also personal and emotional investment in, "a young, attractive girl" whom she expected to become a single mother. The husband's frank admission in court that he would repeatedly abuse again if made to live with his wife prompted the judge to begin divorce proceedings.[61]

The shift in the Eastern European caseworker's opinion of a working-class Hungarian woman who moved to Toronto from Eastern Canada for work and her husband's health (TB) from that of suspicion to sympathy similarly suggests a capacity to really listen to a client. Before the woman's revelation that her husband beat her and spread lies about her having contracted venereal disease as a result of sexual promiscuity, the counsellor described her in unflattering terms, as "a very husky woman" and an unreliable worker who kept annoying potential employers on the Institute's roster by not showing up to clean their houses. Thereafter, she continued to handle the woman's requests for practical assistance, but the tone of her notes changes dramatically. She expresses delight over the news that the woman will spend Christmas with an out-of-town daughter. When she visited the Institute after a ten-month break during which she got divorced, the counsellor calls her "a good old friend" who is "now happy as [her ex-husband] is not pestering her any more." Only a year after landing a "nice" office job at a golf club, she adds, the woman was head of the department and earning "a good pay and a generous bonus." Yet, even this case underscores the precariousness of these women's lives. A year after their happy reunion, the woman was laid off and the counsellor was lining up cleaning jobs. Written after a follow-up call, the final entry indicates the woman's altered emotional state, and hints at the worker's own feelings of disappointment: "Tells me the places were very dirty and is hard work to clean everything up ... a little cheese sandwich she is getting all day for this hard work."[62]

Another of this worker's cases that speaks to a relationship of trust that emerged between differently situated refugee women involved a Hungarian woman of humble (possibly rural) origins who complained about her often-drunk husband's beatings and refusal to support his family. He had also done some jail time for drunk-driving convictions. The worker conducted a home visit to evaluate the woman's eligibility for emergency support from an Institute co-sponsor. In her report (which noted a "clean" home and children) she recorded her conversation with the distraught woman. She recounted depressingly familiar scenarios – he beat her for refusing to let him take the children "for a drive" while "totally drunk" – and dilemmas – she had "to leave the children somewhere" so she could work and help cover the rent and debts, but he threatened to kill her if she contacted the Catholic Children's Aid Society (CCAS). When asked why she thought he acted this way, she said she had "no idea," but that his own explanation – homesickness – was "a lie," as his mother in Hungary said he was "a heavy drinker" back home. Subsequent entries record an ever-escalating situation in which the "almost continually drunk" husband threatened to kill his children, then, "in a rage, damages the furniture and throws things," then, at other times, "cries for no apparent reason." They also track the growing desperation of a woman who, now convinced her husband is mentally ill and likely to get worse, is reaching an emotional breaking point. Convinced that she has good reason to be afraid of her husband, the counsellor, who also appears to have agreed to help her try to get her husband into a mental ward for treatment, gets the woman to promise to call the police the next time he causes trouble.

The woman secured the legal separation a few months later, but facing near-destitution at Christmastime, she returned to ask for a food basket and children's gifts. She also confessed that, unless she could temporarily place the children, she was "afraid she would hit them because of the pressures she was under." She spoke as well of wanting "to get off" welfare, find a job, and "get back on her feet." The confession suggests some trust, or a relationship, however unequal, had developed between counsellor and client. The worker's later entries also indicate her growing anxiety over her client's safety, particularly after she gave in to pressure from the husband, who kept insisting on his fatherly "right" to "look after" his sons, to divulge the name of the CCAS worker. Before she could get hold of the woman to "warn her" about what happened, she learned that he had "tracked" her down, and that, in a "highly intoxicated state," was threatening to beat her. This time, however, the worker recorded, with obvious relief, the woman called the police, who removed him from her flat. And, then, following a four-month gap, the final entry reports that the sobered-up husband was back home and they were saving for a trip to Hungary. The counsellor does not record a response, though she likely worried about the woman's situation. Nor does the outcome negate the trust that the Hungarian woman placed in her female counsellor during an especially trying, and scary, time.[63]

Perhaps the most compelling evidence of the trust established between a female caseworker and her client, or certainly the most overtly emotional text in these files, is the suicide letter sent to the Eastern European counsellor by a Hungarian refugee nurse and long-time wife-assault victim. She is likely the sole author of the letter, which was written a year after she became an Institute client. The counsellor's file entries indicate that, in that time, she had helped the woman find some paid work and located a foster home and a summer camp for her children, and then supported her to secure a divorce in Family Court.

The client's use of the worker's first name in the opening salutation ("Dear *"), a rare occurrence, suggests that a trusting though still hierarchical "professional friendship" had developed between a counsellor-turned-erstwhile-protector and her client/victim. So, too, does the body of the text, which reads: "I am very sorry I was so much trouble to you," but "bodily and spiritually I am breaking down." "I would like to live to see my children grown up," it adds, "but I wouldn't be able to stand losing them." Blaming her plight on her husband's years of cruelty, and expressing hope that God will forgive her (she is Catholic), she asks her worker "to see that my children get loving care from someone who will substitute for the mother they lost this way."[64]

Significantly, the suicide letter, and the relationship it represents, prompt the hospital psychiatrists and doctors to involve the Institute caseworker in the woman's recovery plans, though we do not know what ultimately happened to her. It was not an egalitarian relationship. The women shared a middle-class Eastern European refugee background, but they occupied very different positions within the social work relationship, respectively as an employed knowledge-based professional seeking to protect a wife-assault victim and the other the victim. One of two cases involving attempted suicide, the case also contains entangled narratives of abuse and mental health. But whereas such discussion usually focused on the abusive man's mental health, here the discovery that she used poison brought "from home" prompts speculation of "a pre-existing personality disorder" or a long-time "depressed state" related to her "personal difficulties."[65]

Then and Now

Since the early 2000s, the occurrence of a relatively small number of high-profile "honour killings" involving particularly South Asians in Canada of Muslim and Sikh background has generated debate, including among feminists. On the one hand, some commentators, including some feminists working with women in these communities, distinguish historically observed Western patterns of male abuse of women from the "newer" (for Canada) and supposedly more "culturally driven" violence against women and girls committed by husbands, fathers, or brothers often with the support of women and extended family members.[66] Similar commentary exists for Iraqi, Iranian, Kurdish, and other non-Western immigrants and refugees in Europe, Australia, and other parts of these far-flung diasporas. On the other, leading feminists such as Mojab argue that such a characterization of gender-based violence misses the mark. Honour killing, they note, does differ from most domestic violence in that it is premeditated, planned (sometimes for years), and involves a collective action against women or girls accused of having disgraced the family usually through some sexual transgression. Nevertheless, it is a particular socio-cultural form of the universal phenomenon of violence against women. Furthermore, essentializing this honour-based crime – defined as such because male murder of "deviant" female members supposedly restores the family's honour within the community – in terms of a particular religion, culture, race, nation, or immigrant community lets Western cultures, where men who kill their intimate partners are treated as an aberration, off the hook. It also serves to enhance racism and xenophobia in the hostland.[67]

Even my admittedly limited research base of predominantly pre-1970 wife-assault cases supports a de-culturalized (or de-exoticized) explanation of honour-based crimes that situates them instead within the broad spectrum of violence against women. One or two cases do not a pattern make, and trying to measure degrees of abuse is risky. But let us juxtapose the actions of Mrs G.'s Indian husband, who stole her passport in the hopes of getting her deported, to that of the two European men, one Ukrainian, the other Hungarian, who tried to kill the wife they accused of infidelity. Their modus operandi was hanging by rope and a crushing hammer blow to the head, respectively. The six-month sentence the first man received for an assault conviction – he avoided a murder charge because his 12-year-old son found his mother before it was too late – still speaks volumes on the era's indifference to wife battery. The second husband, who had used flowers and an apology for an earlier beating as a ruse to get into the neighbour's house to which his pregnant wife had earlier fled, got five years for fracturing her skull. After recovering, she faced a whopping $900 hospital bill, though she successfully filed for divorce. The European men's allegations and attacks also fit a narrative of male honour restored.[68]

Indeed, the honour-shame complex that today is discussed primarily with respect to the Middle East, Africa, and Asia did not disappear from post-1945 Europe. For example, traditions of elopement by abduction, arranged and forced marriages, and honour-based crimes continued to influence gender relations in regions across Southern Europe, though they also came under critique and modification. As feminist readings (as opposed to outdated anthropological models) of the honour-shame complex show, the (modified) code also travelled to immigrant communities abroad, including Toronto, where, again, it underwent revision, including by youths, in hostland contexts.[69] The Eastern European cases documenting marital rape and gruesome beatings of wives can be understood not only as male ill-adjustment due to wartime loss and refugee experiences, but also in terms of homeland politics and culture. As a matter of social policy, Communist authorities, note feminist gender scholars, largely ignored domestic violence and the prevailing popular view of this taboo subject was that women were largely to blame for its occurrence. The absence of social services to support female victims and the chronic housing shortages also made it almost impossible for women to escape the violence.

Nor did the women's movements in Eastern Bloc states raise the subject, as they did in the West.[70]

There are a few noteworthy European cases in the database involving meddling and abusive in-laws who participated, not in a premediated murder of a daughter- or sister-in-law, but in a planned abduction of her children. At least two mothers-in-law refused to let an estranged daughter-in-law see her children.[71] Now, as in the past, the media focus on sensational court cases of femicide, but pay comparatively little attention to the efforts of women who seek out the limited resources available to help them reduce or escape an abusive marriage.[72]

There are also differences. Many post-1945 European immigrants experienced anti-immigrant discrimination, and the struggles of abused women to house and care for their children attest to the material deprivations and humiliations endured. Still, the reality of systemic racism means that racialized women from non-Western cultures are more likely than white Western women to be disbelieved by officials and to be refused housing by landlords. At shelters and social agencies, they encounter social workers who blame the violence on their "culture," thus further stigmatizing the victim. Feminist critiques of the male leaders and community members who, consciously exploiting multiculturalism-inspired fears among Canadians of appearing racist, defend honour-based crimes on the grounds of cultural traditions, religious values, and community norms surely expose one of the greatest ironies of this liberal ideology.[73]

Conclusion

At once highly mediated and revealing sources, the case files on marital conflict illuminate the paradoxical nature of the Toronto Institute's social work practices. On the one hand, the value of its pluralist approach is underscored by the recommendations of women's groups and settlement service activists working with today's immigrant wife-assault victims that agencies recruit front-line staff from the women's immigrant communities and provide linguistically and culturally "appropriate" services. Most of the Institute's front-line immigrant and refugee counsellors, and all but one of the women, were not professional social workers with university credentials but rather community practitioners. While training and debriefing sessions emphasized its value, the file entries and occasional casework reports particularly of the female workers suggest they did not consistently practice empathy. Sometimes, though, a sympathetic ear led to helping a woman get what she wanted. The wife-assault cases highlight in particular not only counsellors' sympathy towards abused women but the meaningful if temporary and still asymmetrical relationships that sometimes developed between the European female counsellors and their mostly European female clients.

This is not to suggest that the efficacy of the interventions necessarily required the profile of counsellor and client to be a perfect match, since, as some experts warn, a woman will not always wish to speak with a member of her "community."[74] The Hungarian nurse who survived her suicide attempt might well have preferred a Hungarian-speaking woman counsellor who was not Hungarian to a male Hungarian counsellor on staff, whether because she thought a woman more likely to be sympathetic or that it would give her some protection from community gossip. Violated by a family "friend" as well as her husband, the one South Asian client may have preferred a white European female worker to the Institute's lone South Asian male counsellor.

Institute social workers claimed that their insight into the group-based culture of clients offered them a valuable diagnostic tool and a roadmap towards treatment. In practice, however, a counsellor's possession of the necessary linguistic skills, a basic familiarity with a client's social and cultural background, and a respectful approach, rather than a detailed typology of the supposed ethno-cultural traits of the client's ethnic group, helped to establish a rapport with a client. And it was the advice or action taken by a counsellor to support a woman stuck in a miserable or violent marriage that best helped to build trust. On occasion, an Institute male counsellor also lent a sympathetic ear. Still, the stress involved evidently took more of a toll on the female workers who handled more of these difficult cases. Or at least the male workers' notes are not forthcoming on this point.

There are some parallels between Institute efforts to reform the behaviour of abusive husbands along the lines of the celebrated companionate Canadian model – which assumed a breadwinning and authoritative but domesticated and supportive husband – and the recommendation issued by those who attribute male violence against women in today's racialized communities to non-Western cultures for a systematic acceleration of Canadianization. In both cases, the call to indoctrinate the "foreign" men into the hostland values assumes that all but the exceptionally deviant Canadian (or North American) men respect their wives as their equal.[75] Such calls underscore the slipperiness of notions of integration and assimilation, echoing as it does the Institute leaders and social work consultants who advanced the paradoxical argument that immigrants could be assimilated into the dominant values of the host society while maintaining their distinct cultural traditions. Furthermore, cultures are not static entities, and, as Mojab and other feminist antiracist scholars note, the notion that non-Western immigrant families must emulate Western standards ignores the fact that the homelands in question have in some cases been the site of century-long feminist struggles for gender equity and rights.[76]

The product of multicultural encounters that occurred within a predominantly white European context, the Institute files say little about the (mis) treatment that non-English-speaking European women may have experienced at the hands of employers, court officials, or agency staff. By contrast, today's front-line counsellors are taught to appreciate that their racialized client's efforts to access legal and social support systems will be constrained by the systemic racism that infuses every sector of the wider society, including housing, the justice system, and social welfare services.[77] Finally, front-line workers today are advised to assume violence rather than force a woman, who has probably faced multiple traumas prior to her current situation, to (repeatedly) share her "abuse narrative." By contrast, the Institute counsellors belonged to a long line of social workers who traded in narrative: they wanted and required compelling and corroborating stories. It begs the question whether, the staff's sympathy notwithstanding, the social work encounter played a role in further traumatizing the already victimized.

Chapter Six

Generational Conflict: Intimacy, Money, and "Miniskirt" Feminism

In 1970, the Ontario Economic Council (OEC)[1] declared that the "cultural mosaic model" had failed to integrate immigrants into the wider Canadian community and attributed the supposed failure to the persistence of both self-contained ethnic communities that perpetuated "different" values and the cultural "gap" between immigrant parents and their children, particularly those of Southern European origin. Foreshadowing the racist backlash against the seventies-era immigrants, the OEC report also predicted a worsening of the gap as immigration from South Asia and the Caribbean increased, possibly resulting in violence.[2] It came close to advocating assimilation with its call for "a new approach somewhere between the traditional Canadian cultural mosaic and the U.S. melting pot."[3]

The report's author was Edith Ferguson, a social worker who in the 1960s had led two community projects undertaken by the International Institute of Metropolitan Toronto. Aimed at improving, respectively, the health and the occupational profile of Southern European immigrants, the projects reflected a mix of community organizing and liberal uplift. Ferguson's progressive pluralist agenda had included proposals intended to improve the material lives of low-income immigrants and to foster multiculturalism. Correctly predicting that the wives and mothers of formerly peasant families would become lifelong workers, she had, for example, advocated more training programs that would increase skill levels and improve wages. She supported heritage and language classes for all children on the grounds that it would encourage a greater respect for all cultures and foster a pluralist society (see chapter 8).

Four years after leaving the Institute, and one year before Prime Minister Pierre Elliott Trudeau would adopt multiculturalism as official state policy, Ferguson was calling herself a "middle-of-the-roader" in the melting pot vs cultural mosaic debate. Asked to elaborate, she said she saw "no real harm in the fact that many ethnic groups continue to hang on to their own cultures and values long after they come to Canada." But, she added, "it wouldn't upset her" if they "took on a more Canadian aspect" because "the development of a strong Canadian identity" was essential to "maintaining democratic institutions and liberal cultural traditions."[4] Ferguson's 1970 report coincided with growing public awareness of a "third force" vision of multiculturalism being promoted by ethno-Canadian leaders during the recently completed proceedings of the Royal Commission on Bilingualism and Biculturalism.[5] Ultimately, however, her ambiguous reply reflected less an abandonment of her principles as the tendency within Institute pluralism to blur the lines between integration, Canadianization, and assimilation.

The OEC's proposals for a "comprehensive" program of integration, such as English classes and counselling services, were not new. But the OEC did claim as innovative its rejection of "the popular concept that immigrants enrich Canada by maintaining their cultural identity in ethnic communities." In other words, multiculturalism. The newspaper coverage homed in on the "special integration problem" posed by immigrant youth on account of the separateness of their ethnic communities from Canadian life. Journalists focused on parents from "remote" rural villages who disapproved of their children adopting a "Canadian style of life." They wrote about boys made to quit high school in order to earn money. And how the pressure to direct their earnings towards the family mortgage rather than a much-desired car or motorcycle led them to commit "auto theft" and other crimes.[6] As for teenage girls, they wanted "to wear cosmetics and mini-skirts," attend parties and date without supervision "as Canadian girls do," but instead were cloistered, chaperoned, and forced by parents to marry men whom they hated.[7]

Did such media portraits fully capture the range of generational conflict in immigrant families? What role did the International Institute of Metropolitan Toronto play in mediating such conflicts? Drawing on newspapers as well as confidential case files, this chapter examines how Institute counsellors understood and responded to the "problem" of generational conflict within immigrant families in late 1960s and early 1970s Toronto. It highlights parent-teen tensions, but also considers conflicts between parents and older children. I probe the counsellors' observations of their clients' emotional state as well as their own sometimes emotional reactions. The primary focus, however, is the counselling staff's differing response to the teenagers facing parental dictates to leave school and earn money to help support the family and to those accused of transgressing the transplanted moral codes of their parents. In playing ally to teens in the first instance, and to parents in the second, Institute workers responded in both prescriptive and contradictory ways to the embattled immigrant teens they encountered. In the first case, they sought to mediate and reduce parental influence and encourage, albeit within limits, the youngsters' participation in an urban modernity that promised them more individual freedom, self-realization, and the accoutrements of a more affluent life. Many of the relevant case files contain professional Canadianization narratives of potential redemption, or modest upward mobility, that ultimately foundered in the face of parental opposition. In the second, counsellors supported parental efforts to exert control over teenagers who challenged their parents' moral and social codes. Told of an alleged or court-deemed "incorrigible" son or daughter, workers turned into sleuths who (indiscriminately) gathered evidence of bad behaviour from various sources. These files took on the character of detection tales characterized by a contradictory mix of facts, gossip, and hearsay evidence that might nevertheless hold sway in juvenile court.[8] Significantly, in handling both types of parent-teen conflict, female counsellors' actions did not differ from those of their male counterparts.[9]

Scholarship and Cases

Historians and other scholars have approached the issue of generational conflict in a variety of ways. A large and diverse literature produced by family historians and historians of women and sexuality has examined the conflicts and negotiations between parents and adult children over money, property, and customary obligations, including those with respect to courtship and marriage, amid periods of continuity as well as change.[10] While sympathetic to the immigrant generation's strategies of survival and security, particularly through homeownership, feminist histories of urban working-class immigrant families have explored the struggles, modest workplace mobility, and cultural aspirations of the sons and daughters negotiating conflicting cultures.[11] A key focus of the theoretical and historical research within moral regulation studies and on the socialized justice meted out by family and juvenile courts is youthful transgressions of parental and societal moral and legal codes of behaviour.[12] Studies with an immigrant focus, such as Mary Odem's *Delinquent Daughters*, highlight the roles played by the rural codes of immigrant and migrant parents and by Anglo-Protestantism in shaping understandings of delinquency and parental interactions with the courts.[13] Also important are analyses that highlight social work theories and interventions with pregnant teens.[14]

Bringing together insights from these various literatures, I highlight both the range of conflict within immigrant families in late-sixties and early-seventies Toronto and the differing social work responses they engendered. My analysis of the popular media portraits of immigrant youth in conflict with their parents, and deemed in danger of acting up, breaking down, and dropping out of high school is informed by an assessment of a subset of 150 case files related to the theme from my Toronto Institute database of 7,000 case files. In contrast to the media focus on Southern Europeans, the subset represents twenty-two ethnic groups, though Portuguese, Italians, and Greeks, along with Hungarians, account for two-thirds of the clients. There is also a sprinkling of German,

Yugoslavian, Czech, and Slovakian cases, but, again, few non-European ones.[15] Two-thirds of the parent-child conflicts involve teenagers (100) and one-third (50) adults[16] between their mid-twenties and early forties. Four-fifths of the teen-related cases concern wage-earning, while one-fifth deal with transgressions against parental codes. A dozen different counsellors handled the subset of cases under review. The Portuguese-, Italian-, and Greek-speaking workers handled close to two-thirds of them while the Eastern and Northern European workers covered most of the rest.

The Institute became involved with most of the families because one or more members turned to its Department of Individual Services for assistance, but a few of the "juvenile delinquency" cases are Family Court referrals. Female clients slightly outnumber male ones. Most parents are married, but some are widowed, divorced, or separated. Mothers or mothers-in-law slightly outnumber their male counterparts. Most cases involve recent arrivals, but the presence of families with longer Canadian residency reflects conflicts that arose as the children grew older.

Adult Children and Older Parents

Some conflict was bound to occur within Toronto's many multi-generational and financially strapped immigrant households. One type not captured in the media's focus on youth involved adult children and the parents they supported. Feelings of guilt, worry, or sense of personal diminishment led some of the parents in this cluster of one dozen cases to ask the Institute for help in finding a job or securing welfare support so they could better contribute towards their own upkeep. The relevant entries contain descriptors such as "worried" or "anxious" and note tears and crying. As with the three mothers over the age of 60 who asked about applying for a Canadian widow's pension or welfare support in order to help a daughter or son with the rent, the strategy usually failed because either the parents were the sponsored "dependants" of their adult child or they did not meet the specific residency requirements.[17] The one reportedly "optimistic and cheerful" parent in this group was also the youngest: a 56-year-old Hungarian man living with the daughters who sponsored him wanted to find work so that he could in turn sponsor his wife and youngest child. He was placed as a dishwasher in a hotel restaurant.[18]

The narrative contents of the files reveal the toll that the emotional and physical stress of supporting parents took on certain adult children. At one end of the age spectrum, a 25-year-old Italian son who for three years was breadwinner to his unemployed father and sick mother ended up hospitalized for ulcers attributed to prolonged stress. In terms of educational achievement, he was an unusual Italian client, but his family troubles killed his dream of being a teacher when the hospitalization forced him to abandon teacher's college. At his request, the Institute supported an application for a scholarship for him to begin a program in social services work at Toronto's Ryerson Polytechnical Institute. This dutiful son's plans did not mean abandoning his customary family obligations: the letter notes that "illness and overcrowding at home" adversely affected his marks in teacher's college, but that he was now healthy and employed (in a store stockroom), and ready to return to school part-time. At the other, a 42-year-old Greek married father of two who had supported his parents for a decade turned to the Institute after his father had a stroke and he lost his own job. The parents' lengthy residency in Canada did qualify them for welfare support, but a small glitch in the application process perhaps underscores the son's emotional state. He reported on his father cashing an additional Department of Welfare (DPW) cheque that did not belong to him out of fear that it would jeopardize their support. The problem was resolved.[19]

Similar cases involving single mothers and single daughters shed light on how the emotional (feelings) interacted with the material (money) to produce different scenarios. In an example where mother and daughter evidently wished to stay together, the Hungarian mother, age 64, explained that, unless she could come up with a little more than $10 per month, her divorced daughter would be "forced" to rent to someone who could. With a teenager as well as a mother to support, and an ex-husband reneging on his child-support payments, the daughter, who was enrolled in a training course and so receiving only a modest weekly stipend ($55), was struggling to make ends meet. The mother, having fled an abusive marriage, wanted to stay put. The sympathetic European male counsellor suggested she ask the DPW office for some additional support, but no outcome is recorded in the file.[20]

The two widowed mothers who claimed they could avoid being evicted by a hostile daughter only by paying more rent offer a sharp contrast. The first case ends with a call to a mission shelter, suggesting the worker thought the Hungarian mother might end up homeless.[21] In the second, lengthier, case from 1967, the conflict between mother (a university-educated Czech refugee who came to Canada a decade earlier) and daughter was compounded by a diagnosis of schizophrenia and competing narratives of the mother's actions. The European female counsellor immediately noted the woman's odd behaviour – she notes that the woman kept accusing the Czech Masaryk Hall, a community centre where she had worked, of pocketing the bingo profits, a major source of hall funds, and other nefarious activities – and went into detective mode.[22] She reports that investigation into the woman's claim that she left a long-term typist position after being refused a salary increase revealed that she was dismissed for perennial lateness. Then, she reports, the DPW staffer contacted said she had illegally cashed some UIC (Unemployment Insurance Commission) cheques while working as a casual typist. In pursuing the woman's request to be shifted to a psychiatric outpatient clinic offering one-on-one therapy because she disliked the hospital's group therapy approach, the worker gathers more damning evidence. A different DPW official claimed the woman was interested "only" in "weeping" for more money, not dealing with her mental health problems or applying for a medical "disability" certificate that might qualify her for long-term welfare support. He added that he had wasted his time visiting the mother about a DPW application because the daughter, who had earlier intimated that her mother used her illness to avoid work, had "slammed the door in his face, saying that she does not need assistance." When the Institute worker followed up with the daughter, she reportedly used "spiced vocabulary" and "called her mother a beggar, etc.," but agreed to let her mother sign the DPW form.

The counsellor grew increasingly exasperated with her difficult client. After hearing she did not show up for job interviews, she writes "I am not able to help her." Told she had approached an Institute co-sponsor for funds, she lectures the woman about "not expect[ing]" money from other agencies when she is already collecting welfare. She then writes, "the idea that she should work is just not understood." The remaining entries suggest a further deterioration in the shaky social welfare relationship. When the woman begs off the latest interview (claiming toothache), the worker writes that "she has every time another excuse," and that "she slammed the telephone at me as she did many times already." Also imbedded in the motley collection of details and opinions, though, is a competing narrative about the woman not getting the medical attention she needs. Her psychiatrist admits to the counsellor that the hospitals have turned to group therapy because it is cheaper than individualized therapy and no one seems to have helped her to become a clinic patient. Meanwhile, she continued to repeat the bingo-related allegations against the Masaryk Hall and, when referred to them for long-term casework, made allegations against Catholic Family Services. And then, to the worker's surprise, the woman secured a "small loan" from a senior Institute female staffer, though this not uncommon break in professional protocol is never explained. As the case ends, the woman appears to have left her daughter's place for a small government-subsidized apartment obtained through the Ontario Housing Corporation.[23]

Property Feuds

The high degree of debt assumed to purchase homes and the steep payments required to pay off mortgages led to inevitable generational tensions over money. Like the issue of wage-earning teens submitting their paycheques to the family patriarch (see below), property-based feuds involved negotiating customary expectations in new contexts. One of the two examples that evolved into legal cases involved a Croatian mother and two adult sons who lost a lawsuit against the husband/father for ownership of the family home on the grounds that he had abdicated his family obligations and not helped with the mortgage payments. The judge had ruled in his favour and ordered the mother and sons to pay him $7,500 plus legal expenses. When they asked the European male counsellor at the Institute whether they should follow their legal aid lawyer's advice to appeal the decision, he told them to keep in mind that, when the 70-year-old man died, "they'll receive the house anyway."[24]

In the second case, which, like the first, occurred a decade after the family's arrival in Canada, a Hungarian mother and her married son fought over a farm they inherited from the now-deceased husband/father. After going into sleuth mode, the counsellor shifted her opinion of who was the troublemaker. The mother came to the Institute seeking legal help in a dispute with her son, who she claimed had reneged on his responsibilities towards her. Both had inherited the farm in 1955 and, a few years later, she purchased a house in Toronto with her son despite his marrying "against her wishes." They signed a legal contract giving the son possession of the farm in exchange for guaranteeing her permanent accommodation and other expenses. The conflict erupted eight years later, when the son "got mad" over his mother's refusal to co-sign his application for a hefty loan ($11,000) and "threw her out of the house," in the course of which he "kicked her," possibly breaking a finger. She retaliated by trying to get the contract revoked in order to take possession of his share of the property.

The case file includes references to mental illness and competing versions of events. The European male caseworker observed that the mother "expressed a great deal of anxiety" about her son plotting to place her in "a mental hospital," adding that it had taken three sessions to help her "overcome this fear." But as the dispute continued, the worker grew impatient with the woman, who also alienated the lawyers with constant threats to fire them unless they produced immediate results. Shifting to the son, who had initially refused to sweeten what he claimed was an already generous live-in contract, the counsellor brokered a new deal. The son agreed to add to the original terms of the contract an entitlement to her own private quarters (a kitchen and two other rooms) and coverage of "quite high" medical bills, and a lump sum of $3,500, "provided she would not interfere in his way of handling his family." The mother claimed to be "touched" by the son's offer and apology for the kicking, but still wanted more money, first suggesting $5,000, then $7,000. She also wanted to change lawyers again.

The mother returned a year later to tell the new counsellor, also a European man, assigned to her case that she was suing the son for lack of support despite her lawyer's warning that it would fail because she had continued to live with her son and daughter-in-law. Even if she did win, the lawyer explained, she would recover only a one-half interest in a farm with no running water or electricity and back taxes owing on it. She accused the lawyer, who had proposed an out-of-court settlement, of plotting with her son to commit her to a mental institution, adding that she had letters attesting to her sanity. She then claimed

108 Narrative, Subjectivities, and Affect

that her husband had once tried to poison her and asked the worker to help her sponsor a son still in Hungary. In response, he referred her to a family service agency, indicating that he thought she needed long-term institutional help.[25]

Meddling Mothers-in-Law

Institute counsellors, not unexpectedly, encountered cases in which married adult children, in a quest for privacy, were motivated to ask or demand that parents or in-laws leave their household. Like marriage and family experts, they advised newlyweds to find separate quarters that would afford them the intimacy needed to get to know and truly understand each other, to grow into their respective roles as wife and husband, and to prepare themselves for parenthood. The ideal itself was of course punctuated with contradictions, not least of them the claim that the modern companionate marriage was an egalitarian relationship in which husbands enjoyed ultimate authority.[26]

All but one of five such cases capture the feelings of abandonment harboured by older mothers even when they accepted some blame for the conflict that led to their ouster. A 71-year-old Estonian refugee renting a room in a private home since getting "into trouble with her daughter-in-law" said she "felt very lonesome." She especially missed her grandchildren, whom she now saw only occasionally when her son brought them over. A heart condition also made it "very difficult" for her to walk up the hill where the house sat, though kind drivers sometimes stopped to give her a lift. The European male worker found her the ground-floor unit she wanted in the vicinity of Estonian House, a community centre where she could meet other Estonians and take English classes.[27]

Generational conflict cases, unlike the Institute case files on marital conflict (see chapter 5), sometimes contained explicit engagement with social-cultural perspectives. Of a Portuguese widow, age 66, facing eviction from the home of her married son, one of the Portuguese female counsellors wrote that, as a rural villager accustomed to dense family networks, she "enjoys spending most of her time" with her son and daughter-in-law. But that, since her son said he "wishes to spend his time alone with his wife," she has felt "depressed and lonely." She tried to help the woman accept the situation by referring to the aspirations of newlyweds in Canada in terms of working hard to realize their nuclear family dreams. The son, she added, wanted to spend his very limited leisure time with his wife. The mother evidently got the point as she accepted a live-in babysitting job. In an effort to cheer her up, the worker noted the benefits of making "her own money," but was silent on the job's disadvantages, including, ironically, a lack of privacy. She does not comment on whether the daughter-in-law played a role in this family drama, though that did apply in other cases.[28]

In a twist to the tale of the ousted meddling mother-in-law, the conflict between an older Polish woman and her daughter-in-law resulted in the son leaving with his mother. The case also offers a rare glimpse of the trust that developed between a male worker, in this instance a European immigrant with social work training, and his male client. A Polish refugee who came to Canada with his parents a decade earlier, the man was referred to the Institute by a psychiatric clinic that thought his "problems" were "related primarily to culture." By then, he had spent eight years with his sick widowed mother in Toronto while his estranged wife and children lived elsewhere. The file entries present a textbook example of casework resulting in diagnosis and solution. First, the worker's assurances that Institute personnel possess an "understanding of his feelings and difficulties" encouraged the initially hostile man "to express his feelings and concerns." Next, a social-cultural analysis explains the man's refusal to heed the hospital's recommendation that, upon her imminent release from psychiatric care, the mother be placed in a home for the elderly. The worker explains that, "according to his cultural values," children are "responsible" for their parents' welfare while "old age homes are ... for the 'poor and rejected' people." In other words, a clear case of (European) group culture "dictating" immigrant behaviour despite the presence of "new" options, namely, modern homes for the aged.

The mother's passing shortly afterwards then allows the focus to shift to family reconciliation. Once the client admits that his wife has asked him to come home, but that he felt "ambivalent" about it, the worker focused on convincing him to do so. In attributing the positive outcome to the "case work" provided, he highlights two factors: expertise ("our counsellor was a former immigrant himself and aware of his culture") and appropriate counselling that considered "past and present cultural environment, ego support and assisting forces of repression." The last point referred to having gotten the man to reflect on and overcome his fear of returning home. In this instance, though, the claim is borne out by the man's cards and letters, which also report on his improved relations with his wife and children.

While the Institute's pro-family approach explains the satisfaction expressed over a patriarch's reinstallation in the family home, equally noteworthy is the wife's apparent role in initiating the reunion and the male bonds of trust that developed between client and caseworker. The mail sent to the worker over the course of a year reflected the client's emotional investment in continuing a now long-distance relationship. The worker's response offers a mix of the professional and the personal. Explaining that he "purposely" held off responding to allow the man "time to solve [his] own problems, without outside help," he reminds the man to be patient and applauds the family for possessing the "courage to tackle the problem." (He also listed some local family agencies just in case.) Obviously replying to the man's personal questions, the worker adds, "We have a lovely time in Europe and enjoyed it to be with our relatives once more" and witness Europe's return to "prosperity." The personal exchange both blurred the private/public line normally drawn between institutions and their clients and underscored the relationship forged.[29]

Parents and Teens

The handwringing that, by the late 1960s, focused on the conflicts between parents who held to "traditional" mores and expectations and their more rapidly Canadianizing teenagers occurred within the wider context of the era's alarmist discourses of spreading juvenile delinquency, with its focus on boys' petty crimes and girls' sexual promiscuity. But immigrant youth were also singled out for special attention.[30]

As social-culturalists, the Institutes viewed the conflict in terms of a clash between different "group-defined" lifeways. The children's entry into the hostland's school system, a major institution of socialization, introduced them to values and behaviour that differed markedly from their parents' moral and social codes, so that by the time they reached puberty, they felt embarrassed by and resentful towards them. The explanations juxtaposed model (middle-class) North American parents, who raised children to be curious and confident, and gave them the freedom to pursue interests and relationships beyond the family, with immigrant parents whose "patrocentric family" model emphasized obedience and discipline. Other contributing factors included the challenge of learning a new language, the inability to maintain friendships because of the family's (local) transiency, and the "acting out" associated with the raging hormones of teenagers. While acknowledging that not every conflict in immigrant families was "caused" by "cultural elements," pluralist social workers, including Institute consultants, argued that the frequency of disputes due to the clashing values of parents and children underscored not only the need to interpret the host society's standards to the parents but also the families' absorption of its core values.[31] In Ontario at least, the experts disagreed over whether television contributed towards immigrant youth alienation (Ferguson's position) or might help in their family's adjustment to modern life.[32] Unlike the Institute's multicultural events, which showed an appreciation for cultural hybridity (see part 4), the sources under review here reveal a pathologizing of rural immigrant cultures and the adoption of a remedy that stood closer to assimilation than to integration.

The media coverage of parent-teen conflict in the wake of the OEC's 1970 report was extensive but varied in tone from the lighthearted to the voyeuristic and foreboding. The focus was on Southern Europeans, but Asian and Caribbean families were also discussed. For example, an early-sixties article featured 19-year-old Victor Chung, who had arrived from Hong Kong with his parents a dozen years earlier. It delivered the oft-made point about immigrant teens who had learned English but, having failed to advance in their "mother-tongue," could not discuss "complex" matters with their non-English-speaking parents.

Using a jocular tone, the reporter notes that Victor "is a full-blown Canadian" who "loves folk singing, movies, hamburgers, long hair and Canadian girls," but that he needs an interpreter (an older brother) to discuss dating non-Chinese girls with his parents, who "still cling to many of the old ways of their country."[33] But the media's main focus was, as liberal journalist Sidney Katz noted, on the conflict "between parents reared in an ancient, impoverished European rural environment and children raised in a modern, affluent North American city." An Italian-born female social worker (Nada Costa) interviewed by Katz for the *Toronto Star* noted the resentment of Italian parents towards the Canadian school system for lacking the rigour of schools in Italy, where "religion, discipline, respect for parents, and other social and moral values are taught as part of the regular curriculum."[34]

The parental practice of turning high school teens into wage earners so they could help pay off the mortgage in a family-linked strategy of homeownership attracted much criticism. While focused on Italians, Costa's explanation of how a corporatist family ethos transplanted from Europe's villages to urban Canada produced generational conflict was seen to apply as well to Portuguese and Greek families. The basis of childrearing in rural village societies was to prepare the child to cope with a hard and insecure life, the safeguards against which meant working collectively, living frugally, and complying with parental demands. In Toronto, however, parents were "dismayed" by their children's "extravagant tastes" in clothes and viewed the Canadian custom of giving children "a regular allowance with no strings attached" as "spoiling" them. Describing a long-standing source of generational conflict within working-class immigrant families, Costa added that young wage-earning Italians resented the expectation that they hand over their entire paycheque to the father, who then provided a small allowance and covered the cost of clothes and other necessities out of the "family treasury." (She failed to note the mother's role as the family's frugal shopper.) An Institute staffer cited an example in which the financial pressure that parents, determined to pay off a mortgage in five years, exerted on their son, who preferred instead "to finish his education," could lead to his "mental breakdown."[35]

The problem of the early (underage) school-leaver caused particular consternation. Under Ontario law children were required to attend school until age 16. In the public and Catholic school systems in Toronto, principals and school board officials frowned on the special work permits that, until 1970, allowed parents to take their 14- and 15-year-olds out of school mainly to earn money. But they often approved the request because of the family's depth of need. Because of Italian concentrations, it happened more frequently in the Catholic schools. The process was also gendered. Given the choice of issuing a permit to a son or daughter, they tended to give it to the girl, whose childminding released the mother to work and allowed the boy, a future breadwinner, to stay in school and complete the Grade 10 required for entry into a trade.[36]

Teenage Workers

Institute counsellors found teens part-time or summer jobs on farms, golf courses, and other workplaces, but full-time work was another matter. Four-fifths of the parent-teen cases of conflict concern a teen's full-time wage-earning. Despite the media trope of the immigrant girl stuck at home until married off, girls slightly outnumber boys. All but five cases involve Southern Europeans.[37] Most youths visited the Institute one or two years after arriving in Canada, had some Canadian schooling, and reportedly spoke "fair" English. Together, the cases show that while counsellors might appreciate the parents' financial struggles, they openly accused them of forfeiting a child's chances for a better future in order to achieve their goal of homeownership. As social workers who by inclination (given their urban middle-class backgrounds) and training promoted the modernization of rural immigrants, they sought to protect their teenage clients from parental dictates sure to doom them to the lowest rungs of the workforce. But there were also class limits on the degree of social uplift they envisioned for them.

Like other historical sources on poor and working-class children, the Institute files on the teens who said "I want [or need] a job to help the family" appeared to adopt a matter-of-fact tone. The boys often invoked their father (as in my father needs my help) and the girls their mother. But we cannot naively read a teen's motive from a counsellor's notations as the phrasing may have reflected a parental directive, even wording, rather than a teen's desire.[38] Some of the teens' families are large, with four to eight children, and in one case, eleven, but many of them are smaller, with two or three children. Reference to large debts, particularly mortgages on a recently purchased house, is common, but hospital bills also come up. The recorded explanations of teens who claim a dislike of school as the reason for wanting to work – such as "lacked confidence in English," "difficulty with teacher," and "laughed at by classmates" – indicate feelings of vulnerability, rejection, and low self-worth. Other narrative traces in the files suggest some teens thought, or hoped, they could use a portion of the earnings for themselves. Overall, the recorded outcomes in these cases aligned with media depictions of parental objectives trumping children's schooling.

The professional narrative shaping the fragments in many of these files is one of potential redemption, or uplift, through Canadianization that fails to materialize because of short-sighted parents. In keeping with US social work cases that tracked and endorsed the Americanization of immigrant teens, the road to redemption is captured in the workers' many recorded attempts to entice the teens (and their parents) into staying in school with the promise of a better working life and future attained through a vocational education. That is, a skilled trade for boys and "nice, clean" office work for girls.[39] At the Institute, it proved a tough sell with parents.

Counsellors were most likely to disparage the parents who yanked underage teens from school in order to help pay off mortgages. A file entry like "but he is only 14" turned a pragmatic strategy to achieve security despite low levels of income and education into a morally reprehensible act.[40] Those tricked by parents skilled at using evasion tactics with outsiders expressed annoyance. The scenario captured in the relevant files went like this. With a sense of professional satisfaction, a worker would record that, during a phone call with a teen's parent, the mother or father would agree to allow them to complete Grade 10 and apply for a government-subsidized training program. Then, in a follow-up call made days, weeks, or months later, the worker would learn, usually from an adult other than the parents, that the teen was working in a factory. The final notation usually referred to the worker having told the relative on the phone to tell the parents that their actions "did not help" or "would hurt" the child's future.[41]

The counsellors' efforts at uplift dominate the case files on older teens age 16 to 19. A European female counsellor advised a 17-year-old Portuguese boy with four siblings who said "he has to work and help his family" because "they bought a house and the father is not earning enough" to remain in school as he already spoke "fluent" English and acquiring a trade would "prepare" him for life. A family member later reported that he was "working in a restaurant and is happy." Even if the positive emotional descriptor accurately conveyed the boy's (as opposed to the parents') feelings, the counsellor's reaction would have been one of disappointment. The effort of one of the Portuguese female workers to try to scare another Portuguese boy, age 17, by asking, rhetorically, "what will be his future if [he] does not learn a trade?" also failed. He said he wanted to "earn money."[42] Her efforts to persuade the father of a boy in Grade 10 who wanted to complete an apprenticeship in motor mechanics was only slightly more effective. He agreed to let his son attend the Institute's nighttime English classes in order to improve his job prospects if she dropped the apprenticeship idea. The boy entered a wood factory.[43]

Institute counsellors understood that the daughters of these struggling families – despite the media image of the housebound immigrant girl – would become wage-earners, and sought to elevate them into the ranks of white-collar workers. Just as they encouraged boys to surpass their father's labouring jobs through acquisition of a trade, they urged girls to advance beyond their mothers' "dirty" factory or cleaning jobs by completing clerical or commercial courses that could lead to respectable office jobs as secretaries, bookkeepers, and bank tellers. As a Portuguese female counsellor explained to one client, training to become a secretary or bank teller "will prepare her future much better than in working in factories." She told another to "finish school" in order to get "a better position" than factory or cleaning work, and yet another to "learn a trade and eventually gain a better salary." As evidenced by the case of a Greek girl who agreed to enrol in a clerical course but then quit school and found a factory job,

Institute counsellors encouraged their young female clients to aspire to a white-collar office job like that held by these two tellers, who worked at a branch of the Canadian Imperial Bank of Commerce. A sign indicates that the bank can serve clients in Italian. 23 February 1962. York University Libraries, Clara Thomas Archives & Special Collections, Toronto Telegram fonds, ASC09105.

counsellors could be equally blunt with the parents. This girl's Greek female counsellor called her home and told the relative who picked up that she "will make better in this country if she will go to school first and then go for a trade." This counsellor, like others, would have also looked for evidence that the girl in question possessed the office job's gendered requirement for pleasant and accommodating personalities.[44] Over time, mothers and daughters would often adopt similar language in describing the latter's advancement.[45]

Among the success stories were the few older teens (ages 18 to 19) who appeared keen to learn a trade. In one such case, another Greek female worker actually advised an anxious Greek boy to "quit" school and attend English classes so he could return to school with the English needed to earn the Grade 10 diploma needed to apply for an apprenticeship course. As the case ended, the strategy appeared to be working: the boy was completing his English program and had been promised a spot in an air-conditioning course in a local high school.[46] Applying a strategy that some teens used to convince parents to allow them to learn a skill, one Portuguese girl told her Portuguese female counsellor that her father would let her complete her high school clerical course if she got a part-time job. A few days later, the girl was back in school.[47] In a similar case, the Portuguese girl reported that she "was taking secretarial, and very happy," providing the emotional descriptor herself.[48] These promising outcomes were nevertheless outnumbered by those where clients quit a program because they felt ill-prepared or overwhelmed by the workload.[49]

Consumerism and Streaming

In a few exceptional cases, the parents' educational ambitions for a teen surpassed those of their teen. The best examples, all of which involve boys refusing to complete Grade 10, speak to the points made by journalists and experts about young immigrant working-class men's attraction to the allure of modern urban culture. A Grade 9 student, Pino, age 17, admitted to being interested in a radio and television repair course, but despite parental and Institute pressure, he refused to complete the Grade 10 requirement. He told his male counsellor, a European immigrant, that he wanted to make money because "so many of his friends work and drive their own cars." The era's car culture promoted modernity under various guises.

The image of cruising in a stylish car, the radio turned on to the latest pop songs, appealed to many teenage boys in North America, including urban immigrant youth, even if it meant buying older used models. But unlike the media portraits, and like many other immigrant boys, Pino was prepared to toil at low-skilled jobs for a paycheque that, provided he could keep some of it, allowed him to participate in an affluent culture that also included fashionable clothes and nightclubs.[50] Ironically, as Gilberto Fernandes notes, these young men were applying the strategy of their parents, who achieved material security not through formal education but "extensive labour and meticulous saving strategies" in order to participate in a consumer culture their parents frowned upon. The greater constraints on girls meant they were less likely to purchase cars or frequent nightclubs, but going to the movies and wearing make-up and fashion items like the miniskirt offered them ways of asserting themselves. Like the Catholic girls who hiked up the skirts of their school uniforms after leaving home, many hid their small but meaningful acts of resistance to Old World restrictions from their parents. But at least some of them did not (see below).[51]

Pino's case, like others, reflected a wider concern about the high rates of high school dropouts among Southern European (as well as Black) teens.[52] Changes began to occur during the seventies era of ethnic revivalism, as the promotion of European-focused heritage language schools and curricular reforms meant to foster a pride in culture and a sense of affirmation eventually translated into lower dropout rates and higher levels of academic achievement.[53] There is also evidence to suggest that daughters of Southern European immigrants would

The allure of car culture extended to motorcycles as well as the convertible in this photograph of young men arriving at a campground at night, August 1965. York University Libraries, Clara Thomas Archives & Special Collections, Toronto Telegram fonds, ASC05661.

become more successful than sons at completing high school and a college or university education.[54] Also by the seventies, a new generation of left-leaning social workers and activists who came of age in the turbulent sixties brought to their organizing efforts among the Portuguese and other immigrant communities the ideals of feminism, the civil rights movement, liberation theology, and/ or labour campaigns aimed at redressing immigrant women's low wages and precarious work.[55]

The final exception to the main pattern captured in the cases involving teen wage-earning is the two Greek fathers, both of them skilled workers, who asked about a son's potential for university. Each time, the female worker dampened their hopes that higher education would give a son access to a middle-class income, by stating, categorically, that a vocational, not university, education was the feasible option.[56] While exceptional in the context of my cases, these two files flag another controversy: the streaming of low-income immigrant and racialized high school students. In the 1970s and 1980s, journalists cited reports and interviews with parents that highlighted the predicament of inner-city Southern European and of Black children and spoke of the racial bias in the school system. Already in the 1970s, Black mothers were lobbying the Toronto Board of Education to hire more Black teachers and address systemic racism, but the problem festered.[57] The 1980s saw some gains for Italian and Portuguese children, as outspoken critics like New Democrat Rosario Marchese, an Italian immigrant who earned a university degree in the late 1970s, became a teacher, and was later elected to the Toronto School Board (and later still to the Ontario Legislature), campaigned against streaming. But this and related practices rooted in systemic racism remain to this day.[58] Eighties-era (and later) research documented the disappointments of low-income immigrant parents who learned too late that the child they thought was university-bound had been placed in a vocational stream.[59]

The Institute's emphasis on vocational training, with its gender-based focus on male trades and low-level white-collar female office-service work, also speaks to the limitations of its liberal pluralism. Despite being applauded for adding "value" to industry, nation, and the prospects of young trainees, vocational education has always suffered from low prestige. From the Institute's liberal perspective, it promised to produce skilled workers for Canadian industry and provide the children, just as it did the parents of low-income families (see chapter 8), with better-paying jobs that would offer them greater protection during periods of economic stagnation. In terms of the "mental-manual divide" that distinguishes an academic from a technical education, the Institute's objective also reflected and reinforced the notion that disadvantaged immigrant youth lacked the potential for more intellectual or rigorous schooling. Not that the universities beckoned. Notwithstanding the democratization of post-secondary education in these years, the Canadian university was at this time still an institution of class, gender, and racial-ethnic privilege. These immigrant youth may have been born around the same time as Anglo-Canadian baby boomers, but they were not necessarily "born at the right time."[60]

Transgressive Teenagers

Alongside the popular image of the carjacking or joyriding Mario or Miguel was that of the cloistered and chaperoned Maria or Rosa whose life offered a stark contrast to the sixties image of the emancipated young woman. In the Toronto newspapers following the release of the OEC's report, social workers and popular pundits alike invoked the miniskirt to highlight the gulf between these immigrant girls and women and their Canadian counterparts. An Institute spokeswoman noted the confusion and resentment of teenage girls whose parents forbade them from wearing miniskirts and make-up only to see their teachers donning the latest fashions. Unable to dress and act like their Canadian friends, she added, they become depressed, as do the boys and girls who cannot accompany their classmates on school activities and other social events.[61]

Explanations for this "girl problem" focused on an honour/shame moral code transplanted from the Mediterranean to Canada. Social worker Nada Costa's version of it went like this: men possess powerful sexual impulses and demonstrate their masculinity through conquests of women, hence, women, being by nature "weak and defenceless," must be placed "under constant surveillance" whenever they are out with a man. The male sexual threat is so strong that even the good girl's virtue "is in jeopardy." As the "carriers of family virtue" (to quote anthropologist Wenona Giles), the woman who engages in premarital sex brings shame to her entire family and disqualifies herself from the marriage market. Regarding marriage, Costa noted that many daughters now selected their own marriage partner but were still obliged not to marry anyone the parents do not approve of. Parental attempts "to impose this code of behavior" on their girls enrolled in Toronto high schools, she added, prompted teachers to ask her "to intervene with Italian parents so that their daughters can attend school dances." She also relayed a disturbing anecdote about an Italian father who cautioned his daughter against being "a loose woman" after one boy walked her home from school, and then called her a "fallen woman" after a second one did, the anger and shame prompting him to sell the house and change neighbourhoods. Writers like Katz noted the situation of the boy who could not date a girl within his ethnic group without her parents assuming he intended to marry her. He also emphasized the plight of girls like the 14-year-old who responded to her father's beating for attending a school dance unescorted by taking an overdose of pills. She was taken to hospital to have her stomach pumped out.[62]

The small number of Institute files related to youth transgressions of parental codes or "delinquent" behaviour reflects in part the tendency of non-English-speaking immigrant parents to deal with such matters privately or within their community.[63] Fathers might mete out corporal punishment, though mothers also did, particularly with daughters, and emotionally distraught mothers might turn to traditional healers such as midwives and sorcerers.[64] Together, the cases include a wide range of European groups as well as Italians and Portuguese. One-third of them were Family Court referrals. As in the cases involving wage-earning, failure to resolve the conflict looms large. But whereas counsellors tried to prevent parents from exercising their right to end prematurely their teens' formal schooling, they supported parents trying to rein in disobedient teens, particularly daughters. Paradoxically, the counselling staff expressed concern about but did not openly advocate for immigrant youth who challenged what they themselves (as middle-class urbanites) thought were overly strict "rural village" codes.

The larger number of girls (13) than boys (7) in the cluster of delinquency cases might well reflect these parents' tendency to view a daughter's transgressions as more serious than a son's, hence the willingness of certain parents to consult outsiders. But misbehaving sons were not given a free ride. Parents who turned to the family and juvenile courts often did so at the suggestion of the school authorities who reported on the problematic behaviour, or at the insistence of police officers who may have caught a teen stealing or who returned a "runaway." Theories of juvenile delinquency drew on a mix of psychological, social, and environmental factors, such as poor parental skills, unstable and transient families, and poor neighbourhood relationships. Counsellors emphasized the role played by ill-adjusted and overly strict parents whose opposition to their children's acculturation to the hostland culture produced hypersensitive, anxious, hostile, and defiant teens. A case in point is a Family Court referral of a 14-year-old Italian boy charged by his father with incorrigibility after a third school, within a period of less than a year, expelled him for disruptive behaviour. This Institute file also illustrates how the application of a social-cultural perspective could confirm rather than challenge theories of delinquency.

The European male counsellor who carried out the court-requested social history on the Italian boy and his family was one of the Institute's multilingual and trained social workers. The boy's incorrigibility was not in doubt, which explains why the focus was not on gathering incriminating evidence to make a case but instead on collecting a life history and on that basis arriving at a diagnosis and solution. Based on interviews conducted with each of the parties, the worker concluded that the family, which had remigrated to Canada for the third time in 1960, fit the juvenile delinquency profile to a tee. The father's shoe repair shop, he noted, was in decline and he was "emotionally" troubled by his reliance on funds sent by an eldest son living in Italy. His preoccupation with his financial difficulties had also made him "withdrawn and irritated." A victim-blaming assessment attributed his failing business to his lack of English and consequent dependency on Italian customers, but said nothing about whether "Canadian" customers would visit the shop even if he spoke English. He also described the father as an "affectionate" but ill-informed parent, and a strict but inconsistent disciplinarian who even admitted that a psychiatrist in Italy had once told him to be less strict with the boy. The mother fit the stock portrait of the Southern European mother who is "very permissive" with her young children, but whose "neurotic possessive relationship" with them means that "she resents their growth." Affectionate towards her youngest children and elderly parents-in-law, she was reportedly "quite submissive" in relation to the husband.[65]

As for the boy, the detailed life history revealed a history of problematic behaviour, from the temper tantrums thrown as a toddler in Italy whenever he was disciplined to the recent cruelty shown towards animals: cutting up a dying dog and a sick cat. While he enjoyed a "good" relationship with some of his siblings, the "very poor" one with his parents explained the repeated lying, refusal to obey his father's demands, and misbehaviour at school. In his defence, the boy, who said he barely understood his teacher, though he claimed to have friends among his classmates, explained that the reason for his most recent expulsion – failing to stay after school to clean up a mess that he and another boy had made – was due to extenuating circumstances. The other boy had gone straight home after school and he was also afraid that his father would "scold him for coming home late."

The caseworker concluded that the boy's problems stemmed from "his emotional deprivation from early childhood," a possible birth injury (he was delivered with forceps), and "a history of disease in the family," a reference to the father and grandfather having contracted syphilis, and that these were compounded by his immigrant family's ill-adjustment. The recommendations included in-depth casework for the parents to help them to improve their "economic and social adjustment" and their parenting skills. Adding that child experts "agree that sometimes deficiency is accompanied by a singular skill in a special line," the caseworker also proposed that the boy's apparent "mechanical ability" – he reportedly showed "some aptitude and interest in automechanics" – be encouraged.[66]

The senior probation officer who requested the life history was pleased with the "excellent" report and the Institute staff was delighted with the endorsement. Both sides agreed that, as the court official put it, "one should avoid speaking of 'a New Canadian problem,'" but "recognize that there are problems which are peculiar to New Canadians" who are "handicapped in receiving service because of language and cultural barriers." Noting that his caseload included other immigrant boys (including Russians, Greeks, and Italians) charged with malicious damage or petty theft whose family circumstances, including a strict father, mirrored the one under review, he proposed a closer relationship.[67] Had the Institute been better-resourced, its staff would probably have conducted many more life histories.

The remaining cases under review, two of which involve 15-year-old boys who left home, are frustratingly brief. The first involved an exceptionally adventurous Ukrainian boy who, having returned from a trip to Britain and Istanbul, wanted a job so he could save for "a trip to South America." At the counsellor's request, he agreed to contact his parents about returning home, but it is not clear that he did so. By the time the second boy, a runaway, and his Jamaican immigrant parents met with the Institute counsellor in the only teen case involving a racialized immigrant boy, he had agreed to return home.[68] Whether closer ties with the court would have improved the Institute's track record is debatable, however, given the Family Court's own paradoxical history of separating racialized and Indigenous families (through a child's removal into a foster home or reform school) rather than "saving" them.[69]

Problematic Fiancés

The cluster of cases involving "transgressive" teens that involved parental disapproval of a "fiancé" featured four daughters and a daughter-in-law; they also capture the emotional reactions of their female counsellors. One Greek girl, age 17, who had booked an appointment to discuss a hairdressing course, reportedly blurted out that she "left home [a] week ago and rejects to see her family" (though she was living with a brother) because the parents disapproved of her fiancé. The female counsellor immediately called the Greek boy's home and spoke with his mother, who said her family "likes" the girl, thus confirming the seriousness of the matter. After speaking with the girl's aunt, who confirmed the marriage plans, she called the girl's mother and advised her "to accept" the situation and return the birth certificate she had hidden in the hopes of preventing the nuptials from taking place. (The daughter met the minimum consent age of 16.) But she also wrote, confidentially, that she "feels sorry" for the distraught mother, thereby indicating her own disapproval of a girl marrying so young.[70]

One of the Portuguese female counsellors was frankly flabbergasted to learn that the man her "very nice" and "mature" 17-year-old Portuguese client was talking about marrying despite her parents' disapproval was an older married father of three. (This case also quickly shifted from a job to a fiancé-related one.) Expressing her feelings of incredulity, the worker writes, "she is not even sure if he is divorcing his wife on account of her." She advised the young woman "to discontinue" seeing him," suggesting a visit to Portugal so she could "be far away from him" and work on forgetting him. A feeling that the "appreciative" girl will follow her advice is erased by the mother's report in a follow-up phone call that "she has tried everything to stop her daughter from loving this man but without success."[71]

The file on the young Korean woman at the centre of the only non-European case of generational conflict involving a slightly older daughter captures her emotional reaction to a broken engagement as well as the European female counsellor's attempt to narrate a potential redemption tale. Her plan to marry the man to whom she became engaged a year earlier in Korea was sabotaged because the fiancé's father and aunt, both of whom arrived in Canada shortly before she did, opposed it. Whether under duress or not, the fiancé broke things off. The worker's observations of her client as "a very nice young girl" who "is unhappy at present and wept bitterly about her situation" speaks to her client's emotional state. They also refer to the cultural reasons for it, specifically a strict code that disadvantaged women within Asian cultures: "she is heartbroken and tells me that she can not marry anymore according to her custom and she can not return to Korea. Her family would not take her back."

Because she was sponsored by her relatives, not her fiancé, this young woman was less vulnerable to the possibility of deportation owing to abandonment and indigency, but the fact that a legal aid lawyer had referred her to the Institute for confirmation of her legal status (as a landed immigrant) suggests it was not an irrational fear.[72] Evidently accepting her status as a single woman, she wanted to move on. At her request, the counsellor registered her for English classes. To help with "socializing," something her lawyer also mentioned in the referral, the counsellor gave her an Institute membership and urged her to contact two Korean nurses, described as "pleasant young ladies" who belonged to a small circle of Koreans at the Institute that included group worker Catherine Lee. A note about the client's appreciation of her efforts contains as well the sort of clichéd "chin up" and "silver-lining" advice that Anglo-Canadian advice experts offered lonely, exploited, and abandoned immigrant women. This client's non-Western origins prompted her worker, an Eastern European who counselled on Canadian values, to declare the superiority of Western culture despite having witnessed the damage done to many women of Western origins. "We are able to explain," she writes, "that she can look forward to more pleasant things if she remains here" because "in this culture she is a free individual and nobody is going to hurt her, or her feelings."[73]

Delinquent Daughters

Despite the media focus on Southern Europeans, the cluster of cases featuring scenarios of exasperated parents seeking to rein in a rebellious daughter suspected of sexual promiscuity by turning to outside authorities is evenly divided between Eastern and Southern Europeans. Most cases were initiated by parents who turned to the Institute, though since counsellors sometimes encouraged parents to contact the police or Family Court, some of these cases may have ended up in the juvenile justice system. This was the advice given to the three fathers, one Yugoslavian, the other Slovakian, and the third Hungarian, who reported on a "missing" teenage daughter. The counsellors sympathized with the fathers, though the European female worker who dealt with the Yugoslavian father and his wife, whom she knew, was better at recording her views. Attributing the girl's delinquency to psychological problems, she described the father as "a nice person" willing to take on any job, the mother as "very upset," and the daughter, who had abandoned a job that she had once found her, as "a very disturbed young girl" who posed an ongoing problem for the parents, who had three other children. But there is no follow-up.[74]

Turning to a case that attracted media attention, the news that a Czech teenager died after jumping in front of a subway train while "high on speed" offered a cautionary tale about the dangers of giving teens too much freedom. For the female counsellor of the teen's mother, it also underscored the need to be vigilant in stamping out unhealthy anxieties bred under Communism. The mother, who was divorced, claimed that she knew her daughter and boyfriend were experimenting with drugs and had even noticed needle marks on their arms, but that she was "too afraid to go to the police" because, having lived in Communist Czechoslovakia, she "did not realize Canadian police actually helped people." Initially, the worker, also Eastern European, thought her client a schemer trying to secure patents for never-explained inventions. When she returned after being fired from her job in a dental lab, the worker observed her altered emotional state, writing that she "was crying all through our conversation" and was "in a very bad condition with her nerves." The woman blamed the instructor of the training course she had taken for not properly preparing her for the job, and the worker referred her to the local employment office. The next time she returned, it was to report on her daughter's tragic death.[75]

In a 1968 Family Court case involving a Hungarian family torn apart by incest, the distraught mother asked the Institute for help in securing visits with her 13-year-old daughter, who had been placed in a foster home after being caught having sex with her 14-year-old brother. At the court's request, the Children's Aid Society (CAS) had placed the son in a foster home. A former secretary now toiling as a hotel chambermaid, the divorced mother told her counsellor that the girl's grandfather had sexually abused her daughter in Hungary when she was 10 years old. Thus, like so many so-called delinquent girls, this daughter was a victim of sexual abuse. The mother was frantic because the CAS would not let her visit her daughter. She was also anxious about her son, who, she said, had been so "scared by the doctor" who assessed him that he subsequently took an overdose of sleeping pills and ended up in hospital for three days. He was given some tranquillizers and sent home. The European male counsellor managed to secure the mother some visits with her daughter, but there is no further follow-up.[76]

The most complicated case of all featured a Hungarian family. The file contains competing narratives of the father who reported his daughter missing and of the 15-year-old teen's alleged transgressions. As soon as the unemployed tradesman and single father (whose estranged wife had remained in Hungary) reported that he had not seen his daughter since she left for work at a local restaurant six days previously, the European female counsellor went into detective mode. She phoned the restaurant and spoke with an employee who said the girl had not worked there for three weeks, but that, a week ago, a girl claiming to be her sister (though she did not have one) collected her pay. Another employee claimed to have seen her the day before walking along the street. The worker then called the local police station and arranged for an officer to come to the Institute to interview the father while she interpreted. Offering a rationale commonly used by parents to explain a teen's delinquent behaviour, the father blamed his daughter's bad behaviour on "bad" influences. He singled out an older "Italian driving a Cadillac" whom he claimed had earlier "tried to befriend his daughter" as the one most likely responsible for his daughter's disappearance.

Many stereotypes contain a bit of truth and the father's story of an Italian man in a fancy car cruising for girls like his daughter initially played nicely into what proved to be his performance as the anxious parent. Told about an aunt, the worker got hold of her, too, and her stories placed both father and daughter in a different light. At age 22, the aunt seemed more like a cousin than an elder to the teen and her anecdotes also cast a shadow on her own moral status. She said that her niece had spent a few nights with her, usually arriving around midnight and then disappearing again. She noted that, when the two of them had worked together at a different restaurant, her niece had been "in [the] company of Italian and Yugoslav speaking men." She said, too, that the restaurant manager, whose name was distinctly Italian, had promised to "secure them better positions" than waitressing "should [they] be his girl-friends," and then intimated that they had agreed to the deal by saying they had gone to Hamilton to work as saleswomen. She added that they then received a "proposition to go to Montreal," the sexual innuendo implied by the city's late-night club scene, but claimed that neither of them did so.

The aunt's story fit with a history of young working-class women who encountered pleasure and danger in the urban spaces they inhabited, including workplaces, and the sexual bartering involved.[77] Then came more explicit claims about the girl's history of sexual deviancy. The aunt said that the girl, at age 12, had run away from home and several months later was picked up by the Hungarian police and hospitalized "to be treated for venereal disease." During the 1956 revolt, she was allegedly partying with friends in Austria. After tracking her daughter down, the father stayed with her in Austria "where apparently all had gay times – the father had friends amongst her girl-friends." The concerned father thus morphed into an unfit father who, according to the aunt, had also found "girl friends" from among his daughter's friends in Toronto. The counsellor did not record her thoughts on the father's alleged behaviour, but her notes on a meeting she held with the police following the girl's return home a few days later reveal a disciplinarian determined to stamp out the bad behaviour. Upon hearing of the girl's return, she walked over to the police station to provide an update and had what she considered a useful conversation with a policewoman on the Morality Squad. Her reference to having "exchanged notes" on the girl with the "charming and very interested and concerned" officer probably meant that she told her everything she knew about the girl and the less-than-stellar father. As the counsellor surely already knew, the officer explained that the case would "take time to investigate" because the girl "would have to be caught in an unlawful [sexual] act," as she was a minor, before any action could be taken. She also reportedly promised to inform her sergeant of the case and keep the Institute informed of any developments. No outcome is recorded, but the case underscores the willingness of Institute counsellors to use the law to curtail delinquent behaviour, even if they did not entirely trust the father, who wanted her back home. Being unemployed, he may well have wanted her back because she was the family breadwinner, thereby making this case about money as well as morality.[78]

More than Miniskirt Feminism

Neither the few Institute case files on transgressive girls nor the newspaper articles that treated the subject comment on the "good girls" who, as historian Vienna Paolantonio shows with respect to Italian Canadians, participated in parish activities, both religious and secular, and did not openly defy their parents.[79] However, some journalists did offer nuanced portraits of girls who did challenge their parents' strict moral codes. In his profile of Portuguese-born Filomena Pavao, age 16, the *Toronto Star*'s Joe Serge repeated a familiar narrative about a "pretty teenager" who was desperate to socialize, but who had "never attended a school dance, been to a party with other high school students or out on a date to a movie" because her parents would not allow her to date until she was ready to marry. He wrote about the "loneliness" of her first year of school because the "'English-speaking students would not associate with me'" and her inability to maintain friends once she learned English because she was prohibited from attending after-school activities. Her closed social life, he added, consisted of visits by relatives, short shopping trips to nearby Kensington Market, and attending church. One can, however, detect a muted expression of resistance to parental codes in Filomena's admission that she did "do things without mother knowing," though she also claimed she would never meet a boy without her mother's approval.[80]

The ruminations of a more rebellious Italian daughter appeared in an article that, like so many others, began by painting the west end Little Italy where she lived as being "closer to Sicily" than to the modern bank tower in the area. But it quickly became clear that, in addition to keeping secrets from her mother, this "girl" openly challenged her parents' moral codes. Part of *Toronto Telegram* reporter Helen Singer's 1971 series on "The Italians," the article featured a conversation between Mrs Chiappetta and her daughters, Emily, age 22, and Ruta, age 19, one that relayed the "compromises" reached as a result of the girls' lobbying efforts, as well as Emily's continuing defiance. Noting that the parents allowed the girls to go out in groups, Singer's additional comment, "or, at least they leave the house that way," identified a common way by which immigrant girls circumvented restrictions. They left home with brothers or male cousins, split up, and then returned home together, swearing they had been together the whole time. The readers who saw this article alongside a related one that featured mothers of Danish, Polish, Italian, Portuguese, and Japanese origins who had taken a "YWCA" program on "Canadian" customs so they could better relate to their children, might have inferred that change was occurring within these households. An Italian woman who explained that she completed the program, itself a response to the OEC report, because she no longer wanted her children to say "mummy is a dummy," was a model subject who earned her driver's licence and became an assistant to the Canadian social worker heading the project. For the daughters of such women, acquiring a driving licence and access to the family car signified a greater participation in a recreational life outside the family home.[81]

Singer's essay on the Chiapetta women is most noteworthy for the public exposure it gave to the nascent feminist views of elder daughter Emily. A recent graduate of the University of Toronto, Emily was an exceptional Southern European immigrant daughter who had clearly won some of her battles for greater autonomy and self-actualization, though her embrace of modernity, or Canadianization, had not meant a complete rejection of her parent's culture. In that regard, she resembled an earlier generation of Italian American daughters who, as Donna Gabaccia documented, showed respect for their mothers even as they opposed their traditional ways. In late 1970s Toronto, Giuliana Colalillo found a similar pattern among second-generation Italian Canadian women. As did Wenona Giles among now adult second-generation Portuguese women who recalled their years growing up in Toronto from the late 1960s until the 1980s.[82]

That Emily is negotiating what some scholars have called a "third space,"[83] somewhere between "traditional" homeland and "modern" hostland cultures, is evident from her answer to Singer's question about the women's views on feminism. Singer called it "women's lib." The mother replies first, saying she prefers her cultural traditions of courtship and marriage to the "wrong" ideal of independent women. Younger sister Ruta, who is also clearly trying to carve out a position, and identity, that can bridge a commitment to family and a desire for personal autonomy, says she expects to marry, but intends to date more than one man before choosing a husband. Emily does not identify as a feminist and says that she, too, will probably marry. But she insists that she will do so only if she finds the "right man at the right time." In another nod to feminist-influenced notions of autonomy, she asserts that "the goal" of marriage "isn't the man," but "the act of becoming whatever you are." Rejecting the code that bound young women to marry their first boyfriend (fiancé), she claims to have no compunction about upsetting her parents over a decision "to break it off" with a boy in whom she loses interest. "'I can't say they like it," she says, "but there's not much they can do about it.'" Her position on employment equity, which also has a feminist ring to it, probably reflected her experience on the job market. She describes it as "'a burning inside you when you know you're as good as the man across the room, and he gets the job.'" Of church teachings about women and procreation, she insists, much like a feminist, that women are "good for more" than procreation, and expresses disdain towards "a tradition that woman has dragged behind her for thousands of years." Again, however, she rejects the feminist label by declaring that tearing down church-sanctioned sexism will need more than "carrying a Women's Lib sign down the street."[84]

Clearly pleased to have found a complex subject, Singer attributes Emily's nascent feminist views entirely to a "WASP university education" that has allowed her to break out of a cultural island on which others were still stranded. No doubt, her university education played a major role in shaping Emily's still-developing views and identity, though, like the Portuguese women interviewed by Giles, "household politics" also mattered. The rebellious acts recalled by two of them ranged from resistance to housework to running away, living on their own, and having a child out of wedlock, while the parental responses included threats and beatings. As Giles observes, these women saw their later choice of non-Portuguese partners as "a rejection of a *machismo* that does not fit with the more equitable visions of gender relations to which, as second-generation Portuguese women, they aspire."[85] Emily's declarations of independence were bolstered by the respectability offered by a university education. We do not know what ultimately happened to the girls, and boys, who are referenced in the Institute case files under review, but they belong to a broader history of immigrant working-class youth whose engagements with urban modernity occurred within highly circumscribed contexts.

Conclusion

The era's newspapers did not fully capture the range of generational conflicts erupting within Toronto's immigrant families during the turbulent late 1960s and early 1970s. The focus on the growing number of Southern European immigrant families and the honour-shame code that was said to have crossed the Atlantic without modification both reinforced stereotypes of patriarchal Mediterranean cultures and sidestepped similar tensions within other European newcomer families. It also ignored generational conflict within Canadian families. Nor were these complexities fully captured by Ferguson as author of a 1970 Ontario government report that critiqued the mosaic model. Her self-description as a "middle-roader" in the integration-assimilation debate did not signify an abandonment of the pluralist principles that were on display during her time with the Institute (see chapter 8). Rather, in significant respects, the ambiguity she expressed with respect to where she stood on the continuum between integration and assimilation – for the two, as Werner Sollors and others note, are not simple opposites[86] – was a constitutive element of the international institute movement's paradoxical pluralism.

Indeed, the (often frustrated) efforts of the Toronto Institute counselling staff to mediate and intervene in conflicts between immigrant parents and their children illustrate the contradictory character of an Institute pluralism that blurred the lines between integration, Canadianization, and assimilation. In advocating for adult children who resented parental intrusions, front-line workers might be sympathetic to older parents but they urged them to appreciate and adapt to Canadian models of nuclear family life. They effectively advocated an accelerated program of Canadianization for the parents of teens who viewed them mainly as family wage-earners. But in neither case did they distinguish between total conformity to and degrees of adaptation to dominant Anglo-Canadian norms. The notations of the mainly European counsellors who handled these cases were often written in broken English, not only because they themselves were new to English. They also had to translate ideologically complex ideals into concrete examples for their clients. In plenty of cases, both counsellor and client were speaking in a language (English) that was not their mother tongue. The result was often simplistic-sounding solutions to complex situations.

The paradoxical nature of Institute pluralism also influenced how front-line workers sought to apply the casework methods central to social work practice (even in brief counselling sessions) – with its repertoire of professional narratives that, in the cases under review, mainly shifted between tales of potential redemption, or mobility, thwarted by backward rural parents – with detective work. The workers' efforts to entice teens into staying in school with the promise of better or cleaner jobs and a more affluent life than their parents reflected the possibilities, but also limits, of a vocational education. Their "tough-love" approach to transgressive teens, particularly girls, suggests the limits of a position that allowed these daughters, and sons, to resist Old World ways through prescription to dominant Canadian gender models that were also, if not equally, confining. It was the handful of articles that featured young Southern European women negotiating a highly fraught moral and social terrain, and in one case articulating a nascent feminist position, not the Institute' social workers, that offered concrete attempts at negotiation and mediation.

PART THREE

Community-Building Experiments, Integration Projects, and Collective Belonging

Chapter Seven

Making Multicultural Community at the Institute

In 1961, Director Nell West boasted that the members who participated in the house programs of the International Institute of Metropolitan Toronto represented sixty different ethnic nationalities.[1] Most of those members were from Europe, though the subsequent arrival of immigrants from the Caribbean, East and South Asia, Latin America, and elsewhere did further diversify, albeit modestly, a multicultural community space whose non-white members initially consisted mainly of a small number of Chinese Canadians and Japanese Canadians. The staff of the Institute's Department of Group Services worked with the membership to run a daily roster of social, recreational, and educational programs intended to encourage identification with the Institute and its pluralist goals, promote intercultural dialogue, and foster a sense of collective belonging.

The sponsored clubs and recreational activities were meant to encourage collaborative and democratic modes of organizing as well as to facilitate cross-cultural friendships and forge self-regulated citizens. In this respect, the Toronto Institute was, to quote Bettina Bradbury and Tamara Myers, an "intermediate" space located at what Leonore Davidoff famously called "the ragged frontiers between the public and private." It was a site where everyday interactions occurred among a culturally diverse collection of social workers, newcomers, and Torontonians. A focus on the members' activities and their interactions with the staff permits an examination of the processes of group-identity formation and collective belonging, as well as matters involving personal agency and resistance to the regulatory features of social work practice.[2]

The membership differed with respect to class, education, age, marital status, and gender, though the majority of members, like most staffers, fit an urban middle-class profile. Eastern European men of professional origins were among the Institute's most active members and its loudest critics. Insofar as member/staff interactions involved differently located actors negotiating hierarchal relations shaped by the agency's rules and broader social welfare policies, the

Toronto Institute was also a contact zone marked by unequal power relations.[3] But we should not exaggerate the degree to which front-line group workers, many of whom were immigrants or refugees with little professional training, could wield Foucault's (in)famous "techniques of power" so as to both discipline members and teach them self-discipline.[4]

Focused on what the Institutes called the lighter, but no less important, techniques of integration, this chapter explores how through sports, games, discussion, dance, trips, storytelling, and humour as well as organized dissent, a collection of women and men engaged in a major but flawed experiment to enact a pluralism rooted in everyday social interactions. The mix of newcomers and Canadians who participated in the member-run recreational activities such as bridge and camping, the staff-run and often citizenship-themed speakers' series and film nights, and the midweek and Sunday socials made the Toronto Institute a lively if neither egalitarian nor racially inclusive pluralist social space. The evidence of conviviality, collaboration, friendships, and (heterosexual) romance suggests a degree of community-building. In defying the social work interventions and protesting the bureaucratic rules that limited their decision-making, the members also asserted their autonomy. Ultimately, however, the potential for building a more racially inclusive and progressive community did not materialize.

In contrast to research that pegs the Institutes as either integrationists or delayed assimilationists – an observation that also applies to the historical literature on the settlement house movement[5] – my analysis of the Toronto Institute's community-building efforts considers the possibilities, limits, and paradoxical features involved. As debates over multiculturalism, hyphenated identities, and accommodation continue unabated in Canada and elsewhere, I consider how, in one urban space, identities based on difference were negotiated and forged on a community scale in a particularly formative period in the creation of an official, if now besieged, category of national belonging.[6] Institute-style pluralism combined more bottom-up approaches rooted in community-based mobilizations with top-down methods of social work regulation. Attention to historical specificity also means focusing on the social site itself, for identities are constructed on different spatial scales, from the body, home, and neighbourhood to the workplace, metropolis, nation-state, and global arena.[7] In probing the community-building efforts that occurred within a culturally pluralist organization that was also a social welfare agency, I am mindful, too, of the critique offered by feminist political theorist Iris Young. While acknowledging the value of mutual friendships and cooperation in localized city spaces, Young considered a vision of face-to-face decentralized units an unrealistic model on which to develop a transformative politics in mass urban society, precisely because "communities" invariably privilege unity over difference, leading people to suppress their differences or to exclude others.[8]

Group Methods and Programs

The Toronto Institute, like its US counterparts, combined the settlement house concept of a neighbourhood place with that of a community centre drawing people from across a metropolitan area. It was envisioned as a place where newcomers and hosts learned through group activities to understand, respect, and trust each other. Distinguishing its work from that of the counsellors focused on individual adjustment, the group work staff said it focused on "the total community" and helped to bridge the gap between newcomers and Canadians in several ways. First, the opportunity to pursue interests with others in a friendly but organized environment fostered friendships that increased an immigrant's personal happiness. Developing programs together and meeting one's responsibilities to one's group also helped to develop "the civic skills necessary for community living." The social contacts made would in turn create opportunities that enabled the newcomer to participate in "social and cultural activity in the broader [Canadian] community" and eventually assume the responsibilities of citizenship.[9] Or, as one staffer put it, "organized or group activity" offered an effective technique by which the immigrant was "re-channeled into the mainstream of the life of his new social environment."[10]

Second, Institute group workers claimed their programs would inculcate the democratic values of an essentially liberal nation into the hearts and minds of the immigrants, thereby encouraging their transformation into productive citizens. The club and group elections would nurture leadership skills and political engagement by enabling members to vote and serve as officers; participation in issue-oriented groups would encourage analysis of domestic and international events and civic engagement.[11] The related claim that cultural diversity fortified liberal capitalist democracies – the citizenship forums, classes on modern life, and fundraising campaigns reinvigorating the host nation's inherently liberal democratic character – fit as well the era's liberal internationalism and Cold War consensus in both Canada and the United States.[12]

Third, the host citizen seeking greater degrees of personal and civic integrity would also benefit from these collaborations. Initially, the Canadian host acted as "a demonstrator ... a catalyzer" whose positive actions signalled society's acceptance of the newcomer, a critical "psychological" prerequisite for their readiness to integrate. Then, both hosts and newcomers would take the key lesson of integration – that it can only be achieved by "mutual acceptance and participation" – back to their respective communities, creating a domino effect. Finally, as more Canadians, "native-born" and naturalized, learned and practised these lessons, they would become enlightened citizens of the nation and wider world.[13] Institute folks believed that collective engagement in a "two-way" process of voluntary integration involving unequal "partners" could usher in a pluralist democracy in which all enjoyed equal respect and rights.

In order to promote cross-cultural as well as cross-class relationships (or, as staff put it, relations between "professionals and workers"), the staff combined the group work method with other types of social work intervention. Drawing on insights regarding the role of groups as sites of socialization which also provide settings where people can problem-solve together, the group method aims to enrich people's lives through interpersonal experiences among peers that are structured around group-defined goals and shared decision-making. The recreational programs, argued Institute staff, introduced newcomers "to the recreation common in Canada." By enabling their participation in activities of their own choosing, these programs both exposed them to "new ways" and provided a bridge by which they would "become integrated into their new community."[14] Historically, the group method reflected more reformist impulses than the casework method, with its focus on individual problems and treatments. The Institutes' liberal, as opposed to radical, social work activism also meant a preoccupation with ensuring social equilibrium through the attainment of socially functioning groups.[15]

As social work practitioners, the Toronto Institute group work staff, like their US counterparts, drew on psychoanalytical and social scientific as well as social-cultural perspectives. Social-cultural advocates recognized that group dynamics are shaped by the cultural backgrounds of its members. The key lesson drawn was the need for sensitivity to both the individual and the social factors that affected immigrant life.[16] As for the community-organization approach – which ranges widely from efforts to combine social service provision and local group mobilizations to radical social justice campaigns that mobilize at the local, regional, and global levels – the Institute stood clearly in the reform stream.[17] As liberal advocates of improved immigrant rights and promoters of cultural diversity, its group workers considered themselves members of a progressive social movement. But as part of a community chest–funded volunteer agency that also received support from all levels of government, Institute personnel rarely criticized the state or addressed underlying causes of inequity.[18] There was also significant overlap between the agenda of political elites to ensure the loyalty of an increasingly diverse population to the nation (or city or province) and the Institute's vision of an orderly and well-functioning multicultural society.

Well aware that the number, size, and shape of the rooms in their building mattered to the success of their house programs, Institute personnel were delighted with the move in fall 1959 to the double building on College Street, though its acquisition and renovation were costly. The Toronto Junior League, an Institute co-sponsor, and the member clubs and groups helped to furnish the rooms and decorate the auditorium and cabaret space. An increase in community chest funds paid for more group work and secretarial staff. A decade later, the Institute would move again, to a building at 321 Davenport Road.[19]

All members bought memberships,[20] but there were three main types of member groups. First, the sponsored clubs and recreational groups were expected to bring together Canadian and "foreign-born" members to pursue shared interests (bridge, camping) and "build relationships" through team activities. They were also obliged to organize or sponsor income-generating events (tournaments, lectures, and dances) to help support the Institute financially and "encourage identification" with its wider goals. These groups enjoyed democratic representation and involvement in programming through the Members Council (or Membership Council). Established in 1960, the Members Council was an elected body of eighteen to twenty members that represented the clubs and groups, and three members each from the members-at-large and the staff. It met monthly and issued recommendations to the Programme Committee, a board-appointed body with final say over programming. Two representatives of the Members Council also sat on the Programme Committee.

Second, the staff ran activities that were open to the public, with nonmembers paying a little more than members to attend. These included speaker series (on such topics as practical psychology and libraries as democratic institutions) and group discussions (on law, citizenship, medicare) meant to encourage a "lively exchange of ideas" and a "meeting of minds."[21] There were also instructional classes in dance (folk, ballroom, and, later, modern), budgeting, and arts and crafts, and a mothers' club. The film series included international films on specific countries with invited speakers, Hollywood films,[22] and documentaries made by the National Film Board of Canada (NFB). The educational NFB films dealt with various Canadian institutions (including *Stampede, 1963*) and immigrant adjustment *(The Immigrant Meets the School,* 1959). The few films on Indigenous peoples included *No Longer Vanishing* (1955), which delivered the Canadian government's position in favour of "residential schooling" and "the desirability and inevitability of assimilation." In an upbeat spin on a now officially acknowledged program of cultural genocide, the film features various scenes showing Indigenous people moving off the reserve and working alongside "Canadians" in such occupations as teaching, nursing, and military service.[23]

The more casual activities included "lounging" (the lounge had a multilingual collection of magazines and journals), record hours, and socials with games and a dance. (The orchestra-led dances were more popular than the recorded music events.). The staff also organized excursions, including spring bus trips to Ottawa for the tulip festival, fall trips to Muskoka for the autumn colours and to Stratford for the theatre, and summer trips to Niagara Falls and Algonquin Park.[24] On offer were educational outings ranging from a walking trip to an exhibit on the history of nineteenth-century Blacks in Ontario held at a Toronto Public Library to the tours of the Martyrs' Shrine at Midland, Ontario, with its narrative of heroic Jesuits bringing Christianity to the heathens.

Institute staff and volunteers enjoy a coffee break while creating posters of scheduled house events. Archives of Ontario, F884-2-9, B427166.

But the Institute hardly challenged the supremacy of Anglo-Canadian Protestant culture. Indeed, an Institute review of a 1963 library exhibit on Blacks in Ontario suggested that nineteenth-century Canadians meted out acts of racism and generosity in equal measure.[25] A few charter flights were booked for European cities like Amsterdam. Staff valued the less-structured activities because they drew more participants than the regular meetings, thus enlarging the pool of people who could spread the Institute message.[26]

Third, there were independent community (Canadian) and ethnic organizations that took out group memberships with the Institute. These affiliated groups were highly welcomed because they provided a source of funds, their meetings "added" more diversity to the evening activities, and they helped to mount the special multi-ethnic cultural events (see part 4). Partially funded by local businesses, the Institute newsletter, the *Intercom*, aimed to facilitate "intercommunication" between the different groups and support the agency through subscriptions. By the mid-1960s, it had evolved from a homemade-looking newsletter with stick figures to a news magazine that covered political and social affairs and featured cover art and sketches by member artists.[27]

There was some overlap between the groups and programs. The chess, bridge, and tennis clubs ran instruction classes as well as tournaments while the dance committee organized the holiday dances and parties as well as its regular classes. Plenty of members belonged to more than one club and any given club might also organize a lecture, course, or dance for others to attend. While the group services staff was primarily responsible for the house programs, a few of the counsellors also became involved. The adult students enrolled in the government-run English classes at the Institute could also obtain additional civic and citizenship information from the documentaries, speakers, and discussion nights. The volunteers, including the English teachers, donated items for fundraising bazaars and helped with posters and holiday decorations.

Multicultural and Intercultural Space

Some urban geographers invoke the term intercultural to define space where cross-cultural dialogue occurs, as distinguished from the term multicultural, which emphasizes cultural difference and an element of containment, or cosmopolitan, which assumes a gradual erosion of cultural difference through inter-ethnic mixture and hybridization.[28] The Institutes, which since the 1920s have called themselves intercultural agencies, similarly understood the term intercultural as denoting an emphasis on facilitating cross-cultural learning and dialogue and cross-cultural collaborations and relationships.[29] According to more recent definitions, multiculturalism describes a society that contains several different cultural or ethnic groups whereas intercultural refers to communities in which there is "a deep understanding and respect for all cultures." Intercultural communication in this context aims for the mutual exchange of ideas and cultural norms and the forging of meaningful relationships.[30]

Taken together, the staff, administrators, members, and others who participated in the house programs made the Institute a multicultural if heavily European and hierarchical gathering place. In 1960, at the start of its most active decade, the professional, semi-professional, and volunteer group work staff together spoke fourteen different, though mostly European, languages. As with the counselling department, women, including the volunteers, outnumbered men overall. The core staff comprised about half a dozen people, though there were sometimes only two full-time group workers. As the Institute's first director, and then as director of services, West was directly involved in shaping the group programs, initially because of the absence of a departmental supervisor and then because of the high turnover rate among supervisors. In 1962, Robert Kreem, an Estonian refugee with a law degree from the American Extension School of Law and two social work degrees from Canadian universities – his

University of Toronto master's thesis was entitled "Aging Problems in Ethnic Groups" – became director of services. He left the Children's Aid Society of Metropolitan Toronto (CAS) to join the Institute, where he had earlier worked on a part-time basis, but resigned after one year over conflicts with the board. The board then eliminated the position, and devolved responsibilities to the supervisor of the group services and counselling departments, respectively.[31]

More men than women figured among the half-dozen people who subsequently held the position of group services supervisor, which also required a social work degree, and involved administering the budget, supervising staff and volunteers, and conducting some community outreach. Apart from Kay Brown, one of the two women to hold the post, no one stayed in the job beyond two years. The men included Richard Kolm, a Detroit Institute alumnus who later returned home, and David Stewart, who also delivered lectures on such topics as personal growth and democracy for the discussion nights. Brown, who held the position in the late 1960s and early 1970s, was the only supervisor to come through the ranks, having first been hired as West's secretary. Besides earlier stints coordinating the volunteers and, later, power-sewing classes for women (see chapter 8), she also edited the *Intercom* in the late 1960s. Maya Tulin, a Russian-born nurse with an English education, filled the supervisory role for one year in the mid-1960s, but was otherwise a group worker.[32]

The front-line group workers, who were mainly women, required a social work degree or equivalent, meaning practical fieldwork experience.[33] One of the first Canadians hired was Violet Head, a graduate of the University of Toronto School of Social Work whose placement with the Institute influenced her post-graduate research. After writing a master's thesis on the Hungarian refugees of 1956, she earned a specialization in recreational social work through the Social Planning Council of Metropolitan Toronto (SPC), an Institute co-sponsor, and the Toronto YMCA (Young Men's Christian Association) before pursuing a doctorate at the University of Chicago. Upon completing it, Head was hired by the Toronto Psychiatric Hospital.[34]

With a few exceptions, the primarily European refugee and immigrant women who served as group workers in the 1960s had incomplete credentials. They included the multilingual Tulin, though she had practical experience, having organized health and welfare programs in the displaced persons camps. Olga Stoian, who organized the bus trips among other duties, and Ida De Voin, a teacher who coordinated the English program, had more varied backgrounds. The exceptions included Margaret Maas (later Hanen), a Dutch immigrant with social work training from the Netherlands, and, in the early 1970s, Catherine Lee. The only racialized group worker, the Seoul-born Lee was multilingual (Korean, Japanese, and English) and had a social work degree from Wayne State University. A former supervisor with Seoul-based agencies handling the international adoption of Korean War orphans, she combined her group work duties with counselling mainly Korean clients. Later, Lee, who also taught English to Korean seniors, became supervisor of the group services department.[35]

The Anglo-Canadian female group workers included Helen Steele, a graduate of the University of Toronto's master's program in Slavic studies who had no social work training, but was multilingual (Russian, French, English) and had lived and worked in Europe. (She had also been a Girl Guide leader.) Those with some social work credentials included Joan Buyers, a former small businessperson with SPC experience who, as a widow, took social work courses at the University Toronto and worked with the CAS, and Lucy Gitow, a social work graduate with CAS fieldwork experience. Buyers' correspondence details the hectic schedule of a group worker tasked with managing volunteers and interpreters, organizing dances and open houses, and attending planning meetings with ethnic and city organizations for the multicultural festivals and concerts. Assessments made of Gitow offer some insight into the struggles of a group worker to maintain an empathetic stance on the job. As her supervisor, Lee praised Gitow's efforts to learn "to help the members objectively without involving her own emotional sympathy." It echoed Gitow's self-assessment about having worked hard to "try to surpass" feeling "emotionally upset" by a low turnout for an event or the difficulty of analysing and interpreting the different "behavior modes" observed, and instead to adopt "a positive and empathetic approach."[36]

The male group workers included Tore Maagaard, a graduate of the new social work program at Toronto's Ryerson Polytechnical Institute, and Torontonian Lloyd Kinnee, who also voiced his environmental and nationalist views in the *Intercom*.[37]

The group services department also housed and administered the government-supported English-language program, which received financial support through a federal-provincial agreement.[38] The majority of the certified teachers hired were women. The often short-staffed department relied on mainly female (and some male) volunteers and student placements to run its English tutorials. They usually received some in-service training with regard to Institute mandates and programs. The multilingual secretaries occasionally carried out group work duties as well.

The adult-focused recreational programs attracted mainly single adults between 25 and 40 years of age, but married couples also participated. The annual membership numbers ranged from a low of about 600 to almost 2,000. The successful Saturday night dances and Sunday socials drew a few hundred people. The majority of the participants were European males. Eastern Europeans outnumbered their Northern and Southern counterparts, but there was also a strong Dutch and German presence, especially early on.[39] All together, the members and participants were more racially as well as ethnically diverse than the group work staff. The clubs and house programs attracted a relatively small number of racialized Canadians and newcomers. A few of the English teachers were Black.[40] After 1967, the English classes became more racially diverse. Since an estimated one-quarter of these adult students became Institute members or participants in house activities, the English program provided a modest but important source of racial diversity during the late sixties and early seventies. Reports indicate that "Canadians" ("native-born" and naturalized) comprised about one-quarter of the membership, though more of them occasionally participated in house activities, and many more attended the special cultural events. Still, given the weighty role accorded to Canadians in Institute strategy, this was a disappointing figure. Another source of perennial frustration was the gender imbalance: newcomer women represented perhaps less than one-quarter of the members, though more of them came to the socials and open houses. The single Anglo-Canadian female volunteers improved the gender imbalance somewhat by attending dances and participating in social and recreational activities, as did smaller numbers of ethno-Canadian women volunteers of European and, in still smaller numbers, Asian origins.

The membership also fluctuated. Certain groups (ski and lawn tennis) were seasonal. Some clubs did well over the holidays while others did not. The recreational clubs varied in size from a handful to 100 members, but the tournaments drew between 200 and 300 participants, as did the chess club's international exhibitions.[41] Apart from the golden age group, which was composed of older German women, the sponsored groups were mixed-gender as well as culturally diverse, though, again, men usually outnumbered women. The all-male winning members at a 1966 table tennis tournament held at the Institute included Wah Shinchiu (Chinese), Herik Gotman (Polish), and A. Ashraf (Pakistani). A dance report illustrated the point about dance bringing people together: As "Leo (Wah Chong) Hong and Margaret Smith representing the 'old' and 'new' Canadian" learn the rhumba, they "are slowly and surely fulfilling" the integration mandate. The others named included participants of Irish, Latvian, Indian, Italian, Korean, and Greek origin.[42]

European groups dominated the independent ethnic and community (Canadian) organizations that took out group memberships, but they also included Anglo-Canadians, Asian Canadians, Black Canadians, and Caribbean immigrants. Photographs of the group activities show some East Asian, South Asian, and Caribbean participants.[43] A mix of Anglo-Canadians and British and European newcomers dominated the *Intercom*'s editorial committee, though a Japanese Canadian and Egyptian appear on the roster. Raymond Greiner was a long-serving editor, but counsellor George Nagy and group workers Brown and Kinnee also took turns as editor. The male members who did nighttime reception duties included Ali El-Laboudy (the Egyptian who worked on the *Intercom*), Otto Koepke (German), and Subramanian Varadaraja, a Tamil immigrant described by Kinnee as an "honest, reliable, good worker who gets along with others."[44]

Overall, women dominated the volunteer pool, lending a female presence to the Institute despite low female memberships.[45] In 1965, male and female volunteers with names like Kapsa, Levy, Branand, Sauve, and Chopra taught the English tutorials for professional and skilled newcomers preparing for certification exams.[46] Immigrant women mainly taught the Italian-, Portuguese-, and Greek-language classes for social welfare personnel, and conversational classes in Italian and French. (A man taught Spanish.) Among the women volunteers who offered classes was a former physical education teacher from Greece who taught outdoor tennis in the late 1960s.[47] By contrast, the Trade English instructors, both Canadian and immigrant, were primarily men of Southern European origin, and the immigrant students were mostly men learning the male trades, though the hairdressing courses brought in women (see chapter 8).

Pluralist Community-Building

The Institute was a multicultural place, but was it an intercultural one? Is there evidence of bonds having forged across ethnicity, race, gender, class, politics, and other social categories of difference? To address the question, I draw on both top-down sources like the minutes of board meetings and staff reports, and more bottom-up ones like the club correspondents' reports, members' announcements in the *Intercom*, and the minutes of the Members Council meetings.

Club leaders were enthusiastic Institute members and their reports sometimes explicitly addressed the agency's pluralist vision. As bridge club chair, German-born Stase Bunker declared that, in the place of outmoded "German-style Deutschland-uber-alles-style nationalism," the Institute brought together people of different cultural backgrounds through enjoyable pursuits to create a different kind of society. He reported on the "remarkable" growth of the bridge club from the handful of players in the 1957 season to the more than 200 people who participated in the games and tournaments at the College Street centre during 1962. Attesting to its wholesomeness, he described bridge as a "clever" and "companionable" game where "boys meet girls at a proper distance" and "many lasting friendships" and "mutually helpful relationships" are "sustained."[48] The shout-outs to team members similarly indicate the formation of cross-cultural relationships. The 1969 outdoor tennis club leader Nick Basco, for instance, praised Ali Zahid (Pakistani) as well as fellow Italian Corrado Bordonaro for their support. A 1960 bridge club announcement that Tony Syckorski (Polish) had won the Olive Macdonald tournament cup, named in honour of the club's first female chair, suggests, too, a

Playing cards (likely duplicate bridge) at the International Institute, c. 1960. Archives of Ontario, F884-2-9, B427166.

certain respect between men and women. The fundraising by club leaders to assist members who became ill – as for refugee artist (and sometime receptionist) Fred Berkenmayer in 1960 – offers evidence, too, of collective loyalties beyond those of family, nationality, or ethnicity.[49] While it slipped into cliché, so, too, did the 1966 report of the International Group's correspondent, who referred to the busload of weekend travellers to Niagara Falls as an "international family" that talked, laughed, sang (sometimes too enthusiastically), and formed "solid friendships."[50]

The Canadian and newcomer club leaders tended to be men of professional or skilled background, though a few women and working-class men also held these posts. While allowing for the embellishment that accompanied recruitment efforts, we need not dismiss as mere rhetoric their depictions of friendly competitions and enjoyable socials. After all, the leaders openly scolded members for failing to vote in a club election or show up for a game. Or for talking instead of concentrating on their game, though the

Outdoor group members enjoy a Sunday swim and picnic at Rice Lake, 10 July 1960. Archives of Ontario, F884-2-9, B427166.

conversations themselves indicate friendly relations. At one point, the bridge club chair, Mark Patamia (Slovakian), admonished the "girls" to stop discussing "hats and hairdo's" at the bridge table, and the "boys" to remember that they were "supposed to be the strong, silent sex." As golden age group chair, Hilda Albrecht scolded the members who did not attend a birthday party held for a long-time member who had travelled by bike, bus, and streetcar to be there.[51] The most consistently positive reports came from the outdoor group and focused on the members' shared love of the outdoors. In any given season, there might be a dozen or so core members, but the weekend outings to picturesque Ontario places (Haliburton Highlands, Georgian Bay) might draw thirty or more people.[52]

The club and group reports offer glimpses into relationships forged through participation in organized activities. The outdoor group correspondents noted the collective excitement of viewing "the northern lights in all of their radiant glory," the "exquisite" group meals made out of basic food supplies,[53] and

144 Community-Building Experiments

the heart-warming singalongs accompanied by flute, accordion, or harmonica. A report on a weekend spent at Nell West's guesthouse in Muskoka called it a "luxury" compared to an earlier washed-out camping trip when heavy rain forced people to sleep on the floor of a deserted house. The descriptions of the weekend bridge games and the "amiable" kitchen relations between the group chef, Jos Ansems (Belgian), and the supper club members suggest successful inter-group events.[54] Some of the historical lessons drawn from trips could be problematic, however. A report on a trip to the rugged country surrounding Lake Muskoka concluded that it "must be mainly the same in appearance as when the Indians had this continent to themselves."[55] The photographs of the various outings show that women, some of whom were married to club members, often comprised half of the group.

Purposeful Humour

Emotions and laughter profoundly affect our psychological and physical well-being. As scholars tell us, there is a demonstrable correlation between humour, laughing, learning, and emotional health, and in the formation of positive relations and community-building. When used appropriately, and not to disparage others, humour, including self-effacing humour, can smooth potentially awkward interactions, enhance participation, and initiate social conversations with others in a positive way. Provided, of course, that everyone gets the joke. Clinical research shows that humour can help people cope with adversity and loss, and that it can be leveraged to make others feel good, to gain intimacy, or to help buffer stress. Together with gratitude, hope, and other positive emotions, humour can also help humans forge connections to the world and provide meaning to life. Finally, historical accounts of the use of humour as a weapon of subversion, as in poking fun at those in authority, have found confirmation in contemporary clinical research.[56]

The group reports and *Intercom* columns reveal the frequent, and purposeful, use of jokes and humorous stories to recruit members, encourage conviviality, and foster group identity. One bridge club joke warned of the danger of possible "addiction" and then assured potential recruits that bridge players were "largely successful" people in their home and work life, and that the proceeds from the 50-cent entry fee went to the Institute.[57] The outdoor group's currency was stories of misadventure, such as making do in a rural hostel without cutlery or enough blankets and pillows, and a boat capsizing in the middle of the lake, forcing everyone to swim ashore.[58]

Significantly, given the ubiquity of sexist humour in this era, much of the humour was not sexist, though it often fit the corny category. Non-sexist limericks on the difficulty of learning the English language because of the many different pronunciations ("sounds like corpse, corps, horse and worse") used humour to put people at ease.[59] Humour was used by an English teacher who shared the incorrect answers that appeared on a recent citizenship exam, though one wonders whether, in this case, everyone understood the joke. Asked to name three Canadian generals, the applicant listed the following US companies: General Electric, General Motors, and General Foods; when asked to name two of the Great Lakes: Lake Superior and Lake Inferior.[60]

A British immigrant volunteer who with his wife taught evening English tutorials at the Institute offered a humorous but mainly heart-warming account of their experiences teaching people who, he said, appreciated being corrected in a friendly manner. He thanked the Institute for its "friendly spirit, its friendly staff, its freedom from red tape," and "practical enthusiasm," and expressed the hope that more "old" Canadians would join the efforts to build "a strong and united community."[61] In one of the few student letters to appear in the *Intercom*, Portuguese immigrant Raul Benerides spoke warmly about the teachers' "kindness and affection" towards each student regardless of colour or politics. As a student who became an Institute member, he also attested to the value of using dance, movies, sports, and group discussions with "people from around the world" to promote integration.[62]

Some of the humour was (mildly) sexist, however. Recruiting efforts aimed at women promised the opportunity to meet young attractive men. A self-described "D.P." told one of the recurring fishing jokes. He mischievously asked who was the Glasgow member who told his wife he spent all summer fishing and caught nothing but fish? Some female club leaders also indulged in the humour. In her 1962 bridge report, Margaret Franzen said the men were "happy" with the addition of several "attractive" women players at recent tournaments held in St Catharines and Buffalo, adding, "I noticed appreciative glances last Monday!"[63]

A number of the punchlines of the jokes published in the *Intercom* derived their humour from the sexism implied in an immigrant's imperfect English. A 1966 entry surely submitted by staff noted a hotel clerk who smiled when the husband asked "whether they had a room where he could put up with his wife," though the humour was likely lost on those with rudimentary English. An exchange reportedly overheard at the Institute between a Hungarian and a Turk over the latter's intention to marry a Hungarian woman with whom he had never spoken may have reinforced stereotypes of "foreign" marriages being shaped by male interests.[64]

The sexist jokes that referenced popular culture included one about a couple ordering dinner in a restaurant. The husband asks his wife "what's the name of that Italian dish I'm so crazy about?" and she answers "Gina Lollobrigida." When it appeared in the *Intercom* in 1962, Lollobrigida was, along with Sophia Loren, one of the highest-profile European actresses with a string of Italian and French films, and an international sex symbol who starred in US films with leading Hollywood men like Errol Flynn and Rock Hudson. At this time, she was living in Toronto, having moved to Canada with her husband and son in 1960 to take advantage of lower taxes and obtain legal status for her Slovenian husband (a refugee from Yugoslavia). The joke, like the comment in the US-based *Life* magazine, which covered Lollobrigida's move to Toronto, that she was "the most fetching argument ever advanced for liberal immigration policies," was a classic case of compliment via objectification. Lollobrigida later returned to Italy and divorced. She made headlines again in 1970, but as a photojournalist who landed an exclusive interview with Fidel Castro.[65]

A "sexpot" narrative submitted by a female counsellor described an actual case in which a "young girl" landed a stenographer's position with neither shorthand nor typing skills because the boss loved her "Marilyn Monroe" looks. "We were afraid to discuss [the case] too widely for fear it would become a common practice" is the punchline. This is not to suggest a total disregard for women contending with aggressive male bosses and co-workers.[66] Another publicity narrative constructed from a case file for potential use in Institute reports featured a similarly unqualified but stunning German "girl," age 18, who received job offers from three top department stores in one afternoon. The final line about life getting "quite complicated with the swarms of young men around" suggests some sensitivity to the issue of sexual harassment.[67]

Intimacy, Marriage, and Old Friends

The marriages that came out of the Institute speak to its character as a site of emotional intimacy and offer examples of cross-cultural unions.[68] Social scientists and philosophers alike generally view the presence of exogamous marriages between different ethnic groups, and those between immigrants and "native-born" hosts, as both a mechanism for and an indicator of integration. They also view increasing rates of "mixed" unions as a measure of social inclusion. Today, "mixed" unions (marital or common-law) usually refer to those in which one or both partners are "visible minorities."[69] In the context of the heterogeneous but mainly white and European population of sixties Toronto, the fact that close to half of the twenty-three Institute marriages uncovered involved couples who wed outside their ethnic group is significant.[70] To be sure, these cross-cultural unions occurred primarily between Europeans. Like Armin Viereck (German) and Tiny Burgersdijk (Dutch), who were married at Toronto's St John's Lutheran Church in 1960, most of the couples did not even cross the West/East divide of European geopolitics. In the two (European) cases where religious affiliation was identified, the couple shared the same (Protestant and Catholic) religion, thus conforming to a contemporary pattern, though my evidence is merely anecdotal.[71]

The evidence also sheds some light on the Institute as a site of romance and courtship. The couples who married usually met initially through the same club or group, and became better acquainted through other house activities (dances, games, discussions). Put another way, their romance played out in the intermediate space of a socially patrolled community centre and through regularly scheduled occasions that were "public" enough to be respectable, but "private" enough for romantic intimacy. The Institute's own stress on ensuring wholesome fun meant that staffers and volunteers doubled as chaperones, especially at the dances. But young people could find in a space like the College Street building plenty of potential sites for romantic encounters, whether it involved a chaste kiss or hand-holding or heavy petting and more. It could be a dark corner of the cabaret space or auditorium during a dance, an empty meeting room, the stairs, a cloakroom, the washrooms, spaces just outside the building, or a parked car.[72]

The two mixed-ethnic weddings that came out of a 1962 ballroom dance course included that of Dutch-born William Lambermont and Dorothy Pattinson of Southhampton, England.[73] The Institute's supervised dance courses offered particularly the women a comparatively safe space in which to engage in short, structured interactions with men. By observing the behaviour of a potential love interest (was he courteous and generous or domineering and aggressive on the dance floor and off?) and how others responded to him, they could use dance classes to decide on compatibility.[74] As dancers, the newly married Lambermonts shared an activity that encouraged socializing as a couple, whether at an outside venue or at home with friends and family. Like some other Institute newlyweds, this couple moved to the suburbs (Don Mills), making them part of a growing movement of earlier British and European immigrants to leave the downtown immigrant core. That some newlyweds remained active members following their move to suburbia also speaks to the Institute's modest success at being more than a strictly neighbourhood meeting place.[75]

In light of the restrictions imposed on young Southern European women by their parents' rigid cultural codes (see chapter 6), the 1966 marriage between an Italian woman and a "Persian" (Iranian) man (no names given) is particularly noteworthy.[76] Some would have disapproved of such a "mixed" union, but group worker Stoian considered it a sign of the success of the international club she had created. She spoke in vivid, if also self-serving, terms about the young members' participation in the weekly schedule of games, movies, discussions, and dance, making the Institute a "colourful and lively" meeting place where those of diverse origins could "meet new friends and compare notes about life."[77] The young Italian bride's decision to marry "out" fits with a pattern identified by gender-and-migration historians, namely that migration often accentuates and confounds what the nation-state and ethnic communities try to fix as appropriate behaviour for women, such as meeting a future husband in extended-family venues chaperoned by women. In (presumably) coming to view as outmoded her parents' sense of "good" behaviour, her decision to marry "out" reflected a young immigrant woman's negotiation with urban modernity and even cosmopolitanism. As for negative repercussions, such as abandonment by the family, she took a greater risk than her husband, though he, too, may have faced family disapproval of the match.[78]

The cross-cultural marriage between an Asian Indian man and a German woman also crossed racial lines. It was also exceptional in a more specific sense: South Asian immigrants record the lowest rates of exogamous marriages in many countries. The collective sentiment expressed by the friends of Ravi Sadana and Johanna Lauber in their announcement of the pending nuptials speaks to the progressive possibilities of pluralism. Unlike Institute counsellors, who generally discouraged mixed-race marriages on the grounds that they would falter in the face of cultural differences and racial prejudice, they celebrated the union as "one instance where love has conquered national barriers."[79]

Finally, there were also some marriages involving staff. Two of the three group workers who married were women and both married within their ethnic group, though one of them, Margaret Maas, married an Institute member, Ted Hanen. Staffer Helen Steele left work immediately upon marrying a local artist, moving with him to the United States, but Margaret Hanen remained on staff for a year before returning with her husband, Ted, to Holland.[80]

If the cross-cultural marriages speak to the social-change potential of pluralism, the descriptions of the weddings and festivities suggest significant alignment with conventional heterosexual norms. The reception for the wedding of two Dutch Catholics who were also Institute charter members – Hank Byllaardt, the agency's "handyman" and a group leader who also served on the Members Council, and Elisa de Langlen – was a breakfast party organized by their friends at the Institute. They had one of the longest engagements, having first met six years previously on the dance committee. The bride's attendant was another Dutch female member. The presence of Institute members at the weddings suggests that bonds of friendship and a sense of community emerged among the young adults. We also find conventional depictions of the bride as lovely, demure. Or, as in the case of Hannelore Duringer, the German bride of Slovakian Patamia, the "charming young lady he met at the I.I." The joking references of some brides losing their freedom or their partner's attention upon marriage struck a bittersweet chord. Canadian member Joan Henderson told her wedding guests that she already missed "buzzing around" in the family car doing Institute business. As she dished out cake, the (unnamed) wife of chess club member Hank Spaans told the Institute friends who attended their wedding party bearing a group gift of a pair of lamps that she refused to become "a bridge widow." To which the correspondent replied, "we shall see."[81]

The occasional birth announcements in the *Intercom* suggest the continuance of some friendships, or at least an interest in keeping in touch with "old

Making Multicultural Community at the Institute   149

A crowded dance floor in the Cabaret Theatre on College Street, c. 1961. The photographer was evidently taken with the white woman in the striped dress and beret. The one Black woman may be a volunteer teacher at the Institute. Archives of Ontario, F884-2-9, B427166.

friends," to use a phrase that peppers the correspondents' reports.[82] That such sentiments were expressed towards Egyptian Ali El-Laboudy (most likely Muslim Egyptian) and his probably Anglo-Canadian wife Claire (an English tutor) is noteworthy given how few Muslims belonged to the Institute. Before their departure for the United States several years after meeting in the outdoor group, the couple were fixtures at the Institute. Ali served as an evening receptionist and promotional director for the *Intercom* while Claire did duty as a daytime receptionist and secretary to the Members Council. Photographs show them at Institute Christmas events and socializing with Institute "friends" in a member's modest living room. The *Intercom* announced the early birth of their first "lovely baby boy, Gamal Abdel" (likely named after Egyptian President Nasser) while on holiday in Toledo, Ohio, in 1961, and, that of their second son a year later in San Francisco. There is little on another Arab couple, described as

The original caption for this photograph, which appeared in the *Intercom* newsletter in September 1960, refers to "well known Institute personalities ... enjoying themselves at a recent party in 'Uncle Fred' Berkenmayer's apartment." Left to right: Barbara Hancock, Margaret Hanen, Berkenmayer, Vi Head, Ali El-Laboudy, and Claire El-Laboudy. Archives of Ontario, F884-2-9, B427166.

"Wednesday night record man" George and "his charming wife Marry," but the announcement of a daughter noted her "very romantic Arabic name – Lila."[83]

A long-distance friendship between former group worker Margaret Hanen and member Henrietta Van Haften, also Dutch, allowed others to follow Hanen's life after she returned to Holland. In a 1962 letter to Van Haften that appeared in the *Intercom*, a wistful Hanen described her "quiet" life as a stay-at-home mother of three in a small rural community. She recalled with fondness her "hectic" life in Toronto and the "nice" Canadian summers and outdoor trips. Her parting comments, that "I am often thinking of [the Institute friends] and missing the work I loved so much," convey the frustration, even sadness, of a professional woman compelled by marriage and motherhood to abandon her career. In a Christmas letter sent to the Institute in 1963, Hanen was more upbeat about her move to Australia, noting that they had quickly bought a house with an ocean view, and had been joined by her brother-in-law's family. She added that she was still receiving her *Intercom* and invited people to write her at her home address.[84]

Like any community newsletter, the *Intercom*'s updates on former staff and members point to friendly ties between certain front-line staff, volunteers, and members. Former staffer Head visited the Institute during her trips home to Toronto while she was a PhD candidate in Chicago. A feature on Mme A. Fortier described her as a "popular" and "enthusiastic" French teacher whose pre-migration experiences in France, Algiers, and Bisra "read like an adventure story."[85] The note of congratulations issued to Kees Vandergraaf, a Dutch chef and restaurant owner who helped with Institute dinners, on the purchase of a tourist lodge on the Trent River near Campbellford, Ontario, expressed appreciation for his generosity. One of the reports on people travelling to see family or enjoy a holiday noted that two female social work students embarking on a backpacking tour of Europe had accepted the offer of a Danish male member returning to Denmark for a lengthy visit to escort them on the first leg of their journey. (No sexist jokes here.)

The few death notices expressed an appreciation for former friends. Golden age group member Albrecht was remembered as an energetic participant who also belonged to the stamp club and who proved "a friendly reliable hostess." (The inclusion of some older women on the hostess roster also lent greater credence to the Institute's portrayal of them as cultural ambassadors.) Stamp club leader Randy Randeriis (Danish) was described as a "cheerful" and "greatly respected" member who was always ready to lend a hand.[86]

Tensions and Conflicts

The process of building an international, or pluralist, community at the Toronto Institute was subject to various challenges and limitations. One key source of tensions was the set of rules governing the relationship of the sponsored groups to the Institute. The Institute goal of promoting a culturally diverse and democratic community rooted in relationships of respect, trust, and collective decision-making bumped up against its obligations as a community chest–funded social welfare agency whose activities and services had to align with its incorporated purpose as well as professional social work practices. Institute personnel did not view these principles as mutually exclusive, but in practice, the paradox of trying to build a community that was not only multicultural in composition but also intercultural in intent and practice within a hierarchal structure proved deeply problematic.

The contradiction in goals was reflected in the constitutional rules regulating the sponsored groups' relationship to the Institute. In line with democratic organizing principles, each group created a mandate and set of bylaws, held regular elections for its usually three-person executive, and arrived at decisions collectively through consensus or a vote. As previously noted, each group also had representation on the elected Members Council. At the same time, each group was assigned a staff (or volunteer) adviser who was given direct authority over the group executive. The adviser was to approve all candidates for election, approve and attend all group meetings, designate the use of equipment, co-sign group mail using Institute stationery, and approve outside publicity for group events. The adviser could also refer new members to a group without consulting the group leaders. Still more authority resided with the group services supervisor, who, for instance, could reject a club executive's request to dissolve their group and instead recruit new members for it. In addition, each club or group was obliged to provide the Institute with financial support, mainly through annual contributions of "surplus" funds earned from membership fees or events.[87]

The Institute's need to generate independent funds to help cover various costs meant frequent membership drives and inspection of individual memberships, both of which annoyed members. Staff concerns about the members' "lack of interest" in the Institute beyond their respective group(s) meant leadership workshops that drilled group leaders on their responsibility to ensure greater identification among their members with the Institute and its goals. Many members resented the pressure to canvass for the annual community chest campaigns. One exception was German member Wolfgang Moritz, who credited the United Appeal and the Institute with his ability to retrain as a bookkeeper following a crippling mining accident.[88]

Institute efforts to enforce the requirement that groups identify with the Institute similarly engendered resentment. The stamp club's international exhibits fit well the Institute's brand of liberal internationalism (see chapter 11), but the group services supervisor castigated the executive for initially publicizing itself as "The United Nations Stamp Club of the International Institute of Metropolitan Toronto Inc." because it sounded too independent. Club leaders removed the UN reference following the dressing-down, but the incident rankled. As did the squabbles over securing funds for the stamp fairs, which drew large crowds.[89]

Similar tensions led to the withdrawal of the highly successful outdoor group from the Institute in 1964. Staff criticized the members for using Institute resources such as camping supplies while refusing to support the Institute through contributions. They also accused the group leaders of breaking the rules by making changes to their bylaws or holding meetings without first securing the adviser's consent. The group leaders retaliated with charges of hypocrisy and accused staff of trampling on their democratic rights by denying them access to their equipment and funds. The group leaders, many of whom were professional Eastern European men quick to denounce any action that smacked of patronizing or authoritarian practices, did play a role in the escalation of tensions.

Insofar as the disputes often occurred between middle-class male members frustrated with their subordinate position and middle-class personnel, some of whom were themselves newcomers, the dynamics differed from the inter-class tensions common to social welfare organizations (which occurred between middle-class social workers and working-class or poor clients). But it still spoke to the inequities and contradictions imbedded in Institute practice. The staff announcement of the outdoor group's departure said it had withdrawn from the Institute, but angry members claimed it had been "pushed out."[90]

The tensions created by front-line staff rivalries over securing members and resources for their respective programs, and the resentment felt by underpaid staff, also hurt the community-building enterprise. Since front-line staff were often female and supervisors mostly male, these were also gendered conflicts. Group worker Buyers responded to her dismissal on grounds of insubordination (specifically, of "selfishly over-identifying" with her programs and neglecting other duties) by accusing her male superiors of trying to harass her into quitting. Following a staff assessment that praised Buyers' co-worker Stoian for effectively navigating "the frustrating conditions created by Mrs. Buyers," the board simply upheld her firing.[91]

The gendered character of members' complaints about controlling or arrogant group workers – the complainants were all men, the targets of their criticism mostly women – reflects both the heavily male membership and the prevailing gender norms that made it easier for men than women to speak out. But explicit sexism also played a role. For example, when member Mike Sosaszny, who was at one point suspended for being rude towards board members, accused Tulin of unfairly removing him from his night receptionist job, he drew up a ten-point list of infractions (which included being unfriendly, unorganized, and manipulative), demanded an immediate enquiry into the charges, and insisted on firm disciplinary action. Her administrators had some concerns about Tulin's less-than-stellar qualifications, but she was vindicated and Sosaszny's vitriolic charges dismissed.[92]

The heavily female staff dealt as well with the sexual tensions that played out at the evening dances between single immigrant men and Canadian women volunteers. Their efforts to educate the men who felt entitled to act aggressively towards unaccompanied single women – on the not entirely accurate cultural grounds that, in their homeland, such women were prostitutes or sexually available – on the inappropriateness of such behaviour in Canada were not especially effective. Nor were their attempts to convince the upset women to return. Without letting the men off the hook, it bears noting that they might have resented the superior tone of voice with which staff declared such behaviour un-Canadian, as though Canadian men never harassed women.[93] Nor should we minimize the admittedly few recorded allegations of staff racism, which Institute administrators also handled badly. One such complaint was issued by

Ahmed Shanty, an Arab immigrant member, who informed the board that a group worker had withdrawn her offer of an evening receptionist job after West had allegedly said "Let's have no more Arabs working here." In response, Director H.C. Forbell expressed "disappointment" in Shanty's accusatory stance but agreed to a meeting, though nothing evidently came of it.[94]

By spring 1964, the build-up of anger and resentment led the Members Council to issue a scathing report of the Programme Committee along with a list of recommendations for change. Charging the Programme Committee (and, hence, the board too) of "not performing effectively," the report highlighted contradictions between the Institute's premise that the integration of Canadians and future Canadians of different cultural backgrounds required "a common interest among people" and its practices, and expressed resentment over their treatment as second-class citizens. It argued that the staff's propensity for likening the relationship within the groups to that of a club (warm), but insisting that the group's relationship to the Institute be "businesslike" (financial), ignored the fact that integration "cannot take place on a business-like basis," but instead requires "harmonious" relations between groups and staff.

In response to what it called the staff's propensity to regard everyone as "irresponsible," the report asserted that, while there are "misfits" in any group, most members were "responsible citizens with a variety of interests and a good education," and that the staff's actions were "detrimental" to the Institute's "reputation." In exchange for the funds and volunteer hours they contributed to the Institute, the members, it added, had a right to expect the Programme Committee and staff to take greater care in carrying out its duties and to show more interest in the groups' activities. Instead, staff "apathy" was pushing members away and making it difficult to attract new members; meanwhile the Programme Committee undermined the Members Council's suggestions and efforts to improve the situation.[95]

The submissions by individual members that accompanied the report reiterated the complaints about the Institute's undemocratic and even dictatorial ways and the demand that member groups be given more control over their funds and activities. An attentiveness to the importance of the social space was evident in the calls to improve the "atmosphere" at the Institute by acting on the repeated requests to paint the "disgrace[ful]" rooms and basement, with their peeling paint and rough floors, to repair the lighting, and to improve the upkeep of the washrooms, particularly in the cabaret space. Still others wrote that simply allowing the lounge radio to be on all week instead of only on Sundays, keeping the record player in good repair, and buying up-to-date records would "encourage [a] feeling of warmth." As would permitting the clubs more time to complete games. There were also suggestions for adding new courses dealing with Canadian life. And for improving the "uninspired and uninspiring"

Intercom by adding a sports and a women's page and columns devoted to the personal experiences of immigrants.[96]

In insisting upon their right to decent surroundings and greater autonomy, and in drawing a connection between the "atmosphere" of a social space and group morale and belonging, Institute members were articulating a version of what has been called "moral geographies." They were negotiating a collective ethics of mutual respect that was rooted in meaningful cross-cultural encounters that occurred at the spatial scale of a community "meeting place" of ethnically diverse people.[97] It was not proximity alone that led certain individuals and groups to mediate differences among previous strangers and develop a sense of group identity, but rather that, as members engaged in purposeful activity, the Members Council constituted what Ash Amin has called a "micropublic of everyday social contact and encounter." Whether theatres, sports clubs, or community groups, micropublics, argues Amin, are more effective at negotiating difference and engendering new ways of being and doing than mounting public festivals. We also see in the members' protest a form of oppositional culture familiar to social historians, wherein the targets of moral regulators both absorb some of the intended values, such as democracy, and seek to shame the regulators for violating their own ideology.[98]

The points about intercultural dialogue and collective belonging should not be exaggerated, however, given the persistence of social inequities and the presence of a clique of professional Eastern European men on the Members Council. The fact that its composition during the revolt was more ethnically diverse, and included more women, than in previous years, does suggest, though, that the principle of respect – not just ethnic male posturing – mattered to the wider membership.[99] The protest led to some reforms, including improvements to the physical space, but little came of the promise of democratic reforms in the governing structure.

Sharing Immigrant Tales

The Members Council's revolt also led to the creation of a column in the *Intercom*, "Tales of an Immigrant," where people shared their personal stories. The predominance of European middle-class authors in the column underscored the heavily white and European character of Institute pluralism. The group of ten men and two women reflected another limitation: women's underrepresentation among Institute members. The authors came from both sides of the Iron Curtain, but most were Eastern Europeans. There were two Southern Europeans of rural origins and one former Dutch (female) farmer. Most everyone expressed a mix of emotions, but concluded with positive assessments of Canada and its opportunities, and in the case of the Eastern Europeans, the political freedoms gained. The essays reflect the willingness of members who

156   Community-Building Experiments

have achieved a degree of success in Canada to share their stories. Some embraced their role as pioneer and a few evidently harboured political ambitions. Together, the articles arguably convey something of what emotion theorist Sara Ahmed has called "multicultural love." That is, the immigrants' willingness to validate a national discourse of multiculturalism (as an open and diverse nation) by meeting a key requirement of that nation's "conditional love" – to take on the new nation as a "love object" through allegiance to its ideals and adherence to its norms – is rewarded with the nation's love in the form of tolerance of their cultural difference.[100]

Most of the essays began with familiar anecdotes about leaving home or arriving in Halifax, the insipid cake-like Canadian white bread, and the anxiety they felt – all themes that likely resonated with readers. Apart from the two men who claimed to have immediately fallen in love with Canada, the authors emphasized that initial struggles meant it took some time to truly appreciate Canada. Dutch-born Martin Weiland explained that while he was lucky enough to have found a warehouse job early on, it was learning English at the Institute that eventually led to a bank job that changed "everything" for him. So that six years after arriving in Canada as a wary immigrant intimidated by Toronto, "I felt that I belonged" and became a "happy citizen." He described his integration in Institute-like terms, as a "subtle process" that did not require "forsaking" his ethnic background. Now an accountant, he added that, having recently bought a house outside Toronto on the "beautiful" Credit River, he had joined the many Canadians who commuted to work by train.[101]

Otto Koepke, a former teacher/interpreter who established a photo and print business in Toronto, similarly expressed "no regrets" about coming to Canada. Identifying himself as a German expellee (refugee) from Eastern Europe, he concludes: "I lost my home province to the East and won a better homeland in the west!" Koepke also recounted his bewilderment as a newcomer in Montreal, when people he addressed in English or French replied to him in German, until someone told him that "my hair and my briefcase" gave him away. An enthusiastic YMCA member, he became involved in the Institute's recreational programs.[102]

The most critical writer was a German-born professional, Wilhelm Pilz, who recalled the despair he felt over living in a dark and dirty Toronto hotel worsening after his first interview in an employment centre. In his version of an oft-told tale, he noted that the promised friendly encounter turned out to be "a game of 'let's push him around.'" He recalled the "poor creatures, cheap alcohol on breath, hanging outside the building, begging for a dime or a cigarette in this 'prosperous land,'" and the many rejection letters that embittered him. His only solace, he wrote, was the English classes at the Institute, which became "my second home." Pilz praised the excellent teachers for going "one step further" by inviting students to house parties, where they could enjoy a beer, meet others, and become more involved in the "North American way of life." Although more wistful in tone that others, Pilz also concluded on a positive note, saying that, with his wife's support, he had returned to university, started a new career, and become accustomed to Canada – and "maybe even grown to like it a little bit."[103]

Ilmar Külvet, an Estonian journalist and writer who had worked with the US radio program "Voice of America" in Soviet-occupied Estonia, and who now edited the Toronto-based Estonian newspaper *Vaba Eestlane* (*Free Estonian,* est. 1952), fit the profile of an ethnic elite.[104] His story about the "somewhat cynical" immigration official he met in Halifax also drew on his skills as a playwright. The official told him he had an honest face, but also that he was "a sucker for honest faces," meaning the honest-looking might yet prove dishonest. He then advised Külvet to elevate his former status as a journalist to that of editor-in-chief in order to land a reporter's job because prospective employers, anticipating exaggeration, "will automatically deduct 25% from your claim." He also warned him that Toronto was "a human jungle" where "only those equipped with claws and sharp teeth have a chance to get ahead." Noting that he was able to resume a career as an (ethnic) journalist in Canada after spending several years as a shipping clerk and a barbed-wire wrapper, Külvet ended on a rueful note. He wrote that while he no longer felt that he lived in a jungle "perhaps because I've ... developed the claws and teeth needed to survive it," it had been a long time since someone told him that he had an honest face. The accompanying sketch by artist Joann Saarniit, another Estonian refugee and Institute member, of an anxious man in the big city, underscored the essay's rueful tone.[105]

The essays penned by the women, Czech refugee Nadine Hradsky, a doctor, and Dutch immigrant Madzi Brender a Brandis, a farmer who obtained a university degree in Canada, were both similar to and different from those of the men. Again, there are stories about early bewilderment and struggle. Brender a Brandis wrote about arriving by train at a small town in northern British Columbia on a frosty cold night in 1947 with a baby and two kids tugging at her skirt, and the family's failure at farming. Hradsky recalled her fear of losing her first (night) job in a candy factory because she could not roll the cellophane wrapper around the candy canes as fast as "the Canadian girls," and waiting for her imprisoned husband to join her in Toronto. The women, too, were ultimately positive about Canada, though Hradsky was more emphatic about loving "this country with a passion that embarrasses our Canadian friends." She thanked the co-workers at the candy factory who shared their lunch and taught her English. For Brender a Brandis, life turned around at the University of British Columbia, where she and her husband felt accepted by professors and students alike, creating "very happy memories."

Both women also provided intimate family details. Brender a Brandis, who moved to Toronto after university, recounted feeling homesick and isolated at home while her school-age children and husband had "Canadian" experiences, and feeling overwhelmed by the latest housekeeping regimes, but also how the Institute night classes, clubs, and outings helped her to understand the Canadian way of life. Indeed, she seems the model immigrant mother, explaining that, having weighed the pros and cons of the "strict" European parenting style with those of "the more permissive society," she realized that, for her children to be happy, their parents had to try to raise them as Canadians. Her occasional slip into the "old fashioned" parenting, she joked, brought some "spice" to their lives. Brender a Brandis was clearly an intelligent and resourceful woman, but, in keeping with contemporary gender norms, she gave her husband the main credit for her successful integration. She signed off by advising other husbands to encourage their wives to join the Institute's English, recreational, and arts and craft classes.

Hradsky's essay included a religiously themed account of the first Christmas Eve spent with her children at Union Station, taking in the "towering trees filled with coloured lights" and praying under the vaulted ceilings for her husband's safe arrival. (He arrived several months later.) It was a well-crafted tale about what became an annual family Christmas ritual, one that Hradsky now included in her talks on the Institute delivered to women's volunteer groups. While Institute staff may have helped to write it, this was a female refugee–shaped narrative that became a publicity narrative used in part to recruit volunteers.[106]

Only Sicilian-born Corrado relayed his story through an interview. Institute volunteer Isabel Jemsen described his life as one "of thought, endurance and will, perseverance, skill and luck." Corrado was far less educated than the other authors, though having trained as a welder, and then having become one of the bilingual welding teachers in the Trade English Programme held at the Institute, he enjoyed a status above that of most Italian immigrants. His story spoke of loneliness and unemployment, but also of his feelings of gratitude towards the Institute. The Institute counsellors, he noted, enabled him, first to secure a Canadian certificate in welding, then to land the teaching contract, and, finally, to attend college and obtain a teacher's certificate. Convinced by a trip home that he had become a Canadian, he obtained Canadian citizenship. In another heartfelt plug for the Institute, he said that his active participation in the clubs and activities was not only about repaying the Institute for its support, but also about "making up" for the many deprivations suffered as a very poor child in Sicily.[107]

Semantics or Slippage?

While the "Tales of an Immigrant" column offers some evidence of community-building through collective storytelling, the scathing critique of the house programs by the supervisor of the Group Services Department indicate continuing staff-member tensions and more. Five years after the members' revolt, and three years after the Institute's move to Davenport Road, Kay Brown excoriated the programs and advocated a new path for the Institute. The Institute's inconvenient location, she argued in a 1969 report, meant they needed high-quality programs to attract newcomers, but the (reduced) recreational programs were "an unmitigated disaster." The current membership numbers (evidently in the low 600s) were deceptive, she claimed, because some programs were being "artificially held together" by certain staff, and the Saturday night dances no longer attracted enough people. The "fairly" successful weekend summer trips had seen "a blaze of glory" in 1967 because of Expo and "the general Centennial fever," but had since petered out. Indeed, they were barely breaking even in terms of cost only because the staffer (not named) spent hours on the phone "cajoling and frequently bullying members to participate." She also accused the international club of using the Institute as a private club.[108]

Brown did not suggest eliminating all programs, but she did recommend the adoption of a "Canadianization" policy while denying its assimilationist overtones. In regard to house activities, she favoured continuing with the chess, bridge, and table tennis nights and the film series as they drew good audiences. She recommended closing the building on weekends in order to reduce staff "waste" over "unnecessary" programs, but allowing the outdoor activities to continue. She wanted the bus trips put on a one-year trial basis. As for overall goals, however, Brown rejected the Institute's long-term dual strategy of combining activities that encouraged Canadianization (such as English and mother's classes and discussion groups) with events (ethnic weeks, folk festivals) that promoted cultural preservation and involved close cooperation with the ethnic organizations. Instead, she argued, the focus should be solely on Canadianization programs. .

Brown justified her controversial recommendation largely by addressing the Institute's difficulty in attracting many new members to its house programs despite the recent increase in the professional immigrants that comprised its main target group. Drawing on the recent findings of several social agencies, she argued that the low rates of ethnic-group affiliation registered among residents in Metropolitan Toronto (8 per cent) despite the recent increase of young (age 20–29) urban immigrants in the "professional and managerial" categories indicated that these newcomers were "not particularly interested" in cultural activities designed to preserve old-country values. Instead, she added, they "cheerfully" join programs offered by Canadian agencies and enjoy "commercial entertainment," and attributed both to the advances in modern communication and the increasing Americanization of Europe, which bred a growing familiarity, at least among urban educated immigrants, with contemporary Western culture (the "same" modern plays, dances, movies) and politics. This exposure, she claimed, lessened the culture shock immigrants felt upon arrival in Canada and thus the need for programs that helped to cushion it by respecting and preserving ethnic (folk) cultures while facilitating adjustment to the new culture. As for the "less educated" and family-sponsored immigrants, she thought them unlikely – except for single men – to seek outside entertainment, and that a continuing failure to attract enough single women to the socials meant that many single men did not return to the Institute.

In defence of her position, Brown claimed that the Institute was already undergoing a change in purpose, from the era of West's "very close relationship" with the ethnic groups to one more focused on delivering social services most relevant to the newcomer's Canadianization. That shift, she argued, made eminent sense for three main reasons: the popularity of the English program (which drew an average of 350 students each season), the recent failure of the house programs to return any profit to the Institute, and the fact that public agencies like the Canadian Folk Arts Council as well as the federal and provincial departments of citizenship and immigration were now actively involved in ethnic culture preservation. Consequently, she concluded, the Institute should focus on "the indoctrination of Canadian values and cultural attributes." Her new emphasis on effectively accelerating the process of Canadianization would inform the expert opinion she relayed a year later to the journalist Sidney Katz about the psychological harm being done to teenagers by rural Southern European parents who sacrificed their children's education and future in order to meet their own goal of home ownership.[109]

Brown's 1969 report also reveals some major contradictions. For example, she claimed the Institute could fulfil its new purpose by severing its ties to the ethnic groups interested in cultural preservation and by forging links with the social service groups within growing immigrant communities like the Southern European and Yugoslavian ones, and with long-standing service agencies like the Jewish Immigrant Aid Society. Yet, one could hardly make incursions into any immigrant community without first developing some association, and building trust, with a range of organizations. Equally problematic was the suggestion that the Institute assume the role of coordinating and assessing social service agencies across the immigrant communities. Brown also dismissed the Institute's once close relationship, again through West, with the ethnic press editors because they never adequately covered its programs, but evidently thought they could easily forge links with the ethnic language radio and television media in order to secure better publicity.[110]

Brown clearly anticipated criticism of her recommendations. She thus tried to deflect attention to the matter by claiming that one could "avoid the problem of being tied up in the semantics of integration, assimilation, melting pots and mosaics" simply by viewing the Institute as a teacher whose role is to equip students with the tools and knowledge necessary for them to make their own decisions. Her attempts to navigate a semantic minefield through resort to a slippery logic was not an isolated act, but rather emulated the US institute movement's paradoxical thinking on these questions. As advocates of a liberal creed that claimed enlightened superiority over historically dominant assimilationist movements, Institute personnel adopted a slippery logic – or paradox – whereby the desire to encourage integration, so as to preserve ethnic cultures and promote a robust pluralist nation, existed in tandem with the perceived necessity to ensure newcomers' "absorption" of "American ideals" (see chapter 3).

Although less tangible than charges of undemocratic behaviour, the confusion caused by the slippage between understandings of integration and assimilation posed a challenge as well to community-building efforts in Toronto. It thus requires further comment. Research into a dozen US Institutes and the central body in New York City reveals differing formulations of the movement's mission. Certainly, most Institute folks subscribed to the integrative approach endorsed by Willette Pierce of the Milwaukee Institute, who claimed that balancing migrants' enriching traditions and "aesthetic values" with exposure to and adoption of American values would allow them and their children to "become Americans without throwing off their past."[111] Others appeared equally comfortable describing their mission as assimilationist even as they understood the term to involve respect for immigrant cultures and for cultural diversity. The same Institutes that spoke of "two-way change" in both American and newcomer, such as the Toledo Institute, talked, too, of ensuring immigrants' "induction into American life and concepts, attitudes," with its necessary "personal and group adjustments" and the "assimilation of the foreign-born into the native population." Related remarks, including by movement founder Edith Terry Bremer, about "the Americanization process" progressing at different speeds for different ethnic groups similarly implied that the Institutes' aim was Americanization.[112]

Toronto Institute personnel used the term integration quite consistently to explain their mission, but, here, too, we find instances of this slippery logic. When group work supervisor Kolm warned of the dangers of remaining in the cramped quarters of the St Andrew's building, he used the word "absorption" to underscore the need for a facility that could support "active" house programs that would bring in "constructive and stable persons." "A substantial number" of desirable middle-class Canadians, he noted, was necessary to ensure that the "rough" and "unstable" types "become absorbed" into a Canadian way of life.[113]

Certain *Intercom* columns used the terms assimilation or integration in ways that may have confused some readers. A 1960 editorial on the Institute's mandate to help newcomers "feeling strange and lost in this huge metropolis" to meet a "friendly voice," receive "helpful advice," and achieve that human "thirst for friendship" claimed that the immigrants' first goal was "to be assimilated quickly." Similarly, an article on the psychological aspects of immigration by a French Canadian priest used "integration" to explain the importance of immigrant reception work, but his depiction of immigrants as mainly uprooted people who had to be transformed into Canadians implied assimilation. As did his language. The immigrants, he wrote, need not sever all ties with their homeland, but they must understand that the "complete integration" of an immigrant family will occur within one or two generations. Further, his depiction of the process – namely, that the children, by attending Canadian schools, catechism classes, apprenticeship workshops, youth activities, and camps, will plant roots in the new soil and absorb the adoptive country's culture to the point that "they are attached to their former country ... only through the memory of stories told at home" – implied assimilation. Such arguments might have conveyed the sense that Institute folks were really "delayed assimilationists."[114] In the end, Brown's report reflected her own rather than the Institute's shift from a sometime contradictory pluralist position to an avowedly assimilationist stance, but its slippery logic was not out of the ordinary.

Missed Opportunities

The records of the Institute's house programs point to missed opportunities to develop a more progressive and inclusive category of belonging based on respect for racial difference and progressive politics as well as gender. One example of how the presence of affiliated ethno-Canadian groups outside the European mainstream could have exerted a positive impact was the presence of Japanese Canadian organizations like the retired members of the Japanese Labourers' Union (est. 1920). An *Intercom* article on the contribution of Japanese Canadian mill workers to the Canadian labour movement featured labour leader Etsu Suzuki and other "pioneers" who fought to raise the consciousness of the mainstream unions with respect to the citizenship rights of all Canadians. They did so, it added, first by obtaining a charter as Local 31 of the Camp and Mill Workers Federal Labour Union (1927), and then by securing the support of the Trades and Labour Congress for a 1931 resolution in favour of enfranchisement. This simplified story of a more complex history was part of the coverage given to a reunion of Local 31 members at Toronto's Nikko Garden, thus also offering a reminder of the Canadian state's wartime internment and postwar dispersal of Japanese Canadians across Canada.[115] In symbolic appreciation of the city's acceptance of relocated Japanese Canadians after the war, the Sakura (Cherry Blossom) Club, also an Institute member, helped with a fundraising campaign to realize the wish of the Japanese Consul to Canada to plant a Japanese garden in High Park, Toronto's biggest public park. Overall, however, the Institute's Japanese Canadian programming largely consisted of a few concerts and some Japanese tea ceremonies, including one held on the University of Toronto campus in 1960 with two Japanese Canadian Institute hostesses. Sponsored by the Society for Oriental Study, the event had both an orientalist and Cold War air about it. The Japanese consul spoke on the topic of "the development of democracy in Japan."[116]

The affiliation of progressive groups among the Portuguese and Caribbean immigrants also held out the possibility of building a more inclusive and activist community. The Portuguese Canadian Democratic Association (PCDA, est. 1959) opposed Portugal's Estado Novo dictatorship and sought to prepare Portuguese immigrants in Canada for their transition to democracy. The PCDA was a heavily working-class organization, though its founding president, Fernando Ciriaco da Cunha, was an agricultural scientist and former civil servant, and other members were either political activists in exile or liberal professionals. The Institute and the Department of Citizenship and Immigration (DCI) collaborated with the PCDA on a community project to encourage Portuguese immigrants in Toronto (and Montreal) to pursue Canadian naturalization. But there was no further collaboration, no doubt because of the PCDA's leftist orientation. That politics was on public display during the so-called Bay Street riot of 1961, when pro- and anti-Salazar immigrants clashed in front of the Portuguese consulate. A *Toronto Star* reporter covering the event quoted a DCI officer who touted the Institute line about immigrants needing to abandon Old World conflicts, adding, "We try to stress Canada is their home during occasional lectures at the International Institute." The pro-Salazarists among Portuguese immigrants would probably have challenged an alliance with the PCDA, but the Institute never really entertained the idea.[117]

The Caribbean presence at the Institute, which included the in some cases overlapping memberships of the West Indian Student Association, the West Indies Independence Committee, and Calypso bands created an opportunity for developing cross-racial bonds. Here, a key figure was Charles Roach, who with his "incomparable" Rio Blanco Trio and other bands headlined the Calypso Nights, delivering "haunting calypso tunes" and some "western music" for 200 and 250 people.[118] Born in Belmont, Trinidad and Tobago, to a trade union organizer father, Roach came to Canada in 1955 to pursue a university education. After graduating from the University of Toronto's law school, he worked as a staff lawyer for the City of Toronto until opening his own practice in 1968. He also owned and operated the Little Trinidad, one of the after-hours clubs that emerged in the sixties to serve the small but growing Caribbean community with calypso and other musical genres from home and provide a space for folk art, drama, and dance.[119]

Some young Caribbean immigrants joined the mainly white audience at the Institute's sixties-era Calypso Nights, and Roach, who later co-founded with other Caribbean businessmen the Caribana festival in 1967, might have played the role of intermediary between at least East Caribbean immigrants and the Institute.[120] There was even some overlap between his views and that of the Institute on promoting cultural diversity (see chapter 10). Yet, with the partial exception of the meetings held to discuss human rights issues (see chapter 11), Institute staff did little to develop more racially inclusive house programs. Admittedly, a closer relationship with the Caribbean or Portuguese groups may not have fully redressed the gender imbalance. In the early 1970s, Royston C. Jones, the Institute's Caribbean counsellor and one-time consultant on Caribana, was featured in an article in the *Toronto Star* discussing the polite racism of Canadians towards Black immigrants.[121]

Conclusion

Despite the Institute's perennial financial problems and ongoing tensions, a culturally diverse group of women and men sought to enact a community-based pluralism rooted in everyday interactions and collaborations – and friendly competition. In contrast to the more explicitly hierarchical nature of the social worker–client interactions that occurred in its counselling department, the Institute's house programs involved more egalitarian relationships among members, and even more collaborative relations between members and staff, though a fully formed democracy proved an elusive goal. Humour, sharing stories, and heterosexual marriage, among other factors, helped to develop a sense of community particularly among the members.

As a social welfare organization, the Institute also faced the challenge of attaining that delicate balance between intervention and empowering people, as well as that between integration and assimilation. The concept of two-way integration gave certain Canadians, especially Anglo-Canadians, the upper hand, but also placed the onus as much on them as the immigrants to make the experiment work. The participation of racialized Canadians and newcomers raised the possibility of building a more racially inclusive community that extended beyond the numerically dominant European groups. In the end, however, the possibilities presented by this pluralist experiment were outweighed by its limitations. The latter ranged from the fundamental contradictions within Institute-style liberal pluralism, which tried to square bottom-up principles of community-organization with top-down principles of social work regulation, to the paralysis that set in as the Institute faced its impending extinction. Finally, my focus here was on one locale in a nation that would adopt official multiculturalism, but the analysis is no less relevant for nation-states that had not historically defined themselves as paradigmatic "nations of immigrants."

Chapter Eight

Community Projects for Rural Villagers: Health and Occupational Training

In the early 1960s, the International Institute of Metropolitan Toronto declared that the earlier urban and educated newcomers from Europe had effectively integrated – a sure sign being their move from the city's poorer immigrant districts to modestly affluent suburbs – and turned their sights on the Southern Europeans of rural origins deemed far less equipped to adapt to modern urban life. The Institute carried out two "special" community projects, the first of which explored ways of improving these immigrants' access to health and welfare services, and the second an educational project that focused on vocational training. There were also several pilot projects related to vocational education and trade-training programs. Lacking formal education, these low-skilled immigrants worked and lived in grim conditions, and the Institute's acknowledgment of this reality speaks to the multifaceted character of its brand of pluralism. Not confined solely to sponsoring organized recreational activities (chapter 7) or folk festivals (part 4), the Institute also addressed economic inequities and sought to improve the material and emotional quality of life of economically vulnerable immigrants. Put another way, the Institute's multi-layered pluralist agenda included an economic and labour reform component that was wholly lacking in the version of multiculturalism that became official policy in Canada in 1971. In practice, however, efforts to improve immigrant access to health and welfare resources and trade-training programs produced mixed results.

Canadian social worker Edith Ferguson directed both of the "special" community projects. Both projects were run out of an extension office that was separate from the main Institute building and referred to as the Branch Office. Both projects recruited field staff from the targeted immigrant communities, but differed in focus, scope, and gender profile. The health project involved Italians and Portuguese in Toronto's west end and an all-female staff who dealt mainly with mothers. Focused on English instruction and skills-upgrading, the educational project included Greeks as well as Italians and Portuguese and operated

166 Community-Building Experiments

on a wider geographical scale. While this project involved mainly male staff and male workers, some of the related pilot projects (specifically the industrial sewing and hairdressing programs) included women counsellors, teachers, and workers. The records generated by the two community projects also differed in quality. Describing the approach as one of "meeting the immigrants at the point of need," Ferguson attributed the successes mainly to the efficacy with which her fieldworkers – who, once again, were not professional social workers but mostly middle-class urban immigrants receiving on-the-job training – fulfilled their role as interpreters and intermediaries.[1] A focus on their front-line activities offers a useful yardstick by which to assess these efforts. Just how effectively did they negotiate interactions between the immigrants and community service providers? How did their efforts compare with those of the main Institute's permanent counsellors who ran the pilot projects? How does the Institute's labour-oriented multicultural activism compare with approaches lauded by today's experts?

This chapter explores the Toronto Institute's efforts to address what it saw as the special needs of a growing number of "rural villagers" who hailed from Southern Italy, the Peloponnese region of Southern Greece and Western Macedonia, and the Azorean Islands located far off the coast of continental Portugal. It addresses two major migration-related themes: immigrant health,[2] particularly that of children,[3] and vocational training for adult immigrant workers.[4] Not meant to challenge the "vertical mosaic," the projects reflected instead a shared belief among liberal social welfare personnel, adult education advocates, and immigrant activists that well-placed reforms can create a greater equality of opportunity in a competitive democratic society.[5] Without ignoring the limitations of creating an immigrant-specific field of health and welfare services and vocational training – such as possible ghettoization in underfunded sectors and preparation for second-class citizenship – I argue that these (uneven) efforts demonstrate the value of a community-based pluralist approach to the provision of social services and educational programs for immigrants. As regards race, these activities predated the significant presence of the post-1967 racialized immigrants. Still, the Institute's efforts to assist Southern Europeans, often ascribed an inferior, or in-between, racial status as a "dark" people with "strange" customs, and "different living habits ... mental attitudes and ... goals," through the recruitment of front-line staff from the immigrant communities reflected an inclusive principle that might have been productively applied to the later arriving racialized immigrants.[6]

A Champion of Immigrants?

First hired by the Institute in 1962, Edith Ferguson was a veteran social worker with experience in social welfare administration. A Welsh Canadian professional woman who, like many other female social work leaders, never married, Ferguson had taught in a one-room schoolhouse before attending Queen's University in the late 1920s. After earning a Bachelor of Arts in English and History in 1931, she earned a teaching certificate and taught high school before enrolling in the University of Toronto's School of Social Work. In Windsor and then Toronto, she worked with a number of social welfare organizations during the 1940s, including the Toronto Children's Aid Society (CAS). At the end of the Second World War, Ferguson, like many Canadian social service personnel, worked overseas with UNRRA (United Nations Relief and Rehabilitation Association), first in France and then as part of a team in Germany supervising activities in the displaced persons (DP) camps.[7]

When asked by a reporter how she became "a champion of immigrants," Ferguson referred to her identity as a bilingual Canadian who grew up speaking English and Welsh in the small town of Dunvegan, Ontario, and to her work with refugees in Europe and North America.[8] Upon returning to Canada from Europe in 1947, she joined the liberal voices calling for a more open-door immigration policy. In the popular news magazine *Saturday Night*, she criticized the high rates of rejection in the recruitment of displaced persons for Canadian industry and called for a more generous refugee policy based on humanitarian grounds. As a signatory to the UN resolution in support of refugee resettlement, Canada, she argued, was obliged to resettle older and sick refugees, including Holocaust survivors and those who contracted TB in the DP camps.[9]

Shortly after returning home, Ferguson spent a year in New York City, where she earned a master's degree in adult education and "rubbed shoulders with immigrants in New York settlements."[10] Back in Canada, she worked for Ontario Radio Forum, a progressive radio program that promoted adult education and social activism among rural families, later joining the staff of the Canadian Association of Adult Education, a progressive organization that also advocated for immigrant rights. Having spent most of the 1950s with the Windsor Community Welfare Council, Ferguson returned to Toronto in 1960, where she soon joined the staff of the Social Planning Council of Metropolitan Toronto (SPC). She left the SPC, an Institute co-sponsor, to work with the Institute on what became the first of two contracts, the second of which ended in 1966.[11] Both sympathetic to immigrants and well-versed in the regulatory features and liberal aspirations of her profession, Ferguson's work with the Institute was also shaped by the paradoxical character of liberal pluralism.

With private grants secured from a few charitable foundations and public funds from the federal and provincial departments of immigration and citizenship, both Branch community projects had a modest but independent budget of about $20,000. (The Institute could not have afforded to finance the projects out of its own operating budget.) The largest concentrations of the three targeted groups, which together comprised a majority of the estimated 255,000 to 265,000 Southern Europeans in mid-1960s Metropolitan Toronto, were in the city's historically important reception areas in the west and east ends, and, in the case of the numerically dominant Italians, in some suburbs as well.[12] As project director, Ferguson enjoyed some autonomy, but also reported to an advisory committee that included representatives from the Institute board. The advisory committee for the health project also included representatives from various social agencies, the Public Welfare Department, the Toronto Board of Education's Child Adjustment Service (a counselling service for students), and the University of Toronto's School of Social Work. The education advisory committee included Joseph Carraro, the progressive immigrant priest (who later left the church) behind COSTI (Centro Organizzativo Scuole Tecniche Italiane, est. 1962), an Italian community organization whose initial mandate to help Italian tradesmen meet Canadian (Ontario) certification requirements expanded into a broader multi-ethnic immigrant job-training program.[13] The other consultants included senior personnel with the provincially funded industrial training programs and trade institutes in Toronto and with the federal and provincial departments of labour.

Health and Welfare Project, 1962–4

The goal of the first Branch project was to explore ways of reducing an identified "gap" between the available health services and their underutilization by disadvantaged immigrants. Working out of an extension office that changed location a few times, the Branch staff, following an initial misstep, chose a neighbourhood not far from the main Institute with many Italians and Portuguese.[14] Once again, the Institute hired a multilingual staff of educated immigrant women thought to possess the appropriate insight and judgment and trained them on the job. The strategy did not eliminate class and other distinctions between staff and clients, so the women expected to break through the "wall of suspicion" and build trust with immigrants leery of "outsiders" still faced a daunting challenge.[15] Still, given the hostility with which many "Anglo" personnel in the city's government departments and agencies treated the Italian and Portuguese clients they dismissed as "backward" and "stubborn," the use of immigrant female fieldworkers represented a progressive measure.[16]

The first fieldworker hired was Maria Cosso, a Northern Italian who spoke French as well as English and Italian. A graduate of the University of Genoa's teacher-training program, she had also dabbled in business and journalism. Marucia Montgomery, a university-educated Brazilian from Rio de Janeiro (who appears to have married a Canadian), became the Portuguese-speaking worker after the search failed to produce an applicant from Portugal. Aware of the division between Portuguese immigrants who supported the Salazar regime and opponents of the dictatorship, Ferguson hoped both sides would regard

Montgomery, whom she felt had the cultural sensitivities required, as politically neutral and trustworthy. Because of the influx of Italian clients, in the project's second year the Institute hired June Zelonka, a recent graduate of the University of Toronto's bachelor's program in psychology and a multilingual Polish refugee whose languages included Italian.[17]

Along with Ferguson, who initially combined front-line interviews with administrative duties, Branch staff advertised their services in the local shops and churches, and conducted home and school visits. Ultimately, they interacted with a few thousand immigrants and accompanied dozens of them to clinics and social welfare offices. Published as *Newcomers in Transition,* Ferguson's final report concluded that the rural immigrants' "special cultural characteristics" largely accounted for their underuse of the adequate if not generous existing social services.

Ferguson acknowledged that these immigrants' "special cultural characteristics" were the product of historical, material, and social factors, but she also traded in stereotypes of rural (primitive) and urban (modern) people. As she explained, an understandable wish to improve a low standard of living "catapulted" many thousands of impoverished peasants from an "underdeveloped agrarian society" and frozen "rural folk society" based on face-to-face relations into a terribly different "industrialized city" where they occupied "the bottom of the economic scale." Further marginalized by language, customs, and physical appearance ("short, with dark complexions, black hair and dark eyes"), these mainly family-sponsored immigrants were turning entire city districts into self-enclosed communities. Just as centuries-old poverty and suspicion of outside authorities explained why in Italy and Portugal they avoided urban doctors and dentists unless in extreme pain, and city hospitals unless critically ill or needing surgery, they were reluctant to tap even free services in Toronto or interact with Canadian personnel in whose presence they felt like country bumpkins. Ferguson understood the preoccupation among former land-hungry peasants with achieving financial security through multiple-family home-ownership strategies that involved large and risky mortgages. But she also portrayed the parents as so cut off from modernity that they did not even think to ask about health services for their children.[18]

Ferguson noted that language was the single greatest disincentive to accessing resources, hence all the staff time spent on translating documents and interpretation. But in issuing a call to "overhaul" the approach taken by Canadian personnel towards these immigrants, she combined insight, stereotype, and contradiction. Arguing that rural villagers could not possibly start "from the same place" as urban immigrants because of their backwardness, she thought it wrong-headed to criticize them for "living in colonies" when at home they lived in small-scale villages, or for not allowing their children to go on summer camping trips organized by the "Y" when "they believe that good parents keep

Institute staff may have winced at the sight of this "peasant-looking" woman carrying a burlap bag of produce (onions?) on her head, but her smile suggests she took pride in her capacity for physically demanding labour. Kensington Market, 22 December 1967. York University Libraries, Clara Thomas Archives & Special Collections, Toronto Telegram fonds, ASC12872.

their children close to home."[19] She preferred an approach that encouraged rather than dictated their transition into modern urban citizens. Also willing to admonish Canadians, she argued, in the immigrants' defence, that, while initially "much more helpless" than people realized, most of them needed well-placed support only temporarily as they adjusted to city life and became more self-sufficient.[20]

Immigrant Children's Health

Ferguson's success in negotiating an arrangement with Toronto's public and Roman Catholic school boards owed much to the fact that the schools were receiving an escalating number of immigrant children whose parents' poor English, long working hours, and distrust of outsiders made communication with them difficult. The influx of Italian and Portuguese students meant overcrowded classrooms in aging buildings that lacked modern facilities. The building of some new public schools took some pressure off the older ones. As for

Community Projects for Rural Villagers 171

Institute staff would have approved of these children eating slices of fruit (melon?) during Greek Orthodox Easter celebrations on "the Danforth" in Toronto's east end "Greektown," 10 April 1965. Note the boy's hockey jacket and the girl's fancy dress and bow. York University Libraries, Clara Thomas Archives & Special Collections, Toronto Telegram fonds, ASC34431.

the (publicly funded) Catholic schools, the provincial government's decision in the 1960s to provide grants to the long under-resourced separate schools allowed them to accept many more Eastern as well as Southern European Catholic pupils.[21] Ill-equipped to deal with the health challenges posed by a huge spike in Italian and Portuguese students, the overcrowded schools in the west end welcomed the Institute's project.

Shortly after Ferguson and Cosso visited some school principals in the project's early weeks to inform them of their health project, Branch staff began receiving requests from the local schools for interpreters to help them communicate with the parents of sick or (medically) neglected children. The Institute then signed a formal agreement with the Toronto Board of Education and its Catholic equivalent to act as intermediaries between the schools and the parents. The agreement covered a dozen elementary schools (kindergarten to Grade 8). Individual teachers or the school nurse might initiate the process, but, with the principal's approval, the school nurse usually contacted the Institute's Branch Office to request assistance. Well aware of the problem of relying on children (their students) to act as interpreters in their dealings with the parents, the school principals and nurses welcomed the project's multilingual female staff. The schools most affected particularly by the incoming Italians were the heaviest users of the service, but requests came from all participating schools.[22]

The Branch staff's closer relationship with the schools meant working more closely with public health nurses. Fieldworkers did plenty of one-off interpreting for visiting public health nurses, relaying information about diagnoses, clinic appointments, or baby formula over the phone, or visiting a hospital to explain a procedure to a patient. It also became increasingly common for them to accompany public health nurses conducting afternoon visits, and to conduct evening visits (as more women than expected were in the workforce) or follow-up visits on their own.[23] The arrangement was mutually beneficial: the overloaded nurses appreciated the assistance and the staff considered the nurse a direct route into an immigrant household, where the bigger picture might be revealed.[24]

The main Institute's "permanent" counsellors also handled cases that were primarily or, far more commonly, partially about health and welfare issues. Together, such cases shed light on the everyday challenges faced by newly arrived adults coping with illness, their own and/or that of others, while dealing with other challenges. Those involving Southern Europeans, for example, confirm what others have found for Toronto's working Italian and Portuguese women: they often withdrew from the workforce in response to a child's illness whereas a husband's illness or injury usually prompted wives at home to seek paid work in order to make up for the lost wages.[25] However, the health project records offer more insight into the Institute's interventions because of the availability of fieldwork notes for 75 cases (60 Italians and 15 Portuguese). While the adult-related cases are valuable insofar as they show how illness complicated or sabotaged the plans of financially vulnerable newcomers, the richest records are the 30 cases of children (under 16 years of age) who were referred to Ferguson and her health project staff.[26]

Most of the 30 referrals came from six of the one dozen participating schools (four public and two Catholic) located in the vicinity of the Institute and its Branch Office.[27] These 30 cases involved 16 girls and 14 boys and fell into four broad and overlapping categories: physical ill health (67 per cent), mental and emotional ill health (33 per cent), parental neglect of medical needs (53 per cent), and "retarded development" (20 per cent). They document overlapping "problems," such as poor attendance/performance (35 per cent), known health problem (11.5 per cent), and transfer to a remedial/vocational school or school for "retarded children" (21 per cent).

Some cases (20 per cent) cite a mix of physical and emotional or psychological factors (such as rheumatic fever and severe loneliness). However, a third of them fall into a grey area of reportedly "slow," inattentive, belligerent, or underperforming children considered in danger of failing or being sent back a grade, and whose difficulties are attributed to the material conditions of their underprivileged lives. The contributing factors included overcrowded and noisy households, poor diets and malnourishment, exhaustion due to part-time jobs that got them up too early (to pick worms, sell newspapers) or kept them up too late (setting pins at a bowling alley), and the absence of parents or siblings to help with homework. In the four cases of "delinquent behavior," all involving boys, poor parenting was added to the mix.

Together, these cases capture Institute involvement with immigrant children and their parents, particularly mothers. The rate of positive outcomes recorded among the health project's child cases was considerably higher than that for the adult health cases handled by the main Institute's permanent counsellors (one-third and under 5 per cent respectively), suggesting that the health project's female fieldworkers achieved a noticeable degree of success with a comparatively small clientele.[28]

Women in the Field

An analysis of the child cases with a positive outcome shows project fieldworkers as effective intermediaries. The first school referral came from a school nurse – also a public health nurse – who asked Cosso to persuade the mother of a 14-year-old Italian girl whose deteriorating eyesight was affecting her studies to get her glasses. The nurse explained that she had been trying for two years to convince the mother to take her daughter to a nearby eye clinic for testing; each time the mother promised to consult a private doctor but did nothing, and then, on a follow-up call, insisted that her daughter was perfectly healthy – a classic strategy of evasion. It took two home visits and at least one phone call, but Cosso secured the mother's permission to make an appointment and escort the girl to the clinic for tests and then to pick up her prescription glasses.[29]

Given the huge gulf between Cosso, a well-educated urban Northerner who spoke the requisite "educated" Italian and the mother, a rural Southerner with little education and a regional dialect, Cosso's effective intervention in this case cannot be attributed solely to the women's shared Italian background. By this time, Cosso had visited 200 Italian and dozens of Portuguese households through the block-by-block home visits conducted during the project's first months,[30] and met yet more clients in the project's Branch Office. In the process, she had honed her skills. Her field notes indicate that, like other home visitors, she quickly applied distinguishing labels to the women she visited with such loaded phrases as "a typically southern peasant type" – as in "wearing a black handkerchief on her head" – or "a more educated" Calabrian or "better-educated northern type." She sized up clients with labels such as "uncommunicative" or "pleasant" as well as "messy house" or "newly repaired [house], clean inside and outside."[31]

Overall, however, the notes reveal that Cosso developed an effective professional style combining polite demeanour and firm diplomacy. Her notes on the block visits contain frequent references to the "friendly" or "very friendly reception" received from women (and a few men) who asked her to join them on the veranda or to come inside, and to visit again. She sometimes claimed that accepting such invitations kept her from meeting her daily quota of visits. As Cosso herself recognized, the women's reactions partially reflected their isolation and loneliness,[32] but they also spoke to her ability to establish a rapport with them. The positive outcome achieved in the school referral just described generated more requests and the agreement with the school boards, resulting in a few dozen Italian and Portuguese children getting their eyes, ears, tonsils, and chests treated.

More illuminating is the case of Mario, a 6-year-old Italian boy. His teacher had initiated the process following the parents' failure to make appointments the school nurse had booked with a clinic. Mario, her report reads, "appears to be neglected physically as well as emotionally," adding: "he has crossed eyes [but] his parents refuse to have them fixed," a "speech defect that requires a doctor's observation or diagnosis," and a problem with daytime wetting. Noting that both parents "work long hours," she concludes, "I think because of this complete neglect it is impossible for Mario to learn."[33]

Ferguson reported that Cosso was so instrumental in convincing Mario's initially hostile father to get him medical attention that she "had some difficulty refusing a gallon of wine, offered in gratitude" by the boy's mother, but left it at that. Cosso's field notes permit more telling observations. That she extracted far more information out of Mario's angry father than could the school nurse underscores her skills of persuasion. The details indicate that, contrary to the school's position, the father had not rejected their medical advice purely out of ignorance. He was initially hostile to Cosso and the nurse, reportedly repeating a rant delivered during an earlier visit about the teachers being preoccupied with "insignificant" matters. But he eventually explained that, as Cosso recorded it, "Mario, as a baby and toddler," had had serious problems, including "a nervous illness" and a severe seizure, but that, after spending "lots of money for doctors and specialists" in Naples, they were told he would grow up "completely normal."

The notes indicate, too, that Cosso persisted in efforts to persuade the father, who seemed better off financially than other clients, partly because she thought him overly concerned with saving money. "I had a hard time to convince Mr G. to have his son's eyes examined and then buy ... glasses," she writes, adding, he "is very stingy; has been in Canada for 5 years – never unemployed, wife working – a nice house and have rented the flat upstairs – have 3 sons between 14 and 5." Using the information extracted from the parents to convince the father to take the advice, Cosso persuaded him in stages, first coaxing him to have the child's eyes examined and then to buy the glasses. And then, in lieu of an eye operation on the impaired eye, which was diagnosed as a "lazy eye," she got him to agree to the doctor's plan "to place an eye-patch over the good eye, to force the lazy eye to work." As both parents worked full-time and spoke little English, Cosso arranged the appointments and accompanied the boy on his trips to the eye clinic attached to Toronto's Hospital for Sick Children. In the end, she felt professionally bound to refuse the offer by the mother – whose role in the negotiations is murky but not her gratitude – of homemade wine, though another staffer might have accepted the gift. The notes are silent, however, on the daytime wetting and speech defect.[34]

One of Montgomery's "successful" Portuguese cases also sheds light on the web of financial and health problems into which many of these families were ensnared. It involved an 8-year-old Portuguese boy who had returned to school after being a TB patient at the Gage Institute,[35] the downtown-based hospital and research centre of the National Sanatorium Association, but was attending only "very irregularly." When repeated notes to the parents, both of whom worked, "produced no results," the school nurse asked Branch staff for help. As Ferguson later informed her advisory committee, Montgomery quickly resolved the initial problem identified by convincing the mother, who had three other children in the same school and was pregnant with a fifth, to quit work so she could accompany her still recovering son to and from school. Like the concern over parental neglect due to a preoccupation with homeownership, a child's health trumped a mother's wage-earning.

Montgomery's entry into this household unveiled financial debts for what she critically described as the "new, expensive furniture and appliances" in the cramped flat as well as the father's frequent unemployment, medical debts owing to an inability to maintain hospital insurance payments – a common problem – and late family allowance cheques.[36] Her follow-up visits reveal, too, that the money and health problems were intertwined, and compounded by a failure to meet follow-up medical appointments. Ferguson attributed the positive outcomes to Montgomery's skills of observation and persuasion, and her ability to build trust with the woman through a series of incremental measures, each of which met a specific need. Montgomery, she reports, escorted mother and son to their appointment for a check-up and impressed upon the woman "the importance of not missing any more check-ups" and of ensuring that her son took his medication.[37]

We do not know whether the mother followed Montgomery's advice, but the field notes track her observational skills and quick response rate. Noticing that the woman herself "urgently needed medical attention," she arranged an appointment and escorted her to a pre-natal clinic soon after the boy's check-up appointment. That she reportedly "promised" to call the clinic to verify that the woman attended it suggests as well that fieldworkers' efforts at persuasion could include threats. Just days after the baby clinic appointment, Montgomery returned to the woman's home with (used) children's clothing from the Institute and a private charity. With some phone calls, she solved the mystery of the missing mother's allowance cheques – the family had moved but not sent a forwarding address. Project staff attributed this problem, also a common one, to the precarious housing of these immigrants, who moved frequently in search of lower rents or, in the case of large families, more accommodating landlords, or as part of kin-linked home ownership strategies.

By providing support for an immigrant boy and his mother at moments of acute need, Montgomery gained the woman's trust. No doubt, the shared language helped, but it alone could not have erased the complex dynamics shaping an exchange between a well-educated woman from Rio de Janeiro and a poorly educated Portuguese woman from the impoverished Azores. While Ferguson hoped that Montgomery's Brazilian origins rendered her politically neutral to her Portuguese clients, she enjoyed a superior class position and more refined urban style than they did. However such factors played out, Montgomery crossed several divides in order to gain the woman's confidence, with positive consequences for her sick son and other children. The result is significant even if Ferguson was right to suspect that the family needed long-term financial counselling.[38]

Zelonka's field notes further illuminate the staff's liaison role, as well as the tangled web of financial and health problems uncovered. Several of her Italian cases underscore the well-documented observation that even when poverty does not directly "cause" ill health, it contributes to it and complicates treatment and recovery. One of them involved Carmella, an Italian girl whose guidance counsellor thought she was recovering far too slowly from an appendix operation: several months later, she still complained about frequent headaches. He requested a visit to Carmella's family – described as "proud [but] poor" with a "poor" diet – partly, it appears, because he did not entirely believe the girl, about whom he wrote: "her head always hurts when the teacher gives her work to do."[39] Zelonka's comments on the first visit begin on a negative note: "the house is very poor and shows the need for repairing" [and] "is not neetly (sic) kept," and the bedroom where the mother was dressing her three younger children "was smelling" (soiled diapers perhaps). But the tone turns decidedly sympathetic as she relays her conversation with the woman, whom she describes as polite but anxious about her daughter's spiralling health problems. Carmella underwent an emergency operation to deal with an attack of appendicitis, but developed an infected peritoneum, a dangerous condition, which required a second operation. The second operation resulted in a hernia, also very painful.[40]

In just one visit, this worker extracted critical medical information that school personnel failed to obtain despite having previously met the family. Clearly moved by the mother's own obviously poor health and her dire situation, Zelonka reported that Mrs S., at age 30, already had lost a child to ill health in Italy. In addition, she was struggling to raise six young children, including another daughter recovering from an operation (to remove her tonsils), on her husband's low wages and while carrying monthly mortgage payments. Social workers criticized parents who placed family finances over children's health (see Chapter 6). However, Zelonka interpreted the women's repeated requests for clothing, food, and a job at home sewing garments as the acts of a mother desperate to ensure her children's health even while she and her husband evidently placed the family in a financially risky situation by buying a house. Zelonka's notes record her efforts to meet the woman's requests, including monitoring the sick daughter, though we do not know whether she found the woman some paid work. An acculturated Eastern European woman of urban middle-class origins, Zelonka similarly crossed several divides to connect with this (and other) Southern European women of peasant origins who appreciated the material support and the concern shown towards their children's well-being.[41]

While a capacity for patience and persuasion combined with a strategy of "meeting immigrants at the point of need" could produce positive outcomes, other factors also mattered. One was the willingness of mothers to accept the advice or assistance offered. Historical analyses of working-class and immigrant women's interactions with dispensers of public health suggest that a shared concern over children's health explains why disadvantaged mothers wary of middle-class "intruders" could be receptive to health professionals without becoming passive targets of the medical establishment. The cases under scrutiny similarly suggest that poor immigrant mothers – and some fathers – were willing to tolerate some outside intrusion when a child's health was at stake.[42] Anxious, exhausted, and repeatedly pregnant, the mothers of five, six, and even twelve children thus initiated additional contacts with a health project fieldworker who not only spoke their language and shared a national origin or immigrant status but provided concrete aid.[43]

A referral to interpret for an Italian mother enrolling her daughter in a downtown "school for retarded children" suggests that serendipity could also play a role. Shortly after Cosso accompanied the "very nervous" mother to the school, she phoned about delivering some second-hand clothing. She reportedly found the woman "distraught" over a call she had just received from the hospital to which she had been referred for "psychiatric treatment" telling her to come in that evening. Evidently seeking help for her mental anguish, the woman was in a panic because her husband was still at work and there was no one to watch the children. Cosso booked a worker with the Visiting Homemaker's Association for that evening and the next day, and accompanied the woman to her hospital visits. As Ferguson noted, Cosso's timely intervention happened by accident, but met a critical need (though we do not know about the treatments). It also underscored the value of follow-up calls and visits.[44]

The art of persuasion could also mask more conspiratorial behaviour. A case in point involved a 14-year-old Italian boy admitted to the city's psychiatric hospital on Queen Street. When the parents informed hospital authorities that they were pulling him out because he was "improving" and they were returning to Italy, the hospital called the Branch Office. Cosso informed the boy's principal and visited the parents to try to convince them to have the boy tested in order to determine the state of his health. When the couple's plan was delayed because the husband took ill, Cosso persuaded the wife to accompany her and the son to the hospital for tests. In summarizing the case in *Newcomers in Transition*, Ferguson wrote with approval that, at the time of Cosso's last visit, the boy was at home "under the care of the family doctor and receiving what medication he needs." But the parents had clearly been treated in a heavy-handed manner.[45]

Also revealing are the cases that ended without a positive outcome. Immigrant parents could be wary of any school or Institute intervention, but the cases that failed to secure an intended outcome (28 per cent), as opposed to those that contain scant information (37 per cent), differed from the ones described above in two main respects. First, most were cases initiated by requests to investigate a child's poor attendance or performance at school. School officials dealing with a truant or underperforming student required the visiting nurse to be more inquisitorial in her dealings with the parent(s), putting the interpreting fieldworker into the unenviable position of delivering the school's stern warning. Cosso did as much to the parents of a boy who, it turned out, was missing a lot of school because the father, an injured construction worker, was using him as an interpreter in his dealings with medical and welfare officials. The parents' plight might well have elicited some sympathy, but this couple's reported failure to heed earlier warnings against taking the boy out of school prompted school authorities to threaten court action, with Cosso the messenger. The encounter did not go well, though she tried to soften the blow by telling the father, a repeat client whom she knew, to instead call her when he was "in difficulty."[46] Montgomery and Zelonka issued similar warnings to parents, though, as in the case just described, the outcome is not recorded.[47]

Second, a handful of "failed" cases involved fieldworkers tasked with persuading an "anxious" and "exhausted" mother to place an intellectually disabled child in a special school or institution usually located a few hours outside Toronto. A few mothers initially agreed to the advice, but all but one of these cases were unresolved. Significantly, the exception involved registering a girl in a city boarding school.[48]

Occupational Training, 1964–8

The Institute's special educational project (1964–6), like the related vocational-training pilot projects that preceded and followed it, reflected the premise that encouraging the "potential talent" in the "rural labour pool" through educational measures would meet two key objectives: filling Canada's need for skilled workers and gaining better economic prospects for the immigrants. A concern over the vulnerability of low-skilled foreign workers, and the burden that mass unemployment would impose on the state, was fuelled as well by anxiety over growing automation. As liberal integrationists, Ferguson and colleagues also viewed skills-building as a means by which the "unskilled," a category that was sometimes applied to semi-skilled and even skilled immigrants,[49] could become working-class citizens of worth.[50] In a more condescending fashion, Ferguson also described the goal as getting people for whom the "idea of overcoming unemployment by education and retraining is a foreign one" into English instruction and skills-upgrading courses.[51]

In targeting Greeks as well as Italians and Portuguese, the education project had a wide territorial reach that included the largest immigrant Greek community in the city's east end and the smaller one in the west end. It also included the Italians living in northern suburbs and in the city's east end, as well as in the largest community based in the west end, where most of the Portuguese lived. Besides the Institute and local schools that provided English classes for immigrants, the project drew on the provincial training institutes, adult training centres, and commercial high schools across the metropolitan area. The community in this community project, then, did not approximate an ethnic neighbourhood, but instead encompassed workers belonging to certain vulnerable immigrant communities and resources spread across a wide urban territory. Male workers were privileged on the grounds that, given existing inequities in wage rates, improving a man's earnings proportionally produced the greatest benefit for the family.

Once again recruiting from the targeted communities, the Institute hired three male fieldworkers. Frank Colantonio was a Southern Italian, but no longer a peasant or greenhorn. In his fourteen years in Canada, he had amassed what Ferguson described as "considerable experience working with his fellow countrymen" in Toronto, first as a union organizer and then as director of the

Italian Immigrant Aid Society (IIAS), which supplied many of the Institute's Italian-speaking volunteers. As a carpenter, he had played a leadership role in the construction strikes of the early 1960s to organize the Italian-dominated residential construction sector. His IIAS post had given him practical experience in social service work, but he did not have any social work credentials. Colantonio was hired for his organizing and recruitment skills, but he was also expected to help with sorting out the confusing array of federal and provincial training programs and with lobbying the educational authorities.[52]

At the time of his hiring, the Greek fieldworker Nicholas Georgakopoulos had been in Canada for only one year, but spoke good English. With a doctorate in international law, he differed markedly from his compatriots, but Ferguson thought his own experience with unemployment, in his case owing to Ontario's strict professional accreditation rules, sensitized him to the issues involved. She also described him as "very interested in this type of work."[53] It took longer to find a bilingual Portuguese worker, but Jorge Fernandes joined the staff a few weeks into the project, initially to conduct evening interviews and then as full-time staff. A four-year resident of Canada with a "business training" background, Fernandes likely hailed from mainland Portugal. Building trust with newcomers would again be essential, not least because determining eligibility for a program meant asking potentially embarrassing personal questions, and Fernandes' good command of English and reported "interest" in the Portuguese community got him hired. Because of the many Italian immigrants, the project also hired an Italian-speaking secretary, Cora Gentile, who doubled as an Italian interviewer in the Institute's Branch Office.[54] Ferguson again threw herself into the job and Gentile handled a large caseload, so the educational project also bore the imprint of women's pluralist activism.

Once again, Ferguson attributed the stated problem, which in this case was the rural immigrant's low occupational profile, to a combination of their "special cultural characteristics" and the factors blocking access to resources. But there was also a major twist. Instead of an emphasis on immigrant underuse of more or less adequate services, Ferguson's final report, *Newcomers and New Learning*, concluded that the immigrants, given the opportunity and some encouragement, showed a clear interest in improving their job skills, but that the facilities were wholly "inadequate" and utterly "unsuitable" to the demanding task at hand.[55]

Although Ferguson and staffer Georgakopoulos interviewed Greek immigrants and "community contacts" (such as club presidents and journalists) for the project, *Newcomers and New Learning* offers few details about them beyond regional origins and residency patterns. Reiterating her group portrait of Southern Europeans, Ferguson stressed that in the Greek stream there was a preponderance of impoverished peasants with centuries-old habits and customs nurtured in rural villages that, apart from the recent introduction of electricity, were cut off from the modern world.[56] As with the Italians and Portuguese, the family work ethic explained a lack of interest in the wider society. A similar obsession with achieving economic security through home ownership similarly increased indebtedness and sacrificed educational pathways to improved income earning. Among the few differences noted was that newly arrived Greeks, like Italians, were somewhat better off than their Portuguese counterparts because they could at least find jobs with entrepreneurial compatriots in the restaurant and construction industries, respectively. (No reference is made to exploitation.) In explaining the absence of education beyond elementary schooling as the predominant pattern among all three groups, Ferguson noted the absence of secondary schools in Southern Europe's remote rural villages and the family's inability to pay for boarding schools, but also an ingrained sense that education was the preserve of prominent people.[57] Only much later does she note that, while still in a minority, there was a larger number of skilled workers in the Greek as compared to the Italian and Portuguese streams.[58]

Ferguson highlighted the sojourning mentality that led many young men to view vocational training as "a waste of time." Many a young Manuel, Giuseppe, and Constantinos, she wrote, was lured by the stories of home-owning relatives who return home bearing expensive gifts into embarking on a temporary sojourn in Canada. Finding themselves "exhilarated by the new experience of accumulating material possessions" and becoming "accustomed to modern conveniences," and seeing their children growing up Canadian and their relatives joining them, they end up remaining in Canada. But having taken "no interest" in learning English or "vocational skills" because they did not expect to stay, they found that by the time they decided to remain, as most did, they were forever stuck in exploitative jobs.[59]

The argument was based in reality, though Ferguson and her Portuguese staffer Fernandes perhaps exaggerated the extent of the phenomenon. Many Southern Europeans were temporary guest workers in post-1945 Europe, but a majority of those who left their impoverished villages for North America intended to settle permanently. More specifically, while proportionally more Portuguese mainlanders may have possessed a sojourner mentality, including young couples, the Azoreans generally moved for good to North America, where they also had family ties. Fernandes may have overgeneralized from interviews with mainlanders. Ferguson probably had more contact with mainlanders, who dominated the secular organizations and who were more explicit about being "Portuguese." As Gilberto Fernandes notes, Azoreans were at this time on the margins of the so-called Portuguese community.[60]

Front-Line Recruiters

Ferguson again applauded her staff as conscientious people who showed "understanding and good judgement" in the field, though the lack of archived fieldwork notes for the education project makes an in-depth analysis difficult. Still, the related materials offer glimpses into the men's front-line activities, including their persistence in the face of indifferent officials. Particularly frustrating was the school board officials' initial resistance to increasing the number of state-subsidized English classes, particularly in the schools in the east end and suburbs, by holding nighttime classes during the spring and summer months when the schools normally closed down their nightly programs. Ferguson wrote that when officials were told about new arrivals keen to take classes in the spring and summer of 1964, they said the prospective students could simply wait until the fall and then learn English within a mere six months, a response she attributed to indifference and ignorance.[61]

Perseverance sometimes paid off, however. Two months of lobbying, for instance, convinced the Ontario Citizenship Division (OCD), which administered the English classes, to allow project staff to interview Portuguese and Italian men already enrolled in six-week accelerated ("crash") English courses being held in two west end high schools so as to assess the level of interest in trade-training. The staff would also determine the type of support needed (as in collecting documents and writing referral letters). Buoyed by the results that a majority of the 1,514 interviewed, most of them young men in low-skilled outdoor jobs and factories,[62] were interested in skills training, project staff persuaded the Toronto School Board (TSB) to open additional summer classes in a number of downtown schools and community centres. The 3,600 students enrolled in classes during summer 1965 represented an increase of 125 per cent from the 1,600 enrolled in summer 1963, with Italians far outnumbering Portuguese and Greeks.[63] The east end remained poorly served, however, in part, claimed Ferguson, because of a failure to place English classes in a community centre located along the main thoroughfare of the Greek community on Danforth Avenue. Another sticking point – the shortage of teachers due to the TSB policy of requiring night-school teachers to come from the regular daytime teaching staff – took longer to address. Throughout the education project, field staff repeated a time-consuming strategy of convincing school authorities to offer a course on the condition of meeting a per-class quota and then recruiting the students.

The project's collaboration with COSTI, whose own motto was "integration through education," led to additional "crash" English courses being offered downtown and to their appearance in the suburbs. COSTI now operated from the west end mansion formerly owned by the Italian government, which set up offices for the delivery of certain services for immigrants and allowed COSTI to use the rest of the premises for free.[64] Colantonio initiated the alliance with COSTI in early summer 1964, after failing to sign up enough Italians (100) for a proposed English program. He passed on his list of 45 registrants to COSTI staff, who secured the permission to run a pilot experiment of ten-week "crash"

English courses for Portuguese as well as Italians. News of the courses spread and the final 140 recruits were divided into seven classes. The four Italian classes were held at COSTI and the three Portuguese ones, which included some Spanish students, at the Institute. Student interest remained strong, with average attendance estimated at almost 78 per cent, even as "work conditions," such as shift work and seasonal hires, interrupted attendance. Suggesting the collaboration offered a model for further efforts, Ferguson attributed its success to several factors, including good-quality teachers and the special attention given the students. (The students were registered by staff and volunteers from their own ethnic group and received follow-up calls when they missed class.) She also noted the informal atmosphere of the classes (the immigrants being "intimidated" by public buildings), the four-night (rather than usual two-night) format, and classes devoted to one language group.[65]

Colantonio now referred all Italian requests for downtown courses to COSTI while he focused on the suburbs. School administrators initially opposed creating classes for the growing number of suburban immigrants who could not make it to downtown night classes after work because they preferred the efficiency of holding several "grading" classes in the larger downtown schools, which also allowed for easier readjustment of classes when drop-outs occurred. Again, persistence paid off. After securing the approval of the Ontario Citizenship Division to recruit students for intensive English courses in North York during 1965, on the condition that teachers as well as students could be found, Colantonio persuaded the North York Board of Education to provide the classroom space at a local high school.

Working through clubs, schools, and worksites, Colantonio's recruitment efforts among Italians exceeded expectations, though the expected Greek recruits did not materialize. (The mistaken assumption that many Greeks had also moved into the area is perplexing.) At one point, the 147 mostly Italian students registered into four classes recorded "exceptionally good" retention rates considering the disruptions caused by shift work and summer holidays. Most students lived or worked nearby, including the restaurant dishwasher who played the accordion at the closing exercises. A few took advantage of the summer rule that let them bring their children to class, including the father of an attentive Italian girl whose mother was taking a power-sewing course (see below). Still later came what Ferguson considered a milestone, the first English classes for new Canadians held in North York during the spring term. Colantonio repeated these efforts in York Township, another area of growing Italian concentration, at one point registering some 300 students (90 per cent Italian) into classes held at a local school, again with good retention rates. All this represented modest but important inroads into immigrant suburbia, particularly North York, which was quickly becoming the municipality with the largest concentration of immigrants in Canada.[66]

Ferguson concluded that "many more immigrants" (perhaps in the few thousands) were attending English classes as a result of the Institute education project. The Italians led, but more Portuguese and Greeks, who were still more concentrated in the city, were also taking English classes, though usually in downtown classes with more mixed populations.[67] Still, the recorded results, which, curiously, did not include some of the 1966 enrolments, were uneven and the numbers modest relative to immigrant totals. Even Ferguson spoke in terms of a constructive beginning rather than stellar results, and noted continuing challenges, such as the confusion caused by the grading systems. Welcoming the TSB's decision to allow teachers other than their own to teach English as a second language (ESL), she argued that many educated people, including immigrants and housewives who were once teachers, could ably fill the role.[68]

Trade Courses

The limited funds, confusing array of regulations, and continuing immigration from Southern Europe explain the education project's poor results among "unskilled" men with little experience outside farming or fishing. The supporting legislation was Programme Five (P5) of the Federal-Provincial Technical and Vocational Agreement (FPTVA), which provided courses for retraining unemployed persons over sixteen years of age who had been out of school for at least one year. One had to be referred by the National Employment Service (NES), pass a health exam, and meet a residency requirement. There was a modest training allowance and some job counselling. The one-year course, which was meant to prepare students for a qualifying exam for entry into an apprenticeship program or for entry into one of the less demanding trades, consisted of two parts. The Phase I English course, which included some Canadian civics or citizenship content, was taught in several locales, while the Phase 2 course, on English trade terminology, took place at one of the adult education centres and certain technical schools.[69] Project staff welcomed the reduction in the Canadian residency requirement, from six months to one, that came midway through the project, but it did not improve the poor results, which were largely due to the low subsidies and the men's need to earn money immediately. Also, those among the growing number of undocumented Portuguese arrivals after 1961 would have avoided contact with officialdom out of fear of being deported.[70]

Branch staff did marginally better with an alternative program that offered short-term credit courses in such trades as welding, electronics, and machine shop as well as in bricklaying and carpentry. Colantonio referred interested Italians, many of whom were learning building-related trades informally on construction sites, to COSTI, which was already providing these courses. Italian recruitment for machine shop courses was disappointing, however, especially in the east end.[71] There were far fewer Portuguese than Greeks in the trades overall and fewer Portuguese than Italians with respect to the building trades. Like the later-arriving Portuguese, Italians faced hostile Canadian unions, but they also benefited from their larger numbers and recent organizing drives. Heavily disadvantaged, the Portuguese fieldworker Fernandes usually failed to secure enough Portuguese recruits to meet the quota required for a given trade course. A partial exception was welding, which Ferguson attributed to her misplaced sojourning thesis. She argued that because welding was one of the "simpler trades," and one that drew the "highest reward for the least effort," even some of the sojourning-oriented men could be convinced to take a welding course.

The education project's best results occurred among Greek immigrant tradesmen who needed to pass the Ontario qualifying exam in order to legally practise their trade in Canada. Many of them could not meet the minimum entry requirements for an apprenticeship in the certified trades, which, in most cases, was Grade 10. A "skills upgrading" (or pre-licensing) course in English and a given trade was supposed to remedy the problem and prepare graduates for the exam. Those with trade certificates from home and documented work experience in their trade could opt to simply write the qualifying exam, which was in English, with the help of an interpreter so long as "he" was not in the trade. The use of relatives unfamiliar with the trade terminology or multiple-question format meant many failures, however, hence the emphasis on a skills-upgrading or pre-licensing course.[72]

Following COSTI's lead, project staff lobbied to hire a bilingual instructor for the courses they helped to establish. Under this initially controversial arrangement, the instructor taught the subject in English, but students could communicate with him in their own language. Most of the tradesmen who enrolled in the pre-licensing courses were Greeks, followed by Italians. The project records highlight the role of the Greek fieldworker Georgakopoulos. Having convinced the provincial institutes of trade to approve a number of short-term pre-licensing courses, he recruited a credentialed tradesman who qualified as the bilingual instructor. The training school paid his salary. The student registration fee of $20 for the twenty-week course helped to cover the cost of teaching a machine-based course. The minimum quota for each class was twelve to fifteen students of the same language group. Upon completing the requisite course(s), the candidate was expected to sit the licensing exam and, if successful, fulfil the "Canadian experience" requirement of three years in order to attain the final certificate.[73]

Georgakopoulos' recruiting efforts were bolstered by a spike during 1963 in the number of Greek men arriving in Canada as open-placement (skilled) workers following a period of time spent working in Germany. In sixteen months, he registered 229 Greek men into fourteen classes, mainly for electricians and auto mechanics. Some classes were composed entirely of secondary-school graduates. In several cases, however, he came up shy of the target.[74]

Georgakopoulos' persistence in the face of limited classroom space and the continuing indifference of school officials is noteworthy. In February 1965, for example, he had signed up enough auto mechanics for a pre-licensing course, only to be told no space was available at the Provincial Institute of Automotive and Allied Trades. Since auto mechanics were reportedly in short supply, he hustled to find another space at Danforth Technical School in the east end, securing it until the end of March, when the night schools closed. He also found a "well-qualified" bilingual mechanic to teach the class. Then, when the school closed after five weeks, he turned to COSTI for space, but without funds to pay the instructor, they declined. When, six months later, space opened up at a provincial institute of trade, he called up the men. But only a few wanted to complete the course. Most of those contacted had tried but failed the exam and did not want to try again because they were busy working in order to support their families. A handful of the men had learned enough English to enrol in a unilingual (English) upgrading course, however, and they were expected to graduate soon after the project ended.[75]

The school administrators' continuing unease over bypassing the regular English-speaking instructors for bilingual tradesmen also meant requests or requirements that the courses incorporate some regular English instruction.[76] The rule was not strictly followed, but Ferguson criticized the underlying assumption that instruction in "one's native language" delayed the English-learning process and perpetuated the existence of foreign-language groups whose presence endangered Canadian unity. She added that the economy could not wait for workers to first learn English and then upgrade their skills. Articulating a principle of adult education, that of building good citizenship, she noted, too, that those prompted to learn English for concrete reasons were more likely to learn faster and, as newly minted skilled workers, to make a greater contribution to Canadian society and be happier members and stronger supporters of its values.[77]

Women Workers

The pilot projects aimed at improving women's occupational skills began while the health and welfare project was in effect and they involved both the permanent counsellors at the main Institute and the female field staff based at the Institute's Branch Office. The projects focused on industrial-sewing courses for Italians and Portuguese, and skills-upgrading (or pre-licensing) courses for Greek hairdressers. Ferguson did not lead but rather participated in one of these projects. Noteworthy is her insight into the high rates of workforce participation among these rural women: "Going out to work is a new experience for most of them although many were accustomed to working in the fields at farm work." Later, feminist historians would similarly argue that these women's wage-earning, while "new," reflected a transplanted family work ethic that required the labour of all its members.[78] But here, too, we find patronizing commentary.

The Institute described the 1962 pilot project to "upgrade" Italian and Portuguese women's sewing skills through a ten-week P5 course providing instruction in English and power-sewing machines as "a pet project" of Mrs J.S. (Margaret) Hill. An IODE volunteer with the main Institute's reception centre, Hill had joined the Institute board and would sit on the education project's advisory committee. The pilot project also represented a victory for the Institute, which had lobbied city councillors and school officials to support the venture for more than a year. Ferguson and her staff became involved with the early recruitment and training.[79] A NES referral was required, but there were no educational or English requirements, and, initially, an interpreter was based in the classroom. One of the adult training centres agreed to teach classes of twenty-five students and oversee their placement in a factory. The modest daily stipend ranged from $3 for single women living with parents to $6 for married women whose husbands earned less than $6 per week.[80]

The course combined some citizenship training with aiding women familiar with hand-sewing and embroidery, including those who had worked in the "textile industries of Europe," but whose unfamiliarity with "modern" power-sewing and buttonhole machines was "holding them back." The course was also expected to facilitate an engagement with modernity, by introducing the women to Canadian (imperial) measurements, the Canadian Bill of Rights (1960), the Ontario minimum wage law, and "a little mathematics" as well as English instruction and the "different operations for making a complete garment."[81]

The Institute's "permanent" female counsellors assigned to the project recruited students through their client lists. The Branch Office female staff did so through their ethnic networks, but particularly through the churches rather than the male-dominated ethnic clubs and media outlets. Both groups escorted women to the NES office. Together, Branch Office staff, the Italian- and Portuguese-speaking permanent counsellors, and some reception centre volunteers ran the orientation session at the main Institute building. They interpreted for the "Anglo" female NES staff, assisted with the P5 applications, and explained the course materials translated by yet other volunteers. They escorted the students to the training centre for eight weeks of classroom instruction and then to the factory for a two-week placement. The six-hour class was divided between English-language and sewing instruction. The in-class interpreter was removed after a few weeks on the grounds that instruction could be given by demonstration. (In a patronizing manner, Ferguson enthused about the women learning such basic phrases as "This is my foot. This is the treadle. I put my foot on the treadle.") Night classes were later added to the daytime schedule, and the course was expanded to sixteen weeks, the last two still in a factory. The placements would have involved negotiations with the garment unions, but nothing is said about them beyond noting that NES staff quickly assumed from them the responsibility for overseeing the factory placement.[82]

Ferguson claimed that the 1962 power-sewing project enabled the women to make a much smoother transition to paid work than would have otherwise been possible. Their experience as better-trained workers, she added, would make them "more independent, more self-confident and more capable of becoming self-supporting Canadian citizens" as well as more informed mothers of children growing up in Canada.[83] The claims, while exaggerated, were not untrue. The interim reports highlight the valuable liaison role that Branch fieldworker Montgomery played among the Portuguese women. Because Portuguese women found it more difficult than their Italian counterparts to access an Institute counsellor who spoke their language – several multilingual counsellors spoke Italian while fewer spoke Portuguese – they gravitated to Montgomery. In handling their requests, which included convincing husbands to let them attend evening classes, Montgomery, noted Ferguson, came "to know the women intimately." The ties that she cultivated likely had some positive effect on the women.[84]

Other details challenge Ferguson's rosy portrait of the program even while underscoring her respect for immigrant women workers dismissed by many as transient wage-earners. The information gathered on about sixty of the (mostly married) women who were employed in some capacity a few months after completing the course revealed that one-third of them had left their sewing posts, mostly for "family" reasons (pregnancy, childcare), and then returned to low-paid jobs in factories or as cleaners in private homes and hospitals. Ferguson understood the garment industry's reliance on the cheap labour of immigrant women. She also generally supported unions, though she rarely criticized the employers or encouraged union certification campaigns. Ferguson emphasized the need to improve the wage levels in these jobs on the (correct) grounds that many of these women would become lifelong workers with recurring interruptions due to family demands, but she basically instructed her staff to persuade the women to be patient and wait for increases as a result of improved work or union contracts.[85]

The women, however, complained and protested with their feet. The first group of factory trainees complained about the hourly wage (65 cents, the minimum wage) being "considerably lower" than expected, and about a dozen of them left their placement despite promises of wage increases once their work improved. Some of them landed better-paying factory jobs or earned more money through the informal economy, whether at house-cleaning jobs, the preferred choice, or stoop labour, picking worms or carrots. Ferguson attributed the better track record among the second group of recruits to the training instructors possessing a better understanding than the unions of the trainees' individual capabilities (to sew a whole garment or conduct a routine job). But the better wages offered as a result of the earlier walkouts and an increase in the minimum wage – which now ranged between 75 cents and $1.10 per hour – also mattered. Even then, however, some women had left their posts. They included a former dressmaker from Italy, supporting an unemployed husband and teenagers, who landed a job in a canning factory that paid ten cents more than her sewing job, and urged others to join her. Others, like the woman who quit because the trouser-sewing machine was "too heavy," protested the working conditions. That only one woman said she quit because of her husband's disapproval underscores the critical wage-earning role of Southern European women in postwar Toronto and Canada.[86]

The recruitment rate improved with the reduction of the residency requirement in 1965, from six months to one, but problems with attendance and dropouts and a lack of classroom space continued. Staff noted many repeat referrals to a course.[87] Having assumed full responsibility for the pilot project in 1963, the Institute's permanent counsellors continued to recruit for power-sewing courses until 1968. By then, perhaps a few hundred women had signed up for the course, though some of them would not have completed it. As their organizations would articulate beginning in the 1970s, working-class immigrant women wanted skills training that did not interfere with their family obligations in order to better contribute to their family's well-being. As the legal dependants of male sponsors (usually their husbands), many also wished to achieve a degree of economic independence, or recognition, as important wage-earners. The P5 program offered one of the few state-funded resources that they, as dependants, could tap. Still, a sober reminder that success did not eliminate financial worry is the handful of files in my Institute database of women who returned to the Institute after securing a garment job through the P5 program and still needed part-time work in order to augment a still-inadequate income.[88]

Greek women dominated the final pilot project, in 1968, to provide skills-upgrading (pre-licensing) courses for immigrant hairdressers. Ferguson was gone by this point, but the project deserves attention as it was the only one to target skilled Southern European women. Its launch followed a similar project involving tradesmen mounted a year earlier in response to two related issues. The first was the high rate of failure on the qualifying exams. The second was the widespread practice among those who had earned their Provisional Certificate of Qualification (PCQ) upon completing a skills-upgrading course of putting off the qualifying exam indefinitely despite having met the three-year Canadian experience requirement.[89] Recruiting efforts focused not only on those with soon-to-expire PCQ certificates (blue cards) who needed "to cram" for the exam, but also those with more time to study on the grounds that, unless pushed, they would keep postponing the exam. It was clear from early on that the women's project was far more successful than the previous male program. The first two hairdressing courses offered in spring 1969 reportedly showed "excellent results." The pass rate for the first class of thirteen students was 77 per cent with dropouts, not failures, accounting for the losses; the figure for the second class of nineteen was 84 per cent. The additional classes brought the total number of women enrolled in the course to about fifty.[90]

Ferguson attributed the program's general success to the fewer "traditional" restrictions placed on the public movement of Greek women as compared to their Italian and Portuguese counterparts. The assertion downplayed the former's employment in family businesses with built-in chaperones (though that did not necessarily protect them from exploitation), and the factory and nighttime cleaning work performed by Italian and Portuguese women, respectively.[91] Still, Greek women dominated the category of Southern European skilled women in my Institute database, and the one dozen cases created on those enrolled in a pre-licensing hairdressing course involved mainly young women, both single (4) and married (8), in their late twenties and early thirties with a highschool or technical school training in hairdressing. Some of them may have gone to the city to train while others may have lived in larger rural towns that allowed them to apprentice in the trade. The cases show counsellors carrying out their duties, which included making follow-up calls. When one course graduate could not write the exam because she fell "very sick," her Greek female counsellor immediately provided the "official letter" of explanation required to arrange a new date. The client passed the exam and landed a position. Another positive outcome involved a single woman who registered in the course thinking her credentials (Grade 9 and one year of hairdressing school) were insufficient – the formal Ontario requirement was Grade 10 – but was told to try the exam anyway. She was exempted from the course on the strength of her test results and then awarded a licence because she already met the Canadian experience requirement. The negative outcomes involved women who lacked sufficient English to qualify for or to finish a course or whose training was disrupted by pregnancy or illness.[92]

The Institute's involvement with vocational training for immigrants ended in 1969, when a new Ontario Training Act shifted responsibility to George Brown College, a community college, and some technical schools. While its decidedly uneven efforts ultimately affected a tiny minority of the rural Southern European "labour pool" (perhaps a few thousand), Ferguson's anecdotal references to formerly unskilled men and women who expressed pride in their new status as skilled worker suggests that, for the beneficiaries, the impact of the English and skills-training courses was significant, both psychologically and economically.

Despite the criticism often made about vocational education creating a preparation in second-class citizenship among young people,[93] Ferguson's positive assessment fits with recent analyses of occupational training among new adult immigrants, namely, that it can empower marginalized workers and improve their income. But qualifications are in order. The power-sewing courses aimed to modestly improve women's wages, not to liberate them from the exploitative garment sector. Also, as workers whose wage-earning trajectory was shaped in large part by family priorities, most women may not have enrolled in long-term courses.[94]

Conclusion

As short-term community integration projects, the Institute's health and welfare project enjoyed comparatively more success than the education project. Both projects traded in rural stereotypes, though the profiles drawn contained some truth. Both also exposed the obstacles blocking access to resources, though as Ferguson noted, the adult vocational training sector of the educational system was particularly "derelict" in meeting its responsibility to provide educational opportunities for immigrants, who were taxpayers too.[95]

More generally, the projects demonstrate the value of community-based pluralist strategies in which immigrants with some links to the communities being served played active roles on the front lines. Equally important was the gender match or near-match between staff and clients. During the health project, fieldworkers like Cosso exhibited a capacity for empathy, though some entries do have a whiff of head-shaking pity about them. They might use guilt-inducing tactics with mothers in order to get children medical help, but the positive outcomes also indicate the importance of the basic respect they showed parents. Generally, so too did Ferguson, who wrote that the findings revealed parents who "have the welfare of their children very much at heart," but who were too caught up in the struggle to survive, or too uninformed, to access resources. Even allowing for exaggeration, the field notes generally support Ferguson's claim that her female staff "possessed the qualities of understanding, sympathy and tact so necessary for dealing with people," and applied "good common sense to the problems presented." Curiously, she did not comment on their capacity for empathy, the trait considered critical to effective social work.[96] The (vocational) education project and the pilot projects in occupational training faced stiffer challenges than the health project, including intransigent school officials, long distances, and a longer investment of time. But the available evidence confirms the value of using front-line staff from the immigrants' own national, or ethnic and linguistic, group to increase immigrant utilization of social services and educational resources.

In this regard, the projects validate the Institute's bridge-building pluralism as well as Ferguson's recommendations, which included language training for

Canadian social service personnel (something the Institute began doing at this time) and large-scale recruitment of educated and capable immigrant women and men with the language skills and knowledge of "the background of the immigrants whom they serve."[97] Applying the flexibility exhibited in the projects as well as support for professional women forced to retire upon marriage, Ferguson recommended hiring married women whose jobs had offered a training in "human relations," such as teaching and nursing as well as social work, as front-line workers in the administration of health and welfare services to immigrants.

As for vocational training, Ferguson emphasized the necessity of placing the whole adult education system on a more professional standing with an expanded network of counselling services staffed by trained multilingual personnel. She called for an increase in the number of year-round training classes and P5 courses and in the number of bilingual tradesmen hired as instructors. In addition to higher stipends, she recommended that more of the qualifying exams be set in the student's "native" language, and that more funds be directed to specialized teacher training in ESL. Meanwhile, the severe shortage of qualified ESL teachers could be met by hiring housewives who were former teachers and educated immigrants. (She noted that the best ESL teacher at present was an Iranian man, but did not elaborate.)[98] Appreciating the impossibility of ensuring that front-line workers always matched the cultural background of their immigrant clientele, Ferguson stressed the importance of striving towards that goal on several grounds, including the prospect that future immigrants "may come from cultures much more alien than those of European rural immigrants."[99]

All these recommendations generally align with today's multicultural approaches to the provision of health and welfare services and English instruction and vocational training for immigrants. They call for counsellors to undertake "multicultural training" that will provide them with a knowledge of the immigrant clients' cultural values and practices, and to possess the multilingual skills to communicate effectively with them. The contemporary social science literature rarely refers to past experiments using anything resembling such approaches in the city or nation being studied, including for Canada.[100] Research into the Institute's community projects and pilot projects partly redresses this historical amnesia by documenting a longer history of community-building approaches to social services and education for immigrants.

The merits of the approach should not be exaggerated, however. For one thing, it took an enormous amount of staff time to carry out project duties, whether visiting homes, escorting children to clinics or women to the NES, or travelling to the suburbs to pitch English or training proposals to school officials. So much so that the Institute board wondered, particularly with the health project, whether the "support work" would eclipse the project's research mandate. A related concern about the projects creating unfair expectations within the immigrant communities that the main Institute's overworked counsellors would not be able to meet points to the difficulty of replicating the Branch, or neighbourhood office, model on a large scale.[101] Also, as recent studies of immigrant children's health and occupational education for immigrants suggest, we cannot naively assume that past approaches that achieved some success will be applied to subsequent waves of migrants even when they exhibit similar challenges; rather, constant vigilance is required.[102] The partial exception is COSTI: due in part to community chest and government funding, it evolved into a multicultural agency that now provides a range of social services and vocational training to immigrants of all backgrounds.[103] In any event, we should not ignore the many failed attempts, disruptions, or dropouts caused by pregnancy, illness, family crises, or changing work shifts because such factors also affect today's immigrants.

Then, too, individual fieldworkers, or community-based social work practitioners, however well-intentioned, cannot overcome the basically intrusive nature of social work or the profession's tendency to equate "good citizenship" with conformity to dominant middle-class norms. The pluralist, or multicultural, approach of recruiting front-line workers acknowledged the importance of language, culture, and ethnicity, but privileged class, or professional, status. Like other liberal reforms, it also drew on a human capital theory framework in which the needs of industry for "a technically proficient labor force" is an overriding priority.[104] The racism that white Canadians, including Torontonians, unleashed on the South Asian and other racialized groups who began arriving in Canada in significant numbers in the 1970s also makes it foolhardy, even dangerous, to overstate the potential of such a strategy for addressing racial inequities. The Institute's efforts to reduce hostility to immigrants and improve their access to resources by trying to close the cultural gap between hostland community-service providers and marginalized immigrants also considered less-than-white deserves some credit. The Institute's financial and other crises precluded its launching similar projects in the 1970s among the rapidly growing South Asian and Caribbean immigrant communities, leaving us to wonder whether an enlarged Caribbean and South Asian staff would have produced equal or more mixed results.

Chapter Nine

Food as Charity, Community-Building, and Cosmopolitanism on a Budget

Critics of mainstream multiculturalism such as urban geographers Kanishka Goonewardena and Stefan Kipfer rightly criticize what they call the "food and festivals" brand of "aestheticized difference." Driven by corporate interests, public-private city-branding efforts, "creative class" chatter, and tourism strategies, such marketing, they note, seeks to sell diversity through superficial or reductionist notions of difference based on the "exotic" pleasures of "visible" and "edible" ethnicity.[1] However, we should not categorically dismiss every form of culinary pluralism as suspect or exploitative as there are community and collaborative contexts in which the consumption of "ethnic" foods can have a more positive impact on those involved.

The International Institute of Metropolitan Toronto used food as a way of promoting immigrant integration and liberal cosmopolitanism in three major ways. One was in social welfare practice aimed at supporting struggling families and avoiding mass maladjustment. Another strategy entailed the group dinners and collaboratively organized banquets meant to foster community through cross-cultural sharing and exchange in festive contexts. As a third strategy, the cookbook projects, like the banquets, bore elements of popular and tourism-oriented spectacle (see chapter 10), as evidenced by the many references to colourfully decorated tables and enticing ethnic dishes. Each type of activity differed in terms of its potential for fostering a cultural pluralism rooted in meaningful cross-cultural interactions and social relationships.

This chapter highlights the role of food in promoting Institute-style pluralism. The discussion of the mix of Anglo, ethno-Canadian, and immigrant women most directly involved in these activities is informed by the literature that explores the multifaceted character of food as material resource, political tool, social practice, cultural marker, and site of contest and negotiation between dominant and less powerful groups.[2] The women in question included the Institute's female group workers and counsellors, and the volunteers recruited through the Catholic Women's League, IODE, Toronto Junior League, and the women's branches of various ethnic organizations. In scrutinizing the character and impact of this female-led reform activism on both the Institute women themselves and the membership and wider public, I draw as well on the literature on im/migrant and hybridized food cultures, national and transnational foodways, and food-as-spectacle.[3] Of particular importance is the multidisciplinary feminist scholarship that has explored women's agency and empowerment within this traditionally female-gendered activity and examined culinary books as literary texts that, like journals or diaries, can reveal much about contemporary social values, economic conditions, and women's engagement with the wider world.[4]

I consider the possibilities and limits of the culinary pluralism enacted by the Institute's differently located women through an engagement with feminist analyses of women as food providers, cookbook writers, and community fundraisers.[5] In carrying out the Institute's various food campaigns, I argue, the participating women, most of whom were of middle-class origins, forged cross-cultural if not cross-class bonds of respect. A related argument concerns the paradoxes and tensions revealed by generally well-intentioned actions that, alongside other efforts and developments, contributed towards a greater public exposure to and acceptance of varied ethnic cuisines, at least among liberal Torontonians, but hardly erased class, gender, and racial-ethnic hierarchies. Finally, I highlight the critical labour performed by women even when male restaurateurs or chefs were involved and draw a few comparisons between the Institute's support for ethnic entrepreneurialism and more recent public/private efforts in food tourism.

Food Charity

As countless studies have detailed, immigrant women have heroically sacrificed their own health and endured multiple indignities to feed their families in challenging Old and New World contexts, and their success or failure has deeply informed their personal identities and affected their status within their family and community.[6] Charity among poor women has a long and enduring history and, as the US Institutes told American audiences in the 1930s, underprivileged immigrant women knew how to make do through preserving and other means.[7] Then, too, food has been a major charitable or welfare item and middle-class women, whether religious or secular, professional or volunteer, have played key roles in distributing food to struggling women and their families.[8] As a social agency serving non-English-speaking immigrants, the Toronto Institute's organized charitable food-related projects both reflected and reinforced class and ethnic hierarchies.

In carrying out their welfare activities, Institute staff prescribed to the professional and bourgeois codes of a mainstream social service agency surveying resources and selecting suitable recipients. They solicited food vouchers from ethnic stores (such as Johnny Lombardi's nearby grocery store), supermarkets (Dominion Stores), and bakeries (Silverstein's), and funds for vouchers from various sources (including Allstate Insurance and the Junior Red Cross), each time thanking the donor for contributing towards "the newcomers' integration into Canadian life."[9] A preference for food vouchers, which, depending on the number of children, ranged from about $8 to $30, over money vouchers or cash reflected a familiar social welfare ethos, namely that they prevented mothers from potentially "squandering" cash on something else, even a cheap trinket meant to cheer up a gloomy flat. The intrusive methods involved in the selection of families was partly tempered by the sympathy shown the mainly European clients, and by the parties organized for Institute members and for the children of struggling clients.

Such dynamics were much in evidence during the Christmas season, a time of heightened charity-giving, when the Institute distributed as many as 100 baskets to poor and struggling immigrant families in the neighbourhood. As supervisor of the Institute reception centre during the early 1960s, the Czech-born counsellor Margarete Streeruwitz assembled and prioritized the lists of potential recipients identified by the counsellors and reception centre volunteers. The mainly female donors recruited through the Christmas Bureau of the Social Planning Council of Metropolitan Toronto (SPC) were primarily Anglo-Canadians, though a few women of European origins also show up. According to Streeruwitz, the Christmas Bureau donors directed to the Institute usually knew nothing about the agency, but once apprised of its goals, most offered "generous" donations of food parcels, hampers, and toys. The few who refused the referral usually said they preferred to help an English-speaking Canadian family.[10]

The Bureau lists indicate that the Institute's individual donors were mostly women, with married women outnumbering single women, and the group donors mainly guide groups (Brownies, Girl Guides), the Junior Red Cross, and local schools. Some Boy Scout troops also appear. As do individual men: a 1961 list included a Mennonite minister, the head of a YMCA group, and a stockbroker. The staff of local government offices such as the Workmen's Compensation Board also appear on the lists. With the usual caveat about the risk of reading ethnicity from names, the preponderance of names such as Harris, Payton, Boland, Smith, Bailey, and Broadhurst suggests a mainly Anglo-Canadian group of donors.[11]

Most donors were located in the west end, but others came from elsewhere in the city and a few from the suburbs. Showing concern for the immigrant recipients of their charity, several donors wanted assurances that adequate refrigeration facilities existed for the turkeys and chickens being purchased. An imbalance in gifts for women and girls meant specific requests for donations for boys or men. Companies such as Bell Telephone donated puppets, dolls, and other toys. On occasion, the Christmas Bureau passed on specific requests, like the one from a "gentleman from India who wanted to be invited by a Canadian family for Christmas." It likely resulted in an invitation to an Institute Christmas dinner.[12]

As truck drivers, troop leaders, teachers, and other donors dropped off items, Institute staff and volunteers filled the baskets with a Christmas turkey or chicken dinner, food vouchers, and toys. Institute staff preferred that families pick up their basket, but when that proved difficult, they delivered them. Senior female administrators such as Nell West and, later, Tine Stewart, who became director in 1968, sometimes participated in these dropoffs. But the task usually went to seasoned workers such as Streeruwitz and Irene Szebeny (the multilingual bookkeeper/home visitor), who checked in on the family and sometimes recorded their conversation with the mother. The work was sufficiently labour-intensive that it interrupted normal duties and programs for several weeks.[13]

Institute staff, like its SPC counterparts, tried to protect the harried women of these "needy families" from intrusive donors, usually Anglo-Canadian women who wished to accompany a delivery and see what an appreciative immigrant family looked like. To discourage them, workers said the children might be confused and disappointed to see strangers rather than their parents bring home Christmas food and gifts, but they also clearly wished to spare mothers and fathers from potentially embarrassing encounters with their donors. One insistent donor, Mrs Payton of Russell Hill Road in the "Anglo" enclave of wealthy Forest Hill, wanted to hand deliver her parcel to an immigrant family with three children who were similar in age to her own. When the Bureau staffer noted that the family members "speak just Italian," Payne said she spoke Italian "fluently," though it is unclear whether it was an educated or tourist Italian. At any rate, she evidently got her way, as did a few others.[14]

The ethnic profile of the family recipients followed the shifting composition of those living in the heavily immigrant west end where the Institute was located for much of its history. The earlier lists of recipients selected for baskets – and in many cases, additional items such as toys, (used) clothing, and, on occasion, (used) furniture – reflected the European arrivals of the late 1940s and the 1950s, namely Eastern European refugees (the largest group of which was the Hungarians of 1956) and some Germans and Southern Europeans.[15] More than half of a list of 23 families selected in 1958 were of Czech, German, Yugoslav, Russian, Ukrainian, and Hungarian origin whereas Italians (41) topped the list of 66 recipients in December 1961. The remainder included a mix of German, Eastern European, and Portuguese families. The donors for that year included Carol Purche and her Girl Guide troop, whose contribution supported several families, including a financially strapped Polish family.[16]

The growing concentration of Italians in the Institute's west end neighbourhood was reflected in the sixties-era lists. It explains the significant presence of Italian Canadian volunteer home visitors from the Italian Immigrant Aid Society (IIAS), the charitable arm of the Canadian Italian Businessmen and Professional Men's Association. Each year, the IIAS selected between 30 and 45 Italian families from the Institute's list, most of whom lived near the Institute.[17] On occasion, the donor was an immigrant who, having achieved some financial stability, showed compassion towards others. In 1961, Streeruwitz praised a Northern European woman now living in the suburb of Weston for her "very very generous donations" for "one large Italian family" and "a German lady who suffers from diabetes."[18]

Staff and home-visit notes on the recipient families show how separation, desertion, or divorce could push struggling mothers to the brink of disaster. A number of the Eastern European families who received Christmas baskets in 1958, for example, were female-headed households where the presence of a young child or children kept a mother without family child-minders from entering the paid workforce. They included a Czech mother of a 13-year-old boy whose husband was still in Czechoslovakia, a Hungarian nurse and mother of a 4-year-old boy who was separated from her husband, and an unmarried Hungarian mother of an 11-month-old baby. Male unemployment explained why other families, including a German mother of three boys under the age of 6, were on the list.[19] The twenty-eight families on a 1960 list included, unusually, a destitute single Hungarian man whose family was still abroad and a childless Italian couple. There were also several large families, including a Serbian family with five children between the ages of 4 and 14, and a Maltese family with ten children between the ages of 1 and 19.[20] The Italian and Portuguese recipients who increasingly dominated the lists usually had large families.[21]

A home visitor's notes on two Portuguese families on a 1964 Christmas list sheds further light on the challenges plaguing large families. One newly arrived family of four children (ages 5 to 15) was described as completely ill-prepared "for the oncoming winter." The couple was renting two sparsely furnished rooms and a kitchen for a monthly rental fee ($60) that swallowed up too much of the husband's weekly wage ($45) and the children had no winter clothing or other items. A "very large family" of eight young children were crammed into "a very modest home" whose monthly rent ($70) could not be met by the construction worker husband come the winter slack period. In both cases, the "X-mas present" would have included a donation of clothing from the supplies provided by local IODE branches. .[22]

The home visitors' reports reveal as well the detrimental impact that illness or injury of a parent, and on occasion both parents, created for financially precarious families, and how an unexpected crisis compounded matters. Examples from 1963 include a Croatian mother with five children whose husband "was ill for years" and whose family was on welfare, and an Italian family with a diabetic father whose hospitalization with a lung infection left them dependent upon the wife's low weekly income ($35).[23] A majority of the families on the 1964 lists were large young families newly arrived from Portugal that were headed by an unemployed father and in debt to sponsors who had paid their voyage. There were also a number of female-headed households, including a few deserted wives and single mothers and a woman with a husband in jail. Another struggling family included parents trying to support a disabled child.[24]

Late-twentieth-century professional social welfare work was no longer steeped in a Victorian language of "deserving" and "undeserving" poor and the Institute records contain statements of principles regarding "Holiday Living" that emphasize the need to give in a manner that "enhanced" the recipient's "independence and self-respect."[25] But like other twentieth-century social workers, Institute staff passed judgments that reflected age-old expectations about the charity recipients being of solid moral character. The mothers were expected to use the modest food vouchers appropriately, and those who made what staff considered impulse or unnecessary purchases came under criticism. This happened to an Italian mother of seven young children deemed irresponsible for using part of her food voucher to buy chestnuts and other unnecessary "merchandise." The criticism ignored the cultural and emotional significance of this holiday treat for Italians. Further, the woman's effort to rekindle nostalgic memories of roasted chestnuts at Christmastime hurt her chances of getting similar help the following year.[26] In addition, the Institute worked with the Christmas Bureau to ensure that families did not double-dip and receive baskets from more than one agency.[27]

Overall, however, the reports reveal plenty of sympathy for struggling newcomer women, albeit sympathy that frequently bordered on class pity. An Anglo-Canadian home visitor was so moved by the plight of a mother of six young children burdened with hospital and mortgage costs that she recommended additional financial support. The parent's work ethic along with their efforts "to keep the children in school" influenced her recommendation for food and clothing. Her Italian immigrant counterpart described a struggling but deserving Italian couple as "proud people" with "good manners"; the sick and "very depressed" wife had recently undergone a very expensive spine operation. She showed sympathy towards non-Italians, too, including a Portuguese mother of five whose husband had recently died in a car accident.[28] When their resources ran out, Institute staff directed "last minute" requests for help to charities such as the Scott Mission, the Fred Victor Mission, and the Salvation Army.[29]

The Institute served primarily recent arrivals, but the wretched situation in which an Italian family found themselves in 1961, a decade after arriving in Toronto, moved the home visitor to recommend support. The husband had developed an incurable illness, was on welfare, and could not afford the expensive medicine that had to be purchased abroad, and the wife was recovering from an operation and could not pay the current medical bills. The recommendation in the file of a Portuguese woman in hospital with a kidney infection conveyed plenty in few words: "she just had her ninth child and is in a state of depression."[30] So, too, did the home visitor's report on a Portuguese mother of seven children all under the age of 12 who had just given birth to a "mongoloid" son. She noted that the children "needed winter clothing" and "one or two beds for the little ones." In this case, the woman had reportedly initiated the visit so that the worker could witness their poverty. The sympathy expressed for an injured Hungarian woman with an unemployed husband and four children may have been enhanced by the political circumstances surrounding her migration: she had "been shot in the hip during the Hungarian Revolution."[31]

The home visitors did recommend support for mothers whom they considered immoral or irresponsible on the grounds that the children truly needed help. This happened to a racialized woman in these records, an unmarried Jamaican mother of four receiving modest unemployment insurance payments. Three of her children, the youngest of whom was 4 months, were living with her, while a daughter, age 7, was in England (presumably with relatives). The Institute's commitment to a pluralist ethos that claimed respect for "other" cultural norms, and its acknowledgment that female-headed households within Caribbean communities faced a lesser degree of disapproval than in the "Canadian community," did not preclude the home visitor from conveying her disapproval of the fact that the children were fathered by different men. But the "desperate" financial situation led to a recommendation for support.[32] Deprecating comments about European mothers also surface, though again need triumphed, as exemplified by an IODE visitor who chastised a Portuguese mother of seven "very poorly dressed children" for not heeding earlier advice to turn to "the Church for help," but recommended support because her family was "certainly one of the most needy."[33]

Home visitors were disposed to help women with unreliable husbands. The brief notes on an Italian mother of five children, two of them teenagers, is typical of these cases. It reads: "Destitute case. Husband lost job through gambling. He gives her no support whatever. She is expecting again – and very hard of hearing."[34] On occasion, visitors recommended particularly desperate cases to the IODE's adopt-a-family program. The paternalistic language notwithstanding, the program provided additional material support to the family through local IODE chapters. One of the three families taken on during Christmas in 1961 had eleven children; the sponsoring chapter provided extra vouchers for food and shoes and, because the mother was expecting her twelfth child, baby layettes. In other cases, the house bills were also covered for a period of time. In 1966, the Charles of Edinburgh Chapter provided a Polish mother on her own with $25 worth of Christmas presents for her children.[35]

Significantly, the Institute women showed considerable cultural sensitivity towards the food preferences of their mostly European recipients. When donors asked which food items to give, they usually said "southern European" foods because they were easily obtained in Toronto's ethnic shops and would appeal to the largest number of families, even non-Southerners. One suggested list included cod, turkey, chicken, a cooked ham, sardines, macaroni, rice, tinned tomatoes and tomato paste, beans, dried peas, fruit, and olive oil.[36] They also lobbied the Visiting Homemaker's Association, whose nutritionists drew up model baskets, to incorporate ethnic items. The suggested list for "Italians, Greeks, Slavic, and Others" included brand names of Italian foods such as Unico or Bravo canned tomatoes and Lancia "macaroni" as well as "Italian Coffee [espresso]." A "Portuguese and Spanish" list added corn flour for making bread.[37] As these examples suggest, the cultural gap between the "Canadian" foods recommended in the Canada Food Guide and "southern European" foods was fairly easy to close, especially in a multi-ethnic city like sixties-era Toronto.[38]

As their correspondence suggests, the Institute's staff and volunteers drew satisfaction from their charity work and also exhibited a mutual respect for each other. Even allowing for an expected degree of politeness, even effusiveness, the letters and messages that refer to helpful, reliable, and even charming colleagues hint at a few budding friendships. Together, they articulate the women's growing sense of themselves as a community, or collective, of women involved in worthy projects, a theme to which I return below.[39] By contrast, their interactions with the overburdened mothers they met were overlaid with a paternalism that reinforced the class and cultural (if not ethnic)[40] divide between them. But while accepting charity likely proved embarrassing for some mothers, no one rejected a basket, a finding that no doubt reflects the Institute's selection process as well as the depth of need.

Charity work made gift-givers of the Institute women and their social welfare colleagues, but the gift came with strings attached. Having met some bar of need, the recipient of charity also becomes in some way beholden to the giver while the giver, feeling virtuous, might yet expect something in return.[41] Institute staff did encourage the mothers to take out memberships and to enrol in their English classes, mother's clubs, and other programs, but did not limit donations to Institute members. However complicated their response to charity, the recipients of the food baskets and vouchers, many of whom already had been forced by war, displacement, and poverty to rely on aid, expressed their appreciation in letters written on cheap cards or scraps of paper, either in their own language or in rudimentary English.

A typical batch of thank-you messages that arrived at the Institute at Christmastime in 1962 came from Italian, Polish, Yugoslav, and Croatian mothers, or their daughters, and most of the writers struggled to say thanks in English. The English letters were brief and riddled with grammatical and spelling errors (as in "takeyou" for thank you), but heartfelt. A Polish girl thanked the Institute women for the "wonderful" and "adorable" doll she received on Christmas Eve," adding that "I put her on the top of the bookshelf so that I can look at her." In one of the longest letters, an Italian mother thanked the Institute for providing her children with such "a memorable day" and "unforgeble [unforgettable] … great avent [event]," adding: "I will prey the God to give you better living and value future together."[42]

For the Institute women, who worked long hours to bring some sustenance and joy into the homes of newcomer mothers struggling during the stressful holiday season, such displays of appreciation affirmed the value of their actions, and the viability of the Institute's dual-pronged commitment to immigrant adjustment and pluralism. Some self-interest operated, too, in that well-adjusted newcomers would more willingly embrace the Institute's philosophy and join its programs. Overall, though, this labour, like all charity work, reinforced rather than bridged class divisions between givers and recipients.

Children's Parties and Adult Meals

Some Institute food-related charitable activities took place within a more festive context and involved a greater degree of cross-ethnic interaction; these were the luncheons, dinners, parties, and dances held to celebrate mainly Christian holidays. By far the busiest holiday was Christmas, when a children's party, afternoon teas, buffet luncheons and dinners, a formal turkey dinner, and dances were organized. With invitations generated by the counselling staff and volunteers, the size of the events ranged from between 60 and 125 people for the adult meals to between 100 and 320 for the children's party.[43] The principle of breaking bread and, in the children's case, enjoying treats, informed these festive events, as did the "wider universality of the Christmas message" of unity, harmony, and good will.[44] That message was also captured in the Christmas cards designed by Hungarian artist Dora de Pédery-Hunt, one of which featured an abstract tree and another a stylized star surrounded by greetings in multiple languages.[45]

The boys and girls who attended the children's Christmas party feasted on cake, ice cream, and milk or chocolate milkshakes in a holiday atmosphere created by colourful balloons, streamers, bells, a decorated tree (or two), and clowns, and took home a gift from a jolly Santa Claus. The entertainment, which was provided free by newcomer or Canadian performers, might include a puppet or variety show. The 1964 variety show featured a folk-dance troupe and was hosted by Bruno Gerussi, the Italian Canadian stage and television actor who became best known for the long-running CBC-TV show *The Beachcombers* (1972–90).[46] As West put it, the parties were meant to bring some "happiness into the lives of little children" of struggling immigrant families "and indeed of their parents."[47] By 1970, organizers noted the importance of welcoming children who, as Streeruwtiz opined, "did not celebrate Xmas" but "have other customs as interesting," though the party remained overwhelmingly European and Christian.[48]

IODE chapters headed by women such as Mrs A. Stermac (Polish Canadian) and Mrs E.H. Hugenholtz (Dutch Canadian) organized the children's Christmas party. Parents could also accompany a child to the party. With an eye to creating fun and a sense of wonder on a budget, the women tapped donors for the ice cream and milk, and for the eggs and butter to bake large, colourful cakes. Companies such as Acme Farmer's Dairy Ltd and Cira Brothers responded to the call to help bring some joy into the lives of deprived children, most of whom were also celebrating their first Christmas in Canada by providing Dixie cups of vanilla ice cream, half-pints of milk, and cake-baking ingredients. The Ideal Toy Company, International Games of Canada, and other companies donated the Santa gifts. The donated trees were decorated with Institute ornaments and were later reused for the adult tree-trimming party.[49]

By the women's own account, organizing the Saturday party was hugely time-consuming. The tasks included collecting and coordinating the information needed to ensure that each child received an appropriate toy for their age and gender (such as dolls for girls and puppets for boys). As a goodwill gesture, the Santa invitation was translated into different European languages, a job that often went to Szebeny, though the absence of the appropriate alphabet on the typewriter meant invitations to Russian and Ukrainian families were issued in English. The Institute provided the Santa suit and recruited the volunteer Santa, usually from among its male members. The Institute and IODE also supplied the music (on vinyl records or tape) for the carolling session. The young hostesses dressed in colourful ethnic costumes reinforced the event's multi-ethnic character, though an IODE suggestion that the children come similarly attired went nowhere, in part, no doubt, because their parents could hardly afford such outfits.[50] National Film Board (NFB) animated cartoons and holiday films were another party staple.

The changing age and ethnic composition of the children largely parallels the immigration shifts. Thus, a more ethnically diverse European group, albeit one with plenty of Hungarian "1956ers," gave way to parties increasingly dominated by Italians and Portuguese though a few Czech, Yugoslavian, and German children attended into the mid-1960s.[51] The decision in 1961 to reduce the maximum age of the partygoers from 14 to 10 likely reflected the presence of large Italian and Portuguese families. The only non-Europeans to attend the 1963 party of 293 children were two "Japanese" children, probably born to Canadian parents.[52] The Portuguese- and Italian-dominated party of 235 children in 1964 included a few children from previously unrepresented groups: thirteen Spanish and three Moroccan children, and one Afrikaans child (white South African). A few Black children appear in the early 1970s (see image 9.1 below). Again, many of the children lived in the vicinity of the Institute nearby, though a few had suburban addresses.[53] The gender was not always specified, but organizers aimed for a roughly equal number of boys and girls, and for more younger (age 10 and under) than older children or young teenagers.[54]

Here, too, we find some evidence of a shared sense of camaraderie and mutual trust and respect among the organizing women, who clearly derived satisfaction, even pleasure, from bringing a little joy into the children's lives. In 1960, Streeruwitiz complimented Tine Stewart, then an IODE volunteer, for once again "work[ing] so hard to make this party possible for our little ones from all over the world." A 1967 report said "the important contributions" made by "Mrs. E.H. Hugenholtz and her team of IODE volunteers" (Alton chapter), and by "Mrs. Kaye, our regular volunteer," had ensured a highly successful party.[55] Such commentary revealed a patronizing attitude towards the parents who were incapable of giving their children a proper Christmas, but also a shared sense of female accomplishment among the mix of Anglo and ethnic organizers. Even allowing for a tendency to gush in thank-you letters sent to donors and volunteers, West and Streeruwitiz' appreciation for the work done by the IODE, and by the Italian Canadian volunteers who helped with translation and home visits, speaks to the presence of cross-ethnic bonds among a mixed group of middle-class women. The Christmas context, with its emphasis on giving and good cheer, likely reinforced such bonds, if only temporarily.[56]

Certainly, the parties reflected Institute paternalism, but the children surely enjoyed them, and delighted in taking a toy home to their sparsely furnished flat or multiple-family household. For a few hours, children who were baffled by their English-speaking teachers, or embarrassed about being sent back a grade or two because of their poor English, or confused by their parents' constant worries stepped into a "make-believe" world of colourful streamers, carol singalongs, dancers, a decorated tree, and a Santa Claus bearing gifts. For those who lived along its downtown route, only that "mile of make-believe" that was the annual Santa Claus parade rivalled it.[57]

The organizers stressed the children's joy. The report on the 1973 party hosted by the IODE Immouna Ephrem chapter described the "spirit of excitement and glee" that filled the "well decorated Recreation Room" of the Davenport Road building as the children met and played with new friends. The folk-dance teachers and the youth volunteers (who were dressed up as clowns) entertained them. They watched three NFB cartoons: "Christmas Cracker," about a young "heroine" who decorates a tree, the "Great Toy Robbery," a western about Santa retrieving the toys stolen by some cowboys, and a third about the "exciting new theme of space travel." Their enthusiastic greeting of Santa Claus, all "waving little hands and little bodies pushing their way to get a closer look at him," was followed by the "peak excitement" of opening their gift, showing it to parents and friends, and seeing what their friends received. The report ended by thanking the student volunteers, who came from Woodbine High School, George S. Henry High School, Oriole Yorkmills United Church, Kawartha Lakes School, and a senior Sunday school class.[58]

Food as Charity, Community-Building, and Cosmopolitanism   205

Santa's arrival at an Institute Christmas party delights the children, c. 1972. Archives of Ontario, F884-2-9, B427166.

The photos of the parties, which attracted some media attention, confirm the positive IODE reports, showing us mostly (but not exclusively) white immigrant children eating cake, clapping, and singing. Or surrounding Santa Claus (usually an Institute member) when he arrived to hand out the gifts.[59] Other children's parties were also held at the Institute, including a 1961 spring party hosted by Havergal College, an elite private girls' school, which treated 40 children to a supper (probably hot dogs) and ice cream, and a gift of little baskets with candy and games.[60] But it was the Christmas parties that stood out.

The Christmas lunch buffets and the dinners held for adults were more collaborative efforts involving Institute members, both newcomer and Canadian, and the staff and volunteers. The size varied according to the venue and resources but, following Institute practice, the mixed-gender groups, who might consume ham (or ham and cheese croissants), Greek pies, and Portuguese wine,[61] were ethnically diverse but overwhelmingly European. Special invitations to Anglo-Torontonians, from reporters to dignitaries,

Nell West hosts a sit-down Christmas dinner with Institute staff and invited members and guests, 25 December 1958. Archives of Ontario, F884-2-9, B427166.

were issued with the hope that the event would also get some wider public attention. The Christmas dinners to which single adults and childless couples were invited – Streerurwitz called them the "lonely ones"[62] – attracted 60 or more people. The Christmas open house buffet drew closer to 100 people and the tree-trimming party about half that number. On occasion the food ran out, suggesting that numbers exceeded expectations. Given the value placed on such feasts as a community-building act, running out of food caused embarrassment.[63]

West and staff also held more intimate sit-down affairs with a "traditional Canadian dinner with turkey and all the trimmings." The photographs of these dinners feature a smiling West, formally attired in dress, pearls, and hat, and the guests, also dressed up but donning more serious expressions, seated at the table. One cannot easily read emotions from such photos, especially since some would have adopted a formal (unsmiling) pose for the camera even if they were enjoying themselves.[64] Writing about the Christmas dinner she attended

A multiracial line-up of performers sing carols during an International Institute Christmas show, c. 1973. Archives of Ontario, F884-2-9, B427166.

in 1969, Elizabeth Dingman of the *Toronto Telegram*'s women's page remarked with approval on the diversity of the guests. She commented on the general "stiffness" of the atmosphere, but added that the mood was lightened by a gregarious Viennese woman who displayed a fondness for the American "Wild West."[65] A degree of awkwardness would be expected of any gathering where most people do not know each other, and Dingman's own anecdote indicated how a shared meal can break the ice among strangers, leading to conversation, lighthearted or otherwise. Even the not entirely comfortable immigrant guests would have registered the importance of the invitation. The Christmas (and other) parties held for the volunteer English teachers at the Institute, and those the teachers held, often in their own homes, for the graduates of their adult English classes, were more relaxed affairs.[66]

The Christmas and New Year's dances drew the largest crowds. The *Intercom* reported on people enjoying themselves at the 1965 Christmas dance, which also featured a "lively and colourful vaudeville of Canada's past and present," a "magnificent" performance by the Hungarian Kodály Choir of Toronto, and

208   Community-Building Experiments

Santa Claus (member Wolfgang Moritz). The New Year's Eve dance for that year was "a complete sell-out." In 1970, though, it drew a "disappointing" crowd, a harbinger of the difficulties that led to the Institute's demise in 1974.[67]

Eating among Equals

The Institute events that held far greater potential for encouraging cross-cultural exchange and a sense of community, albeit on a small scale, were the member-organized dinners. Even with the annoying interference of the supervisory staff (see chapter 7), these intercultural dinners encouraged collaborative organizing and cross-ethnic sociability. An early success was the mixed-gender supper club, whose members met on two Sundays of each month to make and share a meal and enjoy a movie, music, or a lecture, and conversation.[68] Drawing on their own food customs rather than staff menus, the mostly European members of the Supper Club sat down to a meal that was punctuated with storytelling, debate, and entertainment. In short, they clearly understood that sociability could facilitate and reinforce social bonds, and that, to cite food theorists Carole Counihan and Penny Van Esterik, eating is "an evolving enactment of gender, family, and community relationships."[69] Significantly, both women and men organized the suppers, with the "ethnic" cuisine of choice, be it a Portuguese fish dinner or Italian pasta dinner, determining who might "supervise" the meal-making. There were rosters to ensure that everyone did their share of the preparation, cooking, and cleaning up.

The affiliated ethnic groups also held banquets at the Institute. Although mainly single-ethnic group events, the hosts often invited the director or a few board members and a few Canadian members to help create a more diverse gathering. By the mid-1960s, newer groups were also hosting dinners, which in certain cases, including those involving South Asian groups, prompted vegetarian menus. Institute staff showed an open-mindedness towards the "new" post-1967 immigrants by educating themselves about the differing food rules and preferences of Muslim, Hindu, Buddhist, and other non-Christian newcomers. They also made plans to develop non-Western cookbooks, though only an Asian one materialized (see below).

Banquets and Ethnic Entrepreneurs

The Institute's Ethnic Weeks, which showcased an immigrant group's folk and artistic cultures in order to raise public awareness of Toronto's rich ethnic heritage, included a festive banquet, or "nationality dinner." (The Ethnic Nights and Ethnic Sundays also featured a banquet.) These events reflected the Institute's immigrant-gifts form of cultural pluralism – which asserted that immigrant customs enriched the society that embraced them – and its promotion and popularization of the concept through public spectacle (see chapter 10). The description that director West gave of an upcoming banquet for a Latvian Week, where she promised a table set "with the Easter motif used by Latvians in their homeland, fresh birch branches, green stalks of corn and multicoloured Easter eggs," offered an apt "plentiful table" symbol of culinary pluralism. She promised, too, that young Latvian women dressed in their "varied and colourful" ethnic costumes would serve the dishes, and that guests could try "the national bread in which the centre is filled with the whole kernel of wheat."[70]

Such publicity offered an illustration of how Institute-style cultural pluralism simultaneously celebrated and appropriated ethnic customs for larger objectives, in this case, offering Torontonians an opportunity to consume "other" foods in a festive context. Insofar as the Ethnic Weeks were intended to strip the immigrants of any threatening elements, the banquets were a critical ingredient in promoting a therapeutic pluralism. The cooks and chefs filled their role as makers of food that was exotic enough to make people feel adventurous in their own city but not so exotic as to scare them off.[71]

Insofar as they involved the marketing and commodification of Toronto's growing cultural diversity, these banquets prefigured current city-branding strategies that "present multiculturalism as a product for spectacle and consumption."[72] The Toronto à la Cart program launched in 2009, which ignored the needs of immigrant and ethnic food providers, serves as a caution against accepting feel-good analyses of multicultural banquets as necessarily progressive celebrations of urban cosmopolitanism. An entrepreneurial as well as neo-liberal pilot program to use "ethnic" food (here largely understood as the food of racialized immigrants) to attract tourists and investors, it failed to provide the immigrant vendors who competed for and invested in the carts that would prepare the Korean, Thai, Middle Eastern, Caribbean Fusion, and Indian foods with a viable business. Straitjacketed by rigid regulations regarding location, rent, health and safety inspections (for example, they could not cook in their carts), and the types of foods they could sell, vendors faced disappointing sales and accrued major debts.[73]

But, like the concerts and arts and crafts exhibits that were also part of the Institute's Ethnic Weeks, the banquets were not simply top-down events. They involved the active support of ethnic organizations, many of which invited Institute leaders to their own commemorative and holiday banquets, and immigrant and ethno-Canadian chefs, cooks, and restaurateurs. Whether out of mainly business or political interests or ethnocultural pride, or a mix of all three, the ethnic food entrepreneurs clearly saw the banquets as an opportunity to promote their food specialties as well as a more pluralistic Canada.[74]

As advocates of immigrant entrepreneurialism, the Institute women were pleased to assist ethnic bakery owners, chef-restaurateurs, and caterers in establishing or expanding their clientele. The dinner menu for Latvian week in spring 1957, for example, offered a valuable plug for Little Riga Restaurant, which prepared a buffet that included a starter of head cheese with horseradish and rye bread and three entrees: roast ham baked in dough, roast veal, and roast chicken.[75]

The importance of ethnic food purveyors is similarly illustrated by a German Week. As the Canadian sponsors recruited for the event, a Local Council of Women and the Parkdale Travel Club, a group of travel enthusiasts, were instructed to provide (Canadian) "fruitbread or sandwiches" for the opening afternoon tea because their ethnic counterparts, which included the German-Canadian Business and Professional Association (GCBPA) and Club Harmonie, would provide "the nationality cakes and pastries."[76] But the latter did far more than that. Three local German bakeries – Freimann's Pastry, Hilda's Fancy Cake Bar, and Rudolph's Pastry, who probably belonged to the GCBPA – supplied ethnic pastries throughout the week. Presumably, so, too, did the (unnamed) chef or restaurant owner who supplied the banquet menu of "traditional" German fare: consommé with liver dumplings, smoked pork chops, and Swabian veal steak with noodles. The dessert was apple strudel. These small businesses undoubtedly considered their donations and discounts money well spent for the positive exposure and goodwill it created.[77]

There were also some disappointments. The inaugural Polish dinner held in honour of the Institute's first ethnic week in February 1957 was arranged and catered by W. Szymczak, owner of the Parkside Grill, a modest restaurant located at 695 Queen Street West, not far from the Institute. When only 49 of the 60 people who reserved spots showed up for the ($2) dinner, Institute staff resolved to collect the money when reservations were made in order to avoid debts, though it is not clear that they did so. In 1962, the Institute lost one of its most "generous" chefs, Dutch restaurant owner Kees Vandergraaf, who had catered several receptions and dinners, when he left Toronto to run a tourist lodge he bought on the Trent River near Campbellford, Ontario. We do not know how much his subsidized meals for Institute events helped to attract new diners to his restaurant, but this ethnic entrepreneur's move to rural Ontario meant shifting from an ethnic-niche strategy of serving members of one's urban ethnic community and, one hoped, some other Torontonians and tourists, to a more specifically tourist-oriented one.[78]

The gendered dynamics that characterized many of the Ethnic Weeks, where male elites enjoyed pride of place while female members tended to the preparations, applied to the banquets, though the shared labour encouraged some positive bonds between the women. At the Polish Ethnic Week banquet in February 1957, for example, the male president and vice-president of the co-sponsoring Canadian Polish Congress sat with their wives at the head table along with Rev. Claude Mulvihill, current chair of the Institute board. The women directly involved in the preparations received no fanfare, though they did acknowledge each other's contributions. Director West praised Irene Ungar, a member of the Canadian Polish Women's Federation who sat on the Institute board, for being an effective liaison to the various sponsors. Ungar sent a congratulatory box of chocolates to the Institute "Ladies" for pulling off the event. As coordinator of a later Croatian banquet, Mira Ashby, president of the Croatian Women's Organization, received a similarly effusive thank you.[79]

In the 1960s, the Institute featured some "Eastern" events, including an Indonesian exhibit and dinner. For the Japanese Week held in 1969, the flyer, whose cover featured a drawing of wooden female dolls dressed in kimonos, promised a "Buffet of Japanese Delicacies," but no menu is available. Nor is there one for a Canadiana Week that included "Eastern" food.[80]

The banquets involved some cross-gender collaboration. The Institute women worked with both male and female caterers, bakers, and cooks. They took care of logistical details, including seating plans that ensured mixing and ordering tablecloths and napkins. If they used a commercial laundry, they saved themselves hours of washing up.[81] The Institute's pluralist mandate could serve to disguise women's labours as contributions to a greater goal, especially for festive events, but the women's correspondence suggests that they also expected some recognition for all the work.

The Institute's support for small ethnic businesses would not have precluded support for the corporate-friendly and public-private campaigns in culinary tourism that have come under critique in recent years. It was, after all, involved in organizing the 1969 launch of Metro International Caravan, the folk and trade show festival that helped to define Toronto multiculturalism, both in the city and beyond, for more than three decades (see chapter 10). Food and business, and the business of food, were key elements of Metro Caravan. The press releases for the inaugural festival promoted Toronto as a world trade centre and industrial capital with international port facilities, and as home to many rich "international heritages," including culinary ones. Small ethnic shops and large supermarket chains participated in what became a major tourist attraction by setting up displays of their "international foods" and a wide array of ethnic restaurants advertised their "international specials." The organizers even produced a resident celebrity chef, Stephen Vojtech, long-time chef of the posh King Edward Hotel. He was billed as a world-class chef much beloved among Europe's royal families. Vojtech reportedly supervised all the "gourmet menus" on offer "in consultation" with each participating group, though, in truth, Toronto then had few upscale restaurants, and the pavilions, which were ethnic clubs, church basements, community centres, and pubs dressed up as major cities, offered relatively simple (if labour-intensive) specialties, such as perogies (variously named), cabbage rolls, and pizza.[82]

The excitement of playing the culinary tourist in the safety of one's city emerged as a major theme of the media coverage of Metro Caravan '69. Playing

A Croatian dinner at the Institute in February 1964. Archives of Ontario, F884-2-9, B427166.

up this theme, *Toronto Telegram* writer Colin Murray told readers that, at the Budapest pavilion in the city's west end, people could enjoy "gulyas [goulash] and cabbage rolls the Hungarian way" and purchase "wines like Bull's Blood." (The wine's name, Egri Bikavér, referred to a legend about a band of men who defended their town of Eger against an invading Turkish army in the sixteenth-century.)[83] His description of the Rome pavilion located in Toronto's new Little Italy on St Clair Avenue West captured the festival's eclecticism. Visitors could participate in an ancient Roman festival set against a replica of the Forum by shopping in the surrounding boutiques, dancing on the terrace, and consuming "ravioli, lasagna, wine, wine, wine."[84] The Institute's own contribution to Caravan was a Swiss café (Maison Française) that served cheese and beef fondue on tables with checkered tablecloths, an Alps corner where women, dressed in the peasant-inspired *dirndl* consisting of a full skirt and apron and a blouse with short puffy sleeves, sold cheese-and-onion meat pies, and a Scandinavian smorgasbord buffet. At the outdoor dance, they ate

Food as Charity, Community-Building, and Cosmopolitanism 213

In a scene reminiscent of an Institute food festival, two fashionably dressed women take in an array of Greek sweets during a Community Folk Art Council bake sale at the Blue Flame Room, Consumers' Gas Company, 21–23 Toronto Street, January 1967. York University Libraries, Clara Thomas Archives & Special Collections, Toronto Telegram fonds, ASC08808.

"Canadian" hot dogs, maple-syrup sundaes, and apple pie, and drank beer. In the Institute's most noteworthy attraction, a Caribbean festival located in the auditorium with Calypso music, the bar served rum drinks and the kitchen a curried chicken and rice dinner.[85]

Serious reflection of the wide-ranging, but hardly omnipotent, power of food, might well lead us to ask the following question. Have the critics who reject food-and-festival multiculturalism as entirely illusory, and even dangerous, ignored or underestimated the capacity of food, both as a thing imbued with cultural meaning and as a site of consumption, to expose people to new cultures, and even to express defiance? After all, plenty of middle-class Anglo–North American youth in sixties- and seventies-era heterogeneous cities like Toronto expressed their discomfort with bourgeois conformity in part by experimenting with "ethnic" foods.[86] Furthermore, as Warren Belasco and others note, food battles have often accompanied grassroots political struggles, and the counter-cultural movements of the 1960s and 1970s, which included civil

214   Community-Building Experiments

Stephen Vojtech, master chef of Metro Caravan. The original caption for this publicity shot read in part: "Gourmet fare – at a gourmand's fair – may consist of suckling pig ... or stewed squid, marinated herring or kapustnik [Russian cabbage pie]." York University Libraries, Clara Thomas Archives & Special Collections, Toronto Telegram fonds, ASC60823 (photographer Jac Holland, 13 June 1970).

rights, Black power, feminist, hippie, and back-to-the-land groups, used food as a form of political expression.[87]

Community Cookbook Projects

As Donna Gabaccia notes, the interwar US Institutes helped to popularize the idea that food and sociability go together, both at home and in the wider community, and that immigrant foods brought the spice of variety to American society. A popular strategy for promoting such ideas was the production of multicultural cookbooks, examples of which included the International Institute of St Louis' *Menus and Recipes* (1927) and Lowell's *As the World Cooks: Recipes from Many Lands* (1938).[88] While West herself participated in US and Canadian-based conversations about creating multi-ethnic cookbooks,[89] the Toronto Institute's first foray into this activity was creating a column in the *Intercom* called "Let's Exchange Recipes" featuring (mainly simple) ethnic recipes.[90] A more substantial project was the Christmas cookbook, *Season's Greetings in Food – Christmas 1962*. The collaboration encouraged cross-cultural bonds among the female participants, though the final product was hardly free of contradiction.

The Christmas cookbook reflected a general strategy of promoting the Christian season as a time for "re-dedication" to such "higher principles" as "goodwill to men."[91] Ecumenicalism also informed the efforts to diversify the annual International Festival of Carols. This was billed as an evening of carols and stories that represented "the universality of the Christmas message" and "the spirit" of a city "where immigrants from many lands have come together to create a truly Canadian life," by recruiting "clergy and laymen" from a wider array of denominations and ethnic origins.[92] By 1970, the still heavily European performances for this free event included a Korean ensemble, Japanese choir, and the predominantly Black British Methodist Episcopal Church Choir. Organizers were disappointed by turnouts below 100 people – though no one could do much about the flu outbreak that reduced numbers in 1969 – and occasionally complained about an "obstinate" choir, but thought it a worthwhile event. The music writer for the Toronto *Globe and Mail* described the 1970 festival held at the St Lawrence Town Hall thus: "As a musical event, it left much to be desired. As a simple retelling of a familiar tale [the birth of Jesus told in five languages] it was effective and sometimes moving." He also thought "the most exotic performance" was that of the Armenian choir "with its fascinating Mid-Eastern minor key melodies."[93]

Special articles in the *Intercom* similarly used the multiplicity of long-standing Christmas celebrations as proof of the value of practising a modern-day form of pluralism. Oddly, perhaps, the best example is the publication in 1962 of "American Christmas," a feature from a US magazine supplied by Institute headquarters in New York City, though the Toronto staff clearly thought the message travelled easily across the border. Its main point was to lay out the multicultural origins of Christmas, beginning with the first colonials. (No mention is made of Indigenous peoples.) The article praises the immigrants for bringing harmonizing cultures that were "to change and blend during a century and a half of the Republic," citing the Germans for having introduced two now widely popular customs, the first (of Italian origin), setting up a crèche that represented the birth of Christ, and the second, lighting the Christmas tree. The English and other Europeans, it adds, brought the tradition of singing carols in public.[94]

Similarly, the Christmas message in the 1965 *Intercom* asks readers to practise the "understanding, compassion and goodwill that prevails within the family circle at Christmas" throughout the year, and to extend this compassion for others to Toronto's community of diverse religious and ethnic groups, and also to the province, nation, and the international arena. Through its staff, members, and volunteers "of many races, religions, colours and creeds," it adds, the Institute was doing its utmost "to broaden our horizons still more and to extend the spirit of Christmas in time as well."[95]

At times, Toronto Institute personnel used the Christmas season to recognize the city and nation's non-Christians, and to argue that the positive ideals being celebrated were "not the sole prerogative" of Christians.[96] In the early 1960s, the *Intercom* declared that the Institute's members comprised "peoples of almost all lands and of all races and … religions." The list of 65 countries that appeared in the holiday message included, besides the European ones that dominated it, nations that included significant numbers of Hindus and Sikhs (India), Muslims (India, Iran, Iraq, Lebanon, Syria, and Egypt), and Buddhists (India and Japan). The list also included officially atheist Cuba, though the Institute would not have sanctioned Communism.[97]

The Institute's 1962 multi-ethnic Christmas cookbook project was, however, mainly European, and, like the interwar US Institute cookbooks cited above, Christian – there were no Jewish recipes. The aim, however, was not simply to entertain, but to promote a pluralist message, and the process of producing it involved intercultural collaboration. In both respects, it mirrored the 1956 cookbook of recipes of "new and old Americans" compiled by the staff of the Institute's central body in New York City. That book declared, "when we prepare and eat the food of a foreign country we are not only exploring unique gustatory delights but bridging a gap in international understanding."[98] The Toronto cookbook was also an Institute fundraiser that helped to cover the costs of the Christmas baskets and parties. A few men contributed a recipe, including one for Greek turkey stuffing.[99] Donald Bellamy, a professor of social work at the University of Toronto, sold copies to colleagues who "recognize a good thing and a good cause when they see it."[100] But it was the Institute women and their colleagues who were most directly involved in creating and selling the slim and inexpensive ($1) book. The women who peddled it included nuns, social work instructors, and SPC volunteers.[101]

Cookbooks are more than "just recipes" in part because the recipes, even if single-authored, are so often the product of women's personal and community relationships. Cookbooks offer an entry into the worldview or standpoint of the individual or collective cookbook makers, whether related to advancing a particular type of cuisine over another or projecting a particular cultural or ethics-based lifestyle.[102] In addition to the project's obvious pluralist message, the documents generated by the Institute's 1962 project again offer evidence of cross-cultural bonds of community forming among the women involved. For one thing, a number of women, including immigrant members, responded with enthusiasm to West's call for recipes. A Danish immigrant, Mrs R. Jensen, sent in her favourite recipes for Danish Christmas "Goodies" and was delighted that West included them.[103] The friendly note of a contributor of a recipe for Ukrainian cabbage rolls said she hoped "it helps you in your booklet idea." The inclusion of personal references suggest that she and West were on friendly terms.[104] Czech Canadian writer Marie Dymes sent West recipes for Czech fish dishes and yule loaf (vanocka), adding, "I only hope you will be able to decipher them." Although asked to provide personal favourites, Dymes took the project so seriously that she copied the recipes out of an old cookery book "to make them more reliable," but added, wistfully, that "they certainly evoked some old memories."[105]

West is equally friendly in her replies to the contributors, which included Hungarian Canadian staffers Elizabeth Szalowski and Szebeny. Szalowski wanted her borscht and beef stroganoff listed as "everyday recipes" representing "a mixture of old country and Canadian foods, adapted to the needs of a busy Canadian housekeeper, who still loves to cook and serve interesting meals." In both cases, ketchup and a package of dried onion soup mix appeared as the convenient "Canadian" (North American) processed ingredients. The borscht recipe also added wieners to the hamburger, (canned) consommé, diced beets (also tinned), celery, and potatoes. In addition to the familiar emphasis on quick and inexpensive meals is their flexibility: the meal could be prepared in advance and reheated and refrigerated leftovers used for another meal, thereby aiding "the Hostesses' disposition and appearance." Referring to her borscht recipe ("very nice to serve this stew-type soup on cold winter nights"), Szalowksi offered a familiar encouragement to women to be playful with meals and vary the recipe to keep family members from becoming bored eaters. One could use a ham base for borscht or add lima beans, cabbage, or tomatoes. Even more fun, she exclaimed, "for the ones who do not count calories!" was her "quick tasty potato pancakes": "this is excellent for a kitchen party – everybody ready with a plate waiting for the pancakes to be served right off the skillet (or skillets)."[106] Szebeny's recipe for a chicken and rice dish that included convenience items of cream of mushroom soup and condensed milk indicates that busy ethno-Canadian women had adopted quicker versions of Old World dishes. She, too, stressed ease and flexibility. The dish was "excellent" to prepare in advance for "a nice relaxed Sunday – dinner ready – just heat it and serve it," and leftover soup could be made by adding dumplings or fresh vegetables.[107]

A cookbook like *Season's Greetings in Food – Christmas 1962* is a multi-layered cultural, political, and gendered text. Written in the cheery style of the era's food writers, the book was clearly targeted mainly at Canadian and ethno-Canadian women operating in both an English and an ethnically Euro-Canadian milieu.

Institute staff also hoped to sell copies of the book – an English text that promoted culinary pluralism – to immigrant women like those enrolled in Institute classes or programs.

The cookbook offered brief descriptions of the varied European Christmas customs transplanted to Canada, including the Czechs' St Nicholas, who descends "from the heavens accompanied by an angel carrying a bag of gifts for good children and leading the devil who has switches for the bad ones." It noted the more intimate, familial, and less commercial nature of Christmas in Europe, where people enjoy a quiet family meal on Christmas Eve, attend mass, and perhaps exchange a few gifts. The emphasis, however, is on Christmas as a magical time, where children are delighted by golden or flying pigs or talking animals and people tell each other's fortunes. The playful take on pagan rituals continues into the section on New Year's Superstitions: the Irish must have "their lucky Irish bread" and the English believe that "for every mince pie you eat you will have a wish come true." The only reference to non-Europeans is an entry on the Japanese who "drink the first pail of water drawn from a well on New Year's morning" in the belief that it "drives evil spirits from their body."[108] Despite the inclusion of a few quaint "Anglo" customs, the overall emphasis on European villagers' fantastical beliefs veers into a primitive world of simple folk figures and quaint traditions.[109]

All but eight of the book's thirty-six recipes are depicted as popular Christmastime foods. Most are assigned a nationality or ethnic-group label, though some items easily crossed (European) borders. Paradoxically, given the Institute's interest in encouraging Anglo-Torontonians to experiment with "other" food customs, the single largest number of recipes were identified as British (for Christmas cake, pudding, and sauces), followed by four Czech, Italian, Portuguese, and Hungarian recipes, and two each of Lithuanian, Danish, Yugoslavian, and Ukrainian ones. Only two of the eight "year-around recipes" were ethnically marked, namely Finger Frets (Austrian pastry) and German Cake. The remaining "Canadian" recipes would have been familiar to Anglo-Torontonians: pumpkin pie, tuna casserole, and chicken and rice dishes. As Szalowski hoped, the borscht and the beef stroganoff, though European in origin, were also presented as Canadian recipes for the busy mother. (Her cute asides for the borscht and pancake recipes were also included.) Again, the selection of recipes both reflected and reinforced the mainstreaming of economical and nutritious European-origin foods, with commercially prepared ketchup and tinned or packaged soups acting as means of homogenization.

Nevertheless, the recipes were presented as cultural gifts transplanted to Toronto by the latest waves of European immigrants. The book featured "typical" Christmas meals of recent immigrants, including the Portuguese, who reportedly ate cod for Christmas Eve and a turkey dinner for Christmas with turkey soup, stuffed turkey, fish fillets, pumpkin croquettes, flan pudding, salad, jams, oranges and dried fruits. It noted, through a silly joke, that many Toronto Portuguese bought live turkeys (presumably from Kensington Market or neighbouring farms). "Before killing the turkey," the recipe advises the wife to give her husband "a drink of brandy so he gets drunk, then let him rest without food for 24 hours."[110]

Like other multi-ethnic Canadian and US cookbooks, the Institute's Christmas cookbook helped to create a safe cultural terrain on which the dominant "hosts" could be encouraged to accept "difference." Such cultural politics inevitably involved a process of mainstreaming the foreign food until it was no longer considered dangerously foreign yet still retained enough of the exotic to make experimentation worthwhile. Enticed by the fun prospect of experimenting with ethnic foods that, as a bonus, were generally cheap, it was argued, women across class and cultures could engage in mutual cultural exchange and share a healthy respect for culinary diversity. In short, these foods were cultural gifts that could be used to enrich the smorgasbord of Canadian national unity. A few immigrant and working-class women did participate in the project, but West held the reins of cultural power, and she and her middle-class friends decided what made it into the book.

Asian Cookbooks

The Institute's plans for other cookbooks suggest some effort to redress its Eurocentrism, but with a view to modifying ethnic cuisines for Anglo-Canadian palates. One such plan was for a series of "Eastern" cookbooks to be produced in cooperation with Chinese, Japanese, Korean, and other Canadian and immigrant Asian groups. However, the sole Asian cookbook in the Toronto Institute archive is a thin 1961 pamphlet called *Cooking in the Chinese Manner* that says nothing about having consulted anyone. The cover features a drawing of a young attractive Chinese woman in flowing Japanese kimono winking as she blasts off from a cloud, but the contents consist of Chinese recipes "adapted" to Canadian conditions and made easy for the Canadian housewife, who could now conveniently buy such items as bamboo shoots, water chestnuts, and crunchy noodles in her local supermarket. The featured dishes included Cantonese chow mein, egg foo young, barbequed spareribs, and boiled and fried rice.[111]

Another project that did not materialize was one initiated by Stewart, now Institute director, in 1968. The plan was to publish "a truly International Cookbook" that would celebrate the immigrants' culinary gifts to Canadian culture. It would also reflect, she added, the transformation in "Toronto's eating habits" resulting from "the enormous increase of travel" that had acquainted "native-born Canadians with the pleasing variety of European and Eastern dishes at home." Furthermore, it would "enable a hostess to entertain with a variety of foreign dishes" or serve "a whole meal from one country." Despite initial enthusiasm, the idea was dropped amid staff cuts due to declining funds.[112]

Conclusion

The Toronto Institute's record on promoting culinary pluralism was mixed, but, on balance, the women's food activism represented a collective if not fully co-ordinated effort to modestly shift the dominant Anglo-Canadian food culture of 1940s Toronto to that of a more outwardly pluralist society. In that regard, the Christmas cookbook, though slim, cheap, and even amateurish, and the banquets, though limited to about sixty people, were not only vehicles for the exchange of ideas among middle-class liberal women. To borrow from scholars who explore the relationship between gender, food culture, and nationalism, these texts and venues also constituted sites of a gender-influenced production of nationalist ideology that linked culinary experimentation and celebrations of multi-ethnic diets to participation in the new national culture of a more cosmopolitan society.[113]

The strategies or approaches also differed significantly with respect to the potential they held for promoting cultural diversity through culinary experimentation and facilitating a sense of cross-cultural community. The best example of cross-cultural bonds being forged was largely confined to the middle-class Institute female staff, members, and volunteers who worked collaboratively on both charitable and more community-affirming projects. Lofty ideas about food-and-festival pluralism could also serve to obscure the female labour so critical to getting these projects off the ground. In the end, and notwithstanding their celebration of the immigrants' supposed Christmas beliefs, the Institute women never took a leap towards a more radical reimagining of the city (and nation), one in which progressive immigrants reshape everyday life and revitalize politics in big cities.[114] While it contained some positive features, their food reformism instead remained largely within the realm of charity aimed at immigrant adaptation, the promotion of liberal cosmopolitanism on a budget, and the encouragement of ethnic entrepreneurialism. The latter was helped by the fact that a newcomer could enter the restaurant business with a small investment of capital, no professional training, and little knowledge of the hostland language, though one also needed to be able to draw on the labour of family or kin and work extremely long hours. An array of ethnic entrepreneurs (both pre- and post-1945 immigrants) who began initially by catering to their compatriots and local patrons contributed significantly to the proliferation of ethnic restaurants in 1960s Toronto. By the time of the Institute's demise in 1974, the greater willingness on the part of Anglo-Torontonians and others to experiment with eating "ethnic" was internationalizing Toronto's once dominant meat-and-potatoes and fish-and-chips food culture.[115]

PART FOUR

Ethnic Folk Cultures and Modern Multicultural Mandates

Chapter Ten

Immigrant Gifts, Pluralist Spectacles, and Staging the Modern City and Nation

In mid-1960s Toronto, as many as 20,000 people came out for the spectacular Nationbuilders shows that took place on the grandstand stage of the Canadian National Exhibition (CNE) during the last evening of the Labour Day weekend. As a member of the community folk council that mounted what was billed as the "largest folk festival in Canada," the International Institute of Metropolitan Toronto considered this (and other) multi-ethnic extravaganzas an integral part of their cultural mandate. A central goal of that mandate was to encourage Canadian appreciation for the talents and cultural gifts of immigrants and to promote a vision, or reimagining,[1] of a robustly pluralist city and nation.

The eclectic but polished Nationbuilders shows featured a dizzying array of performers. The 1964 program included more than 50 music ensembles and a cast of 1,500 "young Canadians" who delivered performances "in the native costumes of the land of their fathers." Sir Ernest MacMillan, described as the "patriarch" of Canada's conductors, led the "mass choir" of 500 singers from Toronto's many ethnic choirs and choral groups that ended the show. In regard to the emotional impact that such performances could have on an audience, Toronto Institute personnel believed in the unifying and transformative power of music and performance. The Nationbuilders and other events under review invited Anglo-Canadians, ethno-Canadians of all origins, and newcomers to participate in a festive affair intended to lift both the hearts and minds of audiences.

Insofar as the Nationbuilders shows brought an impressive number of newcomers into one of the defining public spaces of the city of Toronto, the CNE, they mark, too, the emergence of Toronto's immigrants as part of a wider culturally consuming public. The success of the shows, the costumes for which cost an estimated $100,000, served, paradoxically, to both reify immigrant folk cultures and legitimize public displays of cultural difference. It also encouraged still bolder experiments in promoting ethnic diversity through popular spectacle. Aided by the wider folk and white-ethnic revivals of the post-1945 and sixties eras, the Toronto Institute coordinated and participated in many collaboratively organized events. These ranged from the performances and arts and crafts exhibits of the Ethnic Weeks and Canadiana Weeks initiated by its first director, Nell West, to the folk festivals and, by 1969, the first iteration of what became Toronto's largest annual multicultural event, Metro International Caravan. In doing so, the Institute played a significant but largely unacknowledged role in helping to solidify Toronto's image as Canada's most culturally diverse city and to broadcast that image nationally in an era when diversity essentially meant the inclusion of white European cultures.[2]

Many Institute folks were involved in mounting these events, but most active were the women. The Institute's female cultural organizers included its middle-class directors, West and, later, Tine Stewart, its well-connected Anglo volunteers, its group work staff, and a variety of ethno-Canadian volunteers. This cultural activism, argued its advocates, contributed to pluralist civic-mindedness and nation-building in at least four ways. First, by bringing together immigrant, ethnic, and Canadian community groups to work collaboratively to help mount these events, the Institute was fostering mutual understanding, respect, and appreciation among old and new Canadians. Second, the events themselves inspired the public audiences, who took in the emotionally moving or lighthearted performances and the uplifting festive cultures of "others," to become enthusiasts of a more inclusive Canadian nation. Third, by taking immigrants out of their isolation or ethnic clusters to perform for, educate, and interact with Canadians, these pluralist spectacles helped to both preserve and promote cherished ethnic traditions and put them to use in the service of the nation. Finally, by encouraging in everyone, including English Canadians, a more cosmopolitan outlook, these popular spectacles were helping to build in Toronto an "international community," or local "United Nations," that could act as a model for the postwar nation.[3]

This chapter highlights the Institute women's efforts to effect a more fully multicultural reimagining of post-1945 Toronto and Canada through a cultural program of immigrant gifts and spectacles. That project was rooted in the paradoxical claim that immigrants could retain their cultural distinctiveness through a celebration of their "traditional" cultures (understood primarily as folk cultures) while simultaneously adopting Canadian values and integrating into the mainstream. In contrast to the health and trade-training campaigns and employment counselling, the cultural activism arguably had a more therapeutic (as in promoting inter-group harmony and keeping harsh realities at bay) than a reform-oriented goal (seeking to improve individual opportunities).[4] To dismiss this cultural activism as simply feel-good multiculturalism would, however, ignore its political aim – to encourage the loyalty of an increasingly heterogeneous population to the dominant liberal ideal of Canada as an enlightened democratic nation further enriched by immigrant gifts – and the contest and negotiation it entailed. Acutely aware that the success of their cultural events required the participation of an array of performers and audiences, the Institute women and their male colleagues courted and negotiated with the city's ethnic male elites and their cultural representatives, who had their own reasons for participating, or not, in these events.

My analysis of this cultural activity engages the scholarship on pageantry, spectacle, and commemoration, as well as that on nation-building. This literature has shed much light on the significant but uneven process of identity formation and cultural belonging and the creation of social meaning – as well as constructed and erased pasts – at different levels and among different groups of participants.[5] It has explored the impact of contemporary politics on commemorative pageantry and examined the cultural assertion of ethnic groups who were "negotiating the terms of their solicited participation" in official pageantry.[6] The Institute's eclectic cultural events contained a paradoxical mix of elements, including those associated with the liberal anti-modernism of cultural promoters whose projection of rural peoples as timeless folk served the modern tourist's nostalgic desire to visit a "quaint" past.[7] Ultimately, however, the Institute sought primarily to harness ethnic folk traditions to a modernist project in pluralist nation-building.

The chapter also traces the cross-border features of the Toronto Institute's popular pluralism, showing how it aligned with a history of US and Canadian efforts to promote a cultural pluralism that both celebrated and appropriated ethnic customs through a mosaic and treasure chest imaginary. In doing so, it contributes as well to the growing historical scholarship on the roots of multiculturalism in North America. Here, the focus is more on its popular manifestations rather than its intellectual attributes.[8] I argue, too, that the Toronto Institute's cultural pluralism informed late-twentieth-century multiculturalism in Canada, though not in any simple or linear fashion. My more bottom-up approach helps to explain why a federal policy forged in part for political reasons, both cynical and strategic, gained support particularly among many ordinary English Canadians within a relatively short period of time.[9]

Populist Predecessors

The immigrant-gifts approach that informed the Toronto Institute's cultural efforts to use immigrant folk traditions to promote immigrant integration and cultural diversity was inscribed in the mission statement accompanying its logo. A stylized Canada goose "winging over the Seven Seas," the logo was designed by Danish Canadian artist and commercial designer Thor Hansen in symbolic reference to the Institute's "work with people from around the world." The accompanying text declared that each newcomer carries with them "an abundance of gifts ... rich with the qualities that make this country great," and that all those "who help the newcomers express their abundant gifts share in enriching our country's future" and "nourish our nation's heart."[10]

This activity drew on both US and Canadian precedents. Toronto's gifts vocabulary echoed that of the wider international institute movement it officially joined in 1956. The US Institutes' pluralism drew inspiration initially from settlement house leaders, the earliest among the Progressive-era reformers to appreciate that Old World cultural forms survived in the immigrant communities. In the 1920s, prominent figures such as Jane Addams and Grace Abbott, both of Chicago, became leading proponents of an immigrant-gifts ideology. Arguing that immigrant customs did not threaten but instead enriched US society, the settlements expanded their offerings beyond English, civics, and educational programs to include ethnic folk events and pageants. The stage at Addams' Hull House regularly featured the Italian tarantella, Irish jig, and other folk performances. The staff occasionally recruited "native-born" Americans to perform in a Greek tragedy or in some other artistic production in order to increase their appreciation for the immigrants' rich cultural heritages.[11]

As US historian Kristin Hoganson notes, many women participated in the interwar era's gifts movement, including professionalizing social workers, teachers, and municipal officials as well as women's and civic groups. In opposition to the dominant assimilationist ethos of the "melting pot" and "100 per-cent American" movements, they argued not only that immigrants brought valuable gifts to America, but also that, far from undermining national loyalty, acknowledging their cultural distinctiveness and celebrating their nostalgic folk cultures fostered greater patriotism among them. This paradoxical mix of celebrating and appropriating ethnic folk cultures endemic to the immigrant-gifts movement was evident in venues across the nation, including in the Fourth of July parades where immigrant and first-generation Americans in ethnic dress pledged allegiance to the US while performing homeland folk songs and dances. Viewed through the conceptual framework of invented (as opposed to primordial) ethnicity, however, the mix of ethnic and hostland elements that marked ethnic celebrations of American holidays signified not a simple march towards Americanization but instead, as Ellen Litwicki notes, "illuminate[d] the dialectical relationship between ethnicity and assimilation." Situated at the intersection of ethnic and hostland cultures, such celebrations "constituted the intertwined products of the traditions and history of immigrants' homelands and their responses and adaptation to life in the United States." The observation also applies to Canada.[12]

Not surprising given the US history of slavery, anti-Asian racism, and imperialism in Latin America, US pluralists were more receptive to the cultural gifts of European derivation than those of African, Asian, or Mexican origins, though public celebrations of these "other" folk cultures certainly occurred. Public schools were major institutions of assimilation, but teachers also joined these efforts, organizing Pageants of Nations and folk-dance performances. Librarians ordered materials and helped with community events, which popular writers applauded as an effective way of bringing people together in friendly cooperation.[13]

The conversion of Edith Terry Bremer to pluralism in the 1920s similarly influenced the international institute movement that she founded in 1910. Aided in part by guidebooks and experts dispatched by the central body in New York City, local Institutes – which also produced homegrown pluralists – quickly adopted an immigrant gifts mandate. They diversified the "native-born" American staff by hiring immigrant and ethnic "nationality workers" to run classes in Old World history and culture. Often college graduates with some social work training, these foreign-born and first-generation US women organized performances and crafts along ethnic themes.[14]

The US Institutes' increasing emphasis on fostering ethnic consciousness and ethnic pride in immigrant heritage distinguished them from immigrant-gifts Americanizers who, like the YWCA that spawned them, adopted a more assimilationist position. By the 1930s, most Institutes, having declared that pluralism and integration could represent complementary rather than contradictory goals, had severed their ties with the YWCA and merged into a national movement that, as Raymond Mohl notes, carried out a paradoxical mandate of "both promoting cultural and ethnic pluralism and seeking better integration of immigrants and their children in American society." A primary means by which they promoted the message that diversity not conformity, and cooperation not conflict, were the essence of US democracy, was through an array of cultural events imbued with an immigrant-gifts philosophy.[15]

Diana Selig has documented the expansion of the interwar gifts movement into the major institutions of US life, including religious institutions and schools. An array of mostly middle-class liberal intellectuals, social scientists, child experts, educators, and Christian and Jewish clerics, as well as African American and various ethnic groups, sought to challenge the era's intensified xenophobia with demonstrations, interfaith events, child-study groups, and other programs promoting an alternative vision of tolerance and acceptance of cultural diversity. That gifts advocates eschewed radical critiques of class inequities or Jim Crow racism attests to the movement's cautious character.[16] The advent of wartime patriotism dampened some of these efforts, though, as Ellen Wu documents, an "Americans All" variant of liberal pluralism propelled Asian American groups to successfully wage a campaign of inclusion through emphasis on loyalty through military service and compatible family values to ultimately project themselves as model minorities. Still, overall, notes Selig, certain key, and limiting, features of this pluralism, such as the privileging of European folk cultures and a reluctance to address "the socio-economic systems that uphold racism" would resurface in late-twentieth-century multiculturalism.[17]

By then, however, very different factors came into play, including the civil rights movement and left-wing interracial urban alliances.[18]

When Toronto joined the institute movement in 1956, pluralism was still very much a minority position in Canada. Like their US interwar predecessors, West and company saw much of value in an immigrant-gifts pluralism. But unlike their post-1945 US counterparts, which initially focused on refugee resettlement cases,[19] Toronto Institute personnel immediately embraced the wide-ranging cultural mandates of the interwar era. They also consulted contemporary materials like the upbeat pamphlet on the Philadelphia Institute's 1960 Folk Fair that spoke of "35 nationalities and 3,000 people" enacting "a global event in the heart of the city of Brotherly Love."[20] An equally optimistic report by Elisabeth Ponafidine, an Italian American director of Buffalo's International Institute, was printed in the Toronto Institute newsletter, the *Intercom*. In it, she portrayed immigrants as talented people whose willingness to have their gifts "poured into the ever-changing framework of American life" would help to "create something new through the fusion of their talents, their homes, and aspirations," thereby laying "the foundations of love and understanding."[21]

The Toronto Institute's immigrant-gifts pluralism also had long roots in Canada even if a US travel writer, Victoria Hayward, coined that quintessential Canadian term, "mosaic." In her 1922 travelogue, *Romantic Canada*, she invoked the term in reference to the diversity she found during her cross-Canada tour, including in the European church architecture of the prairies, and, in orientalist fashion, the Japanese fishermen who plied the Fraser River in British Columbia. She referred to them as men of the "Far East" transplanted to "a river of the Far West." Hayward's patronizing portraits of the friendly Gaelic housewives of the Maritimes, Quebec's "quaint French villages," Abenaki basket makers, and Mennonite villages reflected an American's view that the presence of still culturally distinct immigrants and Indigenous peoples created an exotic landscape.[22]

Kate A. Foster's survey of "New Canadians" for the Dominion Council of the YWCA in 1926, entitled *Our Canadian Mosaic*, is a more slippery text. Some historians place it within a tradition of British Canadian imaginings of a national culture rooted primarily in Anglo-Saxon traditions but "enriched" by the addition of "other national elements." Criticizing a pluralist reading of the text, Susan Bellay argues that, while Foster later accepted a pluralist position, her 1926 book did not praise the cosmopolitanism of an emerging nation, but instead viewed immigration as "a problem in assimilation." And it endorsed Anglo-cultural homogeneity.[23]

The era's exemplary experiment in reimagining the Canadian nation through a populist pluralist frame was the interwar folk festivals that John Murray Gibbon organized on behalf of the Canadian Pacific Railway (CPR). Together, Gibbon's festivals (1927–31) and his 1938 book, *Canadian Mosaic*, popularized the term (mosaic) that would come to exemplify, as Ian McKay notes, post-colonial British Canadian urban modernity. A Scot born in Ceylon, Gibbon wrote *Canadian Mosaic* at a time when he was an influential figure in Canadian culture, having been involved in the founding of the Canadian Authors' Association (1921) and the Governor General's Literary Awards (1936). The book, which snagged the top literary prize in 1938, did much to propel into the mainstream the notion of Canada as a mosaic in which "different cultural identities coexist and contribute to a unified whole," but neither its approach nor its thesis was entirely original.[24]

Like Foster and others, Gibbon profiled the different European immigrant groups (he called them "races"). He listed their common characteristics and assessed them in terms of their compatibility with British ones, whether due to innate traits (as with the Scandinavians) or historical links with Britain (as with the Czechs). Given the importance accorded Gibbon "in the evolution of a bilingual, multicultural, national culture in Canada,"[25] it bears stressing that he excluded Asian, Indigenous, and African Canadian groups from his category of Canadian belonging. In his view, the community-based churches and clubs of the acceptable groups were the cement that would hold together new and old Canadian groups. Like other advocates of a British Canadian pluralism, Gibbon also put great stock in the malleability of the immigrants' children and considered the English Canadian public school system the most efficient means, or adhesive, by which to ensure a new generation of Canadians. Gibbon imagined that a superior because still emphatically Anglo-Saxon Canadian race would emerge from the commingling of the British and the "best" European groups, and his profiles were steeped in the period's race-based theories of biological traits and eugenics. All this fit with early-twentieth-century currents of Anglo-Canadian pluralism.[26]

As McKay and others observe, Gibbon's highly successful folk-festivals-cum-tourist-extravaganzas implemented a strategy of pursuing national unity amid growing ethnic diversity not through political or social engineering, but by "corralling" colourful and supposedly authentic folk cultures into populist celebrations.[27] As a university student at Oxford, Gibbon became enamoured with early twentieth-century romanticism and the nationalist folk revival movement it spawned in Europe. By the time he became chief publicist for the CPR, he was a consummate cultural entrepreneur whose efforts to reimagine a nationalist ideology amid growing diversity reflected his long-time advocacy of the commercial uses of folk culture. Drawing on a concept of immigrants as the bearers of timeless, premodern folk cultures, Gibbon's festivals reflected the view that, when celebrated together, these cultures offered an entertaining, hence unthreatening, assemblage of colourful dress, music, dance, and crafts that "served to minimize differences between cultures while seeming to provide an instance of democratic pluralism."[28] With British, European, and French groups in "picturesque" costumes and quaint handicrafts for sale, the prairie festivals visualized British Canadian pluralism. The performing immigrant groups were the colourful tiles in the mosaic, their complex histories rendered largely irrelevant, while Canada's geography, climate, and "founding" British peoples (with a tokenistic nod to the French co-founders) the "cements" that held the tiles in place.[29]

Like his counterparts at the US Institutes, Gibbon believed in the power of spectacle to change people's views of foreigners. Folk festivals, he argued, nurtured patriotism by encouraging appreciation especially among Anglo-Canadians for the newcomers. Speaking of his first festival in Winnipeg, which highlighted European settlement, he used a gifts vocabulary, saying it would prove "to Anglo-Saxon Canadians" that continental Europeans "have a fine gift of music and artistry for the making of the Canadian nation."[30] As in the United States, the populist advocates of interwar pluralism in Canada were not an entirely monolithic group, however. They also included ethno-cultural impresarios like the Ukrainian émigré, and cross-border folk-dance performer, Vasile Avramenko. As Orest Martynowych documents, the controversial "showman" used folk dance (and later film) to promote Ukraine's struggle for independence to Canadian and US audiences. After arriving in Canada in 1925, Avramenko established a network of Ukrainian folk-dance schools by appealing to Ukrainian immigrants' homeland loyalties and desire for cultural survival. By the mid-1930s, however, he had lost a fortune trying to parlay his success into a career on Broadway (his dance and music spectacles flopped) and then in Hollywood filmmaking. With his career in serious decline after the Second World War, Avramenko would spend the decades before his death in 1981 failing to secure sponsors in Australia, Israel, and elsewhere.[31]

Then, too, there were the organized ethnic groups that mounted their own public spectacles, and that chose to participate, or not, in state agendas to foster nationalism through commemorative pageantry. Here, Robert Cupido's research into the festivities organized in 1927 for the diamond jubilee of Canadian Confederation is particularly noteworthy. His analysis of the Canadian federal state's first major foray into nationwide commemorative organizing highlights how the ethnic groups invited to participate in a British Canadian–defined display of pan-Canadian nationalism disrupted the official narrative by flaunting their ethnic-group identities and histories. The colourful pageants and folk cultures of the city's marginalized Eastern European groups that were on public display in multiethnic Winnipeg, the site of the most elaborate pageant, asserted (in dialectical fashion) an alternative, pluralistic vision of Canadianness.[32]

The Toronto Institute's efforts to promote a popular form of cultural pluralism that could appeal to many "ordinary" Canadians reveal striking parallels with Gibbon's CPR festivals, though my analysis, like Cupido's, also highlights the agency of the ethnic actors involved. Once again, the celebrations of Canada's ever-expanding mosaic, or ever-enriching treasure chest (to use another popular metaphor) represented efforts to calm anxieties provoked by mass migration and urge ethnic harmony and political unity amid growing diversity. In each case, those efforts both drew on and contributed to a contemporary folk revival movement. As for differences, post-1945 immigration contributed even more significantly to the growing ethnic heterogeneity of Canada's population and, beginning in the late 1960s, to its racial diversity as well. Also, Toronto's popular pluralism was part of a more sustained effort that also included social welfare supports, and benefited from its location in the richest and arguably most influential city in Canada.[33]

Old World Bazaars and New World Gifts

The Institute's tourist-oriented fairs and bazaars were both fundraisers and experiments in community-based pluralism. They involved creating the Old World ambience of a European market or carnival where people could encounter different cultures while remaining safely at home. For the first of its bazaars – a four-day fair in 1957 that interrupted normal programs – the newly affiliated Institute used every space in its St Andrew's building on Jarvis Street to set up colourful booths and displays of crafts, games, and food in an effort to create a mix of Old World charm and New World modernity. In the style of a circus barker luring customers with promises of fun and adventure, the flyer announced "expert palmistry, teacup reading and fortune telling" and the chance to "feel rich" by joining a "millionaire's night." Promising a delightfully foreign shopping excursion for minimal cost, it added that, with handicrafts by artists from many ethnic groups, each item with its own "distinctive design and national character," the adventurous shopper could impress family and friends with "distinctive" gifts, from hats to trays. Or the fairgoer could buy "beautiful and unusual Christmas cards of many lands." The flyer also encouraged people to socialize and end the night on the "gaily decorated" dance floor where, thanks to the Institute's professional dance instructors, they could try everything "from ballroom to hulahula."[34]

In claiming that such events helped the ethnic groups "maintain their folk art and handicrafts in Canada" by introducing them to a larger market, Institute staff combined a certain romantic wistfulness with modernist sentiments about nation-building. As such, they exhibited a degree of nostalgic modernism, a form of liberal anti-modernism informed by an uneasy symbiotic relationship between folklore preservation and faith in capitalist progress.[35] But the emphasis was on complementarity: folklore preservation (unique ethnic handicrafts) existed alongside a faith in capitalist modernity (consumption as a nation-building tool). As the agency's Estonian group work supervisor put it,

232   Ethnic Folk Cultures

A woman dressed as a twenties-era flapper poses with a man dressed in a striped prison uniform during Carnival night at the International Institute on Jarvis Street, c. 1958. Archives of Ontario, F884-2-9, B427166.

through their interactions and purchase of traditional folk crafts, the participants were contributing to "building a new and richer society."[36]

The bazaars hardly provide dramatic examples of what Mikhail Bakhtin called the carnivalesque – events that take on a time-out-of-time character, involving elements of social inversion and/or levelling.[37] Muted expressions of it existed in, for example, the references to labouring immigrants playing (with pennies) at being millionaires, but the focus on fun and domestic tourism (literally buying immigrant gifts) meant little risk of subverting hierarchies of any kind. The stronger message was that, as people soaked up the ambience of an Old World market and joined in a folk dance and a modern cha-cha-cha, a sense of collective belonging would replace the instinctual tendency to huddle with one's own kind – a prerequisite for forging a modern enlightened pluralist community. This strategy of mining folk cultures for modernist goals was also captured in an article on the postwar folk revival that appeared at the same time in the Institute's just launched newsletter. Author Anne Von Oesen attributed the recent resurgence in the popularity of "a long time ago folk lore" that "abounds with imaginary heroes and heroines; in gnomes and witches; nymphs and monsters, etc." to the "yearning" of a sophisticated civilization "for its own simple interpretations of beauty and warmth." But she also emphasized that a knowledge of folk art and how it made its way into the poems, plays, and music of great writers and composers would help modern citizens understand much about modern cultures and nations.[38]

Gift Giving and Receiving Spectacles

The Institute's pluralist stance as gifts promoters was especially evident in the two cultural programs that West launched in 1957, the Ethnic Weeks and Canadiana Weeks. A "community project" to showcase the "cultural attributes" of Toronto's "local ethnic communities" and promote "closer understanding between 'New' and 'Old' Canadians,"[39] each Ethnic Week celebrated a given group's culture with concerts, films, lectures, exhibits, music, dance, and food.[40] Insofar as they offered a packaged pageantry of colourful performances, exhibits, and decorated banquet buffets, they underscore Philip Bohlman's insight about folk festivals being institutional vehicles by which "ethnicity is made manageable." And they illustrated precisely what immigrants were to do with their talents and customs: place them in Canada's treasure chest.[41]

An estimated 300 people attended the Sunday afternoon tea that kicked off the inaugural Polish Ethnic Week in February 1957. The Ethnic Week concerts that followed the afternoon teas typically featured classically trained singers and musicians; in this case, it was baritone Roman Severin, violinist Annette Wegiel, and pianist Josephine Jagusia. Overall, however, the week-long program highlighted folk culture, including dance performances, a film on Polish history ("Homeland of My Mother"), and an arts and crafts exhibit.[42] Other Ethnic Weeks mounted that season, including German, Lithuanian, and Latvian ones, delivered similarly folk-dominated but eclectic programs that attracted similarly sized audiences. The audiences were composed of a mix of Institute members and their relatives or friends – volunteers, English teachers, and other staff along with the friends or colleagues to whom they sold tickets – and those who learned about the event in an English- or foreign-language newspaper.[43]

With the limited space at St Andrew's, the Institute also adopted a one-evening format. One of the Ethnic Nights held in spring 1959 was Greek

Sunday, whose musical program included "accordion solos, Classical and popular numbers, Rhythms of Greece." For St George's Day, an English holiday, stage actor and radio personality Charles Hayter sang some Elizabethan and Shakespearian songs as well as regional folk songs in original dialect. The latter included "Cheshire Man" (Cheshire) and "Turnip Hoeing" (Wiltshire).[44] Following the Institute's move shortly afterwards to College Street, with its renovated auditorium (capacity 1,000) and cabaret space (300–50), West and colleagues resumed the week-long programs.

West argued that the Ethnic Weeks "can do much to increase the [Canadian] community support of ethnic organizations, increase inter-ethnic understanding and further promote the cultural contribution that ethnic groups are making to Canada." She knew, too, that the better the Institute could "mirror" the "variety" of Toronto's "cultural heritages," the greater its claim to being a laboratory in multicultural community living. The much bigger space did boost their profile; throughout the College Street years, the special events attracted capacity crowds.[45]

This was true of the successful Hungarian Week held in November 1963. Toronto mayor and folk-culture advocate Donald Summerville opened the program with a ribbon-cutting ceremony at the arts and crafts exhibit. For the concert, the "famed" Hungarian Kodály Ensemble of Toronto, a choral, orchestra, and folk-dance group, drew from their repertoire of peasant and soldier-themed songs and dances. It included music composed by Zoltán Kodály, the twentieth-century Hungarian classical composer and music educator who became an influential folk-song collector and promoter, and that of contemporary colleagues like Béla Bartók. People returned each night to take in films, lectures on Hungarian architecture and history, poetry readings, the Kodály Ensemble again, and, on Saturday night, a Hungarian dance and floor show in the Hungarian-themed cabaret space.[46]

With the help of the well-connected men on the board, the Institute women, along with the male directors, worked hard to recruit dignitaries for the Ethnic Weeks because their presence lent prestige and attracted the mainstream media. For the ethnic media, they tapped the mainly European networks that West particularly nurtured, including through invitations to socials and, at least on one occasion, to her lodge in Muskoka.[47] The Institute's relationship with Summerville, who died shortly after the 1963 Hungarian week, was closer than with most public figures because of their mutual involvement in the founding of the Toronto-based Community Folk Art Council (CFAC). His presence largely explains the coverage the event received in the mainstream press (see below).[48]

The (less demanding) Ethnic Nights or Sundays also grew more frequent on College Street and then became the norm after the move, in 1969, to Davenport Road. There was no Italian or Portuguese Week, but Italian and Portuguese variety nights were held at the Institute and local restaurants. Using a gifts

Immigrant Gifts and Pluralist Spectacles   235

Folk singer George Brown performs North American songs at the Institute, 1961. Archives of Ontario, F884-2-9, B427166.

vocabulary, the flyer for a 1961 Italian "Continental Café" described the performers as "foreign-born professionals ... who – if given the opportunity – are not only able but willing to enrich Canada's cultural life."[49] In her enthusiastic report on the Portuguese Festival held in January 1968, Portuguese counsellor Maria Mota said that those who braved the cold winter night were "well rewarded" with "magnificent performances." She described the featured folk singer Isabel Santos as Toronto's Amália Rodrigues, a celebrated Portuguese singer of *fado* (nostalgic folk songs) whose international reputation was due largely to a forties hit song ("April in Portugal") that enjoyed renewed popularity following its re-recording in the fifties by French and US singers. The night also featured folk dances performed by Rancho Da Nazere and other troupes associated with the city's First Portuguese Canadian Club. People danced to the popular music supplied by the Da Boa Esperança band, also of Toronto.[50]

From the start, the Institute did include cultural performances by racialized groups such as Chinese Canadians. By the 1960s, the cultural gifts of racialized immigrants were celebrated through the Caribbean-themed Calypso evenings and, at decade's end, an India Night with "Classical and Folk Dances," music, and films. In the early 1970s, the Institute promoted the events of its tenant, the Tibetan Cultural Society, and an Asian youth festival.[51] Overall, however, the

Women like these hostesses dressed in Lithuanian national dress made out of colourful textiles welcomed people to the Institute's Ethnic Weeks and other cultural events. Note also the hand-crafted dolls and wood-carved decorative spinning wheel. Archives of Ontario, F884-2-9, B427166.

Institute carried out its experiment in cultural pluralism within a mainly white European and Anglo-Canadian context. The two key ingredients for success were the ethnic groups' "readiness" to "come out of their isolation and present themselves to the [Canadian] community," and the "voluntary, spontaneous interest of the Canadian public" in attending and participating in these events.[52] Even if English Canadians had to be cajoled into attending, their appreciation of the performances was paramount.

If the Institute's Ethnic Weeks and nights created cultural spectacles in which immigrants symbolically offered their talents and gifts to Canada, the Canadiana Weeks served in part to symbolically accept them into an ever-expanding Canadian treasure chest that, through its collection and absorption of the

Immigrant Gifts and Pluralist Spectacles   237

A Latvian folk-dance troupe that performed at the Institute on Jarvis Street in 1958. Archives of Ontario, F884-2-9, B427166.

Young women perform traditional Chinese dances at the Institute on Jarvis Street, 1958. Archives of Ontario, F884-2-9, B427166.

The Chinese dragon dance was part of the line-up of several Institute-sponsored multicultural shows. Here, the performers and spectators are in front of Mon Kuo Trading Co. Ltd., 120 Elizabeth Street in the Ward. York University Libraries, Clara Thomas Archives & Special Collections, Toronto Telegram fonds, ASC02735.

cultures of successive waves of immigrants, became enriched. They were also meant to educate and inspire feelings of loyalty to Canada. As the fall event kicking off a new season of programs, the Canadiana Weeks followed a familiar format but put Canadian, especially Anglo-Canadian, history and culture on display. Canadian folk singers (both traditional and commercial), arts and crafts, and a ceremonial marking of historic events considered key in Canada's evolution from British colony to mature nation, filled the programs. The nationalist narrative contained a pluralist interpretation of Canada as a nation whose two founding races, but especially the British, had learned first to tolerate, then accept, and finally celebrate the cultures of others. This narrative underlay the highly eclectic Anglo-Canadian spectacles, which also stressed the diversity of Scots, Irish, and other groups that comprised Canada and Ontario's British population. There was also some French Canadian, Indigenous, and European content.

More than six hundred people attended the Sunday opening ceremonies of the first Canadiana Week in September 1957 hosted by John Yaremko, a Ukrainian Canadian lawyer and member of the Ontario legislature. One of several Ukrainian Canadian leaders that would claim or receive recognition as a "father" of multiculturalism, Yaremko later returned to the Institute as Ontario's provincial secretary and minister of citizenship. (In the early 1970s, he served on the Institute's board.) The text of Yaremko's speech for the 1957 event is not available, but in other speeches that acknowledged the Institute, he declared that newcomers "enrich themselves and our nation" by preserving their culture and drawing from the "equally rich storehouse of the two cultures which lie at the root of this nation."[53]

Set against a colourful backdrop of flags, the 1957 Canadiana festivities included the Hungarian Kodály Choir's "soaring" rendition of "O Canada" and a "lively" and "festive" recital delivered by a young German pianist, Horst Minkofski-Garrigues.[54] But it was the Canadian content and lessons provided through the performances, films, lectures, books, and paintings that dominated this and subsequent Canadiana Weeks. A reported highlight was a "fascinating" lecture by Eric Morse, executive secretary of the Canadian Clubs movement. A joint event held with the YWCA and the YMCA at the Central "Y" in downtown Toronto, Morse's colour-slide show celebrated his recent escapade with five other "adventurers" who, "guided by maps, air photos, and early diaries," retraced the canoe routes of the early explorers and fur traders. His conclusion – that, 1600 miles later, he could report that Canada's landscape "has hardly changed since the white man first came" – suggests how a colonial gaze erased Indigenous peoples. An NFB film made for tourists featuring "scenic vistas" and "people of many ethnic origins" highlighted the diversity and industry of Canada's settler people as well as the landscape.[55]

The ubiquitous presence of folk music at the Canadiana Weeks was in evidence in the sixties-era programs, whose opening concerts included a mix of European folk songs, African American gospel music, and Canadian folk songs. The immigrant component in 1963 came in the form of some "country dances" performed by the International Folk Troupe at University Settlement House, a west end settlement, led by staffer Ivy Krehm.[56] An eclectic program also characterized the successful opening of Canadiana Week in 1965, when a thousand people filled the auditorium to hear Toronto's first Jewish mayor, Nathan Phillips, accompanied by John Gellner, the Czech Canadian president of the Institute board, praise the ethnic groups for their many contributions to Canada. An Institute group member, Gateway to Entertainment, staged a Continental European Caravan with European folk songs, piano and accordion solos, the Spanish flamenco (with guitar), and the French can-can.[57]

English Canada enjoyed centre stage at the Canadiana Weeks, but some attention was paid to the folk culture of Quebec and francophone Ontario. The organizers sought to instil pride in and loyalty to the nation among mixed audiences through the use of dramatic imagery, the ceremonial marking of achievements, and bold predictions of still further progress. Each year, the Toronto

Nell West hosting John Yaremko (left, holding a small basket with decorated eggs) and a priest during an Institute cultural event, c. 1960. Archives of Ontario, F884-2-9, B427166.

Art Gallery (now the Art Gallery of Ontario) lent paintings by officially celebrated "masters" who, either in traditional (such as Cornelius Krieghoff's peasant-themed "Habitants Sleighing") or modern style (Emily Carr's "Kispiax Village" featuring West Coast totem poles) captured what were heralded as quintessentially Canadian subjects. With their muscular renditions of the Canadian landscape (erased of Indigenous peoples), the paintings by members of the Group of Seven might offer quick nationalist lessons in the beauty and vastness of Canada and the spirit and strength of a white-settler northern people.[58]

The 1965 program featured Confederation Life Insurance Company's collection of commissioned paintings depicting historic Canadian subjects, or, rather, some glossy reproductions. No stranger to nationalist pageantry, Confederation Life had published a brochure of its paintings to encourage schools, service clubs, and local communities to celebrate the approaching hundredth anniversary of Canadian Confederation by providing ideas for "suitable" commemorative histories, pageants, and tableaux.[59] What it meant by "suitable" is suggested by the pamphlet's inclusion of John David Kelly's paintings of the 1885 North-West Rebellion, a Métis and First Nations resistance crushed by an expanding Canadian state but officially touted as a victory for white-settler civilization and a historic achievement in modern nation building.[60] The pamphlet's narrative combined a romantic view of Canada's heroic past and its supposed openness to "other" peoples with an optimistic assessment of the nation's future "greatness." There is plenty of "forgetting" here of less exemplary acts like Canada's Chinese exclusionary regime and the thoroughly discredited church- and government-run residential schools that sought to assimilate Indigenous children to the lowest rungs of white society. The message that "Canada's phenomenal development" reflected the "contributions of the men and races who have followed" the original explorers to this land, fit well the Institute's claims that, having grown stronger from incorporating earlier waves of immigrant talents and cultures, Canada was poised to become a model pluralist nation.[61]

Folk Festivals and Multicultural Extravaganzas

The Institute made its first foray into mega-festival organizing in June 1957 as a founding member of the new Ontario Folk Festival Society – whose goal was to "promote good citizenship" through the advocacy of "the folk arts that are the heritage of Canada's people of every racial and religious background." It did so by piggybacking onto an established venue, the (modestly priced) annual John Madsen Folk Festival, a Saturday stage-show extravaganza involving several thousand people at a folk school based on a farm just outside Toronto. While the performers at Institute events came mainly through the affiliated ethnocultural groups, more commercial ventures like the Madsen Folk Festival, established in 1948 by a Danish Canadian couple, tapped into a wider semi-professional North American circuit. The performers themselves combined or straddled classical and popular traditions. Choral groups, for example, performed folk songs and sacred (liturgical) music as well as choral pieces written or interpreted by classically trained composers influenced by folk traditions. Similarly, gospel singers often had some classical training while opera-trained singers often performed ethnic folk songs.[62]

Described as "perfection!" the 1957 jointly sponsored event involved the usual procession of high school marching bands and "Scottish" bagpipers and a jam-packed show with hundreds of performers belonging to more than twenty groups from across North America. In addition to the English country dances, a few French Canadian folk songs, and many European performances, the Madsen festival typically included a few more "exotic" dances of Indonesian, African, Indigenous, or other origins, though the coverage of the 1957 event contains no such references. But things did end as usual, with a (bring-your-own) picnic supper, mass square-dancing on the greens, and a singalong around a large bonfire.[63] The Institute's entry into mega-festival organizing was also helped, albeit indirectly, by commercial ventures like the CNE's annual Canadiana variety show, which, by the late 1950s, added more ethnic folk content to a mainly Canadian line-up that included the Canadian Armed Forces Drill

Squad or the RCMP Musical Ride, and Canadian folk singers. The hosts were usually American personalities expected to be big draws, such as comedians Danny Kaye and George Gobel.[64]

West's successor as Institute director, H.C. Forbell – who worked with West and others to expand their cultural mandate – articulated the logic behind the large festivals. Toronto, Forbell asserted in 1961, had gained "such cultural talent" and "innumerable artistic treasures" from immigration that it was time to focus on "mount[ing] major multicultural events celebrating the Canadian mosaic." The smaller events staged by the individual ethnic groups, he reasoned, had a role to play in preserving and promoting ethnic customs within the immigrant communities and among subsequent generations. The nation's interests, however, were best served by large venues where the immigrants' "artistic and cultural talents" were enjoyed "by all ethnic groups, by immigrants, by new Canadians and by old Canadians." Furthermore, it was the latter's attendance at such events "that the greatest good can be achieved for all concerned." Capturing the Institute's strategy of harnessing "traditional" ethnic folk cultures to a modern and mainly urban nation-building project, Forbell added that the "artistic and cultural talents with which the various ethnic groups are so richly endowed should not be preserved like diamonds in a jeweller's vault," but had "to be used [and] exercised nationally." By so doing, "they will grow and take on a new vitality," both "retain[ing] all the significance of the country of origin" and "tak[ing] on new and meaningful interpretations of this land."[65]

An example of how the Institute carried out this ambitious strategy through collaboration with others is the Nationbuilders shows held in 1964 and 1965. (Similar shows occurred in 1969 and 1970.) As a founding member of the show's sponsor, the Community Folk Art Council of Metropolitan Toronto (CFAC est. 1963), the Institute committed staff time and resources to organizing them.[66] The show followed the city's Labour Day parade at the CNE, which ended in front of the grandstand. Admission was free with admission to the park. The mass choir that concluded the variety show line-up of performances included members of the Lithuanian Varpas Choir, Santa Cecilia Italian Choir, Irish Choral Society, Polonia Choir, and Prometheus Ukrainian Chorus. Gathered in tribute to the recently deceased mayor and founding CFAC chair, Donald Summerville, the "cosmopolitan" choir also closed the 1965 show. The previous year's performance included a "massive melodic folk song panorama of Canadian folk songs," ranging from the "lively sea shanties of Newfoundland to the plaintive ballads of the Prairies." John Fisher, the Centennial Commissioner in charge of planning the country's hundredth anniversary festivities, narrated the two-hour show in 1964 and came as special guest for the 1965 show.[67] All this fit nicely with the Institute's position that, as one staffer put it, "music was the universal language" and "a great unifying factor" that helps people recognize that "we" have "common interests" that must be nurtured.[68]

While a few people later grumbled about the city not having offered more financial support, the Nationbuilders shows were fully orchestrated events produced with all the stage facilities of the grandstand. Its executive producer, Jack Arthur, produced them along with CFAC chair, Leon Kossar. A Ukrainian Canadian folk-culture advocate and cultural entrepreneur, Kossar was a journalist whose *Toronto Telegram* column "New Canadian Interests" promoted this and other ventures. With audiences that ranged between 17,000 and 20,000 people, these were well-attended shows in a venue with a regular maximum seating of between 21,000 and 22,000. The mix of newcomers, ethno-Canadians, and Anglo-Torontonians in the audience were actively participating in an immigrant-gifts pluralism that, for all of its shortcomings, contributed towards legitimizing public displays of cultural difference in Toronto.[69] (The big-ticket CNE concerts that drew larger audiences to an expanded Exhibition Stadium did not begin until the 1970s.) Their success raised Kossar's profile as a cultural entrepreneur and popularizer along the Gibbon model.[70]

This is not to suggest that the Institute's populist pluralism followed a linear trajectory towards larger venues. Its plans to make Toronto both the driving engine and a shining model of a bold cultural pluralism suffered setbacks. City boosters might boast about Toronto having surpassed Montreal as the nation's financial centre, but no city rivalled Montreal during Expo 67, the multi-million-dollar world fair held to celebrate the one hundredth anniversary of Confederation. Expo 67 attracted the most attendees ever to a world fair.[71] The excitement it generated among immigrants as well as Canadians and tourists was evident at the Toronto Institute, where group work staff worked overtime to organize dozens of weekend bus trips to Expo.[72] The Institute and CFAC pledged to rival Montreal with grand plans for a national choral competition, folk festival, and various ethnic food and music preservation projects, but the final production resembled an Institute-style Canadiana Week in both format and size (perhaps just over a thousand attended).[73]

However, two years later, the Institute, under Tine Stewart's directorship, enjoyed its biggest ever success through its role in launching Metro International Caravan. Taking the immigrant-gifts and domestic tourism approach to another level, Metro Caravan became the splashiest multicultural extravaganza in Toronto's history. A pluralist spectacle that combined the elements of a trade show, city booster campaign, nationalist propaganda event, ethnic-group lobby, and tourist venue, Metro Caravan's inaugural summer festival featured thirty international pavilions, or "ports of call," awaiting discovery by Torontonians and visitors to the city. Playing on the tourist conceit, Metro Caravan had people purchase a passport ($2 in 1969) to visit some of the world's capitals and leading cities, most of which were located in ethnic halls and clubs across the metropolitan area. (Expo 67 had used the same gimmick.) The pavilions bore the colours of their city and country, the performers were dressed in bright costumes, and the hosts, dressed in ethnic regalia, served "authentic national foods, drinks" and "arts and crafts" at reasonable prices. Events were held in the evening so more people could attend. The passport, duly stamped with the cities visited, could be kept as a souvenir or mailed in for a chance to win a trip to an "exotic" locale. In 1969 it was Mexico City.[74]

In keeping with the eclecticism of such events, the opening ceremonies kicking off the five-day festival on 26 June offered a mix of the old and new. City of Toronto Mayor William Allen proclaimed the start of Metro Caravan at Nathan Phillips Square (site of the new City Hall) while flanked by a town crier in medieval regalia. Marching bands played the festival theme song, "The Magic Caravan," an insipid pop tune, and the City Hall performances included a Latvian folk troupe and Irish step dancers. Similar ceremonies took place in all five participating boroughs and special buses moved people across city and suburbs for free. The festivities concluded on Dominion Day (1 July) with a concert at Queen's Park, site of the Ontario legislature, and a parade and street dancing. An immediate success, Metro Caravan attracted 40,000 people in its early years and grew steadily both in duration and number of pavilions. In 1970, some 400,000 people participated. Far outlasting the Institute, it became an integral part of Toronto's multicultural landscape for thirty-five years.[75] Significantly, many middle-class Anglo-Torontonians cite their participation in Metro Caravan as the event that raised their consciousness about the city's growing diversity.[76]

As festival host, Kossar (who also co-wrote the theme song) was the public face of Metro Caravan: wife Zena was centrally involved, too, but reporters named him "Mr. Ethnic Canada." The executive committee both acknowledged that it aimed to replicate the successful "international folk fairs" of US cities such as Toledo, St Paul, Philadelphia, and Detroit – all cities with an International Institute – and boasted about putting on a bigger show "involving 50 civic and community sites." They explained the festival's dual purpose in Institute-style language. One was "to dramatize with quality the many cultural heritages that make up Canada," to ensure the "special participation" of the newcomers, and to provide "a major event that exemplifies the international aspects of Metro Toronto." The other was "to show the public that we have mutual interests in being citizens of Metro Toronto, and proud Canadians no matter what our creed, race, nationality or tradition."[77]

Metro Caravan attracted considerable mainstream media attention from city and national newspapers and newsmagazines. In the 1970s, the *New York Times* and other US publications wrote about Caravan. Most Toronto reporters obliged the organizers of the inaugural Metro Caravan. They played up the cosmopolitan fun and pluralist lessons to be had from a festival that, as *Toronto Telegram* writer Colin Murray claimed, would allow so many to become "a world traveler for six mad carefree days" without the hassle of real travel. "No smallpox vaccinations. No cramped economy seats. No customs inspections. No little brown pills," he wrote, adding, "just soft candlelight dinners, exotic food, wild international drinks, beautiful girls in brilliant costumes, singing, dancing, international cabarets." In their rush to celebrate the immigrants' cultural gifts, reporters like Murray overlooked the fact that some cities, including Mexico City, were on display not because of an immigrant presence in Toronto but because of the backing of companies and tourism boards hoping to drum up business.[78]

Other columnists, including McKenzie Porter, also of the *Telegram,* wrote seriously about the "cosmopolitanism" of Metro Caravan and urged Toronto's "WASPS" to appreciate, indeed embrace, the "bright, modern, more worldly attitude" that was replacing the city's "old Anglo-Saxon provincialism." The retrograde US "melting pot" also made an appearance. Significantly, Porter acknowledged the Asian as well as European pavilions, and the contributions of non-European groups to the nation. Praising them for having "proven themselves good Canadians without losing their individuality," he invoked the former Liberal prime minister, saying that "the ethnic groups" were "giving us what Lester Pearson described as 'unity in diversity.'"[79] While he did not say so explicitly, Porter's comments underscored the fact that Metro Caravan was taking place against the wider backdrop of the hearings, briefs, conferences, and reports generated by the Royal Commission on Bilingualism and Biculturalism (1963–9) that Pearson had launched primarily to address English-French tensions.

As Institute director, Stewart oversaw the plans that turned its new building on Davenport Road into a Caravan pavilion. Paying homage to several nationalities, it offered an eclectic mix of "Steel Bands, Smorgasbord, Swiss Fondues, Canadian Folk Singers!" A "French-Canadian room" featured an exhibit of Quebec sculptures and recordings of folk songs. The room named after the nation's capital, Ottawa, displayed "Indian masks" and "Eskimo prints." A historical exhibit highlighted Canada's growth with maps and photographs. A bigger attraction was the outdoor dance area where people practised square-dance steps accompanied by a fiddler and caller, and danced polkas and modern dances under the twinkling Christmas lights. Every hour, a group of folk singers performed a set of Canadian folk songs. Most noteworthy was the Caribbean festival located in the auditorium, where the "hot rhythm of the Steel Band of Trinidad-Tobago" performed in "an island setting for dancing." Dressed in white billowing blouses, dark skirts, and colourful jewellery, the young Caribbean women of La Petite Musicale of Toronto also performed songs and dances.[80]

The Caribbean musicians recalled the Institute Calypso Nights of the early 1960s (see chapter 7) featuring, among others, Charles Roach, now a civil rights lawyer and co-founder of Caribana, the Caribbean festival launched two years previously as a Canadian Centennial project. If the small but important West Indian presence held out the promise of building a more racially inclusive Institute community, Roach's own belief in the power of music and culture to raise

Of the outdoor Bavarian Beer Garden at the Berlin pavilion (site of the German Canadian Club Harmonie, 410 Sherbourne Street), the Metro Caravan program wrote, "A six-piece oom-pah-pah band provides accompaniment for the visitors' sing-along, and Bavarian dancers entertain." York University Libraries, Clara Thomas Archives & Special Collections, Toronto Telegram fonds, ASC60822 (photographer Jac Holland, 26 June 1971).

the morale particularly of racialized immigrants, facilitate integration, and affect broader social change suggested some common ground with the Institute and Kossar. In a 1965 article published in the *Intercom*, Roach emphasized the need for Toronto's many ethnic groups to shift from creating enclaves of "intense cultural activity on a purely ethnic in-group basis" to transforming a stern Anglo-Saxon city lacking "joie-de-vivre" and "spirit" into a culturally vital place. He thought it would still take some time because, while the immigrants might be impressed by the city's wealth and modern services, and even benefit materially from its educational and job opportunities, alienation and fear of "rocking the boat" created a "feeling of emptiness" that kept these groups, even the numerous Italians, from becoming fully engaged.

Roach's understanding of "joie-de-vivre" as the "public expression of convivial fellowship in day-to-day living, in fashion, music, dance, theatre, art, sports and all leisure time activities" resembled that of the Institute and its cultural allies. But he differed from them in arguing that Torontonians, particularly the well-to-do, would play no role in injecting cultural spirit into the city core because they considered it a place of work and shopping, but not of living (which for them was the suburbs or the cottage). His suggestions for how immigrants accustomed "to a more spirited life-style" could "noticeably" change the city reflected a familiar mix of community-building techniques, such as dance and sports, and tourism-related strategies. Toronto, Roach argued, needed sporting events that reflected homeland cultures (which, in the West Indian case, included cricket matches and its attendant social practices), sidewalk cafes, public art, ethnic neighbourhood festivals in places like Kensington Market, Chinatown, and College Street's Little Italy, carnivals, and band concerts in High Park and Civic Square. Roach got into some semantic gymnastics, noting that "of course, the immigrant must be assimilated," but also that integration must be "a two-way street," thereby approximating the Institute's vision of both old and new Canadians becoming transformed through pluralist community-building.[81] But apart from some individual input, there was no evidence of direct Institute involvement in Caribana. Beyond Metro Caravan's multiracial performances, I did not detect an emerging multiracial alliance among Toronto's cultural entrepreneurs.

Behind the Festival Stage

How did a modestly funded agency mount an impressive array of cultural events? Well aware that their modest budget for cultural programming could hardly support their grand plans, Institute personnel mobilized people and resources in support of these events. Male board members with business, media, or political networks helped in attracting funds or recruiting dignitaries to attend or host an event. Business links also explain more commercialized events; for example, the organizer of a 1970 ski-themed Scandinavian Night owned the travel agency that sold the tickets for the weekend ski package.[82]

But it was the women administrators, staff, and volunteers who repeatedly made requests of everyone, from local ethnic bakeries and department stores (for prizes, decorations, and building supplies) to City Hall, Queen's Park, and Ottawa (for the grandees). Staffers recruited Institute members, both immigrants and "native-born" Canadians, to decorate rooms, make posters, and build booths. The Toronto Junior League and IODE volunteers used their networks to ensure that more "old" Canadians attended the events. Ethno-Canadian volunteers brought novelty items and recorded music for the carnivals. The network of YMCA and YWCA branches, and their Jewish counterparts, offered the Institute space and co-hosted certain cultural events with them. The Institute women tapped the Local Councils of Women and men's service groups (Kiwanis, Rotary) to help with the opening teas and get their people out to the events. The Toronto Historical Board and other local societies provided materials for exhibits. This legwork was critical because the contributions helped to subsidize the events and keep Institute finances afloat. The dignitaries secured included city councillors, mayors, and citizenship judges as well as a few provincial ministers, such as Yaremko, and a few federal ministers, such as J.W. Pickersgill (as minister of immigration).[83]

The support of the Institute's affiliates, however fraught and complex the relationship, was essential to its cultural strategies. The Institute's 1960 roster of thirty affiliated organizations[84] included Anglo-Canadian groups (such as the Toronto Council of Friendship and Toronto Business & Professional Women's Club) and ethno-Canadian ones (including the Dutch Canadian Credit Union and the Italian Immigrant Aid Society). Especially important were the ethnic organizations and cultural groups because, in exchange for the access to Institute space for meetings or rehearsals, they agreed to help with the special cultural events. These heavily European groups included immigrant groups like the Canadian Lithuanian Association and ethno-Canadian ones like the Canadian Polish Congress.[85] Just as the West Indian Student Association's group membership probably helps to explain the Caribbean performances at the Institute, the membership of the Japanese Canadian Citizens Association likely explains the 1969 Japanese Night, which promised "classical Japanese dances," music, films, and dinner. Yet it still took more than two decades after the wartime internment and postwar dispersal to organize this goodwill gesture towards Toronto's Japanese Canadians.[86] Beholden to the "ethnic groups," Institute organizers were drawn into complex negotiations especially with the European groups whose participation they most sought.

Courting and Negotiating

Institute women courted individual immigrant and ethnic organizations, such as the Estonian Association of Toronto and German Canadian Club Harmonie, respectively. They reached out to the Toronto headquarters or branches of national federations that, like the Latvian National Federation in Canada (co-sponsor of 1957 Latvian Week) and the Hungarian Canadian Federation (co-sponsor of 1963 Hungarian Week), represented a variety of constituent groups. These groups' mostly male leaders included middle-class ethno-Canadians rebuilding an associational life dismantled by the war, and newcomers, also mostly middle-class in origin, who, like the Baltic refugees, ran various immigrant organizations. When an umbrella organization like the Canadian Polish Congress (CPC) agreed to co-sponsor an Institute Ethnic

Week, it took greater responsibility than its Canadian counterpart(s) to supply performers and exhibits, usually doing so by securing the participation of its affiliated folk-culture groups. Since the central body may well have helped its cultural affiliates cover the cost of costumes, instruments, and even, perhaps, an honorarium for the choreographers and choirmasters, their endorsement was essential.[87] This hierarchal arrangement was also gendered: ethnic male elites typically asked the women's auxiliary to plan a tea or concert while they came as special guests. The ethnic groups thus heavily subsidized the Toronto Institute's cultural pluralist mandate. Hence, the fulsome thanks issued to leaders like CPC president Z. Jaworski, whose organization co-sponsored the inaugural Polish Week, thus also ensuring the participation of the Canadian Polish Women's Federation as well as various performers, speakers, and arts and crafts groups. The Canadian co-sponsor for the event was the Catholic Women's League.[88]

The male ethnic elites and their cultural counterparts were hardly about to permit the Institute to dictate the terms of their participation in its spectacles. Rather, they used the immigrant-gifts platform to present their own historical narratives at Institute and wider city events. By so doing, they made culturally assertive claims for becoming a "third force" (after but equal to the English and French) in Canadian society and politics, a phrase that gained increasing traction during the B&B Commission discussions.[89] Of course, this is not surprising given their own investment both in matters of cultural preservation and historical commemoration and in the lobbying required to gain greater public recognition. In Toronto as elsewhere, ethnic groups had long used performance, ethnic regalia, and pageantry to commemorate their group's history and to assert their historical narratives and ethnic (as well as political or religious) identity both in their halls and out on the streets. In some respects, the war dampened such activity, but in others, as with the Ukrainian Canadians suspected of "divided loyalties" (to either Nazi Germany or Communist Russia), both the conservative (nationalist) and progressive (left) organizations increased their cultural activity in large part to demonstrate their loyalty to Canada and the Allies.[90]

A combination of factors, which included post-1945 migration, a growing white-ethnic lobby, and folk revival,[91] served to intensify this cultural activity. Some groups, both older ethno-Canadian and recently arrived groups, proved highly adept at asserting their cultural presence. These included both conservatives – such as the nationalist and virulently anti-Communist Ukrainian Canadians and Ukrainian displaced persons who advocated for a Soviet-free Ukraine – and leftists – such as the Greek immigrants who opposed the military junta that ruled Greece during the period 1967–74. Institute leaders like West routinely accepted invitations to attend the cultural events of their affiliated ethnic groups, whether concerts in support of refugees or anniversaries commemorating highly symbolic victories or tragedies. In doing so, they acted as public witnesses to the group's history and proud cultural traditions. For the Eastern European groups, the events often commemorated an uprising against the Soviet Union or celebrations of the persistence of their customs despite Soviet repression.[92] Then, too, the ethnic groups brought to the Institute performances that emphasized an exalted ethnicity. The 1969 Greek Night, for example, saw the wife of the organizer, social work student Alec Economides, and others reciting poems from such Greek classics as Constantine Cavafy's "Waiting for the Barbarians," and from English poet Lord Byron's "The Islands of Greece." The folk troupes included members of a Greek youth club named "Alexander the Great."[93]

The idea that folk festivals offered a therapeutic multiculturalism that glossed over material difficulties is based in some truth. The folklorist Robert Klymasz referred to the "universal ability of folklore to bridge the gaps of time and to meet the needs of today by providing an ever-ready vehicle that, without fail, always leads jaded appetites to an amazingly rich and seemingly limitless source of entertainment, instruction, wonder, and pride."[94] This stance must be tempered, however, by an understanding of the tactical cultural politics involved. The ethnic-group sponsors of Institute events could and did influence the "Canadian" reception of their cultural productions. If, for instance, Mayor Summerville's presence at the start of the 1963 Hungarian Week explains the mainstream news coverage it garnered, Gabor Temesevary, president of the co-sponsoring Hungarian Canadian Federation, largely shaped its Cold War tone and content. In a positive review in the populist *Toronto Telegram*, the reporter quoted Temesevary at length. Those words urged readers to appreciate that "the treasured possessions" and "vital artistic traditions" on display were brought to Canada by people "who loved their art so much" they packed "paintings and art objects into their suitcases" even as they were fleeing the Communists after the war and "the 1956 Hungarian bloodbath." Temesevary's comments captured the Institute goals while placing at centre stage his group's historical narrative of folklore (and art) preservation under Soviet Communism.[95] Latvian, Polish, Byelorussian, and other exhibits at Institute events similarly illustrate how the cultural assertion of ethnic leaders helped to shape Canadian-led public commemorations of their group's place in Canada's history and thus its role in an imagined pluralist future. Their endorsement of the Institute's cultural events gave their respective cultural custodians, both men and women, a pluralist public space in which to showcase their folk cultures while providing an "appropriate" narrative.[96]

The mixed-gender group of choirmasters and choreographers who led the folk troupes and choirs at the Institute's events and the mega folk festivals took seriously their role as cultural guardians of their group's "authentic" folklore customs, and directly helped to shape their troupe's particular repertoire. Some of the (mostly male) cultural impresarios might well offer new but still "authentic" (as in respectful) interpretations of a folk song or dance. (In this regard, folk cultures are hardly static.)[97] One might view these cultural promoters as liberal anti-modernists keen to charm their mixed audiences through nostalgic or enchanting performances invoking a simpler or romantic past. After all, European male choral groups like the Kodály choirs performed a folk repertoire shaped by nationalist composers, such as Kodály and Bartók, who had sought to nurture what they claimed was a pure ancestral culture against the forces of modernization and political upheavals. But they also understood the larger political goals at stake. The Eastern European groups so active in the Institute's programs already imbued their folk culture with deep political meaning. When the struggle for national independence was suppressed in Soviet countries, it fell to the diaspora to pursue national survival. Performing groups like the Kodály Choir saw themselves as engaged in a modern political project of nation rebuilding in Canada, one in which their own histories, and present and future, had to be made to count, both symbolically and politically, in a reimagined city and nation. It was equally true for the other ethnic groups who placed their cultural products, from ceramics to music, on the public stage.[98]

All this made for complicated negotiations. The commitments that ethnic leaders and cultural representatives had to their own community's calendar of events, for example, placed limits on their support for Institute events, leading to postponements or cancellations of plans.[99] Institute leaders were delighted with the large turnout for Metro Caravan '69, but with so many of their usual ethno-cultural contacts busy at their own pavilions, they partnered with less prominent groups like the Swiss Club.[100] Ethnic rivalries also created tensions. The frequent complaints about there being too few or too many of this or that group in a show reflected the political value of folk cultures to the increasing ethnicization of Canadian politics in these decades.[101] It was part of what scholars have described as the dialectical dance of accommodation and resistance the ethnic groups carried out with their Canadian hosts, refusing to be supplanted, and demanding, in exchange for their participation, more political clout.[102] The Cold War context meant that, with the rare exception, pro-Communist groups were not invited to the dance. Ironically, though, the fact that the era's folk music travelled partly through the children of left-wing Ukrainian Canadian and other Euro-Canadian groups, and some leftist newcomers, meant that some left-leaning performers and folklorists undoubtedly participated in the Institute's cultural events.[103]

Significantly, the long-time ethnic rivalries that occasionally erupted into bitter conflict over particular events did not derail the Institute's cultural programs. In 1963, for example, some Slavic groups objected to Hungarian Week on the ground that Hungarians were "totalitarians" with a history of mistreating Slavic minorities (Croatians, Slovenians, Ruthenians, and Slovaks). Denouncing the

Hungarians as "the last of the wild Asians to come from a nation in Europe" and tyrannical perpetrators of a "cruel despotism and terrorism" against Slavic ethnic nationals, the Slavic Ethnic Club demanded a stop to the "propaganda" for this "retrograde race." The Captive Nations Club, a refugee group representing Eastern European nations under Soviet control, declared that Hungarians were "mongolian creatures" who "do not belong to the European mosaic of culture[d] nations."[104] But the Hungarian Week went ahead as planned.

The Institute's success at attracting to its special events a much larger and greater mix of people than its house programs – the major concerts often filled the 1,000-seat auditorium and an average of 300 people attended the opening tea and concert for the Ethnic and Canadiana Weeks – owed much to the ethnic sponsors.[105] It explains why the Institute never planned a special event without consulting with their affiliated (and other) ethnic organizations and the gushing thank-you letters sent to the men who headed them.[106] Even so, Institute folks always wished for more Anglo-Torontonians in the audience, and that more of them came from the "wider public" beyond their own networks.

Overlapping and Competing Pluralisms?

Nations, note theorists and historians of the nation-state, are not natural or primordial entities but rather constructions forged in contested contexts, and they invariably involve the manipulation of historical myths and symbols or the invention of traditions.[107] As middle-class pluralists who, despite some significant differences, shared an interest in harnessing folk cultures to a modern nation-building project, the Institute women and their ethnic collaborators fit a portrait of bourgeois elites whose nationalist ideology reflected not the aspirations of the masses but their own agendas. Those agendas both overlapped – as in the shared Cold War claim that liberal multiculturalism would act as a bulwark against Communism – and competed. In regard to the latter, the Institute women and their male colleagues envisioned an Anglo-Canadian nation repeatedly replenished and enriched but never entirely replaced by immigrant and ethnic folk cultures while the ethnic community leaders with whom they interacted increasingly adopted a third-force thesis in favour of multiculturalism. To that end, ethnic leaders and cultural allies might well adopt a strategy of cultural essentialism: presenting one's folk forms as timeless and unchanging bolstered claims about ethnic distinctiveness and the need to promote ethnic diversity. Within politically polarized groups like the Ukrainian Canadian community, anti-Communist elites used the strategy to condemn the left-wing opponents interested in cultural exchanges with Soviet Ukraine.[108]

Both the Institute and the ethnic groups understood the value of the media in communicating their vision of a multicultural Toronto and Canada to wider publics. Hence, the Institute's frequent requests to mainstream and ethno-Canadian radio and television journalists, producers, and personalities to cover their events. West in particular established a rapport with certain members of the ethnic press club, though their attendance at events was spotty. The biggest catch was mainstream media personality John Collingwood Reade, host of a popular multi-ethnic music and culture program on CFRB Radio called *Canadians All*. An English immigrant proud of his British heritage and a well-travelled man reportedly "curious" about other cultures, Reade's reputation as a "new-style" broadcaster with a talent for personalizing the news received a boost during the war, when he contributed to the BBC's *Britain Speaks* overseas broadcasts. Described as "a skilled writer" who approached the radio as "theatre of the mind," Reade's dramatic delivery made him a popular master of ceremonies. A valued "friend" of the Institute, Reade hosted various Institute shows and folk-festival performances. A 1960 session of *Canadians All* that he broadcast from the Institute had a racially diverse line-up that included European troupes and choirs as well as an Asian Indian dance group, a Japanese judo act, a Chinese dragon dance, and a Black gospel choir.[109] Then, too, the eclecticism of the Institute shows fit well the variety show format that was a staple of 1960s and 1970s television. At a time when CBC Radio featured folk programs and ethnic folk festivals were getting some television coverage, the Institute's efforts to use the media to project a multicultural Toronto to the nation through folk culture was making some headway before the agency's demise.[110]

Equally important was the English Canadian context. Many scholars agree that, by the 1960s (if not earlier), a Canadian national culture rooted primarily in British traditions was in tatters and, in the view of some, that the decade saw a civic understanding of citizenship and growing support for multiculturalism replacing the British heritage model.[111] Others have accorded the multiculturalists, from Pierre Trudeau himself to the ethnic protest lobby that emerged during the 1960s, a more significant role in promoting a social good, however complicated its implementation might have proved.[112] Yet, the shrewd tactics involved cannot be ignored: as still others note, official multiculturalism within a bilingual framework offered a means out of the constitutional and other challenges posed by Quebec nationalism and separatism and by the Red Power, New Left, feminist, and other radical forces that produced the tumultuous 1960s. By placating the leaders of the Ukrainian Canadian–led ethnic lobby that emerged during the B&B Commission, Trudeau sidestepped other demands for equality and self-determination. In exchange for multiculturalism, the mostly European lobby could act as a counterweight to Quebec.[113]

The Toronto Institute's cultural pluralism and that of its allies and collaborators suggest some revision or refinement of these points. First, Institute-style cultural pluralism assumed that, like the expanding treasure chest, immigrant and ethnic folk cultures would enrich the nation culturally – the Institute women truly delighted in the opportunity to create a more cosmopolitan culture (see chapter 11) – but without undermining the core values that owed much to its British heritage. It was not that they wanted non-English-speaking people to be turned into model British ones. Like their colourful and boisterous but scripted shows, they understood multiculturalism as a means of ordering difference and ensuring the loyalty of the many to the nation. As for José Igartua's argument about English Canada's rapid transformation in the 1960s from a British-blood-and-culture to a rights-based definition of citizenship, the Institute's multi-ethnic performances and multicultural spectacles (along with its uneven efforts to promote human rights and liberal internationalist ideals) contributed towards an increasing acceptance particularly of European forms of cultural difference. Even before 1960, Institute personnel embraced a bold and aggressive, though heavily Eurocentric, pluralism. However, as members of an English Canadian middle-class cultural elite, the Institute women – who, after all, included leading IODE members – never abandoned a commitment to a British-defined version of cultural pluralism.[114]

The Institute's Anglo-Canadian cultural pluralism also came up against the ethnic pluralism of its ethnic collaborators and allies, and, to a lesser extent, its heavily European staffers. The affiliated ethnic groups increasingly articulated the terms of their invited participation in Institute events and wider collaborations in the vocabulary of the ethnic lobby that protested the B&B Commission's two-founding nations narrative of Canada. Third-force aspirations affected the Toronto Institute's relations particularly with the Eastern European elites and their ethnocultural representatives, both ethno-Canadians and refugee émigrés, who would participate in or follow the briefs, hearings, and conferences held by the ethnic lobby during the years of the B&B Commission.[115] The non–Eastern European elites also understood the importance of using the Institute's immigrant-gifts platform for inserting their cultural narratives into the mainstream agenda.

This third-force momentum explains not only why so many cultural groups participated in these events, but why their heads urged the Institute to "go big" with the ethnic festivals. A case in point is a 1961 meeting to discuss plans to launch a major "cultural festival." Institute board and CFAC member Stephen Davidovich, yet another nationalist Ukrainian Canadian to promote the third-force thesis in favour of multiculturalism, stressed the ethnic groups' collective "responsibility" to help in "creating a favourable image of the third element to Canadians as a whole," and to do so here by "working together" for "the promotion of a kaleidoscopic image of Canada." Using the Institute's own metaphor of a "United Nations in miniature," still another Ukrainian Canadian representative, Jaroslav Bilak, urged that the "plan should be big," adding, "the Ukrainian and other groups are interested in bigness." The Croatian delegate agreed and advised "exploiting" all the "TV" contacts while his Hungarian counterpart stressed as well the importance of "first class talent of which there was plenty available." Summing up, Kossar proposed "a miniature grandstand show, handcraft, art, and industrial fair."[116] In this, as in similar instances, the Western and Southern European leaders agreed, and, during the 1960s, some of these grand plans materialized.

Conclusion

On the eve of Metro Caravan '72, which took place a year after Canada became the first nation in the world to adopt multiculturalism as official policy, Caravan host Kossar was busy doing interviews. He boasted to reporters that while "the [federal] government relatively recently discovered multi-culturalism," people like himself, his wife Zena, and many other Torontonians already knew that "multiculturalism has been alive and living in Canada for years," and that "Caravan has been making It work for years."[117] The roots of contemporary Toronto's bold, brash, and highly commercialized "super multiculturalism" are diverse, but one set of them lies with the cultural spectacles in which the Institute played a leading or coordinating role, including the Institute Ethnic Weeks and folk festivals, the Nationbuilders shows, and Metro Caravan.[118]

Another striking feature of Canadian multiculturalism is how quickly many Anglo-Canadians evidently accepted Trudeau's 1971 vision statement of a multicultural nation within a bilingual framework.[119] They may well have been ready for the message because of the waning (but still tenacious) British vision of Canadian nationhood, and the need to replace it with something else. The tremendous success of Metro Caravan speaks volumes to the ability of Anglo and ethnic liberal multiculturalists to nudge Anglo-Canadians through non-threatening spectacle and tourism to partake of other cultures. Trudeau's pronouncement would not have gained such quick traction without near-grassroots activism, in Toronto at least. The Institute women and their male colleagues were laying such a groundwork from the 1950s onward, though they could not have done so without the participation of the ethnic elites and ethnocultural groups whose own agendas both overlapped with and diverged from that of the Institute.

More than simply representing a particular kind of post-colonial Canadian pluralist nationalism, the Toronto Institute in the late 1950s, the 1960s, and early 1970s was popularizing its gifts and spectacle pluralism among large numbers of ordinary people. Like earlier iterations of liberal cultural pluralism, that mandate was rooted in a paradoxical strategy of affecting a more pluralistic and integrated society through the celebration and appropriation of the "authentic" cultures (understood mainly as folk cultures) of sequential waves of immigrants and their subsequent descendants. For Toronto Institute folks, the process of Canadianization, which invariably involved some homogenizing of ethnic cultures along dominant Canadian norms, and pluralism existed in symbiotic relationship to each other. In this context, taking in an Institute intercultural or multicultural event involved a positive, indeed enriching, process of absorbing the "other" and rendering it Canadian. While seemingly apolitical folklore was preferred, the politicization of folk culture, especially when it cast a harsh light on Communism, was also acceptable in the Cold War era. Although it folded in 1974, the Toronto Institute, like the US affiliates, and wider cultural gifts movement, influenced late-twentieth-century multiculturalism in both nations, as evidenced by a familiar immigrant-gifts discourse, a privileging of European customs, and an emphasis on cultural celebration that sidesteps the harsh material realities of immigrant life. Nevertheless, this activism helped pave the way for the wider acceptance of a (Eurocentric) multiculturalism in Canada after 1971, that is, multiculturalism in a specifically modernist, nation-building mode. The activism of the Institute women and their male allies belongs alongside other sixties-era developments that, in a positive or negative way, helped to create the ideology of "official" multiculturalism before Trudeau announced it.

Chapter Eleven

Handicrafts, High Art, and Human Rights: Cultural Guardianship and Internationalism

As co-hosts of United Nations Week in 1957, the International Institute of Metropolitan Toronto's director, Nell West, staffer Violet Head, and the well-connected Anglo-Canadian volunteers mounted a multi-ethnic program that celebrated cultural pluralism as the domestic embodiment of the liberal principles championed by the United Nations including an internationally enlightened form of national citizenship, inclusivity, and global peace. At the afternoon tea that kicked off the program meant to raise public awareness about the UN and encourage support for its causes, young women in "nationality costumes" welcomed people and served them "ethnic" pastries. During the evening concert, Toronto harpist Clara Emerson engaged the themes of international cooperation and goodwill by performing "beautiful compositions" of Old World music that "delighted" the capacity audience. For the occasion, the Institute also booked a "treasure van" of "beautiful handicrafts" from the Canadian Handicraft Guild that included "Eskimo" sculptures, Mexican silver objects, Greek jewellery, and Asian Indian brass objects and incense. The International Night that closed the week featured folk dancers who stepped, twirled, and stomped their way through a lively program.[1]

Middle-class women have long been involved in folklore preservation and promotion[2] as well as liberal causes at home and internationally.[3] It is thus not surprising that the Toronto Institute's middle-class Anglo-Canadian women, who embraced the agency's self-image as a local United Nations that offered a model for the nation organized multi-ethnic folk performances and craft exhibits in support of international causes and cosmopolitan citizenship. Or that the content and descriptions of the folk performances and arts and crafts exhibits traded heavily in female stereotypes and otherwise conveyed conservative gender alignments. In mounting these events, Institute directors like West and (Dutch-Canadian) Tine Stewart, along with volunteers such as Margaret Jennings,[4] collaborated with Anglo- and ethno-Canadian women folklorists. These interactions sometimes fostered cross-cultural bonds of respect among mainly middle-class women, but disagreements and tensions also emerged.

The Institute women's strategy of promoting liberal, democratic, and internationalist values through a cultural-pluralist frame reveals paradoxical elements. Certainly, promoting ethnic handicrafts rooted in Old World traditions in order to encourage respect for cultural differences in the present aligned with the institute movement's popular pluralism. But these women also revelled in the "high" art produced by "master" refugee artists and even tried to replicate the exalted atmosphere of the European art gallery. Similarly, their enjoyment of classically rendered folk music performed in an upscale concert hall stood a little uncomfortably alongside the democratic premise of the participatory folk workshops they organized in the more mundane setting of a high school gymnasium or the basement of a local "Y." The wealthier women's participation in the making of a bourgeois aesthetic that traded in ethnic folk performance and arts and crafts bumped up against their democratic ideals. Such tensions reflected the women's class and racial privilege, but other factors also mattered. A consideration of the real and apparent contradictions of a female cultural guardianship that mined high art as well as folk culture, and used elite venues as well as community spaces, in the service of its pluralist goals also sheds light on the immigrant and refugee artists and craftspeople who participated in the Institute's events.

This chapter examines the relations among the women involved in the Toronto Institute's cultural events, the gendered features of folk-craft production and folk-dance performance, and the relationship between pluralism and internationalism. It explores how Institute women both promoted and mobilized pluralism in support of liberal internationalist ideals and civic engagement at the local and national level; it also looks at the nature of their interactions with their female allies and colleagues. Drawing on the feminist and gendered scholarship that highlights the different roles or symbolism assigned to women and men in pageantry, commemoration, and folk performance,[5] the chapter explores gendered practices. My analysis of the folk performances suggests how modern reform movements that traded in folk culture reinforced hegemonic ideals of masculinity and femininity.[6] The discussion of the "pretty hostesses" recruited for the Institute events addresses the era's ethnic beauty pageants and the young women's efforts to negotiate modernity.[7]

The chapter explores, too, how middle-class women used a folk revival and commemoration to insert themselves publicly as defenders of civic values and ideologies that advance a "modern" progressive agenda, even when it involved some conservative elements.[8] The activities under review occurred against the wider context of a folk revival and the insurgence of liberal internationalism. The second North American folk revival movement of the 1950s, 1960s, and early 1970s – named as such to distinguish it from the folk revival of the late-nineteenth and early-twentieth centuries – was, as Gillian Murphy notes, a fluid, multi-dimensional, and contradictory movement containing overlapping as well as parallel and competing strands.[9] Depending on where one looks, this folk revival shared elements in common with its pre-1945 iteration. Earlier debates over whether folk culture represented a "pure" or static thing to be preserved, or a dynamic entity subject to aesthetic revisioning, were also part of the second revival.[10] In both academic folklore circles and in popular music, Canadian activity and careers again benefited from the networks of a more established American folklore industry. But if the first US folk revival helped to encourage the legitimacy of folklore studies in Canada as both a semi-profession and an academic pursuit, the music strand of the second folk revival was particularly important to Canada's folk music scene, which benefited from an expanding North American music industry that launched the careers of progressive folk musicians. A familiar gender hierarchy in folklore studies saw women folklorists still clustered in less prestigious sectors, such as fieldwork, popular publications, radio programs, and folk-based tourism, while men dominated the professional positions in the museums and universities. Once again, large-scale immigration stimulated research in immigrant folklore studies. Like other "second wave" movements, the post-1945 folk revival had long roots, in this case in the thirties and forties. It also included some still-active first-generation revivalists.[11]

Regarding differences, the post-1945 revival, particularly in folk music, whose left-wing roots in the United States lay in Popular Front and New Deal reclamations of the people's music, was a more urban and mass movement than its first iteration. The sixties conjure up images of the large folk music festivals where progressive and commercially successful artists performed for progressive if mainly white, middle-class, and urban (or suburban) audiences.[12] Although widely viewed as "Old World" or "traditional," ethnic folk festivals also underwent change. Among the long-established ethnic groups who over a few generations had adapted to life in North America, selective retentions, accommodations, and outright changes to the form, content, and other features of their folk repertoire of songs, dances, and crafts had, by the 1950s, produced a "streamlined" and "modern" ethnic folk culture complex.[13] These hybrid forms reflected a less linear path towards assimilation in that, in the construction or invention of an ethnic Canadian (or ethnic American) identity, they combined homeland and hostland elements to produce something new.[14]

As liberal pluralists, the Toronto Institute's women shared with other folk music revivalists an optimistic and culturally pluralist conception of the nation, but they felt no affinity for the radical politics of a Pete Seeger. Their strongest ties were to the ethnocultural and anti-Communist European ethnic and immigrant groups who promoted their respective folk cultures in ways similar to their interwar revivalists and impresarios, even as they modified its form and content.[15] The fluidity of the folk revival meant as well that the Institute women occasionally consulted or collaborated with folklorists and performers with left-wing views. One such contact was Ruth Rubin, a Montreal-born but New York–based collector and performer of Yiddish folk songs whose work belongs to a larger history of Jewish left-wing folk movements.[16] Another was Edith Fowke (see below).

Then, too, Toronto Institute events reflected to a modest degree the commercialization of sixties and early-seventies folk music: the performers included Canadian folk singers such as Mary Jane and Winston Young, who were part of Toronto's progressive folk scene in Yorkville and who performed at the Mariposa Folk Festival. The repertoire that the folk trio Lynn Ward, Robin Ward, and Craig Allen performed at the Toronto Institute's 1963 Canadiana Week was typical of such performances. It included "This Land Is Your Land" (described as a "Canadian Folk Song"), "Blowin' in the Wind" ("Song of Protest"), "Auction Block" ("Song of Slavery"), "Un Canadien Errant" (French Canadian Song), and "Joy, Joy" ("American Campfire Tune").[17] Overall, however, the eclecticism of the Toronto Institute's folk events, like that of its US interwar predecessors and postwar counterparts, and like that of contemporaneous Canadian multi-ethnic festival venues such as Metro International Caravan and Winnipeg's Folklorama (first held in summer 1970) stood in for a liberal pluralist nation and more harmonious world order.[18]

Handicrafts and High Art

Handicrafts, whether part of a museum-quality collection like that featured at the 1957 UN Week described above, or the saleable wares of craftspeople using traditional or near-traditional methods to produce rural crafts, are a major staple of folk revival movements. Handicraft revival has also involved the application of new technology, such as the replacement of two-shaft looms with more complex ones, to produce more "aesthetically pleasing" and "commercially viable" items that retain certain traditional patterns or other elements.[19] In contrast to fine art, which is usually credited as a creative and contemplative form of work that expresses human emotions, folk crafts are considered the products of applied skill and experience that go into the creation of objects that fulfil a particular purpose, whether utilitarian or decorative. They also constitute very tangible cultural gifts that more "primitive" rural folk can bestow upon modern urbanites. But if the Institute's strategic use of folk culture for nation-building purposes explains the ubiquity of ethnic handicrafts at its events and exhibits, what explains all the fine art that was also present? Even allowing for the blurring of such lines by generations of artists, the mixing of high (paintings and sculptures) and popular (folk) art requires some comment.[20]

The Institute women's promotion of ethnic handicrafts, a category that also included Indigenous crafts, drew on a form of bourgeois women's cultural activity dating back to the late nineteenth century. The prominence of middle-class "native-born" Anglo-American women in the early-twentieth-century folk revival movement in the United States, observes Kristin Hoganson, "owes much to the belief that women's realm included cultural guardianship," and the protection of "folk culture in particular."[21] Wealthy clubwomen and emerging female folklorists as well as those from regionally based handicraft institutions or city galleries participated in efforts to preserve and promote ethnic folk crafts. As the captions and souvenir programs of the handicraft exhibits mounted in venues such as the Albright-Knox Gallery (Buffalo) and the Boston Museum attest, an immigrant-gifts ethos (see chapter 10) informed this work. The banner that accompanied the Boston Museum's handicraft shows in 1919 read "The Nations Come to America Bringing Gifts."[22]

The late-nineteenth and early-twentieth-century international folk revival movement whose origins were in Europe enhanced its appeal among US women much enamoured with the cosmopolitan world of European elite travel and its exotic entertainments. Such sentiments also spread from Europe to the wider colonial world, including in India, where, as Hoganson notes, British male officials collected Indian arts and crafts and, in a classic example of imperialist nostalgia (lamenting the loss of the way of life they helped destroy), promoted local customs and mounted folklore exhibits. Such staging of folk exhibits in early-twentieth-century Europe, India, and elsewhere represented an "invention of tradition" as much as it did an attempt at cultural preservation.[23]

As pluralism took hold among leading reformers, they promoted ethnic handicrafts as desirable gifts to be poured into the American treasure chest and as a means of earning an income. In Chicago, Jane Addam's Hull House held classes in such crafts as pottery, weaving, and woodworking, and immigrant women demonstrated their traditional craft skills on the stage alongside folk singers and dancers. South End House in Boston had a lacemaking shop and New York's Greenwich House ran a handicraft school. Drawing on the ideas of arts and crafts pioneer William Morris, settlement house workers also sought to preserve handicraft skills in an industrial age by running spinning and weaving classes for younger women, who, they hoped, would develop an appreciation for their ethnic heritage even as they acculturated to the American mainstream. Similar patterns obtained in the interwar international institute movement. Founder and long-time head Edith Terry Bremer dispatched handicraft instructors to Institute affiliates to assist immigrant women in maintaining craft-making traditions. The central body also supplied individual Institutes with instructional materials for producing crafts and costumes for Old World holidays.[24]

In Canada, too, there is a long history of Anglo bourgeois women's involvement in handicraft preservation and promotion. These privileged, accomplished, and well-travelled club women saw their efforts to revive the declining production of domestic crafts (such as hooked rugs and needlework), and to create an urban tourist market that would offer rural women a fair remuneration for their labour, benefiting the women and their impoverished communities as well as retarding rural depopulation. The women who created a handicraft committee within the Montreal branch of the Women's Arts Association of Canada (WAAC, est. 1894) were influenced by the wider British and American handicraft movements in which both leading male artists (like the British socialist William Morris) and female reformers (such as Addams and Bremer) played prominent roles. In 1905, the handicraft committee of WAAC's Montreal branch left the WAAC and formed the Canadian Handicraft Guild.[25] The Guild's middle-class Anglo women combined a sense of noblesse oblige and patriotism with an emerging commitment to cultural pluralism. They sought to retain, encourage, and educate the wider public about the handicraft traditions that new immigrants brought from their homelands, and to sell ethnic crafts, whether Doukhobor embroidery or Czech pottery, to Canadians. They imported specialized materials from Europe and hired immigrant craftswomen to run craft classes for immigrant children and women [26] The Guild's participation in the interwar folk festivals organized by J.M. Gibbon for the Canadian Pacific Railway – and which contained a major ethnic handicraft component both in terms of selling crafts and featuring craftspeople on the stage accompanied by folk singers – boosted its national profile.[27]

The Guild's remit also included Indigenous crafts. According to Ellen Easton McLeod, Guild women played a critical role in encouraging an "Indian" arts and crafts movement through collection and education, and by creating an urban market for the crafts, which settler cultural "experts" had elevated to an art form. By the 1950s, Guild leaders attributed the thriving cooperative arts and crafts industry in the North largely to their efforts. A sculpture-collecting trip through the North led to the Guild's first major Inuit art show in southern Canada, held in Montreal in 1949. To the members' delight, the show sold out in three days.[28] The Institute, as noted at the outset of the chapter, occasionally booked a Guild exhibit for an event, though the featured crafts were usually provided by the ethnocultural organizations, patrons, and the craftspeople themselves.

Men, too, were involved in handicraft revivalism, including J.M. Gibbon. While best known for organizing the interwar folk festivals on behalf of the Canadian Pacific Railway, Gibbon also headed the Guild in the early 1940s. Considered the founder of professional folklore studies in Canada, Marius Barbeau, the Quebec anthropologist and folklorist with the National Museum (now the Canadian Museum of History), played a role in the revival of textile handicrafts in his home province.[29] Similarly, men headed some of the post-1945 immigrant and ethno-Canadian arts and crafts organizations courted by the

Institute women. Nonetheless, as suggested by the examples of the Institute and Guild, women's strong association with handicraft preservation and promotion carried into the period (1950s to 1970s) under review.

Indeed, a familiar gender hierarchy characterized the Institute events that featured ethnic handicrafts, be it an Ethnic Week, a human rights reception, or UN event. For such occasions, lecturers were often recruited to provide the attendees with information both entertaining and edifying. The absence of professional credentials or titles for the ethno-Canadian or immigrant women who gave lectures on the exhibits attests to their rank as community experts. Bronka Michalowska (a painter) provided the historical and cultural context for a Polish Week exhibit featuring handmade dolls from different regions of Poland, as well as rugs, paper cut-outs, wood carvings, embroidery, and fine lacework. Stase Prapuolenis did likewise for a Lithuanian Week exhibit, "Amber Work, Dolls in National Costumes, Embroideries, Handwoven Articles, Leatherwork, Silverwork, Woodwork."[30] While the male heads of the cultural associations who sometimes supplied the crafts might speak to journalists in lofty tones about their homeland's arts and crafts traditions, the women lecturers were community interpreters and instructors who explained the items on display to those in attendance. The (fewer) men who delivered lectures, such as H.N. Milnes, a professor of German literature at the University of Toronto who spoke at a German Week, were academics who addressed more intellectual themes.[31]

The texts of the handicraft lectures delivered by women like Michalowksa and Prapuolenis are not available, but they likely combined information about regional specialties and production methods with references to the remarkable talents and ancient traditions passed on through the ages.[32] The observation applies to today's folkcraft marketing. A 2014 website on Polish crafts pitched at middle-class tourists uses a familiar mix of history, folksy (or anti-modernist) language, and nationalist rhetoric to promote crafts like the crocheted lace that is a regional specialty of the women lacemakers of Koniaków, a village in the Beskid Mountain range in southwest Poland.[33]

West and colleagues similarly emphasized the quality of the handicraft exhibits in their invitations to potential co-sponsors, donors, and hosts. In an invitation to host a Latvian Ethnic Week, West told Mayor Nathan Phillips that, in addition to the hostesses and the banquet, he could expect a "very good" folk art exhibit.[34] When Pearl McCarthy, long-time art critic for the Toronto *Globe and Mail,* praised the handicraft exhibit for a Croatia Week as "one of the best exhibits of folk art" she had seen, a delighted West used it in subsequent efforts to recruit co-sponsors and dignitaries for other events.[35]

Rather than immigrant crafts, the crafts featured during the Canadiana Weeks were more likely to be a mix of rural and Indigenous "Canadian" (though rarely Québécois), their inclusion a visual testimonial to a rich pluralist history of the different peoples, regions, and cultures that came to comprise Canada.[36] The hooked mats exhibited by the Grenfell Mission's Labrador Handicraft Group during the inaugural Canadiana Week showcased the cultural gifts produced by successive female descendants of the English and Irish fishers who settled the remote areas of northern Newfoundland and Labrador in the eighteenth and nineteenth centuries. Wilfred Grenfell, the British medical missionary who arrived in 1892 to bring health services to this poor region, was credited with stimulating industrial development in the region and creating a local handicraft industry that allowed residents to sell their hooked mats made out of silk stockings, knitted items, and other crafts to North American shops. Distinguished by their simple scenes or colourful images, the woman-made Grenfell rugs were now designated an artistically worthy expression of the people of Atlantic Canada.[37] Similarly, a 1962 Canadiana Week exhibit of "patchwork quilts" made by "United Empire Loyalist women 150 and 100 years ago" was a testimony to Canada's lengthy history of accepting refugees, and to the cultural benefits obtained through the acquisition of such delightful handicrafts.[38] In the 1964 Canadiana Week, Indigenous peoples were added to the colonial mix through an "Indian and Eskimo" handicraft display.[39]

The selling and buying of handicrafts bring together the paradoxical elements of tourist-oriented folk festivals that make them such dramatic expressions of what Michael Kammen has called "nostalgic modernism" (and others liberal anti-modernism), representing a simultaneous embrace and suspicion of capitalism. The ethnic crafts were gendered insofar as women generally made the fine lacework, handstitched embroidery, handwoven shawls, and hooked rugs while men tended to produce the larger wood carvings, silverwork, leatherwork, and sculptures. But both women and men produced the jewellery, silhouettes, straw crafts, amber work, small wood carvings, and sculptures. The acquisition of folk crafts also differs from that of "ethnic" food, which is consumed mainly in the moment, though bringing home edible products would become a feature of the middle-class vacation.[40] Still, the purchase of a straw doll, embroidered textile, or crocheted lace as a souvenir can, to paraphrase cultural theorist Arjun Appadurai, imbue the consumable "thing" with a cultural meaning beyond its material constituents. Here, the transaction involves a social interaction between crafts-maker and tourist, and between a (constructed) simpler past and a complicated present filtered through a discourse and politics of authenticity. Depending on whether the souvenir is on permanent display or brought out to punctuate a vacation narrative, it can become an occasional or constant reminder of the tourist's temporary time-travelling into the past.[41]

A 1972 Institute craft show that transferred this cultural exchange to Toronto and a follow-up survey offer some insight into the immigrant craftspeople involved. The impetus came from an Institute craft committee composed mainly of IODE volunteers chaired by Frances Bander, who sat on the Institute board.

Having secured funds from several IODE branches to explore the idea of establishing an annual craft show and permanent shop, the committee held a large craft show in spring 1972. More than forty craftspeople, most of them women, participated in the show, which also included seventies-era "hippie" crafts, including macramé, thus further blurring the lines between traditional and modern. The craftspeople helped with setting-up and the organizers distributed the tickets through their networks, albeit with modest results. The Institute took its usual 15 per cent cut of the total sales.[42]

Most of the twenty-seven people who completed the questionnaire meant to determine the viability of a permanent shop were European women. They included makers of Finnish wooden angels and crocheted caps, Swedish handwoven rugs, Hungarian doilies, Danish ceramic jewellery, and Spanish lace and embroidered cushions. The non-Europeans included a Korean woman (pictures with natural materials), a Ceylonese woman (batik and wall hangings), a Mexican man (flowers and other items), and an Asian Indian man (jewellery). All but two respondents had sold something, the value of which ranged from $9 to over $100. The responses indicated overwhelming support for more craft shows and a "boutique." No one objected to the inclusion of contemporary items of the tie-dye variety. The mostly positive comments – one participant, who made close to $100, said "I enjoyed it!" while another, who made about $25, "was very pleased" – suggests that these craftspeople craved a larger audience and potential market. As do their few critical comments. The Korean woman expressed appreciation for the "opportunity to show my skills," but stressed that "we need more visitor[s]." A Polish woman (earnings of $25) suggested more advertising and limiting the products to "handcrafts made in Canada." Other suggestions included holding an annual Saturday Bazaar before Christmas.[43]

The questionnaire's purpose offered little space for the articulation of broad cultural goals, but the respondents' strong desire for more opportunities to sell their wares certainly spoke to the challenge faced by newcomers who, far from being quaint rural folk figures, were struggling to earn a livelihood in an urban metropolis. It may explain why no one objected to the folksy content of the publicity materials, which conjured images of folk making useful but delightful objects, such as ceramic jugs and shawls, according to Old World specifications. In the end, however, the Institute's own financial crisis kept it from becoming a more active player in the urban craft market.[44]

The significant presence of fine art also on display at many Institute events may have contradicted the institute movement's primarily folk-oriented brand of pluralism, but it underscores my argument about a modern nation-building campaign taking precedence over a consistent commitment to folk revivalism (see chapter 10). The Institute women's comfort at mixing "high" and "low" art reflected a shared assumption among liberal-minded but culturally privileged women, at least some of whom visited museums on their travels abroad, that high art also fell within the purview of their cultural guardianship. It is captured in West's letter to the head of a Kiwanis Club she hoped to recruit as a co-sponsor for a Ukrainian Week: using a circular logic, she promised that both the fine and folk art would be "exceptionally good" because "the Ukrainians have a number of well-known artists and their folk art is advanced and colourful."[45]

The display of fine art, whether produced by academically trained refugee artists (or less-skilled hobbyists), or borrowed from owners and art groups, reflected as well the pronounced Eastern European profile of the Institute's membership and of the ethnic contacts that West and others nurtured. Many of the artists featured in the 1963 Hungarian Week exhibit – which included paintings, miniatures, and sculptures on loan from local art patrons and artist-owned work that was on sale – had earned academic credentials before escaping Hungary following the Second World War or in the aftermath of the failed 1956 revolt. A Hungarian Canadian doctor and his wife lent some of their paintings for the exhibit, the market value for which ranged from $30 to $2,000, the latter for a painting by early-twentieth-century modernist József Rippl-Rónai.[46] The exhibits occasionally included an artist with a left-wing sensibility, though the painting themselves did not necessarily deliver an obvious working-class or radical message. The painting by Russian Canadian Paraskeva Clark featured in the 1963 Canadiana Week exhibit, for example, was entitled *Swamp, 1939*. It depicted a swamp in Haliburton, northeast of Toronto.[47]

As self-perceived aficionados of fine art who also understood its value as a class marker of worldly sophistication, the Institute women's promotion of newcomer artists sometimes verged on the paternalistic. For them, the Canadian treasure chest could absorb the artistic traditions of elite homeland cultures as easily as it did the folk craft. The appropriative element contained in that stance smacked of Anglo snobbery, though the artists' own blurring of high and popular (or commercial) art also played a role.

Consider Dora de Pédery-Hunt (1913–2008), the Hungarian sculptor who became Canada's leading designer of medals and coins. She was the daughter of a Catholic middle-class Budapest family whose physicist father had carried the bronze elephant she sculpted as a master's degree project when they fled Hungary for Germany in 1944 to use as proof of her artistic credentials. In Toronto, de Pédery-Hunt first worked as a live-in domestic and then a high school art teacher. By the time of the Institute's 1963 Hungarian Week, whose arts and crafts exhibit featured two of her sculptures, de Pédery-Hunt was enjoying success as a sculptor, thanks in part to the support of influential friends such as the sculptors Frances Loring and Frances Wylie, and Alan Jarvis, who as director of the National Gallery of Canada purchased one of her sculptures. Having turned to medallion art following a trip to Brussels in 1958, de Pédery-Hunt also designed commissioned medals for cultural and sports organizations. Later, she produced a series of bronze sculptures commemorating leading Canadians, including feminist crusader Nellie McClung.[48] De Pédery-Hunt was also a commercial designer, and West recruited her to design a new Christmas card for an Institute fundraiser in 1963. Announcing it in the *Intercom*, West referred to "the internationally known sculptress" creating "a new, very unusual design" and encouraged people to buy copies of the card.[49]

Just as composers blurred the line between folk and classical music, some of the paintings and fine art objects displayed at Institute events featured folk themes. Certain paintings reportedly shown at the 1963 Hungarian Week contained female folk images. These included *Forest Maidens*, by Béla Iványi-Grünwald (1867–1940), who later abandoned his folk-themed pastoral paintings for impressionist landscapes, and *Peasant Woman*, by Eduard "Ede" Telcs (1872–1948), a Jewish Hungarian artist who became a sculptor and medallist. (Thanks to Raoul Wallenberg, Telcs had escaped deportation to a Nazi death camp.) The exhibit also included *Gypsy Caravan*, by Gyula Rudnay (1878–1957), whose paintings and tapestries hung in the Hungarian Parliament. The exhibit's handicrafts included decorative items lent by their owners, such as a mosaic tray, an antique "bread cutting woman" (breadknife), and "braedery" (scenes made with braided wool).[50]

There were also efforts to replicate the rarefied atmosphere of the European art gallery in specially designated rooms at the Institute. With the support of West and board members such as Irene Ungar, a professionally accomplished woman and prominent figure within the Polish Canadian community, the well-to-do volunteers from the Toronto Junior League took the lead on this endeavour. In 1961, they formed a cultural committee with a mandate to meet "the need for cultural exchange" in "a fast-growing city" by holding monthly shows of "works by new Canadian artists" and to help newcomers "interpret Toronto's "more established cultural forms" through occasional Canadian exhibitions. In promoting pluralism as a means by which to acquire an appreciation of the city's diverse artistic traditions – and a more "cosmopolitan" outlook – the committee both celebrated and appropriated elite European culture for the same reason it did folk culture: to advance a civic and nation-building project. Their efforts, the committee claimed, would help prevent the "unchecked" spread of "misunderstanding and intolerance" and sow "the seeds of a great city whose cultural and social life are the products of the many nationalities represented in its citizens."[51]

As well-heeled cultural matrons from Toronto's upper-class neighbourhoods,[52] these Institute women also promoted commemoration ceremonies in an effort to attract more attention to and elevate artists' work. Beginning in 1961, they mounted art exhibits into the room-turned-gallery-space dedicated to the memory of Arturo Scotti, an intellectual and journalist who had served on the Institute board and supported the idea of using culture to promote inter-group harmony. A refugee of Italian origin from Istria, Scotti co-founded

268 Ethnic Folk Cultures

Women sell candelabras, decorative cards, and knick-knacks at the Institute craft show in 1972. Archives of Ontario, F884-2-9, B427166.

An immigrant craftsman (probably of Mexican origin) selling paper flowers and other handmade decorative items attracts potential customers at the Institute's 1972 craft show. Archives of Ontario, F884-2-9, B427166.

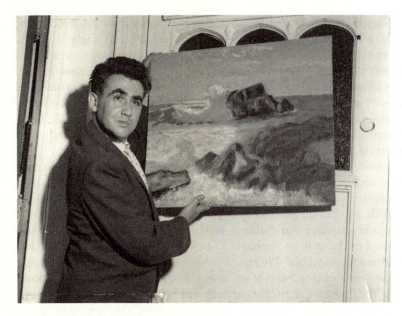

Refugee artist Edward Volkman holds up his painting of a seascape, c. 1963. Archives of Ontario, F884-2-9, B427166.

(with Gianni Grohovas) the Italian-language newspaper *Corriere Canadese*. Scotti's interest in raising the Italian Canadian community's plebeian profile, and uniting the immigrants across regional origin and politics through the promotion of Italy's grand cultural traditions and contributions to the world, clearly resonated with the women and men of the art committee.[53] Two years later, they raised considerably more funds for the dedication of a gallery to the memory of John Collingwood Reade, the popular radio broadcaster who had produced some of the Institute's concerts. Ungar chaired the memorial committee, which commissioned de Pédery-Hunt to create a bronze memorial plaque for the gallery, and established a bursary for a promising new Canadian student to attend the Royal Conservatory of Music. Reade's wife Elizabeth, who had been involved in the fundraising efforts, joined the Institute's arts committees. Later, she chaired the Institute committee for Metro Caravan '69, working closely with Elizabeth Isserstedt, then female president of the Institute board, and others.[54]

The art shows held in these galleries drew between 200 and 350 people on opening night. A Czechoslovakian exhibit co-sponsored with the Toronto Branch of the Czechoslovakian Society of Arts and Sciences featured the art of three "outstanding" refugees of the 1948 Communist takeover, including the diplomat-turned-artist Jaroslav Sehnoha. The Institute art director, Judas Buda, a Hungarian refugee painter who had exhibited in England and Paris before coming to Canada in 1958, surely wrote the enthusiastic review for the *Intercom*. Offering an unusually heavy dose of Canadian boosterism that would have pleased the Institute women, he reported that while Sehnoha had already earned a grand master's pedigree in Europe, his "artistic talents" had been "fully developed in Canada," a country that was supposedly "unfavourable towards all types of cultural endeavour." He ended by noting the "good" attendance and reporting that a number of paintings had sold to "eager buyers."[55]

Overall, the Institute exhibits showed more works by men than women, but there were several one-woman shows. One of them featured Zoya Lisowska, a Ukrainian portrait painter and illustrator who had exhibited in Italy, Geneva, Munich, and Rio de Janeiro before settling in Geneva. A main subject of her European paintings was children, including refugee children.[56] Folk themes featured in the work of Stephania K. Haller, a former professor of Budapest's Academy for Industrial Art and "a proud protagonist of the representational and impressionistic schools of art" who worked mainly in aquarelle (watercolour). The flyer for her 1970 show described her as excelling in "the charming depiction" of "village scenes and national costumes," the "sparkle of light and vibrant color" capturing "the romance and music of Hungary in a manner that only one steeped in its unique traditions may successfully communicate."[57]

One of the few non–Eastern Europeans to get a show in the Scotti gallery was Italian ceramicist Aldo Covello. Unlike most artist biographies, his self-written profile noted that he had completed his training in Canada at Toronto's Ontario College of Art. It also unapologetically reported that he was supporting himself by working as a sign painter.[58] Another Southern European, T.J. Schembri, a modernist painter from Malta who had spent the war in East Africa as an Italian-language interpreter with the British Armed Forces, expressed his appreciation for the public exposure his show received, including on a television show, by donating a Cubist-inspired oil painting to the Institute. He, too, injected a dose of reality by also thanking the Institute counsellors for helping his wife find a job.[59]

The limits on the Institute's support for artists became abundantly evident in 1971, when the Canadian Czechoslovakian Artists Association lobbied director Stewart to mount a "massive" two-week art show in a high-end venue like the O'Keefe Centre with an opening-night concert featuring classical music. Stewart rejected the proposal on the grounds that the fee, which Elizabeth Reade had costed at double the $2,000 estimate given, was "quite beyond our reach."[60]

Concert Halls and Gendered Performances

West and colleagues prioritized modern nation-building goals over a singular pursuit of folk revivalism. But they were deeply enamoured of the European folk music that had been shaped by an elite cadre of classically trained, and politically conservative, nationalist composers claiming, in the face of growing urbanism and industrialization, to have captured the essence of their nation's (rural) folk. As such, they were liberal anti-modernists who revelled in the haunting melodies performed by choral groups and chamber ensembles whose repertoire of folk songs, sacred music, and orchestral arrangements blurred the line between classical and folk.[61] This more elitist form of women's cultural guardianship, like the promotion of fine art, is evidenced by the role played by West, Jennings, and others in bringing certain folk concerts to Massey Hall, an upscale concert hall that was home to the Toronto Symphony Orchestra.

In 1955, West and Jennings, then both with the Institute's precursor, the New Canadians Service Association, helped to organize two sold-out concerts by the Ukrainian Bandurist Chorus. A male ensemble of musicians who sang and played the lute-shaped bandura instrument, the Ukrainian Bandurists entered the United States as refugees in the late 1940s, settling in Detroit. The Detroit Institute joined with prominent Ukrainian American groups to co-sponsor North American tours. A concert poster introduced them as "The Only Chorus of Bandurists in the Free World" whose resettlement "in America" meant their "unusual" music "lives again to delight you and add its beauties to our culture."[62] Besides West and Jennings, the Canadian patrons of the 1955 tour, which involved several Canadian cities, included Jennings's lawyer-husband and James Duncan, head of Massey-Ferguson, a leading agricultural implements manufacturer. The few ethno-Canadian patrons were Jewish Canadian Mayor Nathan Phillips and his wife, and the soon-to-be provincial secretary and minister of citizenship of Ontario, Ukrainian Canadian John Yaremko. The endorsements plastered on the concert poster included one by US Senator Margaret Chase Smith, a moderate Republican best known for a 1950 speech that criticized McCarthyite tactics. Smith, who wrote of the "beautiful" music that emanated from the men's "hearts and souls," also had some immigrant credentials, given her English-born father and French Canadian mother. Another came from Liberal member of Parliament and senior minister Paul Martin Sr., architect of the 1947 Canadian Citizenship Act, who called the concert "a unique and memorable musical experience." West and Jennings's involvement in the 1955 concerts may have also facilitated the founding of the Toronto Institute one year later.[63]

A later example was the 1961 concert, also sold out, by the Kapoustin Ensemble, an international group of 100 European performers. It was funded by Robert Kapoustin, a Yugoslavian businessman whose first venture as a cultural impresario evidently occurred at the behest of his choreographer wife, Tatiana. In an endorsement the Institute women would have loved, the Kapoustins said their "mammoth" ensemble was inspired by the many ethnic folk performances they enjoyed during an earlier visit to Toronto. Tatiana, who evidently initiated the Institute's unusual collaboration with a "Communist" group, held rehearsals for three months at the Institute's College Street auditorium. Echoing Institute views, husband Robert told reporters that, to thrive, the ensemble had to overcome the "hermetic" pride of individual ethnic groups and work together.[64] West said of such concerts that she hoped the emotionally uplifting performances would become a regular feature of the Toronto concert scene.[65]

By transporting an urban middle-class Anglo-Canadian audience to the quaint charms or heroic splendour of an earlier era in Europe, concerts like those given by the all-male Bandurists, the mixed-gender Kapoustin Ensemble, and Liga, a Latvian eight-women choral ensemble, could create a therapeutic space in which the immigrants' complicated past and difficult present were held at bay. Invoking the lyrical and romantic language of the past, the program of the 1955 Bandurists concerts portrayed the Bandurist as "a troubadour" who plays his one-of-a-kind hand-carved and hand-painted wooden instrument as "he sings ballads of an ancient nation in words and melodies handed down for more than a thousand years."[66] The text fit the culturally essentialist position adopted by the anti-Communist Ukrainian Canadian Committee (UCC). In opposition to the left-wing Ukrainian Canadians interested in cultural exchanges with Soviet Ukraine, the UCC, as Kassandra Luciuk explains, declared that only the art that predated Soviet Union control, and not the "living" art produced by artists in the territory of Ukraine, was valued.[67] In their colourful boisterousness, the Kapoustin Ensemble's many troupes projected a kaleidoscope of whirling dervishes that could similarly serve to erase the immigrants' complicated pasts and gloss over the harsh material realities of their lives.[68]

Such performances risked turning the performers into tourist folk figures. Descriptions and images abound of smiling and costumed folk dancers who energetically twirled, clapped, and stomped their way through a folk dance such as the Hungarian csardas, a courting dance of eighteenth-century origins popularized by Roma bands in Hungary and neighbouring regions before being made a national dance of Hungary. With the women dressed in traditional wide skirts of bright red or yellow that swirled as their male partners, dressed in embroidered wide-sleeved shirts and vests, spun them around, the dancers performed to a musical score that shifted from a slow and melancholic opening to an upbeat tempo during which the couples whirled in dramatic fashion. An "elite" rendition of a folk dance occasionally took place in mundane surroundings. Professional Canadian ballet dancers Marilyn Kantor and Michael Drabik performed a ballet csardas to the music of classical composer Léo Delibes's ballet *Coppélia* during an Institute folk pageant held in a high school auditorium.[69]

Like historians of pageantry, scholars of folk-dance performance have documented the markedly different portrayals of male and female figures, whether romanticized heroes and heroines or metaphorical representations.

As ethnomusicologist Henry Spiller notes, staged folk-dance performances can reinforce hegemonic gender ideologies by "making prescribed behavior appear not only essential but aesthetically beautiful as well."[70] With dance performance often coded feminine, one might expect to find homophobic utterances aimed at "foreign" men who pranced on the stage in flowing sleeves and pantaloons made by bigoted Canadian men and youth. But my research generally confirms the argument made by folk-dance performance experts like Marcia Ostashewski that the athletic prowess of male dancers who showed off their acrobatic talents with audience-pleasing jumps, spins, and squats projected an exuberant manliness.[71]

The masculinity projected by the Bandurists was that of the romantic balladeer whose songs of the brave and hypermasculine Cossacks reinforced their own heterosexuality. The 1955 concert program included the compositions of Hnat Khotkevych (1877–1938), the twentieth-century modernist writer, scholar, theatre director, and classical composer credited with saving the "ancient" art of bandura music from decline in the 1920s. The men performed centuries-old songs about freedom-loving Cossacks fighting the oppressive Tatars and Turks, the Russian tsar, and other enemies. As Ostashewski observes, the romanticized Cossack that informed Ukrainian nationalist ideology and the folk performances transplanted to Canada and elsewhere idealized the Cossacks as a democratic "brotherhood" and ignored those who became mercenaries and landowners or otherwise deviated from the heroic Cossack image. The program also featured *dumas*, or epic (rhyming) poems of Cossack origins that were recited or chanted to the accompaniment of the bandura. The "Song of Chumaks," for example, heralded "the men who centuries ago, brought the salt inland from the sea." A song like "The Lone Tavern," a courtship song about a young tavern girl who regrets running off with the Cossacks who had promised that "life will be gayer with us than in your mother's house," reaffirmed the men's heterosexual masculinity while offering them a mild rebuke. The evening ended on a solemn but climactic note with "Play, O, Bandurists" with lyrics by Taras Shevchenko, the nationalist poet revered by Ukrainians across the political spectrum, and whose own poetry contributed to the romanticized image of the Cossack.[72]

The choreographed movements that folk dances assign to women, who usually assume the role of the passive or coquettish but "wholesome" love interest of men, require them to perform gestures coded as submissive and female. In the interwar settlements, workers promoted mainly European folk dances (or American renditions of them) among girls and young women as a safe, healthy, and morally virtuous alternative to the often African American–influenced popular dances of the day. In the many descriptions of female folk dancers who performed in Toronto Institute–related events, it was their slim and lithe young bodies, their smiling and made-up but wholesome-looking faces, and

Greek performers in national costume dance at an outdoor concert at Nathan Phillips Square in front of a large crowd, Toronto City Hall, 14 July 1970. York University Libraries, Clara Thomas Archives & Special Collections, Toronto Telegram fonds, ASC34485.

their hairdos festooned with decorative ribbons, a crown of flowers, or festive kerchiefs, and not their talents or skills, that received most attention.[73]

In ways that echoed the beauty pageants that became popular in this period, audiences informed by the era's heteronormative gaze turned the women performers into what some feminist scholars have called symbols of race (or ethnicity) and nation. Attractive and friendly, these young women were expected to embody the idealized values, concepts, and behaviour of their given group or community.[74]

Folk Workshops

As members of a cultural elite that went to the symphony, theatre, and art galleries, Institute women like West, Jennings, and Bander felt at home in the polished folk performances that occurred in Toronto's bourgeois venues. As popular pluralists, they believed that participatory folk-dance workshops held in community spaces where ordinary people practised each other's folk-dance routines could help to foster mutual trust and a democratic outlook among

Canadians, new and old. Brief presentations on the cultural heritages of the dances, they added, would make the experiment more meaningful for the participants. An awareness of the need to create an environment conducive to making friends explains the related focus on having fun.

The plans that led to the first folk-dance workshop brought together a loose collection of women, and some men, who agreed that folk cultures could promote "good citizenship."[75] West and Jennings began with a proposal to the Co-ordinating Council of Citizenship for Metropolitan Toronto, a multigroup community organization on which they sat as Institute representatives, to organize a folk pageant for the tenth anniversary of Citizenship Day, held each year in honour of the Canadian Citizenship Act. With West as council chair, and Jennings as chair of its citizenship committee, the proposal carried. The familiar allies on the planning committee included social worker Charity Grant, an Institute board member, Jean Kotick of the Canadian Council of Christians and Jews, Ivy Krehm, group worker and folk-dance instructor at University Settlement House, and some YWCA staffers. The men included Institute staffer Richard Kolm, Andrew Thompson, a Liberal member of the Ontario legislature and Institute board member, and some YMCA staff.[76]

The Institute's "ethnic" collaborators included Alma Kopmanis of the Baltic Women's Council, who became an Institute friend, and Betty Madsen, the Danish Canadian owner of a folk school located outside Toronto and organizer of the Madsen folk festivals (see chapter 10). Having arrived in Canada and then married another Dane in 1937, the now-widowed Madsen headed the folk school she founded with husband John in 1945 and had links to the movement in Europe. The Madsen school taught choral singing and handicraft classes in woodcarving, sculpture, ceramics, and leather to people of various backgrounds. Madsen's immigrant-gifts populism mirrored that of the Institute. A typical festival program declared that Canada was "rich beyond imagination in Folk Lore treasures gathered from every part of the world," and that by "weaving these treasures into one colourful tapestry, we will all gain and add to the culture of this new and wonderful country."[77] The school's commitment to using folk activities to help people become "better citizens" capable of making "a real contribution to human relations in Canada"[78] resonated with the Institute's non-denominational but generally Christian worldview, though the organization did not publicly adopt Madsen's explicitly Christian vocabulary.[79]

The biggest recruit was Edith Fowke, then probably the best-known Canadian folklorist in Canada. An ardent nationalist and popularizer who began collecting rural folk songs in southwestern Ontario in the 1940s, the prolific Fowke was at this time broadcasting *Folk Song Time* (1950–63), the first of several popular CBC radio programs she hosted on Canadian folk songs. (In the early 1970s, she began teaching folklore studies at York University.) The Institute women shared with the Saskatchewan-born Fowke an interest in popularizing folk cultures for nationalist ends, but also differed from her in certain respects. For example, the Institute's folk-culture repertoire had no place for the industrial songs and workers' songs of protest that Fowke had begun to collect and publish. As a socialist of the CCF (Co-operative Commonwealth Federation) persuasion, and a feminist, Fowke's politics differed markedly from that of West and colleagues. However, as Pauline Greenhill notes, Fowke was more conventional in her selection and analysis of folk traditions than her involvement in various progressive political and social movements, including pacificism, would suggest. Further, Fowke, whose work was shaped by British and US models of folklore study, did not approve of collecting the folk cultures of immigrants, or what she called "the multicultural groups," because they were first-generation imports. To count as Canadian folklore in her books, the songs had to have survived at least one entire generation in Canada.[80] But she was clearly curious enough to join the planning committee. The Institute women were avowed anti-Communists, but unlike Helen Creighton, the Nova Scotian folklorist who branded Fowke a Communist worth watching,[81] they never red-baited Fowke.

Several months into their work, the planning committee abandoned its initially ambitious plans to celebrate Citizenship Day with a "mass" event. Those plans had involved a "parade of national costumes," a mega-concert in Maple Leaf Gardens, then the city's largest arena, and a dance at the Palais Royale, an imposing Moroccan-style structure on Lake Ontario that housed one of Toronto's few remaining large dance floors. On Jennings's recommendation, the committee agreed to postpone plans until sufficient funds could be raised to mount "an imposing presentation."[82] And she and West pursued alternative plans for a series of dance workshops to be held in venues across the city. The Central YMCA hosted the first one in June 1957. An ethnic- and gender-mixed group of about a dozen folk-dance instructors, choreographers, and choir leaders participated.

The Institute considered the first workshop a success in that 350 people representing two dozen ethnic groups, including folk troupes from Hamilton, Niagara Falls, Buffalo, and Syracuse, had participated despite insufficient publicity. But problems had arisen. The workshop, which the Institute hosted with the YMCA's Square Dance Group, ran an ethnically mixed program of sessions that involved troupe demonstrations and dance-alongs; these included Canadian and US square dances, European folk dances, and some vocal music sessions featuring Serbian and Ukrainian folk songs. Fowke ran a group singalong that featured Canadian songs. But various glitches caused confusion, embarrassment, and tensions, and hampered the dancing. The failure to provide "a prominent Ukrainian choir leader" leading a folk-singing session with the requested mimeographed copies of song lyrics written phonetically so that non-Ukrainians could participate had caused an uproar, prompting a profuse apology to the choirmaster. To make amends, the Institute planned to invite him to repeat the session at their next event. Keen to maintain cordial relations with other folk-culture contacts, the organizers agreed that even those folklorists who, like Rubin, had cancelled at the last minute, be invited to all future events.[83]

The report on the event also criticized the Canadian and ethno-Canadian troupe leaders and members for sticking to themselves following their own dance demonstrations instead of joining in the other group dances, thereby failing to become acquainted with the cultures of "others." For future workshops, it noted, the instructors, interpreters, and demonstrators must be made to understand their role as "the hosts through which the initiated will gain a knowledge, understanding and insight into their ethnic heritage." In short, they were to "help their guests enjoy themselves by learning one of their national dances, rather than performing for a sit-down audience."

The complaints about insufficient media publicity were also pointed. As promised, CBLT-TV (CBC Toronto) sent a cameraman to the event, but his shooting reportedly interfered with the program, creating "problems and jealousies," and the station never used the footage. Leon Kossar, the Ukrainian Canadian journalist and folk festival enthusiast, the report added, had written an "excellent" article on the upcoming workshop in his *Toronto Telegram* column, "New Canadian Interests," but never followed up. At the *Toronto Star*, Eric Geiger, author of the "New Canadians" advice column, gave the workshop only a passing mention despite being sent plenty of material. The conservative *Globe and Mail* ignored the event altogether. The failure of the *Canadian Scene*, a private anti-Communist outfit that distributed translated news items to the ethnic press, to get the materials to the editors in good time furthered hampered the coverage.[84]

The organizers nevertheless agreed that, despite its flaws, the workshop had generated enough goodwill to justify holding additional ones. Meanwhile, measures could be taken to address the problems, such as recruiting people experienced with the ethnic press to handle the publicity. Overall, the folk-dance workshops attracted less attention than the splashy folk festivals and musical extravaganzas. Still, the slim evidence on subsequent workshops, some of which appeared as part of a folk festival program and others independently, suggests that, while difficulties continued, the Institute drew uneven but reasonable crowds in the few hundreds. The folk workshop that kicked off the United Nations Week program at the Central YMCA in the late 1950s involved a larger than usual number of performers and attendees. (No estimates were given, but the numbers may have nudged towards 500 people.) The follow-up report also indicated a higher degree of active participation among the mixed crowd in the square, folk, and ballroom dances.[85]

Debating Scripts

Unlike the workshop goals, which generated consensus, the script of the folk festivals planned by the folk-culture planning (former Citizenship Day) committee caused friction between the Institute members and their female folklore allies. Certainly, there was plenty of agreement: the audiences had to be moved as well as entertained; a prominent host would help attract wider media attention; and some audience participation, such as group singalongs, would help produce "a feeling of identification" with the program. Agreement over ensuring respectable standards of performance and high-quality acts without sacrificing "authenticity" meant recruiting juries and holding auditions to find "professional" productions with "commercial" appeal. There was agreement as well on projecting liberal pluralist themes.

However, the Institute folks disagreed with their folk allies over the script and format. Institute representatives (such as West, Jennings, and Kolm) insisted that only a historical "citizenship pageant" format could properly narrate the story of Canada's steady progress towards modernity as expressed through industry and pluralism. A pageant format, they added, would easily include all the groups by grouping them together as they came to Canada originally, not singly, but in waves that would begin with the English, Scots, Indians (!), and French, then the Western Europeans, followed by the Southern Europeans along with the "Oriental peoples." Having presented Canada's history as a succession of gift-bearing immigrants, the show would then "blend" the individual groups into a large, impressive, and uplifting finale. Institute members also advised working through the "ethnic groups" to secure the performances. Indeed, having already met with some of their affiliated cultural groups, West et al. reported on what was offered. In addition to the European folk-dance troupes, mixed-gender choirs, a gymnastics group, and a children's ballet group, the Chinese Canadian Association promised performers for a Chinese drum dance and lion dance.[86]

Both Fowke and Madsen disliked the idea of working through the Institute's ethnic group members. Fowke suggested they first choose a compelling theme, then find a writer to produce an appropriate script, and only then select the folk acts that best fit the script. This approach, she claimed, would allow the writer to produce a quality script, which would make it easier to convince a director of stature, such as theatre director Dora Mavor Moore, to take on the project. Fowke's emphasis was on professionalism, but it may have also reflected a reluctance to let "the multicultural groups" decide the show's form and content. Madsen's pragmatic approach – to audition the available troupes and select the most appropriate ones, and then build a script around them – leaned towards the Institute's strategy but did not prioritize its ethnic contacts.[87]

Fowke and Madsen also disagreed with the Institute's pageant format and suggested alternative ways of depicting immigrant contributions to Canada. Arguing that the "rigidity" of the pageant formula would "restrict audience appeal," Fowke proposed instead an industry-by-industry approach that highlighted "those groups which contributed most to the particular industries." The proposal likely reflected Fowke's interest in working-class folk songs, though it hardly amounted to a call to celebrate the decidedly left-wing, if also commercial, folk music scene associated with musicians like Pete Seeger or events like the Winnipeg Folk Festival.[88] An Institute friend, Mira Ashby of the Croatian Women's Organization, agreed with Fowke about moving away from the pageant model, but her friendly suggestion of a province-by-province theme fell flat. When Madsen suggested updating the history by turning the stage into "a busy air terminal" and having each group step out of "an enormous plane," one of the male committee members, Herman Geiger-Torel, a German-born television producer, opera director, and sometime Institute collaborator, dismissed it as the same-old mosaic variety approach, but offered no alternative. University Settlement House staffer Krehm, who supported the Institute position, proposed a four-act pageant whose grand finale would offer "a glimpse into the future" by showing how Canadian folk song and dance already had incorporated "new Canadian" culture.[89]

As with other iterations of this debate, the Institute representatives claimed that their surveys of "interested people" showed a clear preference for the historical pageant, and insisted that a historical theme best served everyone's interest.[90] On this, as on later occasions, the Institute position triumphed, but their rigidity over the matter arguably created unnecessary friction with their folklorist allies. Indeed, it appears that, following the first folk-dance workshop and the Institute's one and only participation in the Madsen folk festival, both of which occurred in June 1957, neither Fowke nor Madsen worked closely again with the Institute.

Liberal Internationalism and International Beauties

The interwar US Institutes had supported the League of Nations out of a belief that internationalism offered a remedy for the mistakes that led to the First World War, including the marginalization of ethnic minorities. Likewise, the post-1945 Institutes, including Toronto's, believed that support for the United Nations and its principles of collective security, international diplomacy, and humanitarianism could ensure peace in a postwar world made scarier still by the Cold War and the nuclear arms race. Key Toronto personnel like West provided some continuity between the two periods. The Toronto Institute's position also aligned with that of the post-1945 Canadian government, which supported the United Nations as a way of aiding in the rebuilding of war-torn Europe, establishing security stability, and maintaining allies in an increasingly polarized world. In support of the UN's dual mandate, Canada pledged to participate in interventions meant to avert war and to encourage world peace through a commitment to economic development, social justice, and human rights.[91]

The promotion of a pluralistic Canadian citizenship that also embraced an interest in global affairs and support for international causes informed much

Institute activity. For example, its stamp club did so through its house activities. These included building a library of stamps and journals related to the UN's work, and holding its annual International Stamp Mart, which combined the auctioneering and exchange of stamps with lectures on campaigns aimed at alleviating Cold War tensions and promoting international cooperation and peace. The 1962 event celebrated the Philatelic Crusaders for Peace Organization's campaign aimed at "interjecting something positive into this world of disunity and nuclear threat" by posting "beautiful" stamps commemorating national and regional landmarks on letters sent to heads of state and other world leaders. First launched in Alexandria, Egypt, in 1960, the campaign then shifted to Athens, Rome, and elsewhere. The 1962 event also highlighted a campaign begun a few years earlier to rally support for the combined efforts of Egypt, Sudan, and UNESCO to save the ancient monuments of Nubia and related artifacts before they were flooded by the building of the Aswan High Dam.[92]

A central aspect of the Institute's notion of citizenship was that "native-born" Canadians, and not only newcomers, had to undergo a process of "re-education" that would instil in them a respect for cultural diversity.[93] It found expression in the events organized in support of the United Nations and international charitable organizations like the Save the Children Fund. Likening their efforts to eliminate mutual suspicions and promote harmonious relations "into the social life of [the] metropolis" of Toronto to "the kind of integration that the UN is attempting to effect in the world," Institute leaders endorsed the United Nations Association in Canada (1946), a founding member of the world federation of member nations. Through its central body and local branches, UNA-Canada sought to raise public awareness about the UN and encourage ordinary Canadians to support its goals, including through fundraising efforts for charities like the United Nations Children's Fund (UNICEF). Initially led by James Thompson, moderator of the United Church, the UNA-Canada membership was composed mainly of middle-class Canadians, including civic-minded professors, teachers, clergy, elected politicians, and journalists. As Tara Brookfield notes, men dominated the UNA leadership, but women formed the backbone of many local branches.[94] The Institute women's support of UN causes once again involved working with a cross-cultural and mixed-gender planning committee that included representatives of civic and citizenship groups, settlement houses, ethnocultural groups, the YMCA, and the YWCA and other women's groups.

During its first year of operation, the Institute co-hosted United Nations Week, held each October in honour of the organization's founding, with the Toronto branch of UNA-Canada. The program followed a familiar format of Sunday teas, luncheons, lectures, exhibits, and concerts. (Local UNA branches across Canada mounted a similar set of festivities.) The Institute's 1957 program included lectures by local UN leaders, who delivered the UN's main message about avoiding "future cataclysms of the human race" by "settling our differences through negotiations." UN fieldworkers reported on the distribution of emergency medical supplies to the most recent child victims of war and the development of community-based services to promote long-term health. There were also non-denominational church services as well as films on UN agencies and an exhibition of UN posters that reported on the agency's work.[95]

The concert led by harpist Clara Emerson and the Guild handicraft exhibit borrowed for the Institute's 1957 UN Week (described in the chapter's introduction) suggest how the Institute used UN events to garner support for its immigrant-gifts pluralism. Both concert and exhibit were meant to symbolize (English) Canada's long-standing respect for cultural diversity and inclusivity. The "spectacle" of the woman harpist, who performed Old World music on an instrument of ancient origins, and one whose angelic sound, in the context of Christianity, has long linked it, symbolically, to the sacred, engaged the theme of global harmony through the purifying force of "heavenly" music.[96] The crafts collected from immigrant and Indigenous communities across central Canada provided a familiar, and problematic, representation of Canadian diversity in which the absent white collectors assumed the role of benevolent saviours of endangered traditions. The International Night that closed this UN Week offered a familiar multi-ethnic line-up of classically trained singers and musicians and folk troupes. Ironically, unless an exception was made, a luncheon address held at a local private men's club would have excluded the female organizers.[97]

Canadian support for the UN was, to quote Tara Brookfield, "erratic." Having peaked during the Suez peacekeeping mission promoted by Lester Pearson in 1956, it waned in the 1960s, though many Canadians continued to donate generously to UNICEF.[98] The Institute did not host another UN Week, but it continued to support UN causes including charitable ones. The Institute's most successful fundraising drive came in 1960, but in support of the Toronto Branch of the Canadian Save the Children Fund (SCF, est. 1922), a branch of the international charity. It did so through participation in a Festival of Nations. An international fair initiated by a group of diplomats from SCF member nations, the 1960 festival was modelled after "successful" fairs held in London, Paris, and other "world centres." Overseeing the plans was Canada's first woman senator Cairine Wilson, a liberal and a humanitarian who had long advocated for refugee admissions and the liberalization of immigration laws. The publicity materials described the SCF's services, from family reunification and distribution of "millions of meals and tons of clothing" to needy children, to improved medical aid in hospitals and support for orphanages in Europe and elsewhere. West and colleagues endorsed the SCF's child sponsorship program, which encouraged sponsors to communicate with the child and learn about their family and village, as a fine experiment in compassionate global citizenship. No doubt, they expected Canadians rather than financially strapped newcomers to become sponsors. For the 1960 festival, Senator Wilson convinced Ottawa to permit all "foreign goods" that could be defined as "gifts," such as handicrafts, to enter the country duty-free, which meant lower prices for the items.[99]

The fair was held in Casa Loma, an imposing castle-like mansion in Toronto, and included a familiar line-up of ethnic folk performances and sales booths of "quality articles" reflecting the "national arts and crafts" traditions of the participating groups. In this context, the commodification of handicrafts, or the domestic tourism being promoted, served a higher global goal. To mount the event, the Institute women secured free newspaper advertising, food donations, and building materials, as well as donations from local businessmen, a few companies, including Bell Telephone and British American Oil, and several banks. (Donations ranged from $250 to $1,000.) They also extended the one-day fair by another day after the invited craftspeople refused to participate unless they had more time to sell their crafts. No total is recorded, but the correspondence suggests the fair raised a decent amount (perhaps several hundred dollars).[100]

By the 1960s, the events mounted in support of the United Nations and other liberal causes included beauty pageants. Cultural historians and scholars of sexuality have shed light on the paradox of staging ethnic, multicultural, and interracial beauty contests. The hybridized presence of "non-hegemonic" women conveying such values as inclusivity and international goodwill, they note, was intimately linked to a spectacle that used the allure of attractive young female bodies (a growing staple in the era's popular culture) to attract audiences and make money.[101] The Institute ran neither a Miss UN nor a Miss International Institute beauty contest, but Metro International Caravan, the popular ethnic folk and trade show the Institute helped to launch in 1969, did so (see chapter 10). The "international beauties" representing the "world city" pavilions competed for the title on the festival's final day. Held in the rotunda of the new City Hall, the winner of the first Miss Caravan pageant was twenty-year-old Miss Kiev/Maria Hlushko, a secretary of Ukrainian origins born in Germany who reportedly dazzled in both traditional costume and modern party dress.[102]

The Institute's practice of recruiting, again through the ethnic groups, young women to perform as "hostesses" for their well-intentioned events produced similar results. The in-house photographs and newspaper items capture hundreds of "pretty attendants" in "nationality dress" serving hors d'oeuvres or pastries at a Citizenship Day reception, a UN luncheon, or a dinner for the Ontario Human Rights Commission. Indeed, photos of hostesses were more likely to be published and thus spread news of the Institute events. One of the two photos that accompanied the Toronto *Globe and Mail* coverage of a 1961 SCF fundraiser held in the "handsome house" of Mrs W.D. (Isabel) Ross – an Institute IODE volunteer and widow of a former Lieutenant Govenor of Ontario who lived on Crescent Road in tony Rosedale[103] – shows three women representing

The original caption read in part: "Camera fan Mayor William Dennison makes like an ordinary tourist as the Miss Caravan contestants gather together in Nathan Phillips Square yesterday for the opening night ceremonies of the week-long festival." York University Libraries, Clara Thomas Archives & Special Collections, Toronto Telegram fonds, ASC60821 (photographer Jac Holland, 25 June 1971).

SCF nations. Two of them were married, a Budapest-born woman dressed in a "Hungarian gown" and an Italian woman with an Anglo last name (Macmillan) in "a festive Italian dress." The single woman, Irene Skuba, wore the dress of an unspecified region in Czechoslovakia. The second photo, which showed two women, one of them Dutch, featured one of only two Black attendants uncovered by this research. Similarly attired, she is described as Loretta Lesmond of the West Indies.[104]

That the Institute women ran an active roster of hostesses is not surprising for the period, but, ironically, the transactions commodified them as so many pretty ethnic gifts. Take West's matter-of-fact response to a request from the Ontario Citizenship Branch (OCB) for attendants to host a citizenship exhibit being organized at the Canadian National Exhibition in August-September 1960. After consulting her list of contacts, West noted that her Croatian contact (Ashby described above) had two or three Croatian "girls," her Italian contact (Mrs S. Di Giacomo) a probable "three or four girls," and her Swiss, Dutch, Estonian, Ukrainian, Austrian, and Swedish contacts a few girls each. She also named two "Latvian girls" who could host in September. Her contact in a Lutheran Church–based immigrant aid society, she added, could provide some "German girls," but they would need help in securing costumes. After giving the OCB staffer the information for the contacts from whom she had not yet heard, she expressed disappointment in failing to recruit any girls from her "Chinese contact." The appreciative OCB staffer replied, as did others, that the girls "would bring some much needed colour to the exhibit and stimulate greater interest generally."[105]

The ubiquitous presence of these "pretty attendants" at Institute events had a doubled-edged impact. On the one hand, the familiar sight of these women, who wore conservative ethnic dresses and did not don a bathing suit or walk the runway,[106] arguably contributed to the process of legitimizing the public display of cultural difference and, by extension, internationalism. Expected to strike up conversations with strangers as well as smile and serve the "ethnic pastries," they were considered cultural ambassadors, or intermediaries, in their own right. Indeed, Institute staff encouraged them to become members so they could pick up lessons in pluralism and develop some leadership skills. Occasionally, staff provided these attendants with orientation sessions.

Further, it seems clear that many of these young women volunteers were active, even proud, members of their respective ethnocultural organizations and thus took seriously their role both as representatives of their ethnic heritage and as modern young Canadians participating in a pluralist experiment. The same could be said of the few young male hosts.[107] The women expressed an appreciation for the opportunity to participate in Institute affairs, reportedly saying that it afforded them an opportunity to develop and refine skills relating to "tact, patience, [and] sympathy," and good training for future jobs in the professions or the service industry.[108] In contrast to many, but by no means all, of their middle-class Anglo-Canadian counterparts, these immigrant youth were not experimenting with counter-cultural lifestyles during the sixties and seventies, but rather negotiating a hybridized identity as an ethno-Canadian in a pluralist city.[109]

The strategy of utilizing "pretty attendants" to enhance the attraction of progressive causes was fraught with flawed logic and contradictions. Young women like Susan Borsi, a Hungarian hostess for 1963 Hungarian Week who matched her traditional ethnic costume with a fashionable modern beehive hairdo, embodied a mix of ethnic nostalgia and urban modernity that echoed Institute-style pluralism. Along with the performances described above, she offered a visual example of what happens when, as anthropologist Liisa Malkki argues, an internationalist logic that is assigned a moral quality, such as liberal invocations of internationalism, is projected onto a "local" case of cultural difference, such as post-1945 Toronto and Canada. In effect, it provides a means by which to contain, or domesticate, the offending differences that might otherwise threaten the logic of the nation-state.[110] Or put another way, using "lovely" costumed women to "add colour" to well-intentioned fundraisers did less to focus attention on the global inequities and injustices that produced the "need" being acknowledged than contribute towards the therapeutic function that a gifts-and-spectacle pluralism can perform. The inherent contradictions are perhaps highlighted by a revealing anecdote involving a man who approached a hostess at an Institute event and, upon receiving confirmation that she was indeed a hostess, asked her to sew a loose button onto his jacket.[111]

Far from being static folk (and domestic) figures, young women like Borsi were negotiating the pull of the era's beauty culture within the confines of limited budgets. As Abril Liberatori observes, the era's ethnic beauty pageants combined pageantry and spectacle to display the embedded connection between ethnicity and femininity among immigrant communities abroad while the beauty sections of ethnic newspapers skirted the line between feminine aesthetics and practical exigencies by telling women how to look beautiful for less. Class and other differences also shaped these young women's outlooks. As someone likely of middle-class urban origins, Borsi's engagement with modernity would have differed from the rural Southern Italian women who immigrated to Ontario and Buenos Aires after the Second World War. As Liberatori's research documents, for many of these women, commercial culture abroad signified an escape from the backward and unmodern Old World and an entry into a new commercialized, modern society. Her interview subjects read the popular Italian-language women's magazines (*Donna* in Ontario and *Femirama* in Buenos Aires) and the women's pages in newspapers for ideas, bought sewing patterns, and prided themselves on producing a fashionable wardrobe on a budget.[112]

Still, the juxtaposition of traditional rural folk heritage and urban modernity that these young costumed women embodied could threaten to turn them into anachronistic objects of amusement. That tendency was evident at the folk ball held at the upscale Royal York Hotel to kick off the 1965 Nationbuilders show, a multicultural musical extravaganza held at the CNE grandstand (see chapter 10). The organizers booked a glamorous ballroom in the hopes of attracting more Anglo-Torontonians to the event. The images accompanying the *Globe and Mail*'s coverage of the ball showed traditionally costumed ethnic women gyrating to the latest dances with Canadian men who, dressed in modern suits, moved in more subdued fashion. The photographer who shot a young German woman in ethnic garb dancing the twist with a suited "Anglo" man pumped up the traditional vs modern, or modernist vs anti-modernist, clash by including in the frame two older ethnic women watching the woman's dance moves with obvious disapproval.[113]

Human Rights

The movement for human rights received a major boost in the aftermath of the war and the Holocaust, culminating in the UN's adoption of the Universal Declaration of Human Rights in 1948. The Institute's modest efforts to support the cause by addressing anti-immigrant racism and prejudice in Toronto owe much to the work of Daniel Hill, the African Canadian sociologist, social worker, and human rights pioneer. The son of an African American minister and a social worker, a war veteran, and a graduate of Brown University, Hill arrived in Canada after the war with a strong social conscience. In 1953, he married Donna Mae Bender (Hill), a white US civil rights activist who worked for a time with the Toronto Labour Committee for Human Rights, which documented instances of racial discrimination to pressure the Ontario government to enact more comprehensive anti-discrimination legislation.[114]

With a master's degree in sociology from the University of Toronto in hand, Hill, as research director of the Social Planning Council of Metropolitan Toronto, first spoke at the Institute on the subject of "population trends" in April 1957. After holding other positions in the social welfare field and obtaining his PhD from the University of Toronto (1960) with a groundbreaking dissertation on Blacks in Toronto, Hill became director of the Ontario Human Rights Commission (OHRC) in 1962. The OHRC, which administered the Ontario Human Rights Code (enacted 1962), was the first public agency of its kind in Canada. Under Hill's active leadership, it became a major enterprise, but it began life in a downtown office with a handful of employees.[115]

Unlike the Jewish Canadian, Japanese Canadian, African Canadian, and Caribbean-born human rights and civil rights activists, Institute personnel never became prominent actors in the postwar human rights movement. But they did try to raise an awareness about the Ontario Human Rights Code, which was posted on their bulletin board, by organizing panels, a dinner, and a conference, and by publishing articles on the bill's principles of equity and anti-racism. One such *Intercom* article highlighted the concept of "mutuality" imbedded in the code. It argued that the need to create "at the community level" a climate of understanding and mutual respect in which all people, regardless of racial, religious, or cultural background, are made to feel equal in dignity and rights, applied as much to the new Canadian as the "native-born." Each group, the article added, had "a rich contribution" to make to the province's and the nation's well-being, and permitting them to do so was "a prerequisite for the development of a truly healthy Canadianism."[116]

A dinner held in honour of the Ontario Human Rights Commission on 18 October 1963. Commissioner Daniel Hill (far left) and others stand by an exhibit of Jamaican crafts, embroidered clothing, and a cloth calendar commemorating Jamaican independence (1962). Archives of Ontario, F884-2-9, B427166.

In May 1964, the Institute co-hosted with UNA-Canada a conference that brought together youth groups from across the metropolitan area to address the spread of hate literature and how to eliminate it. Capturing the mood of the conference, one contributor explained that, by means of isolating individuals or groups such as racialized immigrants, hate literature sought to "deny them human rights and dignity that are the common heritage of all Canadians."[117] By the time the *Intercom* published a three-part series on the OHRC's work five years later, Institute director Stewart and colleagues could detect the early signs of a racist backlash against the post-1967 racialized immigrants that would reach crisis proportions in the 1970s. In response, the *Intercom* urged members to apply the code's principles to their everyday life, to inform the Commission of any discriminatory practices observed, and to convince their ethnic organizations to observe the (December) anniversary of the UN's

288   Ethnic Folk Cultures

Invited "ethnic leaders" and members at the Ontario Human Rights Commission dinner at the Institute on 18 October 1963 are listening to a speaker (likely Daniel Hill). Archives of Ontario, F884-2-9, B427166.

Universal Declaration of Human Rights and establish a Human Rights Committee that could educate their members on the issues.[118] But there were no signs of plans to intensify such efforts before crippling problems shut down the Institute in 1974.

Can we attribute the Toronto Institute's disappointing record on human rights activism to the limited, even naive, "handicrafts and human rights" or "multicultural spectacle as democratic internationalism" approach to anti-racist work entirely to cultural pluralist ideology? As US critical race scholars like Ellen Wu note, the growing influence in US society of cultural pluralism – which rejected older biologically determinist racist theories – allowed certain racialized "others," such as Asian Americans, to lay claims of belonging to the nation. Institute acknowledgment that racialized migrants differed in terms of national, regional, or ethnic origins, and, most especially, group-defined cultural practices, reflected progressive thinking. It also aligned with the general shift in the social sciences post-1945 away from biology and towards psychology.[119] One of the articles to appear on the subject in the *Intercom* came from the National Conference of Christians and Jews, a liberal organization and Institute ally that promoted the ideals of "brotherhood," social justice, mutual respect, and dialogue. The author, John Gillin, explained that (anthropological) research had discredited the biological concept of race by showing that human groups do not possess "true hereditary homogeneity" but instead differentiate according to social-cultural features. Using Peru as an example, he noted that Peruvians and Indigenous peoples have been erroneously viewed as separate races on the basis of differences in clothing, language, and customs (the latter being modified versions of Spanish and Indigenous customs) despite the fact that both groups possessed mixed racial ancestries. The differences between them, he stressed, denoted "socio-cultural division." Gillin concluded by stressing the need to educate parents and other child-minders to raise the next generation of children without "building" into them "unnecessary attitudes" towards other human beings.[120] I use Gillin's essay here to suggest that pluralism did allow for the possibility of more incisive anti-racist activity than that engaged in by Toronto Institute personnel.

Not that their US counterparts necessarily did better. In keeping with their view of human behaviour, institutions, and values as group-defined entities, the Institutes used a language of culture, not race, in their assessments of clients. But their practices often reflected dominant racial hierarchies and a colonial gaze. For example, some US Institutes, including Philadelphia's, hosted a club for "American Indians." While the scant references to them suggest inactivity or negligence, the clubs' presence alone speaks to the paradoxical way that Indigenous peoples were both reduced to just another ethnic group and treated as a race that stood outside US life.[121]

Differences in racial status also likely help to explain the differing treatment the Milwaukee Institute meted out to their Dutch members, who arguably enjoyed an uncontested whiteness, and their Puerto Rican members, who did not. A 1958 report praised a newly formed Flying Dutchman Club composed mainly of newcomers who participated in several community events, including the Institute's annual folk ball, where they nominated someone for the Nationality Queen contest. In predicting a rapid adaptation to US life, head group worker Willette Pierce did not explicitly reference their whiteness, but an assessment of her positive evaluation should consider the Institutes' long history of dealing with European groups, and a general perception that, as Western Europeans, the Dutch were "closer" to American values than other groups.[122] By contrast, Pierce's report on the Puerto Rican fiesta her staff mounted with a local "Mexican church" suggests, at best, ineptitude at dealing with racialized migrants. The festival, which included a Puerto Rican orchestra, dancing, and food, followed a familiar format. But Pierce's report on the difficult lessons learned – particularly that Puerto Ricans did not like egg salad sandwiches "for a dance" – indicates the absence of consultation with a group they aimed to integrate into their "democratic" ways.[123] Native Americans and Puerto Ricans, unlike unnaturalized European, Asian, and Latin American clients, were US citizens. However, the Institutes' perception of them, shaped as it was by the colonial gaze of the "Greater United States,"[124] was that of racialized foreigners in need of special attention – though, overall, Puerto Ricans received far more attention than did Native Americans.

Finally, the Toronto Institute's failure to develop a robust anti-racist campaign reflected its limited, and increasingly scarce, resources as well as an evident lack of interest among a still heavily white immigrant membership to actively take up the call.

Conclusion

A focus on the Institute's Anglo-Canadian middle-class women and the cultural events and fundraisers they mounted in support of "good" citizenship, internationalism, human rights, and charitable campaigns reveals their public embrace of a long-standing association of bourgeois women with cultural guardianship and with liberal internationalism. A commitment to modern nation-building goals rooted in pluralist concepts of immigrant integration, international community, and cosmopolitan citizenship fuelled their organizing. Enthusiastic participants in certain strands of the post-1945 folk revival, they seemed equally keen to promote fine art as folk crafts. Their enjoyment of classically influenced folk concerts that occurred in the exalted surroundings of a concert hall was palpable, but, so, too, was their investment in the democracy-building, gym-based folk-dance workshops. Connecting all this activity was an immigrant-gifts pluralism that used the cultural gifts of immigrants, no matter their status, as a means by which to manage ethnic relations and garner support for cultural diversity and a pluralistic Canadian identity. These women also understood the importance of collaborating with Canadian and ethnic folklore allies, though the debates over cultural scripts could put them in conflict with them.

Like the artists and artisans, the performers (ethnic hostesses, dancers, musicians, and beauty contestants) were subjected to a heterosexual and objectifying tourist gaze, but the female performers and hostesses were more likely to be reduced to "pretty" symbols of pluralism. Their own daily struggles to make ends meet explain why the immigrant and ethnic craftswomen and men jumped at the opportunity to sell their wares, though a desire for some recognition of their skills also mattered. Finally, the seeming inability of the Institute women to mount more sustained campaigns in support of human rights exposes the limits of a popular pluralism forged within a white European context.

Conclusion

The Institute's Demise

Plagued by charges of irrelevance and facing the loss of critical funds, the International Institute of Metropolitan Toronto closed its doors for good at the end of 1974. Since the federal government's adoption of multiculturalism as an official policy three years earlier, the Institute had struggled to stay afloat by downsizing staff and services and decentralizing operations, so that, by 1973, it consisted of a small network of four offices spread across the metropolitan area.[1]

A volunteer agency, the Institute throughout its history relied primarily on community chest funds, though it also received occasional government and private charity support. Already by 1970, however, the United Community Fund began to criticize the Institute for "an erosion of services" due to ineffective management and the loss of leadership in the field.[2] In response, the Institute board commissioned a report by Wilson Head, the African American/Canadian sociologist, community planner, and civil rights activist who had been a co-author of the Ontario Human Rights Code in 1962. He now chaired the School of Social Work at Atkinson College, York University (est. 1966).[3] Head's 1973 study along with a major UCF report prompted discussion about the need to develop a "new model" of operations. In this context, Head at one point advised the Institute staff to consider being "more political" in terms of lobbying governments as the tensions between the volunteer and state sectors could lead to "creative possibilities."[4]

Struggling to define a revised role for the embattled Institute, director Tine Stewart proposed developing more expertise in race relations and combatting racism, including, as she put it in reference to the bullying and streaming of Black immigrant students, "bigotry and bias in the schools." Others defended the Institute's record and suggested advocating, in particular, on behalf of poor, elderly, and chronically ill immigrants. A Portuguese counsellor who had recently escorted a client to a government office in order to interpret for him admitted to feeling "humiliated" by the worker who dismissively asked why an

Institute staffer was even there.[5] The Institute's seventies-era correspondence confirms the sense that social agency leaders and funders increasingly viewed the Institute as having lost its leadership in the immigrant and settlement service field. The sentiment was perhaps reinforced by the fact that Stewart, the director since 1968, had been a long-time volunteer rather than a professional social worker.

The growth in the multiculturalism bureaucracy that followed the Liberal government's adoption of official multiculturalism also contributed to the Institute's demise.[6] A number of pluralist-oriented initiatives at both the federal and provincial levels actually predated 1971, but the new infusion of funds expanded the scale of activity. A Multicultural Directorate was created in the Department of the Secretary of State in 1972 to assist in the development of multicultural policies and programs and, a year later, a new Ministry of Multiculturalism began overseeing their implementation within government departments. Civil servants, scholar-consultants, and community leaders deliberated over defining a mandate. Staff developed programs and conducted outreach. They drew up policy criteria for the awarding of public funds to non-governmental citizen and community actors in accordance with a multicultural policy that, at least initially, understood barriers to social adaptation and economic success mainly in cultural terms rather than in terms of economic, gender, or racial inequity. As part of the developments that occurred at the federal and Ontario level, the Toronto Institute was effectively displaced and absorbed by the state.[7]

A provincial initiative that directly threatened the Institute was the Ontario government's move in 1973 to provide settlement services directly to newcomers through its Welcome House. (Four years later, it passed a multicultural policy and, in 1982, created a Ministry of Citizenship and Culture.) Located at 8 York Street in the downtown core, the Welcome House had first focused on the Asian Ugandans expelled by Idi Amin, but later offered services to all newcomers.[8] The Institute had organized some initial services for the Ugandan refugees before the project was passed on to the Ontario government. A model of centralizing reception and settlement services in a single place made sense, but the Institute board and staff feared being made redundant. The news that the English-language classes offered through the Ontario Citizenship Division would be relocated from the Institute to the Welcome House had set off alarm bells because the rental of classroom space had covered a major portion of the Institute's own building-rental costs.[9]

Then came the invitation to move into Welcome House. While accompanied by promises to respect the Institute's autonomy, Stewart articulated the shared fear that accepting the invitation would undermine the Institute's raison d'être. Noting that the Institute had long argued that "we are doing this particular kind of work – services to immigrants – because the Government is not doing it," she called the move risky. Others feared losing "our flexibility" to government directives or losing UCF support altogether, or felt the idea wrong-headed because immigrants were "not *fond* of government buildings." Stewart proposed and then immediately dismissed the idea of trying to ensure the Institute's autonomy by fundraising among the "ethnic groups" on the grounds that the "tremendous division – to the left or to the right – in so many ethnic groups" risked losing "our greatest strength, *neutrality*."[10] She and long-time staffer Margarete Streeruwitz may still have been smarting from the controversy over a fundraising project to make and sell ethnic commercial directories to social agencies. Some Czechoslovakian and other Eastern European groups had decried the inclusion of the Czechoslovakian embassy and consulate in the Czechoslovak directory. The explanation that social service personnel might need to contact these offices for "official matters" had drawn the angry reply that inviting Communist diplomats to interfere in the lives of any Czechoslovakian refugee was "absurd," even possibly leading to their being pressured to return home, with tragic results.[11] Facing UCF pressure, the Institute board arrived at a compromise, and, as part of its decentralization plans, a tiny staff moved into Welcome House. The office offered multilingual counselling services, but little else. The other Institute offices provided a few additional services, such as interpretation, legal aid support, registration for some English classes being run by George Brown College, or modest recreational programs including outdoor excursions.

By this point, the Institute already had lost any edge it had as an organizer of popular folk festivals and spectacles to metropolitan-wide organizations like the Community Folk Art Council. But it did manage to deliver some social services to its clientele until the bitter end. The Christmas parties continued into 1973 as did the volunteer-led conversational English tutorials. There was a small but successful children's "multicultural" summer camp program. In addition to carrying out her group work and counselling duties, Korean social worker Catherine Lee developed ties with some (South) Korean community organizations, including a United Church club, a Catholic club, and a seniors' group.[12] Staff secured some new funds, including a modest Local Initiatives Program (LIP) grant in support of a Greek-language Free Interpreter Service located near the Institute's east end office.[13]

The financial troubles undermined most initiatives, however, including those intended for the post-1967 immigrants. As Caribbean and South Asian staff, Royston C. Jones and Murali Nair juggled their responsibilities to the Institute and other community and social agencies in the face of scarce resources and a mounting racist backlash against Caribbean (particularly Jamaican) and South Asian (particularly Pakistani) immigrants. At the Institute's Weston Branch, which was located in a government-subsidized apartment building that included a significant Black Caribbean population, the priority was "preventing alienation through isolation in impersonal high rises."[14] In addition to running the Institute's Legal Aid Program and heading a committee calling for better working conditions for migrant domestic workers from the Caribbean, Jones was involved in some west end branch projects, including a mothers and tots program, but programming suffered from insufficient funds.[15] In a spring 1974 report that conveyed a sense of impending doom, Institute board member Katharine Symons referred to the establishment of a West Indian Centre in the area as another sign of "the eroding of the Institute's role in the community." Set up to serve Jamaican immigrants, and administered by Beverley Corke, a Jamaican-born social worker, the centre had received UCF and LIP funds.[16] Meantime, Nair's proposal for an "Asians in Transition" community project modelled on the Institute's earlier projects among Southern European immigrants never got off the ground.[17]

Notwithstanding Stewart's exhortation to turn "our sad outlook" into a "cheerful face" for the sake of the communities they served,[18] the financial woes exacerbated tensions among the Institute staff. The few professional social workers complained about being underappreciated and the others of being overworked or harassed – and people left. Having earlier taken out a private loan to cover staff salaries, the board learned in spring 1974 that the UCF's Allocations Committee would provide no further funds. On 31 December, the Institute ceased to exist.[19]

One can speak of an Institute legacy, a problematic and paradoxical one, to be sure, but one that deserves attention given the lack of knowledge of the historical role that women played in launching community pluralist experiments in Canada before official multiculturalism. An understanding of the longer and more bottom-up, if still heavily middle-class, roots of late-twentieth-century multiculturalism both challenges and offers greater insight into the ascendancy of a liberal ideology, and a form of nationalism, long understood as being of recent origin.[20]

The movement of some Institute personnel into the multicultural/citizenship/immigration complex also suggests a more specific legacy. While some remained active in ethnic community politics, others joined a rising class of multicultural experts who landed jobs as consultants and public servants and as citizenship judges at the federal and provincial levels. A journalist, civil servant, and administrator as well as a Polish patriot, long-time Institute volunteer Irene Ungar, for example, became a Canadian citizenship judge. Relocated to Vancouver in the late sixties, volunteer Emily Ostapatch joined the Labour Relations Board of British Columbia with a personal mandate to protect working women from discrimination.[21]

If the state co-opted or absorbed Institute programs and practices, the Institute also helped to inform late twentieth-century multiculturalism in Canada. Toronto's International Institute drew on a long, multifaceted, and blemished history of pluralist ideals, cultural spectacles, community projects, social work practices, and female volunteerism in both Canada and the United States.

Multiculturalism did not achieve official status in the United States as it did in Canada. But in both countries, an array of social agencies, community centres, and grassroots organizations tapped government, community chest, and other funds in order to provide resources and social services to immigrant groups.[22] The Toronto Institute, and the wider international institute movement to which it belonged, were part of a long history of North American conversations and networks that conceived of a white, settler-based model of multiculturalism that did not question the state's continuing colonial relations vis-à-vis Indigenous peoples. This history of colonialism, too, had shaped late-twentieth-century Canadian multiculturalism.

Standing Back

As a left feminist historian's intervention into the massive scholarship on multiculturalism in Canada, North America, and beyond, this study tells the largely neglected history of women's pluralist advocacy and activism in Canada before the advent of official multiculturalism through a case history of the International Institute of Metropolitan Toronto (1952–74). The heavily female profile, multi-ethnic composition, and multifaceted mandate of the Toronto Institute makes in-depth research on its form of liberal multiculturalism a worthwhile exercise. The Institute's profile and the range of activities makes for a compelling case study. And the findings shed light on wider issues and debates.

In contrast to most organizations with a multicultural mandate or orientation, which, then as now, focus either on delivering services to newcomers or mounting cultural events, the Toronto Institute combined these sets of practices with a third focus on community-building and community-organizing projects. Unlike the Anglo-Canadian staff and male administrators who typically staffed the era's government departments and social agencies, the Institute had a multi-ethnic if mainly white and European staff, and women figured prominently among its supervisors and administrators. Indeed, women occupied every position at the Institute, from board member, director, and project or casework supervisor to front-line group and community worker, from counsellor, home visitor, and receptionist to folk culture advocate and festival organizer. Key funders and co-sponsors included women's organizations, and women were conspicuous in the Institute's wide-ranging networks. Its heavily multicultural and female profile also distinguished the Institute from most immigrant and ethno-Canadian organizations, which represented one or a small cluster of groups, and from immigrant reception agencies such as the Italian and Jewish immigrant aid societies.[23] A social centre, too, the Institute's social, recreational, and cultural activities gave rise to a multicultural if inegalitarian community rooted mainly in cross-cultural but also some cross-racial and cross-class relationships.

In fleshing out the longer roots and cross-border networks that have informed late-twentieth-century multiculturalism in Canada, this Toronto study has debunked Canadian myths about the absence of a history of multiculturalism in the United States. Across two centuries, pluralism in both countries moved in varying fashion from a minority to a leading if contested creed. So, let us finally discard the old and hackneyed melting pot vs cultural mosaic trope. Not that multiculturalism in either society has offered a sufficient antidote to racism. As the exploitation of migrant workers and the police killings of Black and Indigenous people in North America during the COVID-19 pandemic tragically revealed, both of these historically self-described liberal and tolerant nations share a history and present of racism.

The Toronto Institute did try to extend its services and activities to the racialized immigrants who arrived after 1967, as evidenced by the hiring of Black Caribbean and Asian staff. Stewart's 1973 comments about possibly developing an anti-racist campaign suggests, too, an awareness of the need to strengthen the Institute's tepid record on promoting human rights and combatting racism. But its demise a year later means we will never know whether Institute personnel would have carried out the consultations and rethinking required to embrace a more inclusive and anti-racist mandate. In interpreting thousands of Institute case files, I demonstrated more by theoretically informed application than by detailed theoretical explication how to interpret case records in ways that avoid the pitfalls of either a strictly empiricist (they capture what actually happened) or postmodern (they are the file-maker's "fiction") stance.

Grim Realities, Possibilities, Radical Imaginaries?

Viewed against the idea of a radically transformative, racially and gender inclusive, anti-colonial, and egalitarian multiculturalism, the limitations of Toronto Institute pluralism are glaring. In light of present-day realities, however, making easy pronouncements about a flawed or failed experiment is simply not enough. Without abandoning a critical lens, my decision to highlight the possibilities and positive features of Institute-style liberal pluralism, as well as its limits and paradoxical nature, was guided by a basic question. Does a flawed multiculturalism still offer any redeeming qualities or useful lessons for our current grim times?

In 2003, Himani Bannerji, one of Canada's leading critics of multiculturalism, raised such a question. The context in which she did so is critical. She was considering the backlash against racialized and non-Christian immigrants in English Canada and in Quebec against the global display of gruesome wars, ethnic genocides, forced migrations, and the "new racism" (or cultural racism) that uses a language of cultural incompatibility to declare

Muslim, Hindu, and other non-Christian im/migrants unfit for life in Western liberal democracies. Instead of excoriating Canadian multiculturalism, she suggested that a completely implemented pluralism-from-below in which "the multicultural others" genuinely attain greater equity and dignity would benefit all Canadians.[24]

Since Bannerji offered what I take to be her proposal for a reassessment of Canadian multiculturalism in 2003 – that is, in an already post 9/11 world in which heightened Muslim-bashing, surveillance, and neo-liberalism also served to silence debate[25] – things have worsened. In 2010–11, state leaders Angela Merkel, Nicolas Sarkozy, and David Cameron declared multiculturalism a failure within their respective European nations. They and other leading figures demanded that the immigrants accept the core values of European societies, two of the most important of which were said to be individual freedom and sexual equality. Political leaders in the Netherlands and elsewhere followed with similar declarations. In the debates that raged within these countries, the gendered stereotypes of the Muslim fanatic/misogynist male and veiled/controlled Muslim female fuelled an anti-immigrant rhetoric that, in some cases, brought together right-wing xenophobes, neo-liberals, and some leftists and feminists.[26]

Historical accounts of the multicultural backlash in Europe shed light on one of the themes of this study, namely that the varied meanings attached to this slippery term creates ambiguity and confusion. Rita Chin's study of how, since the 1950s, political leaders and social agencies in several Western European nations have dealt with the growing presence of non-Western immigrants, shows that European multiculturalism has had little to do with the positive, if contested, connotations historically attached to the term in North America. Rather, it has been about managing the diversity of the (now multigenerational) foreign guest workers – and the family members who joined them and who have since been born on European soil – who did not return "home" as expected when the post-1945 economic boom collapsed in the early 1970s. In France, for example, initial efforts to encourage expressions of religious and cultural identity among these workers were meant to ensure an attachment to their homeland in Algeria and elsewhere, the better to treat them as a reserve army of labour, returning home without difficulty in bust periods and migrating to France when needed. By the time the economic slump occurred, however, permanent but segregated communities of racialized Muslim residents had taken root. In Britain, the management of an increasingly diverse population focused on post-colonials from the Caribbean and South Asia – the so-called empire that struck back – though some progressive advocates of multiculturalism also emerged. While the alarmism over immigrants reared its ugly head well before the more recent arrival of refugees from violence and wartorn places in the Middle East and Africa, their presence both in the United Kingdom and on the Continent has intensified the moral panic over veiled women and Muslim terrorists fuelling the multiculturalism backlash.[27]

While I was writing this book, the declarations of the failure of multiculturalism in Europe – which meant not the failure to create more welcoming societies but that Muslim culture was not compatible with European traditions[28] – continued unabated. They did so amid an on-going refugee crisis, seething xenophobia, the re-emergence of fascism, and the issuing of Muslim bans in the name of the war against terror. The pandemic of 2019–22 exposed and compounded the class, racial, and gender divides within and across nations, and exacerbated the unemployment, poverty, and marginalization of millions of refugees. Highly concentrated in jobs where physical distancing is either difficult or impossible, migrant workers in Canada and other OECD (Organization for Economic Co-operation and Development) nations faced an infection risk at least twice as high as that of the "native-born."[29]

During the writing process I was, however, heartened by the Canadian response to the Syrian refugee crisis. Here, Chancellor Merkel's leading role in confirming the European Union's obligation towards refugees by opening Germany's borders to more than a million Syrians in 2015 was an important precedent. Yet, as Chin notes, a "hesitant welcome" issued as a response to a "humanitarian crisis" emphasizes Western altruism without questioning the highly publicized shift towards an assimilationist model of integration.[30] In Canada, it took the photo of the death of a boy, Alan Kurdi, in 2017 to stir passions and prompt action, but the lauded, and largely community-based, Canadian response to the on-going Syrian refugee crisis arguably fits an Institute-style pluralism.[31]

The Institute's demise before Toronto's racialized immigrants had reached significant numbers means my material on the South Asian, Caribbean, and other immigrants of whom Bannerji spoke most directly in 2003 is frustratingly slim. Still, my assessments have benefited from feminist anti-racist, materialist, and discursive modes of analysis. Without exaggerating its bottom-up or community-based character or radical potential, scrutinizing Institute pluralism illuminates the fundamental tensions within liberal ideologies, including those informing pluralist social work and nation-building practices. On the one hand, there are the democratic ideals of informed and participatory citizenship and collective notions of belonging. On the other, the regulatory and intrusive features of social work and nationalism – both of which demand loyalty to or at least compliance with certain ideals – and the asymmetrical hierarchies of power and influence that shape social interactions and public discourse.

Given my warts-and-all analysis, I might have simply concluded this study by saying that, ultimately, the Toronto Institute women, like Joan Scott's French feminists, had "only paradoxes to offer."[32] However, as underscored by Scott's own study on the politics of the veil in France – which documents how the forces of racism, sexuality, individualism, secularism, and nationalism combined to raise the alarm over veiled Muslim girls and women – the resurgence in anti-im/migrant hate behooves us to consider what might be salvaged from faulty experiments in liberal multiculturalism. The exercise is worthwhile precisely because as critical race scholars such as Bannerji, Stuart Hall, and Rinaldo Walcott note, multiculturalism as an idea of (to quote Walcott) "multiple cultures co-existing" in a mobile but unequal world "is now a fixture of our current times." The claims of white scholars and pundits who declare its demise or its incompatibility with liberal democracy and human rights without acknowledging, let alone engaging, more than thirty-five years of research and debate on the subject, Walcott adds, is "disgraceful."[33] While informed by these and other relevant literatures, my much more modest aim here is to reflect on the value of a case study of Institute-style pluralism to ongoing debates and experimentation. I offer a few brief examples.

The first example relates to the Institute's heavily newcomer, female, multilingual, and multicultural staff. The Institute did lose ground to the Inter-Agency Council of Ontario, created in spring 1970 as a coordinating agency of mostly non-governmental and community-based immigrant- and refugee-serving agencies. Ironically, it had helped to found the Council, which became a project of the Social Planning Council of Metropolitan Toronto, and Stewart had sat on its executive. (In 1978, OCASI, Ontario Council of Agencies Serving Immigrants, assumed this role.)[34] Equally noteworthy, was the Institute's pioneering role in applying such progressive pluralist principles as recruiting front-line workers from the immigrant communities being served. In that regard, the emergence of a grassroots immigrant women's activism during the woman's movement of the 1970s to 1990s offered a more fully realized implementation of this inclusive or bottom-up principle.

In contrast to the Institute's heavily European, middle-class, and staunchly anti-Communist counsellors and fieldworkers, immigrant women activists in 1970s and 1980s Toronto – who included racialized and Latin American women – were feminists or social justice activists with a radical, anti-colonial, and even revolutionary worldview. In their capacity as reception and settlement service staff, their emphasis on providing both practical and culturally appropriate social services for their female clients recalls key aspects of the Institute's social service practices. Whether specific to one group (such as Cleaners' Action, which liaised with Portuguese office cleaners) or groups (such as the YWCA West Indian Women's Program), or multi-community-based (such as the Working Women's Community Centre), these later agencies offered a range of services, including English classes, interpretation and translation of documents, skills-training, counselling, and legal aid support. Here, too, the staff helped clients to meet or comply with the restrictive rules of accreditation regimes and employment legislation, the most notorious of which were the government-created temporary worker schemes. But unlike the Institute's personnel, which always included a core group of bourgeois, Anglo-, and ethno-Canadian women and men who generally accepted the reality of the vertical mosaic, these grassroots agencies were founded and run by immigrant women whose activist and advocacy work was shaped by an egalitarian ethos and by the needs and interests of immigrant women like themselves.[35]

Since its demise, the Institute's on-the-job training of what are now called paraprofessionals – immigrant agency staff who provide services in a client's language – has become more institutionalized in the form of certificate courses and programs. What persists, regrettably, are the funding constraints and the lower status within social work of the immigrant or settlement service field, where many staff are practitioners lacking formal credentials, not professionally trained social workers. The professionalization of these workers may go some way to addressing this second-class status. However, my evidence underscores (in a negative way) what umbrella organizations like OCASI (which today represents more than 200 community groups) well understand: the need to act as a collective force when lobbying for resources and when promoting the right of im/migrants and refugees in Canada.[36]

A second set of observations concerns the value of casework studies. Social workers and other social scientists often treat analytical histories of their profession as so much background "story" rather than offering critical insight into their practices. Given the continuing reliance on practitioners (paraprofessionals) and volunteers in the immigrant settlement services field, my careful reading of thousands of confidential case files created by an earlier generation of immigrant practitioners offers contemporary staff and scholars alike rare access into those practices, both rhetorical and material.[37]

The presence at the Institute of male as well as female immigrant and refugee counsellors permitted some meaningful comparisons based on gender. Female counsellors shared much in common with their male counterparts, including an urban, educated, middle-class background, a refugee or immigrant status, a sense of class superiority towards their poor clients, and varying degrees of social work training. They, too, could be judgmental or impatient with a "difficult" client. Overall, however, female counsellors and project fieldworkers understood better than their male counterparts the struggles of their immigrant female clients, both single and married, even if they sometimes underestimated their capabilities or pitied them. Having visited women in their crowded homes or spartan flats, escorted them or their children to clinics, accompanied them to the hospital or welfare office, and witnessed their angry husbands belittle them in Family Court, these female workers understood better than their male colleagues the "domestic side" of marginalization, poverty, and patriarchy.[38] Like the male social workers studied by Mark Peel, the Institute's male counsellors were more likely to emphasize the loss of men's homeland status and male privilege as both a symptom and cause of their economic and emotional ill-adjustment, or abusive behaviour, and consider "the creation of an appropriately resolute manhood as the goal of social work."[39]

That most of the Toronto Institute's professionally trained counsellors were men surely explains why their case records were far more likely than the female-created ones to emphasize, even exaggerate, their insight into a client's problems and the efficacy of their interventions. Among the richest case files were those in which both counsellor and client were women, in part because female practitioners were more likely than their professional male counterparts to detail and describe in vernacular prose what was said and done. These files offered revealing glimpses of the difficult conversations that took place, and the meaningful relationships or alliances that women counsellors occasionally forged with a female client, however unequal or short-term the relationships may have been.

The evidence suggests that a shared ethnocultural or newcomer background with a client could help a counsellor or project fieldworker establish a degree of trust with a client, but also that a capacity to build rapport and to persuade mattered. The specific issue at hand also mattered. Many clients invited intervention, but on terms that made sense to them, though, of course, they did not always get what they wanted. As refugees and immigrants who had also suffered displacement, war, loss, and downward mobility, the counsellors were not entirely surprised by a lot of what they heard, but the female workers were more likely than the men to "really listen" to a female client suffering from enormous anguish. While the era under review predated the finding of "compassion fatigue" among "helping" professionals, my admittedly slim evidence of worried, harried, and harassed female counsellors underscores the value of viewing social work as a form of caring labour that can take an emotional toll on female workers.[40]

A third set of observations concerns the Toronto Institute's noteworthy efforts to combine a popular cultural mandate with a social change, or reform, agenda. Perhaps the most common criticism that scholars and popular pundits have launched against "multiculturalism," official or otherwise, is that it promotes a colourful and boisterous but banal tourist version of for-profit folk festival–spectacle tourism – or "McMulticulturalism."[41] By delivering a feel-good, therapeutic, or Disney World[42] version of diversity, it denies or erases the structural inequities and systemic racism and sexism that perpetuate an ever-more racialized vertical mosaic. Certainly, as feminist anti-racist critics correctly observe, an exclusive focus on display and consumption of the "exotic" can serve to deny or obfuscate the official and popular "forgetting" of everyday racism and the state's role in creating and perpetuating the obfuscation.[43]

Thinking with and beyond the Institute example, however, suggests at least a modest revision of this position. For one thing, there is evidence that points to the fact that celebrations of food, song, and dance can bring people together and even foster meaningful cross-ethnic and cross-racial experience. Furthermore, as the examples supplied by radical groups such as the Wobblies (Industrial Workers of the World), socialist unions like the International Ladies Garment Workers' Union, and founders of the Winnipeg Folk Festival (e.g., Trotskyist Mitch Podolack) and the Caribbean-themed Notting Hill Carnival (e.g, Communist, feminist, and Black nationalist Claudia Jones), multicultural exchanges of folk storytelling, music, dance, and food can help to create a sense of community or solidarity, including in hostile contexts.[44] In this respect, it is the social and political context, and the uses to which folk culture is put, that largely determine the radical or conservative role it performs.

As for liberal aims, mega-festivals like Metro Caravan did help to legitimize public displays of difference, as evidenced by those middle-class Anglo-Torontonians whose participation in that festival first brought home and then reinforced the fact that their city had indeed changed. It did so largely by drawing them to pavilions located in unfamiliar immigrant and ethnic enclaves of the metropolitan area. In an era before the intensified yuppification of ethnic foods, Metro Caravan is where young and middle-aged Anglo-Torontonians ate their first perogy or samosa and took in their first live performance of a European, Caribbean, or Asian folk performance. Yes, the festive context rendered other cultures non-threatening, but it sometimes also facilitated further cultural experimentation.

For another thing, however analytically useful the concept of liberal or nostalgic anti-modernism is, the assumption that the performers and craftspeople decked out in ethnic regalia allow themselves to be turned into simple quaint folk contains a degree of class condescension. Applying the insights of anthropologist Michael Ashkenazi (who studied the "polysemic" quality of Japanese festivals) and French philosopher Pierre Bourdieu (who noted that commentators' snobbish dismissals of folk or popular culture serves to bolster their own prestige), Paul Bramadat has criticized Canada's educated elites for assuming they know better how ethnic minorities should express their collective identities.[45] My research on the Institute suggests, too, that the costumed performers, craftspeople, and even "pretty attendants," and not only the ethnic elites and cultural impresarios, were involved in their own complex process of negotiating Old and New World cultures. That folk performances exhibited conventional gender norms speaks to the cross-cultural character of gender hierarchies, but they did not necessarily dictate completely the performers' off-stage lives. Like Susan Borsi, the Hungarian Week attendant who combined her traditional costume with a modern beehive hairdo, these young women and men were involved in their own dance of accommodation and resistance to both homeland and hostland cultures.[46]

Then, too, while the Toronto Institute's popular festivals and cultural spectacles certainly contained elements of the "Disneyfication" of cultural diversity, it would be inaccurate, even unfair, to treat them in isolation from the Institute's simultaneous efforts to promote social reforms and improve the material lives of their many clients. Even putting aside the counselling geared towards orientation (housing and first jobs), the Institute women and their colleagues devoted more staff time and resources to the community and pilot projects and the counselling aimed at improving the occupational profile, job opportunities, and wages of low-skilled clients than to the cultural spectacles. In the latter case, the participating ethnocultural groups played a critical role.

As Head quickly learned during his 1973 investigation of the Institute, its personnel did not organize public demonstrations or lobbies to remove or reform restrictive employment and other regulations. However, the immigrant counsellors and fieldworkers who carried out the health and vocational training projects, and their allies (most notably COSTI), successfully convinced a number of medical, school, and employment personnel and officials to expand existing resources or to improve immigrant access to them. The fieldworkers also showed considerable patience and tact in recruiting candidates and getting them to remain in a program. While these efforts privileged the male breadwinner, the fact that serious attention also was paid to women reflected Edith Ferguson's correct prediction that many of the rural Southern European women would become life-long workers.

To be sure, these projects had limited objectives – a modest improvement in workers' skills and wages – and produced mixed and even poor results, though the benefits accrued by the successful candidates could be significant. The point, however, is that Institute-fashioned multiculturalism from the start included a reform and labour agenda, and, like the more radical multicultural campaigns that occurred in the United States, it points to the possibility of envisioning and implementing a more radical multiculturalism-from-below.[47] Other multiracial multicultural alliances might yet envision what Canadian geographers Kanishka Goonewardena and Stefan Kipfer have described as more radical urban agendas.[48] In addition, immigration scholars, myself included, have shown considerable respect for immigrant parents and their transplanted survival strategies, but the Institute counsellors deserve credit for their albeit mostly unsuccessful efforts to keep in school the teenagers of parents willing to forgo their children's high school education in order to realize dreams of home ownership.

Historical Contingencies

Of course, radical imaginaries cannot be implemented in a historical vacuum, and here, too, but in a negative sense, the Toronto Institute case is illustrative. It was not only the contradictions within liberalism that imposed class, gender, racial, and other limits on Institute-style pluralism. Certainly, a key paradox was the assumption that host societies can integrate immigrants into the mainstream – a process that inevitably involves a degree of homogenization to dominant norms – while preserving and promoting "authentic" immigrant cultures understood and utilized primarily as folk cultures. Nevertheless, a convergence of several factors influenced the shape that pluralism took in Toronto. Returning to the cultural mandate, I highlight two related factors. The Cold War and the prominence of the Eastern European groups in the Institute's cultural programs ensured that there would be no leap into a radical multicultural reimagining.

The immigrant-gifts ideology that informed Institute cultural pluralism, and the collaborations and extravaganzas that left their imprint on Toronto and environs, harnessed mainly European folk cultures to an urban, modernist nation-building project that simultaneously sidelined Indigenous and racialized people, even when they were included as performers. The folk festivals were also sites of conflict and contestation, however, and the final pageantry the result of negotiations between the Institute folks and the male elites and cultural impresarios and performers who used the gifts platform to assert their presence, both symbolically and politically, in the city, province, and nation. The ability particularly of the Eastern European groups to impose their narratives on the Institute and the city's wider agenda played a role in the Institute's shift from a more narrowly British to a more pluralistic but still Eurocentric vision of Canada.

The affiliated ethnic groups on which the Institute relied increasingly articulated the terms of their participation in Institute events and wider collaborations in the language of the ethnic lobby that challenged the two founding nations narrative of Canada that had shaped the Royal Commission on Bilingualism and Biculturalism. Those who portray the lobby as a popular ethno-political movement emphasize the role played by Ukrainian Canadian leaders such as Paul Yuzyk – the University of Manitoba historian, nationalist Ukrainian Canadian, and Conservative senator whose maiden speech in the senate in 1964 offered the first treatise on multiculturalism in Parliament – who first resisted and then renegotiated the B&B commission's dual narrative so that it acknowledged the "other" (mostly European) ethnic groups as the "third element" of Canadian society.[49]

When Yuzyk introduced "multiculturalism" into Canadian political debate, he credited the term to an American sociologist who had been active in southern California's pluralist networks before moving to Alberta.[50] Analyses now abound of how Yuzyk and his confrères manipulated the historical myths and symbols of both (a Soviet-oppressed) homeland and hostland for greater political ends: to ensure ethnic-boundary maintenance (as in securing the persistence and revival of distinct ethnic-group identities)[51] and to promote group-based linguistic and cultural rights.[52] Yuzyk et al. advanced a white, conservative, and colonial ideology of nation-building – one that celebrated the Ukrainian "pioneers" who purportedly brought white-settler civilization to the prairies and their successful and assimilated descendants – that could appeal to mainstream English Canadian elites.[53] Racism against the early racialized immigrants who arrived under the points system helped further the white-ethnic cause because, viewed alongside Black and Asian newcomers, the Euro-Canadian groups looked decidedly white and acceptable.[54] The era's white-ethnic consciousness, with its focus on group rights, also helps to account for the Institute's weak record on human rights (despite its commitment to liberal internationalism) and on race relations and anti-racist work.

The benefits that European immigrants accrued from multiculturalism in the years since the Institute's demise, including increasing respectability and even a full-fledged whiteness bolstered by class mobility, were linked as well to the growing racialization of immigration to Canada. The continued privileging of a Eurocentric pluralism despite significant changes in the populations at the city, province, and national level, along with systemic racism and growing racial inequities, help to account for the situation that contemporary feminist and critical race scholars have decried. Notwithstanding the efforts of racialized immigrants and Canadians to reshape a cultural policy into a tool for redressing racial and other inequities, multiculturalism policies, note scholars such as Sunera Thobani, Enakshi Dua, and others, serve to contain racialized immigrants by transforming them into culturally bound others with primitive ethnic traditions while depicting white settlers as modern, superior, progressive, and tolerant of these others.[55] Insofar as it failed to develop a more egalitarian, or consultative, relationship with the racialized Canadian and immigrant groups whose participation it also sought, the Institute ultimately bears responsibility for perpetuating a Eurocentric pluralism.

In comparison to its counterparts in the United States, where a number of individual International Institutes are still in operation today in certain cities,[56] Toronto's International Institute had a short-lived history. But while its demise brought an end to the city's explicit involvement in a twentieth-century US-led movement of pluralist social agencies, its roots extend further back to late-nineteenth and turn-of-the-twentieth-century debates and experiments on both sides of the border.

As the primary agents of an important but flawed Canadian experiment in promoting a liberal multiculturalism as a means by which to reimagine the nation, build community, and ensure the integration of immigrants, the Institute women and their colleagues left behind a mixed and uneven legacy. By recovering the largely neglected history of women's pluralist activism in Canada before the advent of a now half-century-old official multiculturalism, and by assessing their accomplishments and limitations, it is my hope that this study contributes to and invigorates the ongoing research and debate concerning a leading if contested and beleaguered component of Canadian national identity.

Appendix

Database of 7,000 Case Files

The case files from which the database was created are found in the International Institute of Metropolitan Toronto collection at the Archives of Ontario, Toronto. The finding aid gives the agency's dates as 1952–1975, but it ceased to exist on 31 December 1974 and I found no documents that are dated 1975. A more accurate periodization is 1952–74.

The International Institute collection is vast, the materials spanning 18.23 metres. The total number of case files cover the period 1952–72 and make up a significant portion (7.2 metres) of the collection. The case files were generated as follows. When an individual (and on occasion, a couple) came to the Institute seeking assistance with a personal matter (such as finding work, sponsoring the immigration of a child still overseas, or dealing with an elderly mother), a cover form that asked for biographical information and type of "problem" was filled out. (Once established in 1960, the Reception Centre staff carried out this task, though a counsellor or caseworker might also do so.) The subsequent entries on the form and on any additional pages were made by the counsellor during the initial and subsequent appointments with a given client, though a client might meet with more than one counsellor. The secretaries typed up the counsellors' notes, adding pages as they needed, but some counsellors may have sometimes done their own typing. (Some secretaries were also home visitors and probably typed up their own notes.) The database contains 7,000 of these case files for the period 1952–72.

The process of selection combined a sampling technique and a specific strategy. Every tenth case file was included for the period 1952–72. In addition, every lengthy file was added in the expectation that they would be more informative. By lengthy, I mean more than three pages of qualitative text, which might consist of a counsellor or caseworker's entries and/or a report(s) or summary report(s) conducted by the social agency or medical or court authorities that referred the client to the Institute. The numbering of the case files in the endnotes of the relevant chapters in no way reflects where a specific case was located in the records or entered into the database. This final database is the product of a career-long engagement with the Toronto Institute collection, and the work of a dozen research assistants, several of them now established scholars. Ethically, handling such sensitive material requires sensitivity on the historian's part, and I have tried to do just that.

The quality of the case files varies enormously, becoming increasingly scanty by the late 1960s. The record-keeping increasingly eschewed qualitative remarks and many of the later files provide only the most basic information in a standard chart format. The files for the 1970s are particularly terse. I did not sample the files for 1973 and 1974 because they were so slim and appeared unhelpful. Regrettably, the case files for later-arriving clients, including newcomers from Asia, Africa, and the Caribbean, as well as from Central and South America, are the least well-documented cases.

Tables 1 (world regions by nationality/ethnic groups) and 2 (top 15 nationality/ethnic groups) provide information on the clientele in the database, which represents 120 different groups. (All 120 groups could not be displayed in one format.) Most groups were defined by nationality (country of origin) but a handful of them were defined by ethnicity (as in a majority or minority ethnic group from within a given nation). An example of the latter is the Czech group in table 2, which refers to the ethnic Czech group from Czechoslovakia and not both Czechs and Slovaks. As tables 1 and 2 demonstrate, the database is heavily skewed to Europeans who formed the great bulk of the Institute's caseload particularly during the 1950s and 1960s.

As tables 3 (male age groups) and 4 (female age groups) show, men outnumber women in the database. As regards age, a large proportion of both the male and female clients fell into the age 22–34 category. The general youthfulness of the clientele reflects the overall youthfulness of immigrants to Canada (e.g., average age 24.9 in the period 1946–67).

Table 5 shows the types of case files. Referrals to English classes are the single largest group of files, but I did not make explicit use of them because they were so routine. Individuals were assigned to a class and non-counselling staff or volunteers dealt with the enrolments.

Combined, male and female employment made up the largest type of case file: 3,248 or 46.4 per cent of the total number of files. Men significantly outnumber women. In contrast to the records of most social welfare institutions, which rarely "catch" middle-class clients, one third of the files (2,310 cases) involve clients from professional backgrounds. The other two-thirds involve skilled tradespeople and clients variously defined as semi- or low-skilled or of rural origins. Rather than simply rely on a counsellor's initial designation, I decided on the primary designation to assign each file. Many files fit more than one type of case and some files quickly or eventually shift in focus from one theme (such as employment) to another one (such as generational conflict). During the collection phase, my researchers and I attached more than one thematic category to about one-third of the files. Once the database was completed, I determined the primary type of case after carefully reading the entire contents of a file.

Throughout the book, I make use of both brief and lengthy case files, but I rely more heavily on the lengthy files that deal with more complicated cases. My analysis of the examined files is informed by my familiarity with all the cases in the database. Putting aside the referrals for English class, the case files that were examined for this book represent two-thirds of the total files in the database.

The case files, which contain sensitive material, are the only restricted records in the collection. In order to gain access to them, I signed a research agreement in which I agreed to respect the privacy of the clients. I have anonymized each client's identity by using a fictitious name or initials or avoiding both. I have modified or omitted details (such as the exact age, home address, employer, and so on) without altering the ethnicity of individuals or key features of a case. My research agreement did not specifically require me to anonymize the counsellors. They are briefly profiled in chapter 3 on the basis of information contained elsewhere in the collection and in other sources. My detailed analysis of certain case files draws on relevant aspects of a counsellor's profile. However, in order to fully respect their privacy as well, when discussing the contents of a case file, I have not divulged the identity of the counsellors or caseworkers.

Appendix

Table 1. World regions by nationality groups

Africa	103
Asia	1,292
Americas	1,091
Eastern Europe	1,640
Western Europe	2,393
Middle East	414
Other (Australasia)	4
Unknown	63
TOTAL	7,000

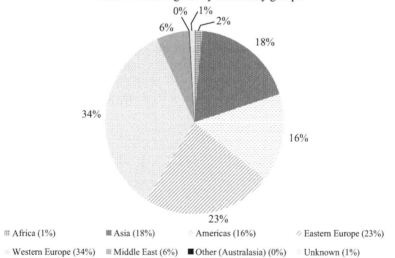

Table 2. Top 15 nationality and ethnic groups

	Count
Hungarian	707
Greek	704
Portuguese	648
Italian	448
Korean	310
Indian	298
Yugoslavian	298
German	254
Chinese	252
Ecuadorian	229
Japanese	213
Czech	194
Polish	182
Uruguayan	158
Colombian	109
TOTAL	5,004

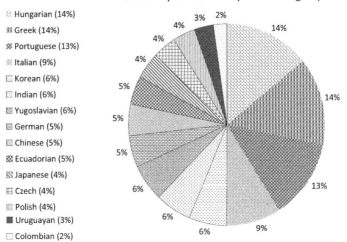

Appendix

Table 3. Male age groups

	Male (Total Database)
13–21	686
22–34	2,650
35–50	883
51–64	211
65–80	34
Unknown	29
TOTAL	4,493

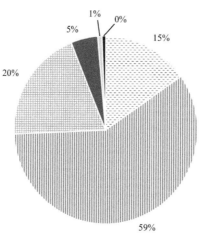

Table 3 Male age groups

Table 3 Male age groups

13–21 (15%)   22–34 (59%)   35–50 (20%)   51–64 (5%)   65–80 (1%)   Unknown (0%)

Table 4. Female age groups

	Female (Total Database)
13–21	531
22–34	1,276
35–50	531
51–64	138
65–80	16
Unknown	15
TOTAL	2,507

Table 4 Female age groups

Age	Count
Unknown	15
65–80	16
51–64	138
35–50	531
22–34	1,276
13–21	531

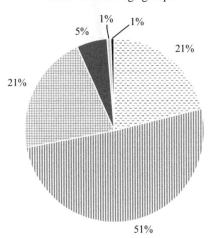

Table 4 Female age groups

13–21 (21%)   22–34 (51%)   35–50 (21%)   51–64 (5%)   65–80 (1%)   Unknown (1%)

314 Appendix

Table 5. Types of case files

	Total
Generational conflict	150
Marital conflict	100
Referred to Institute for English classes	2,728
Referrals to other social agencies	359
Female employment	1,085
Male employment	2,163
Legal aid counselling	177
Health/mental health counselling	98
Other	140
TOTAL	7,000

Table 5 Types of case files

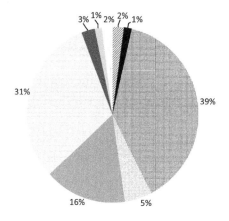

⁒ Generational conflict (2%) ■ Marital conflict (1%)
▦ Referred to Institute for English classes (39%) Referrals to other social agencies (5%)
▩ Female employment (16%) Male employment (31%)
■ Legal aid counselling (3%) Health/mental health counselling (1%)
☐ Other (2%)

Notes

1 The Case Study

1 The quotations used for this vignette come from Archives of Ontario (AO), International Institute of Metropolitan Toronto, Fonds 884, MU6406 (B280543), File: Clippings – International Institute, 1959–70, Ralph Hyman, "They Oil the Hinges of Integration's Door," Toronto *Globe Magazine*, 20 Feb. 1960; MU6422 (B280579), File: Intercom Copies 1957, Nell West, "What Is the Institute?," *Intercom*, April 1957; MU6413, File: Ethnic Occasions 1957, Mrs W.E. West (hereafter West) to Controller Jean Newman, Toronto City Hall, 28 March 1957. Note that issues of the Institute newsletter *Intercom* cited in this chapter are from designated files in MU6422 (B280579) and MU6442.

2 I conducted selective research on a dozen US Institutes and the central body (or headquarters) in New York City. Immigration History Research Center Archives, Elmer L. Andersen Library, University of Minnesota (hereafter IHRCA), American Council for Nationalities Service records, which contain the American Federation of International Institutes (AFII) collection.

3 Benedict Anderson, *Imagined Communities: Reflections on the Origins and Spread of Nationalism* (London: Verso, 1983, 2006). For the critique that Anderson's theorization of an imagined community as a "horizontal comradeship" (7) among members who do not necessarily know each other glossed over the (irreconcilable) divisions of class, race, gender, and ideology in nationalist movements, see, for example, Himani Bannerji, *The Dark Side of the Nation: Essays on Multiculturalism, Nationalism, and Gender* (Toronto: Canadian Scholars Press, 2000), 65–75.

4 Part 4 examines these themes, but a tiny sample of this work includes Bannerji, *Dark Side of the Nation*; Eric Hobsbawm, "Introduction" and "Mass-Producing Traditions: Europe, 1870–1914," in Eric Hobsbawm and Terence Ranger, eds., *The Invention of Tradition* (Cambridge: Cambridge University Press, 1983); 263–308; Geneviève Fabre, Jürgen Heideking, and Kai Dreisch, eds., *Celebrating Ethnicity and Nation: American Festive Culture from the Revolution to the Early Twentieth Century* (New York: Berghahn Books, 2001).

5 A tiny sample of the extensive literature on social work as progressive and regulatory practice includes Judith Ann Trolander, *Professionalism and Social Change from the Settlement House Movement to Neighborhood Centers, 1886 to the Present* (New York: Columbia University Press, 1987); Mark Peel, *Miss Cutler and the Case of the Resurrected Horse: Social Work and the Story of Poverty in America, Australia, and Britain* (Chicago: University of Chicago Press, 2012); Linda Gordon, *Heroes of Their Own Lives: The Politics and History of Family Violence, Boston, 1880–1960* (New York: Penguin Books 1989); and the publications on the US International Institutes discussed below.

6 For a valuable contribution to the genre of institutional studies that focuses on immigrant organizations, see the Theme Issue on Immigrant Organizations, *Journal of Ethnic and Migration Studies* 31, no. 5 (2005), with guest editors Marlou Shrover and Floris Vermeulen. Most essays focus on organizations initiated by immigrants (or their children), but those by Héctor R. Cordero-Guzmán (on New York), Irene Bloemraad (Toronto), and José Moya (a sweeping global overview) examine or refer to community-based organizations that share characteristics with the International Institutes.

7 University of Pittsburgh, Nationality Rooms, https://www.nationalityrooms.pitt.edu/rooms (last accessed 15 April 2022); Royden Loewen and Gerald Friesen, *Immigrants in Prairie Cities: Ethnic Diversity in Twentieth-Century Canada* (Toronto: University of Toronto Press, 2009), 92–4.

8 See, for example, Kanishka Goonewardena and Stefan Kipfer, "Spaces of Difference: Reflections from Toronto on Multiculturalism, Bourgeois Urbanism and the Possibility of Radical Urban Politics," *International Journal of Urban and Regional Research* 29, no. 3 (2005): 670–8; Mariana Valverde, "The Ethic of Diversity: Local Law and the Negotiation of Urban Norms," *Law & Social Inquiry* 33, no. 4 (Fall 2008): 895–923.

9 For just two examples of media references to the Raptors tapping into Toronto's diversity, see Tim Reynolds, "The Raptors Diversity Serves Them Well as Global Champions," *National Post*, 15 June 2019; https://www.si.com/nba/raptors/news/diversity-social-change; Gamal Abdel-Shehid, "Toronto's Multicultural Raptors: Teamwork and Individualism," *The Conversation*, 3 June 2019, https://theconversation.com/torontos-multicultural-raptors-teamwork-and-individualism-118141 (both last accessed 30 April 2021).

10 City of Toronto Archives (CTA), Social Planning Council of Metropolitan Toronto (SPC) SC40, Box 6, File: 25-I, M, EG, Problems of the New Immigrant Co-ordinating Committee, 1951–4, Minutes, 26 Feb. 1953; AO, MU6472, Letters of Appreciation 1959–62, N.S. Bojovic, "The International Institute of Metropolitan Toronto and Its Services," Address to Forest Hill Collegiate, 11 Feb. 1960.

11 J.B. Thomas, "Open Door to Canada," *Food for Thought*, Nov. 1954, 20; AO, MU6381, File: St Andrew's House Study, Toronto Welfare Council Report (TWC), 1954.

12 MU6381, File: St Andrew's House Study, 1954–5, TWC Report 1954 and Report 7 Dec. 1955. Alex Freund, "Troubling Memories in Nation-building: World War II Memories and Germans' Inter-ethnic Encounters in Canada after 1945," *Histoire sociale/Social History* 39, no. 77 (2006): 129–55.
13 CTA, SC40, Box 53, File: 2-A-IIMT [1956–63], Florence Philpott (director) to Clarence Weaver, Community Chest of Niagara Falls, NY, 1 March 1956 (copy to Boston Institute); AO, MU6381, File: Governing Committee Minutes, 1952–6, Minutes, 6 Oct. 1956; Minutes, 14 Dec. 1955, Appendix, Jack Thomas (St Andrew's warden), Report on Detroit Institute; Warden's Report on American Federation of International Institutes, 27 Jan. 1956.
14 "Junior League Sponsors New Canadian Service," *Toronto Star*, 23 Oct. 1954; AO, MU6380, File: Board of Directors, New Canadians Service Association of Ontario (hereafter NCSA), 1952; MU6474, File: Immigrant Assistance, 1957–61, Memorandum Draft – History of Institute (contains errors); MU6380, File: Reports, Report on NCSA, 21 July 1955.
15 Katie Pickles, *Female Imperialism and National Identity: Imperial Order Daughters of the Empire* (Manchester: Manchester University Press, 2002), ch. 7; Franca Iacovetta, *Gatekeepers: Reshaping Immigrant Lives in Cold War Canada*, (Toronto: Between the Lines, 2006), ch. 5. For the debate over the rapid demise or continuing influence of British values in sixties-era English Canada, see, respectively, José Igartua, *The Other Quiet Revolution: National Identities in English Canada, 1945–71* (Vancouver: UBC Press, 2006), and C.P. Champion, *The Strange Demise of British Canada: Liberals and Canadian Nationalism, 1964–1968* (Montreal/Kingston: McGill-Queen's University Press, 2010). My evidence suggests the co-existence of a growing civic nationalism and a continuing commitment to British values.
16 Volunteer quoted in Florence Schill, "Full-Time Organizer Aids Work of New Canadian Services," Toronto *Globe and Mail*, 8 Dec. 1954. On post-1945 and 1960s contexts, see, for example, Aya Fujiwara, *Ethnic Elites and Canadian Identity: Japanese, Ukrainians, and Scots, 1919–1971* (Winnipeg: University of Manitoba Press, 2012), chs. 5–6; Igartua, *Other Quiet Revolution*; Eve Haque, *Multiculturalism within a Bilingual Framework: Language, Race, and Belonging in Canada* (Toronto: University of Toronto Press, 2012), ch. 2; Lara A. Campbell, Dominique Clement, and Gregory S. Kealey, eds., *Debating Dissent: Canada and the Sixties* (Toronto: University of Toronto Press, 2012).
17 On this theme see Margaret Wills, *A Marriage of Convenience: Business and Social Work in Toronto, 1918–1957* (Toronto: University of Toronto Press, 1975), and Shirley Tillotson, *Contributing Citizens: Modern Charitable Funds and the Making of the Welfare State, 1920–1966* (Vancouver: UBC Press, 2008).
18 Personnel files and *Intercom* profiles in Toronto Institute collection at AO; Toronto *Star* 13 Dec. 1960, *The Canadian Encyclopedia*, https://www.thecanadianencyclopedia.ca/en/article/david-croll (R. Bothwell); https://www

318 Notes to pages 10–15

.thecanadianencyclopedia.ca/en/article/james-robbins-kidd (S. Mowat) (both last accessed 29 April 2021).
19 Schill, "Full-Time Organizer." In the sources, married women were referred to by others and referred to themselves by their husband's name. When able to locate a first name, I included it.
20 *Globe and Mail*, 24 Aug. 1957 and 29 Nov. 1984; *The Canadian Encyclopedia*, https://www.thecanadianencyclopedia.ca/en/article/jean-lumb (A. Chan); Polish Language and Literature, University of Toronto, Ungar, https://sites.utoronto.ca/slavic/polish/donors.html (both last accessed 29 April 2021).
21 Personnel files and *Intercom* profiles in Toronto Institute collection at AO; *Globe and Mail*, 8 Dec. 1954, 1 June 1955, 10 Sept. 1956, 25 Feb. and 14 April 1958, 9 July 1963, 27 May 1971, 18 Oct. 1990; on Senathirajah, obituary, https://www.legacy.com/ca/obituaries/thestar/name/nallamma-senathirajah-obituary?pid=190763876 (last accessed 12 Oct. 2021); on McBain/Isserstedt, 1956 Voters List, ancestry.ca. Jennings served as board president during the agency's final year in 1974.
22 British immigrant John de Montfort was fired and the position was eliminated for several years. MU6425, File: Staff Restructuring, West to Marie Rosenberg, 26 March 1963; File: Montfort, resume, notes.
23 Personnel files and *Intercom* profile (April 1957) in Toronto Institute collection at AO; Croll cited in *Intercom* Dec. 1965; Archer cited in *Intercom* 1 Oct. 1968; *Globe and Mail* 1 March 1942, 8 Dec. 1954, 20 Feb. 1960, 1 March and 27 May 1961, 10 Aug. and 13 Oct. 1965.
24 The points system favoured education, job skills, and the ability to speak English or French.
25 MU6410 (B280597), File: Executive Director Correspondence, Mr Philip, 19 Dec. 1967.
26 MU6424, File: Executive Director Personnel, 1956–62, Personnel 1960–1 and Forbell to Gellner, 28 March 1961; *The Canadian Encyclopedia*, https://www.thecanadianencyclopedia.ca/en/article/john-gellner (last accessed 29 April 2021).
27 MU6425 (B280562), File: John Seaman, biographical sketch 1965; *Intercom* Oct. 1965, 12. Edward Roy and Charles Borque served very briefly in 1967 and 1973, respectively.
28 Quoting Jack Jedwab, "Multiculturalism," *The Canadian Encyclopedia*, https://www.thecanadianencyclopedia.ca/en/article/multiculturalism (last accessed 29 April 2021).
29 The Institute's use of the term "nationality group" to refer to the members of a given nation or to an ethnic group creates some ambiguity, but this number likely combined both meanings.
30 Unless otherwise specified, the following summary of the US Institutes draws on Raymond A. Mohl, "The International Institute Movement and Ethnic Pluralism," *Social Science* 56, no.1 (Winter 1998): 14–21; Mohl, "Cultural Pluralism in Immigrant Education: The International Institutes of Boston, Philadelphia, and San

Francisco, 1920–1940," *Journal of American Ethnic History* 1, no. 2 (Spring 1982): 35–58; Raymond A. Mohl and Neil Betten, "Paternalism and Pluralism: Immigrants and Social Welfare in Gary, Indiana, 1906–1940," *American Studies* 15, no. 1 (Spring 1974): 15–26; Kristin L. Hoganson, *Consumers' Imperium: The Global Production of American Domesticity, 1865–1920* (Chapel Hill: University of North Carolina Press, 2007), ch. 5; entry on Bremer in Barbara Sicherman and Carol Hurd Green, *Notable American Women: The Modern Period* (Cambridge MA/London: Radcliffe College, 1980), 105–7.

31 Marilyn Fischer, "Jane Addams on Cultural Pluralism, European Immigrants and African Americans," *The Pluralist* 9, no. 3 (Fall 2014): 38–58, and the more critical Hoganson, *Consumers' Imperium*, ch. 5; Rudolph J. Vecoli, "Louis Adamic and the Contemporary Search for Roots," *Ethnic Studies* 2 (1978): 29–35; Gerald Meyer, "The Cultural Pluralist Response to Americanization: Horace Kallen, Randolph Bourne, Louis Adamic, and Leonard Covello," *Socialism and Democracy* 22, no. 3 (Nov. 2008): 19–51; John P. Enyeart, "Revolutionizing Cultural Pluralism: The Political Odyssey of Louis Adamic, 1932–1951," *Journal of American Ethnic History* 34, no. 3 (Spring 2015): 58–90; and references below.

32 On this theme, see Dorothea Browder, "A 'Christian Solution of the Labor Situation': How Workingwomen Reshaped the YWCA's Religious Mission and Politics," *Journal of Women's History* 19, no. 2 (2007): 85–110.

33 Andrew Urban, "Social Work and Substantive Justice: The International Institutes' Response to Discriminatory Immigration and Naturalization Laws, 1924–1945," *Journal of American Ethnic History* 37, no.1 (Fall 2017): 5–29; Mohl, "Cultural Pluralism," 45–7.

34 Hoganson, *Consumers' Imperium*, ch. 5, esp. 222–9, 240–9.

35 Donna Gabaccia, *Immigration and American Diversity: A Social and Cultural History* (Malden: Blackwell, 2002), 209–16.

36 Elaine Tyler May, *Homeward Bound: American Families in the Cold War Era* (New York: Basic Books, 1988), 16–20, 207; Margot Canaday, *The Straight State: Sexuality and Citizenship in Twentieth-Century America* (Princeton, NJ: Princeton University Press, 2009).

37 Gabaccia, *Immigration*, 202–3; Aristide Zolberg, *A Nation by Design: Immigration Policy in the Fashioning of America* (New York: Russell Sage Foundation, 2006), 303, 321, 580.

38 IHRCA, International Institutes, Box 271, File Folder: 10, Edith Terry Bremer, "Development of Private Social Work with the Foreign Born," *Annals of the American Academy of Political and Social Science* CCLII (March 1949); Box 278, File Folder: 1, William Bernard, "The International Institute Movement and Its Contribution to American Cultural Vitality," 27 Jan. 1956.

39 The International Services in London ran an International House that Toronto Institute folks visited in May 1966. *Intercom*, May–June 1966; Loewen and Friesen, *Immigrants in Prairie Cities*, chs. 3–4.

40 Ninette Kelley and Michael Trebilcock, *Making the Mosaic: A History of Canadian Immigration Policy*, 2nd ed. (Toronto: University of Toronto Press, 2010), 364; Reg Whitaker, *Double Standard: The Secret History of Canadian Immigration* (Toronto: Lester & Orpen Dennys, 1987), 12–13; Jordan Stanger-Ross, *Staying Italian: Urban Change and Ethnic Life in Post-War Toronto and Philadelphia* (University of Chicago Press, 2009), 5–18, 30–2.

41 James Lemon, *Toronto since 1918: An Illustrated History* (Toronto: James Lorimer, 1985), chs. 3–4; Toronto History Museums, "The History of Toronto: An 11,000 Year Journey, The Modern Metropolis from 1951," https://www.toronto.ca/explore-enjoy/history-art-culture/museums/virtual-exhibits/history-of-toronto/the-modern-metropolis-from-1951/ (last accessed 9 April 2021). Between 1951 and 1971, the percentage of Roman Catholics in the city grew from 20 to 39 per cent. For Metropolitan Toronto, the figures were 17 and 34 per cent. Lemon, *Toronto*, 197.

42 The figure for the city was 44 per cent. Lemon, *Toronto*, 196.

43 Kelley and Trebilcock, *Making the Mosaic*, 354, 579n3.

44 Statistics Canada, "100 Years of Immigration," https://www150.statcan.gc.ca/n1/pub/11-630-x/11-630-x2016006-eng.htm (last accessed 9 April 2021).

45 From Michael Ornstein, *Ethno-Racial Groups in Toronto, 1971–2001: A Demographic and Socio-Economic Profile* (Toronto: Institute for Social Research, York University, Jan. 2006), Table 1.1, p. 100.

46 From Ornstein, *Ethno-Racial Groups in Toronto*, Table 1.1, p. 100. The 1981 figures are as follows: South Asia (71,490); Caribbean (54,960); South and Central America (18,790). On Blacks, the total number of 121,875, or just over 4 per cent, is documented in "Overview Report, Demographical Portrait of the Black Community in the GTA, Black Experience Project, Environics Institute," https://www.environicsinstitute.org/docs/default-source/project-documents/black-experience-project-gta/black-experience-project-gta---4-demographic-portrait-of-the-black-community-in-the-gta.pdf?sfvrsn=32b221cd_2 (last accessed 9 April 2021).

47 For a general description of the groups, see Kelley and Trebilcock, *Making the Mosaic*, chs. 8–9.

48 This outburst of racism led to the municipal-sponsored Task Force on Human Relations report, *Now Is Not Too Late* (Toronto: Council of Metropolitan Toronto, 1977). See also Sheyfali Saujani, "Empathy and Authority in Oral Testimony: Feminist Debates, Multicultural Mandates, and Reassessing the Interviewer and Her "Disagreeable" Subjects," *Histoire sociale/Social History* 45, no. 90 (2012): 361–91.

49 Mohl, "Cultural Pluralism," 41–2, 53–4 (which comments on some paradoxical elements of Institute pluralism but does not make paradox a central framing); Mohl, "International Institute Movement and Ethnic Pluralism"; Mohl and Betten, "Paternalism and Pluralism."

50 Victor Greene, "Dealing with Diversity: Milwaukee's Multiethnic Festivals and Urban Identity, 1840–1940," *Journal of Urban History* 31, no. 6 (2005): 839, 842.

51 Hoganson, *Consumers' Imperium*, ch. 5, esp. 222–49.
52 Rita Chin, *The Crisis of Multiculturalism in Europe: A History* (Princeton, NJ: Princeton University Press, 2017), 9–10. For a more detailed discussion, see my conclusion.
53 For the argument that this characterization also applies to the US Institutes, see Franca Iacovetta and Erica Toffoli, "A Double-Edged Pluralism: Paradoxes of Diversity in the International Institute Movement, 1945–1965," *Journal of Social History* (2020) 54, no. 3 (Spring 2021): 897–919.
54 Werner Sollors, "Introduction," in *The Invention of Ethnicity* (New York: Oxford University Press, 1989), ix–xvii; Kathleen Neils Conzen et al., "The Invention of Ethnicity: A Perspective from the USA," *Journal of American Ethnic History* 12, no. 1 (Fall 1992): 3–41; Ellen M. Litwicki, "'Our Hearts Burn with Ardent Love for Two Countries': Ethnicity and Assimilation," *Journal of American Ethnic History* 19, no. 3 (Spring 2000): 3–34.
55 Marjorie Johnstone and Eunjung Lee, "Shaping Canadian Citizens: A Historical Study of Canadian Multiculturalism and Social Work during the Period from 1900 to 1999," *International Journal of Social Welfare* 29, no. 1 (2020): 71–82.
56 Eileen Yeo, cited in Peel, *Miss Cutler*, "Introduction," 5n7, but see also Eileen Yeo, *The Contest for Social Science: Relations and Representations of Gender and Class* (London: Rivers Oram Press, 1996). An insightful discussion of these themes is in Peel *Miss Cutler*, "Introduction" and passim; Karen Tice, *Tales of Wayward Girls and Immoral Women: Case Records and the Professionalization of Social Work* (Urbana: University of Illinois Press, 1998), Introduction, ch. 2, and passim.
57 Leonore Davidoff, "Regarding Some 'Old Husband's Tales': Public and Private in Feminist History," in *Worlds Between: Historical Perspectives on Gender and Class* (Oxford: Blackwell Publishers, 1995), 227–76; Bettina Bradbury and Tamara Myers, "Introduction," in *Negotiating Identities in 19th and 20th Century Montreal* (Vancouver: UBC Press, 2005), 1–21.
58 Mary Louise Pratt, *Imperial Eyes: Travel Writing and Transculturation* (London: Routledge, 1992); Thobani, *Exalted Subjects*; Sara Ahmed, *Strange Encounters: Embodied Others in Post-Coloniality* (London: Routledge, 2000).
59 Edwin N. Wilmsen, "Introduction: Premises of Power in Ethnic Politics," 2–5, and Jan Nedervereen, "Varieties of Ethnic Politics and Ethnicity Discourse," 25–44, in Edwin N. Wilmsen and Patrick McAllister, eds., *The Politics of Difference: Ethnic Premises in a World of Power* (Chicago: University of Chicago Press, 1996); Litwicki, "Our Hearts Burn"; Robert Cupido, "Public Commemoration and Ethno-Cultural Assertion: Winnipeg Celebrates the Diamond Jubilee of Confederation," *Urban History Review* 38, no. 2 (Spring 2010): 64–74 (with thanks for initially introducing me to this work).

2 The Scholarship

1 John Biles, "The Government of Canada's Multiculturalism Program: Key to Canada's Inclusion Reflex?" in Jack Jedwab, ed., The Multiculturalism Question:

Debating Identity in 21st-Century Canada (Montreal/Kingston: McGill-Queen's University Press, 2014), 31–50. The results of Focus Canada surveys conducted by the Environics Institute for Survey Research and other findings contained in Laurence Brosseau and Michael Dewing, Canadian Multiculturalism (15 Sept. 2009; revised 3 Jan. 2018), https://lop.parl.ca/sites/PublicWebsite/default/en_CA/ResearchPublications/200920E (last accessed 22 July 2021). They also report on negative responses, including by pundits, to multiculturalism.

2 David A. Hollinger, *Postethnic America: Beyond Multiculturalism* (New York: Basic Books, 1995), 101 (quotation), 79, 98–101; Werner Sollors, "The Multiculturalism Debate as Cultural Text," in Wendy F. Katkin, Ned Landsman, and Andrea Tyree, eds., *Beyond Pluralism: The Conception of Groups and Group Identities in America* (Urbana: University of Illinois Press, 1998), 63–4; Nathan Glazer, *We Are All Multiculturalists Now* (Cambridge, MA: Harvard University Press, 1997), 5–8, 10; Sarah Miller-Davenport, *Gateway State: Hawai'i and the Cultural Transformation of American Empire* (Princeton, NJ: Princeton University Press, 2019), 14n37. My discussion of American multiculturalism draws heavily on Russell A. Kazal, "Rethinking the Origins of Multiculturalism: New Perspectives on American Pluralist Ideologies" (an article manuscript in preparation for submission to a journal), with thanks to him for generously sharing his unpublished research with me.

3 *Regents of the University of California v. Bakke* 438 U.S. 265 (1978), 316 (quotation), and *Grutter v. Bollinger* 539 U.S. 306 (2003), both cited in Kazal, "Rethinking the Origins of Multiculturalism."

4 Kazal, "Rethinking the Origins of Multiculturalism." For examples of such pairings, see Gary Gerstle, *American Crucible: Race and Nation in the Twentieth Century* (Princeton, NJ: Princeton University Press, 2001), 349–52; Miller-Davenport, *Gateway State*, ch. 6; Hollinger, *Postethnic America*, ch. 4. Gerstle argued that "hard" multiculturalism included both Afrocentrists and advocates of a "cultural hybridity" inclusive of "cosmopolitan" identities (*American Crucible*, 350–1). On what Matthew Frye Jacobson terms the "Third Worldist strain" within a left "brand of multiculturalism," see his *Roots Too: White Ethnic Revival in Post-Civil Rights America* (Cambridge, MA: Harvard University Press, 2006), 229, 208.

5 On conflicts over multiculturalism, see Andrew Hartman, *A War for the Soul of America: A History of the Culture Wars* (Chicago: University of Chicago Press, 2015), chs. 8–9. On late-twentieth-century nativism, see George Sánchez, "Face the Nation: Race, Immigration, and the Rise of Nativism in Late Twentieth Century America," *International Migration Review* 31 (Winter 1997): 1009–30; Juan F. Perea, ed., *Immigrants Out! The New Nativism and the Anti-Immigrant Impulse in the United States* (New York: New York University Press, 1997); David M. Reimers, *Unwelcome Strangers: American Identity and the Turn Against Immigration* (New York: Columbia University Press, 1998); Daniel J. Tichenor, *Dividing Lines: The Politics of Immigration Control in America* (Princeton, NJ: Princeton University Press, 2002), ch. 9.

6 Bruce J. Schulman, *The Seventies: The Great Shift in American Culture, Society, and Politics* (New York: The Free Press, 2001), 58–72 (quotation on p. 72); Gary Gerstle, *American Crucible*, 349–57, 364–8; Jacobson, *Roots Too*, chs. 5–6 and passim (quotations on pp. 243 and 208).

7 Hollinger, *Postethnic America*, 92–101; John Higham, "Ethnic Pluralism in Modern American Thought," in John Higham, *Send These to Me: Immigrants in Urban America*, rev. ed. (Baltimore: Johns Hopkins University Press, 1984), 198–232 (1st ed. 1975); Philip Gleason, "The Odd Couple: Pluralism and Assimilation," in *Speaking of Diversity: Language and Ethnicity in Twentieth-Century America* (Baltimore: Johns Hopkins University Press, 1992), 47–90; Nicholas V. Montalto, *A History of the Intercultural Educational Movement, 1924–1941* (New York: Garland Publishing, 1982). Gerstle did note that the "soft" multiculturalism that continues "to value the nation" so long as it allows for a wide array of ethnic and racial difference was not in fact a new stance. After appearing in Kallen's work, it re-emerged periodically in a wide array of subsequent pronouncements and writings, including the government's Second World War propaganda campaigns, Oscar Handlin's post-1945 scholarship, and the "curricular initiatives" of some urban school districts in the early 1960s. Gerstle, *American Crucible*, 349. On Kallen and contemporaries, see chapter 1.

8 Kazal, "Rethinking the Origins of Multiculturalism"; Russell A. Kazal, "The Lost World of Pennsylvania Pluralism: Immigrants, Regions, and the Early Origins of Pluralist Ideologies in America," *Journal of American Ethnic History* 27 (Spring 2008): 7–42; Russell A. Kazal, "'The United Peoples of the United States': International Socialism and the Transnational Context of American Pluralist Ideologies," paper presented at the Annual Meeting of the Organization of American Historians, New Orleans, LA, April 2017; Daniel Katz, *All Together Different: Yiddish Socialists, Garment Workers, and the Labor Roots of Multiculturalism* (New York: New York University Press, 2011); Diana Selig, *Americans All: The Cultural Gifts Movement* (Cambridge, MA: Harvard University Press, 2008); Daniel Geary, "Carey McWilliams and Antifascism, 1934–1943," *Journal of American History* 90 (December 2003): 912–34; Allison Varzally, *Making a Non-White America: Californians Coloring outside Ethnic Lines, 1925–1955* (Berkeley, CA: University of California Press, 2008); Daniel Hurewitz, *Bohemian Los Angeles and the Making of Modern Politics* (Berkeley, CA: University of California Press, 2007); George J. Sánchez, " 'What's Good for Boyle Heights Is Good for the Jews': Creating Multiculturalism on the Eastside during the 1950s," *American Quarterly* 56, no. 3 (September 2004): 633–61; Matt Garcia, *A World of Its Own: Race, Labor, and Citrus in the Making of Greater Los Angeles, 1900–1970* (Chapel Hill, NC: University of North Carolina Press, 2001); Russell A. Kazal, "Grass-Roots Pluralism: Los Angeles and the Origins of American Multiculturalism" (book manuscript in progress); Russell A. Kazal, "Toward 'a Multi-Cultural Nation': Multiracialism and Languages

of Diversity in Postwar Southern California," paper presented at the Annual Meeting of Social Science History Association, Montreal, November 2017; Russell A. Kazal, "John Anson Ford and Global Interracialism in Mid-Century Los Angeles," paper presented at the Annual Meeting of American Studies Association, San Juan, Puerto Rico, November 2012.

9 See, for example, Peter Cole et al., eds., *Wobblies of the World: A Global History of the IWW* (London: Pluto Press, 2017), esp. Introduction and essays by Kenyon Zimmer, David M. Struthers, and Mark Leier.

10 Hurewitz, *Bohemian Los Angeles*; Miller-Davenport, *Gateway State*; Kazal, "Grass-Roots Pluralism."

11 For differing assessments of Trudeau, see H.D. Forbes, "Trudeau as the First Theorist of Canadian Multiculturalism," in Stephen Tierney, ed., *Multiculturalism and the Canadian Constitution* (Vancouver: UBC Press, 2007), 27–42; Karl Peter, "The Myth of Multiculturalism and Other Political Fables," in Jorgen Dahlie and Tissa Fernando, eds., *Ethnicity, Power and Politics in Canada* (Toronto: Methuen 1981), 56–67; Wsevolod W. Isajiw, "Multiculturalism and the Integration of the Canadian Community," *Canadian Ethnic Studies*, 15, no. 2 (1983): 107–17; May Chazan et al., eds., *Home and Native Land: Unsettling Multiculturalism in Canada* (Toronto: Between the Lines, 2011).

12 For differing assessments of Yuzyk (and Ukrainian Canadian allies), see, for example, Oleh W. Gerus, "Paul Yuzyk (1918–1986): A Personal Reflection," in *In the Footsteps of Nationbuilders*, May 2000, https://yuzyk.com/2019/09/22/paul-yuzyk-1918-1986-a-personal-reflection/ (last accessed 20 April 2022); Julia Lalande, "The Roots of Multiculturalism – Ukrainian-Canadian Involvement in the Multiculturalism Discussion of the 1960s as an Example of the Position of the Third Force," *Canadian Ethnic Studies* 38, no. 1 (2006): 47–64; Aya Fujiwara, *Ethnic Elites and Canadian Identity: Japanese, Ukrainians, and Scots, 1919–1971* (Winnipeg: University of Manitoba Press, 2012), chs. 5–6; and the more critical Eve Haque, *Multiculturalism within a Bilingual Framework: Language, Race, and Belonging in Canada* (Toronto: University of Toronto Press, 2012), 214–20; Kassandra Luciuk, "Making Ukrainian Canadians: Identity, Politics, and Power in Cold War Canada" (PhD diss., University of Toronto, 2021), ch. 4.

13 See chapter 10.

14 Lee Blanding, "Re-branding Canada: The Origins of Canadian Multiculturalism Policy, 1945–1974" (PhD diss., University of Victoria, 2003). The related work on academic advisers is referenced below.

15 A tiny sample containing differing assessments include Manoly R. Lupul, ed., *Ukrainian Canadians, Multiculturalism, and Separatism: An Assessment.* (Edmonton: University of Alberta Press, 1978); William Kaplan, ed., *Belonging: The Meaning and Future of Canadian Citizenship* (Kingston/Montreal: McGill-Queen's University Press, 1993), esp. the essay by Paul Martin Sr. and part 4; Peter H. Russell, *Constitutional Odyssey: Can Canadians Become a Sovereign People?*, 2nd

ed. (Toronto: University of Toronto Press, 1993); Manoly R. Lupul, *The Politics of Multiculturalism: A Ukrainian Canadian Memoir* (Edmonton: Canadian Institute of Ukrainian Studies Press, 2005); Tierney, *Multiculturalism and the Canadian Constitution*.

16 A tiny sample includes Himani Bannerji, *The Dark Side of the Nation: Essays on Multiculturalism, Nationalism, and Gender* (Toronto: Canadian Scholars Press, 2000); Sunera Thobani, *Exalted Subjects: Studies in the Making of Race and Nation in Canada* (Toronto: University of Toronto Press, 2007); essays by Rinaldo Walcott, Glen S. Coulthard, and others in Chazan, *Home and Native Land*; Nadia Jones-Gailani, *Transnational Identity and Memory Making in the Lives of Iraqi Women in Diaspora* (Toronto: University of Toronto Press, 2020*); Eva Mackey, *The House of Difference: Cultural Politics and National Identity in Canada* (Toronto: University of Toronto Press, 2002).

17 Evelyn Kallen, "Multiculturalism: Ideology, Policy and Reality," *Journal of Canadian Studies* 17, no.1 (Spring 1982): 51–63; Michael Temelini, "Multicultural Rights, Multicultural Virtues: A History of Multiculturalism in Canada," in Tierney, *Multiculturalism*, 43–60; José Igartua, *The Other Quiet Revolution: National Identities in English Canada, 1945–71* (Vancouver: UBC Press, 2006); Biles, "Canada's Multiculturalism Program"; Paolo Prosperi, "The Politics of Multiculturalism Reform in Canada: Institutions, Ideas and Public Agendas" (PhD diss., Université de Montréal, 2006), ch. 4.

18 See, for example, Will Kymlicka, *Finding Our Way: Rethinking Ethnocultural Relations in Canada* (London: Oxford University Press, 1998); Will Kymlicka, *Multicultural Citizenship: A Liberal Theory of Minority Rights* (London: Oxford University Press, 2001); Charles Taylor, *Multiculturalism: Examining the Politics of Recognition* (Princeton, NJ: Princeton University Press, 1992) and 1994 edition (with respondents) edited by Amy Gutmann.

19 Besides Blanding, "Re-branding Canada," see Ivana Caccia, *Managing the Canadian Mosaic: Shaping Citizenship Policy* (Kingston/Montreal: McGill-Queen's University Press, 2010); Leslie A. Pal, *Interests of State: The Politics of Language, Multiculturalism, and Feminism in Canada* (Montreal/Kingston: McGill-Queen's University Press, 1993); N.F. Dreisziger, "The Rise of a Bureaucracy for Multiculturalism: The Origins of the Nationalities Branch, 1939–1941," in Norman Hillmer et al., eds., *On Guard for Thee: War, Ethnicity, and the Canadian State, 1939–1945* (Ottawa: Minister of Supply and Services Canada, 1988); Luciuk, "Making Ukrainian Canadians."

20 Neil Bissoondath, *Selling Illusions: The Cult of Multiculturalism in Canada* (Toronto: Penguin, 1994, rev. ed. 2002); Kanishka Goonewardena and Stefan Kipfer, "Spaces of Difference: Reflections from Toronto on Multiculturalism, Bourgeois Urbanism and the Possibility of Radical Urban Politics," *International Journal of Urban and Regional Research* 29, no. 3 (2005): 670–8; Mackey, *House of Difference* On this theme, see also chapter 10 and conclusion.

21 Mackey, *House of Difference*, chs. 5–6.
22 John Porter, *The Vertical Mosaic* (Toronto: University of Toronto Press, 1965); Michael Ornstein, *Ethno-Racial Groups in Toronto, 1971–2001: A Demographic and Socio-Economic Profile* (Toronto: Institute for Social Research, York University, January 2006), 82–9.
23 Grace-Edward Galabuzi, *Canada's Economic Apartheid: The Social Exclusion of Racialized Groups in the New Century* (Toronto: Canadian Scholars Press, 2006), esp. preface, chs. 4–5; see also essays by Galabuzi, Rinaldo Walcott, and Glen Coulthard in Chazan, *Home and Native Land;* Thobani, *Exalted Subjects*, esp. ch. 4.
24 Nandita Sharma, "Canadian Multiculturalism and Its Nationalisms," in Chazan, *Home and Native Land*; Nandita Sharma, *Home Economics: Nationalism and the Making of 'Migrant Workers' in Canada* (Toronto: University of Toronto Press, 2006).
25 Himani Bannerji, "On the Dark Side of the Nation: Politics of Multiculturalism and the State of Canada," *Journal of Canadian Studies* 31, no. 3 (Fall 1996): 103–30; Bannerji, *Dark Side of the Nation*; Richard J.F. Day, *Multiculturalism and the History of Canadian Diversity* (Toronto: University of Toronto Press, 2010).
26 In addition to Kymlicka's and Taylor's many publications, see the following research projects: "Boundaries, Membership and Belonging," https://cifar.ca/research-programs/boundaries-membership-belonging/; "Multiculturalism Policy Index," https://www.queensu.ca/mcp/, and Global Centre for Pluralism ("we believe that societies thrive when differences are valued"), https://www.pluralism.ca/ (all last accessed 15 April 2022).
27 For a recent example involving the angry fallout from a law professor's accusations of racism in Quebec, see https://montrealgazette.com/news/quebec/pq-leader-wants-university-to-tell-professor-to-stop-bashing-quebec (last accessed 6 April 2021). On the commission, which recommended a model of interculturalism, see Gerard Bouchard, *Interculturalism: A View from Quebec*, trans. Howard Scott (Toronto: University of Toronto, 2015).
28 See the discussion of Victoria Hayward, *Romantic Canada* (Toronto: Macmillan Company, 1922), and Kate A. Foster, *Our Canadian Mosaic* (Toronto: Dominion Council of the Young Women's Christian Association, 1926), in chapter 10.
29 Such as lone woman commissioner Gertrude Laing (University of Manitoba) and sociologist Jean Burnet (Glendon College, York University), who was involved in the Canadian Ethnic Studies Research Program. Haque, *Multiculturalism*, 39–40, 257; Biles, "Canada's Multiculturalism Program," 14–16; Maxwell Yalden, "Forward: The B&B Commission 50 Years Later," *Canadian Issues/Thèmes canadiens* (Fall 2013): 9.
30 Others were Beatrice Hayes (National Council of Women of Canada) and Ethel Brant Monture (National Indian Council). Haque, *Multiculturalism*, 99–100.
31 See especially chapter 10.
32 Marlene Epp, *Mennonite Women in Canada: A History* (Winnipeg: University of Manitoba Press, 2008); Laurie Bertram, *The Viking Immigrants: Icelandic North*

Americans (Toronto: University of Toronto Press, 2019); Frances Swyripa, *Wedded to the Cause: Ukrainian Canadian Women and Ethnic Identity, 1891–1991* (Toronto: University of Toronto Press, 1993).
33 Frances Swyripa, *Storied Landscapes: Ethno-religious Identity and the Canadian Prairies* (Winnipeg: University of Manitoba Press, 2010).
34 As in, respectively, Susan Bellay, "Pluralism and Ethnic/Race Relations in Canadian Social Science, 1880–1939" (PhD diss., University of Manitoba, 2001), and Fujiwara, *Ethnic Elites and Canadian Identity*, which covers the period 1919 to 1971. Howard Palmer, "Mosaic Versus Melting Pot: Immigration and Ethnicity in Canada and the United States," *International Journal* 31, no. 3 (1976): 488–528, dates the origins of ethnic pluralism in the 1930s.
35 Chapter 10 contains a more detailed treatment of this theme, but on Gibbon, see, for example, Antonia Smith, "'Cement for the Canadian Mosaic': Performing Canadian Citizenship in the Work of John Murray Gibbon," *Race/Ethnicity* 1, no. 1 (Autumn 2007): 37–60.
36 Robert C. Vipond, *Making a Global City: How One Toronto School Embraced Diversity* (Toronto: University of Toronto Press, 2017); Royden Loewen and Gerald Friesen, *Immigrants in Prairie Cities: Ethnic Diversity in Twentieth-Century Canada* (Toronto: University of Toronto Press, 2009).

3 Toronto Counsellors and International Institute Social Work Theory and Practice

1 Archives of Ontario (AO), International Institute of Metropolitan Toronto, Fonds 884, MU6424, File: Personnel Committee 1965, J.T. Seaman to Effie Tsatsos, Oct. 1965; Kathleen Rex, "The Swallows Mean Happiness," Toronto *Globe and Mail*, 26 Feb. 70, in MU6406 (B280543), File: Clippings 1959–70.
2 MU6425, File: Szebeny, Letter from Streeruwitz and Szebeny to director Tine Stewart, 11 April 1972; MU6474, File: Monthly Reports and Reviews, Department of Individual Services, Annual Report, 1 Oct. 1956–1 Oct. 1957; MU6424, File: Executive Director Personnel 1956–62, West letter dated 4 July 57; Donna Dilschneider, "Metro grant cut could spell trouble for immigrant aid," *Toronto Star* 13 June 1968.
3 On the polarized literature, see chapter 1.
4 On this point, see also Andrew Urban, "Social Work and Substantive Justice: The International Institutes' Response to Discriminatory Immigration and Naturalization Laws, 1924–1945," *Journal of American Ethnic History* 37 no. 1 (Fall 2017): 5–29; Erika Lee and Judy Yung, *Angel Island: Immigrant Gateway to America* (Oxford: Oxford University Press, 2010), 283.
5 A tiny sample includes Elise Franklin, "Defining Family, Delimiting Belonging: Algerian Migration after the End of Empire," *Gender & History* 31, no. 3 (Oct. 2019): 681–98; Mark Peel, *Miss Cutler and the Case of the Resurrected Horse:*

Social Work and the Story of Poverty in America, Australia, and Britain (Chicago: University of Chicago Press, 2012); Ellen Ross, ed., *Slum Travelers: Ladies and London Poverty, 1860–1920* (Berkeley: University of California Press, 2007); Regina Kunzel, *Fallen Women, Problem Girls: Unmarried Mothers and the Professionalization of Social Work, 1890–1945* (New Haven, CT: Yale University Press, 1993); Karen Tice, *Tales of Wayward Girls and Immoral Women: Case Records and the Professionalization of Social Work* (Urbana: University of Illinois Press, 1998); Margaret Little, *No Car, No Radio, No Liquor Permit: The Regulation of Single Mothers in Ontario, 1920–1977* (Toronto: Oxford University Press, 1998); Linda Gordon, *Heroes of Their Own Lives: The Politics and History of Family Violence, Boston 1880–1960* (New York: Viking, 1988); Jaime Wadowiec, "Muslim Algerian Women and the Rights of Man: Islam and Gendered Citizenship in French Algeria at the End of Empire," *French Historical Studies* 36, no. 4 (Fall 2013): 649–76.

6 Raymond Mohl, "The International Institute Movement and Ethnic Pluralism," *Social Science* 56, no. 1 (Winter 1998): 14–21. On racialized social workers and managing diversity in the post-1945 era of decolonization, migration, and emerging multiculturalism in Britain, see Radhika Anita Natarajan, "Organizing Community: Commonwealth Citizens and Social Activism in Britain,1948–1982" (PhD dissertation, University of California Berkeley, 2013); Radhika Anita Natarajan, "Public Intimacy: Pansy Jeffrey and the Politics of Migrant Welfare," paper delivered at the Migration, Institutions, and Intimate Lives Symposium, University of Bristol, 13–14 April 2018.

7 The discussion draws on personnel and staff list files contained in several volumes, including MU6424 and MU6438.

8 Christopher Grafos, "Canada's Greek Moment: Transnational Politics, Activists, and Spies during the Long Sixties" (PhD diss., York University, 2016); Noula Mina, "Homeland Activism, Public Performance, and the Construction of Identity: An Examination of Greek Canadian Transnationalism, 1900s–1990s (PhD diss., University of Toronto, 2014); Gilberto Fernandes, *This Pilgrim Nation: The Making of the Portuguese Diaspora in Postwar North America* (Toronto: University of Toronto Press, 2020); Susana Miranda, ''Not Ashamed or Afraid': Portuguese Immigrant Women in Toronto's Cleaning Industry, 1950–1995 (PhD diss., York University, 2010).

9 Notes on Bojovic in MU6424, File: Executive Director, Personnel 1956–62, N.W. West reference letter for Bojovic, 16 Nov. 1960.

10 Bojovic quotation from MU6474, File: Monthly Reports and Reviews, Department of Individual Services, Annual Report, 1 Oct. 1956–1 Oct. 1957; West quotation from MU6424, File: Executive Director Personnel 1956–62, West letter dated 4 July 57; Mary Jukes, "Once Over Lightly [on clients keen to see Streeruwitz]," *Toronto Star*, 14 Nov. 1960 in MU6406 (B280543), File: Clippings 1959–70.

11 MU6475, File: Statistical and Activity Reports 1958–74, Individual Services Committee, Annual Report, 1960, by Chair, Institute Board (Mrs [J.S.] Margaret Hill).

Notes to pages 35–9   329

12 *Intercom*, Dec. 1965; Peter C. Newman, "The Hungarians," *Maclean's*, 16 Feb. 1957, https://archive.macleans.ca/article/1957/2/16/the-hungarians; Nagy Obituary, https://www.legacy.com/obituaries/theglobeandmail/obituary.aspx?n=george-nagy-felso-eori&pid=189716720&fhid=17701 (both last accessed 11 Oct. 2021).

13 MU6424, File: Personnel 1960s, Director H.C. Forbell to Henry Weisback, Institute Board, Confidential, 28 May 1962; Bojovic resignation letter, 22 May 62; MU6425, File: John Henselmans, Notes.

14 Quotation by director Milton Philip in MU6425, File: Personnel 1960s, note on Henselmans.

15 Quotation by director Tine Stewart in MU6425, File: Szebeny, letter dated April 1974.

16 MU6424, File: Executive Director 1960s, Forbell's comments on Justi's resume, 29 Jan 1962 (Streeruwitz was a reference); MU6475, File: Statistical and Activity Reports 1958–74, Justi to R. Lederer, note for Annual Report, 27 March 1957.

17 MU6424, File: Executive Director Personnel, Vincent G. Castellano resume and notes.

18 MU 6425, File: Thanos Panagiotis, Director's Report, 16 Aug. 1972.

19 MU6425, File: Maria Mota, notes on Mota; postcards and reply, 1970s; quotation from director Tine Stewart's reference letter, 10 Nov. 1969.

20 MU6431 (B280568), File: Staff Minutes 1970, Minutes for Meeting, 7 May 1971; MU6425 (B280562), File: Royston C. Jones, Mrs Douglas Jennings, Acting President, Board, letter dated 4 April 1974; Resume; Consultant to Caribana, Jan. 1973.

21 On Lee, see chapter 7.

22 Betty McBain and Betty Wangenheim are listed as reception centre supervisors. MU6475 (B436179), File: Reception Centre 1964, Monthly Reports; MU6474, File: Statistical and Activity Reports 1958–74, Reception Centre Annual Report 1961 (M. Streeruwitz); MU6389 (B280527), File: Special Committee Casework, Case Work Committee Meeting, 25 Nov. 1959; MU6410 (B280597), File: Executive Director 1964–66, J.T. Seaman reference letter for A. Garcia, 1 Sept. 1966.

23 MU6389 (B280527), File: Special Committee Casework, Case Work Committee Meeting, 25 Nov. 1959, Volunteers, Progress Report (N.S. Bojovic).

24 MU6474, File: Statistical and Activity Reports 1958–74, Reception Centre, Annual Report 1961 (M. Streeruwitz).

25 Tice, *Wayward Girls*, quotation on p. 34, and ch. 2, esp. 50–69; Kunzel, *Fallen Women*, ch. 2, esp. 48–52; Peel, *Miss Cutler*, chs. 2–3, 10, 12, 17, and passim.

26 Susan Bellay, "Pluralism and Race/Ethnic Relations in Canadian Social Science, 1880–1939" (PhD diss., University of Manitoba, 2001), 53–7, 108–21, 414–48. See also Ramsay Cook, *The Regenerators: Social Criticism in Late Victorian English Canada* (Toronto: University of Toronto Press, 1985), 213–29.

27 Quotation from John R. Graham, "A History of the University of Toronto School of Social Work" (PhD diss., University of Toronto, 1996), 217. On Schlesinger,

who also published on elder abuse, single-parent families, Jewish and Canadian families, and child abuse, see also 260–3, 279n11.

28 Benjamin Schlesinger, "Socio-Cultural Content in North American Social Work Journals 1956–1963, An Introduction and Bibliography," *International Social Work* 9, no. 1 (1966): 30–8.

29 Established in 1952, the membership of this professional body of social workers in the United States then included several Canadian social work programs.

30 Quoting Graham, "A History," 263. Schlesinger, "Socio-Cultural Content in North American Social Work Journals," cites Hertha Kraus, "The Newcomer's Orientation to the American Community," and Katherine Newkirk Handley, "Social Casework and Intercultural Problems," both in Family Service Association of America, *New Emphasis on Cultural Factors, Papers Reprinted from Journal of Social Casework, 1946–48*, and Handley, *4 Case Studies in Hawaii* (Honolulu: University of Hawaii Press, 1961). His "The Socio-Cultural Elements in Casework: The Canadian Scene, *Social Worker* 30, no. 1 (Jan. 1962), cites Handley's *Socio-Cultural Elements in Casework: A Case Book of Seven Ethnic Case Studies* (New York: Council on Social Work Education, 1959). On Kraus, see Beate Bussiek, "Hertha Kraus: Quaker Spirit and Competence – Impulses for Professional Social Work," in Sabine Hering and Berteke Waaldijk, eds., *History of Social Work in Europe 1900–1960, Female Pioneers and the Development of International Social Work* (Opladen: Leske & Budrich, 2003). On the Council, see entry by Ray J. Thomlinson in Francis J. Turner, ed., *Encyclopedia of Canadian Social Work* (Waterloo: Wilfrid Laurier University Press, 2005), 85–6.

31 Charles Fine, "Canadian and American Ethnic Viewpoints: A Study in Contrast," *Social Worker* 29 (4 Oct. 1961), which cites William Gioseffi, "The Relationship of Culture to the Principles of Casework, *Social Casework* 34 (July 1954), and Kraus, "The Newcomer's Orientation to the American Community."

32 Fine, "Canadian and American Ethnic Viewpoints."

33 For just one example, see MU6400, File: ACNS [American Council for Nationalities Service, an amalgamation (est. 1959) of the American Federation of International Institutes (AFII) and the educationally oriented American Council for Nationalities Services], Convention, Detroit, 21–24 May 1968, Cases Involving Cultural Factors for Discussion, May 1968 (William Bernard).

34 E.B. Taylor, *Primitive Culture* (vols. 1 and 2) (London: John Murray, 1871), and Ruth Benedict, *Patterns of Culture* (with preface by Margaret Mead) (Boston: Houghton Mifflin, 1946) were cited by Institute-linked social workers like Mary Hurlbutt and Morton Teicher as well as Schlesinger. Immigration History Research Center Archives, Elmer L. Andersen Library, University of Minnesota (hereafter IHRCA), American Council for Nationalities Service records, which contain the American Federation of International Institutes (AFII) collection (hereafter II), Box 275, File: 10, II San Francisco, Mary Hurlbutt, Minutes, "In-Service Training Program," 1–11 May 1945; Morton Teicher, "Concept

of Culture," 15 May 1958; Mary Hurlbutt, "Recognizing Cultural Differences and Using Them Constructively," 29 January 1955, AFII, Convention Address, Detroit; Schlesinger, "Socio-Cultural Elements in Casework."
35 Teicher, "Concept of Culture"; Hurlbutt, "Recognizing Cultural Differences."
36 Revealingly, the Toronto Institute collection contains "Canadianized" notes from Kraus' "The Newcomer's Orientation to the American Community" in MU6405, File: Case Histories, "Extracts" from Kraus, "The Newcomer's Orientation to the "Canadian" Community."
37 Teicher, "Concept of Culture," 15 May 1958; Hurlbutt, "Minutes, In-Service Training Program"; Hurlbutt, "Recognizing Cultural Differences."
38 IHRCA, II, Box 278b, File: 14, II Milwaukee, Frieda Heilberg, "Psycho-Cultural Factors in the Social Adjustment of Newcomers of Foreign Cultural Background," National Conference on Social Welfare, Chicago, 13 May 1958. See also James Leiby, *A History of Social Welfare and Social Work in the United States* (New York: Columbia University Press, 1978).
39 IHRCA, II, Box 2786, File: 14, Heilberg, "Psycho-Cultural Factors"; Boris Clarke, "Social Adjustment of Newcomers," 13 May 1958; Bremer, "Development of Private Social Work."
40 On integrating anti-Communist refugees into American modern democratic life, see, for example, IHRC, II, Box 271, File: 9, S.E. Peabody, Mission Statement, II Boston, 14 June 1950; "They Pour In ... and Family Shows Refugees Can Fit In," *Life*, 7 Jan. 1957, 21, 24–5. On general context, see, for example, Elaine Tyler May, *Homeward Bound: American Families in the Cold War Era* (New York: Basic Books, 1988); Joanne Meyerowitz, ed., *Not June Cleaver: Women and Gender in Postwar America, 1945–1960* (Philadelphia: Temple University Press, 1994); Geoffrey Smith, "National Security and Personal Isolation: Sex, Gender, and Disease in the Cold War United States," *International History Review* 14, no. 2 (1992): 307–35; Margot Canaday, *The Straight State: Sexuality and Citizenship in Twentieth-Century America* (Princeton, NJ: Princeton University Press, 2009); Franca Iacovetta, *Gatekeepers: Reshaping Immigrant Lives in Cold War Canada* (Toronto: Between the Lines, 2006); Gary Kinsman and Patrizia Gentile, *The Canadian War on Queers: National Security as Sexual Regulation* (Vancouver: UBC Press, 2010).
41 IHRCA, II, Box 2786, File: 14, Bremer, "Development of Private Social Work."
42 See chapter 8.
43 IHRCA, II, Box 2786, File: 14, Frieda Heilberg, "Psycho-Cultural Factors in the Social Adjustment of Newcomers of Foreign Cultural Background," National Conference on Social Welfare, Chicago, 13 May 1958.
44 See, for example, AO, MU6447, File: Individual Services Department 1961–4, Report for 1 Oct. 1956–1 Oct. 1957; MU6400, File: International Institute Department, Annual Reports for 1961–2, 1964, 1967; MU6475, File: Statistical and Activity Reports 1958–74, Notes and Report for 1957–8, 1959, 1960; MU6475, File: Selected Special Cases, "Adjustment of Newcomers in Canada by a Social

Worker" (N.S. Bojovic) c. 1960; MU6472, File: Letters of Appreciation 1959–62, N.S. Bojovic, "International Institute of Metropolitan Toronto and Its Services," presented to Forest Hill Collegiate, 11 Feb. 1960.
45 IHRCA, II, Box 275, File: 10, Hurlblutt, "Minutes of In-Service Training Program."
46 Ibid.
47 Ibid.
48 IHRCA, II, Box 2786, File: 14, Heilberg, "Psycho-Cultural Factors."
49 Hurlblutt, "Minutes, In-Service Training Program."
50 IHRCA, II, Box 2786, File: 14, Pierce, "Patterns of Collaboration," 1958.
51 Scholars of whiteness differ with respect to the emphasis placed on either the uncontested whiteness of European immigrants or their in-between status, marginalization, and eventual upward mobility. This is a large literature, but see the useful historiographical essays by Anna Pegler-Gordon, Allison Varzally, David Roediger, Eiichiro Azumo, and Mark Overmyer-Velázquez in the special theme issue, *The Racial Turn in Immigration and Ethnic History*, in *Journal of American Ethnic History* 36, no. 2 (Winter 2017): 40–93; David Roediger, "A Reply to Kaufmann," *Ethnicities* 6, no. 2 (2006): 254–62.
52 Hurlbutt, "Minutes, In-Service Training Program"; Josephine Donovan, *Feminist Theory: The Intellectual Traditions,* 3rd ed. (New York: Continuum, 2000), 171; bell hooks, *Ain't I a Woman? Black Women and Feminism* (Boston: South End, 1981).
53 Like those in, for example, Karen Tice, *Tales of Wayward Girls and Immoral Women: Case Records and the Professionalization of Social Work* (Urbana: University of Illinois Press, 1998).
54 A tiny sample that captures this trajectory within case file scholarship includes Joan Scott/Linda Gordon, Debate, *Signs* 15, no. 4 (1990): 848–60; Tice, *Wayward Girls*; Kunzel, *Fallen Women*; Franca Iacovetta and Wendy Mitchinson eds., *On the Case: Explorations in Social History* (Toronto: University of Toronto Press, 1998); Peel, *Miss Cutler*. See also the other references above.
55 Scholars exploring US Institute social work practice have had to rely on summary reports and presentations rather than actual case files, though the reports, like the instruction materials, often reproduced all or parts of specific case files. See Urban, "Social Work and Substantive Justice."
56 There is now a large literature on empathy in social work, but I found helpful Karen E. Gerdes and Elizabeth Segal, "The Importance of Empathy for Social Work Practice: Integrating New Science," *Social Work* 56, no. 2 (2011): 141–8, and their "A Social Work Model of Empathy," *Advances in Social Work* 1, no. 2 (2009): 114–27. For one front-line worker's optimistic implementation of empathy, see Sharon Lacay, "Breaking Boundaries with Empathy: How the Therapeutic Alliance Can Defy Client/Worker Differences," *The New Social Worker*, https://www.socialworker.com/featurearticles/practice/

Breaking_Boundaries_With_Empathy%3A_How_the_Therapeutic_Alliance_Can_Defy_Client-Worker_Differences/ (last accessed 17 April 2022).
57 Tice, *Wayward Girls*, ch. 2; Kunzel *Fallen Women*, ch. 5;
58 Quotation from Tice, *Wayward Girls*, 201n3.
59 Tice, *Wayward Girls*, 7; Peel also urges the use of our historical imagination in *Miss Cutler*, Introduction and dramatizations, cases 1–6.
60 Tice *Wayward Girls*, quotation on p. 14 and ch. 5.
61 This is a key theme in the studies cited above, and in Ellen Ross, *Love and Toil: Motherhood in Outcast London, 1870–1918* (Oxford: Oxford University Press, 1993), and Franca Iacovetta, "Women Pluralists Negotiate Children's Health in an Era of Mass Migration," *Journal of Migration History* 4 (2018): 161–86, among others. For my detailed treatment of this theme, see chapters 3 and 6.
62 Gordon, *Heroes*, 298. See also Peel, *Miss Cutler*, 8–9 and passim.
63 Mary Louise Pratt developed the neocolonial concept of a contact zone in *Imperial Eyes: Travel Writing and Transculturation* (London: Routledge, 1992), but feminist, anti-racist, and left scholars of multiculturalism, among others, speak in similar terms about interactions within contexts shaped by asymmetrical power relations. Examples include Sunera Thobani, *Exalted Subjects: Studies in the Making of Race and Nation in Canada* (Toronto: University of Toronto Press, 2007); Sara Ahmed, *Strange Encounters: Embodied Others in Post-Coloniality* (London: Routledge, 2000). On intermediate spaces, Leonore Davidoff, "Regarding Some 'Old Husband's Tales': Public and Private in Feminist History," in *Worlds Between: Historical Perspectives on Gender and Class* (Oxford: Blackwell Publishers, 1995), 227–76; Bettina Bradbury and Tamara Myers, *Negotiating Identities in 19th and 20th Century Montreal* (Vancouver: UBC Press, 2005), esp. Introduction, and Myers, "On Probation: The Rise and Fall of Jewish Women's Antidelinquency Work in Interwar Montreal," 175–200. See also Ruth Sandwell, "The Limits of Liberalism: The Liberal Reconnaissance and the History of the Family in Canada," *Canadian Historical Review* 84, no. 3 (September 2003): 423–50, and my discussion in chapter 7.
64 Michel Foucault, *Power/Knowledge,* ed. Colin Gordon (London: Harvester 1980); Michel Foucault, *History of Sexuality,* vol. 1, *An Introduction,* trans. R. Hurley (London: Allan Lane, 1979), and for some examples of feminist critical engagements with Foucault, see Irene Diamond and Lee Quinby, eds., *Feminism and Foucault: Reflections on Resistance* (Boston: Northeastern University Press, 1988). On the glance, see Franca Iacovetta, "Gossip, Contest and Power in the Making of Postwar Suburban Bad Girls: Toronto 1940s–1950s," *Canadian Historical Review* 80, no. 4 (Dec. 1999): 608 (with thanks to Ellen Ross for the initial insight).
65 Peel, *Miss Cutler*, 5, citing Eileen Yeo, *The Contest for Social Science: Relations and Representations of Gender and Class* (London: Rivers Oram Press, 1996), 249.
66 Davidoff, "Public and Private in Feminist History."

4 Professionals, Narrative, and Gendered Middle-Class Subjectivities

1 Archives of Ontario (AO), International Institute of Metropolitan Toronto, Fonds 884, MU6472, File: Letters of Appreciation 1959–62, contains original handwritten letter addressed to N.S. Bojovic (1959) and improved, typed version cited here.
2 MU6474, File: Statistical and Activity Reports, 1958–74, Reception Centre, Annual Report 1961 (M. Streeruwitz); on speaking stories, Mark Peel, *Miss Cutler and the Case of the Resurrected Horse: Social Work and the Story of Poverty in America, Australia, and Britain* (Chicago: University of Chicago Press, 2012), 3–5, 153–5, 189–90, 267–8, and *passim*; Karen Tice, *Tales of Wayward Girls and Immoral Women: Case Records and the Professionalization of Social Work* (Urbana: University of Illinois Press, 1998), Introduction and ch. 6, esp. 176–80.
3 Eileen Yeo cited in Peel, *Miss Cutler,* Introduction, 5n7, but see also Eileen Yeo, *The Contest for Social Science: Relations and Representations of Gender and Class* (London: Rivers Oram Press, 1996). See also Ellen Ross, *Slum Journeys: Lady Explorers in Darkest London* (Berkeley: University of California Press, 2007).
4 Trish Luker, "Performance Anxieties: Interpellation of the Refugee Subject in Law," *Canadian Journal of Law and Society* 30, no. 1 (2015): 91–107; Stephen Paskey, "Telling Refugee Stories: Trauma, Credibility and the Adversarial Adjudication of Claims for Asylum," *Digital Commons@University at Buffalo School of Law* 56 (2016); Shulamit Almog, "Healing Stories in Law and Literature," in Austin Sarat et al., eds., *Trauma and Memory: Reading, Healing and Making Law* (Stanford: Stanford University Press, 2007). See also Canadian Council for Refugees, "Raising Refugee Voices," https://ccrweb.ca/en/refugee-voices (last accessed 14 April 2022).
5 For just two examples involving recent newcomers, see Nadia Jones-Gailani, *Transnational Identity and Memory Making in the Lives of Iraqi Women in Diaspora* (Toronto: University of Toronto Press, 2020); Stéphane Martelly, "'This thing we are doing here': Listening and Writing within Montreal's Haitian Community," in Katrina Srigley , Stacey Zembrzycki, and Franca Iacovetta, eds., *Beyond Women's Words: Feminisms and the Practices of Oral History in the Twenty-first Century* (London/New York: Routledge, 2018), 184–91.
6 For example, Irwin Cotler, "Bringing Nazi War Criminals in Canada to Justice: A Case Study," *American Society of International Law Proceedings* 91 (April 1997): 262–9.
7 See also chapter 3.
8 A tiny sample includes Peter Gossage and Robert Rutherdale, eds., *Making Men, Making History: Canadian Masculinities across Time and Place* (Vancouver: UBC Press, 2018); Kathryn McPherson, Cecilia Morgan, and Nancy Forestell, eds., *Gendered Pasts: Historical Essays in Femininity and Masculinity* (Toronto: Oxford University Press, 1999); Joan Scott, "Gender: A Useful Category of Historical Analysis," *American Historical Review* 91, no. 5 (1985): 1053–75; and her

reassessment, "Gender: Still a Useful Category of Analysis," *Diogenes* 57, no. 1 (2010): 7–14; Joy Parr, "Gender History and Historical Practice," *Canadian Historical Review* 76, no. 3 (1995): 354–76; R.W. Connell, *Masculinities* (Cambridge, UK: Polity, 2005); R.W. Connell and James W. Messerschmidt, "Hegemonic Masculinity: Rethinking the Concept," *Gender and Society* 19, no. 6 (2005): 829–59; John Tosh, "What Should Historians Do with Masculinity?" in *Manliness and Masculinity in Nineteenth-Century Britain: Essays on Gender, Family, and Empire* (Harlow, UK: Pearson Education, 2005); Sonya O. Rose, *What Is Gender History?* (Cambridge, UK: Polity, 2010).

9 Such as Karen Flynn, *Moving beyond Borders: A History of Black Canadian and Caribbean Women in the Diaspora* (Toronto: University of Toronto Press, 2011); C. Meares, "A Fine Balance: Women, Work and Skilled Migration," *Women's Studies International Forum* (2010): 473–81. See also Naila Meraj, "A Scoping Review of Settlement Experiences of Professional Immigrant Women in Canada, USA, UK and Australia and Their Influence on Health and Well Being" (MA thesis, Western University, 2015).

10 Shibao Guo, "Difference, Deficiency, and Devaluation: Tracing the Roots of Non-Recognition of Foreign Credentials for Immigrant Professionals in Canada," *Canadian Journal for the Study of Adult Education* 22, no. 1 (2009): 37–52; Rosalie K. Hilde and Albert Mills, "Making Critical Sense of Discriminatory Practices in the Canadian Workplace: Case Study of Hong Kong Chinese Professional Immigrants, Experience, Voice and Reflection," *Critical Perspectives on International Business* 11, no. 2 (2015): 173–88; Gurcharn S. Basran and Li Zong, "Devaluation of Foreign Credentials as Perceived by Visible Minority Professional Immigrants," *Canadian Ethnic Studies* 30, no. 3 (1998): 7–23; Judith T. Shuval, "The Reconstruction of Professional Identity among Immigrant Physicians in Three Societies," *Journal of Immigrant and Minority Health* 2, no. 4 (2000): 191–202; Maitra Srabani, "Creating Enterprising Workers through Career Training among Canada's South Asian Professional Immigrants," *Studies in Education of Adults* 49, no. 2 (2017): 196–213; Mai B. Phan et al., "Family Dynamics and the Integration of Professional Immigrants in Canada," *Journal of Ethnic and Migration Studies* 14, no. 13 (2015): 2061–80.

11 Milda Danys, *DP: Lithuanian Immigration to Canada after the Second World War* (Toronto: Multicultural History Society of Ontario, 1986), chs. 13–14 (quotation p. 254); Jan Raska, *Czech Refugees in Cold War Canada* (Winnipeg: University of Manitoba Press, 2018).

12 Danys, *DP*, 273; Raska, *Czech Refugees*.

13 Guo, "Difference, Deficiency"; Hilde and Mills, "Discriminatory Practices"; Srabani, "Creating Enterprising Workers"; Basran and Zong, "Devaluation." See also Grace-Edward Galabuzi, *Canada's Economic Apartheid: The Social Exclusion of Racialized Groups in the New Century* (Toronto: Canadian Scholars Press, 2006), chs. 3–5.

14 Shezan Muhammedi, "'Gifts from Amin': The Resettlement, Integration, and Identities of Ugandan Asian Refugees in Canada" (PhD diss., Western University, 2017). Julie Gilmour, "The kind of people Canada wants: Canada and the Displaced Persons, 1943–53 (PhD diss., University of Toronto, 2006)," and Laura Madokoro's *Elusive Refuge: Chinese Migrants in the Cold War* (Cambridge, MA: Harvard University Press, 2016), contain material on professionals, although that is not their primary focus. Marlene Epp, *Refugees in Canada: A Brief History* (Ottawa: Canadian Historical Association, 2017).

15 H. Bauder, "Brain Abuse, or the Devaluation of Immigrant Labour in Canada," *Antipode* 35, no. 4 (2003): 699–717; Tara Kennedy and Charles P. Chen, "Career Counselling and New and Professional Immigrants: Theories into Practice [Canada]," *Australian Journal of Career Development* 21, no. 2 (Winter 2012): 36–45; Hilde and Mills, "Discriminatory Practices," 179–81.

16 Quotation from MU6419 (B280556), File: Human Interest Stories, Individual Services Department document (n.d.).

17 MU6472, File: Letters of Appreciation 1959–62, N.S. Bojovic, Notes for Conference on Employment, 27 Jan. 1960, and "Observation of Effect of Mass Unemployment on Immigrant Worker," both for *Toronto Star* editor Ron Lowman, 9 Feb. 1961; A.G. Gilham, Toronto Employment Committee, to W.E. West, 15 Jan. 1961; MU6474, File: Reports to Director 1959–60, Further Programme Planning as indicated n.d. (c. 1960).

18 MU6474, File: Statistical and Activity Reports 1958–74, Reception Centre, Annual Report 1961 (M. Streeruwitz).

19 Quotations from Peel, *Miss Cutler*, 4, 133, and 45.

20 Some two dozen speaking stories are in MU6405, File: Case Histories and MU6419 (B280556), File: Human Interest Stories. Additional stories appear or are referenced in other files.

21 In MU6405, File: Case Histories, n.d.

22 Ibid.

23 In MU6419 (B280556), File: Human Interest Stories, n.d.

24 Ibid.

25 In MU6405, File: Case Histories, n.d.

26 In MU6419 (B280556), File: Human Interest Stories, n.d. On humour, Tice, *Wayward Girls*, 176–7.

27 Archives of Ontario (AO), International Institute of Metropolitan Toronto, Sub-series E-3, MU6507-MU6567 (case files); on 7,000 case-file database, see Appendix. Of the total number of 2,310 professional cases in the 7,000-file database, men and Eastern Europeans dominate overall, and Eastern Europeans dominate the most prestigious occupations, such as law and medicine.

28 The national/ethnic group and gender breakdown for the subset of 335 files (composed of 197 men and 138 women): German (M40, F28); Hungarian (M37, F27); Czechoslovakian (Czech M32, F25, Slovak M18, F11); Polish (M14, F11); Ukrainian (M10, F5); Yugoslavian (Yugoslav M13, F8, Serbian M6, F5); Lithuanian (M6,

F4); Latvian (M3, F5); Bulgarian (M4, F3); Dutch (M3, F2); Ugandan Asian (M4, F0); Chinese (M3, F2); Chilean (M2, F2); Indian (M2, F0).

29 For more on these groups, see Ninette Kelley and Michael Trebilcock, *The Making the Mosaic: A History of Canadian Immigration Policy* (Toronto: University of Toronto, 1998), ch. 9; Julie Gilmour, "'The kind of people Canada wants'"; Franca Iacovetta, *Gatekeepers; Reshaping Immigrant Lives in Cold War Canada* (Toronto: Between the Lines, 2006); Lubomyr Luciuk, *Searching for Place: Ukrainian Displaced Persons, Canada, and the Migration of Memory* (Toronto: University of Toronto Press, 2000); Raska, *Czech Refugees*, chs. 5–7; Laura Madokoro, "Good Material: Canada and the Prague Spring Refugees," *Refuge* 26, no. 1 (2009): 161–71; Jeremi Suri, "The Promise and Failure of 'Developed Socialism': The Soviet Thaw and the Crucible of the Prague Spring, 1964–1972," *Contemporary European History* 15, no. 2 (2006): 133–58; Gerhard P. Bassler, "German Immigration to Canada," https://www.thecanadianencyclopedia.ca/en/article/german-canadians (last accessed 9 Oct. 2020); Alex Freund, "Troubling Memories in Nation-building: World War II Memories and Germans' Inter-ethnic Encounters in Canada after 1945," *Histoire sociale/ Social History* 39, no. 77 (2006): 129–55.

30 Quotation from MU6475, File: Statistical and Activity Reports 1958–74, A.D. Justi to Mrs Jennings, 1972, Report on Help Program for Chilean Refugees, Reception Centre Report, 12 Jan. 1974. On the main group of 1973 coup refugees, Francis Peddie, *Young, Well-Educated, and Adaptable: Chilean Exiles in Ontario and Quebec, 1973–2010* (Winnipeg: University of Manitoba Press, 2018); Reg Whittaker, *Double Standard: The Secret History of Canadian Immigration* (Toronto: Lester & Orpen Dennys, 1987), 255–61; Jan Raska, "1973: Canada's Response to Chilean Refugees," *Pier 21*, https://pier21.ca/research/immigration-history/canada-s-response-to-the-1973-chilean-crisis (last accessed 15 May 2021).

31 Muhammedi, "'Gifts from Amin.'"

32 Kelley and Trebilcock, *Making the Mosaic*, ch. 9; Jin Tan and Patricial E. Roy, *The Chinese in Canada* (Ottawa: Canadian Historical Association, 1985), 15–16; Norman Buchignani et al., *Continuous Journey: A Social History of South Asians in Canada* (Toronto: McClelland and Stewart, 1985), part 3; Sunera Thobani, *Exalted Subjects: Studies in the Making of Race and Nation in Canada* (Toronto: University of Toronto Press, 2007); Sheyfali Saujani, "Empathy and Authority in Oral Testimony: Feminist Debates, Multicultural Mandates, and Reassessing the Interviewer and Her 'Disagreeable Subjects,'" *Histoire sociale/Social history* 45, no. 90 (2012): 361–91.

33 The occupational breakdown for the 197 men: engineer (21%); university academic (10%); doctors/radiologist (7%); lawyers/judge (7%); architect (6.5%); draftsperson (6.5%); teacher (5.5%); university graduate (5%); agricultural and forestry expert (4.5%); artist (4%); dentist (4%); accountant (3.5%); veterinarian (3.5%); journalist (3%); pharmacist (2.5%); banker (2.5%); other (4.5%).

34 Raska, *Czech Refugees,* 157–9, esp. 160.
35 The occupational breakdown for the 138 women: teacher (27.5%); nurse (23%); lawyer/doctor/academic/dentist (11%); pharmacist/technician (7%); engineer (6%); artist (5%); draftsperson (5%); agricultural/forestry/economics expert (4%); university graduate/student (5%); other (geologist/psychologist/librarian/social worker/business person) (6.5%).
36 MU6382 File: Board and Committee Minutes: 1958 Correspondence, First Annual Report, Counselling Service, 1 Oct. 1956–1 Oct. 1957.
37 Case #391.
38 Case #2738.
39 See also chapter 7.
40 Quotation from MU6474, File: Reports to the Director 1959–60, Further Programme Planning n.d. (circa 1960); Minutes of Meeting, Professional & Skilled Immigrant-Volunteer Committee 1956 Report (chair Elizabeth Szalowksi).
41 MU6419 (B280556), File: Human Interest Stories, Individual Services Department document (n.d.); MU6474, File: Monthly Reports and Reviews, Individual Services, Annual Report, Oct. 1956–Oct 1957; letter in case #3061 sent to a charitable foundation.
42 MU6382, File: Board and Committee Minutes 1958 Correspondence, Annual Report – Counselling Service, Oct. 1956–Oct. 1957.
43 Case #918 (he suggests over $30 per week); case #3043.
44 Case #2980.
45 Quotation from Case #940 (German). On narrative traces, see chapter 3.
46 Case #681.
47 Case #3001.
48 Case #2133. Case #307. An example includes Ukrainian immigrant Jaroslav Rudnyckyj, who became a Slavic studies professor at the University of Manitoba and an influential commissioner on the Royal Commission on Bilingualism and Biculturalism. See https://www.slideshare.net/ThomasMPrymak/j-b-rudnyckyj-and-canada?qid=3d0b3213-3158-473a-855b-c2c82b34e242&v=&b=&from_search=1 (last accessed 22 May 2021); Eve Haque, *Multiculturalism within a Bilingual Framework: Language, Race, and Belonging in Canada* (Toronto: University of Toronto Press, 2012), 56–205; Aya Fujiwara, *Ethnic Elites and Canadian Identity: Japanese, Ukrainians, and Scots, 1919–1971* (Winnipeg: University of Manitoba Press, 2012), 157–70.
49 Case #3043. On nationalist Ukrainians who mobilized in support of a Ukrainian homeland rid of Soviet control, see Iacovetta, *Gatekeepers*, ch. 5; Luciuk, *Searching for Place,* chs. 6–8; Kassandra Luciuk, "Making Ukrainian Canadians: Identity, Politics, and Power in Cold War Canada" (PhD diss., University of Toronto, 2021).
50 Case #346.
51 Case #6368. MU6467 (B280604), Newspaper Clippings, Lois Wallace, "Hydro solicitor aids Ugandan new Canadians," *Toronto Star,* 2 Feb. 1973, and Final Report

on Uganda Committee of Toronto and Toronto Institute, Mrs K.M. Fletcher, 20 March 1973; MU6411, File: Executive Director Correspondence 1972, Mrs M.D. Stewart to *Toronto Star*, letter "Love for Immigrants"; on Freda Hawkins, one of the "architects" of the Ugandan refugee operation, MU6419 (B280556), File: 13 Immigration Program Development, clipping, Norman Hartley, "Immigration expert favors orientation for new Canadians," n.d.; Muhammedi, "'Gifts from Amin,'" 183–230. On Institute efforts to counter racism, see also chapter 7.

52 Kennedy and Chen, "Career Counselling," which draws on social cognitive career theory developed in R. Lent et al., "Social Cognitive Career Theory," in D. Brown, ed., *Career Choice and Development*, 4th ed. (San Francisco: Jossey-Bass, 2002), 255–311, and narrative career-counselling approach developed in L. Cochran, "Career Counseling: A Narrative Approach," in R. Sharf, ed., *Applying Career Development Theory to Counseling*, 5th ed. (Pacific Grove, CA: Brooks/Cole, 1997), 315–45.

53 MU6472, File: Letters of Appreciation 1959–62, N.S. Bojovic, "International Institute of Metropolitan Toronto and Its Services," Forest Hill Collegiate, 11 Feb. 1960. Points repeated elsewhere, including in letters written on behalf of a client. On immigrant stories circulated through the Institute newsletter, see chapter 7.

54 My discussion of client types (see chapter 3) draws on 51 cases and is informed by such studies as Connell and Messerschmidt, "Hegemonic Masculinity," 836–8, 847–52; Danys, *DP*; Luciuk, *Searching for Place*, chs. 6–8; Raska, *Czech Refugees*; Suri, "Promise and Failure of Developed Socialism."

55 Case #2267; on male breadwinning see discussion below.

56 Case #2967; case #2957.

57 Twenty-one cases.

58 In the first instance, 62 per cent of total (42) engineer cases; in the second, 9 cases involving engineers of European (5), Indian (2), and Chinese (1) origin.

59 Christopher Dummitt *The Manly Modern: Masculinity in Modern Canada* (Vancouver: UBC Press, 2007), but see also Magda Farhni's more nuanced essay on "expert" masculinities in post-1945 Quebec in Gossage and Rutherford, *Making Men*. Written before the "masculinity turn," valuable information on refugee engineers and others is contained in Danys, *DP*, ch. 13.

60 Case #2996; three cases involving engineers. Freund, "Troubling Memories."

61 Case #3027 of seven files.

62 Case #2948. On the IRC, https://www.rescue.org/page/history-international-rescue-committee. (last accessed 9 Oct. 2020).

63 Case #3061.

64 Newspaper clipping in Case #3061; https://www.heliconsociety.com/html/about_us.html (last accessed 9 Oct. 2020).

65 Letter in case #3061.

66 Case #3061.

67 Case #3068. On stories as a rhetorical act, James Phelan and Peter J. Rabinowitz, "Narrative as Rhetoric," in David Herman et al., eds., *Narrative Theory: Core*

Concepts and Critical Debates (Columbus: Ohio State University Press, 2012); Natalie Davis, *Fiction in the Archives* (Stanford, CA: Stanford University Press, 1987).
68 Case #2366.
69 Case #2321. A recent example of the "human capital" argument applied to post-1991 Eastern European professionals in North America is Nina Michalikova, "Segmented Socioeconomic Adaptation of New Eastern European Professionals in the United States," *Comparative Migration Studies* 6, no. 8 (2019): 1–27. For a critique of how the approach neglects the impact of gendered social roles in post-migration outcomes, see Bandana Purkayastha, "Skilled Migration and Cumulative Disadvantage: The Case of Highly Qualified Asian Indian Immigrant Women in the U.S.," *Geoforum* 36, no. 2 (2005):181–96.
70 Case #2750 of four cases.
71 Case #2268.
72 Case #2975.
73 Case #2195.
74 Case #102 and case #929.
75 Case #899.
76 Case #5546; case #6875. I found no reference to female staff identifying as a feminist, but counsellors referred clients to feminist-organized clinics and agencies. On Planned Parenthood – the Toronto clinic was founded in 1961 see Percy Skuy, "Canadian Pioneers in Family Planning," *History of Medicine Blog*, 1998, https://www.jogc.com/article/S0849-5831(16)30075-1/pdf (last accessed 15 May 2021).
77 Case #300. Canadian Council for Refugees, "A Hundred Years of Immigration to Canada, 1900–1999 (Pt 2)," https://ccrweb.ca/en/hundred-years-immigration-canada-part-2 (last accessed 22 May 2021).
78 The respective totals are four and three.
79 Case #3024.
80 Case #2160 (of five employment letters).
81 Case #2958.
82 Case #2286.
83 Case #3030; case #976; case #398.
84 Case #2959.
85 Case #286; case #995.
86 Note, too, that, though limited, the gender analysis in such studies as Danys, *DP*; Raska, *Czech Refugees*; Peddie, *Young, Well-educated, Adaptable* distinguishes them from the treatment of professionals in the books in the Generation Series on the *Peoples of Canada* publications funded by the federal Department of the Secretary of State, such as Henry Radecki and Benedykt Heydenkorn, *A Member of a Distinguished Family: The Polish Group in Canada* (Toronto: McClelland and Stewart, 1976).
87 Phan et al., "Family Dynamics," 2063–75.
88 Nine of fifteen case files; Raska, *Czech Refugees*, 160. See also Jarmila L.A. Horna, "The Entrance Status of Czech and Slovak Immigrant Women," in Jean Leonard

Elliott, ed., *Two Nations, Many Cultures: Ethnic Groups in Canada* (Scarborough, ON: Prentice-Hall, 1979); on feminist daycare lobbies, Susan Prentice, "Workers, Mothers, Reds: Toronto's Postwar Daycare Fight," *Studies in Political Economy* 30, no. 1 (1989): 115–41; *Day Care for Everyone* (Daycare Organizing Committee, Toronto, 1973–4), and *Good Daycare* (Daycare Reform Action Alliance), both in *Rise Up! A Digital Archive of Feminist Activism*, https://riseupfeministarchive.ca/ (last accessed 9 Oct. 2020).

89 Case #4911; general observation drawn from 82 files in the female professional group.
90 Case #337.
91 Case #3054.
92 Case #3054; case #315.
93 Flynn, *Moving beyond Borders*; Danys, *DP* 252; cluster of 21 cases.
94 Case #813.
95 MU6472, Files: Letters of Appreciation 1959–62, Letter, Olga Fedeyko, 20 March 1960.
96 Alas, these files shed little light on how women maintained a sense of professionalism and dignity in work contexts where they were devalued and belittled. On this theme, and how racism significantly shaped the context, see Flynn, *Moving Beyond Borders*.
97 Case #4746.
98 Case #1857.
99 Case #4894.

5 Marital Conflict, Emotions, and "De-culturalizing" Violence

1 Archives of Ontario (AO), International Institute of Metropolitan Toronto, Fonds 884, Sub-series E-3, MU6507-MU6567 (case files), case #4263 of a 7,000-casefile database (see Appendix). Dorothy Chunn, "Reshaping Deviant Families through Family Courts: The Birth of 'Socialized Justice' in Ontario, 1920–40," *International Journal of the Sociology of Law* 16 (1988): 137–58.
2 Case #4263. On Greek immigrants, who, like other Southern Europeans, were mainly humble rural people with some primary schooling, see chapter 8.
3 Shahrzad Mojab, "The Politics of Culture, Racism, and Nationalism in Honour Killing," *Canadian Criminal Law Review* 16, no. 2 (2012): 115–34, esp. 127–30. See also her "The Particularity of 'Honour' and the Universality of 'Killing': From Early Warning Signs to Feminist Pedagogy," in S. Mojab and N. Abdo, eds., *Violence in the Name of Honour: Theoretical and Political Challenges* (Istanbul: Bilgi University Press, 2004), 15–37.
4 There are many histories that document social welfare encounters, but among the few examples that relate to the material at hand are Linda Gordon, *Heroes of Their Own Lives: The Politics and History of Family Violence, Boston 1880–1960*

(New York: Viking, 1988); Mark Peel, *Miss Cutler and the Case of the Resurrected Horse: Social Work and the Story of Poverty in America, Australia, and Britain* (Chicago: University of Chicago Press, 2012); essays by Margaret Little and others in Franca Iacovetta and Wendy Mitchinson, *On the Case: Explorations in Social History* (Toronto: University of Toronto Press, 1998); David Peterson del Mar, *What Troubles I Have Seen: A History of Violence against Wives* (Cambridge, MA: Harvard University Press, 1996); Joan Sangster, *Regulating Girls and Women: Sexuality, Family, and the Law in Ontario, 1920–1960* (Don Mills, ON: Oxford University Press, 2001); Margaret Little, *No Car, No Radio, No Liquor Permit: The Moral Regulation of Single Mothers in Ontario, 1920–1997* (Toronto: Oxford University Press, 1998).

5 Peel, *Miss Cutler*, 8–9 and passim. See also Gordon, *Heroes*, 298.
6 See Sarah Pinto, "The History of Emotions in Australia," *Australian Historical Studies* 48 (2017): 103–14 and references below.
7 Peel, *Miss Cutler*, 5, citing Eileen Yeo, *The Contest for Social Science: Relations and Representations of Gender and Class* (London: Rivers Oram Press, 1996), 249.
8 For example, for *Gatekeepers: Reshaping Immigrant Lives in Cold War Canada* (Toronto: Between the Lines, 2006), I drew on one dozen mostly wife-assault cases involving mostly Eastern Europeans, particularly Hungarian "1956ers" from a set of 1,105 files (222–31; 252–5). A preliminary article in Franca Iacovetta and Mariana Valverde, eds., *Gender Conflicts* (Toronto: University of Toronto Press, 1992), drew on only 320 files across a six-year period (1956–62).
9 On the more specific debate over whether to view honour-based violence as distinct from domestic violence but in alignment with violence against women more broadly, or as falling within the spectrum of domestic violence, see, in the first instance, Shahrzad Mojab, "Politics of Culture"; Mohammad Mazher Idriss, "Not Domestic Violence or Cultural Tradition: Is Honour-based Violence Distinct from Domestic Violence? *Journal of Social Welfare and Family Law* 39, no. 1 (2017): 3–21; and, in second, Wendy Aujla and Aisha K. Gill, "Conceptualizing 'Honour' Killings in Canada: An Extreme Form of Domestic Violence?" *International Journal of Criminal Justice Sciences* 9, no. 1 (2014): 153–66; Aruna Papp, *Culturally Driven Violence against Women: A Growing Problem in Canada's Immigrant Communities* (Winnipeg: Manitoba Frontier Centre for Public Policy, 2010).
10 See, for example, *Learning Network*, issue 26, *Intimate Partner Violence against Immigrant and Refugee Women*, https://www.vawlearningnetwork.ca/issue-26-intimate-partner-violence-against-immigrant-and-refugee-women (last accessed 30 May 2021), and discussion below.
11 This discussion draws on several sources, including N. Eustace et al., "AHR Conversations: The Historical Study of Emotions," *American Historical Review* 117 (2012): 1487–531; Barbara H. Rosenwein, "Worrying about Emotions in History," *American Historical Review* 107, no. 3 (June 2002): 821–45; Barbara H. Rosenwein, "Problems and Methods in the History of Emotions," *Passions in Context* 1

(2010): 1–32; Peter N. Stearns and Carol Z. Stearns, "'Emotionology'": Clarifying the History of Emotion and Emotional Standards," *American Historical Review* 90, no. 4 (Oct. 1985): 813–36; Jan Plamper, *The History of Emotions: An Introduction*, trans. Keith Tribe (New York: Oxford University Press, 2015); William M. Reddy, "Against Constructionism: The Historical Ethnology of Emotions," *Current Anthropology* 38 (1997): 327–51.

12 Ann Laura Stoler, "Tense and Tender Ties: The Politics of Comparison in North American History and (Post) Colonial Studies," *Journal of American History* 88 (2001): 829–65 and responses, 893–897; Rhacel Salazar Parreñas, "Mothering from a Distance: Emotions, Gender, and Intergenerational Relations in Filipino Transnational Families," *Feminist Studies* 27 no. 2 (Summer 2001): 361–90.

13 Eustace et al., "AHR Conversations," 1525–6.

14 As in Joan Scott's position in the debate with Linda Gordon over *Heroes* in *Signs* 15 (1990). See also chapter 3.

15 Reddy, "Against Constructionism"; Frank Biess, "'Everybody Has a Chance': Nuclear Angst, Civil Defense, and the History of Emotions in Postwar West Germany," *German History* 27, no. 2 (2009): 215–43.

16 As in "social groups whose members adhere to the same valuations of emotions and their expression." Rosenwein, "Problems and Methods," 1.

17 Ibid., 10–24; Barbara H. Rosenwein and Riccardo Cristiani, *What Is the History of Emotions?* (Cambridge, UK: Polity Press, 2018).

18 A tiny sample of the large body of multidisciplinary work on immigrant women and violence includes Mojab, "Politics of Culture"; Shahrzad Mojab, "'Honor Killing': Culture, Politics and Theory," *Middle East Women's Studies Review* 17, no. 1 (2002): 1–7; Aisha K. Gill et al., eds., *"Honour" Killing and Violence; Theory, Policy and Practice* (New York: Palgrave Macmillan, 2014); Papp, *Culturally Driven Violence*; Gordon, *Heroes*; Karen Dubinsky and Franca Iacovetta, "Murder, Womanly Virtue and Motherhood: The Case of Angelina Napolitano, 1911–22," *Canadian Historical Review* 72, no. 4 (Dec 1991): 505–31; Himani Bannerji, *The Dark Side of the Nation: Essays on Multiculturalism, Nationalism, and Gender* (Toronto: Canadian Scholars Press, 2000), ch. 5; and references below.

19 These are Hungarians (26), Portuguese (11), Greeks (10), Italians (7), Yugoslavians (7), and Germans (5). Other groups represented include Polish, Ukrainian, Spanish, Dutch, Czech, Slovak, Belgian, Austrian, French, Indian, Jamaican, Colombian, and Filipino.

20 The breakdown is Hungarian (21), Greek (9), Portuguese (7), Yugoslavian (7), Italian (5), German (5), Polish (3), Ukrainian (3), Slovak (3), Dutch (2), Czech (2), and 1 each of Austrian, Belgian, Colombian, French, Indian, Jamaican, Filipino, Spanish. Those from better-off backgrounds (56%) slightly outnumber those of plebian origin (44%).

21 The breakdown is Hungarian (5), Portuguese (4), Italian (2), Ukrainian (2), Czech (2), Yugoslavian (2), Greek (2), and 1 each of Austrian, Dutch, French, Indian,

Polish, Slovakian. Those of better-off origins (58%) outnumber those of plebeian backgrounds (42%).
22 A sample of the extensive literature includes Katharine Harvey, "To Love, Honour and Obey: Wife Battering in Working Class Montreal, 1869–79," *Urban history Review* 19 no. 2 (Oct. 1992): 128–40; Carolyn Strange, "Historical Perspectives on Wife Assault," in Mariana Valverde et al., eds., *Wife Assault and the Canadian Criminal Justice System* (Toronto: Centre for Criminology, University of Toronto, 1995): 293–304; Annalee Goltz, "Uncovering and Reconstructing Family Violence: Ontario Criminal Case Files," in Iacovetta and Mitchinson, *On the Case*; Judith Fingard, "The Prevention of Cruelty, Marital Breakdown and the Rights of Wives, 1880–1920," *Acadiensis* 22, no. 2 (1993): 131–48; Dubinsky and Iacovetta, "Murder, Womanly Virtue, and Motherhood"; Sangster, *Regulating Girls and Women*; Tracy Chapman, "'Till Death Do Us Part: Wife Beating in Alberta, 1905–20," *Alberta History* 36, no. 4 (1998); James Snell, "Marital Cruelty: Women and the Nova Scotia Divorce Court, 1900–39," *Acadiensis* 18 (Autumn 1988): 3–32.
23 Besides Gordon, *Heroes*, see, for example, Lynn Abrams, "Whores, Whore-Chasers, and Swine: The Regulation of Sexuality in Nineteenth-Century German Divorce Court," *Journal of Family History* 21, no. 3 (1996): 267–80; Elizabeth Pleck, *Domestic Tyranny* (Oxford: Oxford University Press, 1987); del Mar, *What Troubles I Have Seen*; Ellen Ross, "Fierce Questions and Taunts: Married Life in Working-Class London, 1870–1914," *Feminist Studies* 8, no. 3 (Fall 1982): 575–602; Nancy Tomes, "A Torrent of Abuse: Crimes and Violence between Working-class Men and Women in London, 1840–75," *Journal of Social History* 11, no. 3 (1978): 328–45; Jeffrey S. Adler, "'We've got a right to fight; we're married': Domestic Homicide in Chicago, 1875–1920," *Journal of Interdisciplinary History* 34, no. 1 (2003): 27–48.
24 On this theme, Roxanna Ng, "Gendering Policy Research on Immigration," in *Gendering Immigration/Integration Policy Research* (Ottawa: Status of Women, 1998); Iacovetta, *Gatekeepers*, 264–70; Ju Hui Judy Han, "Safety for Immigrant, Refugee and Non-status Women: A Literature Review," in *Immigrant Women's Project: Safety of Immigrant, Refugee, and Non-status Women* (Vancouver: Ending Violence Association of British Columbia, Vancouver, Mosaic, & Lower Mainland Multicultural Family Support Services Society, 2011), https://endingviolence.org/wp-content/uploads/2014/03/IWP_Resource_Guide_FINAL.pdf, 11–15 and passim (last accessed 6 Aug. 2020).
25 Besides *Gatekeepers*, see Franca Iacovetta, "The Sexual Politics of Moral Citizenship and Containing Dangerous Foreign Men in Cold War Canada," *Histoire Sociale/Social History* 33, no. 66 (2002): 361–81.
26 Case #2174; case #458.
27 Case #147; case #5440.
28 Case #146; case #4351.
29 Case #5981.

30 Case #1459.
31 Case #325. For one example, see Immigration History Research Center Archives, Elmer L. Andersen Library, University of Minnesota, American Council for Nationalities Service records, which contain the American Federation of International Institutes collection, Box 2786, File: 14, Peter Sandi, "Contrasts and Comparisons in American and Italian Concepts and Practices in Social Work," 15 May 1958.
32 Case #325.
33 Case #4297.
34 Case #4093.
35 Case #2897.
36 Case #3887. A reference to the Ontario Medical Services Insurance Plan, or OMSIP, Ontario's first government-run health plan, established in 1966, and precursor to today's medicare plan.
37 Only one man, a Czech tradesman, 37, admitted that his refusal to change his "bachelor" ways had driven his wife away, though he claimed they remained friends and he visited his son. An artist, he had come to the Institute for help in registering in an art school. Case #837.
38 Case #2747; case #1654.
39 Case #2355.
40 Case #2168. On the rarity of mother's sexual abuse of children, especially daughters, see, for example, David Finkelhor, *Sexually Victimized Children* (New York: Free Press, 1979), 93–4; Gordon, *Heroes*, ch. 7.
41 These cases – #2911 and #4577 – attracted media attention, and are also discussed below.
42 Golz, "Family Violence," 300.
43 Case #4482 of four cases.
44 Arlie Russell Hochschild, *The Managed Heart, Commercialization of Human Feeling* (Berkeley: University of California Press, 1983). See also Paul Brook, "In Critical Defence of 'Emotional Labor': Refuting Bolton's Critique of Hochschild's Concept," *Work, Employment and Society* 23, no. 3 (2009): 531–48.
45 Front-line female social workers also perform caring labour, which involves a "care penalty" that takes various forms, including a loss of personal time and missed-out experiences. Nancy Folbre, *The Invisible Heart: Economics and Family Values* (New York: The New Press, 2012).
46 Brian E. Bride, "Prevalence of Secondary Traumatic Stress among Social Workers," *Social Work* 52, no. 1 (2007): 63–70; April Naturale, "Secondary Traumatic Stress in Social Workers Responding to Disasters, *Clinical Social Work Journal* 35 (2007): 173–81; Nicky James, "Care = organisation + physical labour + emotional labour," *Sociology of Health & Illness* 14, no. 4 (1992): 488–509.
47 Case #3059.
48 See chapters 3 and 7.

346 Notes to pages 90–7

49 Together, they handled 14 of the 19 cases handled by women counsellors in the minority group of 25 cases.
50 As I explain in the Appendix, for privacy reasons, I do not reveal the identity of the counsellor whose case file I am examining, but a general profile of the counselling staff is in chapter 3.
51 Case #4078 and case #301 of 10 cases.
52 Case #4184 of 4 cases. Migration scholars have interpreted the term or idea of emotional transnationalism in different ways, but my meaning parallels that of Parreñas, "Mothering from a Distance."
53 Case #4196.
54 Case #4115. On this theme, see, for example, Karen Tice, *Tales of Wayward Girls and Immoral Women: Case Records and the Professionalization of Social Work* (Urbana: University of Illinois Press, 1998),129–34.
55 Case #2477. On this theme, see also Little, *No Car, No Radio.*
56 Case #2815.
57 On this theme, see chapter 4.
58 Case #4292.
59 The cluster of 14 cases includes 6 lengthy cases.
60 For a detailed treatment of these patterns and themes, see Iacovetta, "Sexual Politics of Moral Citizenship."
61 Case #3653.
62 Case #3095.
63 Case #2918.
64 On professional relationships, see, for example, Tice, *Wayword Girls*, ch. 5, which, like most social work histories, focuses on cross-class relationships.
65 Case #2233. The case ends on that point.
66 One example is Papp, *Culturally Driven Violence*, esp. 15–16. See also the discussion of the debate in Aujla and Gill, "Conceptualizing 'Honour' Killings."
67 Mojab, "Politics of Culture"; Idriss, "Not Domestic Violence or Cultural Tradition."
68 Case #2911; case #4577 (both case files contain newspaper clippings but I have not cited them here for privacy reasons). See also Adler, "'We've got a right to fight.'"
69 This discussion draws on a range of sources, including Maria Kalogeropoulou, "Columns of the House, Proud Workers, Greek Immigrant Women in Vancouver, 1954–1975" (PhD diss., Simon Fraser University, 2015), esp. chs. 1–3; Efi Avdela, "'Corrupting and Uncontrollable Activities': Moral Panic about Youth in Post-Civil-War Greece," *Journal of Contemporary History* 43, no. 1 (2008): 25–44; Noula Mina, "Taming and Training Greek 'Peasant Girls' and the Gender Politics of Whiteness in Postwar Canada: Canadian Bureaucrats and Greek Domestics, 1950s–1960s," *Canadian Historical Review* 94, no. 4 (2013): 514–39; Donna Gabaccia, "Honor and Shame in a Mobile World," unpublished paper, 2003, and

subject of a 2009 conference at the Rockefeller Center in Bellagio, Italy, in 2009; Franca Iacovetta, *Such Hardworking People: Italians in Postwar Toronto* (Montreal/Kingston: McGill-Queen's University Press, 1992), ch. 5; Loretta Baldassar, "Marias and Marriage: Ethnicity, Gender and Sexuality among Italo-Australian Youth in Perth," *Journal of Sociology* 35, no. 1 (1999): 1–22; Wenona Giles, *Portuguese Women in Toronto* (Toronto: University of Toronto Press, 2002), 10–11, 39–40; 58–61, 73–4.

70 Janet Elise Johnson, "Contesting Violence, Contesting Gender Crisis Centers: Encountering Local Government in Barnaul, Russia," in Janet Elise Johnson and Jean C. Robinson, eds., *Living Gender after Communism* (Bloomington: Indiana University Press, 2007), 40–1; L. Shelley, "Inter-personal Violence in the USSR," *Violence, Aggression and Terrorism* 1, no. 2 (1987): 41–67; V. Sperling, "Rape and Domestic Violence in the USSR: Response to the Victimization of Women and Children," *Journal of the Center for Women Policy Studies* 13, no. 3 (1990): 16–22. See also the Introduction and the essay on multiculturalism and honour killings by Marlou Schrover in Marlou Schrover and Deirdre M. Moloney, eds., *Gender, Migration and Categorisation: Making Distinctions between Migrants in Western Countries, 1945–2010* (Amsterdam: Amsterdam University Press, 2013).

71 Case #3653; case #985; and case #239.

72 Papp, *Culturally Driven Violence*; https://www.vawlearningnetwork.ca/issue-26-intimate-partner-violence-against-immigrant-and-refugee-women (last accessed 30 May 2021).

73 Papp, *Culturally Driven Violence*, 8–10. See also Holly Maguigan, "Cultural Evidence and Male Violence: Are Feminists and Multicultural Reformists on a Collision Course in Criminal Courts?" *New York University Law Review* (1995): 36–99 (on South East Asian cases in the United States). For a comprehensive report that draws on studies from across Canada, see *The Safety of Immigrant, Refugee, and Non-Status Women Project: Ending Violence* (Vancouver: Association of BC, MOSAIC, & Vancouver & Lower Mainland Multicultural Family Support Services Society, 2014), https://endingviolence.org/wp-content/uploads/2014/03/IWP_Resource_Guide_FINAL.pdf (last accessed 30 May 2021).

74 https://www.vawlearningnetwork.ca/issue-26-intimate-partner-violence-against-immigrant-and-refugee-women (last accessed 30 May 2021).

75 Papp, *Culturally Driven Violence*, 10, 17–18.

76 Sharzad, "Politics of Culture," 124.

77 https://www.vawlearningnetwork.ca/issue-26-intimate-partner-violence-against-immigrant-and-refugee-women (last accessed 30 May 2021).

6 Generational Conflict: Intimacy, Money, and "Miniskirt" Feminism

1 The OEC (1968–85) advised the cabinet of the Ontario government on raising public awareness in regard to major socioeconomic issues. See https://

thecanadianencyclopedia.ca/en/article/ontario-economic-council/ (last accessed 28 Aug. 2020).
2 Cited in Chris Braithwaite, "Somewhere between Mosaic and Melting Pot: Program to Help Immigrants Adjust to Canadian Ways Urged," Archives of Ontario (AO), International Institute of Metropolitan Toronto, Fonds 884, MU6406, File: Clippings, Immigration.
3 *Toronto Telegram*, 24 July 1970, editorial, "Immigrant policies condemned," in MU6406, File: Clippings, Immigration.
4 Cited in "Report's author a 'middle-roader,'" no author, in MU6406, File: Clippings, Immigration.
5 On this theme, see chapter 2 and part 4.
6 Braithwaite, "Somewhere between Mosaic."
7 Braithwaite, "Somewhere between Mosaic." See also Michael Cobden, "Pretty twins feel stifled at home," *Toronto Star*, in MU6406, File: Clippings, Immigration.
8 Many studies of juvenile delinquency and child protection agencies, including those cited in this chapter, make similar points, but on redemption and detective tales, and on gossip and hearsay evidence, see Karen Tice, *Tales of Wayward Girls and Immoral Women: Case Records and the Professionalization of Social Work* (Urbana: University of Illinois Press, 1998), ch. 4; Mark Peel, *Miss Cutler and the Case of the Resurrected Horse: Social Work and the Theory of Poverty in America, Australia, and Britain* (Chicago: University of Chicago Press, 2012), ch. 4 and passim; Franca Iacovetta, "Gossip, Contest and Power in the Making of Postwar Suburban Bad Girls: Toronto 1940s–1950s," *Canadian Historical Review* 80, no. 4 (1999): 585–623.
9 On this theme, see also Abril Liberatori, "'Family Is Really All Over the Place': Ethnic Identity Formation within a Transnational Network" (PhD diss., York University, 2017), ch. 3.
10 This admittedly eclectic list includes Joan Scott and Louise Tilly, *Women, Work and Family* (Holt, Rinehart and Winston, 1978); David L. Kertzer and Mario Barbaglia, eds., *The History of the European Family*, vol. 2, *Family Life in the Long Nineteenth Century 1789–1913* (New Haven, CT: Yale University Press 2002); Enrico T. Carlson Cumbo, "As the Twig Is Bent, the Tree's Inclined": Growing Up Italian in Toronto, 1905–1940" (PhD diss., University of Toronto, 1996); Karen Dubinsky, *Improper Advances: Rape and Heterosexual Conflict in Ontario, 1880–1929* (Chicago: University of Chicago Press, 1993).
11 Examples include Elizabeth Ewen, *Immigrant Women in the Land of Dollars: Life and Culture on the Lower East Side, 1890–1925* (New York: Monthly Review Press, 1985); Judith E. Smith, *Family Connections: A History of Italian and Jewish Immigrant Lives in Providence, Rhode Island 1900–1940* (Albany: State University of New York Press, 1985); Donna Gabaccia, *From the Other Side: Women, Gender, and Immigrant Life in the U.S., 1820–1990* (Bloomington: Indiana University Press, 1994); Loretta Baldassar and Donna Gabaccia, eds., *Intimacy and Italian*

Notes to pages 103–5 349

Migration: Gender and Domestic Lives in a Mobile World (New York: Fordham University Press, 2011); M. Gail Hickey, "'Go to College, Get a Job, and Don't Leave the House without Your Brother': Oral Histories with Immigrant Women and Their Daughters," *Oral History Review* 23, no. 2 (1996): 63–92; Cumbo, "Twig Is Bent."

12 A few North American examples include Dorothy Chunn, *From Punishment to Doing Good: Family Courts and Socialized Justice in Ontario, 1880–1940* (Toronto: University of Toronto Press, 1992); Ellen Ryerson, *The Best-Laid Plans: America's Juvenile Court Experiment* (New York: Hill and Wang, 1978); Iacovetta, "Gossip, Contest and Power"; Joan Sangster, *Girl Trouble: Female Delinquency in English Canada* (Toronto: Between the Lines, 2002); Bryan Hogeveen, "'The Evils with Which We Are Called to Grapple': Elite Reformers, Eugenicists, Environmental Psychologists, and the Construction of Toronto's Working-Class Boy Problem, 1860–1930," *Labour/LeTravail* 55 (Spring 2005): 37–68; Michael Boudreau, "'Delinquents Often Become Criminals': Juvenile Delinquency in Halifax, 1918–1935," *Acadiensis* 39, no. 1 (2010): 108–32.

13 Mary Odem, *Delinquent Daughters: Protecting and Policing Adolescent Female Sexuality in the United States, 1885–1920* (Chapel Hill: University of North Carolina Press, 1995). An important correction to the valuable but heavily Protestant-skewed English Canadian literature is Tamara Myers, *Caught: Montreal's Modern Girls and the Law* (Toronto: University of Toronto Press, 2006), which also makes effective use of a large number of case files.

14 Besides those already noted, see, for example, Regina K. Kunzel, *Fallen Women, Problem Girls: Unmarried Mothers and the Professionalization of Social Work, 1890 to 1945* (New Haven, CT: Yale University, 1993); Sharon Wall, "Some thought they were 'in Love': Sex, White Teenagehood, and Unmarried Pregnancy in Early Postwar Canada," *Journal of the Canadian Historical Association/Revue de la Société historique du Canada* 25, no. 1 (2014): 207–41.

15 Archives of Ontario (AO), International Institute of Metropolitan Toronto, Fonds 884, Sub-series E-3, MU6507-MU6525 (case files), on 7,000-case file database see Appendix. The ethnic breakdown for the 150 cases is Italians (20%), Portuguese (18%), Hungarian (17%), Greek (15%), German (5%), Yugoslavian (5%), Czech (3%), Slovak (3%), Russian (2%), Polish (2%), 1% for Armenian, Spanish, Ukrainian, Jamaican; and just under 1% for Austrian, Croatian, Serb, Estonian, Egyptian, Colombian, Korean, and British.

16 Adult defined as 25 years and over for singletons; 21 and over for married children.

17 Case #4919; case #7; case #222 of 12 cases. For a widow's pension, the residency requirement was five years.

18 Case #85.

19 Case #865; case #4814.

20 Case #3990. On my use of an emotions approach, see chapter 5.

21 Case #2143.
22 On the centre's history, https://masaryktown.ca/?page_id=231 (last accessed 22 Sept. 2020).
23 Case #728. The OHC was established in 1964 to provide socialized housing. C. Valkii-Zad, "Privatizing Public Housing in Canada, A Public Policy Agenda," *Housing and the Built Environment* 11, no. 1 (1996): 47–68.
24 Case #896.
25 Case #2813.
26 For just two Canadian examples, Mona Gleason, *Normalizing the Ideal: Psychology, Schooling, and the Family in Postwar Canada* (Toronto: University of Toronto Press, 1999); Franca Iacovetta, *Gatekeepers: Reshaping Immigrant Lives in Cold War Canada* (Toronto: Between the Lines, 2006), ch. 7. See also chapter 5.
27 Case #190. chapter 3 discusses Institute applications of social-cultural analyses.
28 Case #4044.
29 Case #2829. On male social workers, see Peel, *Miss Cutler*, part 6, chs. 27–30.
30 Mary Louise Adams, *The Trouble with Normal: Postwar Youth and the Making of Heterosexuality* (Toronto: University of Toronto Press, 1997); Iacovetta, *Gatekeepers*, ch. 5, esp. 195–99; Mariana Valverde, "Building Anti-Delinquent Communities: Morality, Gender, and Generation in the City," in Joy Parr, ed., *A Diversity of Women: Ontario, 1945–80* (Toronto: University of Toronto Press, 1995).
31 Benjamin Schlesinger, "The Social Cultural Elements in Casework: The Canadian Scene," *Social Worker* 30, no. 1 (1962); Edith Ferguson, *Newcomers and New Learning* (hereafter *NNL*) (Toronto: International Institute of Metropolitan Toronto, 1964–6), 2–4, 33–8, 50, 68–70. On the multicultural programming, see part 4.
32 "Idiot's Machine or Educational Split over TV," *Globe and Mail*, 8 July 1965.
33 "Boy needs interpreter in own home," *Toronto Star* (photo of Victor and parents), in MU6406, File: Clippings, Immigration. They would have been among the small number of Hong Kongers who immigrated to Canada in the 1950s and 1960s.
34 Costa and Katz in Sidney Katz, "Canadian way of life splits the generations in immigrant families," *Toronto Star*, 4 July 1970; Christie Blatchford, "Generation Gap Splitting Greeks," *Globe and Mail*, 27 Feb. 1973, and critical letter by George Papadatos, 7 March 1973. On this theme, see also Cumbo, "Twig Is Bent," ch. 1. Beginning in the mid-1970s, daughter/mother relations were attracting the attention of social scientists. See Kurt Danziger, "The Acculturation of Italian Immigrant Girls in Canada," *International Journal of Psychology* 9, no. 2 (1974): 129–37; Giuliana Colalillo, "Patterns of Socialization among Italian Adolescent Girls, *Journal of Baltic Studies* 10, no. 1 (Spring 1979): 43–50; Wenona Giles, *Portuguese Women in Toronto: Gender, Immigration, and Nationalism* (Toronto: University of Toronto Press, 2002); Judith Nagata, "Adaptation and Integration of Greek Working-Class Immigrants in Toronto, Canada: A Situational Approach," *International Migration Review* 4, no. 1 (1969): 44–70.

35 Cited in Katz, "Canadian way of life"; Serge, "Immigrants' mental ills."
36 City of Toronto Archives, Social Planning Council of Metropolitan Toronto, SC40, Box 56, File 13 I/M/E/G: Newcomers' Research: Experiment in Bringing Services [1960–6], Edith Ferguson, Notes on Interview with Chief Attendance Officer, Metropolitan Toronto Separate School Board, 1 Sept. 1960.
37 These 80 cases involved 42 girls and 38 boys. The ethnic breakdown is Italian (36), Portuguese (23), Greek (16), and one each for Polish, Hungarian, Russian, German, and Ukrainian. The age breakdown is 14–15 (20) and 16–19 (60).
38 Mona Gleason, "Avoiding the Agency Trap: Caveats for Historians of Children, Youth and Education," *History of Education* 45, no. 4 (2016): 448.
39 See Peel, *Miss Cutler*, part 3, esp. case 3 and ch. 15; Tice, *Wayward Girls*, 66–7.
40 Case #1624. Twenty-five per cent of the wage-earning teens were under 16. On homeownership, see also chapter 8; for other groups, John Bodnar, "Immigration and Modernization: The Case of Slavic Peasants in America," *Journal of Social History* (Fall 1974): 44–71.
41 Case #4113, case #4731, and case #1624 of five cases. On these themes, see also Miriam Cohen, *Workshop to Office: Two Generations of Italian Women in New York City, 1900–1950* (Ithaca, NY: Cornell University Press, 1993), chs. 4–5; Bodnar, "Immigration and Modernization; Peel, *Miss Cutler*, chs. 15–19.
42 Case #4692; case #4702. On emotional descriptors, see chapter 5.
43 Case #4178. See also Cumbo, "Twig Is Bent," 100, 170, 288.
44 Case #4537 and case #4151; case #1916 of 17 cases. See also Cohen, *Workshop to Office*, 161–3, 178–82.
45 Giles, *Portuguese Women in Toronto*, 37, 81–5; author conversation with three Italian Canadian informants.
46 Case #4526.
47 Case #4168 of five cases.
48 Case #1145.
49 Seven such cases.
50 Case #51. Doug Owram, *Born at the Right Time: A History of the Baby Boom Generation* (Toronto: University of Toronto Press, 1996); Margaret Walsh, "Gender and the Automobile in the United States," https://www.autolife.umd.umich.edu/Gender/Walsh/G_Overview3.htm (last accessed 22 Sept. 2020); Steve Penfold, "'Are we to go literally to the hotdogs': Parking Lots, Drive-ins, and the Critique of Progress in Toronto's Suburbs, 1965–1975," *Urban History Review/Revue d'histoire urbaine* 33, no. 1 (Fall 2004): 8–16; Christopher Dummitt, The Manly Modern: Masculinity in Postwar Canada (Vancouver: UBC Press, 2007), 125–31; Catherine Genovese, "T-Bucket Terror to Respectable Races in Vancouver, B.C., 1948–1965," in Jim Conley and Arlene Tigar McLaren, eds., *Car Troubles: Critical Studies of Automobility and Auto-mobility* (Farnham: Ashgate Publishing, 2009), 21–36. On cars in the delinquency literature, see, for example, Iacovetta, "Gossip, Context, and Power"; Wall, "Some thought they were 'in Love.'"

352 Notes to pages 115–18

51 Liberatori, "'Family Is Really All Over the Place,'" ch. 3; Karen Elizabeth Ross, "Deconstructing the 'Good Catholic Girl': A Critique of Sexual Pedagogies for Young Women in Catholic Ethics" (PhD diss., Loyola University, Chicago, 2018), ch. 3.
52 See, for example, Martin Schiff's series on marginalized teens, "The Long Wait for Development," parts 2 and 3, *Globe and Mail*, 11 and 12 July 1961.
53 Gilberto Fernandes, *This Pilgrim Nation: The Making of the Portuguese Diaspora in Postwar North America* (Toronto: University of Toronto Press, 2020), ch. 7; Vienna Paolantonio, "Good Friday on College Street: Urban Space and Changing Italian Identity" (PhD diss., York University, 2020), 132, 182–4; Marcel Danesi and Alberto Di Giovanni, "Italian as a Heritage Language in Ontario: A Historical Sketch," *Polyphony* 11, nos. 1–2 (1989): 91–4. See also Clifford Jansen, *Factbook on Italians in Canada* (Institute for Behavioural Research, York University, 1981); Nagata, "Greek Working-Class Immigrants." On folk culture ethnic revivalism, see part 4.
54 Giles, *Portuguese Women in Toronto*, 9–10.
55 Fernandes, *Pilgrim Nation*, 280–5; Susana Miranda, "'Not Ashamed or Afraid': Portuguese Immigrant Women in Toronto's Cleaning Industry, 1950–1995 (PhD diss., York University, 2010), ch. 4, esp., 195–261.
56 Case #3993; case #4091.
57 See, for example, "Downtown children aren't dumb – they need a better program (Park School Parents' Brief), *Toronto Star*, 16 Nov. 1971; Harvey Schachter, "Why poor kids never catch up with the wealthy," Special Report, *Toronto Star*, 25 Feb. 1978; James Royson and Leslie Papp, "School system fails to educate black children, parents charge," *Toronto Star*, 17 Jan. 1989.
58 Sandro Contenta, *Rituals of Failure: What Schools Really Teach* (Toronto: Between the Lines, 1993). In summer 1990, the Ontario government pledged to phase out Grade 9 streaming of students into academic and applied tracks in 2021, but it remains to be seen. See https://toronto.ctvnews.ca/ontario-to-begin-phasing-out-grade-9-applied-and-academic-streaming-in-2021-1.5017071 (last accessed 13 Nov. 2021).
59 Joseph Hall, "*Marchese tries to meet needs of immigrants*," *Toronto Star*, 24 Sept. 1990.
60 Aaron Benavot, "The Rise and Decline of Vocational Education," *Sociology of Education* 56, no. 2 (1983); a play on Owram, *Born at the Right Time;* Gillian Mitchell, *The North American Folk Music Revival: Nation and Identity in the United States and Canada, 1945–1980*, 2nd ed. (Abingdon: Routledge, 2016). On vocational training for immigrant adults, see chapter 8.
61 Joe Serge, "Immigrants' mental ills blamed on pace," *Toronto Star*, 23 May 1970. See also Leslie Scrivener, "Immigrant kids in cultural clash," *Toronto Star*, 23 Aug. 1980. Such images long predated this period; see, for Toronto, Cumbo, "Twig Is Bent," ch. 2.

62 Costa in Katz, "Canadian way of life." See also Giles, *Portuguese Women in Toronto*, 39–41, 57–8.
63 The ethnic breakdown of the 20 cases in question is Hungarian (3), Italian (3), Portuguese (3), Greek (2), and 1 each for Czech, German, Jamaican, Korean, Polish, Serbian, Slovakian, Ukrainian, Yugoslavian. There are 13 girls and 7 boys. Most cases are very brief.
64 Conversation with three Italian Canadian informants; see also Cumbo, "Twig Is Bent," ch. 1. Similar points are made in the delinquency literature cited above.
65 Case #2465. For a detailed treatment of equally revealing cases involving an Italian and a Mexican mother and their "delinquent" daughters discussed during a 1945 training session at the International Institute of San Francisco, see Franca Iacovetta and Erica Toffoli, "A Double-Edged Pluralism: Paradoxes of Diversity in the International Institute Movement, 1945–1965," *Journal of Social History* 54, no. 3 (2021): 897–919.
66 Case #2465.
67 Ibid., Probation officer to Institute, 29 Sept. 60. See also MU6472, Files: Letters of Appreciation 1959–62, excerpts on work of Department of Individual Services (Dec. 1960). See also Cumbo, "Twig Is Bent," ch. 3.
68 Case #856; case #6725.
69 Allyson D. Stevenson, *Intimate Integration: A History of the Sixties Scoop and the Colonization of Indigenous Kinship* (Toronto: University of Toronto Press, 2020). On the now widely denounced form of child apprehension – the residential school system – see J.R. Miller, *Shingwauk's Vision* (Toronto: University of Toronto Press, 1996); Royal Commission on Indigenous Peoples, *Report of the Royal Commission on Indigenous Peoples,* vol. 1, *Looking Forward, Looking Back*, ch. 10 on "Residential Schools" (Ottawa: Supply and Services Canada, 1996).
70 Case #4371 of seven cases.
71 Case #4220.
72 See chapter 5.
73 Case #4191. Although the client was in her early twenties, I included this case because of the social-cultural issues it illuminates. On immigrant advice columns, see Iacovetta, *Gatekeepers*, 174–84.
74 Case #3859.
75 Case #4974 (and newspaper clipping not cited for privacy reasons).
76 Case #1435. Many female delinquency studies note the cruel irony of sexual abuse victims being dubbed delinquents, but an analysis that highlights immigrants is Odem, *Delinquent Daughters*, ch. 2.
77 Odem, *Delinquent Daughters*, ch. 2.
78 Case #2733.
79 Paolantonio, "Good Friday on College Street," chs. 4–5.
80 Joe Serge, "She's 16, pretty, but can't go on dates," *Toronto Star* in MU6406, File: Clippings, Immigration.

81 Yvonne Crittenden, "Communication Gap: YWCA Aids Immigrants," *Toronto Telegram*, 26 June 1970. On this theme among forties-era Italian Americans, see Cohen, *Workshop to Office*, 178–82.
82 Gabaccia, *From the Other Side*, 120–5; Colalillo, "Patterns of Socialization"; Giles, *Portuguese Women in Toronto*, 9–10, 68–78.
83 Nadia Jones-Gailani, "Feminist Oral History and Assessing the Duelling Narratives of Iraqi Women in Diaspora," in Marlene Epp and Franca Iacovetta, eds., *Sisters or Strangers? Immigrant, Ethnic, and Racialized Women in Canadian History*, 2nd ed. (Toronto: University of Toronto Press, 2016), 584–602; Nadia Jones-Gailani, *Transnational Identity and Memory Making in the Lives of Iraqi Women in Diaspora* (Toronto: University of Toronto Press, 2020), which also addresses the issue of female modesty in relation to recent and contemporary Iraqi women in North America.
84 Helen Singer, "Courage takes root in a strange land," *Toronto Telegram*, 17 July 1971. On immigrant daughters challenging traditional stereotypes in new urban contexts, see also Ewen, *Immigrant Women*; Smith, *Family Connections*; Hickey, "'Go to College'"; Odem, *Delinquent Daughters*, ch. 6.
85 Giles, *Portuguese Women in Toronto*, quotation on p. 61, interviews in ch. 3, esp. 48–65.
86 Werner Sollors, "Introduction," in *The Invention of Ethnicity* (New York: Oxford University Press, 1989); Kathleen Neils Conzen et al., "The Invention of Ethnicity: A Perspective from the USA," *Journal of American Ethnic History* 12, no. 1 (Fall 1992): 3–41.

7 Making Multicultural Community at the Institute

1 Archives of Ontario (AO), International Institute of Metropolitan Toronto, Fonds 884, MU6442 (B280559), File: Members Council [hereafter MC] 1960–65, Minutes of MC Meeting, 17 Aug. 1961.
2 Bettina Bradbury and Tamara Myers, eds., "Introduction," in *Negotiating Identities in 19th and 20th Century Montreal* (Vancouver: UBC Press, 2005), 1–21; Leonore Davidoff, "Regarding Some 'Old Husband's Tales': Public and Private in Feminist History," in *Worlds Between: Historical Perspectives on Gender and Class* (Oxford: Blackwell Publishers, 1995), 257–8. See also Peter Gossage and Robert Rutherdale, "Introduction," in *Making Men, Making History: Canadian Masculinities across Time and Place* (Vancouver: UBC Press, 2018), 3–25.
3 Mary Louise Pratt, *Imperial Eyes: Travel Writing and Transculturation* (London: Routledge, 1992); Sunera Thobani, *Exalted Subjects: Studies in the Making of Race and Nation in Canada* (Toronto: University of Toronto Press, 2007); Sara Ahmed, *Strange Encounters: Embodied Others in Post-Coloniality* (London: Routledge, 2000).
4 Michel Foucault, *History of Sexuality*, vol. l, *An Introduction*, trans. R. Hurley (London: Allan Lane 1979); Bradbury and Myers, *Negotiating Identities*, 7. See also part 2.

5 Sympathetic studies include Allen F. Davis, *Spearheads for Reform: The Social Settlements and the Progressive Movement 1890–1914* (New York: Oxford University Press, 1967) and Judith Ann Trolander, *Professionalism and Social Change from the Settlement House Movement to Neighborhood Centres, 1886 to the Present* (New York: Columbia University Press, 1987). Critical studies include Rivka Shpak Lissak, *Pluralism and Progressives: Hull House and the New Immigrants, 1980–1919* (Chicago: University of Chicago Press, 1989), which labels Jane Addams an assimilationist and Hull House a failure, despite offering examples of their successes; and Elizabeth Lasch-Quinn, *Black Neighbors: Race and the Limits of Reform in the American Settlement House Movement, 1980–1945* (Chapel Hill: University of North Carolina Press, 1993), which documents the movement's failure to engage African Americans and reclaims Black community organizing as settlement work.
6 See my discussion of these themes in part 1 and conclusion.
7 Examples include Linda McDowell, *Gender, Identity and Place: Understanding Feminist Geographies* (Minneapolis: University of Minnesota Press, 1999); Kanishka Goonewardena and Stefan Kipfer, "Spaces of Difference: Reflections from Toronto on Multiculturalism and the Possibility of Radical Urban Politics," *International Journal of Urban and Regional Research* 29, no. 3 (Sept. 2005): 670–8; Helen F. Wilson, "Collective Life: Parents, Playground Encounters and the Multicultural City," *Social and Cultural Geography* 14, no. 6 (2013): 625–48.
8 Iris Marion Young, "The Ideal of Community and the Politics of Difference," in Linda J. Nicholson, ed., *Feminism/Postmodernism* (London: Routledge, 1990), 300–23. On the ironic silencing of women and ethnic minorities within some postmodernist radical geography, see Liz Bondi, "Feminism, Postmodernism, and Geography: Space for Women? *Antipode* 22, no. 2 (1990): 156–67.
9 MU6422 (B280579), File: Intercom Copies 1957, *Intercom*, April 1957, Richard Kolm "Purpose through Programme." Note that *Intercom* copies cited in this chapter are contained in marked files in MU6442 and MU6442 (B280579).
10 MU6382 (B280521), File: Board and Committee Minutes 1958, Richard Kolm, Evaluation of Department Work, Oct. 1956–Oct. 1957.
11 *Intercom*, April 1957, Nell West, "What Is the Institute?"; Immigration History Research Center Archives (hereafter IHRCA), Elmer L. Andersen Library, University of Minnesota, American Council for Nationalities Service records, which contain the American Federation of International Institutes Collection (hereafter II), Box 275, Folder: 12, Survey of Need of Service; IHRCA; II, Box 271, File: 9, Edith Terry Bremer, "Why an International Institute?"
12 On liberal internationalism, see chapter 11.
13 AO, *Intercom*, April 1957, Kolm, "Purpose through Programme." See also *Intercom*, June 1957, Kolm "Purpose through Programme."
14 MU6525 (B280562), File: Tom Robertson, "The Need for Programs," n.d.
15 O.W. Farley et al., *Introduction to Social Work*, 10th ed. (Boston: Pearson Education, 2006), 5–8; R. Ambrosino et al., *Social Work and Social Welfare: An*

Introduction, 7th ed. (Canada: Brooks/Cole, 2012); N. Chukwu et al., "Methods of Social Practice," in U. Okoye et al., eds., *Social Work* (Nsukka: University of Nigeria Press Ltd.), ch. 4.

16 MU6425 (B2800562), File: Robert Kreem, "Social Work: Renewed Focus upon the Social Environment."
17 C. Das et al., "Re-engaging with Community Work as a Method of Practice in Social Work: A View from Northern Ireland," *Journal of Social Work* 18, no. 4 (2018): 376–7.
18 For the argument that state welfarism blunts social work's radical potential see Das, "Re-engaging with Community Work."
19 Kolm, Evaluation of Department Work, Oct. 1956–Oct. 1957; *Intercom*, Feb. 1967, Dec. 1968.
20 The individual fee increased from $2 to $3 and later to $5.
21 *Intercom*, April 1957.
22 Such as Paul Newman in *The Young Philadelphians* and Cary Grant and Ingrid Bergman in *Indiscreet*. *Intercom*, Oct. 1960, Nov. 1960.
23 MU6438, File: Correspondence, film lists (I found no record of the discussions); Truth and Reconciliation Commission of Canada, *Honouring the Truth, Reconciling for the Future: Summary of the Final Report of the Truth and Reconciliation Commission of Canada* (Ottawa: Truth and Reconciliation Commission of Canada, 2015), 1–2 and passim.
24 For example, *Intercom*, Sept. 1963, Dec. 1965, Jan. 1967, April 1968.
25 *Intercom*, Dec. 1963.
26 David A. Stewart (Services Supervisor), Annual Report, 1958–9.
27 On artists, see chapter 11.
28 Ash Amin, "Ethnicity and the Multicultural City: Living with Diversity," *Environment and Planning A*, 34 (2002): 959–80, esp. 967.
29 Raymond A. Mohl, "The International Institute Movement and Ethnic Pluralism," *Social Science* 56, no. 1 (Winter 1998): 14–21, ch. 1.
30 Paula Schriefer, "What's the Difference between Multicultural, Intercultural, and Cross-cultural Communication?" *Spring Institute*, 18 April 2016, at https://springinstitute.org/whats-difference-multicultural-intercultural-cross-cultural-communication/ (last accessed 11 Oct. 2021). On tensions between promoting multiculturalism within state institutions and promoting interculturalism between individual citizens, see Will Kymlicka, "Multicultural States and Intercultural Citizens," *Theory and Research in Education* 1, no. 2 (2003): 147–69. The Bouchard-Taylor Commission's model of interculturalism focuses more particularly on how to maintain Quebec's distinctive francophone culture while being open to the cultural contributions of ethnic and religious minorities. See Gerard Bouchard, *Interculturalism: A View from Quebec*, trans. Howard Scott (Toronto: University of Toronto Press, 2015).
31 MU6425 (B280562), File: Robert Kreem, profile in *Intercom*, Oct. 1965; resignation letter, 14 May 1966.

32 Other short-lived supervisors included social worker A. Sandberg and Gordon Row, a former YMCA worker from Montreal and Sault Ste Marie. MU6431 (B280568), File: Staff Lists 1960–8; Staff Salaries 1968, Personnel Files.
33 MU6410, File: Executive Director Correspondence 1961–2, H.C. Forbell to Julia Kay, 15 Aug. 1962.
34 Kolm, Evaluation of Department Work, Oct. 1956–Oct. 1957; MU 6424, File: Executive Director Personnel, 1956–62, Jean Sheck to Nell West, 22 June 1959; *Intercom*, Nov. 1962, Sept. 1963.
35 Details from files on Executive Director, on Personnel, and on Correspondence regarding group work staff in MU6424, MU6410, and MU6438.
36 MU6425 (B280562), File: Lucy Gitow, Evaluation by C. Lee, 8 Aug. 1972; Gitow Self-evaluation, 27 July 1972. On empathy, see also chapter 3.
37 Files on Kinnee and on group workers in MU6425 (B280562).
38 The classes were offered under the auspices of the Citizenship Division of the Ontario government. They used a rotating system that allowed students to enrol in a class at a time during the year when they could so. For hosting the classes, the Institute received $3 for the initial class and $1.50 for each additional class. See designated files in MU6458 (B280595), MU6412, and MU6447 (B280584).
39 Observations based on club and house program statistics in various files in MU6444 (B280581) and MU6430 (B280567).
40 The one Black woman teacher identified in the *Intercom* is Joan Cumberbatch. *Intercom*, Oct. 1968 (photo); "A Tribute to Our Volunteer Teachers" (list of names), *Intercom*, June–July 1971.
41 Estimates based on statistics in files in MU6444 (B280581) and MU6430 (B280567), and in club reports in *Intercom*, 1957–72.
42 *Intercom*, May–June 1966; *Intercom*, March 1962, "To Dance Is to Integrate."
43 For example, *Intercom*, Oct. 1968.
44 MU6438, File: Correspondence, notes regarding staff; MU6425 (B280562), File: Lloyd Kinnee, reference letter for Varadaraja, 27 March 1969.
45 *Intercom*, Sept. 1968 and Summer Edition 1969. In the sixties, the numbers appear to hover between 40 and 60 volunteers in a given year.
46 List from MU6438, File: Correspondence, regarding group work staff.
47 *Intercom*, Oct. 1965 and March 1969.
48 *Intercom*, March 1962, "Building a Bridge" (S. Bunker).
49 *Intercom*, Summer Edition 1969 (N. Basco); Minutes of MC Meeting, 19 May 1960.
50 *Intercom*, May–June 1966. The unnamed correspondent also thanked Stoian for her friendly support; on photos showing a mixed-race group, see *Intercom*, Feb. 1966.
51 *Intercom*, July 1962 (Patamia); *Intercom*, June 1961 (H. Albrecht).
52 *Intercom*, June 1957, "A Day at Dagmar" (near Peterborough).
53 *Intercom*, June 1957, "Outdoors-Ho!" On food, see chapter 9.

54 *Intercom*, June 1957 "Outdoors-Ho!" and "Dagmar" and regular reports in *Intercom*, June 1961 (G. Fitzpatrick), May–June 1963 (A. Godschalk); Oct. 1961, Sept. 1962 (no author). On the supper club, see chapter 9.
55 *Intercom*, Outdoor Group, June 1961 (G. Fitzpatrick).
56 Brandon M. Savage et al., "Humor, laughter, learning, and health!," *Advances in Physiology Education* 41 (2017): 341–7; Janet M. Gibson, "Getting Serious about Funny: Psychologists see Humor as a Character Strength, https://theconversation.com/getting-serious-about-funny-psychologists-see-humor-as-a-character-strength-61552; Peter McGraw, "The Importance of Humor Research: A Serious Non-serious Research Topic," *Psychology Today*, 14 Sept. 2011, https://www.psychologytoday.com/us/blog/the-humor-code/201109/the-importance-humor-research; Disa A. Sauter et al., "Cross-cultural Recognition of Basic Emotions through Nonverbal Emotional Vocalizations," *Proceedings of the National Academy of Sciences* 107, no. 6 (Feb. 2010): 2408–12, https://doi.org/10.1073/pnas.0908239106 (all last accessed 10/11/2021).
57 *Intercom*, March 1962.
58 *Intercom*, June 1957, June 1961, Sept. 1962, and Oct. 1962 (D. Viereck).
59 *Intercom*, June 1957, "English Is Tough Stuff."
60 *Intercom*, May–June 1966 (C.W. Martin).
61 *Intercom*, April 1962, "Impressions of an Amateur Language Teacher" (unnamed).
62 Letter in *Intercom*, May–June 1966.
63 *Intercom*, Nov. 1960, Oct. 1962, April 1962 (M. Franzen).
64 Both in *Intercom*, May–June 1966.
65 *Intercom*, March 1962; Eliza Berman, "The Italian Bombshell Who Proved That Life is about Much More Than Curves," *Time Life Magazine*, 22 July 2015, https://time.com/3957219/gina-lollobrigida/. Peter Stackpole's 1960 photographs at https://fromthebygone.wordpress.com/2018/03/13/gina-lollobrigida-in-toronto-1960/ (both last accessed 11 Oct. 2021).
66 *Intercom*, June 1957.
67 MU6419 (B280556), File: Human Interest Stories, "The Looker"; Naomi Klein, *The Beauty Myth* (New York: Perennial, 2002 [1990]). On publicity narratives, see chapter 4.
68 A. Celeste Gara, "Understanding Emotional Intimacy: A Review of Conceptualization, Assessment and the Role of Gender," *International Social Science Review* 77, nos. 3–4 (2002): 151–70.
69 Anne Milan, Hélène Maheux, and Tina Chui, "A Portrait of Couples in Mixed Unions," *Statistics Canada*, 2006, https://www150.statcan.gc.ca/n1/pub/11-008-x/2010001/article/11143-eng.htm#a6 (last accessed 11 Oct. 2021); Hill Kulu and Tina Hannemann, "Mixed Marriage among Immigrants and Their Descendants in the United Kingdom," *Population Studies* 73, no. 2 (2019): 181–4; Leo Lucassen and Charlotte Laarman, "Immigration, Intermarriage and the Changing Face of Europe in the Post War Period," *History of the Family* 14, no. 1

(2009): 52–68; Will Kymlicka, *The Current State of Multiculturalism in Canada and Research Themes on Canadian Multiculturalism, 2008–2010* (Ottawa, Government of Canada, 2010), 21.

70 Ten of the 23 cases drawn mostly from the *Intercom* (1957–72), but also staff reports and counselling files, involved partners who belonged to a different ethnic group.

71 *Intercom*, Oct. 1960. Contemporary studies cited above indicate that a shared religious identity can be a positive factor influencing mixed unions.

72 Outdoor group marriages such as Jos Ansems and Stanley Trochonowicz speak to the opportunities for intimacy during weekend trips.

73 *Intercom*, Dec. 1962.

74 Rachel Cassandra, "Falling in Love on the Dance Floor," https://socialdancecommunity.com/falling-in-love-on-the-dance-floor/ (last accessed 11 Oct. 2021). See also Judith Lynne Hanna, "Dance and Sexuality: Many Moves," *Journal of Sex Research* 47, nos. 2–3 (2010): 212–41.

75 *Intercom*, Dec. 1962; Cassandra, "Falling in Love on the Dance Floor." Many English class students also came from outside the immediate neighbourhood.

76 On this theme, see also chapters 5–6.

77 *Intercom*, Dec. 1967, Olga Stoian, International Group report (photos).

78 Loretta Baldassar and Donna R. Gabaccia, eds., "Introduction," in *Intimacy and Italian Migration: Gender and Domestic Lives in a Mobile World* (New York: Fordham University Press, 2011), 1–24; Gabaccia, "Honor and Shame in a Mobile World" (unpublished paper, 2003, and subject of a 2009 conference at the Rockefeller Center in Bellagio, Italy); Abril Liberatori, "'Family Is Really All Over the Place': Ethnic Identity Formation within a Transnational Network" (PhD diss., York University, 2017), 105–8. See also Davar Ardalan, "How a Persian-American Love Story Got Its Start in Harlem, in *Code Switch: Race and Identity Remixed*, https://www.npr.org/sections/codeswitch/2014/05/09/310094118/how-a-persian-american-love-story-got-its-start-in-harlem (last accessed 11 Oct. 2021).

79 *Intercom*, June 1957. On South Asians see Kulu and Hannemann, "Mixed Marriage," which cites several other contemporary studies.

80 *Intercom*, April 1961; on Hanen, see discussion below.

81 *Intercom*, Nov. 1960.

82 As in reports in *Intercom*, Oct. 1960 (on a folk-dancing series); *Intercom*, Oct. 1961 (on the outdoor group); *Intercom*, Oct. 1968 (on a recent Open House).

83 *Intercom*, Sept. 1961, Oct. 1961, April 1962, Sept. 1962; on Lila, *Intercom*, Oct. 1961. My thanks to Michael Akladios for helping me to situate the El-Laboudy couple. See his "Heteroglossia: Interpretation and the Experiences of Coptic Immigrants from Egypt in North America, 1955–1975," *Histoire sociale/Social History* 53, no. 109 (2020): 646–7.

84 *Intercom*, April 1962, Sept. 1962, Dec. 1963.

85 *Intercom*, Nov. 1960, April 1961.

86 Both in *Intercom*, April 1962.
87 MU6444 (B280581), File: Groups: Bylaws and Special Memorandum on Relationship of Groups to the Institute, August 1958, and "Constitution" form filled out by members; Minutes of MC Meeting, Feb. 1963 on managing group finances.
88 MU6382 (B280521), File: Board and Committee Minutes [1958], Minutes of Board Meeting, 14 Dec. 1959, 9 May 1960, 18 Aug. 1960, 20 April 1961; *Intercom*, Sept. 1960, Nov. 1960; Minutes of MC Meeting, 18 Aug. 1960.
89 Minutes of MC Meeting, 26 Dec. 1962. On internationalism, see chapter 11.
90 MU6442 (B280559), File: Membership Council 1960–5, Minutes of MC Meeting, Feb. 1963, 16 May 1963, 18 April 1963; File: General Membership Meeting, 15 Nov. 1964, Report to PC from MC, 28 May 1964; *Intercom*, May 1964.
91 MU6425 (B280562), File: Group Services Staff, Evaluation of Buyers, 28 Feb. 1966; Joan Buyers to David Jones (board), 19 April 1966. She named the current director, J.T. Seaman, Kreem, and his replacement as group services supervisor (Row).
92 MU6410 (B280547), File: Executive Director Correspondence 1961–2, H.C. Forbell to C.D Milani (board), 11 April 1962; Mike Sosaszny to H.C. Forbell, 28 Oct. 1962; Forbell to Sosaszny, 2 Nov. 1962; MU6410, File: Executive Director Correspondence 1961–2, Forbell to Henry Weisbach (Personnel Committee), 26 June 1962.
93 MU6442 (B280559), File: Members Council 1960–5, Minutes of MC Meetings, 19 May 1960, 18 Jan. 1962, 19 April 1962, 15 Nov. 1962; MU 6410 (B280597), File: Executive Director Correspondence 1964–6, J.T. Seaman to Fred Brett, 22 Aug. 1966, blaming "the odd Italian or Yugoslavian male."
94 MU6410 (B280547), File: Executive Director Correspondence 1961–2, Ahmed Shanty to T.M. West, Chair, Board of Directors, 11 Oct. 1961, Forbell to Shanty, 16 Oct. 1962.
95 MU6442 (B280559), File: General Membership Meeting 1964, Report to Programming Committee from MC, 28 May 1964.
96 Ibid. On mediating difference, G. Valentine, "Living with Difference: Reflections on Geographies of Encounter," *Progress in Human Geography* 32, no. 3 (2008): 323–37.
97 The literature on moral geographies is extensive, but studies relevant to this discussion include Sarah Miller's "Jives, Jeans and Jewishness: Moral Geographies, Atmospheres, and the Politics of Mixing at the Jewish Lads' Brigade Club, 1954–1969," *Environment and Planning D: Society and Space* 34, no. 6 (2016): 1098–112; Valentine, "Living with Difference"; Matt Finn, "Atmospheres of Progress in a Data-based School," *Cultural Geographies* 23, no. 1 (2016): 29–49, esp. 32–3.
98 Amin, "Ethnicity and the Multicultural City." The relevant social histories are too numerous to mention, but see Bradbury and Myer's Introduction to *Negotiating Identities*.
99 The men included a few Italians and Canadians and one Franco-Ontarian man; the women included the chair, a Dutch woman, and the wife of bridge club veteran Bunker. Minutes of MC Meetings, January 1964–May 1964.

100 Sara Ahmed, *The Cultural Politics of Emotion* (Edinburgh: Edinburgh University Press, 2014), ch. 6, esp. 133–9.
101 *Intercom*, June–July 1971, Martin Weiland, "Country of Promise Becomes Home."
102 *Intercom*, Sept. and Oct. 1970, O. Koepke, "Unknown Shores."
103 *Intercom*, Nov. 1970, Wilhelm Pilz, "High Priority."
104 On VOA, see https://www.insidevoa.com/a/history-voa-75th-anniversary/3700428.html; on Külvet, see Aarne H. Vahtra, "Man of Letters Ilmar Külvet 85," *Estonian World Review*, 28 Oct. 2005, https://www.eesti.ca/man-of-letters-ilmar-kulvet-85/article11540 (both last accessed 18 April 2022).
105 *Intercom*, Oct. 1965, Ilmar Kulvet, "An Honest Face in the Jungle."
106 *Intercom*, March 1971, Madzi Brender a Brandis, "A Real Surprise"; *Intercom*, Dec. (Christmas issue) 1965, Dr Nadine Hradsky, "Our First Christmas."
107 *Intercom*, April and May 1971, "The Institute Did the Trick," by Corrado as told to Isabel Jemsen; on the Trade English Programme, see chapter 8.
108 MU6444 (B280581), File: Programme Report 1969, Kay Brown, Group Services Report, Programme Evaluation, May 1969.
109 See my reference to an Institute spokeswoman in chapter 6.
110 Brown, Programme Evaluation, May 1969.
111 IHRCA, II, Box 278b, File: 14, II Milwaukee, May 1958, Pierce, "Patterns of Collaboration in the Practice of Group Work, Casework and Community Organization"; ibid., Box 271, File: 9, American Federation of International Institutes, Edith Terry Bremer, "Forecast of Post War Problems of the Nationality Communities," June 1945.
112 Quotation from IHRCA, II, Box 275, Folder 12, II Toledo, Steven Markowski to Merwyn Leatherman, 1 Sept. 1953.
113 AO, MU6382 (B280521), File: Board and Committee Minutes 1958, Richard Kolm, Evaluation of Department Work, Oct. 1956–Oct. 1957.
114 *Intercom*, Feb. 1963, Precis of "Psychology and the Immigrant" by Very Reverend Georges de Rochau in recent *Migration News*. On the US Institutes as delayed assimilationists, see part 1 and passim.
115 *Intercom*, May 1964, "Japanese Canadian Workers' Contribution to the Labor Movement in Vancouver"; Gillian Creese, "Exclusion or Solidarity? Vancouver Workers confront the 'Oriental Problem,'" *BC Studies* 80 (Winter 1988–9): 24–51.
116 *Intercom*, Nov. 1960 (chair Ken Marshall); *Intercom*, July 1962; https://highparknaturecentre.com/2/cherry-blossom-history (last accessed 11 Oct. 2021); *Globe and Mail*, 26 April 1957.
117 Gilberto Fernandes, *This Pilgrim Nation: The Making of the Portuguese Diaspora in Postwar North America* (Toronto: University of Toronto Press, 2020), 235–42 (quotation p. 240).
118 Quotation from *Intercom*, July 1962; *Intercom*, July 1961, with photo of "Calypso Capers" night, 24 June 1961, featuring Roach's West Indian Band. The caption read in part: "A record crowd of 250 including many new faces participated

in some live dancing and enjoyed the music and songs of C. Roach and D. Campbell."

119 On Roach, see obituaries at https://nowtoronto.com/news/remembering-charlie-roach/; https://www.thestar.com/news/gta/2012/10/03/charles_roach_toronto_lawyer_and_human_rights_advocate_dies_at_79.html; Kevin Plummer, "Afterhours clubs and the West Indian music scene of the 1960s," *Torontoist*, 28 Dec. 2013, https://torontoist.com/2013/12/historicist-sounds-of-home-ii/ (all last accessed 11 Oct. 2021).

120 On Caribana, see, for example, B. Denham Jolly, *In the Black: My Life* (Toronto: ECW Press, 2017), ch. 10; Peter Jackson, "The Politics of the Street: A Geography of Caribana," *Political Geography* 11, no. 2 (March 1992): 131–51; and chapter 10.

121 MU6425 (B280562), File: Royston C. Jones, interviewed for *Toronto Star*, "As Immigrants See Us" column, "Canadians are too sophisticated to display prejudice" (news clipping, n.d.). See also Sidney Katz, "Toronto blacks unite to squelch that ghetto image," *Toronto Star*, 26 Dec. 1970.

8 Community Projects for Rural Villagers: Health and Occupational Training

1 Archives of Ontario (AO), International Institute of Metropolitan Toronto, Fonds 884, MU6470 (B436174), File: Newcomers in Transition 1964, Application; Edith Ferguson, *Newcomers in Transition* (A Project of the International Institute of Metropolitan Toronto, 1962–4) (hereafter *NT*), 109.

2 One useful overview is Ilene Hyman, "Setting the Stage: Reviewing Current Knowledge on the Health of Canadian Immigrants: What Is the Evidence and Where Are the Gaps?" *Canadian Journal of Public Health* 95, no. 3 (May–June 2004): 14–18.

3 See, for example, M.A. George and C. Bassani, "The Health of Immigrant Children Who Live in Areas of High Immigrant Concentration," *Ethnicity and Health* 21, no. 5 (2016): 426–38; Sylvia Guendelman et al., "Overcoming the Odds: Access to Care for Immigrant Children in Working Poor Families in California," *Maternal and Child Health Journal* 9, no. 4 (Dec. 2005): 351–62; Sonia Morano Foadi, "Children and Migration in the EU: The Impact of Family Breakdown on the Children of European Families," *Journal of Social Welfare and Family Law* 24, no. 3 (2002): 363–75; Staffan Mjones, "Refugee Children – A Concern for European Paediatricians," *European Journal of Pediatrics* 164, no. 9 (2005): 535–38; and references below.

4 A small sample includes Ann Valentin Kvist, "Immigrant Groups, Vocational Training, and Employment," *European Journal of Training and Development* 36, no. 8 (2012): 809–26; Ya-Ling Wu, "Applying Culturally Responsive Pedagogy to the InVocational Training of Immigrants," *Journal of Educational and Training Studies* 4, no. 2 (2016): 177–81; John E. Lyons, Bikkar S. Randhawa, and Neil A. Paulson, "The Development of Vocational Education in Canada," *Canadian*

Journal of Education 16, no. 2 (1991): 137–50; Håvard Helland and Liv Anne Støren, "Vocational Education and the Allocation of Apprenticeships: Equal Chances for Applicants Regardless of Immigrant Background?," *European Sociological Review* 22, no. 3 (July 2006): 339–51; Lisa Y. Flores, Catherine Hsieh, and Hung Chiao, "Vocational Psychology and Assessment with Immigrants in the United States: Future Directions for Training, Research, and Practice," *Journal of Career Assessment* 19, no. 3 (2011): 323–32.

5 John Porter, *The Vertical Mosaic* (Toronto: University of Toronto Press, 1965).

6 MU6470 (B436174), File: Newcomers in Transition, Edith Ferguson, *NT*, 24. The same could be said of her suggestion in *NT* that all children, including Anglo-Canadian children, take heritage classes where everyone can learn about each other's heritage (ch. 10, recommendations).

7 Ron Lowman, "She travelled long, hard road to write report on immigrants," *Toronto Star*, 25 July 1970; Susan Armstrong-Reid and David Murray, *Armies of Peace: Canada and the UNRRA Years* (Toronto: University of Toronto Press, 2008); Ben Lappin, *The Redeemed Children* (Toronto: University of Toronto Press, 1963).

8 Lowman, "She travelled long."

9 Edith Ferguson, "Large Source of Labor in Europe's D.P.'s," *Toronto Star*, 13 Dec. 1947; Ferguson, "Most D.P.'s Pick Canada for New Homeland," *Saturday Night*, 8 Nov. 1947.

10 Lowman, "She travelled long."

11 Ibid.; Ruth Sandwell, "'Read, Listen, Discuss, Act': Adult Education, Rural Citizenship and the Canadian National Farm Radio Forum 1941–1965," *Historical Studies in Education/Revue d'histoire de l'éducation* (2012): 170–94; Franca Iacovetta, *Gatekeepers Reshaping Immigrant Lives in Cold War Canada* (Toronto: Between the Lines, 2006), ch. 2.

12 Group estimates were Italians (200,000), Greeks (35,000–40,000), Portuguese (20,000–25,000).

13 *COSTI, Integration through Education* (Toronto: COSTI Italian Community Education Centre, 1973), COSTI: History in Progress, https://www.costi.org/downloads/COSTI_HISTORY_IN_PROGRESS_EXCERPTS.pdf (last accessed 12 Nov. 2021).

14 The "neighbourhood" was bound by Ossington Avenue on the west, Harbord Street on the north, Bathurst Street on the east, and Dundas Street at the south, with College Street the main thoroughfare. The first choice was dropped because it was more heterogeneous than expected; the original Parkdale name was dropped because the new boundaries did not include that area of the city. City of Toronto Archives (CTA), Social Planning Council of Metropolitan Toronto (SPC), SC40, Box 53, File: 1A International Institute (hereafter II) 1961–3, Ferguson, Project Director's Interim Report, 24 April 1962.

15 Ferguson, *NT*, 18; MU6469 (B436173), File: Correspondence 1962–3, several Interim Reports, 1 March to 31 Dec. 1962.

16 Ferguson, *NT*, ch. 4; Susana Miranda, "'Not Ashamed or Afraid': Portuguese Immigrant Women in Toronto's Cleaning Industry, 1950–1995" (PhD diss., York University, 2010); Gilberto Fernandes, *This Pilgrim Nation: The Making of the Portuguese Diaspora in Postwar North America* (Toronto: University of Toronto Press, 2020); Franca Iacovetta, "Recipes for Democracy? Gender, Family, and Making Female Citizens in Cold War Canada," *Canadian Woman Studies* 20, no. 2 (Summer 2000): 12–21; Franca Iacovetta, *Such Hardworking People: Italian Immigrants in Postwar Toronto* (Montreal/Kingston: McGill-Queen's University Press, 1992).
17 CTA, SPC, SC40, Box 53, File: 1A II 1961–3, File: 3A II Parkdale Branch [Branch Office] 1961–3, Ferguson, Interim Reports, 1962–3 (hereafter Interim Reports); Ferguson, *NT*, 18; Fernandes, *Pilgrim Nation*, esp. ch 6.
18 Ferguson, *NT*, ch. 3.
19 Ferguson, *NT*, 109–10; Interim Reports.
20 Ferguson, *NT*, 109.
21 Ferguson, *NT*, 109–12; Robert C. Vipond, *Making a Global City: How One Toronto School Embraced Diversity* (Toronto: University of Toronto Press, 2017), 86–9; Mark McGowan, A Short History of Roman Catholic Schools in Ontario," https://docplayer.net/25423386-A-short-history-of-catholic-schools-in-ontario-dr-mark-g-mcgowan-professor-of-history-st-michael-s-college-university-of-toronto.html (last accessed 18 April 2022).
22 Interim Report, 13 Nov. 1962; MU6403 (B280540), File: Branch Office, Parkdale Branch [Branch Office] Year-End Report, March 1962–March 1963. Estimates of "Italian-heavy" schools ranged from "40–70%" to "90–95% Italian."
23 Ferguson, *NT*, ch. 5, 66–8, 71. Heather MacDougall, *Activists and Advocates: Toronto's Health Department, 1883–1983* (Toronto: Dundurn, 1990), 60–167; Christopher Rutty and Sue C. Sullivan, *This Is Public Health: A Canadian History* (Ottawa: Canadian Public Health Association, 2010), https://www.google.com/search?channel=trow5&client=firefox-b-d&q=this+is+public+health+a+canadian+history (last accessed 18 April 2022).
24 Interim Report, 13 Nov. 1962; Ferguson, *NT*, 72. Access to acute hospital services was guaranteed through the 1957 *Hospital Insurance and Diagnostic Services Act*. The 1966 *Medical Care Act* afforded access to insured medical services. https://www.phac-aspc.gc.ca/cphorsphc-respcacsp/2008/fr-rc/cphorsphc-respcacsp11-eng.php#59 (8 May 2022).
25 My 7,000-file database (1952–72) lists 98 cases that deal primarily or exclusively with health issues (see Appendix), but some 1,800 case files involving Europeans contain some health-related content. My few observations here draw on the 800 Southern European cases.
26 The workers' field notes and reports in: AO, MU6470 (B436173), File: Little Italy Interviews 1962; File: Neighbourhood Visits, 1962; File: Italian Records 1962–3; File: School Interviews; File: Italian Records 1962–3; MU6470 (B436174), File: Portugal Records 1962–3, Fieldworker Cases; MU6470 (B436173), File: School

Notes to pages 172–9   365

Interviews; MU6470 (B436174), File: Portuguese Records 1962–3, Montgomery home visits, 1962–3; School Referrals, 1962–3, Referral Forms; School Interviews (3 lists), List of Interviews; Branch Director to Project Committee summary reports. See also Ferguson, *NT*, ch. 6 and Appendix A (76 school cases for the period 1 Oct. 1962–15 Oct. 1963, pp. 119–22).

27 Ferguson, *NT*, 119; Interim Reports. The public schools were Grace, Alexander Muir, Charles E. Fraser, and Clinton, and the separate ones were St Patrick and St Francis of Assisi.
28 Percentages based on a comparison of the 30 child cases from the health project and the 800 Southern European cases containing a health component in my Institute database.
29 Case #1 in 30 child health cases and one of the few cases discussed in Ferguson, *NT*, ch. 5.
30 She worked from city directories and a volunteers' list of "needy families."
31 Examples from AO, MU6469 (B436173), File: Neighbourhood Visits 1962. On reading case files, see part 2.
32 MU6469 (B436173), File: Dundas Interviews; File: Neighbourhood Interviews, Block Interviews (Cosso); Second call, Ossington etc., 1962–3 etc.
33 Case 17 of 30 child health cases.
34 Case #17.
35 Case #11.
36 Landed immigrants could qualify for family allowance, a universal program (introduced in 1944) of the Canadian government that provided modest monthly funds to mothers based on the number of children.
37 CTA, SPC, SC 40, Box 53, File 3: II Parkdale Branch, 1961–3, Ferguson, Report on School Referrals, 24 Jan. 1963.
38 Case #11.
39 Case # 21.
40 Today, an infected peritoneum is treated with strong antibiotics.
41 Case #21; a similar case is #29.
42 Cynthia Comacchio, *Nations Are Built of Babies: Saving Ontario's Mothers and Children, 1900–1940* (Montreal/Kingston: McGill-Queen's University Press, 1993); Ellen Ross, *Love and Toil: Motherhood in Outcast London* (New York: Oxford University Press, 1993); Iacovetta, *Gatekeepers*, ch. 7.
43 Cases #4, #24, and 28.
44 Case #19; Ferguson, *NT*, 73
45 Case #30; Ferguson, *NT*, 67.
46 Case #3.
47 Cases #2, #8, and #26.
48 Cases #6, #19, and #30; Ferguson, *NT*, 73.
49 Iacovetta, *Such Hardworking People*; Fernandes, *Pilgrim Nation*, Noula Mina, "Taming and Training Greek 'Peasant Girls' and the Gendered Politics of

Whiteness in Postwar Canada: Canadian Bureaucrats and Immigrant Domestics, 1950s–1960s, *Canadian Historical Review* 94, no. 4 (Dec. 2013): 514–39.
50 AO, MU6459-MU6470 contains materials on what the Institute called its Educational (or Vocational) Guidance Project, including versions of Ferguson's final report, but I also cite from a personal copy of the published report: Edith Ferguson, *Newcomers and New Learning* (hereafter *NNL*) (Toronto: International Institute of Metropolitan Toronto, 1964-6), 2, 8–11.
51 Ferguson, *NNL*, 9–10.
52 Ferguson, *NNL*, 22, 112. On Colantonio and the strikes, see his *From the Ground Up: An Italian Immigrant's Story* (Toronto: Between the Lines, 1997); Iacovetta, *Such Hardworking People*, ch. 7.
53 Ferguson, *NNL*, 31.
54 Ferguson, *NNL*, 31–2.
55 Ferguson, *NNL*, 5, passim.
56 Ferguson, *NNL*, 19, 2. For a contrasting pattern, see Lina Venturas, "Greek Immigrants in Belgium, Community and Identity Formation Processes," *Journal of the Hellenic Diaspora*, 28, no.1 (2002): 33–72.
57 Ferguson, *NNL*, 17, and 12–21.
58 Ferguson, *NNL*, 12–21, 62–6. Noula Mina, "Homeland Activism, Public Performance and the Construction of Identity: An Examination of Greek Canadian Transnationalism, 1900s–1990s" (PhD diss., University of Toronto, 2014), chs. 2–4; Fernandes, *Pilgrim Nation*, ch. 3; Iacovetta, *Such Hardworking People*, chs. 2–3.
59 Ferguson, *NNL*, 15–16.
60 Quotation from Ferguson, *NNL*, 57; Fernandes, *Pilgrim Nation*, ch 3; Miranda, "'Not Ashamed or Afraid,'" ch. 3; Iacovetta, *Such Hardworking People*; Mina, "Taming and Training."
61 Ferguson, *NNL*, 23–9.
62 The group consisted of 804 Italians, 259 Greeks, and 229 Portuguese. The schools were Central Technical School and Harbord Collegiate. Ferguson, *NNL*, 35–9.
63 Ferguson, *NNL*, 76. My calculations based on Ferguson's charts and reports.
64 In 1966, COSTI also became involved in retraining injured workers. See https://www.costi.org/whoweare/history.php (last accessed 28 April 2020).
65 Ferguson, *NNL*, 43–5.
66 Ferguson, *NNL*, 42–6. The North York school was George Harvey Secondary School. On suburban Italians, see Vienna Paolantonio, "From College Street to Woodbridge: Postwar Italian Immigrants and Ethnic Expression in Urban and Suburban Spaces" (unpublished paper delivered to the Toronto Immigration Group, 2017).
67 Ferguson, *NNL*, 78, 81–4.
68 Ferguson, *NNL*, 48–9.
69 Ferguson, *NNL*; reports in MU6470 (B436174), File: Education Project Liaison 1963; MU6458 (B280595), File: Trade English Classes 1969; MU6400 (B280537), File: Adult Retraining, *Adult Retraining Counselling Centre* (20 pp.).

Notes to pages 184–9   367

70 Ferguson, *NNL*, 52; Correspondence with Gilberto Fernandes, 22 May 2020 (email).
71 Ferguson, *NNL*, 53–6.
72 Ferguson, *NNL*, 62–3.
73 Ferguson, *NNL*, 53–5; MU6410 (B280541), File: Executive Director Correspondence, Jan.–June 1964, Charles Caccia, Vice-President, COSTI, to H.C. Forbell, 1964, Statistics on Men and Women in Various Programs, 1961–4.
74 Ferguson, *NNL*, 66–9.
75 Ibid.
76 Ferguson, *NNL*, 104.
77 Ferguson, *NNL*, 55.
78 Ferguson, *NT*. This topic has an extensive literature, but for Toronto examples, see Iacovetta, *Such Hardworking People*; Miranda, "Not Ashamed or Afraid"; Mina, "Taming and Training."
79 MU6474, File: Reception Centre Monthly Reports 1962, Reception Centre Report (M. Streeruwitz), 1–30 Nov. 1962; MU6447, File: Individual Services Department 1961–4, Report on Individual Services, n.d.
80 Ferguson, *NNL*, 59–62, 104.
81 MU6474, File: Reception Centre Monthly Report 1962, Report 20 Dec. 1962; Minutes of Meeting (M. Streeruwitz) on Adult Retraining Courses, Power Sewing, 7 Nov. 1962.
82 Ferguson, *NT*, ch. 7 and 123–7 (quotation from p. 123); Ferguson's interim and year-end reports, 1962–3, in MU6470 (B436174), File: Parkdale Branch [Branch Office] 1962–5; MU6403 (B280540), File: Branch Office International Institute; MU6474, File: Reception Centre Monthly Report 1962, Streeruwitz' reports on project groups dated 7 Nov. to 7 Dec. 1962; MU6470 (B436174), File: Parkdale Branch 1962–5, Ferguson, "Report on Sewing Course Trainees, 18 Sept. 1963. Those receiving unemployment insurance received a smaller stipend.
83 Ferguson, *NT*, 127. On this theme, see also Ya-Ling Wu, "A Socio-cultural Approach to Understanding the Learning Experiences of Vocational Training among Vietnamese Immigrant Women in Taiwan," *Women's Studies International Forum* 44 (May–June 2014): 80–8.
84 Ferguson, *NT*, 128–9; MU6474, File: Reception Centre Monthly Report 1962, Reception Centre (M. Streeruwitz), reports on pilot project, first groups, 7, 22, 27, 28 Nov. and 7 Dec. 1962.
85 MU6470 (B436174), Parkdale Branch, 1962–5, Ferguson, Report on Sewing Course Trainees, 18 Sept. 1963; Ferguson, *NT*, 124–5. On this theme, see also Ana Alberro and Gloria Montero, "The Immigrant Woman," *Women in the Canadian Mosaic* (1976): 131–48; Sunera Thobani, *Exalted Subjects: Studies in the Making of Race and Nation in Canada* (Toronto: University of Toronto Press, 2007); Margaret Little, Lynne Marks, et al., "Family Matters: Immigrant Women's Activism in Ontario and British Columbia, 1960s–1980s" *Atlantis* 41, no. 1 (2020): 105–23.
86 MU6470 (B436174), File: Parkdale Branch 1962–5, Reports on Groups 1–5, 10 Dec. 1962 to June 1963, in Ferguson, "Report on Sewing Course Trainees, 18

Sept. 1963; MU6458 (B280595), File: Power-Sewing Course 1962–3, Details of Meeting, 7 Nov. 1962; Ferguson, *NT*, 123. See labour force statistics in Iacovetta, *Such Hardworking People*, Appendix 1; Monica Boyd, "The Status of Immigrant Women in Canada," *Canadian Review of Sociology*, 12, no. 4 (1975): 406–16.
87 Ferguson, *NNL*, 59–60; MU6458 (B280595), File: Power-Sewing Course 1962–3.
88 Seven cases from my database. On this subject, see also Karen Charnow Lior, ed., *Making the City: Women Who Made a Difference* (Working Women Community Centre, Toronto) (Halifax/Winnipeg: Fernwood, 2012), 35–6, 69–83; Tania Das Gupta, *Learning from Our History: Community Development by Immigrant Women in Ontario, 1958–1986* (Toronto: Cross Cultural Communication Centre, 1986).
89 MU6442, File: Intercom 1961–72, *Intercom*, Sept. 1968.
90 MU6467 (B280604), File: Pilot Project–Trade English Classes, Kay Brown, Staff Minutes, 14 June 1968; MU6458 (B280595), File: Trade English Courses 1969; MU6431 (B280568), File: Occupations and Trades, Brown to L. Gorge, Industrial Trades Chief, Department of Labour, 14 March 1969; Brown to Walker, 14 March 1969.
91 Ferguson, *NNL*; Miranda, "'Not Ashamed or Afraid,'" chs. 3–4; Iacovetta, *Such Hardworking People*, 93.
92 Eleven cases in my database, of which four indicate a positive outcome.
93 Harry Smaller, "Vocational Education in Ontario's Secondary Schools: Past, Present – and Future? Training Matters: Works in Progress (WIP #2000-04) (Toronto: Labour Education and Training Research Network Centre for Research on Work and Society, York University, n.d.).
94 Ferguson, *NNL*, 59, 31; Lior, *Making the City*, 36–40; Little and Marks, "Family Matters."
95 Ferguson, *NT*, 110.
96 Ferguson, *NT*, 18.
97 Ferguson, *NT*, 111, ch. 10 (recommendations).
98 Ferguson, *NT*, 48–58, ch. 10 (recommendations).
99 Ferguson, *NT*, 118.
100 Two examples are Flores et al., "Vocational Psychology and Assessment with Immigrants in the United States"; Wu, "Applying Culturally Responsive Pedagogy."
101 CTA, SPC, SC40, Box 53, File 3A Parkdale Branch 1961–3, Interim Report 15 May 1963; H.C. Knight to Leon Kumove, Report on International Institute, 21 June 1962, 5 Sept. 1963.
102 Regarding health, see, for example, Frances M. Marks, "Symptoms in Children of British and of Bangladeshi Parents measured by the Rutter B2 Questionnaire," *Ethnicity and Health* 2, no. 3 (1997): 255–9; Elizabeth L. McGarvey et al., "Using Focus Group Results to Inform Preschool Childhood Obesity Prevention Programming," *Ethnicity and Health* 11, no. 3 (2006): 265–85.
103 Ferguson, *NNL*, 9–80; COSTI, https://www.costi.org/whoweare/history.php (last accessed 28 April 2020).

104 See, for example, Aaron Benavot, "The Rise and Decline of Vocational Education," *Sociology of Education* 56, no. 2 (1983): 63–76; Smaller, "Vocational Education."

9 Food as Charity, Community-Building, and Cosmopolitanism on a Budget

1 Kanishka Goonewardena and Stefan Kipfer, "Spaces of Difference: Reflections from Toronto on Multiculturalism, Bourgeois Urbanism and the Possibility of Radical Urban Politics," *International Journal of Urban and Regional Research* 29, no. 3 (2005): 670–8.

2 Examples include Stephen Mennell, Anne Murcott, and Anneke H. van Otterloo, *The Sociology of Food: Eating, Diet and Culture* (Newbury Park, CA: Sage, 1992); Mary Douglas, ed., *Food in the Social Order: Studies of Food and Festivals in Three American Communities* (New York: Basic Books, 1984); Carol F. Helstosky, "Fascist Food Politics: Mussolini's Policy of Alimentary Sovereignty," *Journal of Modern Italian Studies* 9, no. 1 (2004): 1–26; R.W. Davies and S.G. Wheatcroft, "The Soviet Famine of 1932–33," in R.W. Wheatcroft, ed., *Challenging Traditional Views of Russian History* (London: Palgrave Macmillan, 2002), ch. 4; Harvey Levenstein, *Paradox of Plenty: A Social History of Eating in Modern America* (New York: Oxford University Press, 1993); Ian Mosby, "Administering Colonial Science: Nutrition Research and Human Biomedical Experimentation in Aboriginal Communities and Residential Schools, 1942–1952," *Histoire social/ Social History* 46, no. 91 (2013): 145–72.

3 A sample includes Hasia R. Diner, *Hungering for America: Italian, Irish, and Jewish Foodways in the Age of Migration* (Cambridge, MA: Harvard University Press, 2001); Krishnendu Ray, *The Migrant's Table: Meals and Memories in Bengali-American Households* (Philadelphia: Temple University Press, 2004); Donna Gabaccia, *We Are What We Eat: Ethnic Food and the Making of Americans* (Cambridge, MA: Harvard University Press, 1998); Viranjini Munasinghe, *Callaloo or Tossed Salad? East Indians and the Cultural Politics of Identity in Trinidad* (Ithaca: Cornell University Press, 2001); Arjun Appadurai, "How to Make a National Cuisine: Cookbooks in Contemporary India," *Comparative Studies in Society and History* 30, no. 1 (1988): 3–24; Molly Ungar, "Nationalism on the Menu: Three Banquets on the 1939 Royal Tour," in Franca Iacovetta, Valerie Korinek, and Marlene Epp, eds., *Edible Histories Cultural Politics: Towards a Canadian Food History* (Toronto: University of Toronto Press, 2012), 351–8; Nathalie Cook, ed., *What's to Eat? Entrees in Canadian Food History* (Montreal/Kingston: McGill-Queen's University Press, 2009); Elizabeth Zanoni, *Migrant Marketplaces: Food and Italians in North and South America* (Urbana: University of Illinois Press, 2018).

4 See, for example, Carole Counihan and Penny Van Esterik, eds., *Food and Culture: A Reader* (New York: Routledge, 1997); Arlene Voski Avakian and Barbara Haber, eds., *From Betty Crocker to Feminist Food Studies: Critical Perspectives on Women and Food* (Amherst: University of Massachusetts Press, 2005); Frances

Swyripa, *Wedded to the Cause: Ukrainian Canadian Women and Ethnic Identity* (Toronto: University of Toronto Press, 1993), 195–260; Valerie J. Korinek, *Roughing It in Suburbia: Reading Chatelaine in the Fifties and Sixties* (Toronto: University of Toronto Press, 2000); Franca Iacovetta and Valerie J. Korinek, "Jell-O Salads, One-Stop Shopping, and Maria the Homemaker: The Gender Politics of Food," Marlene Epp, "The Semiotics of Zwieback: Feast and Famine in the Narratives of Mennonite Refugee Women," and Helen Vallanatos and Kim Raine, "Consuming Food and Constructing Identities among Arabic and South Asian Immigrant Women," all in Marlene Epp and Franca Iacovetta, eds., *Sisters or Strangers? Immigrant, Ethnic, and Racialized Women in Canadian History*, 2nd ed., (Toronto: University of Toronto Press, 2016), 190–230; Julie Guard, *Radical Housewives: Price Wars and Food Politics in Mid-Twentieth-Century Canada* (Toronto: University of Toronto Press, 2019).

5 See, for example: Avakian and Haber, *From Betty Crocker to Feminist Food Studies*; Mary A. Procida, "No Longer Half-Baked: Food Studies and Women's History," *Journal of Women's History* 16, no. 3 (2004): 197–205; Marlene Epp, "More Than 'Just Recipes': Mennonite Cookbooks in Mid-Twentieth-Century North America," and Andrea Eidinger, "Gefilte Fish and Roast Duck with Orange Slices: A Treasure for My Daughter and the Creation of a Jewish Cultural Orthodoxy in Postwar Montreal," both in Iacovetta et al., *Edible Histories*, 173–88; Laurie Bertram, *The Viking Immigrants: Icelandic North Americans* (Toronto: University of Toronto Press, 2019), ch. 5.

6 In addition to the references above, examples include Stacey Zembryzski, "We Didn't Have a Lot of Money but We Had Food: Ukrainians and Their Depression-Era Food Memories," in Iacovetta et al., *Edible Histories*, 131–9; Marlene Epp, "'The dumpling in my soup was lonely just like me': Food in the Memories of Mennonite Women Refugees," *Women's History Review* 25, no. 3 (May 2016): 365–81; Nadia Jones-Gailani, "Qahwa and Kleiche: Drinking Coffee in Oral History Interviews with Iraqi Women in Diaspora," *Global Food History* 3, no. 1 (2017): 84–100.

7 Ellen Ross, *Love and Toil: Women of Outcast London* (London: Oxford University Press, 1992); on International Institutes, see Donna Gabaccia, *We Are What We Eat*, 137–8.

8 A few North American modern-era histories include Cathy James, "Reforming Reform: Toronto's Settlement House Movement, 1900–20," *Canadian Historical Review* 82, no. 1 (March 2001): 55–90; Linda Gordon, *Pitied but Not Entitled: Single Mothers and the History of Welfare, 1890–1935* (Cambridge, MA: Harvard University Press, 1994); Margaret Little, *No Car, No Radio, No Liquor Permit: The Moral Regulation of Single Mothers in Ontario, 1920–1977* (Toronto: Oxford University Press, 1998); Mark Peel, *Miss Cutler and the Case of the Resurrected Horse: Social Work and the Story of Poverty in America, Australia, and Britain* (Chicago: University of Chicago Press, 2012).

9 Thank you letters in Archives of Ontario (AO), International Institute of Metropolitan Toronto, Fonds 884, MU6406 (B280543), File: Christmas 1959 and MU6472, File: Christmas List for Clients 1966.
10 MU6474 (B436178), File: Reception Centre 1961, Reception Centre (hereafter RC) Report, 1 Dec. 1961 (M. Streeruwitz); MU 6471, File: Xmas Donors 1961, Report 15 Jan. 1962.
11 MU6474 (B436178), File: Reception Centre 1961, RC Report, Dec. 1961 (Streeruwitz).
12 MU6471, File: Xmas Donors 1961, X-mas Bureau Donors, 14 Dec. 1961; MU6474 (B436178), File: Reception Centre 1961, Donors, 1 Dec. 1961 and 15 Jan. 1962.
13 For example, MU6444, File: Current Programme 1963-5, RC Report, 1963.
14 MU6471, File: Xmas Donors 1961, Notes on Meeting of Christmas Bureau, 4 Nov. 1958; Xmas Bureau Donors Report, 1 Dec. 1961 (Mrs Payton).
15 MU6471, File: Christmas 1961, 1958 List of Families (23).
16 MU6471, File: Xmas Donors, Social Planning Council of Metropolitan Toronto (SPC), 29 Dec. 1961.
17 MU6471, File: Xmas Donors, RC Report 15 Jan. 1962, Jan. 1963, and others.
18 MU6471, File: Xmas Donors, Notes for Dec. 1961.
19 MU6471, 1958 List. See also MU6472, File: Letters Oct. 1953-64.
20 MU6471, File: Christmas 1961, List of Families (28) 1960 (N.S. Bojovic). Most families had between two and four children.
21 As in between three and six children. MU6471, File: Christmas 1961, Xmas list (72) 13-14 Nov. 1963.
22 MU6471, File: Christmas 1961, Lists, Portuguese Families, 10 Dec. 1964. On IODE clothing donations, see, for example, MU6474, File: IODE Thank You Letters '66, M. Streeruwitz to Mrs R. Kerr, Hon. George S. Henry Chapter, 7 Nov. 1966 and 12 Jan .1968, and to Mrs Tiffin, Mississauga Chapter, 16 Jan. 1967.
23 MU6471, File: Christmas 1961, Xmas list (72) 13-14 Nov. 1963.
24 MU6471, File: Christmas 1961, List of Families 1964.
25 MU6472, File: Christmas List for Clients 1966, Canadian Welfare Council, Principles of Holiday Giving, from SPC Oct. 1966.
26 MU6471, File: Christmas 1961, Xmas List 14 Nov. 1963. The home visitor (Mrs Armstrong, possibly an IODE volunteer) put down "maybe" for a basket for next year. On this theme, see, for example, Gordon, *Pitied but Not Entitled*; Peel, *Miss Cutler.*
27 MU6472, File: 12 Nov. 1968, Xmas List, Note to Xmas Bureau attached.
28 MU6471, File: Christmas 1961, 1963 Xmas List (72) 13-14 Nov. 1963.
29 MU6472, File: 12 Nov. 1968 Xmas List, Report Xmas 1968.
30 MU6471, File: Christmas 1961, List of Families (72), 13-14 Nov. 1963.
31 Ibid., Xmas Needy Family Lists 1964.
32 Ibid., Xmas Needy Families Lists 1964/65.
33 Quotation in MU6471, File: Christmas 1961, List of Families (72) 13-14 Nov. 1963.

34 Quotation in MU6471, File: Xmas List 1962, Xmas List, Reception Centre, 27 Nov. 1962.
35 MU6474 (B436178), File: Reception Centre 1961, RC Report; MU6474, File: IODE Thank You Letters '66, Streeruwitz to Mrs Keys, IODE, 14 Nov. 1966.
36 MU6471, File: Christmas 1961, List starting 16 Dec. 1964 (M.S.).
37 MU6471, File: Xmas Lists 1962, Memorandum Diana Wilson to Streeruwitz, 29 Nov. 1962; Reception Centre Xmas 1965, Food Gifts Suggested for Italians; Spanish; Portuguese, 17 Nov. 1965. On nutrition as socially constructed, see, for example, Ian Mosby, *Food Will Win the War: The Politics, Culture and Science of Food on Canada's Home Front* (Vancouver: UBC Press, 2014); Caroline Durand, "Rational Meals for the Traditional Family: Nutrition in Quebec's School Manuals, 1900–1960," in Iacovetta et al., *Edible Histories*, 109–30.
38 On Canada Food Guide, Mosby, *Food Will Win the War*.
39 For examples, MU6474, File: IODE Thank You Letters from M. Streeruwitz to Mrs E.H. Hugenholtz, 12 May 1965, Mrs A. Stermac, Glen Alton Chapter, IODE, 11 May 1965 (calling Hugenholtz "a charming person"), Mrs H.J. Heslop, 10 Jan. 1964, Mrs W.L. Smart, 17 Dec. 1962, S. Perri, 19 July 1962. I draw on Valerie Korinek's discussion of how *Chatelaine*'s readers and writers forged a "community of women" in her *Roughing It in Suburbia*.
40 As in encounters between acculturated ethno-Canadian women and newcomers who came from the same country or belonged to the same ethnic group.
41 Gareth Stedman Jones, *Outcast London: A Study in the Relationship between Classes in Victorian Society* (Harmondsworth: Penguin, 1984), 251–71.
42 MU6476, File: Thank You Letters 1961.
43 Calculations based on annual statistics from the relevant files.
44 MU6473 (B436177), File: Letters Oct. 1970, Report 1970 (M. Streeruwitz). See also Christmas issues of *Intercom*, Dec. 1962 to Dec. 1969; and items in MU6406, File: Christmas 1969. Note that *Intercom* issues are found in designated files in MU6400, MU6406, MU6407, MU6442, and MU6472.
45 Details in MU6406, File: Christmas Card 1963/4 and File: Christmas 1965. For more on the artist, see chapter 11.
46 MU6444, File: Jan. 1965, Newsletters, Report by IODE Municipal Chapter 1964; on Gerussi, entry by James V. Defelice, https://www.thecanadianencyclopedia.ca/en/article/bruno-gerussi; and https://vancouversun.com/news/local-news/canada-150-bruno-gerussi-was-noted-shakespearean-actor-before-becoming-a-beachcomber/ (both last accessed 19 April 2022).
47 MU6404 (B380543), File: Christmas 1961, Notes by Nell West, Dec. 1961.
48 MU6473 (B436177), File: Letters Oct. 1970, Notes about Christmas by M. Streeruwitz. The document also includes descriptions of ethnic group Christmas traditions, including those written by Portuguese and Croatian counsellors and English teachers originally from Chile and Ecuador. The few Chinese children who attended the 1966 party may have been Christian. MU6472, File: Children's Christmas Party 1966, drafts of articles for *Intercom*.

Notes to pages 203–8   373

49   See, for example, Jennings and other IODE women's correspondence with donor companies in MU6471, File: Christmas 1957 Party and MU6474, File: Meetings–Reception Centre 1957–63, Notes on Christmas Activities.
50   MU6441 (B280578), File: Prospective Memberships 1958–65, Notes 18 Oct. 1965; MU6430 (B280567), File: Staff Meeting Minutes 1966, Notes Dec. 1965.
51   Observations based on available lists of children, 1958–68.
52   Calculations based on MU6471, File: Xmas 1963, Children's Party, RC Lists for 12 and 18 Nov. 1963 and updated lists. Two-thirds of the 293 children were Italian and Portuguese.
53   MU6471, File: Xmas 1964, Children's Party, List for 5 Dec. 1964 (Streeruwitz).
54   Observation based on available lists for 1958–68.
55   *Intercom*, Jan. 1967. See also thank you letters in MU6474 File: IODE Thank You Letters '66.
56   See notes and drafts of articles for *Intercom* in MU6472, File: Children's Christmas Party 1966, and examples below.
57   Steve Penfold, *A Mile of Make-Believe: A History of the Eaton's Santa Claus Parade* (Toronto: University of Toronto Press, 2014), esp. ch. 2.
58   MU6473 (B436177), File: Letters Out 1973, Christmas Party Report, IODE Immouna Ephrem, 1 Jan. 1973.
59   MU6471, File: Xmas 1963, Children's Party, news clippings, *Toronto Daily Star* and image in text.
60   MU6471, File: Xmas Lists 1961, Memorandum and List for Havergal College Party, 22 March 1961.
61   MU6339, File: Kay Brown, Staff Meetings 1966–7, Minutes of Meeting 16 Dec. 1966.
62   Quotation from MU6474 (B436178), File: Reception Centre 1961, RC Report, Dec. 1961 (Streeruwitz).
63   This discussion draws on items in MU6471, File: Christmas 1961; File: Xmas Donors 1961; MU6406, File: Christmas 1962; File: Xmas 1958, Children's Party; File: Christmas 1963; and Xmas Lists for 1962–8. On wider context, Franca Iacovetta, *Gatekeeepers: Reshaping Immigrant Lives in Cold War Canada* (Toronto: Between the Lines, 2006), chs. 4 and 6.
64   See, for example, MU6474 (B436178), File: Reception Centre 1961, Statistical Monthly Report, Dec. 1961 (Streeruwitz); Administrator's Report, Nov.–Dec. 1961 (H.C. Forbell); MU6563, File: Executive Minutes, Stephen Davidovich, Chair, Programme Committee, 3 Jan. 1961.
65   MU6406 (B280543), File: Clippings 1959–70, clipping dated 27 Dec. 1969.
66   See chapter 7.
67   MU6444 (B280581), File: Newsletter, Feb. 1965; MU6406 (B280543), File: Clippings, 1959–70, Executive Director's Report, 14 Jan. 1970 (no estimates).
68   MU6382, File: Board Minutes 1956–7, Minutes of Programme Committee, 13 March 1957.

69 Counihan and Van Esterik, "Introduction," in *Food and Culture*.
70 Quotations from MU6413, File: Ethnic Occasions 1957, W.E West to Jean Newman, Toronto City Hall, 28 March 1957; MU6415, File: Latvian Federation 1957, West to Ian McIntosh, CBC television news editor, Memoranda on Latvian Week, 1957.
71 On this and related themes, see part 4.
72 Marilena Liguori, "Toronto à la Cart: Promoting Cultural Diversity through Food" (Appendix 8), in "Finding Meaning in (The) Diverse-City: The Competitive City and Immigration in Toronto" (PhD diss., Université du Québec, 2015), 154–6.
73 Ibid. See also Goonewardena and Kipfer, "Spaces of Difference."
74 Drawing on the few unearthed cases, these outfits were headed by men, but, given that many immigrant businesses were family-run enterprises, at least some wives and perhaps other female kin would have been involved. Anne Smith Catering (1957 Irish banquet) was the only woman caterer named. On this theme, see also Diane C. Vecchio, *Merchants, Midwives, and Laboring Women: Italian Migrants in Urban America* (Urbana: University of Illinois Press, 2006), chs. 3–4. On the (mainly craft-oriented) entrepreneurialism among Mennonite women, see Marlene Epp, *Mennonite Women in Canada: A History* (Winnipeg: University of Manitoba Press, 2008), 234–6.
75 MU6413, File: Ethnic Occasions 1957, Flyer – Latvian Week, March–April 1957; Thelma Barer-Stein, You *Eat What You Are: A Study of Ethnic Food Traditions* (Toronto: McClelland and Stewart, 1979), 54–60.
76 See, for example, MU6413, File: Ethnic Occasions 1957, West to T.W. Lovet, Kiwanis Club (Ukrainian Week), 28 March 1957.
77 MU6413, File: Ethnic Occasions 1957, Flyer – German Week, Feb. 1957; Barer-Stein, *You Eat What You Are*, 218–32.
78 MU6413, File: Ethnic Occasions 1957, Polish Dinner Notes, 15 Feb. 1957; *Intercom*, Nov. 1962. On the role of ethnic entrepreneurs in sustaining and enlivening Toronto's food cultures, see Joel Dickau, Jeffrey M. Pilcher, and Samantha K. Young, "'If You Wanted Garlic, You Had to Go to Kensington': Culinary Infrastructure and Immigrant Entrepreneurship in Toronto's Food Markets before Official Canadian Multiculturalism," *Food, Culture and Society* 24, no. 1 (2021): 31–48.
79 MU6413, File: Ethnic Occasions 1957, Polish Dinner Notes, 15 Feb. 1957; West to Z. Jaworski, president, Toronto Branch, Canadian Polish Congress, 6 March 1957; West to Mrs M. Ashby, Croatian Women's Organization, "Kat. Zrinskh," Toronto, 27 March 1957; MU6414, File: Canadian Polish Congress 1957, Irene Ungar to Dear Ladies, n.d. (1957). On Mulvihill, see chapter 1.
80 MU6400, File: Administration 1958–66, "Fact Sheet 1964."
81 Ibid., "Points to Be Arranged 24 Hours before the Dinner."
82 MU6385 (B280523), File: Metro International Caravan, Community Folk Arts Council (hereafter CFAC), 1969 Details; Executive Committee, 1969 Plans; Final Instructions Re: Operations, 26–30 June 1969. See also chapter 10.

83 See https://www.the-buyer.net/people/producer/elizabeth-gabay-egri-bikaver-bulls-blood/ (last accessed 19 April 2022).
84 MU6407, File: CFAC 1963–74, news clippings, Colin Murray, "Metro International Caravan: Toronto's at Home to the World," *Toronto Telegram Weekend/The Good Life*, 21 June 1969.
85 Ibid., Press Release, 12 June 1969, Board of Directors, Memoranda, 11 and 27 June 1969; Report of Caravan Committee, 21 May 1969; *Intercom*, July 1969; other press releases.
86 This theme has emerged in countless conversations with colleagues and friends of this generation; Dickau et al., "'If You Wanted Garlic.'"
87 Warren J. Belasco, *Appetite for Change: How the Counterculture Took on the Food Industry 1966–1988* (New York: Pantheon Books, 1989); Sandra Johnson, "Edible Activism: Food and the Counterculture of the 1960s and 1970s" (Honours thesis, Colby College, 2012); Catherine Carstairs, "Food, Fear, and the Environment in the Long 1960s," in Lara Campbell, Dominique Clement, and Gregory S. Kealey, eds., *Debating Dissent: The 1960s in Canada* (Toronto: University of Toronto Press, 2012), 29–45.
88 Gabaccia, *We Are What We Eat*, 137–8.
89 MU6415, File: Ethnic Recipes 1956–63, West correspondence (June 1961) with William Kaufman about a US-based Catholic cookbook featuring holiday recipes from around the world, and with Katherine Caldwell Bayley, Director, Home Bureau, *Canadian Home Journal*, Jan. and Feb. 1956.
90 Such as "Jugo-Slav Goulash" and "French Canadian Cretons" (pork pâté). See recipes flagged for *Intercom* in MU6415, File: Ethnic Recipes 1956–63.
91 *Intercom*, Dec. 1963.
92 *Intercom*, Dec. 1969; MU6406, File: 1968 Christmas, Director's Report, Jan. 1969.
93 Quotation from MU6446 (B280583), File: International Festival/Cards 1970, news clippings, John Kraglund, "Festival of Carols effective retelling of an old tale," Toronto *Globe and Mail*, 18 Dec. 1970. Also see To-Do List and Preparations in this file and in MU6446 (B280583), File: Intl Festival/Cards 1971 and File: Intl Festival Carols 1972.
94 *Intercom*, Dec. 1962.
95 *Intercom*, Dec. 1965. On Christian multicultural food practices since 1960, see Michel Desjardins and Ellen Desjardins, "The Role of Food in Canadian Expressions of Christianity," in Iacovetta et al., *Edible Histories*, 70–82.
96 *Intercom*, Dec. 1963.
97 *Intercom*, Dec. 1963.
98 Immigration History Research Center Archives, Elmer L. Andersen Library, University of Minnesota, American Council for Nationalities Service records, which contain the American Federation of International Institutes collection, Box 265, File 7: Cookbook Orders. Cookbook (draft, c. 1955, front page). See also Gabaccia, *We Are What We Eat*.

99 AO, MU6415, File: Ethnic Recipes 1956–63, Joe Vatileroti(?) to West, 26 Nov. 1962 (with minced meat, wine, turkey livers, heart, onions, bread crumbs, tomato paste, sweet butter).
100 Ibid., Don Bellamy to West, 21 Dec. 1962 and West to Bellamy, 27 Dec. 1962.
101 Ibid., Lists of women selling copies of book; correspondence with Mrs Casey, SPC, Christmas Bureau, and others.
102 Epp, "More Than 'Just Recipes'"; Eidinger, Gefilte Fish and Orange Duck"; and other references above.
103 MU6415, File: Ethnic Recipes 1956–63, West to Mrs R. Jensen, Scarborough, 14 Nov. 1962.
104 Ibid., "Olia" to West, 3 Nov. 1962.
105 Ibid., Mrs Marie Dymes to West, 5 Nov. 1962.
106 Ibid., I determined that the messily written signature referring to a Mrs Schalasky or Schalosky is Szalowski. See Everyday Recipes, n.d. (1962). (The potato pancake recipe involved basic items of potatoes, flour, and egg, but notes that the traditional sour cream could be substituted with cranberry sauce, presumably tinned.)
107 Ibid., Szebeny recipe for chicken and rice; final entry in *Season's Greetings in Food – Christmas 1962* (International Institute of Metropolitan Toronto), 19.
108 Ibid., 4 (and to make "lucky" tea).
109 For a detailed discussion of this theme, see part 4.
110 *Season's Greetings in Food – Christmas 1962*, 10–11
111 MU6415, File: Ethnic Recipes 1956–63, "Cooking in the Chinese Manner" cookbook launched at "The Moon Festival," Sept. 1961 (signed Nell West). The debate over authentic versus Canadianized Chinese food has shifted, with recent writers making a case for a distinctive hybrid rather than "fake" Chinese dishes. See Ann Hui, *Chop Suey Nation* (Madeira Park, BC: Douglas and McIntyre, 2019). Also, Lily Cho, *Eating Chinese: Culture on the Menu in Small Town Canada* (Toronto: University of Toronto Press, 2010).
112 *Intercom*, April 1968; "International flavor in cook book project," *Toronto Telegram*, 24 July 1968. On the project and its eventual failure, MU6410 (B280547), File: Cookbook Project 1968–71.
113 A few examples include Appadurai, "How to Make a National Cuisine"; Ilaria Porciani, ed., *Food Heritage and Nationalism in Europe* (London/New York: Routledge, 2019), ch. 1; Cook, *What's to Eat?*
114 See Goonewardena and Kipfer, "Spaces of Difference," especially their discussion of Mike Davis' *Magical Urbanism: Latinos Reinvent the US City* (London: Verso, 2001), on how Latinos in the United States are reshaping everyday life and revitalizing left politics in big cities.
115 Peter D. Chimbos, *The Canadian Odyssey: The Greek Experience in Canada* (Toronto: McClelland and Stewart, 1980) 44, 52–6; David Wencer, "Historicist: Greektown on the Danforth," *Torontoist*, 15 Oct. 2016, https://torontoist

.com/2016/10/historicist-greektown-on-the-danforth/ (last accessed 19 April 2022); Dickau et al., "'If You Wanted Garlic.'"

10 Immigrant Gifts, Pluralist Spectacles, and Staging the Modern City and Nation

1 Benedict Anderson, *Imagined Communities: Reflections on the Origin and Spread of Nationalism* (London: Verso, 1991).
2 This summary draws on the following: Archives of Ontario (AO), International Institute of Metropolitan Toronto, Fonds 884, MU6407, File: Community Folk Art Council (hereafter CFAC) 1963–74, *Community Folk Art Council Newsletter* 2 (1964); Jesse Munroe Personal Archive, Canadian National Exhibition Association (CNEA), *Canadian National Exhibition (CNE) Souvenir Catalogue and Programme* for 1964 and 1965 (with special thanks to Jesse Munroe for sharing these materials with me); Robert Kreem, "The Community Groups at the Institute," *Intercom*, July 1961 [referencing Canadiana Week concert]. On festive ethnic culture, Barbara Lorenzkowski, *Sounds of Ethnicity: Listening to German North America, 1850–1914* (Winnipeg: University of Manitoba Press, 2010), ch. 4, esp. 121–7; Paul A. Bramadat, "Shows, Selves, and Solidarity: Ethnic Identity and Cultural Spectacles in Canada," *Canadian Ethnic Studies* 33, no. 2 (2001): 78–98. Note that *Intercom* issues cited here are found in designated files in MU6407; MU6442, and MU6415. On nation-building, see discussion below. On folk revival, see chapter 11.
3 MU6413, File: Ethnic Occasions 1957, "Ethnic Weeks" and "Suggested Schedule for Ethnic Weeks"; Mrs W.E. West (hereafter West) to Controller Jean Newman, Toronto City Hall, 28 March 1957; MU6403 (B280540), File: Brochure, *The International Institute* 1960; MU6416, File: 1957 Folk Festival (Minutes of Meetings), West to Reliable Toy Co., 29 May 1957.
4 On scholars' (different) use of the notion of a therapeutic pluralism, see, for example, Ian McKay, *The Quest of the Folk: Antimodernism and Cultural Selection in Twentieth-Century Nova Scotia* (Montreal/Kingston: McGill-Queen's University Press, 2009), ch. 1 and passim; Robert B. Klymasz, "From Immigrant to Ethnic Folklore: A Canadian View of Process and Transition," *Journal of the Folklore Institute* 10, no. 3 (Dec. 1973): 131–9; Daryl Michael Scott, "Postwar Pluralism, *Brown v. Board of Education*, and the Origins of Multicultural Education," *Journal of American History* 91, no. 1 (2004): 69–82.
5 A North American sample includes Susan G. Davis, *Parades and Power: Street Theatre in Nineteenth Century Philadelphia* (Philadelphia: Temple University Press, 1985); Ian Radforth, *Royal Spectacle* (Toronto: University of Toronto Press, 2004); H.V. Nelles, *The Art of Nation Building: Pageantry and Spectacle at Quebec's Tercentenary* (Toronto: University of Toronto Press, 1999); Ronald Rudin, *Founding Fathers: The Celebrations of Champlain and Laval in the Streets of*

Quebec, 1878–1908 (Toronto: University of Toronto Press, 2003); John R. Gillis, ed., *Commemorations: The Politics of National Identity* (Princeton, NJ: Princeton University Press, 1994); John Bodnar, *Remaking America: Public Memory, Commemoration and Patriotism in the Twentieth Century* (Princeton, NJ: Princeton University Press, 1992); Craig Heron and Steve Penfold, *The Workers' Festival: Labour Day Parades* (Toronto: University of Toronto Press, 2006); Michael Kammen, *Mystic Chords of Memory: The Transformation of Tradition in American Culture* (New York: Knopf, 1991); Eric Hobsbawm and Terrence Ranger, eds., *The Invention of Tradition* (Cambridge: Cambridge University Press, 1990); Eva Mackey, *The House of Difference: Cultural Politics and National Identity in Canada* (Toronto: University of Toronto Press, 2002).

6 Robert Cupido, "Public Commemoration and the Politics of Cultural Assertion: Winnipeg Celebrates the Diamond Jubilee of Confederation," *Urban History Review* 38, no. 2 (Spring 2010): 64–74 (quotation on p. 65); Edwin N. Wilmsen and Patrick McAllister, eds., *The Politics of Difference: Ethnic Premises in a World of Power* (Chicago: University of Chicago Press, 1998); Ellen M. Litwicki, "'Our Hearts Burn with Ardent Love for Two Countries': Ethnicity and Assimilation," *Journal of American Ethnic History* 19, no. 3 (Spring 2000): 3–34; Laurie Bertram, *The Viking Immigrants: Icelandic North Americans* (Toronto: University of Toronto Press, 2019); Geneviève Fabre, Jürgen Heideking, and Kai Dreisch, eds., *Celebrating Ethnicity and Nation: American Festive Culture from the Revolution to the Early Twentieth Century* (New York: Berghahn Books, 2001).

7 McKay, *The Quest of the Folk*, 13–154. See also chapter 11.

8 See my discussion on this theme in part 1.

9 A sample of this extensive literature includes the following: Jack Jedwab, *The Multiculturalism Question: Debating Identity in 21st Century Canada* (Montreal/Kingston: McGill-Queen's University Press, 2014); Eve Haque, *Multiculturalism within a Bilingual Framework: Language, Race, and Belonging in Canada* (Toronto: University of Toronto Press, 2012); Aya Fujiwara, *Ethnic Elites and Canadian Identity: Japanese, Ukrainians, and Scots, 1919–1971* (Winnipeg: University of Manitoba Press, 2012); Manoly Lupul, *The Politics of Multiculturalism: A Ukrainian-Canadian Memoir* (Edmonton: Canadian Institute of Ukrainian Studies, 2005); Julia Lalande, "The Roots of Multiculturalism – Ukrainian-Canadian Involvement in the Multiculturalism Discussion of the 1960s as an Example of the Position of the Third Force," *Canadian Ethnic Studies* 38, no. 1 (2006): 47–64; Richard J.F. Day, *Multiculturalism and the History of Canadian Diversity* (Toronto: University of Toronto Press, 2000); Lee Blanding, "Re-branding Canada: The Origins of Canadian Multiculturalism Policy, 1945–1974" (PhD diss., University of Victoria, 2013); Robert F. Harney, "'So Great a Heritage as Ours': Immigration and Survival of the Canadian Polity," *Daedalus* 117 (Fall 1988): 51–97; Manoly Lupul, "The Political Implementation of Multiculturalism," *Journal of Canadian Studies* 17, no. 1 (1982): 93–102; Manoly Lupul, "The Tragedy of Canada's White Ethnics: A

Constitutional Post-Mortem," *Journal of Ukrainian Studies* 7, no. 1 (1982): 3–15; Wsevolod Isajiw, "Multiculturalism and the Integration of the Canadian Community," *Canadian Ethnic Studies* 15, no. 2 (1983): 107–17; Evelyn Kallen, "Multiculturalism: Ideology, Policy, and Reality," *Journal of Canadian Studies* 17, no. 1 (1982): 51–63; Stella Hryniuk, ed., *Twenty Years of Multiculturalism: Successes and Failures* (Winnipeg: St John's College, 1992); Stella Hryniuk and Lubomyr Luciuk, eds., *Multiculturalism and Ukrainian Canadians* (Toronto: Multicultural History Society of Ontario, 1993). See also my discussion of contemporary debates in chapter 2.

10 See, for example, flyers in MU6413, File: Ethnic Occasions 1957. On Hanson, see Rachel Gotlieb and Michael Prokopow, "Scandinavian Design Comes to Canada," and "Everything Cold Is New Again," in *True Nordic: How Scandinavia Influenced Design in Canada* (London: Black Dog, 2016), https://www.gardinermuseum.on.ca/wp-content/uploads/True-Nordic-English.pdf; "Thor Hansen, 1903–1976," in *Feckless*, https://www.fecklesscollection.ca/thor-hansen; "Designer Thor Hansen – Huronia Museum Show," in *Huronia Museum*, https://huroniamuseum.com/category/thor-hansen/; Stephen Dale, "Redesigning the Canadian Identity: The Influence of Scandinavian Style," 16 Oct .2016, *National Gallery of Canada*, https://www.gallery.ca/magazine/your-collection/redesigning-the-canadian-identity-the-influence-of-scandinavian-style (all last accessed 28 Feb. 2020).

11 Kristin L. Hoganson, *Consumers' Imperium: The Global Production of American Domesticity, 1865–1920* (Chapel Hill: University of North Carolina Press, 2007), 230–5; Mina Carson, *Settlement Folk: Social Thought and the American Settlement Movement, 1895–1930* (Chicago: University of Chicago Press, 1990). On the importance of shared language to nation-building, see Benedict Anderson, *Imagined Community*, ch. 5, whose comments about vernacular language and newspapers can be applied to the dissemination of multicultural vocabulary, concepts, and images through print and other media.

12 Litwicki, "Our Hearts Burn," 5–6. See also Werner Sollors, "Introduction," in *The Invention of Ethnicity* (New York: Oxford University Press, 1989); Kathleen Neils Conzen et al., "The Invention of Ethnicity: A Perspective from the USA," *Journal of American Ethnic History* 12, no. 1 (Fall 1992): 3–41.

13 Examples from Hoganson, *Consumers' Imperium*, 209, 218–29.

14 Ibid., 222–6. See also the discussion of handicrafts in chapter 11.

15 Raymond A. Mohl, "Cultural Pluralism in Immigrant Education: The International Institutes of Boston, Philadelphia, and San Francisco, 1920–1940," *Journal of American Ethnic History* 1, no. 2 (Spring 1982): quotation on p. 41; 38, 50–1.

16 Diana Selig, *Americans All: The Cultural Gifts Movement* (Cambridge, MA: Harvard University Press, 2008), chs. 2–5, conclusion.

17 Selig, *Americans All,* epilogue, 275–6; Ellen D. Wu, *The Color of Success: Asian Americans and the Origins of the Model Minority* (Princeton, NJ: Princeton University Press, 2014).

18 See, for example, George J. Sánchez, "'What's Good for Boyle Heights Is Good for the Jews': Creating Multiculturalism on the Eastside during the 1950s," *American Quarterly* 56, no. 3 (Sept. 2004): 633-61, and my discussion in chapter 2.
19 Franca Iacovetta and Erica Toffoli, "A Double-Edged Pluralism: Paradoxes of Diversity in the United States International Institute Movement, 1945-1965," *Journal of Social History* 54, no. 3 (Spring 2021): 897-919.
20 MU6400, File: Administration 1958-66, Philadelphia Folk Fair pamphlet.
21 Ibid., Annual Report, Elisabeth Ponafidine, Director, International Institute of Buffalo, 21 April 1965; *Intercom*, Oct. 1965.
22 Victoria Hayward, *Romantic Canada* (Toronto: Macmillan, 1922), 239, 23-5, 70, chs. 20--28; Ryan McKenney and Benjamin Bryce, "Creating the Canadian Mosaic," *Active History*, 16 May 2016, https://activehistory.ca/2016/05/creating-the-canadian-moasic/ (last accessed 10 June 2020).
23 Kate A. Foster, *Our Canadian Mosaic* (Toronto: Dominion Council of the Young Women's Christian Association, 1926); pluralist readings by Allan Smith, "Metaphor and "Metaphor and Nationality in North America," in *Canada - An American Nation? Essays on Continentalism, Identity and the Canadian Frame of Mind* (Montreal/Kingston: McGill-Queen's University Press, 1994), 139 (cited by Bellay), and McKenney and Bryce, "Creating the Canadian Mosaic"; Susan Bellay, "Pluralism and Ethnic/Race Relations in Canadian Social Science, 1880-1939" (PhD diss., University of Manitoba, 2001), 409-10.
24 McKay, *The Quest of the Folk*, 57-60; quotation from Andrew McIntosh, Ruth Pincoe, and Donald J.C. Phillipson, "John Murray Gibbon," *Canadian Encyclopedia*, 28 June 2007, https://www.thecanadianencyclopedia.ca/en/article/john-murray-gibbon-emc (last accessed 21 Nov. 2019).
25 McIntosh et al. call Murray the first Canadian to conceptualize Canada as a mosaic: https://www.thecanadianencyclopedia.ca/en/article/john-murray-gibbon-emc (accessed 21 Nov. 2019).
26 McKenny and Bryce, "Creating the Canadian Mosaic."
27 McKay, *The Quest of the Folk*, 57. See also Day, *Multiculturalism*, 147-8; Stuart Henderson, "'While There Is Still Time ...': J. Murray Gibbon and the Spectacle of Difference in Three CPR Folk Festivals, 1928- 31," *Journal of Canadian Studies* 39 (2005): 139-74; Gibbon, *Making of a Northern Nation*. On handicrafts, see chapter 11.
28 McKay, *The Quest of the Folk*, 57. See also John Murray Gibbon, *Canadian Mosaic: The Making of a Northern Nation* (Toronto: McClelland & Stewart, 1938), 413, 424-5.
29 Henderson, "'While There Is Still Time," 141-52. See also Gordana Lazarevich, "The Role of the CPR in Promoting Canadian Culture," in Glen Carruthers, ed., *A Celebration of Canada's Arts, 1930-1970* (Toronto: Canadian Scholars Press, 1996), 3-13.
30 Advertisement in Manitoba *Free Press* cited in Henderson, "'While There Is Still Time,'" 151.

31 Orest T. Martynowych, *The Showman and the Ukrainian Cause: Folk Dance, Film, and the Life of Vasile Avramenko* (Winnipeg: University of Manitoba Press, 2015). On US ethnic pluralism, see also chapter 2.
32 Cupido, "Public Commemoration and Politics of Cultural Assertion," 64–74, which draws on Litwicki and others. See also his "Appropriating the Past: Pageants, Politics and the Diamond Jubilee of Confederation," *Journal of the Canadian Historical Association* 9, no. 1 (1998): 155–86, and his "Competing Pasts, Multiple Identities: The Diamond Jubilee of Confederation and the Politics of Commemoration," in Matthew Hayday and Raymond B. Blake, eds., *Celebrating Canada*, vol. 2, *Commemorations, Anniversaries, and National Symbols* (Toronto: University of Toronto Press, 2018), 97–144. On rival commemoration involving immigrant/ethnic groups, see, for example, Lianbi Zhu and Timothy Baycroft, "A Chinese Counterpart to Dominion Day: Chinese Humiliation Day in Interwar Canada, 1924–1930," in Hayday and Blake, *Celebrating Canada*, vol. 1, 244–73.
33 Along with National Film Board films, wartime propaganda included Watson Kirkconnell's *Canadians All: A Primer of National Unity* (Ottawa: Director of Public Information, 1941), which used the metaphor of the "huge mixing bowl" and likened the Canadian peoples to the spiciest of mincemeat. McKay, *The Quest of the Folk*, 79; Ivana Caccia, *Managing the Canadian Mosaic in Wartime: Shaping Citizenship Policy, 1939–1945* (Montreal/Kingston: McGill-Queen's University Press, 2010); Franca Iacovetta, *Gatekeepers: Reshaping Immigrant Lives in Cold War Canada*, (Toronto: Between the Lines, 2006), ch. 4.
34 MU6472, File: Letters of Appreciation, Flyer, "Bazaar" n.d.
35 Kammen, *Mystic Chords of Memory*, 300–2, 533–6, 547–8; Stuart Patternson, "The Dream Then and Now: Democratic Nostalgia and the Living Museum at Arthurdale, West Virginia," in Amy K. Levin, ed., *Local Museums and the Construction of History in America's Changing Communities* (Lanham, MD: Rowman & Littlefield, 2007), 111.
36 MU6472, File: Letters of Appreciation 1959–62, *International Institute News* [before named *Intercom*], "Old World Bazaar," 1957.
37 Mikhail Bakhtin, *Rabelais and His World* (Bloomington: Indiana University Press, 1941) . By virtue of its quality of inversion or levelling, such an event could act as a safety valve allowing for a reversion to a status quo or contained elements that in time would engender significant change.
38 MU6442 (B280579), File: Intercom Copies, *International Institute News*, April 1957, Anne Von Oesen, "Folklore – Rehabilitated."
39 MU6413, File: Ethnic Occasions 1957, "Ethnic Weeks."
40 MU6411, File: Cultural Festival (Member Organizations), West/Forbell notes; MU6415, File: Latvian Federation 1957, notes.
41 Philip V. Bohlman, *The Study of Folk Music in the Modern World* (Bloomington: Indiana University Press, 1988), 59; see also Matthew Frye Jacobson, *Whiteness of a Different Color: European Immigrants and the Alchemy of Race* (Cambridge,

MA: Harvard University Press, 1998); Matthew Frye Jacobson, *Special Sorrows: The Diasporic Imagination of Irish, Polish, and Jewish Immigrants in the United States* (Berkeley: University of California Press, 2002).
42 Berkenmayer, *Intercom,* Oct. 1957.
43 MU6413, File: Ethnic Federations 1957-64, Flyer German Week, Feb. 1957; Flyer Latvian Week, March-April 1957; MU6416, File: Institute Folders/Pamphlets 1957-59, Lithuanian Week, Feb. 1957.
44 MU6416, File Institute Folders/Pamphlets 1957-59, Programme, St George's Day.
45 MU6413, File: Ethnic Occasions 1957, West's template letter, 29 Oct. 1959, to potential donors.
46 MU6414, File: Canadian Hungarian Federation 1963, 1968, Flyer and Programme for Hungarian Ethnic Week, Nov. 1963, Opening Programme; MU6666, File: Director Correspondence, File, Memo Mayor Don Summerville, n.d., lecturers Mr I.J.J. Koroknay (architecture) and Mr Bacsalmasy (minority groups in Hungary). On Kodály, see Percy M. Young, *Zoltan Kodaly: A Hungarian Musician* (London: E. Bern, 1964); Rita Gero, "Music," *Hungarian Presence in Canada,* https://hungarianpresence.ca/arts-and-culture/music/; "Zoltán Kodály (1882-1967)," *Classical Archives,* https://www.classicalarchives.com/composer/2806.html (both last accessed 19 April 2022).
47 MU6415, File: Ethnic Press 1955-62, West to Julius Baier [A Conservative and owner of *Zeitung*], *Toronto Zeitung,* 1 Sept. 1960.
48 MU6666, File: Director Correspondence, H.C. Forbell to Mrs Donald Summerville, 23 Dec. 1963.
49 MU6442 (B280579), File: Intercom, Flyer, Continental Canadiana, Oct. 1961; MU6446 (B280583), File: Recreational Activity, Notices, 1969, Flyers, Italian Variety Night, Serata Italiana, Continental Café; *Intercom,* Portuguese Festival, 28 Jan. 1968.
50 MU6415, File: Portuguese Information Centre, April 1972-3. Portuguese press and radio covered the event and Portuguese bakeries supplied pastries. On Rodrigues, see Gilberto Fernandes, *This Pilgrim Nation: The Making of the Portuguese Diaspora in Postwar North America* (Toronto: University of Toronto Press, 2020), 157, 275.
51 MU6446 (B280583), File: Recreational Activity, Notices, 1969, Flyer, India Night, 23 Feb.; Flyer, Japanese Night, March 1969; On Calypso Capers, *Intercom,* July 1961; MU6415, File: Tibetan Cultural Society 1972-3; MU6454 (B280591), File: Cultural Festival, Flyer, Asian Immigrant Youth Centre, Festival, 1973.
52 City of Toronto Archives (CTA), Social Planning Council of Metropolitan Toronto (SPC), SC40, Box 53, File: IIMT, R. Kolm, Evaluation of Department, Oct. 1956-Oct. 1958.
53 Excerpt from Yaremko speech (Feb. 1961) in Ontario Legislature, *Intercom,* Aug. 1961; Yaremko address (May 1966) acknowledging graduates of English classes at Institute, *Intercom,* May-June 1966. See also G. Laing and Celine Cooper, "Royal

Commission on Bilingualism and Biculturalism," 12 Aug. 2013, in *The Canadian Encyclopedia*, https://www.thecanadianencyclopedia.ca/en/article/royal-commission-on-bilingualism-and-biculturalism (July 2019); "John Yaremko," Obituaries, *Toronto Star*, 9 Aug. 2010. https://www.legacy.com/obituaries/thestar/obituary.aspx?n=john-yaremko&pid=144586284&fhid=7523 (both last accessed 19 April 2022).

54 MU6472, Letters of Appreciation 1959–62, *Newsletter* 1957–8, "Canadiana Week" and "Our Special Thanks"; MU6414, File: Institute Folders/Pamphlets 1957–9, Flyer/Programme Open House, Canadian Week Sept.–Oct. 1957.

55 MU6414, File: Institute Folders/Pamphlets 1957–9, Flyer/Programme, Canadian Week Sept.–Oct. 1957.

56 MU6404, File: Canadiana Week 1961–5, Flyer/Programme, Canadiana Week Sept.–Oct. 1963.

57 *Intercom*, Dec. 1965, review as news clipping in file; MU6404, File: Canadiana Week 1961–5, J.T. Seaman, Director to H.J. Boakes, 21 Oct. 1965.

58 MU6415, File: Canadiana Week 1961–5, Invitation, Sept.–Oct. 1964, with Programme; Flyer, Canadiana Week, Canadian Paintings. On the theme's longevity, see Carl Berger, "The True North Strong and Free," in Peter Russell, ed., *Nationalism in Canada* (Toronto: McGraw-Hill, 1966), 3–26; Carl Berger, *The Writing of Canadian History: Aspects of English-Canadian Historical Writing, 1900–1970* (Toronto: University of Toronto Press, 1986); on Group of Seven, see Mackey, *House of Difference*, 52–9.

59 MU6415, File: Canadiana Week 1961–5, Brochure, *Confederation Life's Gallery of Canadian History*. The paintings hung in a gallery in the company's Toronto headquarters. A current example is Royal Bank of Canada, "The Canadian Shield," *Corporate Responsibility Publications* 62, no. 6 (1981), https://www.rbc.com/aboutus/letter/nov_dec1981.html (last accessed 19 April 2022).

60 Canadian historian George Stanley's imperialist *Birth of Western Canada: A History of the Riel Rebellions* (London: Longmans, 1936; republished by University of Toronto Press, 1966) was for many years the standard academic text on the subject.

61 MU6415, File: Canadiana Week 1961–5, Robert Kreem to Public Relations Department, Confederation Life, 1 Oct. 1965. On institutional forgetting, Kammen, *Mystic Chords of Memory*; Nelles, *Art of Nation*; McKay, *The Quest of the Folk*; Mackey, *House of Difference*; among others.

62 MU6416, File: Folk Festival Minutes of Meetings, Flyer/Programme, 8th Annual John Madsen Folk Festival, 25 June 1955 (admission: adults 75 cents, children 25 cents); Flyer/Programme, 9th Annual John Madsen Folk Festival, Cherry Hill Farm, 23 June 1956; *Intercom*, June 1957, "Cherry Hill Festival" and "Lesson in Understanding." See also Robert Klymasz, "'Sounds You Never Heard Before': Ukrainian Country Music in Western Canada," *Ethnomusicology* 16 (1972): 372–80.

63 *Intercom*, June 1957, "Cherry Hill Festival" and "Lesson in Understanding." My general discussion draws on other flyers in MU6416, File: Folk Festival Minutes of Meetings, Flyer/Programme. See also Robert B. Klymasz, "From Immigrant to Ethnic Folklore: A Canadian View of Process and Transition," *Journal of the Folklore Institute* 10, no. 3 (Dec. 1973): 131–9.

64 CNE Grandstand Performers, 1948–94, https://concerts.fandom.com/wiki/Canadian_National_Exhibition_Stadium (last accessed 5 July 2021).

65 Quoted in MU6409 (B280540), File: Board of Directors Meetings 1961, IIMT, Memo re:Establishments of an Annual Cultural Festival, 26 Oct. 1961.

66 MU6407, File: Community Folk Art Council (hereafter CFAC) 1963–74, *Community Folk Art Council Newsletter* 2 (1964); on Kossar, see Andrew Gregorovich, "Leon Kossar," *Infoukes*, https://www.infoukes.com/newpathway/Page131.htm (last accessed 1 Dec. 2019); Kassandra Luciuk, "Making Ukrainian Canadians: Identity, Politics, and Power in Cold War Canada" (PhD diss., University of Toronto, 2021), ch. 4.

67 Jesse Munroe Personal Archive, Canadian National Exhibition Association (CNEA), *Canadian National Exhibition (CNE) Souvenir Catalogue and Programme*, 1964 and 1965 (Toronto).

68 AO, R. Kreem, "The Community Groups at the Institute," *Intercom*, July 1961 [referencing a Canadiana Week concert]; MU6382, File: Board of Directors Minutes, 12 June 1956, Dec. 1957, Minutes of Programme Committee Meeting, 1 May 1957, Program Committee Report. See also Lorenzkowski, *Sounds of Ethnicity* 121–7.

69 Michael Cobden, "$2,000,000 Metro festival hinges on Ottawa approval," *Toronto Star*, 28 May 1970. Drawing on figures provided by Munroe, I (not Munroe) issued these estimates.

70 Leon Kossar, "New Canadian Interests," news clipping in MU6385 (B280523), File: Metro International Caravan. See also obituary, "Caravan co-founder Leon Kossar dies," Toronto *Globe and Mail*, 7 Aug. 2001, https://www.theglobeandmail.com/news/national/caravan-co-founder-leon-kossar-dies/article4150951/ (last accessed 1 Dec. 2019).

71 On Expo 67, see, for example, Maude-Emmanuelle Lambert's entry in *The Canadian Encyclopedia*, https://www.thecanadianencyclopedia.ca/en/article/expo-67 (last accessed 1 Dec. 2019); John Lownsbrough, *The Best Place to Be: Expo 67 and Its Time* (Toronto: Allen Lane, 2012); Rhona Richman Kenneally and Johanne Sloan, eds., *Expo 67: Not Just a Souvenir* (Toronto: University of Toronto Press, 2010).

72 Stoian cited in *Intercom*, May–June 1966.

73 MU6407, File: CFAC, 1963–74, CFAC Brief to Centennial Commission for 1967 Canada Day, and notes.

74 MU6385 (B280523), File: Metro International Caravan, CFAC, 1969 Details; Executive Committee, 1969 Plans; Final Instructions Re: Operations, 26–30 June 1969. On food, see chapter 9.

75 MU6407, File: CFAC, 1963–74, news clippings, 1969, 1970, 1972.
76 In conversations with 25 Anglo-Torontonians, my mention of Metro Caravan immediately elicited stories about it prompting their first foray into "unknown" ethnic neighbourhoods.
77 MU6385 (B280523), File: Metro International Caravan, Executive Committee, 1969 Plans, later materials, n.d.; CFAC "Metro International Caravan '69 Details" (6 pp). See also David Wencer, "Historicist: The Caravan Is on Its Way," *Torontoist*, 24 June 2017, https://torontoist.com/2017/06/historicist-caravan-way/ ; Noor Javed, "The couple who put Toronto on the map," *Toronto Star*, 4 April 2009, https://www.thestar.com/news/gta/2009/04/04/the_couple_who_put_toronto_on_the_map.html (both last accessed 19 April 2022).
78 MU6407, File: CFAC 1963–74, news clippings, Colin Murray, "Metro International Caravan Toronto's at home to the world," *Toronto Telegram Weekend/The Good Life*, 21 June 1969. On US media attention in the seventies, Javed, "The Couple."
79 MU6407, File: CFAC 1963–74, news clippings, McKenzie Porter, "Caravan Will Give Me a Chance to Dance in the Open," n.d.; quotation from his "Reckless of WASPs to Ignore Caravan," 4 July 1969 (reprinted in *Torontoer* German-language newspaper).
80 Ibid., "'Nina Rosada' Alive in Canada," *Carribean Chronicle* 2, no. 4 (June 1969); Press Release, 12 June 1969, Board of Directors Reminder Memoranda, 11 and 27 June 1969; Report of Caravan Committee, 21 May 1969; *Intercom*, July 1969; other press releases. On food, see chapter 9.
81 Charles Roach, "Some Thoughts on Immigrant Cultural Expression in Toronto," *Intercom*, Sept.–Oct. 1965. On history of Caribana, see, for example, B. Denham Jolly, *In the Black: My Life* (Toronto: ECW Press, 2017), ch. 10; Peter Jackson, "The Politics of the Street: A Geography of Caribana," *Political Geography* 11, no. 2 (March 1992): 130–51.
82 MU6446 (B280383), File: Recreational Activity, Notices, 1969, Scandinavian Night, 7 Feb. 1970, organizer Tore Maagaard.
83 See, for example, planning details, invitations, thank you letters in MU6413, File: Ethnic Occasions 1957; MU6404, File: Canadiana Week 1961–5; and MU6415, File: Canadiana Week 1961–5.
84 On group memberships, see chapter 7.
85 MU6432 (B280569), File: UCF (United Community Fund), IIMT 1960 Analysis to UCF. The folk groups with their own group memberships included the Canadian Polish Dancers Group and Serbian Assembly Folk Dancers.
86 MU6446 (B280583), File: Recreational Activity 1969, Flyer, Japanese Night, March 1969.
87 Of course, group resources varied. On the underfunded Portuguese folk groups, see Fernandes, *This Pilgrim Nation*, ch. 4.
88 MU6413, File: Ethnic Occasions, West to Mr Z. Jaworski, 6 March 1957.

386 Notes to pages 249–51

89 For example, its use during folk festival planning meetings in MU6411, File: Cultural Festival 1961–2, Agenda of Meeting, 8 Nov. 1961.
90 This literature (which includes the references above) is extensive, but pertinent Toronto studies include the following: Ian Radforth, "Collective Rights, Liberal Discourse, and Public Order: The Clash over Catholic Processions in Mid-Victorian Toronto," *Canadian Historical Review* 95, no. 4, (Dec. 2014): 511–44; Noula Mina, "Homeland Activism, Public Performance, and the Construction of Identity: An Examination of Greek Canadian Transnationalism, 1900s–1990s (PhD diss., University of Toronto, 2014); Jordan Stanger-Ross, *Staying Italian: Urban Change and Ethnic Life in Postwar Toronto and Philadelphia* (Chicago: University of Chicago Press, 2009), esp. ch. 3; Fernandes, *This Pilgrim Nation*, ch. 4; Vienna Paolantonio, "Good Friday on College Street: Urban Space and Changing Italian Identity" (PhD diss., York University, 2020); Luciuk, "Making Ukrainian Canadians," ch. 4; Christopher Grafos, "Canada's Greek Moment: Transnational Politics, Activists, and Spies during the Long Sixties" (PhD diss., York University, 2016), chs. 4–5.
91 I discuss the folk movement in chapter 11, but see Gillian Mitchell, *The North American Folk Music Revival: Nation and Identity in the United States and Canada, 1945–1980*, 2nd ed. (Abingdon: Routledge, 2016).
92 For examples, see invitations in MU6413, File: Ethnic Occasions; MU6414, File: Byelorussian 1955–66.
93 MU6446 (B280583), File: Recreational Activity 1969, Flyers Greek Night/Sunday, 23 Nov. 1969.
94 Klymasz, "From Immigrant to Ethnic Folklore," 139.
95 MU6473, File: Hungarian Art and Exhibition 1963, *Telegram* news clipping.
96 MU6415, File: Latvian Federation in Canada, pamphlet "Latvian Arts and Crafts." MU6414, File: Byelorussian 1955–66, Byelorussian Alliance in Canada.
97 See, for example, Klymasz, "From Immigrant to Ethnic Folklore," 131–9.
98 See, for example, Janos Buda (art director) review of Kodály Concert in *Intercom*, July 1961, and references to Kodály above. On art patrons, see chapter 11.
99 For example, MU6416, File: Folk Festival Minutes of Meetings, Minutes of Meeting 29 March 1957, Minutes of Interim Folk Festival Committee Meeting, 12 April 1957.
100 MU6385 (B280523), File: Metro International Caravan, Participating Organizations, June 1969.
101 For example, MU6414, File: Byelorussian 1955–66, Anton Markievich, Secretary General, Byelorussian Alliance in Canada, Toronto, to West, Director of Services, 30 Aug. 1961; 23 Aug. 1961, 18 Jan. 1964; West to Markievich, 19 March 1963.
102 Litwicki, "Our Hearts Burn"; Edwin N. Wilmsen, "Introduction: Premises of Power in Ethnic Politics," 2–5, and Jan Nederveen, "Varieties of Ethnic Politics and Ethnicity Discourse," 25–44, both in Edwin N. Wilmsen and Patrick McAllister, eds., *The Politics of Difference: Ethnicity Premises in a World of Power*

(Chicago: University of Chicago Press, 1996); Cupido, "Public Commemoration and Ethno-Cultural Assertion."
103 Gary Cristall, "A History of Folk Music in Canada: The People's Music," 5-part documentary, CBC Radio, 2008, https://folkmusichistory.com/itmschedule.shtml (last accessed 1 Dec. 2019); Rhonda Hinther, *Perogies and Politics: Canada's Ukrainian Left* (Toronto: University of Toronto Press, 2018), 83–212; Luciuk, "Making Ukrainian Canadians," ch. 4, and references in previous note.
104 MU6416, File; Canadian Hungarian Federation 1963, 1968, Invitation returned, 12 Nov. 63, Slavic Ethnic Club; Invitation returned, Nov. 1963, Captive Nations Club, T.B. Cavlas Yanolcracy.
105 It appears that one hundred or so people typically attended the Saturday ethnic nights at the Davenport Road building.
106 For just one example, MU6413, File: Ethnic Occasions 1957. W.E. West, Director to Mr Z. Jaworski, president Toronto Branch, Canadian Polish Congress, 6 March 1957.
107 Anderson, *Imagined Community*, ch. 3; Eric Hobsbawm, "Introduction" and "Mass-Producing Traditions: Europe, 1870–1914," in Hobsbawm and Ranger, *Invention of Tradition*, 263–308; On ethnic groups, symbolism, and emotional draw of nationalism, see Anthony D. Smith, *Nations and Nationalism in a Global Era* (Cambridge, UK: Polity, 1995). For Canada, see, for example, Himani Bannerji, *The Dark Side of the Nation: Essays on Multiculturalism, Nationalism, and Gender* (Toronto: Canadian Scholars Press, 2000); Fujiwara, *Ethic Elites*.
108 On this strategy, see, besides Litwicki, "Our Hearts Burn," Paul A. Bramadat, "Shows, Selves, and Solidarity: Ethnic Identity and Cultural Spectacles in Canada," *Canadian Ethnic Studies* 33, no. 2 (2001): 78–98; and for a critique of its homogenizing effect, see Audrey Kobayashi, "Multiculturalism: Representing a Canadian Institution," in J. Duncan and D. Ley, eds., *Place/Culture/Representation* (New York: Routledge, 1993), 205–31. On using the strategy against left opponents, see Luciuk, "Making Ukrainian Canadians," ch. 4. See also my discussion in the conclusion
109 MU6416, File: Folk Festival Minutes of Meetings Only, General Invitation/Program, May 1960; *Intercom*, July 1961. See also "John Collingwood Reade," in *History of Canadian Broadcasting*, https://www.broadcasting-history.ca/personalities/reade-john-collingwood (last accessed 2 Dec. 2019); Anderson, *Imagined Community*, ch. 3, esp. 44–6.
110 Mathew Hayday, "Fireworks, Folk-dancing, and Fostering a National Identity: The Politics of Canada Day," *Canadian Historical Review* 91, no. 2 (June 2010): 298–305; CBC Radio, *Folk Song Time* (1950s); and *Folk Sounds* (1960s, hosted by Edith Fowke) and 1970s (more commercial fare).
111 Without intending to flatten the differences in nuance or emphasis among them, here I would include the following examples: Matthew Hayday, "Canada's National Day: Inventing a Tradition, Defining a Culture," in Matthew Hayday and

Raymond Blake, eds., *Celebrating Canada*, vol. 1, *Holidays, National Days and the Crafting of Identities* (Toronto: University of Toronto Press, 2016), 274–305; José E. Igartua, *The Other Quiet Revolution: National Identities in English Canada, 1945–71* (Vancouver: UBC Press, 2006); Royden Loewen and Gerald Friesen, *Immigrants in Prairie Cities: Ethnic Diversity in Twentieth-Century Canada* (Toronto: University of Toronto Press, 2009); Robert C. Vipond, *Making a Global City: How One Toronto School Embraced Diversity* (Toronto: University of Toronto Press, 2017); Wsevolod W. Isajiw, "Multiculturalism and the Integration of the Canadian Community," *Canadian Ethnic Studies* 15, no. 2 (1983): 107–17; Fujiwara, *Ethnic Elites*, esp. chs. 5–6.

112 H.D. Forbes, "Trudeau as the First Theorist of Canadian Multiculturalism," 27–42, and Michael Temelini, "Multicultural Rights, Multicultural Virtues: A History of Multiculturalism in Canada," 43–60, respectively, both in Stephen Tierney, ed., *Multiculturalism and the Canadian Constitution* (Vancouver: UBC Press, 2007). And, with a focus on Ukrainian Canadians, Lalande, "Roots of Multiculturalism," 47–64; Bohdan Bociurkiw, "The Federal Policy of Multiculturalism and the Ukrainian-Canadian Community," in Lupul, *Ukrainian Canadians*, 98–121. See also Bohdan S. Kordan, "The Intelligentsia and the Development of Ukrainian Ethnic Consciousness in Canada," *Canadian Ethnic Studies* 17, no. 1 (1985): 22–32.

113 Again, there are differences of emphasis, but I include among the critiques the following: Karl Peter, "The Myth of Multiculturalism and Other Political Fables," in Jorgen Dahlie and Tissa Fernando, eds., *Ethnicity, Power and Politics in Canada* (Toronto: Methuen 1981), 56–67; Luciuk, "Making Ukrainian Canadians," ch. 4; Bannerji, *Dark Side of the Nation*; essays by Grace-Edward Galabuzi, Rinaldo Walcott, and others in May Chazan et al., eds., *Home and Native Land: Unsettling Multiculturalism in Canada* (Toronto: Between the Lines, 2011); Haque, *Multiculturalism*. On militant movements, see, for example, Lara Campbell, Dominique Clement, and Gregory S. Kealey, eds., *Debating Dissent Canada and the Sixties* (Toronto: University of Toronto Press, 2012); Scott Rutherford, *Canada's Other Red Scare: Indigenous Protest and Colonial Encounters during the Global Sixties* (Montreal/Kingston: McGill-Queen's University Press, 2020). By contrast, Manoly Lupul blames the "failure" of multiculturalism on Trudeau's indifference to the policy. See his "Political Implementation."

114 On the latter, see C.P. Champion, *The Strange Demise of British Canada: Liberals and Canadian Nationalism, 1964–1968* (Montreal/Kingston: McGill-Queen's University Press, 2010). See also Katie Pickles, *Female Imperialism and National Identity: Imperial Order Daughters of the Empire* (Manchester: Manchester University Press, 2002), ch. 7.

115 Such as the Canadian Polish Congress. On the hearings, see Haque, *Multiculturalism*, esp. ch. 2.

116 MU6411, File: Cultural Festival 1961-2, Minutes of Meeting of Presidents of Ethnic Organizations re: Establishment of Annual Cultural Festival, 8 Nov. 1961; and

succinct summary in File: Cultural Festival 1961–2, Minutes of Meeting, 8 Nov. 1961, Scotti Room.
117 Quoted in MU6407, File: CFAC 1963–74, news clipping, *Toronto Star Week* magazine cover story, Peter Goddard, "Visit 42 cities in eight days during Metro Caravan," n.d., but the date is 24 June 1972.
118 On Toronto's importance, see James Lemon, *Toronto since 1918: An Illustrated History* (Toronto: James Lorimer, 1985).
119 I am referring to the 1970s and 1980s and the popularity of folk festivals like Metro Caravan. But see, too, Jedwab, "Introduction," in *Multiculturalism Question*, esp. 1–5. In 1998, Will Kymlicka used increasing rates of intermarriage, naturalization, and political participation as well as approval of mixed-race marriages and friendships since 1971 as indicators of successful integration and multiculturalism in *Finding Our Way: Rethinking Ethnocultural Relations in Canada* (Toronto: Oxford University Press, 1998), 15–24, 187–90. Scholarly critics have also defended the policy; see, for example, Yasmeen Abu-Laban and Daiva Stasilius, "Ethnic Pluralism under Siege: Popular and Partisan Opposition to Multiculturalism, *Canadian Public Policy* 18, no. 4 (1992): 365–86.

11 Handicrafts, High Art, and Human Rights: Cultural Guardianship and Internationalism

1 Archives of Ontario (AO), International Institute of Metropolitan Toronto, Fonds 884, MU6423 (B280560), File: Old World Bazaar 1957–9, United Nations Week 1957.
2 A small sample of the relevant scholarship includes Kristin L. Hoganson, *Consumers' Imperium: The Global Production of American Domesticity, 1865–1920* (Chapel Hill: University of North Carolina Press, 2007), ch. 5, esp. 230–5; Jane Addams, *Twenty Years at Hull House* (New York: Bedford/St. Martins, 1998), ch. 16; Ian McKay, *The Quest of the Folk: Antimodernism and Cultural Selection in Twentieth-Century Nova Scotia* (Montreal/Kingston: McGill-Queen's University Press, 1994); Allana C. Lundgren, "Amy Sternberg's Historical Pageant (1927): The Performance of IODE Ideology during Canada's Diamond Jubilee," *Theatre Research* 32, no. 1 (2011): 1–29; Janet McNaughton, "A Study of the CPR-Sponsored Quebec Folk Song and Handicraft Festivals" (MA thesis, Memorial University, 1982), ch. 1; Cecilia Morgan and Colin M. Coates, *Heroines and History: Representations of Madeleine de Verchères and Laura Secord* (Toronto: University of Toronto Press, 2002); Pauline Greenhill, "Radical? Feminist? Nationalist? The Canadian Paradox of Edith Fowke," *Canada Folk Music* 37, no. 3 (2003): 4, https://www.canfolkmusic.ca/index.php/cfmb/article/view/262/256 (last accessed 5 Nov. 2020).
3 On North American women's internationalism, see, for example, Leila Rupp, *Worlds of Women: The Making of an International Women's Movement* (Princeton,

NJ: Princeton University Press, 1997); Marilyn Fischer, "Addams's Internationalist Pacifism and the Rhetoric of Maternalism," *National Women's Studies Association Journal* 18, no. 3 (Fall 2006): 1–19; Nancy Forestell with Maureen Moynagh, eds., *Documenting First Wave Feminisms*, vol.2, *Canada – National and Transnational Contexts* (Toronto: University of Toronto Press, 2013); Veronica Strong-Boag, *Liberal Hearts and Coronets: The Lives and Times of Ishbel Marjoribanks Gordon and John Campbell Gordon, The Aberdeens* (Toronto: University of Toronto Press, 2015); Valerie Knowles, *First Person: A Biography of Cairine Wilson, Canada's First Woman Senator* (Toronto: Dundurn, 1987). On rethinking the scholarship, Mrinalini Sinha, Donna J. Guy, and Angela Woollacott, guest eds., Introduction and essays in Theme Issue on Feminisms and Internationalism, *Gender & History* 10, no. 3 (1998).

4 See chapter 1.

5 In addition to the references in note 2, see April R. Schultz, *Ethnicity on Parade: Inventing the Norwegian American through Celebration* (Amherst: University of Massachusetts Press, 1994); Jane Nicholas, "Gendering the Jubilee: Gender and Modernity in the Diamond Jubilee Confederation Celebrations, 1927," *Canadian Historical Review* 90, no. 2 (June 2009): 247–74; Geneviève Fabre, Jürgen Heideking, and Kai Dreisch eds., *Celebrating Ethnicity and Nation: American Festive Culture from the Revolution to the Early Twentieth Century* (New York: Berghahn Books, 2001); Frances Swyripa, *Wedded to the Cause: Ukrainian Canadian Women and Ethnic Identity, 1891–1991* (Toronto: University of Toronto Press, 1993); Laurie Bertram, *The Viking Immigrants: Icelandic North Americans* (Toronto: University of Toronto Press, 2020), esp. chs. 3–4.

6 See, for example, the essays in "Music, Movement, and Masculinities," special issue, *The World of Music* 3, no. 2 (2014); Jessica Ray Herzogenrath, "Authenticity and Ethnicity: Folk Dance, Americanization, and the Immigrant Body in Early Twentieth Century America," in Anthony Shay and Barbara Sellers-Young, eds., *Oxford Handbook of Dance and Ethnicity* (New York: Oxford University Press, 2016), ch. 12; Nihal Ötken, "Women in Folk Dances from the Gender Aspects," *Journal of Human Sciences* 8, no. 1 (2011): 268–76; Angela M. Yarbery, *Embodying the Feminine in the Dances of the World's Religions* (New York: Peter Lang, 2011); Daniel J. Walkowitz, "The Cultural Turn and a New Social History: Folk Dance and the Renovation of Class in Social History," *Journal of Social History* 39, no. 3 (Spring 2006): 781–802; Joann W. Kealiinohomoku, "The Expansion of Folk Dance Experiences," *Britannica*, https://www.britannica.com/art/folk-dance/The-expansion-of-folk-dance-experiences (last accessed 5 Nov. 2020). On cross-dressing, see Petri Hoppu, "Folk Dancers Cross-Dressed: Performing Gender in the Early Nordic Folk Dance Movement," *Journal of Folklore Research* 51, no. 3 (2014): 311–35.

7 Such as Colleen Ballerino Cohen, Richard Wilk, and Beverly Stoeltje, *Beauty Queens and the Global Stage: Gender, Contests, and Power* (London: Routledge,

1996); Patrizia Gentile, *Queen of the Maple Leaf: Beauty Contests and Settler Femininity* (Vancouver: UBC Press, 2020), and references below.

8 Such as Lundgren, "Amy Sternberg's Historical Pageant (1927)"; McNaughton, "Folk Song and Handicraft Festivals," esp. ch. 6; Paula Laverty, *Silk Stocking Mats: Hooked Mats of the Grenfell Mission* (Montreal/Kingston: McGill-Queen's University Press, 2005).

9 A small sample of the diverse scholarship on the post-1945 North American folk revival that focuses on or includes Canada reflects the revival's own multifaceted character. It includes Gillian Mitchell, *The North American Folk Music Revival in the United States and Canada*, 2nd ed. (London/New York, Routledge, 2016); Michael MacDonald, "'This Is Important!: Mitch Podolak, The Revolutionary Establishment, and the Founding of the Winnipeg Folk Festival" (MA thesis, Carleton University, 2006); Robert Klymasz, "'Sounds You Never Heard Before': Ukrainian Country Music in Western Canada," *Ethnomusicology* 16 (1972): 372–80; Robert Klymasz, "From Immigrant to Ethnic Folklore: A Canadian View of Process and Transition," *Journal of the Folklore Institute* 10, no. 3 (Dec. 1973): 131–9. See also my discussion of folk festivals in chapter 10.

10 Murphy, *Folk Music Revival*, 46–54. On how these debates played on right and left sides of a politically polarized ethnic community like the Ukrainian Canadians, see Kassandra Luciuk, "Making Ukrainian Canadians: Identity, Politics, and Power in Cold War Canada" (PhD diss., University of Toronto, 2021), ch. 4.

11 McKay, *The Quest of the Folk*, ch. 2; Murphy, *Folk Music Revival*, 33–4; Diane Tye, "'A Very Lone Worker': Woman-Centred Thoughts on Helen Creighton's Career as a Folklorist," *Canadian Folklore Canadien* 15, no. 2 (1993): 107–17.

12 While the US and wider North American network remained important, the nationalist-motivated Canadian content legislation of 1971 would prove a boon to Canadian folk and other musicians. Murphy, *Folk Music Revival*, esp. chs. 2–4, which also discuss the left-wing roots; Macdonald, "This Is Important!"

13 Klymasz, "From Immigrant to Ethnic Folklore."

14 Ellen M. Litwicki, "'Our Hearts Burn with Ardent Love for Two Countries': Ethnicity and Assimilation," *Journal of American Ethnic History* 19, no. 3 (Spring 2000): 3–34; Werner Sollors, "Introduction," to *The Invention of Ethnicity* (New York: Oxford University Press, 1989), ix–xvii; Kathleen Neils Conzen et al., "The Invention of Ethnicity: A Perspective from the USA," *Journal of American Ethnic History* 12, no. 1 (Fall 1992): 3–41; Schultz, *Ethnicity on Parade*, 10–20.

15 Klymasz, "From Immigrant to Ethnic Folklore."

16 Hankus Netsky, "Ruth Rubin, a Life In Song," *Pakn Treger* 57, no. 60 (Fall 2011): 5771, https://www.yiddishbookcenter.org/pakn-treger/12-09/ruth-rubin-a-life-song; Carolyn Blackman, "Camp Naivelt Celebrates 75 Years," *Canadian Jewish News*, 20 July 2000, https://web.archive.org/web/20050910135317/http://www.cjnews.com/pastIssues/00/july20-00/front3.asp (both last accessed 10 July 2021); Murphy, *Folk Music Revival*, 62–5, 170–2.

17 Also known as Ward-Allen Trio. MU6404, File: Canadiana Week 1961–5, Flyer/ Programme Canadiana Week 1963. For context, see Murphy, *Folk Music Revival*, esp. ch. 3; Nicholas Jennings, *Before the Gold Rush: Flashbacks to the Dawn of the Canadian Sound* (Toronto: Viking, 1997).

18 My comments refer to the historical period under review. Historical work on folklorama includes Royden Loewen and Gerald Friesen, *Immigrants in Prairie Cities: Ethnic Diversity in Twentieth-Century Canada* (Toronto: University of Toronto Press, 2009), 146–55, 181; Luciuk, "Making Ukrainian Canadians," ch. 4. For (differing) contemporary analyses, which note an emphasis on commonalities among groups as well as profits and standardization, see Paul A. Bramadat, "Shows, Selves, and Solidarity: Ethnic Identity and Cultural Spectacles in Canada," *Canadian Ethnic Studies* 33, no. 2 (2001): 78–98; and Bramadat, "For Ourselves, Our Neighbours, Our Homelands: Religion in Folklorama's Israel Pavilion," and Cynthia Thoroski and Pauline Greenhill, "Putting a Price on Culture: Ethnic Organisations, Volunteers, and the Marketing of Multicultural Festivals," both in *Ethnologies* 23, no. 1 (2001): 211–32. Other examples are in chapter 10.

19 McNaughton, "Folk Song and Handicraft Festivals," ch. 6. See also McKay, *The Quest of the Folk*, ch. 3, on Mary Black, portrayed as a liberal progressive professional, not an antimodernist, whose role in inventing (rather than reviving) a handicraft industry benefited Nova Scotian women and their families and communities both economically and in terms of "moral therapy."

20 On the distinction, and critiques of it, see, for example, S. Surbhi, "Differences between Art and Craft," *Key Differences*, 6 April 2016, https://keydifferences.com /difference-between-art-and-craft.html; Margo Jefferson, "Beyond Cultural Labeling, Beyond Art Versus Craft," *New York Times*, 22 March 2005, https://www .nytimes.com/2005/03/22/arts/design/beyond-cultural-labeling-beyond-art -versus-craft.html; Laura Morelli, "Is There a Difference Between Art and Craft?," *TEDed*, https://ed.ted.com/lessons/is-there-a-difference-between-art-and-craft -laura-morelli (all last accessed 5 Nov. 2020).

21 Quotation from Hoganson, *Consumers' Imperium*, 241.

22 Cited in ibid., 242.

23 Ibid., 241. Hoganson draws on Eric Hobsbawm and Terrence Ranger's influential *The Invention of Tradition* (New York: Cambridge University Press, 1983).

24 Hoganson, *Consumers' Imperium*, 222–3; Allen F. Davis, *Spearheads for Reform: The Social Settlements and the Progressive Movement 1890–1914* (New York: Oxford University Press, 1967), 46–53.

25 McNaughton, "Folk Song and Handicraft Festivals," 224–30; Ellen Easton McLeod, *In Good Hands: The Women of the Canadian Handicrafts Guild* (Montreal: McGill-Queen's University Press, 1999); Canadian Guild of Crafts, *La Guild, Our Story*, https://laguilde.com/en/blogs/a-propos/notre-histoire; and *Going North: A Beautiful Endeavour*, https://laguilde.com/en/blogs/saviez-vous-que /vers-le-nord (both last accessed 20 April 2022).

26 McLeod, *In Good Hands*, ch. 9 and passim. McLeod acknowledges the women's history of paternalism towards other cultures, but emphasizes that they consciously fostered an inclusive national feeling by exhibiting and selling crafts of all Canadians on an equal footing. See also her "Alice Peck, May Phillips, and the Canadian Handicrafts Guild," in Sharon Anne Cook, Lorna R. McLean, and Kate O'Rourke, eds., *Framing Our Past: Constructing Canadian Women's History in the Twentieth Century* (Montreal/Kingston: McGill-Queen's University Press, 2001), 54–6.
27 McNaughton, "Folk Song and Handicraft Festivals," 224–30.
28 McLeod, *In Good Hands*, ch. 8; Canadian Guild of Crafts, *La Guild, Our Story* and *Going North: A Beautiful Endeavour*, https://laguilde.com/en/blogs/saviez-vous-que/vers-le-nord (last accessed 20 April 2022).
29 McLeod, *In Good Hands*, 246, 307–8; Andrew McIntosh, Ruth Pincoe, and Donald J.C. Phillipson, "John Murray Gibbon," in *The Canadian Encyclopedia*, 28 June 2007, https://www.thecanadianencyclopedia.ca/en/article/john-murray-gibbon-emc (last accessed 20 April 2022); McNaughton, "Folk Song and Handicraft Festivals," ch. 6.
30 MU6413, File: Lists Ethnic Federations 1957–64, Flyer/Programme Polish Week Feb. 1957; Betty Stapleton, "First of Four Ethnic Weeks to Be Polish," *Toronto Star*, 9 Feb. 1957; MU6416, File: Institute Folders/Pamphlets 1957–9, Flyer/Programme Lithuanian Week Feb. 1957. I found no additional information on Prapuolenis.
31 MU 6413, File: Ethnic Federations 1957–64, Flyer/Programme German Week Feb. 1957, 1959.
32 Ibid., Flyer/Programme Polish Week, Feb 1957; Flyer/Programme Lithuanian Week Feb. 1957.
33 The accompanying folksy but high-production image shows crochet hook operators, dressed in elegant ethnic costume while seated at the foot of a picturesque mountain, their "talented hands" producing the items that are "the awe of ethnographers" while accompanied by a mountaineer playing the "bagpipes." This and other descriptions in Anna Legierska, "Handicrafts Made in Poland," 8 April 2014, *Culture*, https://culture.pl/en/article/handicrafts-made-in-poland (last accessed 20 April 2022).
34 MU6413, File: Ethnic Occasions 1957, W.E. West (hereafter West), Director, to Mayor Phillips, Toronto City Hall, 1 April 1957.
35 Ibid., West to T.W. Lovett, Kiwanis Club of Don Mills, 28 March 1957 (Ukrainian Week); Beth Greenhorn, "An Art Critic at the Ringside: Mapping the Public and Private Lives of Pearl McCarthy" (MA thesis, Carleton University, 1996).
36 MU6472, File: Letters of Appreciation 1959–62, Institute *Newsletter* 1957–8, "Canadian Week" and "Our Special Thanks."
37 MU6414, File: Institute Folders/Pamphlets 1957–9, Flyer/Programme, Canadiana Week Sept.–Oct. 1957; Paula Laverty, "Silk Stocking Mats: The Hooked Mats of the Grenfell Mission of Newfoundland and Labrador," *Heritage: Newfoundland &*

Labrador, 1998, 2013, https://www.heritage.nf.ca/articles/arts/silk-mats.php) (last accessed 20 April 2022; Sandra M. Flood, "Canadian Craft and Museum Practice 1900–1950 (PhD diss., University of Manchester, 1998), 152–99.

38 MU6442, File: *Intercom* Copies 1962, *Intercom,* Nov. 1962. See also McKay, *The Quest of the Folk.*
39 MU6404, File: Canadiana Week 1961–5, Flyer for 1963; *Intercom,* 1963.
40 Michael Kammen, *Mystic Chords of Memory: The Transformation of Tradition in American Culture* (New York: Knopf, 1991), 300–2; 533–6; 547–8. On liberal anti-modernism, see my discussion in chapter 10.
41 Arjun Appadurai: "The Thing Itself," *Public Culture* 18, no. 1 (2006): 15–21. For an application of the concept, or conceit, that things, like persons, have social lives, to high-level and "Oriental" crafts, see Brian Spooner, "Weavers and Dealers: The Authenticity of an Oriental Carpet," in Arjun Appadurai, ed., *Social Life of Things: Commodities in Cultural Production* (Cambridge: Cambridge University Press, 1986), 195–235.
42 MU6389 (B280527), File: Programme Committee 1969–71, International Crafts and Needlework Fair, 1971; MU6411, File: Craft File, 1972 Craft Show, List of Participants, Invitations. The file contains 27 filled-out Questionnaires.
43 MU6411, File: Craft File, 1972, Questionnaires.
44 Ibid., Questionnaires.
45 She also promised that the work would not be arduous. MU6413, File: Ethnic Occasions 1957, West to Lovett, 28 March 1957.
46 MU6473, File: Hungarian Art Exhibition 1963, Receipt of Ojects d'Art, signed Dr Paul Rekai and others; on Rippl-Róna see *Fine Arts in Hungary,* https://www.hung-art.hu/index-en.html (last accessed 20 April 2022).
47 MU6415, File: Canadiana Week 1961–5, Flyer/Programme Canadiana Week Sept.–Oct. 1963. On Clark, https://www.aci-iac.ca/art-books/paraskeva-clark/biography/ (last accessed 20 April 2022).
48 MU6473, File: Hungarian Art Exhibition 1963, Biographical Notes of Artists, List of Paintings and Sculptures; Obituary by Sandra Martin, *Globe and Mail,* 4 Oct. 2008; Clara Hargittay entry on Pédery-Hunt in *The Canadian Encyclopedia,* 2 Nov. 2009, https://www.thecanadianencyclopedia.ca/en/article/dora-de-pedery-hunt; Del Newbigging, "In Memoriam: Dora Pédery-Hunt," 2008, *Fidem,* https://www.fidem-medals.org/pdf/in%20memoriam%20arc/2008.pdf (all last accessed 20 April 2022).
49 MU6442, File: Intercom Copies 1963, *Intercom,* Oct. 1963. *Intercom* copies cited in this chapter are found in the designated files in MU6406 and MU6442.
50 MU6473, File: Hungarian Art and Exhibition 1963, Exhibition and Applied Art list. On decorative folk items, see also "Folk Arts" in *Britannica,* https://www.britannica.com/art/folk-art/Style (last accessed 20 April 2022).
51 MU6386 (B280524), File: Cultural Committee 1961, Arts Committee Statement (n.d.), Memo 27 Jan. 1961.

52 MU6386 (B280524), File: Cultural Committee 1961, Memo 27 Jan. 1961. Mrs Hugh Allan, Mrs G.W. Lawrence, Mrs R. Gaby, Mrs Fraser Grant, and Mrs George Walsh.
53 MU6386 (B280524), File: Cultural Committee, Memo 27 Jan. 1961; MU 6406 (B280543), File: News Clippings, "Arturo Scotti Commemorato Dall'International Institute," *Corriere Canadese* (n.d.); *Toronto Star*, 6 Feb. 1960. Dignitaries such as Minister of Citizenship and Immigration Ellen Fairclough attended the unveiling of the plaque. On Scotti, see Paul Baxa, "La Festa della Fratellanza Italiana: Gianni Grohovas and the Celebrations of Italian Memorial Day in Toronto, 1960–1975," *Quaderni d'italianistica* 30, no. 1 (2010): 202, 218n74; Franca Iacovetta, *Such Hardworking People: Italian Immigrants in Postwar Toronto* (Toronto: University of Toronto Press, 1990), 142, 148.
54 Details contained in MU6428 (B280565), File: John Collingwood Reade Memorial 1963, and File: John Collingwood Reade Room – Auditorium 1968. When the Institute moved to Davenport Road, the plaque and dedication were transferred to the auditorium. See also chapter 10.
55 Sehnoha became best-known for his painting of the wife of Paul Martin Sr. *Intercom*, July 1961. Pavel Onderka, "Jaroslav Šejnoha and Egypt," *Annals of the Náprstek Museum* 38, no. 2 (2017): 53–74.
56 MU6476, File: Ukrainian 1955–65, Biography and Catalogue in file (n.d.).
57 MU6400, File: Art Exhibition Oct. 1970; flyer includes biography of Haller.
58 MU6406, File: Christmas 1963, News from the Scotti Room, Aldo Covello; Report/Month in Retrospect.
59 *Intercom* 1962, Review of Exhibit, *Intercom*, Oct. 1962; MU6400, File: Art Exhibition, T.J. Schembri to H.C. Forbell, 14 Nov. 1962; Forbell to Schembri, 19 Nov. 1962; Ivone Kirkpatrick, *Mussolini: A Study in Power* (New York: Avon, 1964), ch. 13.
60 MU6407, File: Programme Committee 1969–72, Report for Board Meeting, 29 July 1970; Proposal to Committee from J.V. Zelina, 13 Aug. 1970; M.D. Stewart, Director, to M. Zlamal, Director, CSASA Toronto, 19 Nov. 1969.
61 I discuss liberal anti-modernism in more detail in chapter 10.
62 Quoted in MU6476, File: Ukrainians 1955–65, Concert Poster, Massey Hall, 1 Oct. 1955; and in Souvenir Book/Program, *Ukrainian Bandurists Chorus*, Wasyl Wytwycky, "With Bandura across the World" (20 pp., not paginated, with photographs) (Detroit, 1955); *Toronto Star*, 7 Dec. 1949.
63 Martin may have attended the first concert the Bandurists performed in Toronto in 1949. On Smith, "First Woman Elected to Both Houses of Congress," https://www.senate.gov/artandhistory/history/minute/First_Woman_Both_Houses.htm (last accessed 5 Nov. 2020).
64 Quotations from Antony Ferry, "Mammoth Dance Group Impresario's Ambition," *Toronto Star*, 11 March 1961. The ensemble also performed in Montreal.
65 West in *Intercom*, April 1961.

66 Wytwycky, "With Bandura across the World."
67 Luciuk, "Making Ukrainian Canadians," ch. 4. See also my discussion of cultural essentialism in chapter 10.
68 Ferry, "Mammoth Dance Group." On therapeutic space, see my discussion in chapter 10.
69 MU6416, File: Institute Folders, Pamphlets 1957–9. Folk pageant finale to Old World Bazaar, 16 Nov. 1957, Harbord Collegiate. On renditions of the csardas by classical composers (e.g., Brahms, Strauss) see Angelica Frey, "Six Famous Csardas You Must Listen To," *CMUSE* https://www.cmuse.org/csardas/ (last accessed 11 May 2022).
70 Henry Spiller, "Introduction: Music, Movement and Masculinities," *World of Music* 3, no. 2 (2014): 8, 5–13.
71 Marcia Ostashewski, "A Song and Dance of Hypermasculinity: Performing Ukrainian Cossacks in Canada," *World of Music* 3, no. 2 (2014): 15–38; see also references in note 2. Numerous Institute and newspaper photographs capture men in mid-air jumps or squats, and the descriptions and captions refer to the men's athletic prowess.
72 Ostashewski, "Hypermasculinity"; Souvenir Book/Program, *Ukrainian Bandurists Chorus*, Wytwycky, "Banduras"; additional background from *Encyclopedia of Ukraine,* https://www.encyclopediaofukraine.com (last accessed 5 Nov. 2020). On left-right commemorations of Shevchenko among Ukrainian Canadians, see Luciuk, "Making Ukrainian Canadian," ch. 5.
73 This insight is based on hundreds of Institute and newspaper-based descriptions, photos, and captions uncovered by my research. On settlements and folk dance as moral regulation, Jessica Ray Herzogenrath, "Authenticity and Ethnicity: Folk Dance, Americanization, and the Immigrant Body in Early Twentieth Century America," in Anthony Shay and Barbara Sellers-Young, eds., *Oxford Handbook of Dance and Ethnicity* (New York: Oxford University Press, 2016), ch. 12.
74 Cohen et al., *Beauty Queens,* 2–5; Christine Reiko Yano, *Crowning the Nice Girl: Gender, Ethnicity, And Culture in Hawaii's Cherry Blossom Festival* (Honolulu: University of Hawai'i Press, 2006), 24–30; Tarah Brookfield, "Modelling the U.N.'s Mission in Semi-Formal Wear: Edmonton's Miss United Nations Pageants of the 1960s," in Patrizia Gentile and Jane Nicholas, eds., *Contesting Bodies and Nation in Canadian History* (Toronto: University of Toronto Press, 2013), 247–66.
75 For examples, see references to Citizenship Day and Citizenship Week in MU6382, File: Board of Directors Minutes, 1956 to 1967; MU6472, File: Letters of Appreciation 1959–62; and *Toronto Star,* 10 May 1955, 16 March 1959, 23 May 1962.
76 MU6457 (B280594), File: Cultural Sub-Committee, Report of Cultural Committee, April 1956.
77 MU6416, File: Folk Festival Minutes of Meetings, Flyer/Programme, 8th Annual Madsen Folk Festival, 23 June 1956. See also ibid., Flyer, "All about Folk Schools in Ontario."

78 Ibid., Flyer/Programme, Seventh Annual John Madsen Folk Festival, 25 June 1955.
79 Ibid.
80 Quotation cited in Greenhill, "Fowke," 4.
81 McKay, *The Quest of the Folk*, 145–50.
82 MU6382, File: Board of Directors Minutes, June 1956–Dec. 1957, Minutes of Meeting of Programme Committee on Ontario Folk Festival, 12 March 1957, and 3 April and 2 May 1957.
83 MU6416, File: Folk Festival Minutes of Meetings, Report on Workshop Folk Festival at YMCA, 21 June 1957.
84 Ibid.
85 MU6416, File: Folk Festival Minutes, Minutes of Ontario Folk Festival Society, 14 Oct. 1957; MU6413, File: Ethnic Occasions, West, Memorandum, 29 Oct. 1959; MU6472, File: Letters of Appreciation 1959–62; *Intercom*, Nov. 1962.
86 MU6416, File: Folk Festival Minutes of Meetings, Minutes of Meeting for Citizenship Day, 29 March, 11 May, and 12 April 1957 and Minutes of Program Sub-Committee, 3 April 1957.
87 Ibid. On Moore, see entry by David Gardiner in *The Canadian Encyclopedia*, 15 August 2007, https://www.thecanadianencyclopedia.ca/en/article/dora-mavor-moore; and "Dora Mavor Moore (1888–1979)," tribute given at the Association for Canadian Theatre History, Saskatoon, 24 May 1979, https://journals.lib.unb.ca/index.php/TRIC/article/view/7537/8596 (both last accessed 11 May 2020).
88 The literature on this topic is large, but for a valuable discussion of the left-wing urban folk revival movement of the late 1960s and the 1970s that paradoxically drew on a radical tradition but attracted a heavily middle-class white audience and enjoyed success within the North American mass-based music industry, see MacDonald, "This Is Important!"
89 MU6382, File: Board of Directors Minutes, June 1956–Dec. 1957, Minutes of Meeting of Programme Committee of [potential] Ontario Folk Festival, 12 March 1957. On Geiger-Torel, see the entry in *The Canadian Encyclopedia* (Canadian Opera Company Archives), 29 April 2007, https://www.thecanadianencyclopedia.ca/en/article/herman-geiger-torel-emc (last accessed 4 April 2022).
90 MU6382, File: Board of Directors Minutes, June 1956–Dec. 1957, Minutes of Meeting of Programme Committee of [potential] Ontario Folk Festival, 12 March 1957.
91 Hoganson, *Consumers' Imperium*, ch. 5; Raymond A. Mohl, "Cultural Pluralism in Immigrant Education: The International Institutes of Boston, Philadelphia, and San Francisco, 1920–1940," *Journal of American Ethnic History* 1, no. 2 (1982): 46–8; Costas Melakopides, *Pragmatic Idealism: Canadian Foreign Policy 1945–1999* (Montreal/Kingston: McGill-Queen's University Press, 1988), 37–51; Adam Chapnick, *The Middle Power Project: Canada and the Founding of the United Nations* (Vancouver: UBC Press, 2005).

92 Quotation from Werner Jabramek, "Philatelic Crusaders for Peace Organization," *Intercom*, Feb. 1962. Other details in MU6442 (B280559), File: Members Council 1960–5, Stamp Club entries, letters, and *Intercom*, April 1961, Feb. 1963. On Nubia, Shehata Adam Mohamed, "Victory in Nubia: Egypt," *UNESCO Courier* 33, nos. 2 and 3 (1980): 5–15.

93 West interview with Ralph Hyman, "They Oil the Hinges of Integration's Door," *Globe Magazine*, 20 Feb. 1960 in MU6406 (B280543), File: Clippings – International Institute 1959–70.

94 Brookfield, "Modelling the U.N.'s Mission," 248–9.

95 Details are interspersed in several files, including in MU6382, File: Board of Directors, Minutes, 12 June 1956–5 Dec. 1957, Minutes of Programme Committee, Embassy, 5 June 1957; MU6423 (B280560), File: Old World Bazaar 1957–9; MU6415, File: Latvian Federation 1957, West to Ian McIntosh, CBC, Toronto, Oct. 1957. See also *Toronto Star*, 22 Oct. 1955, 18 Oct. 1965.

96 MU6423 (B280560), File: Old World Bazaar 1957–9, United Nations Week 1957; on the harp, John Shepherd et al., eds., *Continuum Encyclopedia of Popular Music of the World*, vol. 2, *Performance and Production* (London: Continuum, 2003), 429–30.

97 MU6382, File: Board of Directors Minutes, June 1956–Dec. 1957, Minutes of Programme Committee, 5 June 1957, and Memorandum, 8 Oct. 1957; details in MU6423 (B280560), File: Old World Bazaar 1957–9.

98 Brookfield, "Modelling the U.N.'s Mission," 249–50 (quotation on 249). See also Michael K. Carrol, *Pearson's Peacekeepers: Canada and the United Nations Emergency Force, 1956–67* (Vancouver: UBC Press, 2009).

99 M6400, File: Administration 1958–66, Festival of Nations Flyer, Information, Publicity, 1960, and Report on Festival of Nations, 11 Jan. 1961; Knowles, *First Person*.

100 Ibid. On the organization see "About Us," *Save the Children*, https://www.savethechildren.org.uk/about-us/our-history (last accessed 5 Nov. 2020)

101 Brookfield, "Modelling the UN"; Gentile, *Queen of the Maple Leaf*, esp. ch. 4; Cohen et al., *Beauty Queens*.

102 MU6407, File: Community Folk Art Council (CFAC), 1963–74, clippings of *Toronto Star Week* cover story, Peter Goddard, "Visit 42 cities in eight days during Metro Caravan," n.d., but date is 24 June 1972; CFAC Report, 9 Nov. 1970, to A.M. Campbell, Chair, Municipality of Toronto; Press release 15 Jan. 1970; "Thousands Dance at City Hall Birthday," *Toronto Star*, 2 July 1969.

103 Ross Skoggard, "Mary Jean MacKay Ross Skoggard, 1917–2003," 4 May 2004, https://section15.ca/features/people/2004/05/04/mary_skoggard/; obituary, *Montreal Gazette*, 29 March 1967 (both last accessed 13 Nov. 2021).

104 Photos in *Globe and Mail*, 15 Feb. 1961.

105 MU6413, File: Lists of Ethnic Federations 1957–64, Director West to Godfrey Barrass, Citizenship Branch, Queen's Park, 28 July 1960 (with correspondence).

106 A partial exception was 1970 Scandinavian Night, which included a ski-fashion show. MU6446 (B280583), File: Recreational Activity, Notices, 1969, Flyer Scandinavian Night, 7 Feb. 1970.
107 See clippings in MU6427, File: Publicity Scrapbook; MU6413, File: Ethnic Groups – Clippings, 1971–4; MU6398, File: Croatian Organizations, File: Bulgarian 1961–4; MU6411, File: Mrs Stewart's Log; MU6413, File: Ethnic Organization Lists, Godfrey Barrass to West, 27 June 1960; on male hosts, MU6446 (B280583), File: Recreational Activity, Notices, 1969, Flyers, Greek Night, 23 Nov. 1969; MU5405, File: Xmas 1957/8, Flyer, Christmas Tea, 21 Dec. 1958.
108 *Intercom*, Feb. 1963.
109 On challenging sixties stereotypes, see, for example, Lara Campbell, Dominique Clement, and Gregory S. Kealey, eds., *Debating Dissent: Canada and the Sixties* (Toronto: University of Toronto Press, 2012).
110 Liisa Malkki, "Citizens of Humanity: Internationalism and Imagined Community of Nations," *Diaspora* 3, no. 1 (1994), 41–68 (esp. p. 60).
111 *Intercom*, Feb. 1963.
112 Abril Liberatori, "'Family Is Really All Over the Place': Ethnic Identity Formation within a Transnational Network" (PhD diss., York University, 2017), 105–8.
113 Images and captions from *Globe and Mail*, 31 May 1965.
114 On Hill, see, for example, "Daniel Grafton Hill III, 1923–2003," *Ontario Archives*, https://www.archives.gov.on.ca/en/explore/online/dan_hill/introduction.aspx; entry by James Walker in *The Canadian Encyclopedia*, 21 Feb. 2008, https://www.thecanadianencyclopedia.ca/en/article/daniel-grafton-hill (both last accessed 5 Nov. 2020); entry in Frances J. Turner, ed., *Canadian Encyclopedia of Social Work* (Waterloo: Wilfrid Laurier University Press, 2005), 76.
115 The thesis was entitled "Negroes in Toronto: A Sociological Study of a Minority Group" (Department of Political Economy, University of Toronto, 1960). On Hill's own experiences with racism at this time, see Lawrence Hill, "My Pain Was Your Pain: On Wrestling with My Racial Inheritance at a Moment of Reckoning," https://www.theglobeandmail.com/opinion/article-my-pain-was-your-pain-on-wrestling-with-my-racial-inheritance-at-a/ (last accesed 7 July 2021).
116 "The Ontario Human Rights Code," *Intercom*, Oct. 1962; Carmela Patrias and Ruth Frager, "'This is our country, these are our rights': Minorities and the Origins of Ontario's Human Rights Campaigns," *Canadian Historical Review* 82, no. 1 (March 2001): 1–35; and their "Human Rights Activists and the Question of Sex Discrimination in Postwar Ontario," *Canadian Historical Review*, 93, no. 4 (Dec. 2012): 583–610.
117 "Toronto Youth for Human Rights," *Intercom*, May 1964.
118 "Ontario Human Rights Commission, *Intercom*, Summer 1969.
119 Ellen D. Wu, *The Color of Success: Asian Americans and the Origins of the Model Minority* (Princeton, NJ: Princeton University Press, 2014), ch. 3. On this theme, see also Russel Kazal, "Rethinking the Origins of Multiculturalism: New

Perspectives on American Pluralist Ideologies" (an article manuscript in preparation for submission to a journal); and chapter 2.
120 *Intercom*, Nov. 1962, John Gillin, "Race." On its ideals, see "National Conference on Christians and Jews," *Social Networks and Archival Context*, https://snaccooperative.org/view/31617957 (last accessed 11 May 2020).
121 Immigration History Research Center Archives, Elmer L. Andersen Library, University of Minnesota (hereafter IHRCA), American Council for Nationalities Service records, which contain the American Federation of International Institutes (AFII) collection (hereafter II), Box 271, File: 2, II Philadelphia, Clarence King et al., 1943 and 1946 Reports. On the subject, see Kevin Bruyneel, *The Third Space of Sovereignty: The Postcolonial Politics of U.S.-Indigenous Relations* (Minneapolis: University of Minnesota Press, 2007).
122 IHRCA, II Milwaukee, Box 278b, File: 14, Willette Pierce, "Group Work, Casework and Community Organization Practices with Ninety-two Newly Arrived Dutch Immigrants," May 1958.
123 Ibid., Willette Pierce, "Potential Impact of Puerto Rican Americans Eased by Community Planning," 21 May 1957.
124 Daniel Immerwahr, "The Greater United States: Territory and Empire in U.S. History," *Diplomatic History* 40, no. 3 (2016): 373–91.

Conclusion

1 After vacating 321 Davenport Road, the Institute set up a central downtown office (2084 Yonge Street), an east end branch (1985 Danforth Avenue), the Weston Branch (based in an Ontario Housing Corporation building at 5 Bellevue Crescent), and the Welcome House Branch (8 York Street).
2 Archives of Ontario (AO), International Institute of Metropolitan Toronto, Fonds 884, MU6431 (B280568), File: Staff, Minutes 1970, Memorandum, M.D. Stewart, Director, to Staff, 6 April 1971; MU6384, File: Board Minutes 1973–4, Minutes of Board of Directors, 18 March 1974, 4 and 21 Feb. 1974.
3 Established in 1966. On Head, see https://blackthen.com/wilson-head-american-canadian-sociologist-community-planner/ and https://peoplepill.com/people/wilson-a-head/ (both last accessed 15 Nov. 2021).
4 MU6409 (B2800546), File: Seminar/Board and Staff, Notes on Seminar, York University, 12 May 1973, led by Head; MU6384, File: Annual Reports 1962–73, Director's Report, 4 April 1974.
5 Notes on Seminar, York University, 12 May 1973 in MU6409 (B2800546), File: Seminar/Board and Staff.
6 The policy would later be enshrined in law with the Canadian Multiculturalism Act of 1988.
7 Laurence Brosseau and Michael Dewing, *Canadian Multiculturalism: Background Paper*, Library of Parliament, Research Publications, no. 2009-20-E, 15 Sept. 2009/rev.

3 Jan. 2018, https://lop.parl.ca/sites/PublicWebsite/default/en_CA/ResearchPublications/200920E (last accessed 20 April 2022); Sheyfali Saujani, "'Kind of Like a Bible.' Book IV & the White Paper: A Road Map for the Multiculturalism Directorate," paper presented to the Toronto Immigration Group, April 2016.
8 The Welcome House model would be replicated by other governments, though the provincial government ended the program in Ontario in 1995.
9 MU6431 (B280568), File: Staff, Minutes 1970, Staff Minutes, 2 March 1973.
10 Ibid. See also ibid., Staff Minutes, 23 Feb. 1973.
11 MU6411 (B280548), File: Director Correspondence 1970, J.G. Korn, Secretary-General, Czechoslovak National Association of Canada, 2 Oct. 1970, and M.D. Stewart, Director, 16 Oct. 1970; MU6411 (B280548), File: Mrs M.D. Stewart 1970–2, translated excerpt from "*Hlas Novych*," 15 Oct. 1970 (incorrectly says 1979). The directories otherwise received a positive reception. MU6384, File: Annual Reports 1975 [1973–4], Annual Report, M. Streeruwitz, 29 March 1974; File: Annual Reports 1962–73, Report by M. Streeruwitz, 1973.
12 See, for example, MU6468 (B436172), File: Catherine Lee 1973, Weekly Reports, 22 and 23 May 1973; MU6384, File: Annual Reports 1975, Report by C. Lee, 1974.
13 MU6431 (B280568), File: Staff, Minutes 1970, Staff Minutes, 18 Jan. 1973. The LIP was a federal program established by the Liberal government in 1971 to provide grants to community and cultural projects. Billed as part of Pierre Trudeau's effort to create "a just society," Conservatives criticized it as a program that funded radical causes: https://www.connexions.org/CxLibrary/Docs/CxP-LocalInitiativesProgram.htm (accessed 15 Nov. 2021); Donald E. Blake, "LIP and Partisanship: An Analysis of the Local Initiatives Program," *Canadian Public Policy/Analyse de Politiques* 1, no. 1 (Winter 1976): 17–32.
14 MU6384, File: Annual Report 1975, Director's Report, 17 Jan. 1974.
15 Ibid., Report on Involvement with Black Community, 29 March 1974. The social worker–dominated domestic workers' committee also included Bromley Armstrong, president of the Jamaican Canadian Association. *Montreal Gazette*, 20 Sept. 1972.
16 The new centre was located in St Thomas Aquinas Roman Catholic School on Glenholm Avenue, east of Dufferin Street. MU6384, File: Board Minutes 1973–4, Report by K. Symons, 1 March 1974. As chair of the National Black Coalition (Ontario region), Canadian broadcaster and activist Kay Livingstone had earlier criticized the Secretary of State for providing funds to the Institute for a Black social worker rather than to community-based organizations like the NBC. MU6417, File: Department of Manpower and Immigration (Mr. A.A. Ewen, From 1971), Otto E. Lang to Kathleen Livingstone, 6 May 1971. On Livingstone, a founder of the Canadian Negro Women's Association (1951), later Congress of Black Women of Canada (1973), see *Canadian Encyclopedia* entry by Eli Yarhi, 5 March 2019, https://www.thecanadianencyclopedia.ca/en/article/kay-livingstone,

and *Rise Up! A Digital Archive of Feminist Activism*, https://riseupfeministarchive.ca/activism/organizations/congress-of-black-women-of-canada-cbwc/?highlight=Kay%20Livingstone (both last accessed 15 Nov. 2021).

17 On Nair's commitments, which included preparing professional resumes and meeting with the Indian Immigrant Aid Group, see MU6431 (B280568), File: Staff, Minutes 1970, Staff Minutes, 15 and 23 Feb. 1973.

18 Ibid., Staff Minutes, 18 Jan. 1973.

19 MU6384, File: Board Minutes 1973-4, Minutes of Board Meeting, 21 Feb. 1974, Minutes of Emergency Meeting, 4 Feb. 1974; MU6384, File: Annual Report 1975 [1973-4], Director's Report, 17 Jan. 1974. (Stewart herself retired on 1 April 1974.)

20 Scholarly exceptions include Richard J.F. Day, *Multiculturalism and the History of Canadian Diversity* (Toronto: University of Toronto Press, 2010).

21 Polish Language & Literature, University of Toronto, Donor Irene Ungar, https://sites.utoronto.ca/slavic/polish/donors.html (last accessed 12 Nov. 2021); Janet Morris, "Appointment Delights," *Vancouver Sun*, 23 Jan. 1969; "New citizenship judge started life in Canada as a domestic," *Toronto Star*, 25 Sept. 1973.

22 This is my emphasis, but see, for example, Will Kymlicka, Multiculturalism Policy Index, Multiculturalism Policies in Contemporary Democracies, Entries for United States and Canada, https://www.queensu.ca/mcp/immigrant-minorities/ (last accessed 15April 2022); John Biles, "The Government of Canada's Multiculturalism Program: Key to Canada's Inclusion Reflex?," in Jack Jedwab, ed., *The Multiculturalism Question: Debating Identity in 21st-Century Canada* (Montreal/Kingston: McGill-Queen's University Press, 2014), 31-50; Theme Issue on Immigrant Organizations, *Journal of Ethnic and Migration Studies* 31, no. 5 (2005), with guest editors Marlou Shrover and Floris Vermeulen, esp. the essays by Héctor R. Cordero-Guzmán (New York City) and Irene Bloemraad (Toronto); David A. Hollinger, *Postethnic America: Beyond Multiculturalism* (New York: Basic Books, 1995), 79, 101; Russell A. Kazal, "Rethinking the Origins of Multiculturalism: New Perspectives on American Pluralist Ideologies" (an article manuscript in preparation for submission to a journal); and my chapter 2.

23 On the IIAS, see https://www.costi.org/whoweare/history.php (last accessed 15 Nov. 2021); on JIAS, Jack Lipinsky, *Imposing Their Will: An Organizational History of Jewish Toronto, 1933-1948* (Montreal/Kingston: McGill-Queen's University Press, 2011), ch. 4.

24 Himani Bannerji, "Multiple Multiculturalisms and Charles Taylor's Politics of Recognition," in Barbara Saunders and David Haljan Leuven, eds., *Whither Multiculturalism? A Politics of Dissensus* (Belgium: Leuven University Press, 2003), 35-45, esp. 35, 44. On the new racism, see, for example, Rita Chin, *The Crisis of Multiculturalism in Europe: A History* (Princeton, NJ: Princeton University Press, 2017), 140-66; Centre for Contemporary Cultural Studies, *Empire Strikes Back: Race and Racism in 70's Britain* (London: Routledge, 2004); Paul Gilroy et al., "A

Diagnosis of Contemporary Forms of Racism, Race and Nationalism: A Conversation with Professor Paul Gilroy," *Cultural Studies* 33, no. 2 (2019): 173–97, esp. 181–3.

25 See, for example, Rafeef Ziadah, "Disciplining Dissent: Multicultural Policy and the Silencing of Arab Canadians," *Race & Class* 58, no. 4 (2017): 7–22; Alan Sears and Mary-Jo Nadeau, "This Is What Complicity Looks Like: Palestine and the Silencing Campaign on Campus Social Movements," *The Bullet*, 5 March 2011, https://socialistproject.ca/2011/03/b475/ (last accessed 25 June 2020).

26 Chin, *Crisis of Multiculturalism in Europe*, ch. 4 and passim; Joan W. Scott, "The Culture Veil: The Real Crisis on European Multiculturalism," *The Nation* (a review of three books, including Chin's, on the multicultural backlash in Europe), https://www.thenation.com/article/archive/the-culture-veil/ (last accessed 21 July 2021). See also Steven Vertovec and Susanne Wessendork, eds., *The Multiculturalism Backlash: European Discourses and Practices* (London: Routledge, 2010), esp. their Introduction. See also the Introduction and essay on multiculturalism and honour killings by Marlou Schrover in Marlou Schrover and Deirdre M. Moloney, eds., *Gender, Migration and Categorisation: Making Distinctions between Migrants in Western Countries, 1945–2010* (Amsterdam: Amsterdam University Press, 2013).

27 Chin, *Crisis of Multiculturalism in Europe*.

28 Ibid.; Scott, "The Culture Veil."

29 See, for example, "Compounding Misfortunes: Changes in Poverty since the Onset of COVID-19 on Syrian Refugees and Host Communities in Jordan, the Kurdistan Region of Iraq and Lebanon," Dec. 2020, https://World%20Bank%20-%20UNHCR%20MENA-%20COVID%20Compounding%20Misfortunes%20-2-1.pdf; "OECD Policy Responses to Coronavirus (COVID-19), What Is the Impact of the COVID-19 Pandemic on Immigrants and Their Children?," 19 Oct. 2020, https://www.oecd.org/coronavirus/policy-responses/what-is-the-impact-of-the-covid-19-pandemic-on-immigrants-and-their-children-e7cbb7de/; Migrant Workers Alliance, *Unheeded Warnings: COVID-19 and Migrant Workers in Canada*, June 2020, https://migrantworkersalliance.org/wp-content/uploads/2020/06/Unheeded-Warnings-COVID19-and-Migrant-Workers.pdf (all last accessed 14 April 2021).

30 Chin, *Crisis of Multiculturalism in Europe*, 298, 299–302.

31 See the assessment by Audrey Macklin et al., *The Kinship between Refugee and Family Sponsorship*, Working Paper No. 2020, 4 Aug. 2020, Working Papers Series (Ryerson Centre for Immigration and Settlement and Canadian Excellence Research Chair in Migration and Integration), https://www.ryerson.ca/content/dam/centre-for-immigration-and-settlement/RCIS/publications/workingpapers/2020_4_Macklin_Audrey_et_al._The_Kinship_between_Refugee_and_Family_Sponsorship.pdf (last accessed 23 July 2021).

32 Joan Wallach Scott, *Only Paradoxes to Offer: French Feminists and the Rights of Man* (Cambridge, MA: Harvard University Press, 1996), which argues that the

paradox of "the need both to accept and to refuse 'sexual difference' was the constitutive condition of feminism as a political movement throughout its long history" (3–4); Scott, "The Culture Veil."

33 Rinaldo Walcott, "Disgraceful: Intellectual Dishonesty, White Anxieties, and Multicultural Critique 36 Years Later," in May Chazan et al., eds., *Home and Native Land: Unsettling Multiculturalism in Canada* (Toronto: Between the Lines, 2011), ch. 1, 11–26. On migration and multiculturalism, see, for example, Stuart Hall, "Cosmopolitan Promises, Multicultural Realities," in Richard Scholar, ed., *Divided Cities: The Oxford Amnesty Lectures* 2003 (Oxford: Oxford University Press, 2006), 20–51.

34 MU6384, File: Annual Meetings, Minutes of Annual General Meeting, 15 April 1971; on OCASI, https://ocasi.org/about-us (accessed last accessed 22 July 2021).

35 This discussion draws on several sources, including Karen Charnow Lior, ed., *Making the City: Women Who Made a Difference* (Halifax/Winnipeg: Fernwood, 2012); Tania Das Gupta, *Learning from Our History: Community Development by Immigrant Women in Ontario, 1958–86* (Toronto: Cross Cultural Communication Centre, 1986); Margaret Little and Lynne Marks et al., "Family Matters: Immigrant Women Activists and Mainstream Feminists in Ontario and BC, 1960s–1980s," *Atlantis* 41, no. 1 (2021): 105–23; and following interviews with *Rise Up! A Digital Archive of Feminist Activism*, "Women Unite: Toronto Feminist Activists, 1970s–1990s: Portuguese Workers/Birth of Cleaners' Action 1975" (Marcie Ponte and Sidney Pratt); "Founding of Wages for Housework" (Judith Ramirez); "Organizing Domestic Workers: INTERCEDE" (Martha Ocampo, Cenen Bagon, Genie Policarpio, and Anita Fortuno); and "Immigrant Women Create the Working Women's Community Centre 1975" (Marcie Ponte). I conducted the first three interviews and Sue Colley the fourth one. See https://riseupfeministarchive.ca/collection-women-unite/ (last accessed 15 Nov. 2021).

36 Adnan Turegun, "Immigrant Settlement Work in Canada: Limits and Possibilities for Professionalization," *Canadian Sociological Association* 50, no. 4 (2013): 387–411; https://ocasi.org/about-us (last accessed 22 July 2021).

37 On the importance of social welfare interactions to understanding social welfare regimes, Stephen Pimpare, "Toward a New Welfare History," *Journal of Welfare History* 19 (2007): 234–52; Mark Peel, *Miss Cutler and the Case of the Resurrected Horse: Social Work and the Story of Poverty in America, Australia, and Britain* (Chicago: University of Chicago Press, 2012), 278 (citing Pimpare), conclusion, and passim.

38 On this theme, see, for example, Peel, *Miss Cutler*; Karen Tice, *Tales of Wayward Girls and Immoral Women: Case Records and the Professionalization of Social Work* (Urbana: University of Illinois Press, 1998); Linda Gordon, *Heroes of Their Own Lives: The Politics and History of Family Violence, Boston, 1880–1960* (New York: Penguin Books 1989).

39 Peel, *Miss Cutler*, 278 (quotation), chs. 27–9, and conclusion.

40 On this theme, see my discussion in chapter 5.

41 Cynthia Thoroski, "Adventures in Ethnicity: Consuming Performances of Cultural Identity in Winnipeg's Folklorama," *Canadian Folklore Canadien* 19, no. 2 (1997): 105–12 (quotation on p. 111).
42 The term "Disneyfication" is from Neil Bissoondath, *Selling Illusions: The Cult of Multiculturalism in Canada* (Toronto: Penguin Books, 1984), 83.
43 Sunera Thobani, *Exalted Subjects: Studies in the Making of Race and Nation in Canada* (Toronto: University of Toronto Press, 2007), 143–78. See also Sara Ahmed, *Strange Encounters: Embodied Others in Post-Coloniality* (London: Routledge, 2000).
44 On Jones, see Sagal Mohammed, "Marxist, Feminist, Revolutionary: Remembering Notting Hill Founder Claudia Jones," https://www.vogue.co.uk/arts-and-lifestyle/article/claudia-jones-notting-hill-carnival (last accessed 14 Nov. 2021); Carol Boyce Davies, *Left of Karl Marx: The Political Life of Black Communist Claudia Jones* (Durham: Duke University Press 2007), ch. 5. For the other examples, see chapter 1.
45 Paul A. Bramadat, "Shows, Selves, and Solidarity: Ethnic Identity and Cultural Spectacles in Canada," *Canadian Ethnic Studies* 33, no. 2 (2001): 78–98, which cites Pierre Bourdieu, *The Field of Cultural Production* (New York: Columbia University Press, 1993); Michael Ashkenazi, "Cultural Tensions as Factors in the Structure of a Festival Parade," *Asian Folklore Studies* 46 (1987): 35–54.
46 Kathleen Neils Conzen et al., "The Invention of Ethnicity: A Perspective from the USA," *Journal of American Ethnic History* 12, no. 1 (Fall 1992): 3–41. See also the reflections of Kassandra Luciuk, a folk-dance-performer-turned-leftist-intellectual, in "Making Ukrainian Canadians: Identity, Politics, and Power in Cold War Canada" (PhD diss., University of Toronto, 2021).
47 See my discussion in chapter 2.
48 Kanishka Goonewardena and Stefan Kipfer, "Spaces of Difference: Reflections from Toronto on Multiculturalism, Bourgeois Urbanism and the Possibility of Radical Urban Politics," *International Journal of Urban and Regional Research* 29 no. 3 (2005): 670–8, particularly the discussion of Mike Davis, *Magical Urbanism: Latinos Reinvent the US City* (London: Verso, 2001), on how Latinos are reshaping everyday life and revitalizing left politics in big American cities.
49 As in Michael Temelini, "Multicultural Rights, Multicultural Virtues: A History of Multiculturalism in Canada," in Stephen Tierney, ed., *Multiculturalism and the Canadian Constitution* (Vancouver: UBC Press, 2007), 43–60; Julia Lalande, "The Roots of Multiculturalism – Ukrainian-Canadian Involvement in the Multiculturalism Discussion of the 1960s as an Example of the Position of the Third Force," *Canadian Ethnic Studies* 38, no. 1 (2006): 47–64.
50 Russell A. Kazal, "Rethinking the Origins of Multiculturalism: New Perspectives on American Pluralist Ideologies" (article manuscript in preparation).
51 Fredrik Barth, *Ethnic Groups and Boundaries: The Social Organisation of Culture Difference* (Bergen: Waveland Press, 1969); Eloise Hummell, "Standing the Test of

Time – Barth and Ethnicity," *Coolabah* 13 (2014): 46–60. Canadian applications include Aya Fujiwara, *Ethnic Elites and Canadian Identity: Japanese, Ukrainians, and Scots, 1919–1971 (*Winnipeg: University of Manitoba Press, 2012), 13–19, 35–48; Royden Loewen and Gerald Friesen, *Immigrants in Prairie Cities: Ethnic Diversity in Twentieth-Century Canada* (Toronto: University of Toronto Press, 2009), 4–5, 35, 155.

52 On Yuzyk as father of multiculturalism, see *Honourable Senator Paul Yuzyk: In the Footsteps of Nationbuilders*, https://www.yuzyk.com/ucc2000-e.shtml (last accessed 5 July 2021). Scholarly work on Yuzyk and the lobby includes Lalande, "Roots of Multiculturalism," and the following more critical studies: Eve Haque, *Multiculturalism within a Bilingual Framework: Language, Race, and Belonging in Canada* (Toronto: University of Toronto Press, 2012), 56–222; Luciuk, "Making Ukrainian Canadians," ch. 4; Anna Seccombe, "Canadian Ethnic Elites and Multiculturalism: Accommodation, Resistance and the Politics of History" (MA thesis, University of Toronto, 2018).

53 Haque, *Multiculturalism*, 214–22; Luciuk, "Making Ukrainian Canadians," ch. 4.

54 Jean Burnet, "Multiculturalism, Immigration, and Racism: A Comment on the Canadian Immigration and Population Study, *Canadian Ethnic Studies* 7, no. 1 (1975): 35–9.

55 Thobani, *Exalted Subjects*; Sherene Razack, Malinda Smith, and Sunera Thobani, eds., *States of Race: Critical Race Feminism for the 21st Century* (Toronto: Between the Lines, 2010); Enakshi Dua and Angela Robertson, eds., *Scratching the Surface: Canadian Anti-Racist Feminist Thought* (Toronto: Women's Press, 1999).

56 For example, in Detroit, Los Angeles, Milwaukee, and Akron, Ohio. See https://www.iimd.org/; https://www.iilosangeles.org/; iiwisconsin.org; and https://www.iiakron.org/ (all last accessed 4 April 2022).

Index

Page numbers in *italics* refer to illustrations and tables

Abbott, Edith, 11, 15
Abbott, Grace, 15, 226
Adamic, Louis, 15–16
Addams, Jane, 15, 226, 262
affirmative action, 24
Allen, William, 244
American Federation of International Institutes (AFII), 8, 15–17, 19, 161, 226–8. *See also* International Institute of Metropolitan Toronto
Americanization, 15, 17, 32, 38, 43, 112, 161
Amin, Ash, 155
Anderson, Benedict, 5
Anglo-Americans, 43, 261
Anglo-Protestant profile, Toronto's, 18, 103
anti-Communism: *Canadian Scene* (media organization), 277; Captive Nations Club, 252; Cold War, 17, 251, 256, 304; Czechoslovak directory controversy, 293; of Eastern European professionals, 50, 57, 59, 62, 63, 65, 69; Hungarian Week narrative of, 250; of Institute staff, 34, 58, 276; of IODE members, 8; politicization of folk culture and the arts, 249–50, 252, 256, 269–70, 272
anti-racism, 288–90, 291–2, 296. *See also* racialized immigrants
Appadurai, Arjun, 264
Archer, William, 10, 11
Arthur, Jack, 243
art shows, 269–70
Ashby, Mira, 211, 279, 284
Ashkenazi, Michael, 302
assault. *See* violence against women
assimilation: Anglo-conformity ideology of, 23; confusion over term's meaning, 32, 44, 161–2; expectation of, 15, 17. *See also* Canadianization; Imperial Order Daughters of the Empire (IODE); melting pot vs. mosaic approach to immigration
assimilationist-integrationist tension, 20, 24, 32, 38, 43–4
Avramenko, Vasile, 230

Bakhtin, Mikhail, 232
Bander, Frances, 264–5
Bannerji, Himani, 27, 296–7, 298, 299
Barbeau, Marius, 262

Bay Street riot of 1961, 163
beauty pageants, 20, 282, *283,* 285
Beiss, Frank, 79
Belasco, Warren J., 213
Bellamy, Donald, 216
Bellay, Susan, 38, 228
Benedict, Ruth, *Patterns of Culture* (1946), 40
Benerides, Raul, 145
Berkenmayer, Fred, 142, *150*
Berkson, Isaac B., 15–16
Bernard, William, 17
Bertram, Laurie, 27
Bilak, Jaroslav, 254
Black Power movement, 24
Bohlman, Philip V., 233
Bojovic, N.S., 34, 35
Bordonaro, Corrado, 141, 158
Borsi, Susan, 284–5
Bouchard-Taylor Commission, 27, 356n30
Bourdieu, Pierre, 302
Bourne, Randolph, 16
Bradbury, Bettina, 131
Bramadat, Paul, 302
breadwinner anxiety, 62, 65, 67
Bremer, Edith Terry, 15–16, 17, 41–2, 161, 227, 261, 262
Brender a Brandis, Madzi, 157–8
bridge club, 137, 141–2, *142,* 143, 144, 145
Brookfield, Tara, 280, 281
Brown, Kay, 12, 138, 140, 159–60, 162
Buda, Judas, 270
Bunker, Stase, 141
Buyers, Joan, 139, 153

Calypso Nights, 163, 245
Canada Manpower Centres, CMP (formerly the NES), 60–1
Canadian Association of Adult Education, 167
Canadiana Week, 224, 233, 236, 238–41, 252, 263–4, 266
"*Canadian* Canadian," 26
Canadian Citizenship Act, 271, 275
Canadian Citizenship Branch, 10, 26
Canadian Confederation diamond jubilee celebration, 230, 240
Canadian Czechoslovakian Artists Association, 270
Canadian Folk Arts Council, 160
Canadian Handicraft Guild, 257, 262
Canadianization: blurring of lines between integration, assimilation, and, 20, 32, 99, 102, 127–8; Kay Brown's recommendation to adopt as policy, 159, 160–1; as liberal assimilationist model, 38
Canadian Mosaic (Gibbon), 28, 228–9
Canadian Multiculturalism Act (1988), 23
Canadian National Exhibition (CNE), 223, 241, 242, 243, 283
Canadian Pacific Railway (CPR) interwar folk festivals, 228, 229–30, 262
Canadian Polish Congress (Toronto District), 10, 210, 248
Canadian Polish Women's Federation, 10, 211, 249
Canadians All (radio program), 253
Captive Nations Club, 252
car culture, 115, *116*
Caribana festival, 163, 245, 247
Caribbean festival, 213, 245
Caribbean groups, 140, 163–4
Carraro, Joseph, 168
case files: interpreting, 46–9; overview of, 14, 307–9, *310–14*; for teaching, 44–6; ways to create, discussion around, 37–8. *See also* casework method; counsellors

casework method, 31–2, 37–8, 39, 43.
    See also counsellors
Castellano, Vincent G., 35
Catholic Family Services, 91, 106
Catholic population in Toronto, 18, 320n41
Catholic Women's League (CWL), 10, 12, 36–7, 194–5, 249
Charter of Rights and Freedoms, 23
chess club, 137, 140, 148, 159
Chiappetta, Emily, 125, 126–7
Chiappetta, Mrs., 125, 126
Chiappetta, Ruta, 125, 126
childcare, lack of access to, 70–1
Children's Aid Society (CAS), 123, 138, 167
children's parties, 202–5, *205*
Chin, Rita, 297, 298
Chinese Canadian Association, 4, 278
Chinese Canadians, 131, 235, *237, 238*
Christmas Bureau, 196, 197, 199
Christmas season events and promotion, 202–5, *205, 206,* 206–8, 215–19, 220. *See also* food, use of by Institute
Chung, Victor, 110–11
Citizenship Day celebrations, 275, 276
civil rights mobilizations, 25
Clark, Paraskeva, 266
Clarke, Boris, 42
class: downward mobility, 34, 62, 65, 68, 72, 75; of Toronto Institute clientele and members, 14, 78, 131, 142; of Toronto Institute staff and volunteers, 12, 33, 34, 47, 112, 131. *See also* professionals
Colalillo, Giuliana, 126
Colantonio, Frank, 179–80, 182–3, 184
Cold War. *See* anti-Communism
community building and group work: approach to and conclusions on, 131–2, 164; charity work, 201–2, 204; cross-cultural exchange, 208, 216–17, 220; cross-cultural marriages, 146–9; cross-cultural relationships, forming, 141–4, *143*; English-language program, 139, 140; group identity formation, 144, 155; groups, types of, 135–7, 140; group workers, 134, *136,* 137–40, 141; group work method, purpose and benefits of, 133–4; humour, role in, 144–6; intercultural groups, 7; Kay Brown on Institute programs, 159–61; keeping in touch with "old friends," 148–51; members participating in, 131–2, 135, 140–1; missed opportunities, 162–4; sponsored groups, tensions with Institute, 151–5. *See also* food, use of by Institute; *Intercom;* specific clubs
Community Chest of Greater Toronto. *See* United Community Fund (UCF) and United Appeal Campaign
Community Folk Art Council (CFAC), *213,* 234, 242, 243, 293
community projects: approach to and conclusions on, 165–6, 191–3; Branch Office, 165; children's health, 170–3, 174, 175, 178–9; Edith Ferguson's recommendations for, 191–2; funding for, 167; goals, health and welfare project, 168; goals, occupational training project, 179; industrial-sewing courses, 186, 187–9, 191; *Newcomers and New Learning,* 180–1; *Newcomers in Transition,* 169–70, 178; recruiting students for programs, 181–2; rural Southern Europeans, target audience for, 165–6, 167–8, 179–80; skills-upgrading (pre-licensing) course for hairdressers, 186, 189–90; staff-client gender match, 165–6, 191; staff recruitment from immigrant community, 166, 168–9, 179–80, 191, 192, 193;

community projects (*cont.*)
vocational training, 184–6. *See also* English classes; Southern Europeans
compassion fatigue. *See* secondary trauma syndrome (STS)
concerts. *See* folk dance and folk music
Confederation Life Insurance Company, 240
cookbook projects, 214–19
Cooking in the Chinese Manner, 219
Co-ordinating Council of Citizenship for Metropolitan Toronto, 275
Corke, Beverley, 294
Corriere Canadese, 269
cosmopolitanism, liberal, 194, 209, 220, 224. *See also* food, use of by Institute; public events
Cosso, Maria, 35, 168, 171, 173–5, 177–8, 191
Costa, Nada, 111, 118
COSTI (Centro Organizzativo Scuole Tecniche Italiane), 168, 182–3, 184, 186, 193, 303
Council on Social Work Education, 39
Counihan, Carole, 208
counsellors: bonds of trust with assault victims, 93–6, 98, 99; class-based biases of, 77–8; emotional responses to assault victims, 89, 90–2; ineffectual responses to assault cases, 92–3; male, trust relationship with client, 109–10; men's vs. women's case files comparison, 46–8, 58, 64, 103, 300–1; politics, and recruitment of, 34; profile of, 32–7; recruitment from immigrant communities, 9, 16, 33, 36, 51, 74, 98; secondary trauma syndrome (STS), 89–90; sexist assumptions of male, 83; typologies, use of, 37, 61–2, 74. *See also* case files; socio-cultural approach to social work
Covello, Aldo, 270

COVID-19 pandemic, 27, 296, 298
Creighton, Helen, 276
Croll, David Arnold, 10, 11
cultural apartheid, 26
cultural gifts. *See* immigrant gifts ideology
cultural or "new" racism, 296–7
cultural pluralism, 16. *See also* pluralism
cultural relativism, 38, 40
Cunha, Fernando Ciriaco da, 163
Cupido, Robert, 230
Czechoslovakian Society of Arts and Sciences exhibit, 269–70

dance classes, 135, 137, 140, 147
Danys, Milda, 52
Davidovich, Stephen, 10, 254
Day, Richard J.F., 27
"deficient self," 53, 55–6
Delibes, Léo, 272
Delinquent Daughters (Odem), 103
Department of Citizenship and Immigration (DCI), 163
Department of Public Welfare (DPW), 86, 92, 105–6
de Pédery-Hunt, Dora, 202, 266–7, 269
depression. *See* emotional suffering
De Voin, Ida, 138
Di Giacomo, (Mrs. S.), 10, 284
Dingman, Elizabeth, 207
diversity, American version of, 24. *See also* ethnic diversity; racial diversity
Drabik, Michael, 272
Dua, Enakshi, 305
Duncan, James, 271
Dymes, Marie, 217

Eastern Europeans: anti-Communism of, 50, 57, 59, 62–3, 65, 69; charity recipients, 197, 198; generational conflict cases, 122; Institute groups, 249–50, 251, 252; marital conflict

cases, 80, 97–8; suburbanization, 18. *See also* professionals
Economides, Alec, 250
education, vocational for youth, 112, 113, *114,* 116–17, 128
El-Laboudy, Ali, 140, 149, *150*
El-Laboudy, Claire, 149, *150*
Emerson, Clara, 257, 281
emotional abuse, 77
emotional suffering: and depression, 66–8, 73, 82, 83, 84; expression of, 81, 83; health effects of, 84–5; husbands damaged by, 86–8; in-laws as cause of, 76, 77, 81, 93, 98, 108–10; mentally ill spouses and, 85–6, 89; respecting cultural norms of expression, 87; suicide attempts, 82, 83, 87, 95–6
emotions, framework for understanding, 78–9
English Canada, 7–8, 27, 239, 253–4, 281, 296–7
English classes, 4, 137, 139, 140, 141, 182–4, 192. *See also* Trade English program
Epp, Marlene, 27
ESL (English as a second language). *See* English classes
Estonian Association of Toronto, 248
ethnic diversity: among Toronto Institute clientele, 14, 19; among Toronto Institute directors, 11, 12; among Toronto Institute members, 19, 131, 139–40; among Toronto Institute staff and volunteers, 9, 12, 33, 140–1; in metropolitan Toronto, 18–19, 224; promotion through popular spectacle, 223–4
ethnic entrepreneurialism, 209–10, 220. *See also* food, use of by Institute
ethnic groups, 246–7, 249–52
ethnicity, invented, 20, 226
ethnicization of Canadian politics, 251

ethnic revivalism, 24–5, 115
Ethnic Weeks, 208–11, 224, 233–6, *236, 237,* 252
Eustace, Nicole, 79
events. *See* public events
exogamous marriages, 146–8
Expo 67, 159, 243

fairs and bazaars, 231–3, *232*
Federal-Provincial Technical and Vocational Agreement (FPTVA), 184
feminism, and immigrant daughters, 125–7
Ferguson, Edith: 1970 OEC report, 42, 101–2, 110, 127, 303; assimilation-integration views, ambiguity on, 101–2, 127; background and education, 166–7; as community projects director, 12, 165–6, 168–71, 174–6, 178, 179–81, 190–1; *Newcomers and New Learning,* 180–1; *Newcomers in Transition,* 169–70, 178; project recommendations, 191–2; on skills-building and English instruction, 179, 182, 183–4; on the sojourning mentality, 181, 185; on women's training projects, 186–91. *See also* community projects
Fernandes, Gilberto, 115, 181
Fernandes, Jorge, 180, 181, 185
Festival of Nations international fair, 281–2
film series, at Toronto Institute, 135, 159
Fine, Charles, 39, 40
fine art. *See* handicrafts and high art
First Nations, 240. *See also* Indigenous peoples
Fisher, John, 242
folk crafts. *See* handicrafts and high art
folk dance and folk music: approach to, 258; in Canadiana Weeks, 239; gender stereotypes and, 272–4, *274,* 290, 302; organizing, 270–2;

folk dance and folk music (*cont.*)
second folk revival movement and, 259–60; Ukrainian schools of, 230; workshops, 274–7
Folk Fair pamphlet (1960), 228
folk festivals: Canadiana Week, 224, 233, 236, 238–41, 252, 263–4, 266; Canadian Pacific Railway interwar, 228, 229–30, 262; ethnic, changes to, 259; John Madsen Folk Festival, 241, 279; scripts and formats for, debates on, 277–9. *See also* public events
Folklorama, 260
folklore studies, 259, 263
folk music. *See* folk dance and folk music
folk revival movement (second North American), 258–60
Folk Song Time (radio program), 275
food, use of by Institute: approach to and conclusions on, 194–5, 220; as charity or welfare, 194, 195–6; charity work and forming community, 201–2, 204; children's Christmas parties, 202–5, 205; Christmas and New Year's dances, 207–8; Christmas buffets and dinners, 205–7; Christmas donations and donors, 196–7; Christmas donations recipients, 197–202; cookbook projects, 208, 214–19; *Cooking in the Chinese Manner,* 219; ethnic, as political expression, 213–14; Ethnic Weeks, 208–11, 224, 233–6, *236, 237,* 252; member-organized dinners and banquets, 208, *212;* Metro International Caravan, 5, 211–13, 224, 243–5, 255, 282, 302; *Season's Greetings in Food – Christmas 1962* (Toronto Institute), 215, 216–19, 220; vouchers, 196, 199, 201. *See also* community building and group work
Forbell, H.C., 12, 154, 242
Foster, Kate A., 228
Foucault, Michel, 49, 79, 132

Fowke, Edith, 260, 275–6, 278–9
Frank, Lawrence, 41
Franzen, Margaret, 145
Friesen, Gerald, 28

Gabaccia, Donna, 17, 126, 214
Garcia, Anna, 37
Gateway to Entertainment, 239
Geiger, Eric, 277
Geiger-Torel, Herman, 279
Gellner, John, 12, 239
gender imbalances: among Toronto Institute clientele, 14, 141; among Toronto Institute membership, 9, 14, 140, 164; among Toronto Institute staff and volunteers, 9, 10, 12, 33, 141
gender norms and women's careers, 69–71
generational conflict in immigrant families: approach to and conclusions on, 101–3, 127–8; between adult children and older parents, 104–6; car culture, 115, *116;* Family Court referrals, 104, 118, 119; fiancés of teens, family disapproval of, 121–2; girls challenging strict moral codes, 125–7; high school dropout rates, 115–16; honour/shame moral code, 118, 127; in-laws, conflict with, 108–10; miniskirt as symbol of cultural gulf, 117–18; parent-teen conflicts, 110–11; property-related disputes, 106–8; scholarship and cases overview, 103–4; school vs. full-time work for teens, 111, 112–15; streaming youth into vocational track, 117, 291; teen delinquency, 118–20, 122–5
Gentile, Cora, 180
Georgakopoulos, Nicholas, 180, 185–6
George Brown College, 190, 293
German Canadian Club Harmonie, 210, *246,* 248

Gerstle, Gary, 24, 322n4, 323n7
Gerussi, Bruno, 202
Gibbon, John Murray: *Canadian Mosaic*, 28, 228–30; as folk festival organizer, 228, 229–30, 262
Giles, Wenona, 118, 126, 127
Gillin, John, 289
Gioseffi, William, 39
Gitow, Lucy, 139
Globe and Mail, 215, 263, 277, 282, 285
Golz, Annalee, 89
Goonewardena, Kanishka, 194, 303
Gordon, Linda, 48
Graham, John R., 39
Grant, Charity, 10, 275
Greek community. *See* community projects; Southern Europeans
Greek community political divisions, 34, 249
Greek Night, 250
Greek Sunday, 233–4
Greenhill, Pauline, 276
Greenwich House, 261
Greiner, Raymond, 140
Grenfell, Wilfred, 264
Grossman, Allan, 10
group identity formation, 144, 155
Group of Seven, 240
group work. *See* community building and group work

Hall, Stuart, 299
Haller, Stephania K., 270
handicrafts and high art: approach to and overview of, 258, 260; 1972 craft show and survey, 264–5, *268*; art shows, 269–70; gender hierarchy at events featuring, 263; Indigenous crafts, 262, 264; mixing "high" and "low" art at events, 265–7; promotion of, in Canada, 261–3
Handley, Katherine Newkirk, 39

Hanen, Margaret (*née* Maas), 138, 148, *150*, 150–1
Hanen, Ted, 148
Hansen, Thor, 225
Hawkins, Freda, 10
Hayter, Charles, 234
Hayward, Victoria, 228
Head, Violet, 138, *150*, 151, 257
Head, Wilson, 291, 303
health and welfare projects. *See* community projects
Heilberg, Frieda, 41, 42, 44
Henselmans, John, 35
high art. *See* handicrafts and high art
Hill, Daniel, 286, *287*
Hill, Donna Mae (*née* Bender), 286
Hill, Margaret, 187
Hochschild, Arlie Russell, 90
Hoganson, Kristin, 15, 17, 226, 261
Hollinger, David, 24
home visits, staff and volunteers performing, 9, 33, 34, 36–7
honour killings, 77, 78, 96–7. *See also* violence against women
honour-shame complex, 97–8, 118, 127
hostesses for Institute events, 282–6, 290
Hradsky, Nadine, 157, 158
Hugenholtz (Mrs. E.H., IODE member), 203, 204
Hull House, 226, 261
human rights, 286–90
Hungarian Canadian Federation, 248, 250
Hungarian Week, 234, 250, 251–2, 266, 267
Hurlbutt, Mary E., 40, 41, 43–4, 45

Igartua, José E., 254
Ignatieff, Helen, 10
ill-adjustment: angry younger men, 62–6; depressed older men, 66–8; determining cause(s) of, 43; gap between aspired-to and achieved employment, 54, 62, 64;

ill-adjustment (*cont.*)
  of immigrant parents, 119; importance of healthy adjustment, 53–4; male counsellors' views on, 300–1; of Milwaukee Institute's Puerto Ricans, 44–5. *See also* professionals
immigrant gifts ideology: approach to and conclusions on, 223–5, 255–6, 304; American precedents and approach to, 16, 226–7; Canadian precedents and approach to, 225–6, 228; Ethnic Weeks events and, 208–9; food and recipes as gifts, 218, 219; handicrafts as gifts, 261–2, 264; pluralism at Toronto Institute and, 228, 243, 281, 290, 304; use of, by ethnic elites, 249, 254. *See also* fairs and bazaars; folk dance and folk music; folk festivals; pluralism; public events
Immigrant Meets the School, The (1959), 135
immigration to Canada: non-Christians, 208, 216, 296–9; points system (nominally race-neutral policy), 12, 57, 305, 318n24; post-1945, 12, 14, 18–19, 56–7, 101, 110, 200; Ugandan Asians, 52, 56, 57, 60–1, 292; white immigrant success, 52
Imperial Order Daughters of the Empire (IODE), 8, 12, *13*, 200, 203–5, 247, 264–5
India Night, 235
Indigenous peoples: crafts, 261, 262, 263–4; erasure of, 239, 240; family separation and residential schools, 120, 135, 241; multiculturalism and, 27; sidelining of, by Institutes, 20; in Toronto metropolitan census area, 18; treated as separate race, 289
Industrial Workers of the World, 25
in-laws, 76, 77, 81, 93, 98, 108–10

integration: Black Power rejection of, 24; confusion over term's meaning, 32, 44, 161–2; exogamous marriages and, 146; IODE's shift to, from assimilation stance, 8; models of, 39–40; two-way, 44, 133, 161, 164, 247. *See also* Programme Committee
integrationist-assimilationist tension, 20, 24, 32, 38, 43–4
Inter-Agency Council of Ontario, 299
Intercom: articles on OHRC and Ontario Human Rights Code, 286, 287–8; birth announcements in, 148–9; Charles Roach, on city transformation by immigrants, 246–7; Christmas reportage, 207–8, 215–16; confusing use of terms "assimilation" and "integration," 161–2; editors and editorial committee, 12, 138, 140; goals for, 136–7; on immigrant gifts, 228; Japanese Canadian mill workers article, 162; jokes, 145–6; "Let's Exchange Recipes" column, 215; letters to, 145, 150–1; Lloyd Kinnee, as contributor, 139; reviews, 270; suggestions for improvement, 154–5; "Tales of an Immigrant" column, 155–8; updates on former staff and members, 150–1
intercultural groups, 7
interculturalism, 137, 356n30
intercultural spaces, 48, 137
intermediate spaces, 48, 131, 148
International Folk Troupe, 239
International Institute of Metropolitan Toronto: introduction to and overview of, 3–5; affiliates of, 4, 163, 248, 249, 251–2, 254, 304; board of directors, 9, 10; Christmas season, promotion of, 215–16; clientele, 14; decline and demise of, 291–4; Department of Group Services, 9, 131; Department

of Individual Services, 9, 31, 50, 76, 104; directors, 11–12; funding for, 7, 8–9, 50, 134, 152, 291, 293–4; legacy of, 20, 294–5; logo, 225–6; mandate/mission statement, 17–18, 160, 223, 225; members, 7, 9, 14, 131–2, 135, 140–1; Members Council (or Membership Council), 135, 141, 152, 154, 155; missed opportunities for community building, 162–4; New Canadians Service Agency of Ontario (NCSA), 7–8, 31, 33, 37; Old St Andrew's Church Memorial House, 7, 8, 9, 161, 231, 233; origins, and affiliation with US-based AFII, 3, 6–7, 8, 17; paradoxical nature of pluralism at, 20, 44, 127–8, 224; Programme Committee, 135, 154–5; services and programs, 16–17, 35; staff, 9, 14, 16, 137–9; volunteers, 9, 12, 33, 36–7, 137, 139, 140. *See also* case files; community building and group work; community projects; counsellors; *specific names of board members and directors*

international institutes movement, 7, 9, 15–17, 43, 226, 227–8, 305. *See also* American Federation of International Institutes (AFII)

internationalism. *See* liberal internationalism

International Ladies Garment Workers Union, 25

IODE (Imperial Order Daughters of the Empire), 8, 12, *13*, 200, 203–5, 247, 264–5

Isserstedt, Elizabeth ("Betty," *née* McBain), 10, 269

Italian community. *See* COSTI; Southern Europeans

Italian Immigrant Aid Society (IIAS), 180, 198, 248

Italian variety nights, 234–5

Iványi-Grünwald, Béla, 267

Jacobson, Matthew, 25

Japanese Canadian Citizens Association, 248

Japanese Canadian programming, 162–3, 211, 248

Japanese Labourers' Union, 162

Jarvis, Alan, 266

Jaworski, Z., 249

Jemsen, Isabel, 158

Jennings, Margaret (Peggy), 10, 257, 271, 274–5, 276, 278

Jensen, Mrs. R. (cookbook contributor), 217

Jewish Immigrant Aid Society, 14, 160

John Madsen Folk Festival, 241, 279

Jones, Royston C., 36, 164, 293–4

Justi, Anton, 35

Kallen, Horace, 16, 25, 323n7

Kammen, Michael, 264

Kantor, Marilyn, 272

Kapoustin, Robert and Tatiana, 271–2

Kapoustin Ensemble, 271–2

Katz, Sidney, 111, 118, 160

Kazal, Russell A., 24, 25

Kelly, John David, 240

Khotkevych, Hnat, 273

Kidd, J. Roby, 10

Kinnee, Lloyd, 139, 140, 141

Kipfer, Stefan, 194, 303

Klymasz, Robert B., 250

Kodály Choir, 239, 251

Kodály Ensemble of Toronto, 234

Koepke, Otto, 140, 156

Kolm, Richard, 138, 161, 275, 278

Kopmanis, Alma, 275

Kossar, Leon, 10, 243, 244, 246, 254–5, 277

Kossar, Zena, 244, 255

Kotick, Jean, 275
Kraus, Hertha, 39, 41
Kreem, Robert, 137–8
Krehm, Ivy, 239, 275, 279
Külvet, Ilmar, 157
Kymlicka, Will, 26, 389n119

Labrador Handicraft Group, 264
Latvian National Federation in Canada, 248
Lee, Catherine, 36, 122, 138–9, 293
liberal anti-modernism, 225, 231, 251, 264, 271
liberal internationalism, 20, 22, 258, 279–80, 284–5
Liberatori, Abril, 285
Liga (Latvian choral ensemble), 272
Lisowska, Zoya, 270
Litwicki, Ellen, 226
Local Initiatives Program (LIP), 293, 294
Loewen, Royden, 28
Loring, Frances, 266
Luciuk, Kassandra, 272
Lumb, Jean, 10

Maagaard, Tore, 139
MacMillan, Sir Ernest, 223
Madsen, Betty, 275, 278–9
maladjustment. *See* ill-adjustment
Malkki, Liisa, 284–5
Marchese, Rosario, 117
marital conflict: approach to and conclusions on, 76–8, 98–100; abuse, patterns of, 80–1; assault cases, counsellors' ineffectual responses to, 92–3; assault victims, counsellors' bonds of trust with, 93–6; assault victims, counsellors' emotional responses to, 89, 90–2; emotional investment, shedding, 82; failed love affairs, 82–3; fear of deportation, effects of, 81; non-violent disputes, 81–4; patriarchy and, 79, 80–1; sexist assumptions of male counsellors, 83; sexual conflict, 83–4; sexual misconduct, 87–8; wife assault cases, 88–9. *See also* counsellors; emotional abuse; emotional suffering; violence against women
Martin, Paul, Sr., 271, 395n55
Martynowych, Orest T., 230
masculinity and masculine subjectivities. *See* men; professionals
McCarthy, Pearl, 263
McClung, Nellie, 11, 266–7
McKay, Ian, 229
media: ethnic, 160, 234; event publicity and, 211–12, 234, 244–5, 252–3, 277; reporting on immigrants, 102, 110–11, 122–3, 125–7; women's stories, focus on sensational, 98. *See also specific names of media outlets*
melting pot vs. mosaic approach to immigration, 16, 23, 24, 101–2. *See also* assimilation; integration
Members Council (or Membership Council), 135, 141, 152, 154, 155
men: emotional abuse of, 77; emotionally damaged, 86–8; status and identity, desire to re-establish, 50, 55, 62–3, 64, 67–8, 71–2, 74; stereotypes of "foreign," 81. *See also* professionals
mental health effects of underemployment, 53, 54, 59, 65–6
mental illness, 85–6, 89, 106, 107–8
Mertz, Ida, 34
Metro International Caravan, 5, 211–13, 224, 243–5, 255, 282, 302
Michalowska, Bronka, 263
Milani, C.D., 10
Milnes, H.N., 263
Milwaukee Institute, 44–5, 289–90
Minkofski-Garrigues, Horst, 239
"mixed" unions, 82–3, 146, 147–8, 359n71

Mohl, Raymond, 15, 227
Mojab, Shahrzad, 77, 96, 99
Montgomery, Marucia, 168-9, 175-6, 178, 188
"moral geographies," 155
Moritz, Wolfgang, 152, 208
Morse, Eric, 239
mosaic vs. melting pot approach to immigration, 16, 23, 24, 101-2. *See also* assimilation; integration
Mota, Maria, 36, 235
Muhammedi, Shezan, 52
multiculturalism: American ideologies of, 23-5; backlash against in Europe, 19-20, 296-8; Canadian ideologies of, 25-7; Canadian Multiculturalism Act (1988), 23; definition, 137; "hard" vs. "soft," 24, 322n4, 323n7; "multicultural love," 156; and pluralism, contrasts, 19-20, 25; as state policy (1971), 23, 253; third-force argument of, 25-6, 102, 249, 252, 254, 304; Toronto style of, 6; white-settler version of, 26, 240-1, 295, 304-5. *See also* interculturalism; pluralism
Mulvihill, Claude J., 10, 210
Murphy, Gillian, 259
Murray, Colin, 212, 244-5
Muslims, 26, 52, 96, 149, 208, 216, 296-9. *See also* non-Christian immigrants
Myers, Tamara, 131

Nagy, George, 35, 140
Nair, Murali, 36, 293, 294
Nathan Phillips Square, 244, *274, 283*
National Conference of Christians and Jews, 289
National Employment Service (NES), 54, 184, 187, 188
National Film Board of Canada (NFB), 4, 135, 203, 204, 239
Nationbuilders shows, 223, 242-3, 255, 285

nation-building, 3, 5, 20, 224
NCSA. *See* New Canadians Service Agency of Ontario (NCSA)
"New Canadian Interests" (newspaper column), 243, 277
"New Canadians" (advice column), 277
New Canadians Service Agency of Ontario (NCSA), 7-8, 31, 33, 37
Newcomers and New Learning, 180-1
Newcomers in Transition, 169-70, 178
No Longer Vanishing (1955), 135
non-Christian immigrants, 208, 216, 296-9
"nostalgic modernism," 231, 264
nurses, immigrant, 72-3

Odem, Mary: *Delinquent Daughters*, 103
Old St Andrew's Church Memorial House, 7, 8, 9, 161, 231, 233
Ontario Citizenship Branch (OCB), 283, 284
Ontario Citizenship Division (OCD), 182, 183, 292, 357n38
Ontario Council of Agencies Serving Immigrants (OCASI), 299, 300
Ontario Economic Council (OEC), 101-2, 110
Ontario Family Court, 76, 120
Ontario Folk Festival Society, 241
Ontario Housing Corporation, 86, 106
Ontario Human Rights Code, 286, 291
Ontario Human Rights Commission (OHRC), 286, 287, *287, 288*
Ontario Radio Forum, 167
Ontario Training Act, 190
Ostashewski, Marcia, 273
Our Canadian Mosaic (Foster), 228

Panagiotis, Thanos, 36
Paolantonio, Vienna, 125
patriarchy, 79, 80-1
Patterns of Culture (Benedict), 40
Pavao, Filomena, 125

Pearson, Lester, 245, 281
Peel, Mark, 46, 54, 300
People's Republic of China, recognition of (1970), 57
Peruklijevic, Vera, 37
Philip, Milton, 12
Phillips, Nathan, 239, 263, 271
Pickersgill, J.W., 248
Pickles, Katie, 8
Pierce, Willette, 44, 161, 289–90
Pilz, Wilhelm, 156–7
pluralism: double-edged, 20; immigrant gifts version, at Toronto Institute, 228, 243, 281, 290, 304; integration, assimilation, and Canadianization, blurring of lines between, 20, 32, 99, 102, 127–8; and liberal internationalism, relationship between, 20, 22, 258, 279–80, 284–5; and multiculturalism, contrasts, 19–20, 25; paradoxical nature of Toronto Institute's, 20, 44, 127–8, 224; pre-1960s ideologies, 25; rejection of determinist racist theories, 16, 32, 288–9; and social order, 5, 10; Toronto's style of, 6; in the United States, 15–16, 226–8. *See also* International Institute of Metropolitan Toronto; multiculturalism; sociocultural approach to social work
points system, 12, 57, 305, 318n24
Polish Week, 210–11, 233, 249, 263
Ponafidine, Elisabeth, 228
Porter, John, 26–7
Porter, McKenzie, 245
Portuguese Canadian Democratic Association (PCDA), 163
Portuguese community. *See* Portuguese Canadian Democratic Association (PCDA); Salazar dictatorship; Southern Europeans
Portuguese Festival and variety nights, 234–5

Prapuolenis, Stase, 263
Primitive Culture (Taylor), 40
professionals: approach to and conclusions on, 47–8, 51–2, 74–5; anti-Communism of, 50, 57, 59, 62, 63, 65, 69; breadwinner anxiety, 62, 65, 67; career/identity re-establishment, contemporary insights on, 52–3; case files, overview of, 56–8; certification rules, 58–9, 60–1, 63–4, 70, 75; compliance, counsellors' emphasis on, 52, 64, 74; "deficient self," 53, 55–6; deskilling and reducing expectations, 51, 52, 59–60, 66–7, 71–2, 75; downward mobility, 65, 68–9, 72, 75; dual-career marriages, 72–4; female vs. male counsellors' approaches to, 48; masculinities, finding in case files, 51–2, 59, 62; men, angry younger (typology), 62–6; men, depressed older (typology), 66–8; mental health effects of under-employment, 53, 54, 59, 65–6; publicity/human-interest narratives, 50–1, 53–6; sexism and gendered expectations, 69–71; speaking stories, 54; status and identity, desire to re-establish, 50, 55, 62–3, 64, 67–8, 71–2, 74; subjectivities, finding in case files, 21, 47–8, 51; trailing spouses, 72–4; white-collar job strategy, promotion of, 59, 64, 66, 71, 73, 75. *See also* counsellors; ill-adjustment
Programme Committee, 135, 154–5
Provisional Certificate of Qualification (PCQ), 189, 190
public events: approach to and conclusions on, 223–5, 255–6; commemoration ceremonies, 267, 269; ethnic rivalries and, 251–2; Ethnic Weeks, 208–11, 224, 233–6, *236, 237,* 252; Festival of Nations

international fair, 281–2; Forbell, on the importance of, 242; funding and support for, 247–8; hostesses for, 282–6, 290; as immigrant-gifts pluralism, 243; Institute and ethnic group agendas for, 252; International Stamp Mart, 280; media coverage, 252–3; Metro International Caravan, 5, 211–13, 224, 243–5, 255, 282, 302; Miss Caravan pageant, 282, *283*; as nation- and community-building, 224, 246–7; Nationbuilders shows, 223, 242–3, 255, 285; negotiating partner group participation, 248–9, 252; shaping cultural narratives via, 249–52; third-force argument of multiculturalism, 25–6, 102, 249, 252, 254, 304. *See also* folk dance and folk music; folk festivals; handicrafts and high art; *specific names of festivals*
public health nurses, 172, 173
Puerto Ricans, 17, 42, 44–5, 289–90

Quebec, 23, 27, 239, 245. *See also* Royal Commission on Bilingualism and Biculturalism

racial diversity: among Toronto Institute members, 139–40; among Toronto Institute staff and volunteers, 9, 33, 140
racial inclusivity, missed opportunities for, 162–4
racialized immigrants: backlash against, 19, 101, 287, 293, 296–7; cultural pluralism, effects on some, 288–9; in economic apartheid, 27; Family Court and, 120; mixed-race unions, 82–3, 147–8; professionals, 55–6, 60–1, 74; racism towards, from Institute staff, 153–4; South Asians, 14, 19, 52, 56, 57, 60–1, 193; streaming of Black students, 117, 291; "universal" measurements and deskilling, 52. *See also* anti-racism; Milwaukee Institute
racism, cultural or "new," 296–7
racism, systemic, and violence against women, 78
Raska, Jan, 52, 71
Reade, Elizabeth, 269, 270
Reade, John Collingwood, 253, 269
Reddy, William M., 79
re-education, 4, 11, 280
Rio Blanco Trio, 163
Rippl-Rónai, József, 266
Roach, Charles, 163, 245–7
Romantic Canada (Hayward), 228
Rosenwein, Barbara H., 79
Ross, Isabel, 282
Royal Commission on Bilingualism and Biculturalism, 12, 27, 102, 245, 249, 253, 254, 304
Rubin, Ruth, 260
Rudnay, Gyula, 267
rural villagers. *See* community projects; Southern Europeans
Ryerson Polytechnical Institute, 105, 139

Saarniit, Joann, 157
Sakura (Cherry Blossom) Club, 162
Salazar dictatorship, divisions over, 34, 163, 168–9
San Martin, Javier, 36
Santos, Isabel, 235
Saturday Night (news magazine), 167
Save the Children Fund (SCF), 281–2
Schembri, T.J., 270
Schlesinger, Benjamin, 39
School of Social Work (University of Toronto), 39, 138, 167, 168, 216
Schulman, Bruce, 24
Scott, Joan, 298–9
Scotti, Arturo, 267, 269, 270
Seaman, John T., 12

Season's Greetings in Food – Christmas 1962 (Toronto Institute), 215, 216–19, 220
secondary trauma syndrome (STS), 89–90
Sehnoha, Jaroslav, 269–70
Selig, Diana, 227
Senathirajah, Nalla (Nallamma) Subramaniam, 10
Serge, Joe, 125
settlement houses, 133, 226, 239, 261, 275
settlement movement, 9, 11, 38, 132
sexism and sexist behaviours: in the professions, for immigrant clients, 69–70; towards female staff and volunteers, 153
sexual conflict, 83–4
Shanty, Ahmed, 154
Shevchenko, Taras, 273
Silva, Ezequiel Pereira da, 36
Singer, Helen, 125, 126–7
Slavic Ethnic Club, 251–2
Smith, Margaret Chase, 271
socialized justice, 76, 103
Social Planning Council of Metropolitan Toronto (SPC): projects, education support, and work experience at, 7, 138, 139, 167, 196, 286, 299; volunteers with, 10, 12, 216. *See also* Ontario Council of Agencies Serving Immigrants (OCASI)
socio-cultural approach to social work: approach to and overview of, 31–2; Canadian and American models of, 38–40; caseworkers and counsellors, profile of, 32–7; casework method, 31–2, 37–8, 39, 43; central paradox of, 32; in generational conflict cases, 108–9, 110; instruction on and theory of, 40–3, 44–6; pro-family stance at Toronto Institute, 76, 91, 93, 109; respecting cultural norms of emotional expression, 87; storytelling (as counselling practice), 51, 61. *See also* case files; casework method; counsellors; professionals
Sollors, Werner, 127
Sommerville, Donald, 242
Sosaszny, Mike, 153
South End House, 261
Southern Europeans: Azoreans, 166, 176, 181; food baskets, preferences for, 201; in health and welfare cases (Institute case files), 172; *Newcomers and New Learning*, 180–1; politics, 34, 163, 168–9, 249; of rural origins, 7, 19, 42, 165, 166, 167–8, 169–70; socio-economic status effects on, 42; workforce participation of rural women, 186–7, 190. *See also* community projects
Spaajkovic, Olga, 37
speaking stories, 54
Spiller, Henry, 273
stamp club, 151, 152, 280
Stampede (1963 film), 4, 135
status anxiety. *See* professionals
Steele, Helen, 139, 148
Stermac, Mrs. A. (IODE member), 203
Stewart, David A., 138
Stewart, Tine: demise of Toronto Institute, 291–4; event organization, 224, 257, 270, 274; as Institute director, 12, 197, 219, 243, 245, 287; as IODE volunteer, 204
Stoian, Olga, 138, 147, 153, 159
storytelling (as counselling practice), 51, 61
Strangers within Our Gates (1909 tract), 38
streaming, educational, 117, 291
Streeruwitz, Margarete: Christmas charity and events, organizing, 196, 197, 198, 202–3, 204, 206; Czechoslovak directory controversy,

293; social work with Toronto Institute, 31–2, 34–5, 54
suburbanization, 18, 147, 165, 168, 182–3
suicide attempts. *See* emotional suffering
Summerville, Donald, 234
Supper Club, 208
Suzuki, Etsu, 162
Swyripa, Frances, 27–8
Symons, Katharine, 294
Szalowski, Elizabeth, 217, 218
Szebeny, Irene, 35, 197, 203, 217

table tennis club, 140, 159
Taveres, Zia, 36
Taylor, Charles, 26
Taylor, E.B., *Primitive Culture* (1895), 40
teenagers. *See* generational conflict in immigrant families
Teicher, Morton, 40, 41
Telcs, Eduard "Ede," 267
Temesevary, Gabor, 250
tennis club, 137, 140, 141
third-force argument of multiculturalism, 25–6, 102, 249, 252, 254, 304
"third space," 126
Thobani, Sunera, 305
Thompson, Andrew, 275
Thompson, James, 280
Tibetan Cultural Society, 235
Tice, Karen, 37, 48
Tirkantis, Clara, 35
Toronto, metropolitan, 6, 18–19, 103, 224
Toronto à la Cart program (2009), 209
Toronto Art Gallery (now Art Gallery of Ontario), 239–40
Toronto Board of Education, 35, 117, 168, 172
Toronto Institute. *See* International Institute of Metropolitan Toronto

Toronto Junior League, 8, 10, 37, 134, 194–5, 247, 267
Toronto Labour Committee for Human Rights, 286
Toronto Raptors, 6
Toronto School Board (TSB), 117, 182
Toronto Star, 111, 125, 163, 164, 277
Toronto Telegram, 125, 207, 212, 243, 244, 250, 277
Toronto Welfare Council (TWC), 7. *See also* Social Planning Council of Metropolitan Toronto (SPC)
Trade English program, 141, 158. *See also* English classes
Trudeau, Pierre Elliott, 12, 25, 253, 255
Tsatsos, Effie, 31–2, 36
Tulin, Maya, 138, 153
two-way integration, 44, 133, 161, 164, 247

Uganda Committee of Toronto, 61
Ugandan Asians, 52, 56, 57, 60–1, 292
Ukrainian Bandurists, 271, 272, 273
Ukrainian Canadian Committee (UCC), 272
Ukrainian Canadians, 249, 252, 253
Ukrainian folk-dance schools, 230
Ungar, Irene, 10, 211, 267, 269, 294
United Community Fund (UCF) and United Appeal Campaign, 7, 8, 152, 291, 293, 294
United Nations Association in Canada (UNA-Canada), 280, 287
United Nations Children's Fund (UNICEF), 280, 281
United Nations Relief and Rehabilitation Administration (UNRRA), 11, 167
United Nations Universal Declaration of Human Rights, 286
United Nations Week, 257, 277, 280–1
University Settlement House, 239, 275
Urban, Andrew, 17

Vaba Eestlane (Free Estonian), 157
Van Esterik, Penny, 208
Varadaraja, Subramanian, 140–1
vertical mosaic, 26–7, 301
violence against women, 77, 88–9, 96–7, 99. *See also* honour killings; honour-shame complex; marital conflict
Vipond, Robert C., 28
Visiting Homemaker's Association, 178, 201
vocational education for youth, 112, 113, *114,* 116–17, 128
vocational training projects. *See* community projects
Vojtech, Stephen, 211, *214*
Von Oesen, Anne, 233
vouchers, food, 196, 199, 201

Walcott, Rinaldo, 299
Weiland, Martin, 156
Welcome House, 292, 293
West, Nell ("Nellie," *née* Wark): Christmas cookbook, 215, 216–17, 219; Christmas events at Toronto Institute, 202, 204, 206, *206,* 267; close relationship with ethnic groups, 160, 209, 211, 249; Ethnic Weeks, 209, 234, *240,* 263; and event hostesses, 283–4; event organization, 224, 270–1, 272, 274–5, 276, 278; Institute clientele, contact with, 197; racism complaint against, 153–4; relationship with press, 253; as Toronto Institute director, 3–4, 8, 11, *13,* 31, 131, 137; United Nations Week program, 257
West Indian community in Toronto, 163, 293–4
West Indian Student Association, 4, 163, 248
West Indies Independence Committee, 163
white ethnic revivalism, 24, 25
whiteness, 25, 45, 289, 305, 332n51
white-settler model of multiculturalism, 26, 240–1, 295, 304–5
Wilson, Cairine, 281, 282
Wobblies, 25
women: courtship, safe space for, 147; as cultural guardians, 258, 261, 265–6, 271, 290; feminism, and immigrant daughters, 125–7; immigrant activists in 1970s/1980s Toronto, 299–300; labour, gendered dynamics of, 210–11; lack of childcare, 70–1; in literature of multiculturalism and pluralism, 27–8; migration effects on, 70, 147–8; negotiating modernity, 285–6; sexism, gender norms and careers, 69–71; silencing of, 79; social workers at Toronto Institute, 46–8; "Tales of an Immigrant" (*Intercom*), essays by, 155–8; as trailing professional spouses, 72–4; underemployment in Canada, 71–2. *See also* community projects; counsellors; marital conflict; professionals; violence against women
Women's Arts Association of Canada (WAAC), 262
women's pluralism in Toronto: approach to, overview of and concluding thoughts on, 5–6, 14, 20, 21–2, 290, 295–305; case files database, 14, 46, 48–9, 307–9, *310–14;* scholarship overview, 23–8. *See also* community building and group work; community projects; counsellors; folk dance and folk music; folk festivals; food, use of by Institute; generational conflict in immigrant families; handicrafts and high art; immigrant gifts ideology; International Institute of Metropolitan Toronto; marital conflict; multiculturalism; pluralism; professionals; public events; socio-cultural approach to social work

Woodsworth, J.S., 38
Wu, Ellen D., 227, 288
Wylie, Frances, 266

Yaremko, John, 238–9, *240*, 248, 271
YMCA (Young Men's Christian Association), 247–8, 276, 277, 280

Young, Iris Marion, 132
Yuzyk, Paul, 25–6, 304–5
YWCA (Young Women's Christian Association), 15, 16, 125–6, 227, 228, 247–8, 280

Zelonka, June, 169, 176–7, 178

STUDIES IN GENDER AND HISTORY

General Editors: Franca Iacovetta and Karen Dubinsky

1. Suzanne Morton, *Ideal Surroundings: Domestic Life in a Working-Class Suburb in the 1920s*
2. Joan Sangster, *Earning Respect: The Lives of Working Women in Small-Town Ontario, 1920–1960*
3. Carolyn Strange, *Toronto's Girl Problem: The Perils and Pleasures of the City, 1880–1930*
4. Sara Z. Burke, *Seeking the Highest Good: Social Service and Gender at the University of Toronto, 1888–1937*
5. Lynne Marks, *Revivals and Roller Rinks: Religion, Leisure, and Identity in Late-Nineteenth-Century Small-Town Ontario*
6. Cecilia Morgan, *Public Men and Virtuous Women: The Gendered Languages of Religion and Politics in Upper Canada, 1791–1850*
7. Mary Louise Adams, *The Trouble with Normal: Postwar Youth and the Making of Heterosexuality*
8. Linda Kealey, *Enlisting Women for the Cause: Women, Labour, and the Left in Canada, 1890–1920*
9. Christina Burr, *Spreading the Light: Work and Labour Reform in Late-Nineteenth-Century Toronto*
10. Mona Gleason, *Normalizing the Ideal: Psychology, Schooling, and the Family in Postwar Canada*
11. Deborah Gorham, *Vera Brittain: A Feminist Life*
12. Marlene Epp, *Women without Men: Mennonite Refugees of the Second World War*
13. Shirley Tillotson, *The Public at Play: Gender and the Politics of Recreation in Postwar Ontario*
14. Veronica Strong-Boag and Carole Gerson, *Paddling Her Own Canoe: The Times and Texts of E. Pauline Johnson (Tekahionwake)*
15. Stephen Heathorn, *For Home, Country, and Race: Constructing Gender, Class, and Englishness in the Elementary School, 1880–1914*

16 Valerie J. Korinek, *Roughing It in the Suburbs: Reading* Chatelaine *Magazine in the Fifties and Sixties*
17 Adele Perry, *On the Edge of Empire: Gender, Race, and the Making of British Columbia, 1849–1871*
18 Robert A. Campbell, *Sit Down and Drink Your Beer: Regulating Vancouver's Beer Parlours, 1925–1954*
19 Wendy Mitchinson, *Giving Birth in Canada, 1900–1950*
20 Roberta Hamilton, *Setting the Agenda: Jean Royce and the Shaping of Queen's University*
21 Donna Gabaccia and Franca Iacovetta, eds, *Women, Gender, and Transnational Lives: Italian Workers of the World*
22 Linda Reeder, *Widows in White: Migration and the Transformation of Rural Women, Sicily, 1880–1920*
23 Terry Crowley, *Marriage of Minds: Isabel and Oscar Skelton Re-inventing Canada*
24 Marlene Epp, Franca Iacovetta, and Frances Swyripa, eds, *Sisters or Strangers? Immigrant, Ethnic, and Racialized Women in Canadian History*
25 John G. Reid, *Viola Florence Barnes, 1885–1979: A Historian's Biography*
26 Catherine Carstairs, *Jailed for Possession: Illegal Drug Use Regulation and Power in Canada, 1920–1961*
27 Magda Fahrni, *Household Politics: Montreal Families and Postwar Reconstruction*
28 Tamara Myers, *Caught: Montreal Girls and the Law, 1869–1945*
29 Jennifer A. Stephen, *Pick One Intelligent Girl: Employability, Domesticity, and the Gendering of Canada's Welfare State, 1939–1947*
30 Lisa Chilton, *Agents of Empire: British Female Migration to Canada and Australia, 1860s–1930*
31 Esyllt W. Jones, *Influenza 1918: Disease, Death, and Struggle in Winnipeg*
32 Elise Chenier, *Strangers in Our Midst: Sexual Deviancy in Postwar Ontario*
33 Lara Campbell, *Respectable Citizens: Gender, Family, and Unemployment in the Great Depression, Ontario, 1929–1939*
34 Katrina Srigley, *Breadwinning Daughters: Young Working Women in a Depression-era city, 1929–1939*
35 Maureen Moynagh with Nancy Forestell, eds., *Documenting First Wave Feminisms, Volume 1: Transnational Collaborations and Crosscurrents*
36 Mona Oikawa, *Cartographies of Violence: Women, Memory, and the Subject(s) of the "Internment"*
37 Karen Flynn, *Moving beyond Borders: A History of Black Canadian and Caribbean Women in the Diaspora*
38 Karen Balcom, *The Traffic in Babies: Cross Border Adoption and Baby-Selling Between the United States and Canada, 1930–1972*

39 Nancy M. Forestell with Maureen Moynagh, eds., *Documenting First Wave Feminisms, Volume II: Canada – National and Transnational Contexts*
40 Patrizia Gentile and Jane Nicholas, eds., *Contesting Bodies and Nation in Canadian History*
41 Suzanne Morton, *Wisdom, Justice and Charity: Canadian Social Welfare through the life of Jane B. Wisdom, 1884–1975*
42 Jane Nicholas, *The Modern Girl: Feminine Modernities, the Body, and Commodities in the 1920s*
43 Pauline A. Phipps, *Constance Maynard's Passions: Religion, Sexuality, and an English Educational Pioneer, 1849–1935*
44 Marlene Epp and Franca Iacovetta, eds. *Sisters or Strangers? Immigrant, Ethnic, and Racialized Women in Canadian History, Second Edition*
45 Rhonda L. Hinther, *Perogies and Politics: Radical Ukrainians in Canada, 1891–1991*
46 Valerie J. Korinek, *Prairie Fairies: A History of Queer Communities and People in Western Canada, 1930–1985*
47 Julie Guard, *Radical Housewives: Price Wars and Food Politics in Mid-Twentieth Canada*
48 Nancy Janovicek and Carmen Nielson, *Reading Canadian Women's and Gender History*
49 L.K. Bertram, *The Viking Immigrants: Icelandic North Americans*
50 Donica Belisle, *Purchasing Power: Women and the Rise of Canadian Consumer Culture*
51 Allyson D. Stevenson, *Intimate Integration: A History of the Sixties Scoop in Saskatchewan and the Colonization of Indigenous Kinship*
52 Nadia Jones-Gailani, *Transnational Identity and Memory Making in the Lives of Iraqi Women in Diaspora*
53 Franca Iacovetta, *Before Official Multiculturalism: Women's Pluralism in Toronto 1950s–1970s*